Lecture Notes in Computer Science 16361

Founding Editors

Gerhard Goos
Juris Hartmanis

Editorial Board Members

Elisa Bertino, *Purdue University, West Lafayette, IN, USA*
Wen Gao, *Peking University, Beijing, China*
Bernhard Steffen, *TU Dortmund University, Dortmund, Germany*
Moti Yung, *Columbia University, New York, NY, USA*

The series Lecture Notes in Computer Science (LNCS), including its subseries Lecture Notes in Artificial Intelligence (LNAI) and Lecture Notes in Bioinformatics (LNBI), has established itself as a medium for the publication of new developments in computer science and information technology research, teaching, and education.

LNCS enjoys close cooperation with the computer science R & D community, the series counts many renowned academics among its volume editors and paper authors, and collaborates with prestigious societies. Its mission is to serve this international community by providing an invaluable service, mainly focused on the publication of conference and workshop proceedings and postproceedings. LNCS commenced publication in 1973.

Giuseppe Scanniello · Valentina Lenarduzzi ·
Simone Romano · Sira Vegas · Rita Francese
Editors

Product-Focused Software Process Improvement

26th International Conference, PROFES 2025
Salerno, Italy, December 1–3, 2025
Proceedings

 Springer

Editors
Giuseppe Scanniello
University of Salerno
Fisciano, Italy

Valentina Lenarduzzi
University of Oulu
Oulu, Finland

Simone Romano
University of Salerno
Fisciano, Italy

Sira Vegas
Universidad Politécnica de Madrid
Madrid, Spain

Rita Francese
University of Salerno
Fisciano, Italy

ISSN 0302-9743   ISSN 1611-3349 (electronic)
Lecture Notes in Computer Science
ISBN 978-3-032-12088-5   ISBN 978-3-032-12089-2 (eBook)
https://doi.org/10.1007/978-3-032-12089-2

Preface

On behalf of the PROFES Organizing Committee, we are delighted to present the proceedings of the 26th International Conference on Product-Focused Software Process Improvement (PROFES 2025). The conference took place during December, 1–3, 2025, in Salerno (Italy). Consistent with its long-standing tradition, PROFES 2025 centered on professional Software Process Improvement (SPI) motivated by product, process, and service quality needs. The technical program was curated by a committee of distinguished experts in software process improvement, software process modeling, and empirical software engineering.

This year, the conference received a total of 101 submissions, comprising 62 full research papers, 20 industry papers, and 19 short research papers. Following a rigorous evaluation process, 23 full research papers, nine industry papers (two of them initially submitted as full research papers), and 20 short research papers (seven of them initially submitted as full research papers) were accepted for inclusion in the program. Each submission underwent a single-blind review process conducted by at least three members of the PROFES 2025 Program Committee.

Alongside the main technical program, PROFES 2025 hosted a doctoral symposium, a tutorial, and three workshops. One paper was accepted for the doctoral symposium. The tutorial focused on quantum software engineering. The 1st International Workshop on Analytics for Software Product and Process Improvement (A-SPPI 20205) aimed to explore how software analytics can provide actionable insights for improving the quality of software products and processes. Six papers were selected for A-SPPI 2025. The 1st International Workshop on Promoting and Dealing with Advanced Technology in Healthcare (PATH 2025) aimed to explore the application of advanced technologies, such as artificial intelligence, in the healthcare sector, focusing on their potential to address key challenges related to clinical outcomes, while preserving data security, patient privacy, and system reliability. Eight papers were selected for PATH 2025. The 1st International Workshop on Quality Evaluation of ML-based Software Systems (QUEMALES 2025) aimed to bring together software-quality experts and practitioners to share experiences, new ideas, and solutions to face the challenges related to ML-based software quality evaluation. Five papers were selected for QUEMALES 2025.

We express our sincere gratitude for the privilege of serving as chairs for PROFES 2025. We extend our appreciation to the members of the Program Committee and additional reviewers for their rigorous and invaluable efforts in the evaluation of submitted papers. We are likewise indebted to all authors, presenters, keynote speakers, and session chairs for their contributions, which were essential to the success of PROFES 2025.

Finally, we acknowledge the guidance and support provided by the PROFES Steering Committee throughout the organizational process.

December 2025

Giuseppe Scanniello
Valentina Lenarduzzi
Simone Romano
Sira Vegas
Rita Francese

Organization

General Chairs

Giuseppe Scanniello	University of Salerno, Italy
Valentina Lenarduzzi	University of Oulu, Finland

Program Chairs

Simone Romano	University of Salerno, Italy
Sira Vegas	Universidad Politécnica de Madrid, Spain

Short-Paper Track Chairs

Marcela Fabiana Genero Bocco	University of Castilla-La Mancha, Spain
Miroslaw Staron	Chalmers University of Technology and University of Gothenburg, Sweden

Industry-Paper Track Chairs

Javier Gonzalez Huerta	Blekinge Institute of Technology, Sweden
Daniela Soares Cruzes	Norwegian University of Science and Technology, and Visma, Norway

Doctoral Symposium Chairs

Andreas Jedlitschka	Fraunhofer IESE, Germany
Emilia Mendes	Aarhus University, Denmark

Workshop and Tutorial Chair

Marco Torchiano	Politecnico di Torino, Italy

Publication Chair

Rita Francese   University of Salerno, Italy

Social Media Chair

Pietro Cassieri   University of Salerno, Italy

Web Chair

Sabato Nocera   University of Salerno, Italy

Local Organization Chair

Olimpia Perisano   Palazzo Innovazione, Italy

Program Committee - Full Research Papers

Sousuke Amasaki   Nanzan University, Japan
Hina Anwar   University of Tartu, Estonia
Beatriz Bernárdez   University of Seville, Spain
Stefan Biffl   Vienna University of Technology, Austria
Matteo Camilli   Politecnico di Milano, Italy
Panagiota Chatzipetrou   Örebro University, Sweden
Nelly Condori-Fernández   Universidad Santiago de Compostela, Spain
Anna Corazza   University of Naples "Federico II", Italy
Oscar Dieste   Universidad Politécnica de Madrid, Spain
Michal Dolezel   Prague University of Economics and Business,
                                         Czechia
Fabian Fagerholm   Aalto University, Finland
Anna Rita Fasolino   University of Naples "Federico II", Italy
Michael Felderer   German Aerospace Center (DLR) and University
                                         of Cologne, Germany
Julian Frattini   Chalmers University of Technology and
                                         University of Gothenburg, Sweden
Javier Gonzalez Huerta   Blekinge Institute of Technology, Sweden
Carmine Gravino   University of Salerno, Italy
Helena Holmström Olsson   Malmö University, Sweden

Emilio Insfran	Universitat Politècnica de València, Spain
Andrea Janes	Free University of Bozen-Bolzano, Italy
Slinger Jansen	Utrecht University, The Netherlands
Eriks Klotins	Blekinge Institute of Technology, Sweden
Jil Klünder	University of Applied Sciences and FHDW Hannover, Germany
Marco Kuhrmann	Reutlingen University, Germany
Patricia Lago	Vrije Universiteit Amsterdam, The Netherlands
Jingyue Li	Norwegian University of Science and Technology, Norway
Xiaozhou Li	Free University of Bozen-Bolzano, Italy
Alessandro Marchetto	University of Trento, Italy
Antonio Martini	University of Oslo, Norway
Shinsuke Matsumoto	Osaka University, Japan
Daniel Mendez	Blekinge Institute of Technology and fortiss, Sweden
Manoel Mendonça	Federal University of Bahia, Brazil
Tommi Mikkonen	University of Jyväskylä, Finland
Sandro Morasca	Università degli Studi dell'Insubria, Italy
Maurizio Morisio	Politecnico di Torino, Italy
Jürgen Münch	Reutlingen University, Germany
Marc Oriol Hilari	Universitat Politècnica de Catalunya, Spain
Dietmar Pfahl	University of Tartu, Estonia
Rudolf Ramler	Software Competence Center Hagenberg GmbH, Austria
Filippo Ricca	Università di Genova, Italy
Daniel Rodríguez	University of Alcalá, Spain
Pilar Rodríguez	Universidad Politécnica de Madrid, Spain
Iflaah Salman	Lappeenranta-Lahti University of Technology, Finland
Stefan Sauer	University of Paderborn, Germany
Kari Smolander	Lappeenranta-Lahti University of Technology, Finland
Martin Solari	Universidad ORT Uruguay, Uruguay
Kari Systä	Tampere University, Finland
Paolo Tell	IT University of Copenhagen, Denmark

Program Committee - Short Research Papers

Srijita Basu	Chalmers University of Technology and University of Gothenburg, Sweden

Luigi Buglione   DXC Technology, Italy
Priscila Cedillo   Universidad de Cuenca, Ecuador
Panagiota Chatzipetrou   Örebro University, Sweden
Maya Daneva   University of Twente, The Netherlands
Jakob Droste   Leibniz Universität Hannover, Germany
Jens Heidrich   Fraunhofer IESE, Germany
Emanuel Agustin Irrazábal   Universidad Nacional del Nordeste, Argentina
Sushant Kumar Pandey   University of Groningen, The Netherlands
Sandeep Kumar   Indian Institute of Technology, Roorkee, India
Emilia Mendes   Aarhus University, Denmark
Thamizhiniyan Natarajan   University of Limerick, Ireland
Nicolas Paez   Universidad Nacional de Tres de Febrero,
                                         Argentina
Francis Palma   University of New Brunswick, Canada
Dietmar Pfahl   University of Tartu, Estonia
Sheila Reinehr   Pontifícia Universidade Católica do Paraná, Brazil
Daniel Rodríguez   University of Alcalá, Spain
Gleison Santos   Universidade Federal do Estado do Rio de
                                         Janeiro, Brazil
Faiz Ali Shah   University of Tartu, Estonia
Damiano Torre   University of Washington Tacoma, USA
Ehsan Zabardast   Nordea and Blekinge Institute of Technology,
                                         Sweden

Program Committee - Industry Papers

Thomas Bach   SAP, Germany
Ricardo Britto   Ericsson and Blekinge Institute of Technology,
                                         Sweden
Lukas Fischer   Software Competence Center Hagenberg GmbH,
                                         Austria
Stephan Flake   S&N CQM Consulting & Services GmbH,
                                         Germany
Helena Holmström Olsson   Malmö University, Sweden
Eriks Klotins   Blekinge Institute of Technology, Sweden
Lukas Linsbauer   ABB Corporate Research, Germany
Stefan Marksteiner   AVL List GmbH and Mälardalen University,
                                         Austria
Fredrik Milani   University of Tartu, Estonia
Torvald Mårtensson   Saab AB, Sweden
Antonio Piccinno   University of Bari, Italy

Rudolf Ramler	Software Competence Center Hagenberg GmbH, Austria
Daniel Rodríguez	University of Alcalá, Spain
Dag Sjøberg	University of Oslo, Norway
Anders Sundelin	Ericsson Mobile Financial Services AB and Blekinge Institute of Technology, Sweden
Sahar Tahvili	Einride AB, Sweden
Jan Van den Bergh	Hasselt University and tUL and iMinds, Belgium
Andreas Wübbeke	South Westphalia University of Applied Sciences, Germany
Ehsan Zabardast	Nordea and Blekinge Institute of Technology, Sweden

Additional Reviewers

Maria Fernanda Granda	Universidad de Cuenca, Ecuador
Marius Irgens	University of Oslo, Norway
Karthik Shivashankar	University of Oslo, Norway

Contents

Full Research Papers

Coverage Isn't Enough: SBFL-Driven Insights into Manually Created vs.
Automatically Generated Tests 3
Sasara Shimizu and Yoshiki Higo

AI Alignment for Ethical Compliance and Risk Mitigation in Industrial
Applications 20
*Rushali Gupta, Qunying Song, Matthias Wagner, Emelie Engström,
Emma Söderberg, Markus Borg, and Per Runeson*

In-House Experimentation Platforms Motivations, Implementation
Characteristics and Challenges 36
Nils Stotz and Paul Drews

Writing Aids for Agile Requirements Engineering - A Comparative Study
Between Natural Language Processing and Machine Learning 52
Fabian Gilson, Ella Calder, and Daniel Neal

A Robust LSTM-Based Test Selection Method for Self-Driving Cars 69
Ali Ihsan Güllü, Faiz Ali Shah, and Dietmar Pfahl

FOSS-Chain: Using Blockchain for Open Source Software License
Compliance 86
Kypros Iacovou, Georgia Kapitsaki, and Evangelia Vanezi

Improving the Writing Quality of User Stories: A Canonical Action
Research Study 102
Sabine Molenaar and Fabiano Dalpiaz

From Machine Learning Documentation to Requirements: Bridging
Processes with Requirements Languages 119
Yi Peng, Hans-Martin Heyn, and Jennifer Horkoff

Enhancing Python Code Maintainability Through Large Language
Model-Based Approaches 137
Karthik Shivashankar and Antonio Martini

xiv   Contents

Enhancing Software Maintainability Through LLM-Assisted Code
Refactoring   153
Tommaso Fulcini, Riccardo Coppola, Flavio Giobergia,
Amirali Changizi, Meelad Dashti, Kimia Dorrani,
Domenico Amalfitano, Damiano Distante, and Filippo Ricca

An Investigation of Low-Code Development Adoption in a Finnish IT
Consulting Firm   169
Dongmei Gao and Fabian Fagerholm

Serverless Adoption in Practice: A Socio-Technical Investigation
of Motivations, Challenges, and Strategies   186
Muhammad Hamza, Wardah Naeem Awan,
and Muhammad Waheed Sabir

Generative AI in Simulation-Based Test Environments for Large-Scale
Cyber-Physical Systems: An Industrial Study   203
Masoud Sadrnezhaad, José Antonio Hernández López,
Torvald Mårtensson, and Dániel Varró

Pipelines Under Pressure: An Empirical Study of Security
Misconfigurations of GitHub Workflows   220
Edoardo Riggio and Cesare Pautasso

Towards Effective Automation of Issue–Commit Link Recovery:
An Empirical Investigation   237
Risha Parveen, Zheying Zhang, Kari Systä, Terhi Kilamo, and Ali Mehraj

Policy-Driven Software Bill of Materials on GitHub: An Empirical Study   253
Oleksii Novikov, Davide Fucci, Oleksandr Adamov, and Daniel Mendez

Generating Business Process Models with Open Source Large Language
Models Using Instruction Tuning   269
Gökberk Çelikmasat, Atay Özgövde, and Fatma Başak Aydemir

Temporal Evolution of Architectural Complexity and Technical Debt
in Microservices: An Exploratory Case Study   285
Bhuwan Paudel, Javier Gonzalez-Huerta, and Ehsan Zabardast

Improving Behavior-Driven Development Scenarios: Empirical Evaluation
of a Quality Assessment Framework   303
Dillan Wyatt Sears, Konstantinos Tsilionis, and Yves Wautelet

Application of Large Language Models in Product Management:
A Systematic Literature Review 319
    Vitor Mori Serra, Jan Bosch, and Helena Holmström Olsson

Detecting Technical Debt in Source Code Changes Using Large Language
Models 334
    Merve Astekin, Arda Goknil, Sagar Sen, Simeon Tverdal, and Phu Nguyen

Towards Understanding Team Congestion in Large-Scale Software
Development 353
    Javier Gonzalez-Huerta and Ehsan Zabardast

Influence of LLM Prioritizations on Human Decisions in Requirements
Engineering 369
    Amna Pir Muhammad, Richard Berntsson Svensson, and Irum Inayat

Short Research Papers

Lab Package Development as a Means for Educating Software Engineering
Students 387
    Eliisabet Kaasik, Faiz Ali Shah, and Dietmar Pfahl

A Model-Driven Engineering Method for the Development of Digital Twins ... 397
    Emilio Carrión, Pedro Valderas, and Óscar Pastor

LLM-Based Multi-agent System for Intelligent Refactoring of Haskell
Code 408
    Shahbaz Siddeeq, Muhammad Waseem, Zeeshan Rasheed,
    Md Mahade Hasan, Jussi Rasku, Mika Saari, Henri Terho,
    Kalle Mäkelä, Kai-Kristian Kemell, and Pekka Abrahamsson

Learning Observability Tracing Through Experiential Learning 419
    Anders Sundelin

Privacy-Enhanced Software Design: Purpose-Aware UML Diagrams 429
    Evangelia Vanezi, Georgia Kapitsaki, and Anna Philippou

Requirements Communication at the Intersection Between RE and UX 440
    Anne Hess, Gerald Heller, Hartmut Schmitt, Cornelia Seraphin,
    and Oliver Karras

Architecture Degradation at Scale: Challenges and Insights from Practice 451
    Ehsan Zabardast, Bhuwan Paudel, and Javier Gonzalez-Huerta

From Scenario Selection to Simulation: Safety Testing of an Automated
Driving System 461
　Fauzia Khan, Ali Ihsan Gullu, Hina Anwar, and Dietmar Pfahl

Prompts as Software Engineering Artifacts: A Research Agenda
and Preliminary Findings 470
　Hugo Villamizar, Jannik Fischbach, Alexander Korn,
　Andreas Vogelsang, and Daniel Mendez

An Application of Program Mutations for Generating Negative Test
Scripts Mimicking Human Errors on Web Applications 479
　Tomoya Yamashita, Hirohisa Aman, Sousuke Amasaki,
　Tomoyuki Yokogawa, and Minoru Kawahara

MAPS-AI – A Tool for AI-Assisted Model-Driven Generation of IT
Project Plan and Scope 489
　Oksana Nikiforova, Rihards Bobkovs, Megija Krista Miļūne,
　Kristaps Babris, Oscar Pastor, and Jānis Grabis

Ticket-Augmented Just-In-Time Defect Prediction 498
　Emanuele Gentili, Daniele LaProva, and Davide Falessi

How Well Small Language Models Can Be Adapted for Software
Maintenance and Refactoring Tasks 506
　Gabija Asvydyte, Sushant Kumar Pandey, and Sivajeet Chand

Cost of Artificial Intelligence: A Survey in Finnish Software Companies 516
　Antti Klemetti, Anssi Sorvisto, Mikko Raatikainen,
　and Jukka K. Nurminen

Exploring the Performance of ML Model Size for Classification
in Relation to Energy Consumption 525
　Andreas Bexell, Lo Gullstrand Heander, Emma Söderberg, Sigrid Eldh,
　and Per Runeson

Towards Understanding the Developer Experience in Quantum Software
Development 533
　Ronja Heikkinen, Majid Haghparast, and Tommi Mikkonen

On the Use of Agentic Coding Manifests: An Empirical Study of Claude
Code 543
　Worawalan Chatlatanagulchai, Kundjanasith Thonglek, Brittany Reid,
　Yutaro Kashiwa, Pattara Leelaprute, Arnon Rungsawang,
　Bundit Manaskasemsak, and Hajimu Iida

Detecting and Characterizing Low and No Functionality Packages
in the NPM Ecosystem 552
    Napasorn Tevarut, Brittany Reid, Yutaro Kashiwa, Pattara Leelaprute,
    Arnon Rungsawang, Bundit Manaskasemsak, and Hajimu Iida

PostItFlow: An Early Study on Agent-Based Workflow for Enhancing
and Visualizing User Stories 561
    Oshani Weerakoon, Juuso Rytilahti, Tuomas Mäkilä, Erkki Kaila,
    and Shola Oyedeji

An Empirical Study of Security-Policy Related Issues in Open Source
Projects 571
    Rintaro Kanaji, Brittany Reid, Yutaro Kashiwa, Raula Gaikovina Kula,
    and Hajimu Iida

Author Index 581

Full Research Papers

Coverage Isn't Enough: SBFL-Driven Insights into Manually Created vs. Automatically Generated Tests

Sasara Shimizu$^{(\boxtimes)}$ and Yoshiki Higo

The University of Osaka, Osaka, Japan
`{simizu-s,higo}@ist.osaka-u.ac.jp`

Abstract. The testing phase is an essential part of software development, but manually creating test cases can be time-consuming. Consequently, there is a growing need for more efficient testing methods. To reduce the burden on developers, various automated test generation tools have been developed, and several studies have been conducted to evaluate the effectiveness of the tests they produce. However, most of these studies focus primarily on coverage metrics, and only a few examine how well the tests support fault localization—particularly using artificial faults introduced through mutation testing. In this study, we compare the SBFL (Spectrum-Based Fault Localization) score and code coverage of automatically generated tests with those of manually created tests. The SBFL score indicates how accurately faults can be localized using SBFL techniques. By employing SBFL score as an evaluation metric—an approach rarely used in prior studies on test generation—we aim to provide new insights into the respective strengths and weaknesses of manually created and automatically generated tests. Our experimental results show that automatically generated tests achieve higher branch coverage than manually created tests, but their SBFL score is lower, especially for code with deeply nested structures. These findings offer guidance on how to effectively combine automatically generated and manually created testing approaches.

Keywords: Automated test case generation · Spectrum-based Fault Localization · Mutation Testing · Code Coverage

1 Introduction

In software development, unit testing is essential for improving code quality and detecting bugs early. However, manually creating unit tests is time-consuming and challenging, especially under tight deadlines and limited human resources. In large-scale projects, achieving comprehensive test coverage is often impractical.

To address these challenges, various automated unit test generation tools have been developed. These tools analyze program code to automatically generate test cases, thereby reducing the burden on developers. Notable examples include EvoSuite [4], Randoop [10], and Agitar [1].

G. Scanniello et al. (Eds.): PROFES 2025, LNCS 16361, pp. 3–19, 2026.
https://doi.org/10.1007/978-3-032-12089-2_1

Recent advances in test generation have shown that combining different tools can improve fault detection [5]. Several studies have evaluated such tools from multiple perspectives, including code coverage, mutation score, and bug detection [12,15].

While automatically generated tests perform well in terms of coverage and mutation analysis, they often struggle to identify real faults. This has led to the suggestion that combining manually created and automatically generated tests yields better outcomes. For example, EvoSuite$_{Amp}$ [11], which leverages developer-written tests as seeds, has demonstrated improved fault detection, albeit at the cost of readability. Other studies have identified the limitations of test generation tools, such as challenges in object construction, large search spaces, and handling multithreaded code [6,17].

Spectrum-Based Fault Localization (SBFL) is a technique used to identify defect locations within a program. The SBFL score indicates how accurately faults can be localized using SBFL techniques. In the following sections, we refer to manually created tests as MC-tests and automatically generated tests as AG-tests.

While AG-tests have been widely studied, few works directly compare them with MC-tests using real-world programs. Moreover, their effectiveness has rarely been evaluated from the perspective of fault localization. In particular, no prior study has investigated the use of SBFL score derived from mutation-based artificial faults to compare these test types.

In this study, we compare MC-tests and AG-tests from two perspectives: SBFL score and code coverage. Our objective is to analyze the performance of each test type to identify their respective strengths and weaknesses. Through this comparison, we aim to provide insights into how MC-tests and AG-tests can be effectively combined and under what circumstances each is most appropriate.

We address the following research questions: **RQ1:**Which test type achieves better code coverage—AG-tests or MC-tests? **RQ2:** Which test type performs better in terms of SBFL score?

The results of RQ1 indicate that AG-tests are effective for testing simple conditional branches and structural patterns. They are particularly well suited for achieving broad coverage with minimal manual effort.

However, RQ2 reveals that high coverage does not necessarily imply effective fault localization. In particular, for code with deeply nested logic, the SBFL performance of AG-tests tends to degrade, and they are often outperformed by MC-tests. This suggests that simply maximizing coverage is insufficient. When code complexity increases, SBFL score tends to decline, limiting the utility of AG-tests.

These findings suggest that combining MC-tests with AG-tests can leverage the strengths of both, enabling the construction of more effective and comprehensive test suites.

2   Background

Herein, we describe the background and the research objectives of this study.

2.1   Unit Test

In software development, software testing is conducted to verify whether a program functions as intended. Software testing is performed at multiple stages, depending on the level of testing. Unit testing is performed on the smallest unit of code, such as functions or methods. Since this process is performed early in the development cycle, it helps to identify bugs and issues at an early stage. As a result, unit testing has become an essential practice in software development.

To improve the efficiency of unit testing, test automation frameworks are widely used. A test automation framework provides the necessary environment and utilities for writing and executing test cases. It offers features such as test execution automation and result reporting. For example, JUnit is a widely used test automation framework for Java and is supported by integrated development environments (IDEs) such as Eclipse and IntelliJ IDEA.

To conduct unit testing, a test suite corresponding to the target code must be prepared. A test suite is a collection of test cases designed to achieve specific testing objectives. On the other hand, a test case is the smallest unit of testing and consists of specific inputs to the target code and the expected results.

2.2   Automated Test Generation

Manually creating a unit test suite requires a significant amount of effort. To address this challenge, research has been conducted on automatic unit test generation. Notable tools in this field include EvoSuite and Randoop. In this study, we utilize EvoSuite [4].

EvoSuite is a tool designed to automatically generate unit tests for Java projects. It generates JUnit-format test suites for individual Java classes, leveraging exploratory approaches such as hybrid search, dynamic symbolic execution, and testability transformation to maximize code coverage. Initially, multiple random test cases are generated, which are then iteratively refined through exploratory approaches. The resulting test suite is minimized while maintaining coverage criteria, ensuring that the generated unit tests remain as concise as possible. EvoSuite has been widely used in existing research.

2.3   Research Objective

In this study, we compare tests created by developers with those generated by automated tools from two perspectives: SBFL (Spectrum-Based Fault Localization) score and code coverage. Our objective is to analyze the performance of manually created and automatically generated test cases to identify their respective strengths and weaknesses. By employing the SBFL score, which has rarely been addressed in previous research, we expect to reveal new insights into the characteristics of each testing approach.

Through this comparison, we aim to provide insights into how to effectively combine MC-tests and AG-tests and determine the appropriate scenarios for their use. Ultimately, this research is expected to help improve the test design process in software development environments.

3   Experiment Setup

Herein, we describe the research questions, the evaluation metrics, the target programs, and the experimental procedure used in this study.

3.1   Research Questions

In this experiment, we address the following research questions.

RQ1 Which tests perform better in code coverage between AG-tests and MC-tests?

RQ2 Which tests perform better in SBFL score between AG-tests and MC-tests?

3.2   Evaluation Metrics

This section explains the code coverage and SBFL score used as evaluation metrics.

Code Coverage. Code coverage is a metric that indicates the proportion of code exercised by tests. Coverage criteria define the methods used to measure this coverage, with statement coverage and branch coverage being among the most widely adopted. In this study, we employ both statement and branch coverage, as described below.

Statement Coverage: This metric measures the proportion of executable lines of code in the target code that are executed by the test suite. When calculating code coverage using statement coverage, the following formula is used:

$$\text{Statement Coverage} = \frac{\text{Number of lines executed by the test suite}}{\text{Number of executable lines in the target code}} \quad (1)$$

Branch coverage measures whether the test suite covers both the true and false outcomes of branch conditions within the target code. When calculating code coverage using branch coverage, the following formula is used:

$$\text{Branch Coverage} = \frac{\text{Number of branches executed by the test suite}}{\text{Number of branches in the target code}} \quad (2)$$

SBFL. One technique for estimating defect locations in a program is Spectrum-Based Fault Localization (SBFL) [16]. This technique makes use of execution path information recorded during test execution. The underlying idea is that statements executed in failed test cases are more likely to contain defects, while statements executed in successful test cases are less likely to be defective.

First, all tests are executed, and both the test results (pass/fail) and execution path information are recorded. Based on this information, a suspiciousness score, which indicates the likelihood of a statement containing a defect, is calculated for each statement. The suspiciousness score, $susp(s)$, is calculated using the Ochiai [2] formula, as shown in Eq. 3:

$$susp(s) = \frac{fail(s)}{\sqrt{totalFail \times (fail(s) + pass(s))}} \tag{3}$$

- $fail(s)$: the number of failed test cases that executed statement s
- $pass(s)$: the number of successful test cases that executed statement s
- $totalFail$: the total number of failed test cases

The suspiciousness score $susp(s)$ is computed for all statements, and statements with higher scores are more likely to contain defects.

SBFL Score. Sasaki et al. proposed SBFL Suitability [14], a metric that indicates how suitable a program is for Spectrum-Based Fault Localization (SBFL). The SBFL score is defined as the numerical value representing this suitability, ranging from 0 to 1, where higher values indicate greater suitability for SBFL.

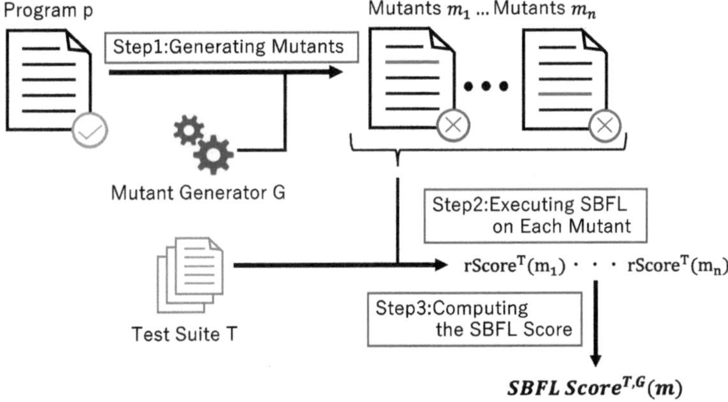

Fig. 1. How to get SBFL Score.

The SBFL score for a program p depends on the test suite T and the mutant generator G, and is denoted as $SBFLScore^{T,G}(p)$. Figure 1 illustrates the process of calculating the SBFL score, which consists of the following three steps:

Step1 Generating mutants from the program p
Step2 Executing SBFL on each mutant and ranking suspiciousness values of the artificial faults
Step3 Computing the SBFL score based on the rankings of the artificial faults in each mutant

Step1. Generating Mutants

A target program and its test suite are prepared. Mutants are generated using a mutant generator, with each mutant differing from the original program by only a single modification. Since there can be multiple modifiable locations in a program, multiple mutants are generated. The set of mutants generated by G from P is denoted as $M^G(P)$.

Step2. Executing SBFL on Mutants

SBFL is executed on each mutant in $M^G(P)$ using the test suite T, and the suspiciousness values for each statement are calculated. For a given mutant $m \in M^G(P)$, the following are defined:

- $susp^T(s)$: Suspiciousness value of statement s
- $rank^T(s)$: Rank of the suspiciousness value for statement s
- $rScore^T(s)$: Normalized rank of the suspiciousness value for statement s

The Ochiai formula is used to calculate suspiciousness values. We chose the Ochiai formula because it is one of the most widely used metrics in the field of SBFL. Many prior studies have demonstrated its effectiveness, and it has become a de facto standard in evaluating suspiciousness [13]. Therefore, in this study, we also adopt the Ochiai formula as a standard approach to ensure comparability with existing work.

The ranking of suspiciousness values is determined by sorting statements in descending order of suspiciousness. If two statements have the same highest suspiciousness value (e.g., two statements with $susp = 1.0$), they are both ranked second, and the next highest (e.g., $susp = 0.8$) is ranked third.

Since the meaning of rank values depends on the total number of statements, ranks are normalized within the range of 0 to 1. For example, ranking 10th out of 10 statements differs from ranking 10th out of 100 statements, with the latter having a higher significance. The normalized rank $rScore^T(s)$ of a statement s is computed as follows:

$$rScore^T(s) = 1 - \frac{rank^T(s) - 1}{totalStatements^T - 1} \tag{4}$$

where $totalStatements^T$ represents the total number of statements executed by test suite T. A value of 1 represents the highest rank (most useful), while 0 represents the lowest.

The normalized suspiciousness rank for a mutant m, denoted as $rScore^T(m)$, is defined as the normalized rank of the artificial fault statement s^m_{fault} within the mutant:

$$rScore^T(m) = rScore^T(s^m_{fault}) \tag{5}$$

Step3. Computing the SBFL Score

The SBFL score is computed as the average $rScore$ over all generated mutants in $|M^G(P)|$. The total number of mutants is denoted as $|M^G(P)|$, and the final SBFL score is calculated as:

$$SBFLScore^{T,G}(P) = \frac{1}{|M^G(P)|} \sum_{m \in M} rScore^T(m) \qquad (6)$$

A higher SBFL score indicates that the program is well-suited for fault localization using SBFL.

3.3 Experimental Targets

In this experiment, we measured statement and branch coverage as well as SBFL score for tests written in Java, and compared the test cases.

We used Defects4J (version 3.0.1) [7] for this experiment, a dataset that collects real-world bugs from Java projects. Defects4J contains buggy code, fixed code, and developer-created tests. We measured coverage and SBFL score on 167 datasets from the Lang and Math projects in Defects4J, which have few dependencies and can be compiled relatively easily.

3.4 Experimental Procedure

In this experiment, we compare MC-tests, which are the developer-written tests included in Defects4J, with AG-tests produced by EvoSuite (version 1.2.0). For each bug, AG-tests were generated for the fixed version of the class where the bug originally existed. Specifically, EvoSuite was run on the fixed code to ensure that generated tests could exercise the corrected behavior and reach all relevant code paths. The target classes were therefore the ones that contained bugs and had been fixed in Defects4J; these are the same classes used during test generation with EvoSuite.

We acknowledge that this procedure differs from the process developers follow when writing tests manually, as developers typically write tests against buggy or evolving code rather than a fully fixed version. Our choice to use the fixed version was intended to ensure that EvoSuite-generated tests would fully exercise the intended functionality and allow a fair evaluation of coverage and SBFL metrics. While this setup may not exactly mimic the original developer workflow, it provides a consistent basis for comparing AG-tests with MC-tests in terms of their coverage and fault localization effectiveness.

To evaluate the tests, we measured both code coverage and SBFL score. For coverage, we used JaCoCo[1], focusing on the class files where the bugs occurred and were fixed—that is, the same class files targeted by EvoSuite. We integrated JaCoCo using the Ant task framework provided by Defects4J. JaCoCo calculates both statement and branch coverage.

For mutation-based fault localization, we followed the procedure described in Sect. 3.2, Steps 1 through 3. Mutants were generated using Mutanerator[2], targeting the same fixed class files. The mutation operators used are listed in

---

[1] https://www.jacoco.org/jacoco/.
[2] https://github.com/kusumotolab/Mutanerator.

Table 1. Mutation operators

Mutation operators	Original conditional	Mutated conditional
Conditionals Boundary	`a<b`	`a<=b`
Increments	`n++`	`n--`
Invert Negatives	`-n`	`n`
Math	`a+b`	`a-b`
Negate Conditionals	`a==b`	`a!=b`
Void Method Calls	`method();`	`;`
Primitive Returns	`return 5;`	`return 0;`

Table 1. To obtain the information necessary for computing the SBFL score, we employed Gzoltar[3].

It should be clarified that Gzoltar itself is not specifically designed to directly provide the final SBFL score for our evaluation. Instead, Gzoltar is a tool for test execution and for calculating suspiciousness values of program elements. In our study, we used Gzoltar to obtain these suspiciousness values and ranking information, and then used this intermediate data to derive the SBFL score required for our evaluation.

For the MC-tests, the number of test cases ranged from 3 to 2,447, with a mean of 102.58. For the AG-tests, the number of test cases ranged from 4 to 642, with a mean of 112.14. Although the maximum size of the MC-tests was considerably larger due to a small number of outlier projects, the overall averages of the two types of test suites are comparable.

As for the mutation analysis, a total of 13,444 mutants were generated in our study. The mutation operators used are listed in Table 1.

Analysis Approach for RQ1. In RQ1, we measure coverage and visualize the overall results using box plots to compare AG-tests and MC-tests. Furthermore, we conduct the Wilcoxon signed-rank test to examine whether there is a statistically significant difference between the two types of tests. We also analyze specific examples of source code and test cases to better understand the differences between AG-tests and MC-tests.

Analysis Approach for RQ2. In RQ2, we perform the Wilcoxon signed-rank test on the overall results to investigate whether there is a statistically significant difference between the two types of tests. Additionally, we analyze the results for each generated mutant based on the nesting depth of the code. This includes visualization using box plots and calculation of the effect size r from the Wilcoxon test. Furthermore, we analyze the results by mutation operator and visualize the distributions using box plots.

---

[3] https://github.com/GZoltar/gzoltar.

4   Experimental Result

We compare and analyze the results of coverage and SBFL score for MC-tests and AG-tests.

4.1   RQ1: Coverage Comparison Results

Bugs that failed to build in Java 11 were excluded. As a result, coverage data was obtained for 133 out of 167 bugs.

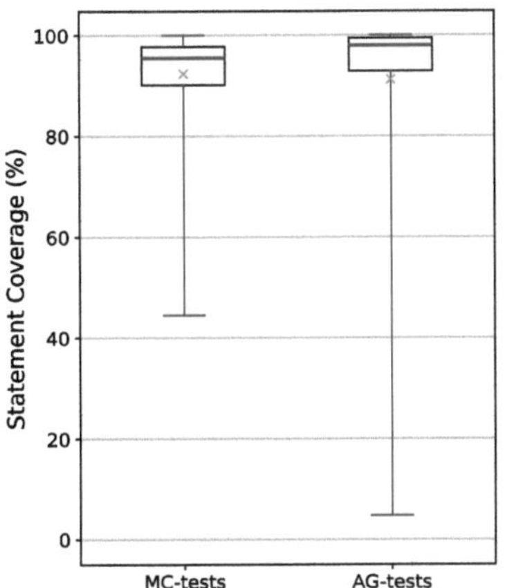

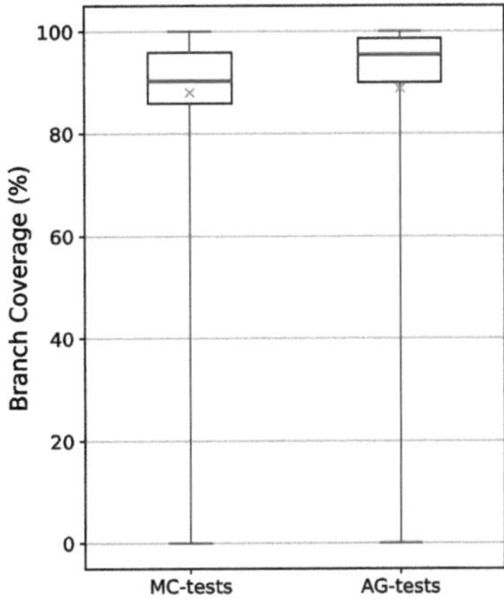

Fig. 2. Statement Coverage Comparison.

Fig. 3. Branch Coverage Comparison.

The results of statement coverage are shown in Fig. 2, and those of branch coverage are shown in Fig. 3. The average coverage values are summarized in Table 2. The red line in each box plot represents the median, while the cross mark ($\times$) indicates the mean. For statement coverage, the range of values is wider for AG-tests than for MC-tests. In contrast, branch coverage shows no significant difference between the two.

Table 2. Comparison of average coverage

	MC-tests	AG-tests
Statement Coverage (%)	92.3	91.0
Branch Coverage (%)	87.9	88.7

We conducted a Wilcoxon signed-rank test to examine whether there were statistically significant differences between MC-tests and AG-tests in terms of statement and branch coverage. The test yielded a p-value of 0.19 for statement coverage and 0.030 for branch coverage. Thus, there was no significant difference in statement coverage, while a significant difference was found in branch coverage.

Furthermore, we conducted a one-sided Wilcoxon signed-rank test for branch coverage, setting the null hypothesis that AG-tests are not superior to MC-tests, and the alternative hypothesis that AG-tests are superior. The result yielded a p-value of 0.015, leading to the rejection of the null hypothesis at the 5% significance level. Therefore, AG-tests significantly outperformed MC-tests in branch coverage.

To further interpret these results, the distinction between statement and branch coverage is important. The absence of a significant difference in statement coverage indicates that both MC-tests and AG-tests are generally effective at covering executable lines of code. However, the significant difference in branch coverage suggests that AG-tests have a particular advantage in covering both true and false paths of conditional statements. Therefore, AG-tests tend to explore a wider set of branch conditions, leading to higher branch coverage even when statement coverage is comparable.

We examined the source code of bugs where MC-tests achieved higher coverage and those where AG-tests had higher coverage. Additionally, we compared the number of MC-tests and AG-tests cases.

Code 1.1. Code of bugID Math-6

```
1   public class LevenbergMarquardtOptimizer
2       extends AbstractLeastSquaresOptimizer {
3       ...
4       @Override
5       protected PointVectorValuePair doOptimize() {
6           checkParameters();
7           final int nR = getTarget().length;
8           final double[] currentPoint = getStartPoint();
9           final int nC = currentPoint.length;
10      ...
```

In the Math project, bug ID 6 exhibits a significant difference in coverage between the MC-tests and AG-tests. The MC-tests achieve 94% statement coverage and 86% branch coverage. In contrast, the AG-tests achieve only 10% statement coverage and 9% branch coverage, resulting in a coverage difference of over 77%. According to the source code (Code 1.1), the issue is caused by a failure to properly set the required `OptimizationData` for the `doOptimize()` method. Although `doOptimize()` is invoked directly, the required data is missing, which results in a `NullPointerException`. Similar large differences (over 77%) are observed for Math-38, Math-64, and Math-68, all of which involve the `doOptimize()` method. This result is consistent with the problem of object construction described in the existing study [6].

Our answer to RQ1 is that AG-tests outperform MC-tests in terms of branch coverage.

4.2   RQ2: SBFL Score Comparison Results

Tests that failed to build in Java 11 were excluded. As a result, SBFL score was obtained for 157 out of 167 bug IDs. The average SBFL score was 0.683 for manually created tests and 0.640 for generated tests.

We conducted a Wilcoxon signed-rank test to evaluate whether there was a statistically significant difference in SBFL score between MC-tests and AG-tests. The test yielded a p-value of 0.027, indicating a significant difference between the two test types.

Furthermore, we performed a one-sided Wilcoxon signed-rank test under the alternative hypothesis that MC-tests outperform AG-tests. The result yielded a p-value of 0.013, leading to the rejection of the null hypothesis at the 5% significance level. Therefore, we conclude that MC-tests significantly outperform AG-tests in terms of SBFL score.

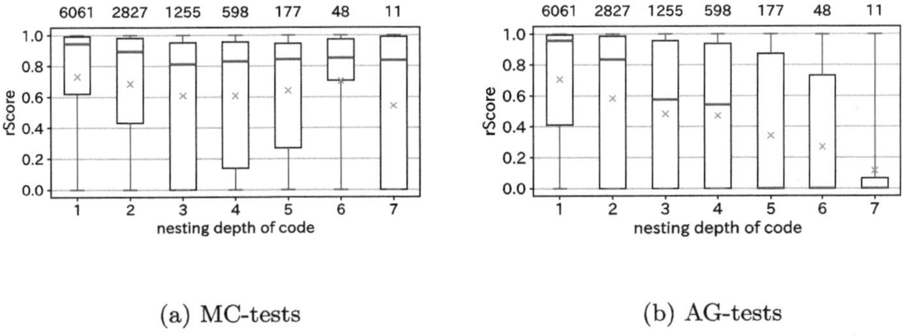

(a) MC-tests   (b) AG-tests

Fig. 4. Relationship between $rScore$ and nesting depth of code.

Figures 4a and b show box plots illustrating the relationship between the nesting depth of mutated code and the $rScore$. The plots correspond to MC-tests and AG-tests, respectively. The x-axis represents the nesting depth, while the y-axis shows the value of $rScore^T(s)$, calculated using Eq. 4, which is used in computing the SBFL score. The value $rScore^T(s)$ indicates the accuracy with which the bug location in each mutant was identified. The total number of data points is 10,977, and the number of elements for each nesting depth is shown at the top of the graph. When focusing on the medians, we observe that in MC-tests, the median remains nearly constant regardless of the nesting depth. In contrast, the median in AG-tests tends to decrease as the nesting depth increases.

We conducted Wilcoxon signed-rank tests at each nesting depth to examine whether the differences in $rScore$ between MC-tests and AG-tests were statistically significant. Additionally, we calculated the effect size r-value for each nesting level, as shown in Table 3. The effect size r-value indicates the magnitude of the observed difference, with larger absolute values representing a stronger effect. As shown in Table 3, the difference in $rScore$ between MC-tests and AG-tests tends to increase with greater nesting depth. This suggests that AG-tests become less effective at accurately identifying faults in deeply nested code structures.

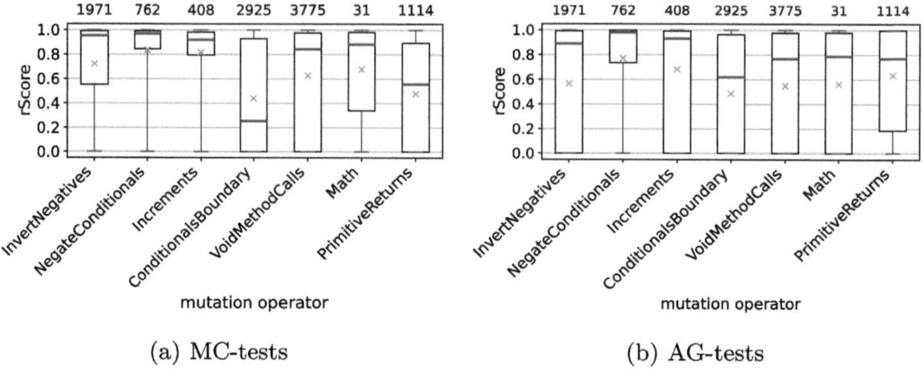

(a) MC-tests   (b) AG-tests

Fig. 5. Relationship between $rScore$ and mutation operators.

Figures 5a and b show box plots for MC-tests and AG-tests, respectively, illustrating the relationship between $rScore$ and the applied mutation operators. Examples of the modifications introduced by each mutation operator are provided in Table 1. When focusing on the medians, we observed a notable difference between MC-tests and AG-tests for the ConditionalsBoundary mutation operator.

Our answer to RQ2 is that MC-tests perform better than AG-tests in SBFL score.

5   Discussion

From the results of RQ1, we found that there was no significant difference between MC-tests and AG-tests in terms of statement coverage. Moreover, AG-tests achieved higher branch coverage than MC-tests. On the other hand, the results of RQ2 revealed that AG-tests tended to yield lower SBFL score compared to MC-tests. Furthermore, the difference in SBFL score between AG-tests and MC-tests increased as the nesting depth of the code became deeper, indicating that AG-tests became less effective for fault localization in deeply nested code.

Table 3. r-value at each nesting depth

Depth of nest	1	2	3	4	5	6	7
r-value	−0.095	0.12	0.21	0.28	0.55	0.67	0.65

These findings highlight a fundamental difference in the strengths of MC-tests and AG-tests, indicating that each has distinct advantages depending on the structure of the code being tested. While AG-tests are effective in achieving high coverage—particularly for simple conditions and control-flow patterns—they often struggle with fault localization in deeply nested or semantically complex code.

In contrast, MC-tests—crafted with human insight and an understanding of the program's intent—tend to perform better in fault localization, especially in structurally complex scenarios. These tests are often designed to target edge cases, semantic nuances, or logically challenging paths that automated tools may overlook.

This trend underscores the limitations of automated test generation, which primarily targets structural coverage but may fail to produce semantically meaningful test cases in complex contexts.

These findings suggest that neither MC-tests nor AG-tests alone are sufficient. Rather, an effective testing strategy should adopt a hybrid approach that leverages the strengths of both.

- AG-tests are well-suited to achieving broad coverage in shallow or syntactically simple code.
- MC-tests are crucial for fault localization in complex or deeply nested code, where human reasoning can more effectively guide test design.
- A combined strategy allows testers to balance efficiency (through automation) and diagnostic power (through manual insight), resulting in more reliable and informative test suites.

Future work should explore intelligent test generation frameworks that dynamically analyze the structural and semantic characteristics of the code and recommend an optimal mix of MC-tests and AG-tests. Such adaptive strategies could significantly improve both testing efficiency and fault localization accuracy.

6   Threats to Validity

In this section, we discuss the potential threats to the validity of our study and describe the measures taken to mitigate them.

6.1   Internal Validity

Our results may be influenced by factors such as the selection of EvoSuite configuration options, the parameters used for mutant generation, and the process of test execution. We used the default settings for EvoSuite and Mutanerator to ensure reproducibility; however, different configurations or versions may yield different results. Additionally, the quality of developer-written tests in Defects4J may vary from project to project, potentially affecting the fairness of the comparison.

6.2 External Validity

The generalizability of our findings may be limited by the scope of our experimental subjects. We focused on two Java projects (Lang and Math) from the Defects4J dataset, which may not represent all types of real-world software. Furthermore, we considered only Java programs and one automatically test generation tool (EvoSuite). Our conclusions may not directly extend to other programming languages, software domains, or test generation tools.

6.3 Construct Validity

The study uses code coverage (statement and branch coverage) and the SBFL score as evaluation metrics. While these are widely used and accepted metrics, they may not capture all aspects of test effectiveness, such as the ability to detect real faults or the maintainability of the test suites. In addition, the SBFL score, while providing insight into fault localization suitability, does not necessarily reflect real-world debugging effort or developer productivity.

6.4 Conclusion Validity

We applied statistical tests (Wilcoxon signed-rank test) to compare MC-tests and AG-tests. However, the statistical power of these tests may be limited by the sample size and the characteristics of the datasets used. The possibility of Type I and Type II errors remains, and the conclusions should be interpreted with caution.

Despite these threats, we believe that our study provides useful insights into the comparative strengths and weaknesses of manually and automatically generated test suites. Future work should include a broader range of projects, tools, and evaluation metrics to further strengthen the validity and generalizability of the findings.

7 Related Work

Fraser et al. investigated the extent to which multiple test automation tools can help identify fault locations [5]. Their study focused on three tools: Randoop, EvoSuite, and Agitar [1]. The results showed that while each tool individually detected no more than 19.9% of faults, the combined use of these tools allowed for the detection of 55.7% of faults. This highlights the complementary nature of different tools in improving fault detection effectiveness.

In line with this idea of complementarity, Serra et al. conducted a comparative study between manually created test cases (MC-tests) and automatically generated test cases [15]. Their evaluation involved tests generated by EvoSuite, Randoop, and JTExpert [12], and was conducted from three perspectives: code coverage, mutation score, and bug detection capability. The results revealed that automatically generated tests performed well in terms of coverage and mutation score, but fell short compared to manually created tests in detecting real bugs. The authors suggested that combining MC-tests and automatically generated tests could help mitigate the limitations of each.

Building on this notion, Roslan et al. proposed an enhanced version of Evo-Suite, called EvoSuite$_{Amp}$, which uses developer-written tests as seeds to guide test amplification [11]. In a comparative evaluation with DSpot across 42 versions in the Defects4J dataset, EvoSuite$_{Amp}$ achieved higher mutation scores and killed more mutants in many cases. However, the generated tests were often large and suffered from reduced readability, indicating a trade-off between test strength and maintainability.

In addition to improvements in methodology, several studies have investigated the limitations of current test generation tools. Herlim et al. conducted an empirical study on EvoSuite using the SBFT 2020 tool competition benchmark [6]. They analyzed the branches that EvoSuite failed to cover and classified the causes into four categories: object construction issues, object-oriented design constraints, large search spaces, and miscellaneous issues. This classification highlighted the technical challenges that limit EvoSuite's coverage.

Watanabe et al. further examined how the structure of the program under test affects the effectiveness of automatically generated test suites [17]. Their study analyzed test suites generated by EvoSuite and identified four main causes of low coverage: specific value requirements, type constraints, unreachable code, and multi-threaded processing. While they proposed mitigation strategies such as inserting dummy branches, they noted that challenges like multi-threaded processing would require improvements in the test generation tools themselves.

More recently, large language models (LLMs) have emerged as a novel approach to test generation. Bhatia et al. explored the use of ChatGPT to generate unit tests for Python programs and compared its performance to that of Pynguin [3] [8]. Their evaluation considered coverage, accuracy, and readability. ChatGPT achieved coverage comparable to or better than Pynguin in some cases but produced incorrect assertions in approximately one-third of the generated tests. Moreover, the uncovered statements differed significantly between the two tools, suggesting that combining them could improve overall test suite completeness.

Finally, some studies have investigated the downstream impact of test suite composition. Matsuda et al. examined how the composition of test cases affects the performance of automated program repair [9]. They manipulated test suites for five types of bug patterns and evaluated the number and correctness of generated patches, as well as the time required for repair. Their findings indicated that adjusting the ratio of passing and failing test cases according to the bug type is critical, and that increasing the number of successful test cases was particularly effective in preventing overfitting during repair.

8   Conclusion

In this study, we compared the SBFL score and coverage of manually created tests and automatically generated tests. We used Java projects from the open-source repository Defects4J, employing developer-created test cases as MC-tests and EvoSuite for automated test generation.

The objective of this study was to compare manually created and automatically generated tests from two perspectives: coverage and SBFL score, in order to identify their respective strengths and weaknesses. Through this comparison, we aimed to gain insights into how MC-tests and AG-tests should be combined and in what scenarios each should be utilized.

This study reveals that MC-tests and AG-tests exhibit different strengths depending on the complexity of the code. While AG-tests are effective at achieving high coverage in simple code, they are less reliable for fault localization when applied to deeply nested structures. In contrast, MC-tests perform better in such complex scenarios, thanks to human reasoning and contextual understanding.

These findings suggest that an effective testing strategy should combine both approaches. AG-tests contribute to broad structural coverage, whereas MC-tests improve diagnostic accuracy. Future work should focus on developing tools that can intelligently suggest the appropriate balance between MC-tests and AG-tests, based on the structural and semantic characteristics of the code.

Acknowledgments. This research was supported by JSPS KAKENHI Japan (JP24H00692, JP23K24823, JP22K11985)

References

1. Agitar one. http://www.agitar.com/solutions/products/automated_junit_generation.html (2014). Accessed 08 Jan 2024
2. Abreu, R., Zoeteweij, P., Van Gemund, A.J.: An evaluation of similarity coefficients for software fault localization. In: 2006 12th Pacific Rim International Symposium on Dependable Computing, PRDC 2006, pp. 39–46 (2006)
3. Bhatia, S., Gandhi, T., Kumar, D., Jalote, P.: Unit test generation using generative AI: a comparative performance analysis of autogeneration tools. In: Proceedings of the 1st International Workshop on Large Language Models for Code, LLM4Code 2024, pp. 54–61. Association for Computing Machinery, New York, NY, USA (2024)
4. Fraser, G., Arcuri, A.: Evosuite: automatic test suite generation for object-oriented software. In: Proceedings of the 19th ACM SIGSOFT Symposium on Foundations of Software Engineering, SIGSOFT/FSE 2011, pp. 416–419, November 2011
5. Fraser, G., Staats, M., McMinn, P., Arcuri, A., Padberg, F.: Does automated unit test generation really help software testers? A controlled empirical study. ACM Trans. Softw. Eng. Methodol. **24**, 1–49 (2015)
6. Herlim, R.S., Hong, S., Kim, Y., Kim, M.: Empirical study of effectiveness of evosuite on the SBST 2020 tool competition benchmark. In: Search-Based Software Engineering: 13th International Symposium, SSBSE 2021, Bari, Italy, 11–12 October 2021, Proceedings, pp. 121–135. Springer-Verlag, Heidelberg (2021)
7. Just, R., Jalali, D., Ernst, M.D.: Defects4J: a database of existing faults to enable controlled testing studies for java programs. In: Proceedings of the 2014 International Symposium on Software Testing and Analysis, ISSTA 2014ISSTA 2014, pp. 437–440. Association for Computing Machinery, New York, NY, USA (2014)

8. Lukasczyk, S., Fraser, G.: Pynguin: automated unit test generation for Python. In: Proceedings of the ACM/IEEE 44th International Conference on Software Engineering: Companion Proceedings, ICSE '22, pp. 168–172. Association for Computing Machinery, New York, NY, USA (2022)
9. Matsuda, N., Maruyama, K.: Investigation of the impact of test cases on automated bug fixes. Comput. Softw. **37**(4), 31–37 (in Japanese)
10. Pacheco, C., Ernst, M.D.: Randoop: feedback-directed random testing for Java. In: Companion to the 22nd ACM SIGPLAN Conference on Object-Oriented Programming Systems and Applications Companion, OOPSLA '07, pp. 815–816. Association for Computing Machinery, New York, NY, USA (2007)
11. Roslan, M.F., Rojas, J.M., McMinn, P.: An empirical comparison of EvoSuite and DSpot for improving developer-written test suites with respect to mutation score. In: Papadakis, M., Vergilio, S.R. (eds.) Search-Based Software Engineering, pp. 19–34. Springer, Cham (2022)
12. Sakti, A., Pesant, G., Guéhéneuc, Y.G.: Instance generator and problem representation to improve object oriented code coverage. IEEE Trans. Softw. Eng. **41**(3), 294–313 (2015)
13. Sarhan, Q.I., Besz des, A.: A survey of challenges in spectrum-based software fault localization. IEEE Access **10**, 10618–10639 (2022)
14. Sasaki, Y., Higo, Y., Matsumoto, S., Kusumoto, S.: SBFL-suitability: a software characteristic for fault localization. In: 2020 IEEE International Conference on Software Maintenance and Evolution (ICSME), pp. 702–706 (2020)
15. Serra, D., Grano, G., Palomba, F., Ferrucci, F., Gall, H.C., Bacchelli, A.: On the effectiveness of manual and automatic unit test generation: ten years later. In: 2019 IEEE/ACM 16th International Conference on Mining Software Repositories (MSR), pp. 121–125 (2019)
16. Souza, H., Chaim, M., Kon, F.: Spectrum-based software fault localization: a survey of techniques, advances, and challenges, July 2016
17. Watanabe, R., Higo, Y., Kusumoto, S.: Impacts of program structures on code coverage of generated test suites. In: Product-Focused Software Process Improvement: 24th International Conference (PROFES), pp. 355–362 (2023). https://doi.org/10.1007/978-3-031-49266-2_24

AI Alignment for Ethical Compliance and Risk Mitigation in Industrial Applications

Rushali Gupta$^{(\boxtimes)}$, Qunying Song, Matthias Wagner,
Emelie Engström, Emma Söderberg, Markus Borg, and Per Runeson

Department of Computer Science, Lund University, P.O. Box 118, 221 00 Lund,
Sweden
`rushali.gupta@cs.ith.se`

Abstract. *Context:* AI technologies are increasingly embedded in products and software engineering processes of industrial IoT, autonomous systems, and cyber-physical systems. It is therefore essential to ensure alignment with safety, reliability, and ethical standards. However, practical software engineering methods for managing misalignment risks remain underdeveloped. *Objective:* This study aims to explore industry awareness of misalignment risks and current practices for monitoring them within real-world software engineering contexts. *Method:* We conducted seven interviews with industry professionals to examine perceptions of misalignment risks, gather insights into existing practices, and understand approaches to alignment across various industrial settings. Three recently proposed taxonomies guided our discussions: one on ethical guidelines for trustworthy AI published by the EU, another summarizing identified AI risks, and a third addressing "double-edged components" (aspects of AI systems that can simultaneously yield positive and negative effects.) *Results:* Our analysis identified common misalignment risks across these settings and revealed limited use of dedicated testing or monitoring for AI alignment. Most organizations rely on general oversight rather than specialized tools. *Conclusion:* These findings highlight the need to develop tailored governance practices for alignment in industrial software engineering settings.

Keywords: AI alignment · ethics · testing

1 Introduction

The use of AI in industry is widespread and is growing at a fast pace. Recent studies have reported the success of using AI in various application domains, such as automotive, healthcare, and industry automation, to perform a wide range of tasks [19]. However, the extensive adoption of AI in different domains also raises general ethical concerns regarding, for example, their technical robustness, safety, transparency, privacy, fairness, and accountability [7,17].

G. Scanniello et al. (Eds.): PROFES 2025, LNCS 16361, pp. 20–35, 2026.
https://doi.org/10.1007/978-3-032-12089-2_2

AI alignment refers to how well an AI system aligns with the values and intentions of its stakeholders [12]. Essentially, AI alignment aims to ensure that AI systems' goals and behaviors reflect human values and ethical principles [9, 18]. How those values are incorporated in industrial applications is reported to a very limited extent, the level of awareness is unclear, and information is missing about countermeasures to mitigate misalignment risks.

The objective of this expert judgment study [23] is to explore AI alignment from the point of view of industry practitioners and to identify potential risks of AI misalignment in their products and development processes. To achieve this goal, we interviewed seven practitioners from six companies in a wide range of industry domains. We structured the interviews around three existing frameworks related to AI alignment, 1) the ethical guidelines for trustworthy AI by the European Commission's high-level expert group on AI [7], 2) a domain taxonomy of AI risks [21], and 3) factors related to AI components' *double edge* [12]. Specifically, we looked into which ethical requirements are perceived the most important and challenging, which alignment risks are most relevant and how risk factors and related misalignment are perceived. In addition, we explored current practices in relation to the monitoring and testing of AI misalignment. The following four research questions guided the study:

RQ1 Which of the key requirements for trustworthy AI [7], are considered most important and most challenging in different application context?
RQ2 Which AI misalignment risks [21] have been identified already and what could be other potential misalignment risks?
RQ3 How can double-edge components [12] be identified, i.e., which characteristics of the AI systems are considered risky from an AI alignment perspective and which are the unintended potential misaligned behaviors due to these risks?
RQ4 How can you assess or measure AI misalignment risks?

The contributions of this paper are threefold. First, we demonstrate the practical application of three recently proposed frameworks for reasoning about AI alignment [7, 12, 21], using real-world software engineering cases to illustrate their utility and limitations in industry contexts. Second, by applying these frameworks to seven real-world cases, we explore specific alignment risks within practical software engineering contexts. Third, we identify current gaps in industry practices for testing and monitoring AI misalignment risks, noting a reliance on basic statistical checks and human oversight. This highlights the need for dedicated tools and methods as AI alignment practices evolve.

2   Background and Related Work

The study of human values originates from cognitive and social psychology and is explanatory (empirical) in nature. Ethics on the other hand originates from moral philosophy and is normative (analytical/theoretical) in nature. Both deal with questions of what is good and valuable, but with different purposes. Studies of human values are often descriptive, explaining what is valued by individuals and cultures, while ethics is prescriptive, providing normative guidelines on how people should act. Digital transformation, such as AI, impacts both fields [15].

Several ethical guidelines have been developed related to AI [7,13]. Similarly, many frameworks have been proposed to support reasoning about AI alignment [5,7,11], AI risks [21], and levels of AI alignment [11]. A few initiatives, to support the incorporation of ethics and measurement of value alignment in the software engineering process, have also been taken [8]. Ferrario and Winter introduced practical tools to obtain and measure human values in software engineering [8]. The Values Q-Sort (V-QS) tool can help participants prioritize values specific to AI alignment. Hou and Green proposed a framework to address the complex and multi-faceted challenge of aligning AI systems with human values and ethical principles at various levels of society [11]. The framework addresses the ethical implications of AI actions and decisions, aiming to ensure that AI systems contribute positively to the society and do not cause harm.

In this study, we used the following three existing frameworks to explore AI alignment based on their relevance and comprehensiveness.

Ethical Guidelines for Trustworthy AI by EU. EU published its guidelines on ethics in AI in 2019, targeting a 'human-centric' approach for AI with respect to European values and principles [7]. The guidelines set seven key ethical requirements recommended for designing, implementing, deploying, and using AI: *Human agency and oversight, Technical robustness and safety, Privacy and data governance, Transparency, Accountability, Diversity, non-discrimination, fairness*, and *Environmental and societal well-being*.

Domain Taxonomy of AI Risks. Slattery et al. performed a systematic review and extracted 777 AI risks from 43 taxonomies [21]. The extracted AI risks are then classified into 7 domains: *Discrimination and toxicity, Privacy and security, Misinformation, Malicious actors and misuse, Human-computer interaction, Socioeconomic and environmental harms*, and *AI system safety, failures and limitations*. These domains are then further structured into 23 subdomains, using experts and a best-fit approach. Unlike the EU guidelines [7], which represents a top-down approach and sets the ethical recommendations for trustworthy AI, this domain taxonomy is synthesized in a bottom-up manner and classifies the risks associated with AI. Nevertheless, they share significant similarities and overlapping themes, such as discrimination, privacy, safety, and societal and environmental concerns.

Double Edge Components. Ji et al. [12] provide a comprehensive survey of alignment research, highlighting key failure modes such as reward hacking, goal misgeneralization, and feedback-induced misalignment. They introduce the concept of double edge components, i.e. features like situational awareness and broadly scoped goals that enhance AI capabilities but also increase misalignment risks. For example, an AI system might take undesirable actions to achieve human happiness, such as persuading individuals to take on high-pressure jobs. In our study, we refer to AI capabilities increasing misalignment risks: *Situational awareness, Broadly scoped goals, Mesa-optimization objectives*, and *Access*

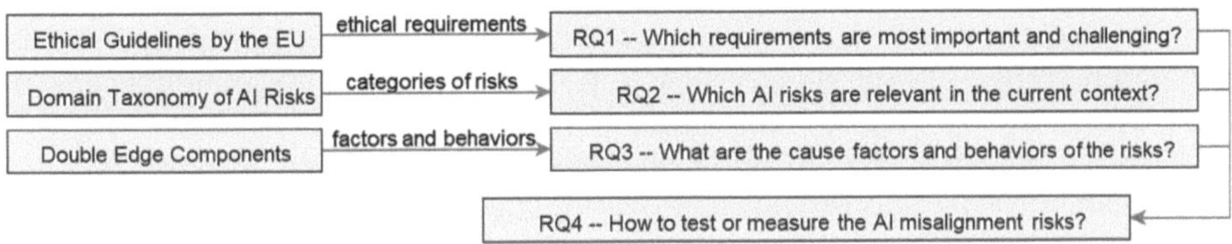

Fig. 1. An overview of relations between the frameworks used and research questions.

to increased resources; and potential misaligned behaviors: *Power-seeking behaviors, Untruthful output, Violation of ethics, Deceptive alignment and manipulation resources*, and *Collectively harmful behaviors*.

These frameworks are complementary and support in exploring different perspectives of AI alignment, as illustrated in Fig. 1. Specifically, the EU guidelines [7] present visions and ethical considerations for trustworthy AI. The domain taxonomy of Slattery et al. [21] collects and classifies the risks posed by AI in a domain taxonomy. The double edge components work by Ji et al. [12] provides a framework of the causing factors and possible behaviors of AI misalignment risks.

The companies in our study engage mainly in domains of advanced IoT and autonomous systems, where alignment is essential for safety and reliability. These systems are often collectively referred to as Cyber-Physical Systems (CPS). The challenges of double-edge components introduced by Ji et al. [12] are particularly relevant in CPS, where the integration of software and hardware components increases the complexity of alignment. In our study, we explored how these theoretical risks were perceived in practice. Radanliev et al. [19] present a conceptual framework for analyzing the evolution of AI decision-making in CPS, highlighting the risk of integrating AI with such systems. Our study complements their work by providing empirical insights into how practitioners approach alignment in CPS contexts. Alexandra et al. [1] review the use of AI in CPS applications in water management and governance, arguing that integrating the social and ecosystem dimensions will be essential in the design of smart and sustainable CPS in this context. Although their work focuses on water governance, the challenges they highlight apply to many CPS domains, stressing the need for alignment in complex, multi-stakeholder settings. Our study further explores how practitioners address similar challenges in other CPS contexts.

AI alignment involves addressing both ethical and practical challenges to ensure that systems behave as intended while minimizing risks. Ji et al. [12] highlight ethical dimensions such as fairness, interpretability, and accountability through their RICE framework (Robustness, Interpretability, Controllability, Ethicality). Kamila and Jasrotia [14] explore these issues through a grounded-theory approach, identifying five major ethical concerns: *Privacy and security, Bias and fairness, Trust and reliability, Transparency*, and *Human-AI interactions*. However, their work addresses general AI applications and does not focus on domain-specific challenges in CPS. Bruinsma et al. [3] analyze the framing of AI risks in Swedish media, highlighting the growing focus on short-term risks, such as the ethical implications of generative AI, since the release of ChatGPT.

They highlight a gap in political engagement compared to academic and industrial actors, reflecting the uneven distribution of responsibility in addressing AI risks. Our study investigates how ethical and practical challenges are perceived by industry practitioners. In addition, we provide empirical insights into the concrete monitoring and testing practices of such challenges.

Testing and monitoring practices are critical for ensuring the alignment of AI systems in CPS. Existing techniques often fail to address the unique challenges posed by AI-enabled systems, necessitating the development of new approaches. Song et al. [22] reveal shortcomings in the testing of CPS, particularly when evaluating AI controllers based on state-of-the-art deep reinforcement learning methods against traditional controllers. Our study builds on their findings by exploring how practitioners adapt existing testing techniques or develop new approaches to ensure alignment in real-world CPS projects.

Arrieta et al. [2] present a preliminary evaluation of how deep learning faults affect CPS in operation, using a robot as a case study. Their results suggest that such faults are more difficult to detect in operation than in off-line testing. Their work highlights the need for empirical insights into how practitioners address these gaps, particularly in operational contexts where alignment challenges manifest differently. Our study contributes to addressing this gap by exploring how practitioners manage and mitigate such issues in practice.

3   Research Method

We launched an expert judgment study [23] and selected interviewees based on their roles and their companies' experience and characteristics. The primary data collection method is semi-structured interviews [20] and the analysis is based primarily on categorical coding [6].

The study was conducted in the context of a recently started industry-academia collaboration program with 15 corporate and non-profit partners, which our university is leading. The scope of this 10-year program is next-generation communication and computational infrastructures and applications (NextG2Com). The application domains include telecommunications, robotics, healthcare, production, automotive, and rescue operations.

3.1   Data Collection

We designed an interview guide (publicly available on Zenodo [10]), comprising 15 semi-structured questions. The interview guide also included short presentations of the frameworks. We conducted a pilot interview with a practitioner to make sure the interview questions are relevant and comprehensible. Based on the feedback from the pilot interview, we then iterated the interview questions and interview instrument design.

We conducted seven semi-structured interviews during September 2024 online via Microsoft Teams. As shown in Table 1. We reached out to our contact network for recommendation of their best candidates, working with AI-related projects

Table 1. Overview of the interviewees and companies involved in this study. A unique identifier is assigned to each interviewee (PID) and company (CID). AI application purposes refer to the intentions an AI application (developed by the interviewee's company) is designed for. Company industry and size (the two rightmost columns) are adopted from their LinkedIn profiles.

PID	Role	AI Application Purposes	CID	Industry	Size
P1	Lead Architect AI Engineering	Transportation, Software Engineering	C1	Software Development	10,001+
P2	Head of Engineering Excellence	Transportation			
P3	Principal Technology	Cybersecurity, Other	C2	Semiconductor Manufacturing	1,001–5,000
P4	Director of Vision and AI Systems,	Wireless Communication, Software Engineering, Other	C3	Wireless Communication	10,001+
P5	Manager	Software Engineering	C4	Automation Machinery Manufacturing	201–500
P6	CEO and co-founder	Transportation, Other	C5	Software Development	11–50
P7	Manager	Production, Other	C6	Packaging and Containers	10,001+

and knowledgeable about AI alignment. We selected the seven interviewees from six companies, based on their interest and availability, covering a wide range of industry domains and company sizes. In particular, four of them were directly or indirectly involved in the discussion of AI risks, ethics, governance, or policy making. Among the interviewees, two have a role in development/design, and five in management. They work with AI applications designed to serve different purposes. The interviews, conducted in English, had an average duration of approximately 55 min.

Before the scheduled interviews, materials to pre-read and a consent form were sent to all the interviewees. The materials included a list of the used frameworks with some description of the taxonomies, see Sect. 2 , to help interviewees get an idea of the discussions that would follow in the interviews. During the interview, we followed the interview guide [10]. We started by introducing the NextG2Com program and the purpose of this study. Then, we briefly described the concept of AI alignment and gave some real-world examples of AI misalignment. After that, we introduced the frameworks and went through the interview questions. We saved the video recordings and interview transcripts generated by MS Teams for subsequent analysis.

3.2   Data Analysis

We used a hybrid coding method for data analysis. For RQ1–3, we used *deductive coding*, based on the three frameworks, to label the interview data. In addition, we designed some codes primarily for analyzing interviewee demographics, such as the types and purposes of AI applications. The list of codes was initially designed by Author 1 and Author 4, and the rest of the authors reviewed and provided feedback to finalize the codes in a few iterations. Together, these formed the foundation of our coding scheme, which is available as a supplementary material [10]. To ensure the codes were suitable and comprehensive, we conducted a pilot coding exercise in which all authors coded the same interview transcript, followed by discussions and code iterations. We maintained an open and iterative approach, continuously reviewing and refining our codes throughout the entire data analysis stage, particularly when new codes or conflicts emerged.

For RQ4, we used an *inductive coding* method in which we analyzed the interview data and annotated relevant text segments using the best codes that summarize them during the coding process. Inductive coding is suitable for RQ4, being an open question to explore the current practices in relation to monitoring and testing of AI misalignment risks from our interviewees.

Prior to the actual coding, the transcripts generated by MS Teams were transferred to an Excel sheet and validated with the interview recordings. If discrepancies were found, they were corrected manually. After validating the transcripts, one author performed the coding, and another performed the coding validation for the same transcript.

3.3 Threats to Validity

With this exploratory study, our aim is to collect and aggregate views and insights from our set of interviewees on AI alignment. All validity threats are not considered equal [24] and, consequently, we focus mainly on the construct validity and reliability of the study. We discuss our consideration in relation to these and the external validity. Internal validity threats are not relevant for this study as we do not look for causal relations [20].

Construct validity refers to the degree to which a study measures the concept it is intended to measure [20]. In this study, we focus on exploring the construct "AI alignment". One threat concerns whether we select interviewees who have a good understanding of the construct under study. To mitigate that, we approached relevant companies in our contact network and the companies recommended the best suitable candidates as described in Sect. 3. Another threat pertains to how interviewees align with us on the concept of AI alignment and alignment risks. To ensure a similar understanding, we sent relevant frameworks to interviewees prior to interviews, as introduced in Sect. 2. To avoid placing too much of a burden on the interviewees, we extracted and sent only parts relevant to this study, rather than full documents. Still, we walked through those taxonomies, guidelines, and frameworks and gave real examples of the risks they comprise during the interviews. In addition, we conducted a pilot interview to make sure the questions were comprehensible and valid.

Reliability refers to the repeatability of research procedures [20]. One threat concerns whether we accurately analyze and synthesize the interview data. To maximize the reliability, we first validated each interview transcript with the corresponding video record to make sure it is correct and comprehensible, as described in Sect. 3.2. Then, we adopted an iterative and cross-validation strategy to ensure consistent coding of the interview transcripts. In the first iteration, we selected three interview transcripts to establish a common ground for coding among the authors. In the second iteration, we continued to code the remaining transcripts with the principles agreed on in the previous stage. For each interview transcript, we assigned one author to code it and another author to validate the codes. Although some subjectivity may still exist, leading to incompleteness or inaccuracy, we minimized it by using an iterative and cross-reviewed process for analyzing the interview data.

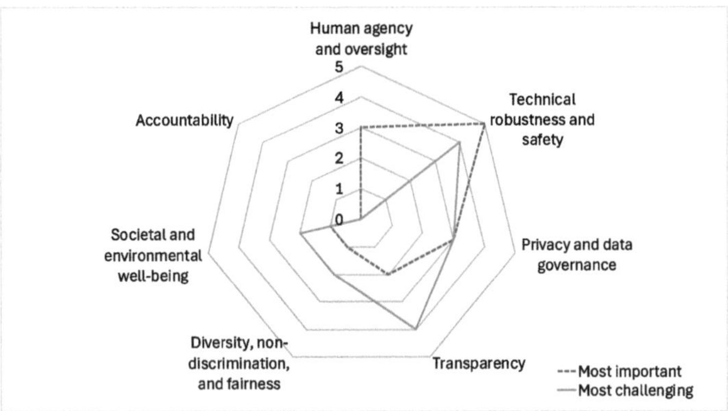

Fig. 2. Comparison of key requirements for trustworthy AI considered most important and most challenging.

Regarding *external validity*, our selected companies and interviewees are example experts who work in relevant industries in relation to AI alignment. This makes them a good source of information for exploring the AI alignment concepts in an industrial context. As this study includes one participant from Germany and the rest of them from Sweden, this work is situated within the broader framework of European Union legislation.

4   Results and Analysis

Here we discuss the findings for all the research questions, RQ1–RQ4.

4.1   Requirements for Trustworthy AI RQ1

The first research question explores which of the EU's seven key ethical require- ments for trustworthy AI [7] are perceived as most important and most challeng- ing within the interviewees' application context. The interviewees selected the two most important and the two most challenging requirements from the list. The responses are summarized in Fig. 2.

Technical robustness and safety stand out as the most frequently mentioned and emphasized aspect by the interviewees (P1, P3, P4, P6, P7). P3 highlighted it as a particularly challenging and significant topic for their work, while P4, P6, and P7 also acknowledged its difficulty, identifying it as a critical area for improvement in their AI efforts. *Privacy and data governance* (P3–P5) and *human agency and oversight* (P1, P2, P7) were also commonly discussed as key ethical concerns. As P5 described, their organization stores a substantial amount of customer data, making careful handling crucial. Governance measures, such as anonymization and filtering during pre-processing, are used to mitigate pri- vacy risks, though P5 acknowledged concerns might still persist. For example, in a system using git commit messages, even anonymized author information may allow identity inference, posing a privacy risk. To address this, they chose to develop and use the system internally. P1, P2, and P7 emphasized integrating *human agency and oversight* into the process.

An interesting observation is that *accountability* was not selected by any interviewee among their main priorities. Similarly, both *societal and environmental well-being* and *diversity, non-discrimination, and fairness* were viewed as less critical. Only P6 shared thoughts beyond their own application contexts, stating that *"societal and environmental well-being; and diversity, non-discrimination, and fairness are important from a societal perspective"*.

Although respondents paid more attention to *transparency*, it ranks quite low in importance (P2, P6). However, one respondent (P6) was more concerned with the transparency of the techniques and algorithms behind AI, and it was considered highly challenging (P2, P5–P7) alongside *technical robustness and safety* (P1–P3, P5). On several occasions these aspects were discussed in tandem. As P5 articulated: *"I think the most challenging [objective/requirement] is to have technical robustness and safety. When AI makes a decision, sometimes it feels like it's just flipping a coin because it has no reason for making that decision, and this relates to transparency or explainable AI. So, if you have a solid decision and then you can motivate it. If you can't motivate it, then you are making a poor decision."* P5 further elaborated their view that integrating AI systems poses greater challenges than developing them due to robustness and transparency concerns. They explained, *"We will not really integrate such systems because we don't see them as robust, and we don't trust the verdicts of their decisions."*

In comparison, *privacy and data governance* was considered slightly less challenging but still received considerable attention (from P3, P6, P7). P6 explained their preference for this requirement by expressing uncertainty as to whether their data is being appropriately handled for AI in their current context. They also shared concerns about the data they provide to large language models and other AI-related models, ensuring that it complies with privacy.

The degree of correlation between perceived importance and difficulty varies across the ethical requirements. At one end, we see strong alignment, such as with *technical robustness and safety* and *privacy and data governance*, which are perceived as both important and challenging, and the other way around *accountability* was seen as neither important nor challenging. Alignment is also prevalent between *societal and environmental well-being* and *diversity, non-discrimination, and fairness*, both being on the low end. The greatest divergence can be observed for *human agency and oversight*. It was ranked moderately important, but at the same time, no interviewee saw it as challenging. This indicates a requirement that could likely be implemented with relatively low effort while still being important for the application context. This is in line with our findings from RQ4 in terms of the perceived need for a human in the loop to monitor and test for AI misalignment risks.

4.2   AI Misalignment Risks RQ2

We presented the interviewees with the domain taxonomy of AI misalignment risks (see Fig. 3) and asked about which risks they consider relevant to their domain and which potential risks they foresee. The category of *privacy and security* emerged as the most frequently selected by the interviewees, with the leading subcategory being *compromise of privacy through obtaining, leaking, or correctly inferring sensitive information* (P1–P4, P7). For instance, P1 emphasized this concern, stating: *"When we are using [AI] models for our development processes, we have to be very careful about what information we share with these models and also about what we are actually using from these models and how we use them."* Similarly, P2 identified the same risk subcategory, highlighting the potential for data leakage due to the use of large datasets in their context. The subcategory of *AI system security vulnerabilities and attacks* is also commonly recognized by our interviewees (P3, P4, P6, P7) under the same category. Indeed, like P4 articulated: *"Of course we need to be aware of whether our systems can be hacked and whether our AI components can be hacked or manipulated in certain ways."* In general, privacy and security risks associated with AI are significant issues to address for our interviewees.

Human-computer interaction emerged as the second most frequently selected risk category among interviewees (P1, P3–6), which encompasses subcategories such as *loss of human agency and autonomy* and *overreliance and unsafe use.* P5 provided an intriguing perspective, stating: *"[...] I think it doesn't have to do with AI. This has to do with automation in general. If you have an automated system, it does something, and you just accept it. After a while, you might lose the skill to do it yourself."* P5 illustrated this view with a concrete yet hypothetical example: When an autopilot system encounters an extreme, hazardous, and complex condition, it might hand control back to the (human) pilot with short notice. In such a scenario, the pilot may struggle to respond effectively due to the dangerous situation and a potential lack of practice.

In addition to the two categories discussed earlier, several other categories of risks were identified, though they were less frequently mentioned by our interviewees, as shown in Fig. 3. For instance, risks related to *AI system safety, failures, and limitations* (P1, P2, P4, P7), which encompass potential issues regarding their robustness, transparency, and interpretability. AI was also identified as a potential source of *misinformation* (P3) or *discrimination and toxicity* (P2, P4, P5). An example of misinformation, provided by P3, involved the misestimation or incorrect estimation of angles or distances in their indoor positioning systems. Such inaccuracies could lead to significant issues in their products, posing real risks. Another example of discrimination, provided by P5, involved a (prototype) test prioritization system that utilizes large language models to identify code changes and analyze test execution logs, thereby prioritizing the most important test cases. However, the system exhibited biases toward specific developers, leading to the elevation or de-elevation of their code changes, which introduces fairness issues. Additionally, concerns were raised about *malicious*

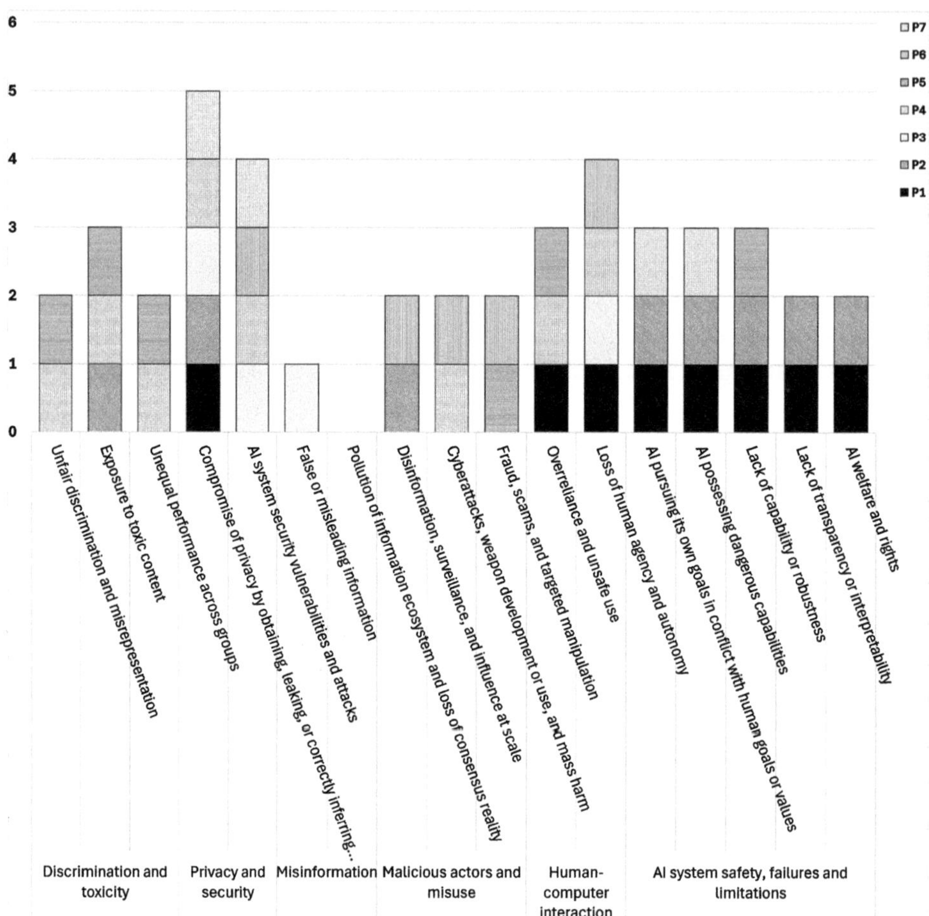

Fig. 3. Distribution of AI misalignment risks considered important by interviewees. In cases where interviewees have only selected a category and no specific subcategory, all the subcategories have been marked as selected.

actors and misuse (P2, P4, P5, P6), indicating the illegal use of AI for purposes such as fraud, scams, or cyberattacks.

Overall, there is a wide spectrum of risks (as defined in Slattery et al. [21]) that are relevant to our interviewees, and we observe that RQ2 responses about key misalignment risks reinforce the trustworthy AI requirements deemed most challenging in RQ1 and *transparency*, to some extent. For example, failure to achieve *technical robustness and safety* may result in risks of *loss of human agency and autonomy* in human-computer interaction.

4.3　AI Misalignment Risk Factors and Behaviors – RQ3

In the context of the interviewees' application domains, we investigated the primary factors contributing to AI misalignment risks and different potential misaligned behaviors, i.e. double-edge components [12]. Two of the seven interviewees did not provide input to the cause factors and one chose not to comment on potential misaligned behaviors. This reluctance may stem from the limited adoption or awareness of taxonomies and analytical frameworks for misalignment in current industry practice. Among the five respondents who answered the most recognized cause factors was *situational awareness* (P2, P5, P6) and *broadly scoped goals* (P2, P5, P7), while *mesa-optimization objectives* (P3) and *access to increased resources* (P7) were selected less often.

Situational awareness means that knowing the situation can help the AI model better adapt to the human intent, complete its tasks, and look for outliers if needed, but at the same time, also pave the way for methods of reward hacking or similarly [12]. P5 provided an example of a chatbot they used at work, explaining that retaining more conversations in its memory can be beneficial in guiding it toward a desired state on certain occasions. However, they noted the risk that AI might prioritize satisfying long-term user goals over providing accurate or good responses. P2 elaborated on this point, attributing part of the issue to the increased complexity of the system. As they put it, *"[...] if you increase the complexity, you can start to get more of this situation into the analysis."*

Broadly scoped goals refers to AI systems designed to develop objectives that span longer time frames, handle complex tasks, and operate in open environments. However, such goals can introduce risks, including the potential for manipulative behaviors by AI [12]. P7 acknowledged it as a primary cause of potential misalignment risks and shared their perspective: *"[...] when you try to generalize on one level, you provide more information than necessary, which allows the model to generalize further and further. We have long-term ambitions for certain AI products, and we are creating a roadmap to consider what might happen in 10 years or so regarding our equipment. At the same time, we observe smaller, day-to-day actions that, organizationally speaking, are not toxic."*

Mesa-optimization objectives refers to situations where a model begins to optimize for goals that differ from the objectives initially set, resulting in a phenomenon known as "double optimization" [12]. Only P3 elaborated on this cause factor, stating: *"When we talk about our models, we need to integrate incremental or adaptive learning so that a system can improve its performance based on the information it receives during its runtime or lifetime. This is what we refer to as incremental learning in a standard embedded environment. However, this approach faces difficulties, such as model drift, where the model might deviate towards outcomes that are not aligned with our intended goals. It has been a significant focus of discussion within our development and research teams. We have been working on how to implement such self-optimizing and self-learning systems in our products, particularly those operating at the edge of these systems."*

When presented with the question about potential misaligned behaviors, i.e. outcomes of misalignment risks, among the given options, most of the respondents recognized *untruthful output,* followed by *violation of ethics.* Among other options presented, *power seeking behaviors* and *collectively harmful behaviors* were discussed by one respondent each.

Most of the interviewees (P1, P3, P5–P7) identified *untruthful output* as the primary misalignment behaviour, referring to AI systems producing incorrect or fabricated information, often referred to as hallucinations. This is a widely recognized issue in AI systems. As P1 noted: *"[...] hallucinations are something we continuously try to address."* Similarly, P6 emphasized the difficulty of resolving untruthful output in their context, highlighting the challenge of first identifying hallucinations before attempting to address them.

Violation of ethics is another behavior identified by P4 and P5, where AI systems perform or lead to unethical actions. P4 elaborated in a real example: *"We develop entertainment products where a human being can interact with the system in a free environment [...], and you want the [real-time generated character] to respond to you in an engaging and appropriate way. If it goes off track with bad words or other inappropriate language, it becomes untruthful and unethical. I think that, in our context, would be a significant issue to manage."*

Other potential misalignment behaviors discussed by our interviewees include *power seeking behaviors*, as raised by P5, such as manipulating the market, and *collectively harmful behaviors*, as highlighted by P1, where AI systems may take actions that appear benign in isolation but become problematic when considered in multi-agent or societal contexts.

4.4   AI Misalignment Risk Monitoring Practices RQ4

We experienced mixed responses to how the interviewees' organizations could assess and monitor existing misalignment risks with their AI products or services. The common theme was that, at the time of the interview, none of the organizations had testing specifically for AI misalignment risks already in place.

P4 figured that *"[...] it would have to be researched specifically for each and every case and developed with specific knowledge for each and every design and use case."* For AI monitoring already done today at our participants' companies, only basic statistical monitoring of model output and some general human oversight were mentioned. For example, P3 reported: *"[...] we do some drift analysis, and we check of course whether the models are still working as intended."*

Interviewees P5 and P7 deemed a human in the loop necessary to monitor and test for AI misalignment risks. With that said, P7 expects that human oversight will primarily be needed in the beginning and become less in the future when we have better techniques available – *"I think having the human in the loop as much as possible when it comes to at least the first phases of deployment would really help detect this kind of misalignments. [...] A little bit in the future we may have more control thanks to this valuable feedback that we have in this first phase where the human is in the loop."*

Two respondents reported on challenges specifically for generative AI applications, for example, Large Language Models (LLMs). P7 highlighted a lack of metrics in this context and P5 emphasized the challenge of testing for factual correctness of LLM output.

Overall, testing and monitoring AI misalignment risks are still in their infancy. This is reinforced by the fact that including a human in the loop was among the proposed approaches from the interviewees. Our finding that none of the organizations had testing specifically for AI misalignment risks in place is likely due to organizations not having considered AI alignment yet. Thus, looking for instances of testing is too early. One would expect organizations first to use some checklists or internal training and only implement testing at a higher maturity level.

5   Discussion

In general, as discussed in the related work section, most existing studies highlight current gaps in AI alignment and serve as a foundation for our work. These studies collectively emphasize the relevance of our research, which explores AI alignment in practice and builds upon their findings and theoretical frameworks to provide both practical insights.

Our findings align closely with existing studies, as reported in the Sect. 2. Specifically, the perceptions of AI alignment (RQ1) and potential misalignment risks (RQ2) expressed by our interviewees are consistent with the challenges and risks identified in studies such as those by Radanliev et al. [19] and Alexandra et al. [1], with a predominant focus on the *technical robustness and safety*, and *transparency* of the systems. However, the causal factors and potential behaviors of misalignment risks (RQ3) are not sufficiently understood, and not all interviewees provided significant insights into these aspects. Some interviewees highlighted *situational awareness* and *broadly scoped goals* as root causes, and *untruthful output* and *violation of ethics* as potential outcomes. These opinions are in line with findings as outlined by Ji et al. [12]. Furthermore, we observed limited practices among our interviewees in monitoring and testing for AI misalignment risks (RQ4), which is consistent with the findings by Song et al. [22] and Arrieta et al. [2]. This can be attributed in part to the theoretical frameworks that we used in this study, which we reflect on in terms of their usefulness in Sect. 5. Nonetheless, we offer empirical insights and real-world examples of AI alignment in addition to the theoretical frameworks previously presented.

Reflections on the Method: We used semi-structured interviews in this study to explore AI alignment from our interviewees. During the interview, we used several frameworks, as presented in Sect. 2, to explain related concepts and facilitate the discussion on AI alignment, as illustrated in Fig. 1. In general, these frameworks were useful and provided a good basis for the discussion. However, the taxonomies in those frameworks were not fully self-explanatory, leading to potential ambiguities. To help the interviewees better understand those taxonomies and related concepts, we used real-world examples, such as the ethical issues reported for Amazon's AI recruitment tool [4] and Google Photo's auto-tagging function [16]. Considering that AI alignment is an emerging topic, our observation is that the taxonomies used in the study, despite their ambiguities, facilitated the interviews to a large extent.

Future Work: We identified several future improvements, based on the results and analysis. One future work item is to expand the study with more interviewees to expand on more perspectives about AI alignment. Another item is studying the individual and organizational level alignment [11], to understand how the thought process about AI alignment varies across the hierarchies within and across organizations and roles. For example, the divergence of different roles, such as developers and managers, on AI alignment, especially how the background and responsibilities of practitioners impact their views and considerations on AI alignment and potential risks. In addition, we are also interested in developing viable frameworks and guidelines for "AI alignment assurance", to support the development and testing of more ethically aligned AI systems. For example, how to monitor and test misalignment risks in Sect. 4.4 for RQ4.

6   Conclusion

We interviewed practitioners to explore AI alignment and its associated risks using several existing frameworks. In general, the interviewees emphasized the importance of developing ethically aligned AI systems that adhere to fundamental human values and principles, such as reliability and safety. Misaligned AI systems may pose risks to its stakeholders, including owners, designers, and users, ranging from privacy breaches to the potential loss of human life.

However, while the significance of AI misalignment is widely acknowledged by our interviewees, the methods for monitoring and mitigating such risks remain under-explored, indicating a lack of sufficient practices for testing AI misalignment risks. Therefore, we view AI alignment as a critical research area and an emerging industry need that requires significant advancements in tools, approaches, and techniques to monitor, test, and address potential misalignment risks, to fill an evident gap in ensuring ethically aligned AI systems.

Acknowledgments. This work was supported in part by the Wallenberg AI, Autonomous Systems and Software Program (WASP) and in part by the NextG2Com Competence Centre – Next-Generation Communication and Computing Infrastructures and Applications – under the Vinnova grant 2023-00541.

Disclosure of Interests. The authors have no competing interests.

References

1. Alexandra, C., Daniell, K.A., Guillaume, J., Saraswat, C., Feldman, H.R.: Cyber-physical systems in water management and governance. Curr. Opin. Environ. Sustain. **62**, 101290 (2023)
2. Arrieta, A., Valle, P., Iriarte, A., Illarramendi, M.: How do deep learning faults affect AI-enabled cyber-physical systems in operation? A preliminary study based on DeepCrime mutation operators. In: ACM/IEEE International Symposium on Empirical Software Engineering and Measurement (ESEM), pp. 1–7 (2023)

3. Bruinsma, B., Fredén, A., Hansson, K., Johansson, M., Kisić-Merino, P., Saynova, D.: Setting the AI agenda – evidence from Sweden in the ChatGPT era. In: Workshop on Fairness and Bias in AI, AEQUITAS 2024, vol. 3808, pp. 1–14 (2024)
4. Chang, X.: Gender bias in hiring: an analysis of the impact of Amazon's recruiting algorithm. Adv. Econ. Manage. Polit. Sci. **23**(1), 134–140 (2023)
5. Chui, M., et al.: Notes from the AI frontier: insights from hundreds of use cases. McKinsey Glob. Inst. **2**(267), 1–31 (2018)
6. Cruzes, D.S., Dyb , T.: Recommended steps for thematic synthesis in software engineering. In: ACM/IEEE International Symposium on Empirical Software Engineering and Measurement, pp. 275–284. IEEE (2011)
7. European Commission: Ethics guidelines for trustworthy AI – high-level expert group on artificial intelligence. Technical report (2019)
8. Ferrario, M.A., Winter, E.: Applying human values theory to software engineering practice: lessons and implications. IEEE Trans. Softw. Eng. **49**(3), 973–990 (2023)
9. Gabriel, I.: Artificial intelligence, values, and alignment. Mind. Mach. **30**(3), 411–437 (2020)
10. Gupta, R., et al.: Materials, November 2024. https://doi.org/10.5281/zenodo.14233495
11. Hou, B.L., Green, B.P.: A multi-level framework for the AI alignment problem. arXiv arXiv:2301.03740 (2023)
12. Ji, J., et al.: AI alignment: a comprehensive survey. arXiv arXiv:2310.19852 (2023)
13. Jobin, A., Ienca, M., Vayena, E.: The global landscape of AI ethics guidelines. Nat. Mach. Intell. **1**(9), 389–399 (2019)
14. Kamila, M.K., Jasrotia, S.S.: Ethical issues in the development of artificial intelligence: recognizing the risks. Int. J. Ethics Syst. **41**(1), 45–63 (2023)
15. Kirchschläger, P.G.: Digital transformation and ethics: ethical considerations on the robotization and automation of society and the economy and the use of artificial intelligence. Nomos Verlag (2021)
16. Monea, A.: Race and computer vision. The Democratization of Artificial Intelligence: Net Politics in the Era of Learning Algorithms **1**, 189 (2019)
17. Müller, V.C.: Ethics of artificial intelligence and robotics. In: The Stanford Encyclopedia of Philosophy. Stanford University (2020)
18. Nasir, S., Khan, R.A., Bai, S.: Ethical framework for harnessing the power of AI in healthcare and beyond. IEEE Access **12**, 31014–31035 (2024)
19. Radanliev, P., De Roure, D., Van Kleek, M., Santos, O., Ani, U.: Artificial intelligence in cyber physical systems. AI Soc. **36**(3), 783–796 (2021)
20. Runeson, P., Höst, M., Rainer, A., Regnell, B.: Case Study Research in Software Engineering – Guidelines and Examples. Wiley (2012)
21. Slattery, P., et al.: The AI risk repository: a comprehensive meta-review, database, and taxonomy of risks from artificial intelligence. AGI - Artif. Gen. Intell. - Robot. - Saf. Align. **1**(1) (2024)
22. Song, J., Lyu, D., Zhang, Z., Wang, Z., Zhang, T., Ma, L.: When cyber-physical systems meet AI: a benchmark, an evaluation, and a way forward. In: Proceedings of the 44th International Conference on Software Engineering: Software Engineering in Practice, pp. 343–352. ACM (2022)
23. Storey, M.-A., Ernst, N.A., Williams, C., Kalliamvakou, E.: The who, what, how of software engineering research: a socio-technical framework. Empir. Softw. Eng. **25**(5), 4097–4129 (2020). https://doi.org/10.1007/s10664-020-09858-z
24. Verdecchia, R., Engström, E., Lago, P., Runeson, P., Song, Q.: Threats to validity in software engineering research: a critical reflection. Inf. Softw. Technol. **164**, 107329 (2023)

In-House Experimentation Platforms Motivations, Implementation Characteristics and Challenges

Nils Stotz[✉][iD] and Paul Drews[iD]

Institute of Information Systems, Leuphana University Lüneburg,
Lüneburg, Germany
`nils.stotz@stud.leuphana.de`, `paul.drews@leuphana.de`

Abstract. In-house experimentation platforms are increasingly used to support continuous, data-driven product development. While prior research outlines general infrastructure requirements, it offers limited insight into why companies build their own platforms, how they design them, and what challenges emerge. This study examines publicly available industry reports and engineering blogs to identify recurring motivations, implementation patterns, and organizational challenges. Companies pursue in-house solutions to gain context-specific functionality, ensure compliance, and embed experimentation into workflows. These efforts lead to modular architectures, custom metrics pipelines, and self-service tooling—but also introduce challenges such as scalability limits, knowledge silos, and cultural resistance. A process model illustrates how motivations shape implementation and how challenges drive iterative refinement. The findings position platforms not as neutral tools but as evolving socio-technical systems embedded in organizational context. The study distinguishes in-house platforms from off-the-shelf solutions and offers practical insights into build-vs-buy decisions, design trade-offs, and long-term experimentation strategy.

Keywords: Continuous Experimentation · Experimentation Platform · Hypothesis Testing · Continuous Discovery · A/B Testing

1 Introduction

In the era of data-driven product development, the ability to make informed decisions based on real-time user behavior has become a defining capability for digital organizations. One of the most powerful tools supporting such decisions is the online controlled experiment, often referred to as A/B testing. In the context of this study, experimentation is scoped specifically to online controlled experiments such as A/B and multivariate tests, and does not include observational analyses, synthetic controls, or other quasi-experimental methods. By enabling randomized comparisons of product variants, experimentation allows organizations to isolate causal effects, validate hypotheses, and drive iterative

G. Scanniello et al. (Eds.): PROFES 2025, LNCS 16361, pp. 36–51, 2026.
https://doi.org/10.1007/978-3-032-12089-2_3

product improvement at scale [1,6]. As companies increasingly pursue agility and responsiveness in product development, experimentation has evolved from a specialized analytics task into a strategic function embedded in the daily operations of technology firms.

To enable this transformation, companies rely on experimentation platforms or software systems designed to manage the lifecycle of experiments, from traffic allocation and exposure control to metric tracking and results analysis. These platforms are essential enablers of what is commonly described as continuous experimentation: the systematic and ongoing integration of experimentation into all stages of product development [13,15]. Existing literature emphasizes that platforms enhance experimentation velocity, reliability, and business impact [7,8] while supporting the integration of experimentation into daily operations.

Alongside these benefits, researchers have explored the technical and organizational prerequisites for successful experimentation. Auer et al. [13] distinguish between the infrastructural and cultural requirements of continuous experimentation, while Mattos et al. [14] stress the importance of metric design and alignment with business objectives. Bojinov and Gupta [15] add that organizational learning and hypothesis-driven innovation depend not only on tools, but also on the processes and values that shape how those tools are used. Despite these contributions, the literature often treats experimentation platforms as functionally similar or externally sourced, offering limited insight into the diverse ways in which companies develop and adapt such systems internally.

In recent years, however, a growing number of companies have opted to develop their own proprietary experimentation platforms. These in-house systems are often motivated by limitations in third-party tools—such as inflexible metric frameworks, lack of integration with internal data systems, or concerns about compliance and autonomy. While these platforms are playing an increasingly central role in experimentation at scale, there is a striking absence of scholarly attention to how and why companies build them, what design decisions they face, and what challenges arise in the process. The phenomenon of in-house experimentation platforms remains largely unexamined in academic research, despite its growing prevalence and practical significance.

To address this gap, the present study investigates the development and operation of in-house experimentation platforms. We define these as software systems developed and maintained internally within an organization to support online controlled experiments. Such platforms are tailored to an organization's infrastructure, product logic, metrics, and compliance needs, and operate independently from third-party providers, including customized or internally forked tools.

Against this background, the guiding research question of this study is:

What drives companies to build in-house experimentation platforms, and what implementation characteristics and challenges emerge as a result?

The paper addresses this question through a systematic grey literature review, drawing on publicly available, non-academic sources such as engineering blogs, technical talks, and internal postmortems. By applying a grounded theory approach, we inductively identify recurring patterns in the motivations, implementation characteristics, and challenges associated with in-house platform development across diverse organizational contexts.

This study advances current understanding in several important ways. Theoretically, it contributes to the literature on experimentation and digital product development by positioning experimentation platforms not as neutral enablers, but as socio-technical systems that co-evolve with organizational structures, cultural norms, and strategic priorities. While prior research has outlined general maturity models and architectural principles, our findings offer a more granular view of how platform capabilities are shaped by internal use cases and how they, in turn, shape experimentation practices. The study also extends the notion of experimentation infrastructure by highlighting its role in knowledge retention and institutional memory, particularly in fast-scaling environments where tacit knowledge is easily lost. Empirically, the paper synthesizes practitioner perspectives that are largely absent from peer-reviewed literature, offering a structured analysis of real-world platform implementations across a wide range of companies. This helps illuminate the practical reasoning behind build-versus-buy decisions and the architectural, organizational, and cultural trade-offs involved in platform development. Practically, the findings offer actionable insights for organizations considering in-house experimentation solutions. These include concrete implementation characteristics, examples of common pitfalls, and reflections on how in-house platforms can support long-term experimentation maturity when properly aligned with organizational processes. In doing so, the study supports both academic inquiry and managerial decision-making by clarifying how experimentation infrastructure can be adapted and scaled to fit distinct organizational needs.

2   Background and Related Work

Online controlled experiments have emerged as a critical mechanism for enabling data-informed decision-making in digital product development. By randomly assigning users to different variants of a product or feature, organizations can isolate causal effects and evaluate the impact of changes with high internal validity [6]. This method, commonly referred to as A/B testing, underpins much of the modern experimentation culture in technology companies and has been credited with improving product performance, user experience, and organizational learning. To support the increasing scale and complexity of such experiments, companies rely on experimentation platforms—software systems designed to automate and orchestrate the lifecycle of experiments. These platforms manage tasks such as traffic allocation, metrics computation, variant deployment, and statistical analysis. Several authors have emphasized their strategic relevance. Fabijan et al. [8], for example, highlight how platforms enhance experimentation velocity and result trustworthiness, particularly in large-scale environments. Gupta et al. [7] further demonstrate the measurable business value derived from high experimentation throughput when supported by robust platform infrastructure. Academic work has also examined the broader organizational and technical foundations required for experimentation to succeed. Auer et al. [13] divide the enabling conditions for continuous experimentation into technical infrastructure (e.g., logging systems, APIs, analytics) and organizational infrastructure (e.g., workflows, roles, incentives). Mattos et al. [14] add a business perspective by focusing on how companies define and validate experimentation metrics to align with strategic goals. Meanwhile, Bojinov and Gupta [15] emphasize the cultural dimension, arguing that an experimentation mindset must be deliberately cultivated across teams in order to support hypothesis-driven development and foster institutional learning. In addition to these foundational elements, the literature has begun to map the specific characteristics and challenges associated with experimentation in practice. Auer, Lee, and Felderer [9] classify experiments by their design complexity and organizational touchpoints, showing that experimentation is rarely a uniform process and often requires alignment across product, engineering, and data teams. Other studies have highlighted the architectural intricacies of experimentation platforms, particularly the trade-offs between flexibility, latency, and observability. For instance, research on platforms like the Windows Experimentation Platform [11] and RIGHT model [12] discusses the need for modular, extensible systems that can evolve with product and organizational demands. A recurring theme in this literature is that experimentation is context-dependent, shaped by constraints such as test volume, segmentation, regulation and scale. However, most existing studies focus either on generalized models of experimentation capability or on illustrative case studies of specific systems. There is relatively limited research on how companies adapt their experimentation infrastructure to meet their individual needs, especially in cases where off-the-shelf platforms may be insufficient. One framework that attempts to quantify experimentation readiness is the experimentation maturity model proposed by Fabijan et al. [16], which assesses organizational capability across several dimensions, including metrics, tooling, coordination, and learning. Their empirical work reveals that while many companies have adopted experimentation as a concept, they often lack the platform-level capabilities necessary to scale experimentation reliably and safely. In particular, deficiencies in statistical robustness, result interpretation, and system integration remain common. Despite these insights, the academic discourse has not yet fully addressed the platform-specific design decisions that organizations face when operationalizing experimentation. While the benefits of experimentation and the enablers of maturity have been explored, there is still a gap in understanding the variation in platform architecture, ownership models, and development paths. Specifically, little attention has been paid to the distinction between experimentation platforms as external services versus those developed and operated internally, even though this distinction may have significant implications for how experimentation is integrated into product development and strategic decision-making.

3   Methodology

This study employs a systematic grey literature review (GLR) following the guidelines proposed by Garousi et al. [17] and adopts a grounded theory-based approach to data analysis as outlined by Wolfswinkel et al. [18]. This combined methodology is well suited to explore underexamined phenomena in rapidly evolving practice domains, particularly where peer-reviewed evidence remains scarce. Grounded Theory in this context served not as a means to generate entirely new theoretical constructs, but as a systematic coding and categorization approach to structure and interpret the grey literature data. It influenced both the inclusion of diverse practitioner sources and the iterative analysis process, ensuring that categories such as motivations, implementation characteristics, and challenges emerged inductively from the material rather than being imposed a priori. The objective is to derive a structured understanding of the motivations, implementation characteristics, and challenges associated with in-house experimentation platforms by synthesizing practitioner-authored, non-academic materials. The GLR was conducted in five iterative steps—define, search, select, analyze, and present—according to the process proposed by Wolfswinkel et al. [18].

In the **define phase**, the scope of the study was delineated to focus on companies that publicly document internally developed experimentation platforms. The research aim was to identify the rationale for building in-house solutions, the architectural and organizational patterns used in their implementation, and the challenges encountered. Based on this scope, we derived inclusion and exclusion criteria and formulated an initial search string.

The **search phase** was carried out via Google, leveraging its capacity to surface diverse types of grey literature such as blog posts, engineering articles, technical conference talks, podcasts, and internal retrospectives.[1] To avoid bias, searches were conducted in a clean browser environment. The final search string was defined as: TITLE("experimentation*" OR "A/B testing*") AND TITLE("in-house"). The search was restricted to English-language content published between 2014 and 2024. During this phase, the search terms were expanded iteratively to reflect variations in terminology observed in the initial results, including synonyms and company-specific platform names.

In the **selection phase**, all hits were collected and assessed based on predefined inclusion and exclusion criteria. Inclusion criteria required that the material (1) be freely accessible, (2) report on a genuinely in-house experimentation platform, (3) align with the thematic scope of the study, and (4) be published within the defined time range. Items were excluded if they were incomplete, non-technical or describing tools relying on third-party providers for core experimentation functionality. After initial screening, all selected sources were entered into an Excel sheet for metadata extraction and verification. The final corpus consisted of 27 documents that met all criteria.

---

[1] A supplemental file to an online resource which provides further information about the articles retrieved can be found here: https://zenodo.org/records/16785118.

For the **analysis phase**, we adopted grounded theory coding techniques to derive patterns from the data in a structured manner. The analysis was conducted using open, axial, and selective coding as described by Wolfswinkel et al. [18]. In open coding, we segmented the textual material to generate preliminary categories such as motivation types, architectural decisions, and reported challenges. Examples included terms like "custom SDKs," "privacy constraints," or "team enablement." These codes were then refined and clustered in the axial coding stage, which involved relating categories to subcategories and identifying interdependencies—e.g., connecting "metric customization" to the broader category of "functional alignment." In the final selective coding step, a coherent narrative was constructed by integrating the most salient categories and identifying recurring themes across the material. This allowed for the emergence of three primary dimensions: motivation, implementation, and challenge.

Throughout the process, the coding remained iterative and comparative. As new materials were added, earlier categorizations were revisited to maintain consistency. The analysis was manually conducted and documented in structured tables, allowing for traceability from source material to emergent themes.

The final step, **present**, was achieved through synthesizing the coded data into a structured findings section, organized according to the motivation, implementation and challenge progression. This structure was selected to mirror both practitioner logic and grounded theory development.

4   Results

This section presents the core findings of the grey literature review. The results are structured following a progression from motivations, through implementation characteristics, to the resulting challenges. This flow reflects the idea that specific reasons for building in-house experimentation platforms lead to corresponding architectural and organizational choices, which in turn generate new sources of friction. While prior academic literature often treats these aspects in isolation, the grey literature offers a more integrated and dynamic view of how they are interrelated in practice.

4.1   Why Companies Build In-House Platforms

The analysis of the selected grey literature sources revealed three major clusters of motivations: the need for functional customization and flexibility, the desire for independence and control, and the strategic aim of tightly integrating experimentation with product development. A significant number of companies emphasized the limitations of off-the-shelf experimentation tools in addressing their unique product logic, decision-making structures, and user behavior patterns. At Just Eat Takeaway, for example, the experimentation team explicitly stated that "tooling has to fit our culture and not the other way around" [22]. This principle is reflected in their decision to design segmentation logic that supports their marketplace model, where experiments must differentiate between customers, couriers and restaurants without disrupting operations. This desire for contextual fit spans several components, such as exposure logic, segmentation and KPI tracking. At Duolingo and Spotify, experimentation processes were shaped by domain-specific needs—language learning progression and music recommendation dynamics, respectively—which demanded modeling approaches that standard tools could not provide [23, 24].

These motivations often led companies to build tailored experimentation platforms aligned with internal needs. This included specialized software development kits (SDKs) that integrated tightly with proprietary backends [20], advanced feature gating systems like Delivery Hero's "Fun with Flags" that enabled more granular rollout patterns [19], and real-time analytics dashboards embedded within existing observability stacks such as Grafana or Kibana [25, 30]. These adaptations were not isolated technical improvements but manifestations of broader product and engineering philosophies. For example, Spotify's integration of its experimentation platform into existing data pipelines ensured that experiment results appeared in the same analytical environment used for music recommendation quality monitoring [24]. This approach favored internal alignment over the flexibility of generic third-party tools.

Beyond functional reasons, many companies cited the need for full operational ownership as a key motivation for building in-house platforms. This included control over data processing, governance, and compliance—particularly in contexts where privacy regulations or internal standards rendered third-party involvement risky or infeasible [27, 30, 31]. WalmartLabs and The New York Times, for instance, developed their own frameworks (e.g., ABRA) to retain sovereignty over sensitive user data, experiment logic, and system behavior [30, 31]. Stitch Fix similarly described its centralized platform as enabling independence from vendor release cycles, service dependencies, and incident protocols [32].

Finally, in-house experimentation platforms were frequently positioned as strategic enablers of continuous product discovery. At LinkedIn, the platform was developed to accelerate decision-making by embedding experimentation directly into product development workflows [39]. Dream11 reported similar motivations, noting that fast iteration in time-critical contexts such as live sports events required an internal solution that could respond at the pace of product needs [35].

In summary, companies build in-house platforms not solely to improve test throughput or functionality, but to ensure that experimentation becomes a deeply integrated and strategically aligned capability—tailored to their technical ecosystems, regulatory conditions, and innovation cadence.

4.2   How Motivations Translate Into Platform Design

The identified motivations are translated into concrete implementation characteristics that span technical architecture, data infrastructure, and organizational processes. The review suggests that in-house platforms are not constructed as static systems, but as evolving infrastructures that reflect and shape the company's experimentation maturity over time. Most in-house platforms share a core of traffic allocation, variant assignment, metric computation and results delivery, but stand out through deeper integration with internal systems, product-specific logic and organizational ownership. While companies tailor their platforms to specific needs, the analysis reveals a set of recurring characteristics—such as modular architecture, custom metrics pipelines, and self-service tooling. These elements appear across diverse contexts, indicating a convergent pattern of implementation rather than fundamentally divergent strategies. The variation lies more in degree and integration depth than in core design principles.

Architecturally, most platforms adopt modular and extensible system designs. At carwow, Holder [20] outlines a five-principle architecture: trustworthiness, usability, extensibility, scalability, and efficiency. These principles informed the company's internal experimentation tooling and were echoed in platforms at DoorDash [26], Delivery Hero [37], and Coupang [38], where modular setups allowed product teams to rapidly iterate while maintaining stability and reproducibility. A defining technical component in nearly all cases was the use of customized feature flagging systems. These systems enabled teams to roll out features and allocate users to experimental variants in real time, while maintaining tight control over exposure conditions [19,20]. Internal libraries were often developed to abstract experiment logic across frontend and backend systems, ensuring consistent implementation and reducing redundant engineering effort [24, 30]. In more advanced setups, such as those at Dream11 and Door-Dash, companies implemented real-time allocation algorithms and parallelization infrastructure to run high-throughput or multi-arm experiments, often in tandem with ML-driven systems [34,35].

A second layer of implementation focused on aligning experimentation outputs with company-specific metric frameworks. Both LinkedIn [39] and Spotify [24] built custom analytics pipelines to integrate experimentation data directly into decision support environments, eliminating disconnects between platform results and strategic metrics. Swiggy and Farfetch developed metric abstraction layers that transformed domain-specific indicators—such as recommendation quality or delivery reliability—into validated experimentation KPIs [21,25]. These integrations enabled faster interpretation, reduced analysis debt, and allowed business teams to rely on experimentation outcomes without bespoke analysis for each test. Organizationally, platform implementation involved developing support processes that allowed for distributed, self-service experimentation while ensuring methodological soundness. Common strategies included automated guardrails to catch faulty test configurations [32,38], role-based access controls for platform components [20], and shared templates for experiment documentation [43]. At Spotify and Zalando, platform capabilities evolved in tandem with organizational restructuring efforts, helping teams maintain coordination and knowledge flow despite growing experimentation complexity [24,41]. Taken together, these implementation characteristics demonstrate how technical, analytical, and organizational components are deliberately engineered to support experimentation at scale. Rather than adopting generalized best practices, companies construct bespoke infrastructures that reflect their unique constraints, strategic goals, and team structures—thereby operationalizing experimentation as a first-class capability.

4.3 Challenges: Where Implementation Meets Friction

Despite the strategic intent and substantial engineering investment behind in-house experimentation platforms, their implementation introduces a range of persistent challenges. These challenges fall into two broad categories: technical limitations and organizational constraints. While many obstacles are familiar from software engineering, their combination in experimentation makes them particularly consequential.

On the technical side, several companies report recurring difficulties in ensuring the integrity and isolation of experimental conditions. For example, Coupang [38] observed instances where unintended changes in the control group logic compromised test validity. To mitigate such risks, some organizations introduced automated monitoring mechanisms and code review bots that detect discrepancies between defined and actual experiment logic—an approach that exceeds the quality control found in many third-party tools.

Scalability presents another common issue. As teams increase the volume and complexity of their experiments, platform performance often begins to degrade. This includes latency problems during parallel experiment execution, as reported at Wolt and DoorDash [29,34], as well as infrastructure bottlenecks caused by tightly coupled or language-specific implementations, particularly in legacy environments [39]. In some cases, platforms struggled to support asynchronous experimentation scenarios, such as experiments involving notifications or background jobs, due to insufficient support for deferred triggers and real-time evaluation pipelines [37].

A further technical concern lies in maintenance overhead and experimentation code hygiene. Several companies noted that deactivating or cleaning up experimental logic post-deployment is often neglected, resulting in long-term technical debt and bloated codebases [26]. These operational shortcomings add friction not only to platform maintenance but also to team productivity, especially in high-velocity development settings.

In parallel with these technical challenges, organizations frequently encounter cultural and coordination barriers. One major issue is the fragmentation of experimentation knowledge. When experimentation practices are undocumented or inconsistently maintained, institutional learning becomes difficult, and valuable insights may be lost when key personnel leave the organization [41]. At the same time, team-specific standards around test design, metric definitions, and statistical analysis contribute to inconsistency and misalignment across departments [28,39].

Cultural resistance to experimentation is another recurring theme. Some organizations reported skepticism from engineers or product managers about the value of controlled experiments, particularly when results contradict intuitive judgments or delay feature rollouts. This lack of experimentation literacy—combined with minimal training opportunities—can lead to underuse or misapplication of the platform [40]. To address this challenge, several companies introduced initiatives to build shared understanding and foster engagement. Spotify and Farfetch, for instance, implemented weekly experimentation review meetings to socialize learnings and reinforce good practices [24,43]. Zalando developed internal statistical libraries to reduce reliance on expert analysts [41], while DoorDash and LinkedIn invested in internal playbooks and bootcamps to train staff in experimentation methods [26,39].

Yet even with such interventions, cultural alignment often lags behind technical progress. As Sherwin [40] notes, a well-designed platform alone is not enough to build a thriving experimentation culture; success depends equally on organizational incentives, leadership support, and long-term knowledge stewardship.

Taken together, these challenges illustrate that in-house experimentation platforms are not merely technical products, but organizational systems embedded in dynamic environments. Their success depends not only on software quality and infrastructure scalability, but also on the organization's ability to institutionalize experimentation practices, maintain shared understanding, and continuously invest in education and process refinement. The friction observed across companies serves as a reminder that experimentation maturity is not guaranteed by tooling alone—it must be cultivated through parallel investments in infrastructure, culture, and coordination.

4.4   Synthesizing the Process: A Conceptual Model

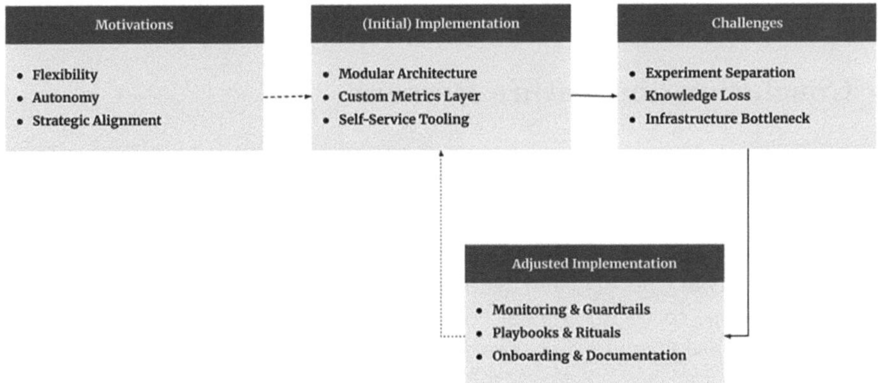

Fig. 1. Iterative model of in-house experimentation platform development: motivations, implementation, challenges, and feedback loops.

To consolidate the findings from the grey literature analysis and illustrate the interplay between the identified themes, we developed a conceptual model (see

Fig. 1) that maps the flow from motivations to implementation characteristics and ultimately to challenges. This model synthesizes how companies operationalize their decision to build in-house experimentation platforms and reveals the recursive nature of platform development in practice.

At the beginning of the process are the core motivations, which cluster around three key drivers: the need for greater flexibility, the desire for autonomy and data sovereignty, and the strategic goal of tightly aligning experimentation capabilities with internal product development cycles. These motivations serve as the impetus for platform development and shape the design goals that teams set at the outset. These motivations are then translated into concrete implementation characteristics, which manifest at multiple levels. Architecturally, companies adopt modular systems that allow for internal extension and customization. In terms of data and analytics, custom metrics layers are introduced to ensure relevance to business-specific KPIs. Organizationally, platforms are structured to promote self-service experimentation, while enforcing quality control through automation and internal standards.

Despite these targeted responses, the implementation of in-house platforms inevitably introduces new challenges. Common issues include difficulty maintaining clean experiment separation, fragmentation of experimentation knowledge when employees leave, and scalability bottlenecks due to technical legacy or capacity constraints. Importantly, these challenges do not signal failure but rather trigger further iteration on the platform. In some cases, they even lead to renewed clarification of motivations—such as revisiting assumptions about platform governance or coordination mechanisms—highlighting the cyclical nature of platform evolution. The model therefore does not depict a linear progression, but a dynamic, iterative process. It illustrates that the development of in-house experimentation platforms is best understood as a recursive feedback system in which technical, organizational, and strategic elements continuously co-evolve.

5   Conclusion and Future Research

This study contributes to the growing field of continuous experimentation by exploring an aspect that has thus far received limited attention in peer-reviewed research: the increasing prevalence and complexity of in-house experimentation platforms. Drawing from a systematic review of 27 grey literature sources, the findings reveal that the decision to develop and operate such platforms is not merely a response to technological constraints, but a deliberate strategic move shaped by use-case specificity, organizational needs, and cultural readiness.

5.1   Research Contributions

In contrast to the academic literature that largely focuses on the benefits and challenges of experimentation as a practice, our findings highlight the infrastructural and organizational consequences of how experimentation is implemented. Prior work has emphasized the importance of experimentation platforms in enabling speed, scale, and trust in test outcomes. Gupta et al. [7] and Fabijan et al. [8] underscore how platforms support decision quality and velocity in digital product development. However, the assumption underlying much of this literature is that such platforms are either universally applicable or externally provided. Prior work often treats experimentation platforms as a generic category, without distinguishing between externally provided tools and internally developed systems. This study addresses that gap by systematically analyzing in-house platforms as a distinct organizational phenomenon. This review challenges that notion by revealing the breadth of motivations behind companies' choices to build these systems in-house. Our analysis shows that the core motivations—ranging from the need for specific functionality, independence from external release cycles, integration with internal data systems, and privacy or compliance considerations—result in highly individualized implementations. This diverges from the more uniform platform architectures often assumed in academic models, such as the experimentation flywheel. While the flywheel metaphor effectively captures how experimentation can create a feedback loop of idea generation and validation, it often abstracts away from the infrastructural mechanisms that enable or constrain that loop.

In contrast, our findings suggest that experimentation infrastructure is not a neutral enabler but an active component that can accelerate, distort, or even block the flywheel if not aligned with context-specific requirements. Theoretically, this positions the experimentation platform not simply as a technical tool, but as a socio-technical system embedded in broader organizational dynamics. The data reveals that platform development co-evolves with the maturation of experimentation capabilities within organizations. Rather than assuming a linear progression from low to high experimentation maturity as in Fabijan et al. [16], we observe a recursive relationship: companies often begin building platforms because their processes have matured to a point where off-the-shelf solutions are insufficient, and the platform itself then enables new organizational practices and experimentation behaviors. This insight invites a more dynamic, contingency-based understanding of experimentation maturity—one that takes into account infrastructure, process, and culture as mutually reinforcing elements. Another theoretical contribution lies in reframing the experimentation platform as a knowledge infrastructure. Bojinov and Gupta [15] already argue that experimentation contributes to organizational learning. What our findings add is the insight that the platform itself plays a central role in institutionalizing that learning. By centralizing test design, metric tracking, and documentation, in-house platforms can serve as repositories of experimentation history, enabling meta-analyses and strategic insights. Yet this potential is only realized when organizational routines support consistent usage, which remains a challenge for many companies. Where such routines are lacking, experimentation knowledge often remains siloed or is lost during personnel turnover—an issue underreported in academic studies to date.

5.2   Practical Contributions

From a practitioner perspective, the findings offer several actionable insights for organizations considering in-house experimentation platforms. Companies should base the build-versus-buy decision not solely on functionality, but on how well external tools align with internal data systems, compliance needs, and strategic priorities. In-house platforms often provide greater flexibility and integration but come with substantial maintenance and coordination requirements. Successful implementations treat platforms not just as infrastructure, but as organizational change mechanisms. This involves embedding shared documentation, standardized test design, and analytics guidance into the platform itself. Such integration helps lower the barrier to entry for non-expert users and ensures consistent experimentation practices across teams. In-house solutions are especially valuable in contexts with regulatory restrictions, high experimentation volume, or complex product architectures. Their effectiveness, however, depends on ongoing investment in education, alignment, and cross-team coordination. Ultimately, the design of an experimentation platform should reflect not only technical goals, but the organization's broader operating model and innovation approach. The reviewed sources rarely mention the effort required to build in-house platforms, yet such systems still demand notable organizational and technical investment.

5.3   Limitations and Future Work

This study is limited by its reliance on grey literature, which may overrepresent successful implementations and lack independent verification. The sample is also skewed toward digitally mature, resource-rich companies in the tech sector, limiting generalizability to smaller firms or different industries. Without triangulation through interviews or usage data, the effectiveness of platform strategies remains inferred rather than measured. Nonetheless, the study offers a grounded view of how experimentation infrastructure is operationalized in leading organizations.

Future research could expand this work in several promising directions. Comparative case studies could explore how platform architecture and process maturity differ across organizational types—for example, between highly regulated industries and consumer-facing digital platforms, or between startups and enterprises. There is also room to study the cost-benefit trade-offs of different platform ownership models, including hybrid approaches that combine in-house control with open-source or third-party components. Moreover, with the increasing adoption of modern data stacks, future studies could examine how architectural choices affect experimentation velocity, flexibility, and reliability. Another opportunity lies in investigating how knowledge generated through experimentation can be more effectively retained, reused, or codified—especially during team transitions or platform migrations. Lastly, as experimentation becomes increasingly automated, the role of AI-assisted analysis and platform intelligence offers an exciting avenue for exploration, raising new questions about human oversight, trust, and experimentation governance. In addition, future research could examine the development processes of in-house experimentation platforms in more depth, tracing how technical and organizational decisions unfold over time. Such work could aim to construct descriptive models that capture common development patterns, trade-offs, and organizational dynamics, providing a richer understanding of how platforms evolve from initial concept to mature, business-critical infrastructure.

References

1. Kohavi, R., Longbotham, R.: Online controlled experiments and A/B tests. In: Sammut, C., Webb, G.I. (eds.) Encyclopedia of Machine Learning and Data Mining, pp. 922–929. Springer (2016). https://doi.org/10.1007/978-1-4899-7687-1_891
2. Wakhlu, S.: Experimentation gets AI to the "real world" (2023). https://www.geteppo.com/blog/experimentation-gets-you-to-the-real-world
3. Google. Google Optimize (2023). https://support.google.com/analytics/answer/12979939?hl=en&sjid=13183120326314837392-EU
4. Singer, T.: Coming soon: confidence — an experimentation platform from Spotify (2023). https://engineering.atspotify.com/2023/08/coming-soon-confidence-an-experimentation-platform-from-spotify/
5. Sharma, C.: A simple "build vs. buy" decision framework for experimentation (2024). https://www.geteppo.com/blog/build-vs-buy-decision-experimentation
6. Imbens, G.W., Rubin, D.B.: Causal Inference: For Statistics, Social, and Biomedical Sciences an Introduction. Cambridge University Press (2015). https://doi.org/10.1017/CBO9781139025751
7. Gupta, S., Ulanova, L., Bhardwaj, S., Dmitriev, P., Raff, P., Fabijan, A.: The anatomy of a large-scale experimentation platform. IEEE ICSA **2018**, 1–109 (2018). https://doi.org/10.1109/ICSA.2018.00009
8. Fabijan, A., Dmitriev, P., Olsson, H.H., Bosch J.: The evolution of continuous experimentation in software product development: from data to a data-driven organization at scale. In: IEEE/ACM 39th International Conference on Software Engineering (ICSE), pp. 770–780 (2017). https://doi.org/10.1109/ICSE.2017.76
9. Auer, F., Lee, C.S., Felderer, M.: Continuous experiment definition characteristics. In: 46th Euromicro Conference on Software Engineering and Advanced Applications (SEAA), pp. 186–190 (2020). https://doi.org/10.1109/SEAA51224.2020.00041
10. Vasthimal, D.K., Srirama, P.K., Akkinapalli, A.K.: Scalable data reporting platform for A/B tests. In: 2019 IEEE 5th International Conference on Big Data Security on Cloud (BigDataSecurity), IEEE International Conference on High Performance and Smart Computing, (HPSC) and IEEE International Conference on Intelligent Data and Security (IDS), pp. 230–238 (2019). https://doi.org/10.1109/BigDataSecurity-HPSC-IDS.2019.00052
11. Li, P.L., et al.: Experimentation in the operating system: the windows experimentation platform. In: ICSE 2019 Software Engineering in Practice, pp. 21–30 (2019). https://doi.org/10.1109/ICSE-SEIP.2019.00011
12. Fagerholm, F., Münch, J., Mäenpää, H.: The RIGHT model for continuous experimentation. J. Syst. Softw. **123**, 292–305 (2017). https://doi.org/10.1016/j.jss.2016.03.034

13. Auer, F., Ros, R., Kaltenbrunner, L., Runeson, P., Felderer, M.: Controlled experimentation in continuous experimentation: knowledge and challenges. Inf. Softw. Technol. **124**, 106551 (2021). https://doi.org/10.1016/j.infsof.2021.106551

14. Mattos, D.I., Bosch, J., Olsson, H.H.: Challenges and strategies for undertaking continuous experimentation to embedded systems: industry and research perspectives. In: Garbajosa, J., Wang, X., Aguiar, A. (eds.) Agile Processes in Software Engineering and Extreme Programming. XP 2018. Lecture Notes in Business Information Processing, pp. 277–292. Springer (2018). https://doi.org/10.1007/978-3-319-91602-6_20

15. Bojinov, I., Gupta, S.: Online experimentation: benefits, operational and methodological challenges, and scaling guide. Harvard Data Sci. Rev. **4**(3), 1–28 (2022). https://doi.org/10.1162/99608f92.a579756e

16. Fabijan, A., Dmitriev, P., Olsson, H.H., Bosch, J.: online controlled experimentation at scale: an empirical survey on the current state of A/B testing. In: Euromicro Conference on Software Engineering and Advanced Applications, pp. 68–72 (2018). https://doi.org/10.1109/SEAA.2018.00021

17. Garousi, V., Felderer, M., Mäntylä, M.: Guidelines for including grey literature and conducting multivocal literature reviews in software engineering. Inf. Softw. Technol. **106**, 101–121 (2019). https://doi.org/10.1016/j.infsof.2018.09.006

18. Wolfswinkel, J.F., Furtmueller, E., Wilderom, C.P.M.: Using grounded theory as a method for rigorously reviewing literature. Eur. J. Inf. Syst. **22**(1), 45–55 (2011). https://doi.org/10.1057/ejis.2011.51

19. Rasch, C., Seretti, F., Latorre, J.G.: Experimentation at delivery hero is fun with flags (2023). https://tech.deliveryhero.com/experimentation-at-delivery-hero-is-fun-with-flags/

20. Holder, G.: Building the future of AB testing at carwow (2022). https://analyticsatcarwow.medium.com/building-the-future-of-ab-testing-at-carwow-ca59aabe7ad9

21. Gomes, N., Ventura, P.: How to swiftly A/B test recommendations from the inside, rocket-style (2021). https://www.farfetchtechblog.com/en/blog/post/how-to-swiftly-a-b-test-recommendations-from-the-inside-rocket-style/

22. AWA Digital: Interview with experimentation lead: Andre Richter at Just Eat Takeaway.com (2021). https://www.awa-digital.com/blog/interview-with-head-of-experimentation-andre-richter-at-just-eat-takeaway-com/

23. Aprameya, L.: Improving Duolingo, one experiment at a time (2020). https://blog.duolingo.com/improving-duolingo-one-experiment-at-a-time/

24. Rydberg, J.: Spotify's New Experimentation Platform (Part 2) (2020). https://engineering.atspotify.com/2020/11/spotifys-new-experimentation-platform-part-2/

25. Amaresh, M.: Experimentation platform (XP) at Swiggy—part 1 (2021). https://bytes.swiggy.com/experimentation-platform-xp-at-swiggy-part-1-e50b7dbdc773

26. Balasubramani, A.: Supporting rapid product iteration with an experimentation analysis platform (2020). https://doordash.engineering/2020/09/09/experimentation-analysis-platform-mvp/

27. Hou, P.: Building the Belfry (2017). https://medium.com/oscar-tech/building-the-belfry-2b93992468ee

28. Wolt Tech Talks. Wolt Tech Talks Podcast — #2 Building Wolt's Experimentation Platform from Scratch [video]. YouTube (2022). https://www.youtube.com/watch?v=Jl-TF3ILEl8

29. Wolt Tech Talks. Developing an experimentation platform using FastAPI — Larissa Leite, Data Engineer at Wolt [video]. YouTube (2021). https://www.youtube.com/watch?v=syHJfo2zTw0
30. Tang, A.: The journey of A/B testing at WalmartLabs (2018). https://medium.com/walmartglobaltech/the-journey-of-a-b-testing-at-walmartlabs-3b9bba8e558f
31. Arak, J., Kaji, K.: ABRA: an enterprise framework for experimentation at The Times (2017). https://open.nytimes.com/abra-an-enterprise-framework-for-experimentation-at-the-times-57f8931449cd
32. Bradley, A.: Building our centralized experimental platform (2019). https://multithreaded.stitchfix.com/blog/2019/07/30/building-centralized-experimental-platform/
33. Ricchiuti, F.: Empowering autonomous experimentation in a scaling enterprise (2021). https://techlab.bol.com/en/blog/empowering-autonomous-experimentation-in-a-distributed-ecosystem/
34. Zhang, J., Thang, Y.: Improving online experiment capacity by 4X with parallelization and increased sensitivity (2020). https://doordash.engineering/2020/10/07/improving-experiment-capacity-by-4x/
35. Jaiswal, S., Gupta, S., Bhardwaj, H., Tyagi, T., Ali, F.: DRS: making high-impact & informed decisions with Dream11's in-house experimentation platform! (2022). https://tech.dream11.in/blog/drs-making-high-impact-informed-decisions-with-dream11s-in-house-experimentation-platform
36. Rydberg, J.: Spotify's new experimentation platform (part 1) (2020). https://engineering.atspotify.com/2020/10/spotifys-new-experimentation-platform-part-1/
37. Luz, M.: Building a global experimentation platform: the technical challenges (2023). https://tech.deliveryhero.com/building-a-global-experimentation-platform-the-technical-challenges/
38. Coupang Engineering. Minimizing technical incidents during A/B testing at scale (2022). https://medium.com/coupang-engineering/minimizing-technical-incidents-during-a-b-testing-at-scale-9615c53fcf4f#1977
39. Ivaniuk, A., Liu, J.: Making the LinkedIn experimentation engine 20x faster (2020). https://engineering.linkedin.com/blog/2020/making-the-linkedin-experimentation-engine-20x-faster
40. Sherwin, G.: Experimentation at Farfetch: an introduction (2020). https://www.farfetchtechblog.com/en/blog/post/experimentation-at-farfetch-an-introduction/
41. Huang, S.: Experimentation Platform at Zalando: Part 1 – Evolution (2021). https://engineering.zalando.com/posts/2021/01/experimentation-platform-part1.html
42. Lam, W.: How Booking.com A/B tests like nobody's business (2023). https://devcycle.com/blog/how-booking-com-a-b-tests-like-nobodys-business
43. Hatt, B., Sherwin, G., Trindade, L.: Digital experimentation at Farfetch (2020). https://www.researchgate.net/publication/381654855_Digital_Experimentation_at_Farfetch

Writing Aids for Agile Requirements Engineering - A Comparative Study Between Natural Language Processing and Machine Learning

Fabian Gilson[(✉)] [iD], Ella Calder, and Daniel Neal

University of Canterbury, Christchurch, New Zealand
`fabian.gilson@canterbury.ac.nz`, `{eca66,dne33}@uclive.ac.nz`

Abstract. In agile software development, user stories (US) and acceptance criteria (AC) are popular ways of recording requirements. While guidelines have been proposed in the literature to assess the quality of US and AC, their correct application remains a manual task. In this work, we designed both a machine learning (ML) and a natural language processing (NLP) classifier for automatically assessing agile software requirements following quality indicators found in the literature. We evaluated their performance to improve the quality of requirements in a user study, as well as the users' perceptions on the usage of such tools as writing aids. While improvements were notable in the quality of requirements written by participants, the improvements were more marginal when using the NLP classifier compared to the ML one. However, participants reported more satisfaction towards the NLP classifier for its "explainability" compared to the ML one.

Keywords: software engineering · agile software development · behaviour-driven development · user stories · acceptance criteria

1 Introduction

Requirements Engineering (RE) is a discipline in which the requirements of a project are elicited and documented [1]. In agile RE, user stories are a common way to document requirements [16,23]. A user story (US) is a short piece of text that describes a user interaction typically following the format *"As <an actor>, I want <action>, so that <rationale>"* [3]. User stories can include acceptance criteria (AC), which define the conditions under which stakeholders judge the completion of a story. These rules sometimes follow the format *"Given <pre-condition>, when <action>, then <post-condition>"*, as influenced by Behaviour-Driven Development practices (BDD) [18].

User stories can lack quality in practice [2], leading to ambiguity or incompleteness in requirements' descriptions [9]. For this reason, frameworks for assessing the quality of user stories (e.g., Wake *et al.*'s INVEST mnemonic [26], Heck

© The Author(s) 2026
G. Scanniello et al. (Eds.): PROFES 2025, LNCS 16361, pp. 52–68, 2026.
https://doi.org/10.1007/978-3-032-12089-2_4

et al.'s guidelines [11], Lucassen *et al.*'s Quality User Story framework [15]) and BDD acceptance criteria (e.g., Wautelet *et al.*'s rules [28]) have been developed.

In this work, we combined the results of two literature reviews identifying Natural Language Processing (NLP), and Machine Learning (ML) techniques designed to assess the quality of US and AC automatically. From the list of identified quality indicators, we implemented both a NLP and a ML classifier, validated on a combined dataset sourced from existing works [4, 28] and in-house product backlogs from software engineering project courses. We then evaluated their ability to improve the quality of requirements and user acceptance in a comparative study with 16 third year software engineering students.

The remaining of this paper is structured as follows. Section 2 introduces the method and results of our literature reviews together with the list of selected quality indicators. We discuss the implementation and performance of both classifiers in Sect. 3. In Sect. 4, we discuss the method and results of our user study. We summarise our contribution and its limitations in Sect. 5 before concluding with future works in Sect. 6.

2   Related Work (Literature Review)

2.1   Method

Two literature reviews were conducted in parallel to identify quality assessment frameworks for user stories and acceptance criteria. The IEEE, ACM, and Scopus digital libraries were searched, as described in Table 1. The initial queries were augmented by manual searches on Google Scholar[1].

Table 1. Queries, and result export dates for the literature reviews.

NLP	`"( "user stories" OR "acceptance criteri*" ) AND`
	`( "quality" OR "assess*" OR "eval*" ) AND`
	`( "nlp" OR "natural language processing" )"`
		6 May 2024

ML	`"( "user stories" OR "acceptance criteri*" ) AND`
	`( "quality" OR "assess*" OR "eval*" ) AND`
	`( "machine learning" OR "deep learning"`
	`  OR "artificial intelligence" )"`
		30 April 2024

For the filtering, the following exclusion criteria were applied: (1) full conference proceedings and books; (2) short papers, extended abstracts or posters with insufficient details; (3) papers written in another language than English.

In the first screening phase, titles and abstracts were then read to further filter the results and identify the pool of potential candidates. On top of the need to propose methods or guidelines for individual stories, papers were kept based on the following inclusion criteria:

---

[1] Reproduction packages available under the https://gitlab.com/ai4seng group.

- Assessment frameworks for user stories or acceptance criteria;
- NLP/ML method used with natural language (NL) requirements;
- NLP/ML method used for assessing the quality of NL requirements;
- NLP/ML method for assessing ambiguity in NL requirements.

After filtering, a further manual search on Google Scholar using the same keywords yielded additional relevant papers about acceptance criteria quality assessment, but none of them used ML techniques. All candidate papers were carefully read by one of the authors to determine the final pool (second author focused on NLP papers, third author focused on ML papers). Cross-checks were made by the first author at all stages of the process for both literature reviews to resolve uncertainties in the filtering assessment, and conduct adjustments to filtering where necessary. The full processes are shown in Fig. 1.

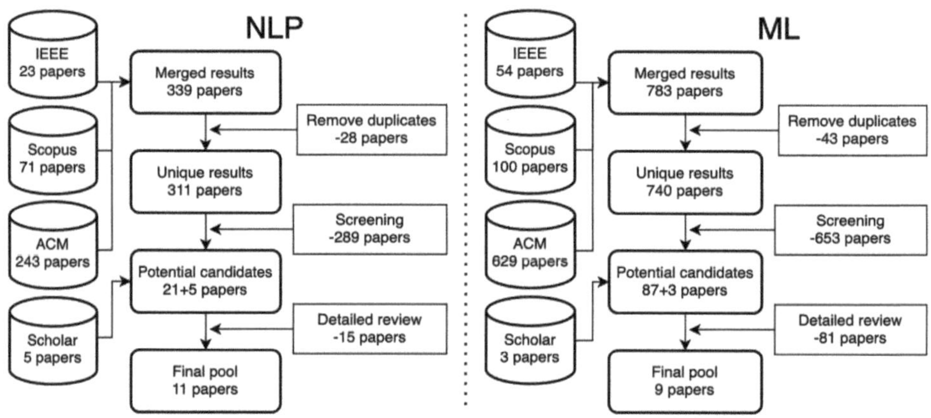

Fig. 1. Literature reviews process; Left: NLP, right: ML.

2.2   Quality Assessment Frameworks

User Story Quality Frameworks. Several frameworks were proposed to assess the quality of user stories, such as Wake *et al.*'s INVEST framework [26], and Heck *et al.*'s guidelines [11]. However the need for an automated process to assess user stories led to more formal frameworks such as QUS [14], later implemented into AQUSA [15], and Jiminéz and Juárez-Ramírez's grammatical framework [13], leading to the USQA prototype [12]. Both later frameworks significantly inspired the implementation of our classifiers, as we will discuss in Sect. 2.4.

Acceptance Criteria Quality Frameworks. Only a couple of exploratory studies on the quality of acceptance criteria used various techniques but ultimately identified a set of quality indicators applicable to both individual and sets of acceptance criteria [19,20]. All indicators related to acceptance criteria had significant overlap with indicators for user stories identified above.

2.3   Automatic Assessment of Quality

NLP for Assessing User Stories. Several works applied NLP techniques to assess the quality of individual user stories. Lucassen *et al.* implemented their QUS framework into AQUSA, resulting in mixed results mainly due to the variety of backlogs used [15]. Dalpiaz *et al.* proposed a tool for finding terminological ambiguity in user stories, but recommended human assessment together with the usage of the tool to improve accuracy [6]. Sarmiento-Calisaya *et al.* implemented a NLP tool to assess structured requirements scenario with a Petri Net generator [22]. While this work deal with different types of requirements, it relies on a similar set of quality indicators, applicable to our context. Wang *et al.* combines user stories with generated iStar models, but focus on inter-backlog qualities, except for the *Estimable* indicator applicable to individual stories [27]. Jiminez *et al.* implemented a partial prototype, but their evaluation focused on grammatical issues or backlog completeness only [12]. Fantechi *et al.* focused their work on ambiguity detection [8]. From all these works, AQUSA, coupled to Fantechi *et al.*'s work revealed to be the most promising as the authors described their rules in details, over a wider range of indicators, which have inspired our work.

ML for Assessing User Stories. Based on Genova *et al.*'s prior work [10], Moreno *et al.* introduce a machine learning technique, specifically rule induction, to create an automatic classifier that replicates expert judgement of requirement quality [17]. Subedi *et al.* propose an approach to identifying user stories that expose the *Testable* and *Valuable* qualities in the INVEST [26] sense [24]. Xu *et al.* establish integrity, consistency (across stories, so out of our scope), and accuracy as criteria for both user stories and acceptance criteria [30]. Fantechi *et al.* compared a NLP process to chatGPT for ambiguity detection, chatGPT showing promising results for short requirements [8].

NLP for Assessing Acceptance Criteria. Based on the results of Oliveira *et al.*'s work [20] as well as the QUS framework [14], Wautelet *et al.* developed a NLP tool to assess the quality of acceptance criteria [28]. This paper also provided information about the rules used for assessing criteria, which are reused in our classifier, and also serves as a baseline for the performance of our classifier.

ML for Assessing Acceptance Criteria. Our literature review did not identify any ML-based approaches for assessing the quality of AC, hence our work is novel, to the best of our knowledge.

2.4   Selected Quality Indicators

From the review of quality indicators for US and AC above, we curated a list of indicators, see Table 2, where we also show which indicators were implemented in which classifier, regardless of their original implementation (e.g., AQUSA relies on NLP, but we followed its rules to annotate our training data set). By construction, the NLP classifier focuses on the quality of the textual structure and the quality of the structure selected to convey the meaning in a requirement. However, such restriction was not necessary for the ML classifier as it relied on manual labelling, but some rules were left out due to poor performance observed during initial evaluation of the trained model, such as full sentences for US and unambiguous AC. It is worth noting that only criteria related to individual requirements were in the scope for this work, and no criteria applying to a full backlog (e.g., redundancy between requirements) were considered.

Table 2. Quality indicators for US and AC requirement specifications, and their implementation in both classifiers.

Rq.	Indicator	Description	NLP Impl.	ML Impl.
US	Well-formed	Structured, with a role, means and a value.	[12, 14, 15, 27]	[12, 14, 15]
US	Uniform	Needs to follow the specified template.	[14, 22, 27]	n/a
US	Full sentences	Needs to be a well-formed full-sentence.	[12, 14, 27]	[12, 17]
US	Atomic	Focus on one feature per story.	[12, 14, 15, 22, 27]	[12, 14, 15, 30]
US	Minimal	Contains **only** a role, a means, and an ends.	[12, 14, 15, 22, 27]	[12, 14, 15, 30]
US	Unambiguous	Needs to have only one meaning.	[5, 6, 8, 12, 14, 22, 27]	[12, 14, 15, 30]
US	Length	Needs to have a maximum length of 70 words.	[10, 12]	n/a
US	Conceptually sound	The means should capture a concrete feature, while the ends expresses the rationale for that feature.	n/a	[12, 14, 15, 24]
US	Problem-oriented	Should specify only the problem. With no discussion of a solution or implementation	n/a	[12, 14, 15]
US	Estimable	A story does not denote a coarse-grained requirement that is difficult to plan and prioritise.	n/a	[14, 15, 27]
AC	Integrity	Needs to contain a context, event, and outcome.	[19, 20, 28]	[19, 20, 28, 30]
AC	Essential	Needs to contain only one context, one event, and one outcome.	[19, 20, 28]	[19, 20, 28]
AC	Singular	Needs to focus on just one flow for the feature.	[19, 20, 28]	[19, 20, 28]
AC	Unambiguous	Needs to have only one meaning.	[5, 6, 8, 19, 20, 28]	n/a
AC	Complete	All necessary elements are interconnected.	n/a	[19, 20, 28]

3 Design and Implementation of Classifiers

3.1 Natural Language Processing Implementation

Overview. Inspired by Sarmiento-Calisaya *et al.* [22], the NLP pipeline uses the NLTK toolkit[2] and works as follow: (1) the preprocessing splits a story, or acceptance criteria in its different parts, e.g., actor - action - value; (2) the classification will then analyse each parts according to rules implementing each relevant quality indicator; and (3) feedback is generated for each unsatisfied rule.

Evaluation of Performance. In order to evaluate the ability of the NLP classifier to cover the indicators described in Sect. 2.4, we compared its results to a human evaluation on a dataset of 201 user stories and 241 acceptance criteria. Part of that dataset was not used as reference to develop the rules in the NLP tool, so that we evaluated the tool on both seen and unseen requirements. The dataset has been annotated by two authors, with cross-checks by the first author, including negotiations on disagreements, so a consensus on the annotation could be reached (see Sect. 3.2 for full annotation process). The dataset came from a selection of Dalpiaz [4] (US), Wautelet *et al.* (US and AC) [28], and backlogs developed in student projects at the *University of Canterbury* (US and AC). Table 3 shows the performance of the NLP tool on the test dataset.

Table 3. Evaluation results for the NLP tool.

Rq.	Indicator	Precision	Recall	F-score
US	Well-formed	1	1	1
US	Uniform	0.85	1	0.92
US	Full sentences	0.85	0.34	0.49
US	Atomic	0.95	0.68	0.79
US	Minimal	0.93	1	0.96
US	Unambiguous	0.7	0.8	0.75
AC	Integrity	0.98	0.95	0.96
AC	Essential	0.98	0.97	0.97
AC	Singular	0.97	0.77	0.86
AC	Unambiguous	0.9	0.5	0.64

Note that the *Length* indicator is left out of the table as this verification is programmatically trivial. *Full sentence* had a very low accuracy, as the complexity of English grammar created issues to cover all possible valid structures as rules. Except for this indicator, the overall performance is in par with the results from AQUSA [15]. In general, the more accurate indicators for both users stories and acceptance criteria were the ones that did not lead to debate when cross-checking the annotations between authors.

---

[2] See https://gitlab.com/ai4seng/nlp4agilerequirements for the source code.

Similarly to the user story evaluation, the *Integrity* and *Essential* indicators were more accurate than those that require more meaning and context, i.e. *Singular* and *Unambiguous*. The prediction of *Unambiguous* AC was similar to a dice roll, highlighting the difficulty to identify ambiguity with naive syntactic rules. This is the only indicator where our tool performs worse than Wautelet *et al.* that showed an average accuracy ≈ 0.7 across indicators [28].

3.2   Machine Learning Implementation

Overview. Various machine learning models have been trained on a subset of our dataset to identify the best performing model for our objective. We decided to follow the prior work by Subedi *et al.* for the initial pool of candidate models as their objectives also encompassed multi-label classification on a similar dataset [24][3]. Before training the models, the text data needed two preprocessing steps using DistilBERT, chosen for its performance in a real-time context so that we can reuse the same approach for real-time feedback [21]: (1) the text is tokenised; and (2) semantic embeddings are generated, so that each word in the raw text is kept with its relationships to other words in the sentence.

Selection and Annotation of Dataset. In a first pass, we annotated 386 US and 493 AC, from the same dataset as described in Sect. 3.1. After independent annotations from two authors, Cohen's Kappa agreement scores were calculated, and all disagreements settled. Prior resolving disagreements, the lowest Kappa scores appeared for: *Well-formed* $k = 0.49$, *Essential* $k = 0.24$, and *Singular* $k = 0.25$, where all other scores were above $k \geq 0.82$. A further 185 US and 252 AC were independently annotated by the third author, following the updated annotation guidelines resulting from the agreement discussions. Punctual cross-checks were applied on these new annotations, with no disagreements observed.

We reserved 20% of this dataset as a held-out test set for final evaluation of the selected models' performance. This stratification ensured that the final performance metrics were calculated on truly unseen data, reducing the risk of over-fitting and therefore providing a more reliable estimate of the models' generalisation capabilities.

Selection and Evaluation of Machine Learning Models. For the model selection phase, we employed a 10-fold cross-validation strategy on the 80% subset for each dataset. The dataset was divided into 10 approximately equal-sized folds, with care taken to maintain the class distribution across folds and runs using an iterative stratification algorithm [25], addressing the multi-class nature of our dataset. The model exhibiting the highest average *F-score* across the 10 folds was selected as the best performer, then retrained on the entire 80% subset to leverage all available training data, and evaluated on the held-out 20% test set. Table 4 summarises the performance achieved by the best performing

---

[3] See https://gitlab.com/ai4seng/ml4agilerequirements for the source code.

models on all quality indicators, namely *Logistic Regression Model* for US, and *Linear Support Vector Classifier* for acceptance criteria.

Table 4. Evaluation of best performing ML models: Logistic Regression (US) and Linear SVC (AC).

Rq.	Indicator	Precision	Recall	F-score
US	Well-formed	0.96	0.76	0.85
US	Atomic	0.90	1.00	0.95
US	Minimal	0.94	0.89	0.91
US	Conceptually sound	0.89	0.99	0.94
US	Problem-oriented	0.97	1.00	0.98
US	Unambiguous	0.74	0.88	0.80
US	Estimable	0.83	0.98	0.90
AC	Complete	0.94	0.94	0.94
AC	Essential	0.94	0.96	0.95
AC	Singular	0.87	0.96	0.91
AC	Integrity	0.87	0.95	0.91

The majority of indicators showed *F-scores* ≥ 0.9, which are close to or better performance when compared to related works [17,19,28]. However, some criteria like *Conceptually sound*, *Problem-oriented* and *Complete* show significant class imbalance, potentially artificially skewing the *F-score* to high values (see reproduction package).

4   User Evaluation

4.1   Context, Demographics, and Method

To compare the ability of the classifiers to assist software engineers in writing software requirements, we conducted a user study. We recruited participants from a software engineering team project course at the *University of Canterbury* using the course notification service (Moodle). Students were incentivised to participate with mall vouchers, and participation was voluntary with no incidence to students' grades as the identity of participants was kept secret from the course coordinator. The study was approved by the Human Research Ethics Committee of the University (ref: 2024/73/LR), and all participants signed consent forms.

There were 7 participants identified as women, and 9 as men, with a range of prior performance in the course (9 A-level students, 4 B-level, and 3 C-level). All students had prior knowledge in software engineering, including on the textual formats used to describe user stories and acceptance criteria as used in this work. However students were not familiar with all indicators highlighted in Sect. 2.4.

The user study was conducted from the 20th to 24th September 2024 and typically took one hour per participant. It involved the following steps: (1) one author (experimenter) introduced the participant into a room set up with a computer, and explained the purpose and timing of the study; (2) the participant received a short brief of fictitious small-scale software system to develop, depicting a few features in free text; (3) the participant wrote 2 stories and 3 acceptance criteria per story, supported by either the NLP or the ML classifier, receiving feedback on demand; (4) the experimenter conducted a structured interview to capture the participant's feedback (see Table 5); and (5) steps 3 and 4 were repeated with the other classifier. Half of the participants started with a different classifier, and the features to develop were randomised between participants to minimise order bias and maturation effect. Participants could move on to the next story at any time, potentially leaving indicators unsatisfied[4].

Table 5. Interview questions for the user study.

ID	Question	Format
1	Rate from 1 to 5 how useful the tips for improving user stories were and provide reasoning.	1–5
2	Was the feedback provided by the tool about user stories helpful or a hindrance, and why?	text
3	Rate from 1 to 5 how useful the tips for improving acceptance criteria were and provide reasoning.	1–5
4	Was the feedback provided by the tool about acceptance criteria helpful or a hindrance, and why?	text
5	What do you think could be improved about the tool's feedback and accuracy?	text

While participants were working on the scenarios, a dedicated logging system recorded the timestamp for each attempt, the scenario number the participant was working on, the input from the participant, and the feedback the classifier displayed for that input. Participants were also encouraged to "think aloud" as they executed their tasks for the experimenter to capture additional observations.

4.2   User Interface

To present interactive feedback to users, a client application was developed, depicted in Fig. 2. The left panel displays the indicators with their definitions, the participants interact with the middle panel where they write their user stories and acceptance criteria, and the right panel displays the assessment by the tool, including which indicator and rules (for the NLP classifier) were unsatisfied by

---

[4] See the full study protocol and source code at https://gitlab.com/ai4seng/ai4agilerequirements-ui.

the participants' attempts. The same interface was consistently used during the full experiment, switching from one classifier to the other after the first interview.

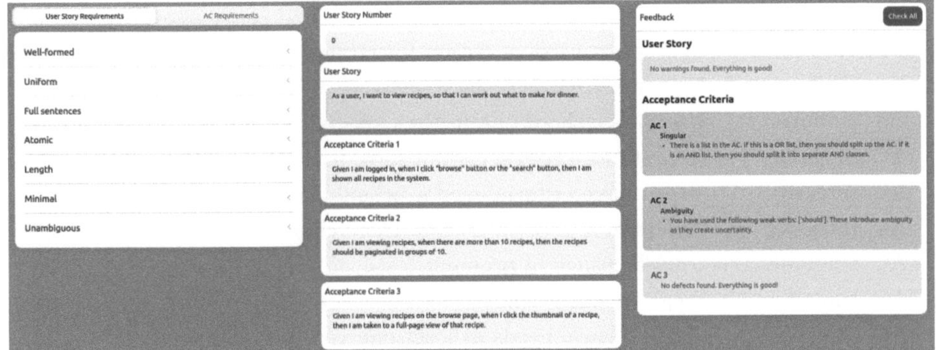

Fig. 2. User interface for interactive feedback.

4.3 Evaluation of Indicators

Commonly Unsatisfied Indicators from NLP Classification. In Table 6 we report on rules that were repeated to the same participant more than once for the same scenario, but not necessarily in a row, alongside the quality indicator the rule relates to. Only rules that were repeated more than 10 times overall are displayed in the table.

The number of occurrences for the two top rules for user stories have been influenced by two sets of false positives observed during the user experiment: (1) when using user types instead of persona (i.e. proper noun), the classifier flagged these attempts as missing an actor in the story; and (2) the classifier falsely flagged some stories written in a single sentences as being multiple. This limitation will be discussed in more details in Sect. 5.2. Still, we observed that rules around well-formedness were commonly violated, either showing a misusage of Cohn's template for user stories, or, from direct observations during the study, a tendency from participants to copy-paste listed features as-is instead of rewriting them in the expected format for their first try.

For acceptance criteria, two types of rules were commonly unsatisfied. First, for ambiguity checks, 88 repeated attempts contained a list instead of splitting conditions in multiple criteria; 25 repeated attempts used pronouns; and 21 used weak modal verbs. Second, the expected format or grammar were not met with either missing parts in the *given-when-then* scenario, or non-verbal sentences.

Commonly Unsatisfied Indicators from ML Classification. Where the NLP classfier relies on manually written rules, we cannot offer the same insights

Table 6. Occurrences of commonly unsatisfied NLP rules per indicator.

Rq.	Indicator	Rule	Count
US	Well-formed	User story must specify who is requesting the feature.	49
US	Minimal	User story must be one sentence.	43
US	Well-formed	User story needs a reason for requesting a feature.	34
US	Well-formed	User story needs to be requesting a feature.	22
US	Uniform	User story should be in the expected format.	15
AC	Singular	Acceptance criteria cannot have lists.	88
AC	Integrity	Acceptance criteria need a 'when' clause.	36
AC	Integrity	Acceptance criteria need a 'then' clause.	27
AC	Unambiguous	Unclear usage of pronoun.	25
AC	Unambiguous	Weak modal verb.	21
AC	Integrity	'Then' clause needs at least one verb and one noun.	13
AC	Integrity	'Given' clause needs at least one verb and one noun.	11
AC	Integrity	Acceptance criterion needs a 'given' clause.	10

Table 7. Occurrences of commonly unsatisfied ML indicators.

Rq.	Indicator	Count
US	Well-formed	131
US	Unambiguous	96
US	Minimal	6
AC	Complete	69
AC	Essential	53
AC	Integrity	50
AC	Singular	2

regarding unsatisfied rules with the ML classifier, being a black-box. Table 7 lists all unsatisfied indicators identified by the ML models during the study.

For user stories, while the results regarding well-formedness are comparable, the ML classifier identified many ambiguities, where the NLP ambiguity rules were never triggered. This may demonstrate the superior ability of machine learning models to detect ambiguity in user stories, similar to Fantechi *et al.* [8].

Regarding acceptance criteria, both classifiers flagged a comparable number of violations of the *Integrity* indicator. The ability for the ML classifier to implement verifications of the *Complete* indicator, i.e. semantic connection between all parts of the *given-when-then* scenario, is somehow in par with the results of the NLP tool flagging missing parts.

Disagreement with Indicators (NLP Classifier). To get insights on the perceived accuracy of the classifiers by participants, we look into how often they disagreed with the classifications, leaving indicators or rules unsatisfied. Table 8 summarises the rules and indicators that participants decided to ignore when using the NLP classifier.

Table 8. Number of indicators left unsatisfied by participants using the NLP classifier.

Rq.	Indicator	Rule	Count
US	Well-formed	User stories need to specify who is requesting the feature	7
US	Minimal	User stories should be just one sentence	3
AC	Singular	Acceptance criteria cannot have lists	10
AC	Integrity	Acceptance criteria need a 'when' clause	2

For user stories, the two rules that were most disagreed with were the rules that contained defects, that we will address in Sect. 5.2. For acceptance criteria, the rules that were most disagreed with were the requirement that acceptance criteria have lists and the requirement that acceptance criteria must have a **when** clause, despite the participants' knowledge about the expected format.

Disagreement with Indicators (ML Classifier). Similarly, Table 9 summarises the participants' disagreements with the ML classifier.

Table 9. Number of indicators left unsatisfied by participants using the ML classifier.

Rq.	Indicator	Count
US	Well-formed	9
US	Unambiguous	8
AC	Complete	12
AC	Essential	10
AC	Integrity	4

Overall, more indicators were left unsatisfied by participants when using the ML classifier. This is especially true for *Complete* (i.e. interconnected parts) and *Essential* (i.e. only one of each parts of the *GWT* format) acceptance criteria. It is worth noting that the classification for *Complete* was not implemented into the NLP tool as deemed too complicated for a rule-based approach. Also the *Essential* indicator was often triggered (see Table 6), but was never left unsatisfied by participants when using the NLP classifier.

Manual Evaluation of Final Attempts. To gauge the efficacy of the classifier to encourage participants to write better US and AC, we conducted a manual assessment of all final attempts following the indicators defined in Table 2 of Sect. 2.4, supplemented by an expert quality review ensuring the written requirements were accurate translations of the expected features. We found that, for requirements written with the aid of the NLP classifier, 69% of US, and 55% of AC passed our expert review, but respectively 70% and 75% passed our review when written with the ML classifier. All failed attempts related to either the *Conceptually sound* or *Complete* indicators.

4.4   Summary of Interview Results

As part of the interview, we asked the students to assess the usefulness of the classifier (see questions 1 and 3, Table 5). Table 10 shows the average ratings given by participants. Note that 2 interview recordings were corrupted and non-recoverable, so we present the results for 14 participants in this section.

Table 10. Average usefulness ratings given by participants.

Rq.	Order during study	NLP avg rating	ML avg rating
US	NLP assessed before ML	3.8	2.2
US	ML assessed before NLP	3.5	3.5
AC	NLP assessed before ML	3.8	2.6
AC	ML assessed before NLP	4.3	3.6

We can note that generally, participants gave higher ratings to the NLP classifier, with an even more pronounced difference for AC when the NLP classifier was evaluated after the ML one. The participants explained this effect by the lack of explainability of the ML classification, compared to the ability of the NLP tool to pinpoint particular rules, something that black-box ML models similar to the chosen ones (Logistic Regression and Linear SVC) can't offer.

In terms of helpfulness of the indicators, we summarise in Table 11 the participants' perception of the classifiers' helpfulness, from their free text responses.

Table 11. Participants' perception of helpfulness of feedback on indicators.

Classifier	Rq.	Useful	Hindrance	Both	Did not say
NLP	US	7	2	1	4
	AC	10	0	2	2
ML	US	8	3	2	1
	AC	7	4	1	2

We can observe a slightly more negative perception towards the ML tool, but participants still majoritarily found both classifiers helpful, even if some participants noted that they may feel "forced" to adhere to the classifiers' assessments when writing their requirements.

5   Discussion

5.1   Summary of Results and Implications

Informed by two literature reviews, we developed both a rule-based NLP, and a ML classifier to assess quality indicators in agile requirements. Both classifiers showed good performance compared to the literature on our mixed dataset (see Sect. 3). We identified that, for many indicators, NLP rules could be developed efficiently to provide explainable feedback to improve the quality of requirements. Additionally, we observed that a ML model performs better to detect ambiguity.

While participants to our user study found the classifiers useful and helpful, the study also highlighted that users may overly rely on the classifiers to tell them how to write *"good"* requirements. Furthermore, participants may stop as soon as the classifier is satisfied, regardless of the fidelity to the expected feature, i.e. the requirement is an accurate translation of the free form feature, leading to sub-optimal requirements, especially when combined to the NLP classifier.

Therefore, the combination of participants' over-reliance on NLP rules to tell them how to improve their requirements, and the observed better quality when using the ML classifier may indicate **that participants engaged more intellectually when facing a black-box classification, leading to more accurate, higher-quality, requirements.**

5.2   Limitations and Threats to Validity

Despite relevant knowledge in agile requirements engineering, participants were not all familiar with the body of knowledge regarding the quality indicators summarised in our literature reviews. Therefore many participants showed lack of practice when they had to write requirements by themselves, hence some decided to ignore parts in *given-when-then* scenarios, for example.

Two rules mentioned in Sect. 4 showed disproportionally large false positive rates leading to some feedback given to participants being erroneous, and influencing the results regarding common mistakes made by participants. This may also have had an impact on participants' perceptions of the NLP classifier.

In terms of threats to validity [29], we particularly note the following:

- *Internal validity:* selection and maturation biases were counter-balanced by the intertwined schedule between the two classifiers, and randomisation of features. Additionally, the annotation of the datasets, and literature reviews were cross-checked by multiple authors.

- *Construct validity:* to draw conclusions, we combined the analysis of the logs produced by the UI tool, notes taken during the think-aloud process, and recordings of interviews, so objective data were used from multiple sources. We also lowered social threats by removing the course coordinator from the experimentation setting.
- *External validity:* due to the experimentation setting, the population, the small sample size, and the imbalance of students' profiles, the generalisability of these results remains low beyond similar (educational) environment. However, both classifiers showed promising experimental results.

6   Conclusions and Future Work

Quality assessment frameworks and tools have been proposed to improve the quality of requirements, especially user stories and acceptance criteria. In this work, we aimed to compare two classifiers: a natural language processing, and a combination of two machine learning models, for assessing user stories and acceptance criteria against state-of-the-art quality assessment frameworks. We also evaluated the performance and usefulness of both classifiers for improving the quality of requirements written by software engineering students. The user study highlighted that participants generally found the classifiers useful and helpful, but preferred the explainability of the NLP classifier against the ML one. Still, participants generally produced requirements of higher quality when using the ML classifier.

In the future, we plan to explore the possibility to combine both approaches in order to cover indicators where the NLP classifier struggles (typically when semantics is important), as well as using explainable transformer architectures, such as attention mechanisms [7] to provide more detailed feedback to users.

References

1. de Almeida Falbo, R., Braga, C.E.C., Machado, B.N.: Semantic documentation in requirements engineering. In: Ibero-American Conference Software Engineering (CIBSE) (2014)
2. Amna, A.R., Poels, G.: Ambiguity in user stories: a systematic literature review. Inf. Softw. Technol. **145** (2022)
3. Cohn, M.: User Stories Applied: For Agile Software Development. Addison-Wesley Professional (2004)
4. Dalpiaz, F.: Requirements data sets (user stories) (2018). https://doi.org/10.17632/7zbk8zsd8y.1
5. Dalpiaz, F., Van der Schalk, I., Lucassen, G.: Pinpointing ambiguity and incompleteness in requirements engineering via information visualization and NLP. In: International Working Conference on Requirements Engineering: Foundation for Software Quality (REFSQ). Springer (2018)
6. Dalpiaz, F., Van Der Schalk, I., Brinkkemper, S., Aydemir, F.B., Lucassen, G.: Detecting terminological ambiguity in user stories: tool and experimentation. Inf. Softw. Technol. **110** (2019)

7. El Houda Dehimi, N., Tolba, Z.: Attention mechanisms in deep learning: towards explainable artificial intelligence. In: International Conference on Pattern Analysis and Intelligent Systems (PAIS) (2024)
8. Fantechi, A., Gnesi, S., Semini, L., et al.: Rule-based NLP vs ChatGPT in ambiguity detection, a preliminary study. In: International Working Conference on Requirement Engineering: Foundation for Software Quality (REFSQ) Workshops (2023)
9. Gupta, A., Poels, G., Bera, P.: Using conceptual models in agile software development: a possible solution to requirements engineering challenges in agile projects. IEEE Access **10** (2022)
10. G nova, G., Fuentes, J.M., Llorens, J., Hurtado, O., Moreno, V.: A framework to measure and improve the quality of textual requirements. Requirements Eng. **18** (2011)
11. Heck, P., Zaidman, A.: A quality framework for agile requirements: a practitioner's perspective. arXiv preprint arXiv:1406.4692 (2014)
12. Jiménez, S., Alanis, A., Beltrán, C., Juárez-Ramírez, R., Ramírez-Noriega, A., Tona, C.: USQA: a user story quality analyzer prototype for supporting software engineering students. Comput. Appl. Eng. Educ. **31**(4) (2023)
13. Jiménez, S., Juárez-Ramírez, R.: A quality framework for evaluating grammatical structure of user stories to improve external quality. In: International Conference in Software Engineering Research and Innovation (CONISOFT). IEEE (2019)
14. Lucassen, G., Dalpiaz, F., Van Der Werf, J.M.E., Brinkkemper, S.: Forging high-quality user stories: towards a discipline for agile requirements. In: International Requirements Engineering Conference (RE). IEEE (2015)
15. Lucassen, G., Dalpiaz, F., van der Werf, J.M.E., Brinkkemper, S.: Improving agile requirements: the quality user story framework and tool. Requirements Eng. **21** (2016)
16. Lucassen, G., Dalpiaz, F., Werf, J.M.E.V.D., Brinkkemper, S.: The use and effectiveness of user stories in practice. In: Requirements Engineering: Foundation for Software Quality (REFSQ). Springer (2016)
17. Moreno, V., Génova, G., Parra, E., Fraga, A.: Application of machine learning techniques to the flexible assessment and improvement of requirements quality. Softw. Qual. J. **28**(4), 1–30 (2020)
18. North, D.: Introducing BDD (2006). https://dannorth.net/introducing-bdd/
19. Oliveira, G., Marczak, S.: On the empirical evaluation of BDD scenarios quality: preliminary findings of an empirical study. In: International Requirements Engineering Conference Workshops. IEEE (2017)
20. Oliveira, G., Marczak, S., Moralles, C.: How to evaluate BDD scenarios' quality? In: Brazilian Symposium on Software Engineering. ACM (2019)
21. Sanh, V., Debut, L., Chaumond, J., Wolf, T.: DistilBERT, a distilled version of BERT: smaller, faster, cheaper and lighter. arXiv preprint arXiv:1910.01108 (2020)
22. Sarmiento-Calisaya, E., Cárdenas, E.H., Cornejo-Aparicio, V., Alzamora, G.S.: Towards the improvement of natural language requirements descriptions: the C&L tool. In: Annual ACM Symposium on Applied Computing. ACM (2020)
23. Schön, E.M., Thomaschewski, J., Escalona, M.J.: Agile requirements engineering: a systematic literature review. Comput. Stand. Interfaces **49** (2017)
24. Subedi, I.M., Singh, M., Ramasamy, V., Walia, G.S.: Classification of testable and valuable user stories by using supervised machine learning classifiers. In: 2021 IEEE International Symposium on Software Reliability Engineering Workshops (ISSREW) (2021)

25. Szymanski, P., Kajdanowicz, T.: A network perspective on stratification of multi-label data. In: Proceedings of the International Workshop on Learning with Imbalanced Domains: Theory and Applications, vol. 74. PMLR (2017)
26. Wake, B.: Invest in good stories, and smart tasks. online (2003). https://xp123.com/invest-in-good-stories-and-smart-tasks/
27. Wang, T., Wang, C., Li, T., Liu, Z., Zhai, Y.: User story quality assessment based on multi-dimensional perspective: a preliminary framework. In: International iStar Workshop (2022)
28. Wautelet, Y., Nassiri, A.K., Tsilionis, K.: Investigating quality attributes in behavior-driven development scenarios: an evaluation framework and an experimental supporting tool. In: IFIP Working Conference on The Practice of Enterprise Modeling. Springer (2023)
29. Wohlin, C., Runeson, P., Höst, M., Ohlsson, M.C., Regnell, B., Wesslén, A., et al.: Experimentation in Software Engineering. Springer (2012)
30. Xu, X., Dou, Y., Qian, L., Jiang, J., Yang, K., Tan, Y.: Quality improvement method for high-end equipment's functional requirements based on user stories. Adv. Eng. Inform. **56** (2023)

A Robust LSTM-Based Test Selection
Method for Self-Driving Cars

Ali Ihsan Güllü[(✉)] [iD], Faiz Ali Shah [iD], and Dietmar Pfahl [iD]

University of Tartu, Narva mnt 18, 51009 Tartu, Estonia
`{ali.ihsan.gullu,faiz.ali.shah,dietmar.pfahl}@ut.ee`

Abstract. Self-Driving Cars (SDCs) require extensive testing in a simulator, which can be costly in terms of time. To optimize the test process, simple and straightforward test cases should be excluded, while challenging test cases should be selected. This study addresses the test selection problem for lane-keeping systems of self-driving cars. Road segment features, such as angles and lengths, were extracted and treated as sequences, enabling classification of the test cases as PASS or FAIL using a Long Short-Term Memory (LSTM) model, named ITS4SDC. The ITS4SDC model is compared against a range of traditional machine learning-based classifiers. Results indicate that the ITS4SDC model outperforms machine learning-based methods in accuracy and precision while exhibiting comparable performance in recall. A follow-up analysis demonstrated the robustness of the ITS4SDC model regarding changes in the Out-Of-Bound (OOB) measure which was used to distinguish PASS from FAIL cases. This work presents a novel LSTM-based approach that solves the problem of selecting test cases in the context of simulation-based testing of SDCs. The proposed solution is effective and robust.

Keywords: Self-driving cars · Simulation-based test selection · Long short-term memory

1 Introduction

Self-driving cars (SDCs), as key components of cyber-physical systems, should be tested in simulation environments before being deployed in the real world to identify potential accidents, prevent financial losses, and not endanger human and animal lives [22,25]. Various simulation platforms[1], such as MATLAB/Simulink, BeamNG.tech, Gazebo, CarSim, SUMO, PreScan, CARLA, LGSVL, and AirSim, have been developed for testing SDCs in the simulation world [1,16].

Despite the benefits of simulation platforms, testing vehicles in these simulation environments is costly in terms of time. To minimize testing cost, it would be helpful to identify and execute only those tests that are likely to cause failures and exclude overly simple tests from the test suite. To address this problem, a test

---

[1] MATLAB/Simulink, BeamNG.tech, Gazebo, CarSim, SUMO, PreScan, CARLA, LGSVL, and AirSim.

G. Scanniello et al. (Eds.): PROFES 2025, LNCS 16361, pp. 69–85, 2026.
https://doi.org/10.1007/978-3-032-12089-2_5

selection model for lane-keeping scenarios in SDCs is developed. The proposed model, named **I**ntelligent **T**est **S**elector **for** **S**elf-**D**riving **C**ars (**ITS4SDC**), is based on a long short-term memory (LSTM) recurrent neural network [13] that focuses on identifying challenging driving scenarios by selecting failure-triggering roads as test cases. The developed model has also been used in the *Self-Driving Car Testing Tool Competition*, organized as part of the 18th IEEE International Conference on Software Testing, Verification and Validation (ICST) 2025[2].

To generate roads with diverse characteristics, the Frenetic road generation algorithm is used [8]. Frenetic is designed to create challenging roads that make it difficult for vehicles to stay within their lanes. It is one of the tools used in the SBST 2021 conference[3] to produce road types where vehicles most frequently went off-road. The Frenetic algorithm has also been utilized in other contexts, such as [3,6]. To label generated roads as PASS (SAFE) or FAIL (UNSAFE), they are evaluated using the BeamNG.tech simulation platform, which offers realistic soft-body physics-based SDC testing. Its realistic physics, including friction forces and deformation during collisions, make it one of the most realistic simulation platforms for SDCs. A part of the labeled roads is then used as training data for models that aim at correctly classifying previously unseen roads as safe or unsafe. The rest of the labeled roads serve as the validation set.

The evaluation results demonstrate that the new LSTM-based ITS4SDC model outperforms a set of state-of-the-art machine learning models in terms of accuracy and precision while showing comparable performance in recall. Moreover, the ITS4SDC model performance is robust with regards to changes in the definition of FAIL-labels. FAIL-labels are defined based on the Out-Of-Bound (OOB) measure.

The main contributions of this paper are the following:

- Description of the ITS4SDC model, a novel LSTM-based model for effective SDC test road selection [24].
- Presentation of a comprehensive comparison between the ITS4SDC and SDC-Scissor [2], a state-of-the-art set of machine learning models for binary test road classification.
- Curation and public release of a labeled (PASS/FAIL) test road dataset for SDC regression testing [12].

This paper is structured as follows. Section 2 presents the background to the research presented in this paper. Section 3 presents related work on testing SDCs for lane-keeping scenarios. Section 4 covers the generation and labeling of test cases, as well as dataset preparation and model training. Section 6 compares the proposed ITS4SDC model with SDC-Scissor, offering a detailed performance analysis. Section 7 summarizes the threats to validity. Section 8 highlights the advantages of the proposed model and outlines recommendations for future work.

---

[2] ICST 2025.
[3] SBST 2021.

2   Background

SDC Scenarios. An SDC scenario typically includes the SDC itself, its environment, and surrounding factors such as roads, buildings, other vehicles or obstacles, weather conditions, and an intended driving maneuver [17]. These scenarios are generated in simulation environments to evaluate the behavior and performance of SDCs.

Among the fundamental scenarios for SDCs is lane-keeping, which has been extensively studied in previous research [3,4,6,11,14,20]. The lane-keeping scenario focuses on one of the most basic safety functions of SDCs, i.e., preventing the vehicle from leaving the road by considering the geometry of the road and the speed of the vehicle. To ensure that the SDCs can adapt to various road geometries, it is essential to thoroughly test the lane-keeping system. For this purpose, the vehicle must be tested on roads with diverse characteristics, such as varying geometries, features, and lengths, and its behavior must be closely examined. However, it is impractical to test every possible road configuration due to the infinite number of potential features and geometries. Therefore, selecting or prioritizing challenging tests that are likely to cause the SDC under test to fail by leaving the road is crucial.

BeamNG.tech Simulation Environment. The BeamNG.tech simulator was employed to test the lane-keeping system of SDCs. This simulator stands out among others due to its realistic physics engine, which closely models the unique dynamics of each vehicle, including skidding, traction, and braking behavior. These realistic physics provide a more accurate assessment of the performance of SDCs under diverse road conditions.

(a) PASS case   (b) FAIL case

Fig. 1. Vehicle stays in the lane (a) or goes off the lane (b) while taking a turn.

Road Generation for SDC Testing. To make the test selection problem challenging, it is important to generate test roads that adequately test the limits of an SDC's lane-keeping system. To address this, the 2022 SBST Tool Competition was organized, aiming to encourage the development of road generation tools designed to create challenging road scenarios for SDCs [10,21].

The first step in testing the lane-keeping systems of SDCs is generating realistic roads. The (x, y) two-dimensional road coordinates are used to create road textures by extending the coordinates laterally on both sides to form a realistic asphalt surface in the simulation environment. Each test starts with a fresh simulation, and the simulation is terminated immediately if the vehicle either violates the defined out-of-bound (OOB) parameter (e.g., crossing the lane boundaries) or reaches the finish line. An example of a scenario where the vehicle successfully stays within the lane is illustrated in Fig. 1a . Conversely, Fig. 1b illustrates the scenario where the vehicle fails to navigate a curve and starts going off-road. The snapshot in Fig. 1b is captured just before the simulation is terminated.

3   Related Work

Studies have been conducted on the problem of selecting PASS and FAIL test roads for SDCs. A review of these studies is provided in [17], which compares several tools [4,6,9,18,19,21]. Among these tools, the SDC-Scissor tool specifically addresses the lane-keeping problem in SDCs [6]. Since SDC-Scissor represents the state-of-the-art when we conducted our study, it serves as our baseline during evaluation. By analyzing road geometries and extracting relevant features, SDC-Scissor classifies roads as either SAFE (PASS) or UNSAFE (FAIL). When developing SDC-Scissor, Birchler et al. conducted the most comprehensive study on lane-keeping systems for SDCs, focusing on road feature extraction and classification [3]. Road attributes (e.g., the number of left and right turns) and statistical metrics (e.g., segment standard deviation and median) were extracted using a segment-based strategy. These features were then classified using machine learning models such as Random Forest, Gradient Boosting, Support Vector Machine, Gaussian Naïve Bayes, Logistic Regression, and Decision Tree.

The SDC-Scissor approach relies on the assumption that statistical or behavioral differences exist between FAIL and PASS roads, which machine learning algorithms can detect by identifying distinct patterns. Different to SDC-Scissor and other existing approaches, for the development of the ITS4SDC the test road classification and selection problem is formulated in such a way that it becomes suitable for LSTMs, which are known to be good at classifying sequential data. This is achieved by representing roads as a sequence of coordinates (way-points).

4   Development of the ITS4SDC Model

This section describes the configuration of the simulation environment used to generate and automatically label test roads, the preparation of the datasets used to train and validate the ITS4SDC and SDC-Scissor models, and the development of the ITS4SDC model architecture.

4.1 Configuration of the Simulation Environment

BeamNG.tech is used as a simulation environment. A 2D map is used for the vehicle, which does not perform any ascending or descending movements along the z-axis. The vehicle selected by the simulation is the ETK-800 model, which was also chosen by previous SDC test selection studies [2,3,5,6]. The BeamNG.tech simulation environment includes a variety of vehicles [23]. However, each vehicle's road grip varies due to differences in components such as the suspension system, tire characteristics, weight distribution and center of gravity, differential type, Traction Control System (TCS), Anti-lock Braking System (ABS), and Electronic Stability Control (ESC) units. For example, a turn that one vehicle can take at 50km/h may not be possible for another vehicle at the same speed.

In BeamNG.tech, vehicles can be controlled either manually or autonomously. For autonomous control, BeamNG.AI, developed by BeamNG.tech, or a custom-developed driver can be utilized. The BeamNG.AI is capable of performing various tasks such as moving on random roads, pursuing a target vehicle, avoiding a target vehicle, maintaining a safe following distance with a target vehicle, and tracking a predefined path. For this study, the configuration is set to make the vehicle follow a given path. The AI driver drives the vehicle based on specific driving parameters, including Maximum Speed (MaxSpeed), Risk Factor (RF), and OOB tolerance.

The SDCs accelerate to MaxSpeed if there are no obstacles and the road is safe and straight. The RF defines the aggressiveness level of the SDCs. If RF is high (e.g., 2.0), the vehicle maintains a high speed and takes significant risks, often causing it to lose stability in sharp curves. When the RF is moderate (e.g., 1.5), the vehicle tends to approach the edges of the road unless the curve is too sharp, in which case it slows down. A low-risk factor (e.g., 1.0) minimizes risk, allowing the vehicle to maintain maximum speed only on completely straight roads. Even on slightly curved roads, the SDC slows down significantly before entering the curve. OOB tolerance defines the permissible extent (as a percentage) of the vehicle's deviation from the road or lane markings before marking the test as a failure. If the simulation is required to stop and the test labeled as FAIL when 50% of the vehicle goes off the road, the OOB tolerance is set to 0.5.

In the context of this study, by default, MaxSpeed is set to 120 km/h, RF to 1.5, and OOB tolerance to 0.5, consistent with the parameter settings used in the ICST 2025 SDC Testing Tool Competition Track. The BeamNG simulator processes the test cases (roads) using the Test-Execution framework provided by SDC-Scissor [2].

4.2 Dataset Preparation

To test SDCs in a simulation environment, the Frenetic tool, which uses a genetic algorithm, is utilized to generate roads with varying characteristics such as the number of curves, turns, and total distance [8]. However, not all roads generated by the Frenetic algorithm are valid. A valid road cannot contain self-intersections or partially overlapping paths [11]. During preprocessing, such invalid roads were removed from the Frenetic-generated dataset, leaving only valid roads to be used as test cases. In some test cases, when the target coordinate is positioned very close to the starting point, the AI Driver occasionally attempts to reach the target point by reversing or making an abrupt maneuver at the beginning of the test. While these cases were labeled as PASS by the simulator, they were excluded from the test suite as the vehicle did not follow the intended path.

In our study, three new datasets were created. Dataset-1 contains 10,000 test roads of which 3,853 received the label FAIL (38%) and 6,147 received the label PASS. Labels were automatically assigned by running SDC-Scissor's Test-Execution framework. If the SDC under test is not able to follow the road, the FAIL-label is assigned, otherwise the PASS-label. The labeling of Dataset-1 assumed that the AI driver uses the values 120 km/h, 1.5, and 0.5 for MaxSpeed, RF, and OOB tolerance, respectively. These are the settings that were also applied in the creation of the dataset used for the original evaluation of SDC-Scissor. The dataset used to develop and evaluate SDC-Scissor is re-used and named Dataset-2 in this study [7]. Dataset-2 contains 3,559 test roads of which 1,334 received the label FAIL (37%) and 2,225 received the label PASS.

To be able to explore the robustness of ITS4SDC against changes in the core parameters that are used for assigning the PASS and FAIL labels. As a start, the focus was laid exclusively on the OOB tolerance value, which was changed to 0.3 to create Dataset-1–30 and 0.1 to create Dataset-1–10. Dataset-1–30 contains 4,746 test roads of which 1,803 received the label FAIL (38%) and 2,943 received the label PASS. Dataset-1–10 contains 1,324 test roads of which 503 received the label FAIL (38%) and 821 received the label PASS.

4.3 Building the ITS4SDC Model with LSTM

Identifying Road Features. An initial analysis of Dataset-1 was conducted to examine the characteristics and statistical differences between roads labeled as FAIL and PASS, as in [6]. These characteristics and analyses focused on segment-based road examination, where each segment is defined as the line connecting two consecutive road coordinates. Features such as the total number of left/right turns, average turning angles, and turning radius were considered. However, the segment-based analysis revealed no significant feature distinctions between FAIL and PASS test cases. The inability to differentiate directly based on road characteristics is affected by the risk factor considered by the AI Driver of the vehicle. The following examples illustrate the challenges of directly separating FAIL and PASS cases based on road features:

– On roads with very sharp curves, the significant angle changes and increased number of turns often can be considered as a challenging path. However, if the curve is located at the beginning of the road, the vehicle can navigate it before gaining high speed and successfully completing the route.
– In the case of two consecutive curves, the vehicle successfully passes the first non-sharp curve, loses some speed, and safely enters and exits the second curve. However, the presence of multiple curves causes significant fluctuations in the angle statistics of the mentioned road.

– On a road with a low turning angle, if the vehicle starts on a straight path, it fails to navigate the curve and leaves the road due to gained speed during the straight part of the road.
– A vehicle traveling on a straight road successfully navigates a curve located very close to the target coordinate. However, the reason for slowing down is not the curve itself, but the proximity of the target coordinate immediately after the curve, as the AI Driver considers the entire road.

These observations indicate that the road characteristics alone do not determine whether the vehicle will go off the road; the driver's behavior is equally important. Initially, we tried to classify test roads by only using road features, as in [3,6], but these features alone showed no significant distinction across Dataset-1, and the apparent separation observed with a small dataset diminished as the dataset grew to 10,000 test cases.

In segment-based road analysis, it is essential to consider road features as a sequence. Two primary features of the road have been examined:

– Segment Angle: The angular displacement formed between a segment defined by two consecutive road positions and an adjacent segment.
– Segment Length: The length of a segment is defined by an Euclidean distance between two consecutive road positions.

The segment angle provides information about curves on the road. Sudden changes in segment angles represent sharp turns. However, the angle alone is insufficient due to variations in the distances between consecutive road positions. Since the duration of a vehicle's turn is determined by the length of the corresponding segment, segment length has been considered as the second feature. On the other hand, considering only segment length as a sequence lacks information about curves and, therefore, fails to provide meaningful information about the safety of the road.

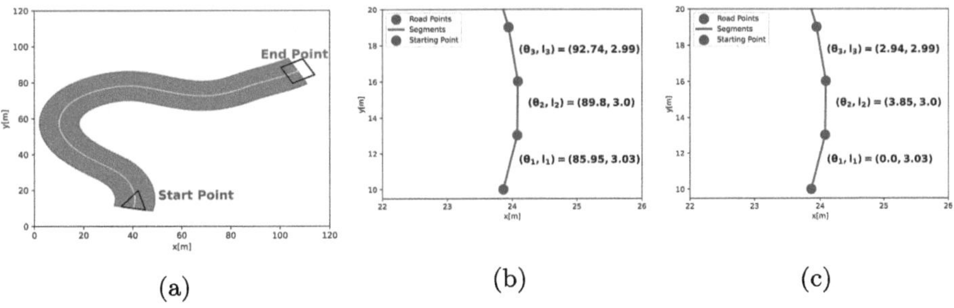

Fig. 2. (a) An example road as a test case. (b) Angle and length pairs corresponding to the road coordinates. (c) Calculated angle information relative to previous reference segments.

The vehicle's ability to stay on the road depends not only on the angle between two consecutive segments but also on the sequential behavior across multiple segments. This makes the problem a sequence classification task, as the sequence characteristics are influenced by both the current road segment and its neighboring segments. Let S_k denote the k-th road segment. Instead of considering only a single segment in isolation, a local neighborhood around the segment is taken into account, as defined in Expression (1). For a given segment S_k, its neighboring segments within a fixed range are also included in the analysis:

$$\{S_{K-w}, S_{K-w+1}, \ldots, S_K, \ldots, S_{K+w}\} \tag{1}$$

where w defines the neighborhood size, meaning that information from w previous and w subsequent segments is incorporated. This formulation ensures that the model captures local dependencies in road geometry.

To address this sequence-based nature of the classification problem, LSTM models are well-suited [15]. The classification labels are binary (0-FAIL and 1-PASS). Initially, the road is represented as a sequence of N coordinate points, as given in Expression (2).

$$\{(x_1, y_1), (x_2, y_2), \ldots, (x_N, y_N)\} \tag{2}$$

where N is the total number of discrete points sampled along the road. From these coordinates, the features (θ_i, l_i), where $i = 1, \ldots, N-1$ denotes the segment index, are computed for each consecutive pair of points. This results in a feature vector of size $(2, N-1)$, as each of the $N-1$ segments is derived from N sampled points along the road. The feature vector serves as the input to the LSTM model, capturing variations in segment angle differences and segment lengths. Figure 2a illustrates an example test case.

Angles are calculated relative to the two-dimensional Cartesian coordinate system. However, the road's initial rotation varies, resulting in high initial angle values (e.g., 200° or 300°). Since the absolute angle values are irrelevant as long as the road remains unchanged, only the angular changes between segments are meaningful. In this representation, the x-axis is considered as the reference direction (0°), meaning that all angles are measured counterclockwise from the x-axis. Figure 2b illustrates the angles and lengths of the first three road segments relative to the x-axis. To avoid very large numerical values in the model's input vector and to speed up training, the angle value of the first segment is initialized to zero. For subsequent segments, the angle difference is calculated by subtracting the angle value of the preceding segment. This difference is then used as the angle information for the current segment. By doing so, the angle values for all segments are adjusted relative to their preceding segments. The recalculated angle values for the road coordinates are shown in Fig. 2c .

Implementation of the ITS4SDC Model. The LSTM model is implemented as a bidirectional LSTM layer. Unlike unidirectional LSTM, bidirectional LSTM processes the sequence from start to end, and then it reprocesses again from end to start. In other words, it not only considers past information but also incorporates future information. Applying reverse sequence processing in the context of roads, the future behavior of the road is as important as its past behavior. Because the AI Driver adjusts its speed and steering angle based on the upcoming curve conditions. Moreover, it has been observed that bidirectional LSTM outperforms unidirectional LSTM when working with smaller dataset sizes (e.g., 1000–3000). However, as the dataset size increases (e.g., 8000–10,000), unidirectional LSTM achieves the same performance as bidirectional LSTM. The conclusion drawn from the experiments is that bidirectional LSTM either provides better results or matches the performance of unidirectional LSTM, which is the primary reason for selecting bidirectional LSTM in this study.

The LSTM model architecture is optimized through experiments. The dataset contained 197 (x, y) coordinates for each road, and the best performance is achieved using a single-layer LSTM model with 220 LSTM cells. Adding more layers or increasing the number of cells did not improve performance and even hindered learning. The activation function used in LSTM cell states and outputs is *tanh*, and a dense layer with a sigmoid activation function is used at the output. Binary cross-entropy is used as the loss function, as it is the standard choice for binary classification tasks and effectively measures the difference between predicted probabilities and actual labels.

To optimize the model architecture, a discrete grid-based hyperparameter search was conducted. The number of LSTM layers was varied from 1 to 10, and the number of LSTM cells was tested with values of 64, 128, 256, and 512. Different optimizers were considered, including Adam, Stochastic Gradient Descent (SGD), RMSprop, and Adagrad. The learning rate was tested at 0.1, 0.01, 0.001, and 0.0001. The best-performing model was determined through experimentation and further fine-tuned, leading to the final selection of 220 LSTM cells while keeping the other parameters fixed.

To prevent overfitting, an early stopping mechanism was implemented with a patience level of 10 epochs. This value was selected as a reasonable heuristic based on typical early stopping settings in deep learning. While it was not systematically tuned, it performed well in practice, ensuring that training stopped before significant overfitting occurred. The final model configuration used for training is as follows:

- Loss function: binary cross-entropy
- Batch size: 1024
- Epoch: 200
- Optimizer: Adam
- Learning rate: 0.001
- Early stopping patience: 10.

The test data processing pipeline of ITS4SDC is presented in Fig. 3. The model takes test road coordinates as input and, in the *Feature Extraction and Angle Adjustment* block, computes the input features required for the LSTM layer. It calculates the angle values as the angular difference between each segment and the preceding segment. At the output of the LSTM layer, a dense layer reduces the information to a single value. The final sigmoid layer outputs the result as a probability between 0 and 1. If the output value of the dense layer is greater than 0.5, the test case is interpreted as PASS, otherwise as FAIL.

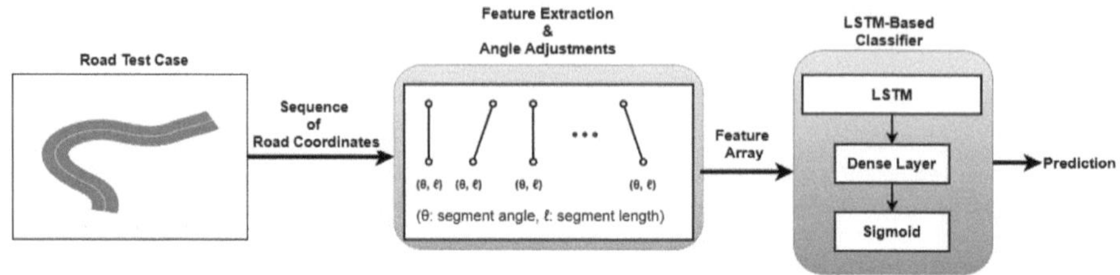

Fig. 3. Test data processing pipeline of ITS4SDC.

5   Evaluation of the ITS4SDC Model

The performance of the ITS4SDC is evaluated by comparing it with SDC-Scissor [6], a machine learning-based model developed specifically for lane-keeping systems in SDCs. Table 1 shows in its first two and last two rows the setups that are used to compare the ITS4SDC with SDC-Scissor. The original versions of each model were developed using different datasets, i.e., Dataset-1, Dataset-2, Dataset-1–30, and Dataset-1–10 respectively. Therefore, to make the comparison between the two models fair, both models are trained and validated on each dataset during the evaluation (Setup 1, Setup 2, Setup 5, and Setup 6). Evaluating the models across datasets that differ regarding quality (e.g., noise level) and definition of FAIL (e.g., chosen OOB threshold) help assess robustness and avoid overfitting or bias towards a single dataset. The total runtime for all experiments conducted on Dataset-1, Dataset-1–30, and Dataset-1–10 was approximately 190 h. For both models, 10-fold cross-validation (10CV) was applied in Setups 1, 2, and 5. However, due to the smaller dataset size, Setup-6 was evaluated using 5-fold cross-validation for both models.

Setup 3 and Setup 4 in Table 1 describe the setups that could only be used to evaluate the ITS4SDC model performance. In these setups, SDC-Scissor's built-in k-fold cross-validation configurations were not modified, and only the ITS4SDC architecture was used without applying cross-validation. Setup-3 corresponds to training the ITS4SDC model on the full Dataset-1 and validating it on Dataset-2, while Setup-4 corresponds to training on the full Dataset-2 and validating on Dataset-1. In contrast, Setups 1, 2, 5 and 6 involve k-fold cross-validation, meaning the full dataset is never used entirely for training.

To facilitate an analysis that checks whether the ITS4SDC model's performance is robust with regards to changes in the definition of what is considered a FAIL, variants of Dataset-1 were generated, i.e., Dataset-1–30 and Dataset-1–10.

Table 1. Setups for Evaluating the Models

	ITS4SDC	SDC-Scissor
Setup	**Trained and Validated on**	**Trained and Validated on**
1	T+V: Dataset-1 (10CV)	T+V: Dataset-1 (10CV)
2	T+V: Dataset-2 (10CV)	T+V: Dataset-2 (10CV)
3	T: Dataset-1 + V: Dataset 2	n/a
4	T: Dataset-2 + V: Dataset-1	n/a
5	T+V: Dataset-1–30 (10CV)	T+V: Dataset-1–30 (10CV)
6	T+V: Dataset-1–10 (5CV)	T+V: Dataset-1–10 (5CV)

In the evaluation the metrics accuracy, precision, recall, and F1-score are used. In formulas shown below, the positive class P corresponds to PASS and the negative class N corresponds to FAIL[4]. True positives, true negatives, false positives, and false negatives are abbreviated as TP, TN, FP, FN, respectively.

$$Accuracy = (|TP| + |TN|)/(|P| + |N|)$$

$$Precision = |TP|/(|TP| + |FP|)$$

$$Recall = |TP|/(|TP| + |FN|)$$

$$F1 - score = 2 * |TP|/(2 * |TP| + |FP| + |FN|)$$

6   Results

Performance of ITS4SDC. In Table 2, Setup-1 to Setup-6 correspond to the definitions given in Table 1. The results show that Setup-1 performs best. This is to be expected, because the model is trained on a large, noiseless dataset (90% of Dataset-1), and predicts correctly labeled data (10% of Dataset-1). Setup-5 and Setup-6 show slightly lower performance than Setup-1, probably due to the smaller sizes of Dataset-1–30 and Dataset-1–10 compared to Dataset-1.

Setup-3 shows the lowest performance. This is surprising at the first glance, because the ITS4SDC model is, like in Setup-1, Setup-5, and Setup-6, trained on noiseless data. Moreover, the size of the training dataset is the largest, because the complete Dataset-1 is used. The reason for the low performance could lie in the fact that the labels of a noisy dataset (Dataset-2) are predicted. One could speculate that the number of FN and FP cases leading to the low performance are actually correctly classified test roads that simply were labeled incorrectly. The drop in performance for Setup-2 and Setup-4 might also be explained by the use of Dataset-2, in this case as training dataset and, in Setup-2, also as validation dataset. Explanations for varying performance often focus on dataset size, data quality, and potential overfitting. The latter can be excluded for ITS4SDC due

---

[4] The positive class has been chosen to be PASS in order to be consistent with [2].

Table 2. ITS4SDC's performance metrics across setups

Setup	Accuracy	Precision	Recall	F1
1	0.88	0.90	0.90	0.90
2	0.66	0.68	0.87	0.76
3	0.65	0.72	0.72	0.72
4	0.70	0.70	0.90	0.78
5	0.76	0.79	0.84	0.81
6	0.73	0.78	0.82	0.79

to the early stopping mechanism used in model training. A full discussion of the mean training and validation loss curves for Setup-1, Setup-2, Setup-5, and Setup-6 can be found in the Materials (see footnote 5). We did not conduct this analysis for Setup-3 and Setup-4 because no cross-validation was done.

Dataset sizes vary strongly between Dataset-1, Dataset-1–30, Dataset-2, and Dataset-1–10, i.e., from 10,000 over 4,746 and 3,559 down to 1,324, respectively. The quality of Dataset-1 is good. It contains a wide range of different test roads and the labels are correct. The quality of Dataset-2 is equally good regarding test road variance, but the manual analysis of a randomly picked sample of 200 test roads from Dataset-2 showed that more than 20% were labeled incorrectly. It is unclear how the noise got into Dataset-2. It is possible that labels were assigned using a version of the BeamNG.tech simulator different to the one used in this study. Overall, ITS4SDC seems to be robust against variations of the OOB threshold but mildly affected by reduced training dataset size and quality.

Comparison Between ITS4SDC and SDC-Scissor. Table 3 shows the results of the comparison between the ITS4SDC and SDC-Scissor. Comparisons A to F refer to six possible combinations of setups as defined in Table 1. The performance metrics show the differences that result when subtracting the average metric value of SDC-Scissor from the corresponding metric value of the ITS4SDC. As mentioned in Sect. 3, SDC-Scissor utilizes six different machine learning models and calculates the accuracy, precision, recall, and F1 score values for each model. The reason for averaging over metric values of the six machine learning models in SDC-Scissor is that none of the models consistently outperformed the others. The absolute values of the performance measures for SDC-Scissor when using Dataset-1, Dataset-2, Dataset-1–30, and Dataset-1–10 can be found in the Materials[5]. Table 3 indicates that, overall, ITS4SDC performs better than SDC-Scissor. However, there is no uniform pattern. Some comparisons show a large difference in performance (e.g., A and C), some show almost equal performance (e.g., B, D, and F), and one is moderate (E). The ITS4SDC model has superior accuracy and precision over SDC-Scissor in comparisons A, C, and

---

[5] URL to Materials: https://zenodo.org/records/15656037.

E, while still performing slightly better in comparisons B, D, and F. F1-score and recall of the ITS4SDC model are better across all comparisons (A to F).

Table 3. Performance Difference ITS4SDC vs. SDC-Scissor

	Setup		$Metric_{ITS4SDC}$ - $Metric_{SDC-Scissor}$			
Comparison	ITS4SDC	SDC-Scissor	Accuracy	Precision	Recall	F1
A	1	1	0.27	0.24	0.13	0.20
B	2	2	0.05	0.04	0.05	0.04
C	1	2	0.27	0.25	0.09	0.18
D	2	1	0.05	0.03	0.10	0.06
E	5	5	0.15	0.13	0.07	0.10
F	6	6	0.02	0.02	0.04	0.02

It seems that ITS4SDC performs better than SDC-Scissor when trained and validated on noiseless datasets, i.e., Dataset-1, Dataset-1–30, and Dataset-1–10. However, the advantage decreases with dataset size. Deep learning models like LSTM are known to require larger datasets for training than the traditional machine learning models used in SDC-Scissor.

Whenever Dataset-2 is involved as training dataset (comparisons B and D), the difference in performance between ITS4SDC and SDC-Scissor is reduced. It is interesting to see that ITS4SDC is still slightly better when predicting noise-less data (D) than when predicting noisy data (B), although in both cases noisy training data is used. It is unclear whether this is due to the fact that in comparison D 100% of Dataset-2 are used for training while in comparison B only 90% of Dataset-2 are used (making it slightly smaller), or whether ITS4SDC is simply more often than SDC-Scissor predicting the positive class (PASS) correctly in noiseless data (relatively higher recall than SDC-Scissor in comparison D) and/or making less mistakes when predicting the positive class in noisy data (relatively higher precision in comparison B). The noisiness of Dataset-2 explains why the performance of the ITS4SDC decreases when using Dataset-2 for training or when classifying roads in Dataset-2. However, it does not explain why the performance of SDC-Scissor models does not improve when using Dataset-1 for training. A possible explanation could be that the SDC-Scissor models are more robust to noise in the training dataset on the one hand, but do not work as well as ITS4SDC on the features extracted during training. Another possible explanation is that the statistical features extracted from the roads used in the SDC-Scissor models are limited in their potential to distinguish between PASS and FAIL cases.

7 Threats to Validity

Internal Validity. A drawback of applying deep learning-based models such as LSTM is the requirement for fixed input feature dimensions. The experiments indicate that the ITS4SDC model is sensitive to parameters such as the activation function and the number of layers. Regarding the road data, input sizes can be adjusted for the LSTM model using interpolation to increase dimensions or sampling to reduce them. The selection of too many points along the road through interpolation creates an obstacle for the model's learning as it leads to a decrease in segment lengths and segment angles. This issue could be avoided by sampling the points along the road and selecting one out of every two or three points. For the dataset used in the competition, the 197 interpolated road coordinates contain learnable segment angle and length data for the model, so no further interpolation or alternative sampling algorithms were deemed necessary.

External Validity. The experiments were conducted in the BeamNG simulation environment using an ETK-800 vehicle on a flat 2D asphalt surface with no slope. Although the BeamNG simulator features soft-body dynamics and can closely model real-world conditions, there may still be discrepancies between the real world and the simulator that should be taken into account. One of the main reasons a vehicle leaves the lane is its dynamic and electronic properties. Therefore, failure-inducing roads vary from vehicle to vehicle, and the dataset used to train the model should be collected based on the target vehicle.

Reliability. ITS4SDC's classification performance might be sensitive to the choice of parameter settings as well as the choice of the simulation environment. For example, OOB (in our experiments set to 50%) defines the threshold that decides how much the lane must be left to classify a test road as unsafe (FAIL). The risk factor RF (in our experiments set to 1.5) strongly influences the driving behavior. How consistent ITS4SDC's performance would be if OOB and RF settings change is unknown and would need to be further explored.

The vehicle's electronic controllers also play an important role. The electronic controllers of the ETK-800, such as the Electronic Stability Controller (ESC) and Anti-lock Braking System (ABS), which activate when the vehicle is about to go off the road and do not always help maintain control in certain situations, might make it easier to keep the vehicle on the road in a different vehicle.

8 Conclusions

Based on our evaluation, we conclude that the ITS4SDC is competitive when compared against the current state-of-the-art classifier SDC-Scissor with the potential to achieve clearly better performance when trained on large and noiseless datasets. The good precision achieved by ITS4SDC makes simulation-based SDC testing more effective because it minimizes the number of false positives, and by doing so prevents the exclusion of unsafe test roads from the test set. The good recall by ITS4SDC makes simulation-based SDC testing more efficient by correctly predicting many PASS cases and by doing so preventing the execution of tests that have a low potential to trigger failures.

Although the ITS4SDC model demonstrates superior performance compared to SDC-Scissor, it has likely not yet reached its optimal performance. Further fine-tuning of hyperparameters could still enhance its accuracy and generalization. In this study, hyperparameters such as the early stopping patience level, learning rate, and dropout rate were not comprehensively optimized.

In the presented work, road coordinates were generated using the Frenetic algorithm. Evaluating the model on datasets generated by other road generation algorithms such as Deeper [20] and Swat [14] could be interesting. Considering that the most critical road feature causing vehicles to leave the road is related to the curve regions, future work might explore attention-based LSTM algorithms by treating these curve regions as attention zones to improve performance.

Acknowledgments. This study was co-funded by the European Union and the Estonian Ministry of Education and Research via project TEM-TA120, by BMK, BMAW, and the State of Upper Austria in the frame of the SCCH competence center INTEGRATE (FFG grant no. 892418) part of the FFG COMET Competence Centers for Excellent Technologies Programme, by grant PRG1226 of the Estonian Research Council, and by Bolt Technology ÖU. We gratefully acknowledge the BeamNG company for providing us with the simulation environment that enabled the test case execution and dataset preparation.

Disclosure of Interests. The authors have no competing interests to declare that are relevant to the content of this article.

References

1. Anagnostopoulos, C., Koulamas, C., Lalos, A., Stylios, C.: Open-source integrated simulation framework for cooperative autonomous vehicles. In: 11th Mediterranean Conf. on Embedded Computing (MECO), pp. 1–4 (2022)
2. Birchler, C.: SDC-Scissor: test execution, 2022–2023. https://tinyurl.com/yfhr3k4a. Accessed 22 Feb 2025
3. Birchler, C., Khatiri, S., Bosshard, B., Gambi, A., Panichella, S.: Machine learning-based test selection for simulation-based testing of self-driving cars software. Empirical Softw. Eng. **28**, 71 (2023)
4. Birchler, C.,Khatiri, S., Derakhshanfar, P., Panichella, S., Panichella, A.: Single and multi-objective test cases prioritization for self-driving cars in virtual environments. ACM Trans. Softw. Eng. Methodol. **32** (2022)
5. Birchler, C., Klikovits, S., Fazzini, M., Panichella, S.: ICST tool competition 2025 - self-driving car testing track. In: 2025 IEEE Conference on Software Testing, Verification and Validation (ICST), pp. 801–804. IEEE (2025)
6. Birchler, C., Ganz, N., Khatiri, S., Gambi, A., Panichella, S.: Cost-effective simulation-based test selection in self-driving cars software. Sci. Comp. Program. **226**, 102926 (2023)

7. Birchler, C., Ganz, N., Khatiri, S., Gambi, A., Panichella, S.: Dataset for cost-effective simulation-based test selection in self-driving cars software with SDC-scissor [data set]. Zenodo. https://doi.org/10.5281/zenodo.5914130
8. Castellano, E., Cetinkaya, A., Thanh, C.H., Klikovits, S., Zhang, X., Arcaini, P.: Frenetic at the SBST 2021 tool competition. In: 2021 IEEE/ACM 14th International Workshop on Search-Based Software Testing (SBST), pp. 36–37 (2021)
9. Deng, Y., Zheng, X., Zhang, M., Lou, G., Zhang, T.: Scenario-based test reduction and prioritization for multi-module autonomous driving systems. In: Proceedings of the 30th ACM Joint European Software Engineering Conference and Symposium on the Foundations of Software Engineering, ESEC/FSE 2022, pp. 82–93, New York, NY, USA. Association for Computing Machinery (2022)
10. Gambi, A., Jahangirova, G., Riccio, V., Zampetti, F.: SBST tool competition 2022. In: 15th IEEE/ACM International Workshop on Search-Based Software Testing, SBST@ICSE 2022, Pittsburgh, PA, USA, May 9, 2022, pp. 25–32. IEEE (2022)
11. Gambi, A., Muller, M., Fraser, G.: Asfault: testing self-driving car software using search-based procedural content generation. In: Proceedings of the 41st International Conference on Software Engineering: Companion Proceedings, ICSE '19, pp. 27–30. IEEE Press (2019)
12. Gullu, A.: Dataset for regression testing of self-driving cars (2025). https://doi.org/10.5281/zenodo.16939865
13. Hochreiter, S., Schmidhuber, J.: Long short-term memory. Neural Comput. **9**, 1735–1780 (1997)
14. Humeniuk, D., Antoniol, G., Khomh, F.: Swat tool at the SBST 2021 tool competition. In: IEEE/ACM 14th International Workshop on Search-Based Software Testing (SBST), pp. 42–43 (2021)
15. Karim, F., Majumdar, S., Darabi, H., Chen, S.: LSTM fully convolutional networks for time series classification. IEEE Access **6**, 1662–1669 (2018)
16. Kaur, P., Taghavi, S., Tian, Z., Shi, W.: A survey on simulators for testing self-driving cars. In: Fourth International Conference on Connected and Autonomous Driving (MetroCAD), pp. 62–70, Los Alamitos, CA, USA. IEEE Computer Society (2021)
17. Khan, F., Anwar, H., Pfahl, D.: Comparing approaches for prioritizing and selecting scenarios in simulation-based safety testing of automated driving systems. WiPiEC J. Works Prog. Embed. Comput. J. **10**(2) (2024)
18. Khan, F., Anwar, H., Pfahl, D.: A process for scenario prioritization and selection in simulation-based safety testing of automated driving systems. In: Product-Focused Soft. Process Improvement, pp. 89–99. Springer, Cham (2024)
19. Lu, C., Zhang, H., Yue, T., Ali, S.: Search-based selection and prioritization of test scenarios for autonomous driving systems. In: O'Reilly, U.-M., Devroey, X. (eds.) SSBSE 2021. LNCS, vol. 12914, pp. 41–55. Springer, Cham (2021). https://doi.org/10.1007/978-3-030-88106-1_4
20. Moghadam, M.H., Borg, M., Mousavirad, J.: Deeper tool (2021). https://github.com/mahshidhelali/tool-competition-av
21. Panichella, S., Gambi, A., Zampetti, F., Riccio, V.: SBST tool competition 2021. In: IEEE/ACM 14th International Workshop on Search-Based Software Testing (SBST), pp. 20–27 (2021)
22. Su, Z., Zhang, H., Zhu, S.: A robotic simulation system combined USARSim and RCS library. In: 2nd Asia-Pacific Conference on Intelligent Robot Systems (ACIRS), pp. 240–243 (2017)
23. BeamNG GmbH 2025. BeamNG official vehicle documentation. https://documentation.beamng.com/. Accessed 24 Jan 2025

24. vatozZ. ITS4SDC Tool (2025). https://github.com/vatozZ/ITS4SDC-Public-Release
25. Wang, S.-H., Lin, C.-X., Tu, C.-H., Jim Huang, C.-C., Juang, J.-C.: Autonomous vehicle simulation for Asia urban areas with a perspective from education. In: 2020 International Computer Symposium (ICS), pp. 454–458 (2020)

FOSS-Chain: Using Blockchain for Open Source Software License Compliance

Kypros Iacovou, Georgia Kapitsaki[(✉)] [iD], and Evangelia Vanezi [iD]

University of Cyprus, Nicosia, Cyprus
{gkapi,vanezi.evangelia}@ucy.ac.cy

Abstract. Open Source Software (OSS) is widely used and carries licenses that indicate the terms under which the software is provided for use, also specifying modification and distribution rules. Ensuring that users are respecting OSS license terms when creating derivative works is a complex process. Compliance issues arising from incompatibilities among licenses may lead to legal disputes. At the same time, the blockchain technology with immutable entries offers a mechanism to provide transparency when it comes to licensing and ensure software changes are recorded. In this work, we are introducing an integration of blockchain and license management when creating derivative works, in order to tackle the issue of OSS license compatibility. We have designed, implemented and performed a preliminary evaluation of *FOSS-chain*, a web platform that uses blockchain and automates the license compliance process, covering 14 OSS licenses. We have evaluated the initial prototype version of the *FOSS-chain* platform via a small scale user study. Our preliminary results are promising, demonstrating the potential of the platform for adaptation on realistic software systems.

Keywords: open source software · blockchain · software licensing · license compatibility

1 Introduction

Open Source Software (OSS) is everywhere, with a large number of OSS repositories being available for reuse online, while there is even participation of commercial companies to OSS development [17]. Open Source Software carries licenses, such as MIT and General Public Licenses (GPL), that regulate the usage, modification and distribution of OSS defining specific licensing terms in their respective legal texts [19]. Nowadays, a vast number of licenses are available for use with the Open Source Initiative (OSI)[1] having approved more than 80 licenses and the Software Package Data Exchange (SPDX) listing more than 550 licenses and exceptions licenses [21]. When creating derivative works, the compatibility between software licenses is important for developers, businesses and the OSS community in general, as it determines whether software components may be

---

[1] https://opensource.org/.

G. Scanniello et al. (Eds.): PROFES 2025, LNCS 16361, pp. 86–101, 2026.
https://doi.org/10.1007/978-3-032-12089-2_6

legally linked without violating licensing terms. This can create challenges for developers who wish to create derivative works of existing software or combine OSS components with different licensing models, particularly when they intend to release proprietary versions of the software.

At the same time, the blockchain technology can be used to build applications for smart contracts, supply chain management and digital identity verification, among others [24]. Blockchain is designed to offer a decentralized, secure and transparent method for recording transactions. Each transaction gets an entry on the distributed ledger and consensus efforts verify it. This makes it extremely challenging for an adversary to alter or manipulate transactions, as anything added to the blockchain is defined immutable [11]. Blockchain's security and transparency properties make it suitable for smart contracts involving OSS license tracking and compliance verification, as they are self-executing and do not require human intervention.

Existing works on license compliance focus on source code analysis to understand licensing information or address license compliance as part of Software Composition Analysis (SCA) processes [15,22]. Such solutions usually require human intervention or provide post-hoc management of licenses. Blockchain can be useful in this respect for proactive management of license compliance, as it can be used to host OSS components and their licensing information, helping developers track software's usage, modification, and distribution over time. Using a blockchain-based system, allows also software contributors to be recognized automatically as contributors of the original software.

Using the above as starting point, in this work we are using a design science approach and are introducing FOSS-chain, a platform that integrates blockchain into license compliance management. *FOSS-chain* relies heavily on smart contracts of blockchain, which are immutable agreements that help in managing and checking the licenses when a developer downloads or uploads software projects. Smart contracts are also very useful when a developer relies on existing software in order to create a derivative work. In order to make the system available for use by OSS developers, we have created a web platform where users can create a new account, search for existing software, download it, and share their own software. *FOSS-chain* performs a license compatibility check, when a user uploads a software that is a derivative work of an existing project on-chain, and currently supports 14 popular OSS licenses. By focusing on proactive enforcement rather than post-distribution audits, *FOSS-chain* shifts the compliance process upstream, reducing legal risk and developers' uncertainty on license management. We have performed a preliminary evaluation of the feasibility of *FOSS-chain* and its initial prototype implementation via a small-scale user study, in order to examine its potential. Users of technical and non-technical background have participated in the evaluation. Most users find the platform useful and easy to use, while they have made suggestions for further improvements. Simple statistical analysis has been employed for this part of the work.

The contribution of this work lies in: 1) the introduction of a blockchain-based smart contracts architecture to enforce OSS compliance and preserve licensing records immutably, and 2) the provision of a web platform that integrates blockchain with license management. **Platform availability.** *FOSS-chain* is available on a GitHub repository online [4].

The remainder of the text is structured as follows. Section 2 presents background concepts, while related work is described in Sect. 3. Section 4 is dedicated to the presence of the *FOSS-chain* architecture and platform, including its design and prototype implementation. The preliminary evaluation performed is presented in Sect. 5, while Sect. 6 briefly discusses main findings and threats to validity. Finally, Sect. 7 concludes the work.

2   Background Concepts

2.1   Open Source Software Licensing

Open Source Software licenses generally fall into three main categories: copyleft and permissive (or non-copyleft) licenses that are further divided into strong and weak copyleft. Strong copyleft licenses, such as the GNU GPL v3.0 (GPL-3.0) and the Affero GPL v3.0 (AGPL-3.0), require that if a work is modified or a derivative incorporating the original software is produced, it must also be released under the same OSS licensing terms. This enables publicly accessible improvements and prevents proprietary versions from being created without sharing modifications. On the other hand, permissive licenses, such as the MIT, the Apache v2.0 (Apache-2.0) and the Berkeley Software Distribution (BSD) licenses (e.g. BSD-2-Clause), have minimal restrictions. They allow developers to modify, use, and distribute the software freely, incorporating it also into proprietary projects. These licenses rely more on community and economic incentives to encourage contributions to the original project. For example, ReactJS carries a MIT License, while TensorFlow is licensed under Apache-2.0. In between, weak copyleft licenses like the GNU Lesser General Public License v2.1 (LGPL-2.1) require the use of the same (or of a compatible) license, when the original software is modified but do not pose these restrictions when the original software remains intact.

License compatibility refers to having different OSS licenses combined in a software project without legal conflicts. A major difference between permissive and copyleft licenses is that permissive-licensed code can be incorporated into copyleft-licensed projects, but that is not always allowed the other way around, due to the stricter sharing requirements of copyleft licenses [10]. For instance, permissive licenses, such as MIT or Apache-2.0, allow code to be used in a software system under any license, including proprietary licenses. Software integrating GPL-licensed components must also be made available under GPL (or under a compatible license). These restrictions can create legal and financial risks for companies that incorporate OSS into their products without being fully aware of the licensing implications, and relevant legal disputes can be found in the literature, e.g. Artifex v. Hancom[2] concerning the Ghostscript project.

---

[2] https://www.fsf.org/blogs/licensing/update-on-artifex-v-hancom-gnu-gpl-compliance-case-1.

2.2 Blockchain

A blockchain is a distributed ledger, which is a decentralized database that records transactions across a computer network. It was first presented as an underlying mechanism for Bitcoin [13]. Unlike traditional databases that are managed by a central authority, such as banks in a financial network, blockchains operate on the peer-to-peer (P2P) network with no single entity controlling the records. Data are being distributed among all participants in the network.

Immutability is a key feature of blockchain: once a transaction gets added to the blockchain and validated by the network, it cannot get changed or deleted. Transactions are collected into blocks, and each subsequent block is cryptographically bound to the previous one, thus creating a chain. Altering any previous record will necessitate altering all subsequent blocks as well, which cannot happen due to network consensus. A key advantage of blockchain is transparency. Due to the public ledger system of blockchains, all transactions are verifiable by the participants of the network which removes the need for any middlemen and chances of fraud. Smart contracts are self-executing contracts with the terms of the agreement directly written into lines of code. By ensuring that all parties adhere to the predefined conditions without ambiguity, administrative overhead is reduced and the potential for human error is eliminated, minimizing the risk of disputes. In terms of license compliance, smart contracts can be used to improve the enforcement of rules, regulations and contracts.

3 Related Work

Most prior works on OSS licensing have focused on tools and frameworks that help developers identify license types, detect conflicts, and ensure license compliance. There are a number of works that assist developers to scan the source code of software systems and extract relevant licenses, such as FOSSology [5] that integrates the Ninka license scanner [3] and ASLA [22]. Other works rely on performing SCA for license compliance [15], such as OSSPolice tailored to mobile applications [2], or on extracting terms from license texts [9], while recommender systems like findOSSLicense [6,7] and online resources (e.g. chooseal-icense,[3] TLDRLegal)[4] for choosing licenses and detecting incompatibilities (e.g. LiDetector, SPDX compatibility check) also exist [8,23]. Such tools assist organizations in identifying issues of non-compliance, but operate usually as reactive mechanisms.

Blockchain has been studied in the past in the context of software engineering. An exploratory study on the smart contracts of Ethereum examined all smart contracts that were created via contract creation transactions [14]. It was found that only a very small percentage of the contracts are used in the majority of transactions, while high-activity contracts have a very small number of source code instructions. When it comes to blockchain transactions processing

---

[3] https://choosealicense.com/.
[4] https://www.tldrlegal.com/.

time, another work found that properties concerning gas pricing behaviors are highly associated with processing times [16]. On the developers side, Rosa et al. examined why and how developers maintain smart contracts using 14 OSS smart contract repositories in Solidity [18]. It was found that developers are mainly making changes to improve the scripts' internal quality and fix bugs.

Existing works in the literature based on blockchain and license compliance are mainly conceptual, or proof-of-concept-based. Blockchain has been suggested as a measure to control software piracy, with smart contracts being used to enforce licensing agreements [20]. In its initial development, this prior work has considered a single software offered by a software vendor who is the owner of the platform and does not consider OSS. The proposed tool does not seem to be available online. Another prior work has introduced the concept of using blockchain for OSS license management similarly as in the current work [12]. The authors used InterPlanetary File System (IPFS), smart contracts, transaction manager (Meta-Mask) and a permissioned blockchain (based on the Ethereum platform) to enforce the conformance of licenses, whereas they also covered commercialization of a software project. Although this later work is very close to our work, it offers a simulation of the concept and does not consider specific OSS licenses and relevant compatibilities. Moreover, in our prototype version of *FOSS-chain* we are providing some additional features to users interacting with the platform (e.g. project search). Overall, the above prior studies focus more on license recording and visibility.

4   The FOSS-Chain Platform

4.1   Platform Overview and Blockchain Use

The core architecture of *FOSS-chain* utilizes smart contracts, storage of licensing information and relevant compatibilities, and function-level hashing to guarantee license compliance. The blockchain ensures the immutability of license acceptance records and function hash logs, which are explained later in the section, providing a transparent and verifiable history of each user's interactions with the platform. Figure 1 illustrates the basic workflow of *FOSS-chain* blockchain. New data, such as software license agreement, are recorded as a new block. This block is then broadcast to all nodes in the decentralized network for validation. If the nodes reach consensus, the block is approved and permanently added to the chain.

Smart contracts in blockchain can store and preserve the data of OSS downloads, including the licensing terms and the function-level structure of the software project that was downloaded. Since users need to use the platform every time they want to make available a new OSS project that may have been created from scratch or may be based on existing projects, they are also required to go via the license compliance process of the platform to ensure they are respecting the licensing terms of the software they are modifying. *FOSS-chain* is envisioned as a platform that manages derivative works of more than one software projects,

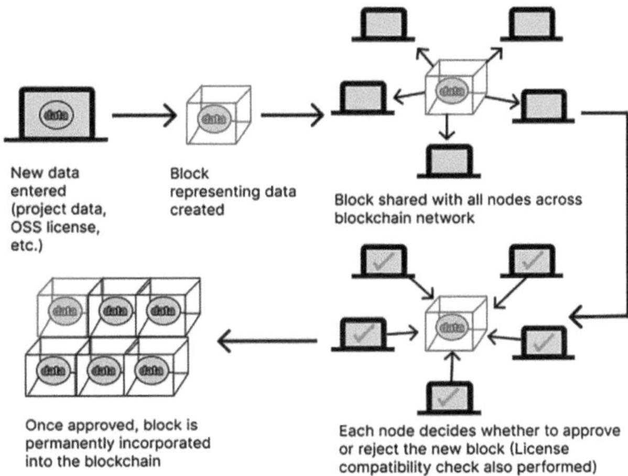

Fig. 1. Main workflow in *FOSS-chain.*

so it is suitable for handling the OSS projects of an organization or even of the OSS community as a whole, although scaling issues arise in that case.

The platform is accompanied with a web application that allows registered users to interact with software projects. Figure 2 depicts the platform architecture with the main interacting components. Once users sign in, they are able to search for software projects, upload a new project or download an existing software project via the front-end UI (User Interface). After the user downloads the project, the front-end initiates a blockchain transaction to record the license agreement. Specifically, a smart contract agreement is triggered via the `DownloadAgreement` contract to ensure license acceptance is recorded immutably on-chain. This contract states the license agreement between the author and the downloader, who acts as licensee, and creates all function hashes of the software downloaded. These hashes uniquely identify the code at the function level. This allows the management system to identify during future uploads whether such functions were previously used.

The upload process of the system contains a verification. When a new project is uploaded, function-level hashes are extracted and are communicated to the back-end for project management and license compatibility checks. *FOSS-chain* queries the blockchain to see if there is a match with any function hashes of all previously downloaded projects by the user. If the system sees equivalence, it obtains the license linked to the original function and runs a compatibility check against the license declared for the new upload. If the licenses are compatible, the project is successfully uploaded on the platform. The upload will stop if there is a license compliance issue; for instance, if a user tries to relicense a GPL code under a non-compatible license, then the user will be notified. Simultaneously, a communication with the `LicenseManager` smart contract on the blockchain is performed in order to verify and store license information.

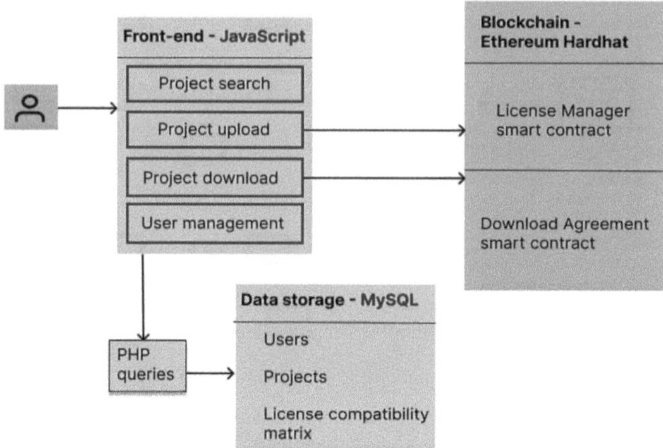

Fig. 2. *FOSS-chain* System architecture.

4.2 Supported OSS Licenses and Compatibility Enforcement

FOSS-chain currently supports 14 OSS licenses, counting also different license versions. These licenses were selected based on their popularity in OSS systems. They are listed in Table 1, whereas their popularity according to the Open Source Initiative top licenses for 2024[5] is also indicated. In GitHub[6], Apache-2.0 was found in 30% of projects in 2021 and MIT in 26%. All licenses are OSI-approved. For compatibility purposes, we have used a license compatibility matrix with the supported licenses, where we indicate for each supported license, the licenses it is compatible with. This matrix is based on a license graph for license compatibility indication from a prior work [10]. More licenses can be added to *FOSS-chain*, if license compatibility information is also available for those licenses.

FOSS-chain is using function-level hashing that generates a distinct hash for every function in the original software systems available in the platform, by applying the SHA-256 algorithm. As aforementioned, hashes are generated for all functions. We have created relevant regular expressions for the three supported languages of the platform: C, Java and Python. In order to detect functions in the software projects, we are using respective regular expressions for each programming language. We are providing as example the regular expression used for the C language (in PHP), while the remaining expressions are available on the GitHub repository of *FOSS-chain* [4]:

```
/(?:function|void|int|char|float|double)\s+(\w+)\s*\([^)]*\)\s
*\{([\s\S]*?)\}/g
```

This allows the system to detect partial reuse in later uploads of the same software project. If there is a match between one or more hashes of the original

---

[5] https://opensource.org/blog/top-open-source-licenses-in-2024.
[6] https://www.mend.io/blog/open-source-licenses-trends-and-predictions/.

Table 1. Supported licenses in FOSS-chain.

License name	SPDX Abbreviation	Category	Rank (OSI)
MIT License	MIT	Permissive	1
BSD 2-Clause "Simplified" License	BSD-2-Clause	Permissive	4
BSD 3-Clause "New" or "Revised" License	BSD-3-Clause	Permissive	2
Apache License 2.0	Apache-2.0	Permissive	3
GNU General Public License v2.0 only	GPL-2.0	Strong-copyl.	5
GNU General Public License v2.0 or later	GPL-2.0-or-later	Strong-copyl.	5
GNU General Public License v3.0 only	GPL-3.0	Strong-copyl.	6
GNU General Public License v3.0 or later	GPL-3.0-or-later	Strong-copyl.	6
GNU Lesser General Public License v2.1 only	LGPL-2.1	Weak-copyl.	8
GNU Lesser General Public License v3.0 only	LGPL-3.0	Weak-copyl.	9
Mozilla Public License 1.1	MPL-1.1	Weak-copyl.	–
Mozilla Public License 2.0	MPL-2.0	Weak-copyl.	11
Affero General Public License v1.0 or later	AGPL-1.0-or-later	Strong-copyl.	–
GNU Affero General Public License v3.0	AGPL-3.0	Strong-copyl.	14

software downloaded and a new software project uploaded on the *FOSS-chain* platform, the back-end detects that the new project is a derivative work of a previous download. This triggers a license compatibility check after retrieving the license of the original software. *FOSS-chain* examines then the compatibility matrix to assess whether the license the user intends to apply on the work is compatible with the license of the original software. This process is repeated for all projects with a match. The upload of the project is permitted on *FOSS-chain* only if the licenses are compatible, or if the same license of the original software is used. Otherwise, the system prevents the upload and informs the user about the license conflict. For instance, a piece of code that is licensed under GPL cannot be relicensed under a permissive license, such as MIT, because this would violate the GPL's copyleft requirements.

4.3   Management of Smart Contracts

As aforementioned, two main smart contracts have been introduced and used for the license compliance enforcement in *FOSS-chain*: `DownloadAgreement` and `LicenseManager` contract. These smart contracts are in charge of storing and managing the licensing agreements, recording the function-level hashes of the downloaded and uploaded projects, and tracking the metadata of these projects.

`DownloadAgreement` is the first contract, which records the acceptance of the software license when the user downloads an existing software project from the platform. When someone downloads the software, this agreement stores the wallet address of the downloader, the unique identifier of the software project in the platform, the name of the license, and the timestamp of the download. These data are stored on-chain, so that they can be retrieved when required in the future for license verification purposes. The record created serves as an immutable indicator of user consent to the specific licensing terms.

The second smart contract, `LicenseManager`, manages the software project uploads, tracks the hashes of functions, and enforces license compatibility. When a user uploads a new software project, this contract will register the metadata of that project including the address of the uploader, the identifier of the project, any parent (i.e. original) project(s) it may be a derivative of, and the license selected by the uploader. More importantly, the contract stores an array of function-level hashes from the uploading project. The project's functional logic is signified by these hashes helping with the precise detection of code reuse on the platform. `LicenseManager` is responsible for enforcing the license verification process. It is not mandatory for the user to indicate one or more parent projects when performing an upload, as the uploaded projects are checked against all projects.

In the current version of the *FOSS-chain* prototype implementation, the wallet addresses are managed manually. Specifically, the wallet addresses of newly registered users are manually entered in a configuration file by the system administrator. Platforms using blockchain usually provide automatic wallet creation and integration of wallets [1]. Future versions of *FOSS-chain* will automate the generation and management of wallets, in order to increase system usability and allow scalability (e.g. for large organizations or popular OSS projects) without administrative actions.

4.4   Implementation Tools and Use Demonstration

For blockchain purposes, Ethereum[7] was used, selected due to its wide popularity and adoption. We have employed the Ethereum Virtual Machine (EVM) that allows the execution of smart contracts. We have also used Hardhat[8] that is a local development environment of Ethereum without needing to use the actual network of Ethereum. Concerning the smart contracts of *FOSS-chain*, they are written in Solidity which is the main programming language for contracts on Ethereum. As depicted in Fig. 2, JavaScript was used for the front-end (e.g. EtherJS library), along with PHP for the back-end, while relevant data are stored on a MySQL database: user profiles, project metadata, blockchain transaction reference, and the license compatibility matrix.

A demonstration of use of the web platform of *FOSS-chain* is depicted in Fig. 3, Fig. 4a and b. A user downloads an existing software project licensed under LGPL-2.1 from the platform after performing a relevant search (Fig. 3) and uploads an updated version of the project (Fig. 4a) that causes a license violation, as the source code has been modified and the user attempts to license the LGPL-licensed original software under the Apache-2.0 permissive license. *FOSS-chain* displays a notification to inform the user and does not allow the project upload on-chain (Fig. 4b). *FOSS-chain* also informs the user about the

---

[7] https://ethereum.org/.
[8] https://hardhat.org/.

compatible licenses that can ne used instead. Note that the *create project* form (Fig. 4a) is the same regardless of whether it concerns a completely new upload or a derivative work.

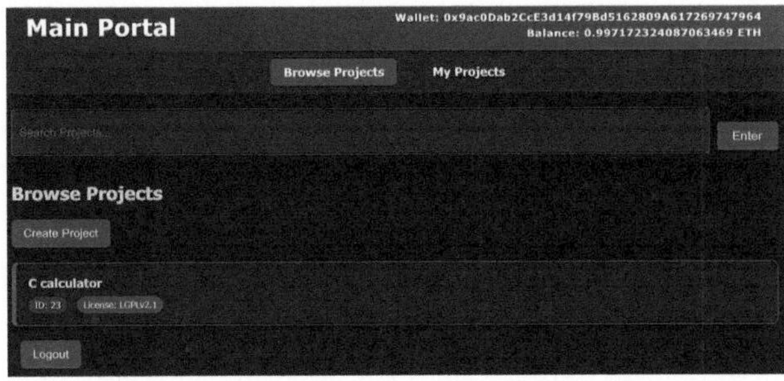

Fig. 3. Browsing of existing projects in *FOSS-chain.*

(a) Upload of a derivative project.   (b) License conflict notification.

Fig. 4. Upload of derivative with conflicting license in *FOSS-chain.*

5   User Evaluation

5.1   Study Design

We have performed a preliminary evaluation of the feasibility of using blockchain for OSS license compliance and the *FOSS-chain* platform with a small scale user evaluation. The questionnaire created for this purpose consists of two main parts: the first part aims to collect users' general perceptions about open source software, licensing, and blockchain technology, while the second part aims to gather technical users' feedback on *FOSS-chain*. Every participant regardless of their technical expertise was first asked to answer a number of general questions that touched on their familiarity and experience with OSS, their opinion on licensing and compliance, and the general concept of *FOSS-chain*. After these more general sections, participants were asked whether they had a software development background. If they gave a positive answer, they were shown a short demonstration video of *FOSS-chain* and after watching this demonstration, these technical participants were presented with a second set of questions aimed at evaluating the tool's clarity and practical potential. They were also invited to share thoughts on the tool's limitations, supported languages, and possible contexts for deployment.

The participants were recruited among personal contacts of the authors via e-mail communication that targeted students and researchers within the University of Cyprus but also software engineers in the software industry in Cyprus, Greece, Germany and Sweden. No personal data were requested from users, while the users were informed that the responses would be used solely for research purposes and for improving *FOSS-chain*. In order to complete the questionnaire, the potential participants gave their consent to the above. The questionnaire consisting of 24 questions is available via Google Forms,[9] and its main sections are shown in Table 2. Most closed form questions are multiple choice or in the 5-Likert scale, while the questionnaire includes also a number of open ended questions. The demonstration video of *FOSS-chain* is also available on YouTube.[10]

Table 2. Parts of *FOSS-chain* evaluation questionnaire.

Section focus	# questions	Example(s)
1. Participants background and OSS use	5	What is your technical level of experience? (*multiple choice*)
2. Software licensing & compliance	4	Do you have experience with Open Source Software licenses? (*multiple choice*)
3. Blockchain understanding	2	How well do you understand how blockchain works? (*multiple choice*)
4. *FOSS-chain* implementation potential	5	Would you support integrating blockchain into open-source software licensing to prevent violations and ensure transparency? (*multiple choice*)
5. *FOSS-chain* feedback	8	Did you find that the tool is easy to use? (*5-Likert scale*)
		In which contexts, do you think the tool could be used? (*checkboxes*)

5.2   Study Results

A total of 34 individuals responded to the questionnaire, with most using free software frequently or every day (85.3%) but only 32.4% having direct experience with OSS licenses (44.1% had limited knowledge and the remaining none). Concerning the biggest challenges in software license compliance, all participants (100%) mentioned that *'people don't read or understand licenses'*, which was one of the options provided. Half of the participants (50%) indicated also the absence of enforcement mechanisms as a reason. 52.9% replied it is because people do not think licenses matter. Most survey participants do not have a good

---

[9] https://shorturl.at/mkk0H.
[10] https://www.youtube.com/watch?v=mcb1ZCnysN8.

understanding of blockchain: only 5.9% understand very well how it works and the remaining do not (64.7%) or have a limited understanding (29.4%). When presented with the potential of *FOSS-chain* (but before watching the respective demonstration video), most participants agreed that integrating blockchain into OSS licensing can assist in preventing violations and ensuring transparency: 67.6% said it is a good idea, while 20.6% were not sure (the remaining 11.8% do not find it necessary). We also presented to users a number of features that would make a blockchain-based software license system more effective and the results are depicted in Fig. 5, with most participants referring to the automation of license compliance.

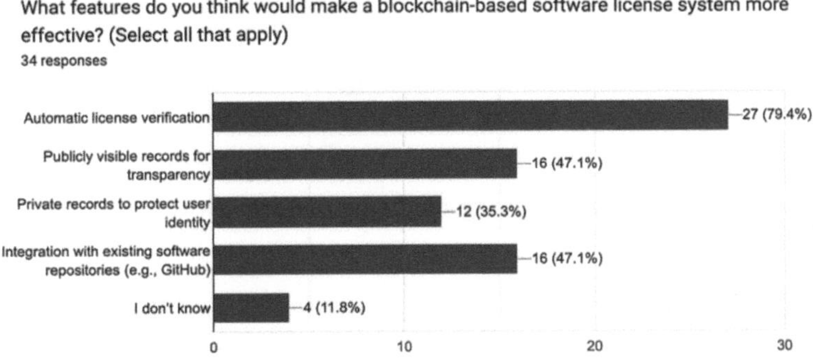

Fig. 5. Useful properties of a blockchain-based software license system (survey results).

In terms of technical roles, the participants pool included: 8 (23.5%) Computer Science bachelor students, 10 (29.4%) bachelor students from non-Computer Science disciplines, 7 (20.6%) researchers or academics and 6 (17.6%) junior software developers. Other participants identified as senior software engineers, or data analysts (3 participants).

Concerning the results on the usage of *FOSS-chain*, we analyzed separately the responses coming from technical users, so non-technical users' responses were excluded from this part of the analysis. 73.5% indicated that they have a software development background, while the remaining 26.5% did not, so the subsequent analysis relies on those 25 participants. We asked technical participants questions on the ease of use and complexity of *FOSS-chain*, using 5 questions in the 5-Likert scale, with the results shown in Fig. 6. The main area of improvement can be found in the navigation of *FOSS-chain*, that some participants found complex. Moreover, more actions are needed to ensure users can trust the provided results. We also asked participants in which contexts they would see the platform being used, with participants results depicted in Fig. 7. According to the participants, *FOSS-chain* is more suitable for independent developers and small organizations. We ran a number of statistical tests (Kruskal-Wallis H rank-based non-parametric test) to examine whether the participants' background (e.g. their technical role or their experience with OSS licenses) affects their experience with *FOSS-chain* but no statistically significant differences were found.

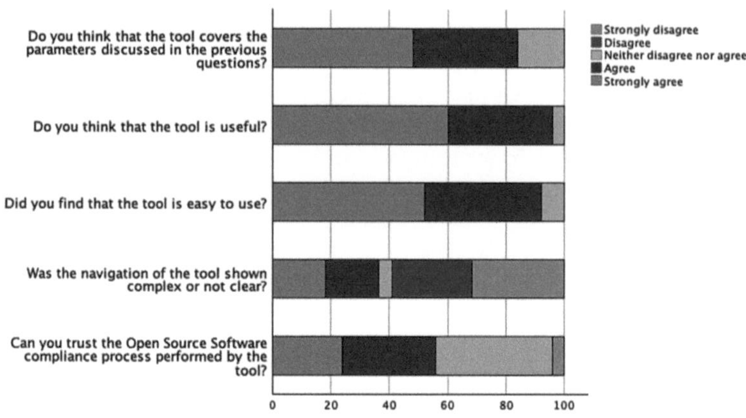

Fig. 6. *FOSS-chain* technical users feedback (results).

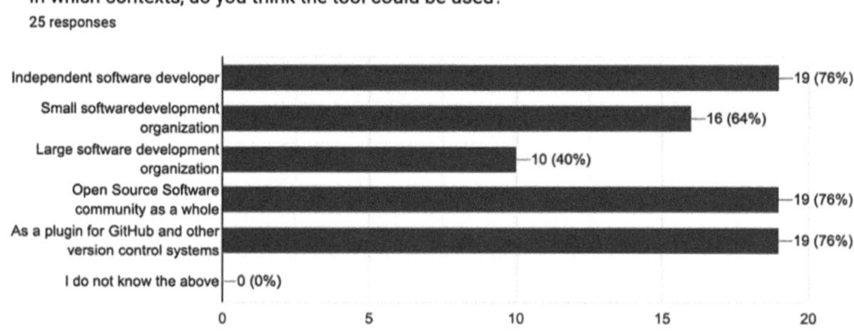

Fig. 7. Appropriate context of use for *FOSS-chain* (survey results).

Technical background participants also indicated a large number of programming languages they would like to see integrated in *FOSS-chain*, including Golang, JavaScript, PHP, C++, C#, R and TypeScript. We finally gathered technical participants' view on how to improve *FOSS-chain*. Seven participants provided such comments. After performing a simple qualitative analysis, the following are the main useful suggestions for future enhancements:

- Integrate the FOSS-chain functionality into an IDE, or software editing tool.
- Add more information on each license indicated in FOSS-chain (e.g. via URL to official license website).

– Explain to the user why an uploaded project has been recognized as a derivative of an existing project on blockchain. This would provide the user the possibility to ask for a review of this decision.

6 Discussion

Main Findings. The prototype implementation of *FOSS-chain* has shown the preliminary usefulness of using blockchain for OSS license compliance purposes. The management process might be long, as the network of nodes expands, so the system might be more applicable organizational-wide and not as a solution for the OSS community as a whole, considering that in this case transaction processing will become very expensive. This is also an outcome of the results of the preliminary evaluation, as most technical background participants find *FOSS-chain* more suitable for independent developers and small organizations. Thus, it might be more meaningful to apply the platform in the framework of small organizations. Its use in a large organization needs to be tested, in order to examine the scalability of the approach, whereas the same needs to be performed across organizations. Although gas pricing of Ethereum did not obstruct testing in the prototype implementation, it does pose a barrier to scaling the system, as investigated in prior work [16]. While the architecture of *FOSS-chain* is tailored to OSS projects, it could be expanded to proprietary software compliance, as suggested in a prior work in the framework of software piracy [20].

Threats to Validity. The current implementation is limited to C, Java and Python languages, but support for additional programming languages like JavaScript, C++ and C# can be added. This might have affected *external validity* referring to the extent we can generalize our findings. A small number of developers participated in the user evaluation that was performed mainly via a video demonstration of the platform and in the framework of the University community, even though developers from the industry were also reached. We should validate our findings with an extended community of software engineers, as the current evaluation entails threats to *conclusion validity*. In terms of *construct validity*, the accuracy of function-level hashing as a tracker of code reuse is a limitation of the approach. While this hashing mechanism is useful to identify identical functions from other projects, it cannot detect cases where the code is altered very slightly but results to the same functionality. Therefore, the current implementation of FOSS-chain might not be able to prevent all cases of intentional license breaches. Future improvements could examine machine learning to detect code similarity. In some cases, slight modifications may not constitute a derivative work and do not require a license compatibility check, so these cases also need to be detected (e.g. if a developer changes only some variable names, or if there is only accidental equivalence of function hashes).

A further limitation is the manual processing of wallet addresses. A system administrator must register the wallet of any user in the configuration file for the user to be able to use the platform. Although this works in a development setting, it is potentially dangerous if mishandled. Future versions must have automated wallets and decentralized identities for improved usability and reduced management costs. At the current implementation, *FOSS-chain* uses a central database that will be replaced with a distributed file system in future versions.

7 Conclusions

In this work, we have presented *FOSS-chain*, a blockchain-based solution for handling OSS license compliance through smart contracts, function-level code analysis and automatic license compliance checks. The users can upload and download a software project, while license compatibility checks are triggered whenever a software project is uploaded that is a derivative work of existing software projects on the platform. The initial user evaluation shows the usefulness of the approach and reveals areas of improvement for future work. Future work will implement the feedback gathered via the user evaluation and will focus on a more precise source code-level comparison integrating abstract syntax tree (AST) analysis or machine learning-based code similarity detection. Support for more programming languages and OSS licenses will also be added, while the consideration of multi-licensing schemes will also be examined.

References

1. Biernacki, K., Plechawska-Wójcik, M.: A comparative analysis of cryptocurrency wallet management tools. J. Comput. Sci. Inst. **21**, 373–377 (2021)
2. Duan, R., Bijlani, A., Xu, M., Kim, T., Lee, W.: Identifying open-source license violation and 1-day security risk at large scale. In: Proceedings of the 2017 ACM SIGSAC Conference on Computer and Communications Security, pp. 2169–2185 (2017)
3. German, D.M., Manabe, Y., Inoue, K.: A sentence-matching method for automatic license identification of source code files. In: Proceedings of the 25th IEEE/ACM International Conference on Automated Software Engineering, pp. 437–446 (2010)
4. Iacovou, K., Kapitsaki, G.: https://github.com/CS-UCY-SEIT-lab/FOSS-chain (2025)
5. Jaeger, M.C., et al.: The FOSSology project: 10 years of license scanning. IFOSS L. Rev. **9**, 9 (2017)
6. Kapitsaki, G.M., Charalambous, G.: Find your open source license now! In: 2016 23rd Asia-Pacific Software Engineering Conference (APSEC), pp. 1–8. IEEE (2016)
7. Kapitsaki, G.M., Charalambous, G.: Modeling and recommending open source licenses with findOSSLicense. IEEE Trans. Softw. Eng. **47**(5), 919–935 (2019)
8. Kapitsaki, G.M., Kramer, F.: Open source license violation check for SPDX files. In: International Conference on Software Reuse, pp. 90–105. Springer (2015)
9. Kapitsaki, G.M., Paschalides, D.: Identifying terms in open source software license texts. In: 2017 24th Asia-Pacific Software Engineering Conference (APSEC), pp. 540–545. IEEE (2017)
10. Kapitsaki, G.M., Tselikas, N.D., Foukarakis, I.E.: An insight into license tools for open source software systems. J. Syst. Softw. **102**, 72–87 (2015)

11. Kshetri, N.: Blockchain's roles in strengthening cybersecurity and protecting privacy. Telecommun. Policy **41**(10), 1027–1038 (2017)
12. Kumar, A., Gupta, A., Sanagavarapu, L.M., Reddy, Y.R.: An approach to open-source software license management using blockchain-based smart-contracts. In: Proceedings of the 15th Innovations in Software Engineering Conference, pp. 1–5 (2022)
13. Nakamoto, S.: Bitcoin: a peer-to-peer electronic cash system (2008)
14. Oliva, G.A., Hassan, A.E., Jiang, Z.M.: An exploratory study of smart contracts in the Ethereum blockchain platform. Empir. Softw. Eng. **25**, 1864–1904 (2020)
15. Ombredanne, P.: Free and open source software license compliance: tools for software composition analysis. Computer **53**(10), 105–109 (2020)
16. Pacheco, M., Oliva, G.A., Rajbahadur, G.K., Hassan, A.E.: What makes Ethereum blockchain transactions be processed fast or slow? An empirical study. Empir. Softw. Eng. **28**(2), 39 (2023)
17. Qin, M., Zhang, Y., Zhou, M., Wang, Z., Li, H., Liu, H.: Developers views on commercial involvement in OSS-a survey from three projects. IEEE Trans. Softw. Eng. (2025)
18. Rosa, G., Scalabrino, S., Mastrostefano, S., Oliveto, R.: Why and how developers maintain smart contracts. Empir. Softw. Eng. **30**(3), 84 (2025)
19. Rosen, L.: Open Source Licensing: Software Freedom and Intellectual Property Law (2005)
20. Shamalka, M., Banujan, K., Kumara, B.: Blockchain and smart contract based approach to mitigate software piracy. In: 2024 4th International Conference on Advanced Research in Computing (ICARC), pp. 247–252. IEEE (2024)
21. Stewart, K., Odence, P., Rockett, E.: Software package data exchange (SPDX) specification. IFOSS L. Rev. **2**, 191 (2010)
22. Tuunanen, T., Koskinen, J., Kärkkäinen, T.: Automated software license analysis. Autom. Softw. Eng. **16**, 455–490 (2009)
23. Xu, S., Gao, Y., Fan, L., Liu, Z., Liu, Y., Ji, H.: LiDetector: license incompatibility detection for open source software. ACM Trans. Softw. Eng. Methodol. **32**(1), 1–28 (2023)
24. Zheng, Z., Xie, S., Dai, H.N., Chen, X., Wang, H.: Blockchain challenges and opportunities: a survey. Int. J. Web Grid Serv. **14**(4), 352–375 (2018)

Improving the Writing Quality of User Stories: A Canonical Action Research Study

Sabine Molenaar[✉] and Fabiano Dalpiaz

Department of Information and Computing Sciences, Utrecht University, Utrecht, The Netherlands
`{s.molenaar,f.dalpiaz}@uu.nl`

Abstract. [Context] User Stories (USs) are a popular notation for writing requirements in Agile software development. USs are often stored in Issue Tracking Systems (ITSs) and are a starting point for defining software development tasks. [Problem] While writing high-quality requirements statements is a typical concern when authoring requirements specification documents, this is less the case when writing USs in an ITS. This may also be the attributed to the fact that practitioners are not familiar with techniques for improving the quality of their USs. [Method] As part of previous research in a large organization, we found that practitioners were eager to learn how to write better USs and asked four Agile teams to participate in a study aimed at improving that practice. We conducted canonical action research where these teams were offered a lightweight intervention in the form of guidelines for writing USs—based on the Quality User Story (QUS) framework—, which they could use to reflect upon the quality of their USs. [Findings] The share of atomic and minimal violations decreased through the use of the intervention and, for the former, the positive effects lasted even after the intervention period ended. However, practitioners did not agree with all the guidelines and argued that violating the criteria can sometimes benefit them in terms of clarity and time spent. These results call for better contextualization of research on user story quality, which we initiate by proposing revised formulations of our guidelines.

Keywords: Requirements Engineering · User stories · Quality User Story framework · Canonical Action Research

1 Introduction

Requirements in Agile software development (ASD) are defined incrementally and iteratively [13], often through the formulation of User Stories (USs), which express a requirement in a compact manner using a simple template such as the Connextra format [3]: *"As a [role], I want to [action], so that [benefit]."*.

In Scrum, the most popular ASD method [23], teams rely largely on information available in their Scrum boards, often stored in issue tracking systems,

G. Scanniello et al. (Eds.): PROFES 2025, LNCS 16361, pp. 102–118, 2026.
https://doi.org/10.1007/978-3-032-12089-2_7

and do not routinely speak to the user [11]. This increases the importance of the quality of USs, as they are a frequently used Agile requirements engineering (RE) practice [11], and are often the only source of information for team members.

Poor requirements can lead to software errors that require rework [5]. This remains a relevant topic, as maintaining requirements quality is considered a challenge in large-scale agile system development. The same is true for time-to-market; teams want to deliver quickly, but still need to achieve requirements with sufficient quality [15].

Several frameworks have been proposed to assess the quality of USs, such as INVEST [24] and Quality User Story (QUS) [16], but their use and effects are rarely tested in practice. In a broader sense, researchers have argued that more empirical studies are needed on the effects of Agile RE and the application of Agile RE practices [4,14].

In a previous study [20], we analyzed the US quality of eight Agile teams by evaluating them on four QUS framework criteria [16]. We found that all four criteria were violated to various degrees. The participants expressed that they were unfamiliar with some of the criteria, but were eager to learn and improve their USs. We invited half of these teams again to participate in this canonical action research (CAR) [6] study to assess whether the quality of their USs could be improved regarding these criteria. In addition, we measured information retention by repeating the analysis after the use of the intervention.

All four teams were given guidelines to use to write their USs for six, two-week sprints. After the period, we interviewed the participating Product Owners (POs) and Scrum Masters (SMs), to get a qualitative perspective on the guidelines' usefulness. In addition, we assessed the written USs on the same four QUS framework criteria and compared the violations to those of the previous study.

We found that the number of violations can be reduced through the use of our lightweight intervention. In addition, the participants stated they would recommend the use of the guidelines to other Agile teams within the organization. However, they disagreed with some guidelines, saying they would make their processes more complex and less time-efficient. Based on their feedback, we propose a reformulation of the guidelines to make them more suitable for use in a real-world Agile development setting, by increasing their pragmatism.

The remainder of this paper is structured as follows. We discuss related literature in Sect. 2. The methods used are described in Sect. 3, followed by the results in Sect. 4. Finally, we present a discussion in Sect. 5 and provide conclusions in Sect. 6.

2   Related Work

We discuss relevant background regarding the QUS framework, as well as studies which evaluate the use of agile requirements in industry settings.

Heck & Zaidman categorized quality criteria for agile requirements (specifications) into three main groups: completeness, uniformity, and consistency &

correctness [10]. The latter category focuses on the correctness of individual requirements and their consistency with others, and an example of this is the INVEST mnemonic [24]. INVEST suggests that USs should be Independent, Negotiable, Valuable, Estimable, Small, and Testable.

Lucassen *et al.* created the QUS framework as a response to limited methods and frameworks for determining and improving the quality of USs. At the time of their study, only INVEST was available. The QUS framework consists of thirteen criteria, which apply to either individual USs or a set of USs [16]. While the authors did experiment with US quality assessment in an industry setting, this required a training session and the use of the AQUSA tool [17], which raises the threshold for participation. Moreover, the training needs to be repeated if new members join the team. Whether the knowledge gained by the practitioners was retained by them after a longer period of time was out of scope. A longitudinal cohort study by Fucci *et al.* showed that it is possible for participants to retain information learned over a period of several months, although they specifically studied Test-Driven Development [9].

Through a survey, Wang *et al.* found that requirements analysts in agile settings discuss requirements once or twice a week with their customers, to confirm new requirements for each sprint or to capture changes to existing requirements [25]. Most respondents used a two-week iteration or sprint, suggesting that requirements need to be captured and documented quickly and often. In addition, high workloads, requirement refinement, creating and estimating USs and requirements ambiguity were among the main challenges in large-scale agile transformation, according to a systematic literature review by Dikert *et al.* [8]. This emphasizes the need for supporting tools, but also shows that these should not be time-consuming to avoid further increasing the workload. This is supported by Kasauli *et al.*, who found that quality and time-to-market are a trade-off large-scale agile systems development often struggles with [15].

Previous studies also evaluated the creation and use of agile requirements through empirical methods. Writing requirements, for example, was investigated by evaluating whether potential POs, people with limited to no experience with writing requirements but who are familiar with the context, are able to write USs [21]. They provided participants with Cohn's US template [3], as well as an example US. They evaluated the output and found that, in general, the participants adhered to the template. Berends & Dalpiaz focused on refinement of USs [2]. Through example mapping, they had team members discuss how the requirement should function in the software; what is allowed and what is not according to the US in question. Their results show that example mapping has a positive impact on the shared understanding of the team [2].

As for the use of requirements, the Requirements Specification for Developers (RSD) approach was developed to tailor the requirements to developers in order to support them in requirements validation [18]; this approach focuses more on the creation and use of acceptance criteria. Medeiros *et al.* evaluated the approach in practice and report that the RSD approach results in a more objective requirements specification, which was deemed more suitable for developers [19]. However, in some cases, multiple requirements were included in one RSD artifact, which negatively affected productivity.

A 2021 study [22] investigated both the creation and use of requirements, by studying how the quality of USs affects the development process, for instance through rework or delays. First, they assessed the quality of 3,414 USs on the well-formed, atomic, minimal, unique and uniform criteria from the QUS framework. The results were expressed as a quality score, which they tested for a correlation with the number of associated bugs, the number of times rework was done and the number of delays. Their results show that lower quality USs correlate with more bugs, increased work, and delays, while high quality USs are less likely to suffer these development problems [22].

3   Research Method

We conducted a Canonical Action Research [6] study to investigate whether US quality can be improved via a not-too-intrusive intervention. Davison defines five main principles for CAR: (i) researcher-client agreement, (ii) cyclical process model, (iii) theory, (iv) change through action, and (v) learning through reflection [6]. In this section, we specify which decisions contribute to which principle, by including them in parentheses (i.e., CAR-i). We selected CAR because the participants in our previous study [20] expressed eagerness to learn and improve (CAR-i/iv). Through CAR, we aim to contribute to the research-industry balance, by making this study relevant to practitioners [12]. We intend to answer the following main research question (MRQ): *How does supporting Agile teams with lightweight guidelines affect the quality of user stories?*

We aimed for a lightweight intervention because (Agile) development teams often have a high workload and therefore cannot always afford to spend time on (additional) training (CAR-iv). Moreover, when a member leaves the team, their knowledge and experience is lost, making training less valuable in the long-term. This is another argument in favor of CAR; only end-users can evaluate whether use of the intervention is viable in the long-term (CAR-iii). Wohlin [26] states that integrating a study into the daily work of the industry is key to the interest and commitment from the industry. We describe the intervention in Sect. 3.2.

We interviewed the practitioners responsible for writing USs for their team to evaluate the intervention and gain insight into their experience (CAR-v). US quality is measured by assessing each US on the four quality criteria at the basis of the intervention: well-formed, atomic, minimal and full sentence. This selection of criteria is in agreement with our previous study and allowed us to compare results; the number of violations of each criterion (CAR-i). We combine qualitative and quantitative methods; the qualitative perspective helps explain patterns found in quantitative data [26].

3.1   Research Design

Figure 1 illustrates our research design.

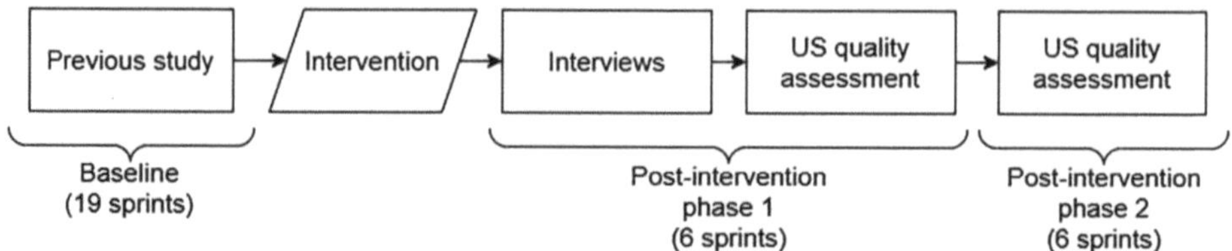

Fig. 1. Research design showing data gathering process.

First, we provided the participating teams with the intervention, the guidelines to use, in the form of a digital one-pager. The practitioners discussed the guidelines at the beginning of the first sprint, and used them to write and refine USs for six sprints, the first post-intervention phase (PI-1), during this time, the researchers and teams did not interact; this also means that we did not enforce the guidelines. After the six sprints were finished, we interviewed the POs and SMs of the participating teams to learn about their experience using the guidelines (CAR-ii). We then assessed the quality of the USs and compared the number of violations from before and after using the guidelines, in absolute numbers and as a share of the USs included. Inspired by Fucci *et al.*. [9], we also assessed the quality of the USs created in the six sprints after that, which we call the second post-intervention phase (PI-2), to see whether any information learned was retained (CAR-iv).

3.2   Intervention: Guidelines for US Writing

We formulated fourteen guidelines for the teams to follow. Each guideline was proposed by the first author and reviewed by the second. We distinguish between practices to follow, "do's", and practices to avoid, "don'ts", when writing a single US. Both Dutch and English versions of the guidelines were made available. Each guideline corresponds to a quality criterion. We summarize the guidelines and the criteria to which they are related in Table 1. The do's are indicated by a P for positive in the ID, while don'ts are indicated by an N for negative.

All guidelines were (i) created using a deductive approach; informed by quality issues encountered in our earlier study [20], in which we objectively assessed each criterion (CAR-ii), and (ii) based on the QUS criteria. We intentionally used theory to inform our guidelines, since we assumed that POs and SMs write US to the best of their ability already and we wished to bring theory and practice together.

The guidelines presented in Table 1 address both 'broad' (violating a criterion) and 'narrow' (improving an element of the US) quality issues. The former are indicated by IDs in **bold**. A US that contains a role and an action does not violate the well-formed criterion, but also does not mean that it contained a 'good' role. For example: *"As [the organization], I want to sort tasks alphabetically."* While this US is well-formed according to QUS, the role could be improved

Table 1. Guidelines presented to participating teams, organized as positive do's (Px) and negative don'ts (Ny), including the corresponding quality criterion.

ID	Description	QUS criterion
P1	Use a specific template	Well-formed
P2	Specify at least a role and an action	Well-formed
P3	Specify a desire for exactly one functionality	Atomic
P4	Formulate a clear benefit or motivation	Minimal
P5	Use a full, grammatically correct sentence	Full sentence
P6	Write in one language (jargon excepted)	Full sentence
P7	Use a function title as a role	Well-formed
N1	Specify the (technical) solution	Minimal
N2	Use negations in actions	Minimal
N3	Add unnecessary information in brackets or at the end	Minimal
N4	Force tasks (e.g., bug fixes, maintenance) into a user story	Well-formed
N5	Specify non-functional requirements in user stories	Well-formed
N6	Refer to other user stories or documents	Minimal
N7	Use a system or application as a role	Well-formed

by mentioning a specific stakeholder instead, we call this a narrow quality issue. Such issues were included in the qualitative findings of our previous study.

While the narrow quality issues are not reflected in the quantitative results, they were discussed in the interviews and part of the qualitative results. Note that the participants were only given the description from Table 1 preceded by "do" or "don't", but were unaware to which criterion a guideline is related. This was done so they could not focus on a single guideline in particular to improve on their violations from the first study.

3.3   Participants

We held our study in a large organization based in the Netherlands; we cannot disclose the identity due to the confidentiality constraints. The organization maintains many applications and over 200 Agile teams are active. The organization and the teams were chosen for convenience, but the researchers were only

Table 2. Demographics of the participating teams.

Team ID	Size in #employees	Type of dev.	Ext. members	Interviewees
T1	8 to 10	Low code	No	2
T2	8 to 10	Full code	Yes	2
T3	12 to 18	Full code	Yes	1
T4	8 to 10	Mix	Yes	3

involved with the teams for the sake of this study (CAR-ii). Six of the teams included in [20] were asked to participate in this study, two of which declined due to high workload. All interviews were held with the POs and/or SMs of the team. A brief description of the teams can be found in Table 2.

3.4   Qualitative Data Gathering

The interviews were semi-structured: interviewees were asked questions, but could share whatever they wanted and ask questions in return. The following questions were asked in every interview:

1. Did you use the guidelines?
2. Were you able to understand the guidelines?
3. What was the most useful guideline?
4. What was the least useful guideline?
5. Was any information new to you?
6. Would you recommend the guidelines to someone else?
7. Is there anything else you would like to share?

We shared no information on the performance of their team with the interviewees before or after the receiving of the guidelines.

3.5   Quantitative Data Gathering

We performed the quality assessment on the USs of the participating teams again after the interviews were conducted. For each team, we gathered the USs of the six sprints that followed right after providing them with the guidelines, the first post-intervention phase. The participants were aware of which criteria their USs would be assessed on. We also gathered the USs of the six sprints that followed after that, the second post-intervention phase, to see if retainment was present; meaning if fewer violations are present after participation in this study has ended. Unfortunately, Team 3 ceased expressing requirements through USs in the second post-intervention phase, as they switched to task descriptions; therefore, for that phase, no data are available for them.

All USs were assessed on the following, adapted, QUS criteria [16] (CAR-iii):

1. Well-formed: A US includes at least a role and an action.
2. Atomic: A US expresses a requirement for exactly one feature.
3. Minimal: A US contains only role, action and benefit.
4. Full sentence: A US is a well-formed, full sentence.

For each US, we manually assessed whether a criterion was met or not, using the same guidelines as described in our previous study [20]. First, for the well-formed criterion, we checked whether a role and an action were included. Second, for atomic, we focused on the use of words such as "and" and "or", indicating enumerations. Third, additional text in USs, such as after the period or included in parentheses, resulted in a minimal violation. Fourth, the full sentence criterion was considered violated if the sentence was syntactically incorrect. The manual assessment was performed by the first author, discussing edge cases with the second. In addition to confidentiality reasons, we made this choice because Wouters *et al.*. [27] reported high inter-rater reliability for the well-formed and atomic criteria.

4 Results

While the quantitative data were collected last, we present these results first in Sect. 4.1, and then use the qualitative results in Sect. 4.2 for triangulation.

4.1 Quantitative Results

We compare the quantitative results of three phases of the study:

1. *Base*: the baseline, the quality and violations observed prior to the intervention (obtained in [20]), which consisted of nineteen sprints;
2. *PI-1*: the first post-intervention phase, focusing on the six sprints during with the participants were asked to use the intervention;
3. *PI-2*: the second post-intervention phase, focusing on the six sprints that immediately follow PI-1.

Based on the number of violations and on the classification from our previous work [20], the USs are divided into three groups: those of high quality (no violations), medium quality (one violation), and low quality (two violations). USs with more than two violations were not observed.

In Table 3, the quality score of the USs written by the teams is shown for each phase. We also include the number of USs assessed. For the baseline, which included more sprints, we include a normalized number of USs in parentheses. Note that in the PI phases, the teams worked with the lower range in number of employees described in Table 2, which explains the decrease in number of USs per sprint per team.

The quality of USs across the teams improved after the intervention; from 74% high quality USs in the baseline to 79% post-intervention. The second post-intervention phase also shows an overall improvement, but of weaker strength (76%). Only team 2 shows a decrease in quality, while teams 1 and 3 show an increase in high quality USs and team 4 only shows an improvement through a reduction in low quality USs (from 2% to 0%).

Table 4 reports the number and share of QUS violations per criteria and team. Again, we also include the number of USs assessed and a normalized number of USs for the baseline.

After the intervention, no well-formed violations were observed, but these numbers were low in the baseline too. The atomic violations decreased from 21% to 14% in PI-1 and are still lower than the baseline in PI-2 (16%). The minimal violations show a slight improvement in PI-1 (5%) compared to the baseline

Table 3. Number and share of USs per quality score and team. The total number for the Base period, over 19 sprints, is also presented in parentheses after normalization to 6 sprints, allowing direct comparison between Base, PI-1, and PI-2.

	Low			Medium			High			n		
	Base	PI-1	PI-2	Base	PI-1	PI-2	Base	PI-1	PI-2	Base	PI-1	PI-2
T1	3	0	0	62	5	4	160	33	35	225 (71)	38	39
	1%	0%	0%	28%	13%	10%	71%	87%	90%	-	-	-
T2	0	1	0	15	14	5	106	32	22	121 (38)	47	27
	0%	2%	0%	12%	30%	19%	88%	68%	81%	-	-	-
T3	5	0	-	47	1	-	133	29	-	185 (58)	30	-
	3%	0%	-	25%	3%	-	72%	97%	-	-	-	-
T4	4	0	2	55	10	15	136	22	25	195 (62)	32	42
	2%	0%	5%	28%	31%	36%	70%	69%	60%	-	-	-
Total	12	1	2	179	30	24	535	116	82	726 (229)	147	108
	2%	1%	2%	25%	20%	22%	74%	79%	76%	-	-	-

Table 4. Number and share of QUS violations per criteria and team.

	Well-formed			Atomic			Minimal			Full sentence			n		
	Base	PI-1	PI-2	Base	PI-1	PI-2	Base	PI-1	PI-2	Base	PI-1	PI-2	Base	PI-1	PI-2
T1	1	0	0	59	5	4	7	0	0	1	0	0	225 (71)	38	39
	0%	0%	0%	26%	13%	10%	3%	0%	0%	0%	0%	0%	-	-	-
T2	0	0	0	11	10	3	4	4	2	0	2	0	121 (38)	47	27
	0%	0%	0%	9%	21%	11%	3%	9%	7%	0%	4%	0%	-	-	-
T3	2	0	-	37	1	-	16	0	-	2	0	-	185 (58)	30	-
	1%	0%	-	20%	3%	-	9%	0%	-	1%	0%	-	-	-	-
T4	0	0	0	46	5	10	15	4	9	2	1	0	195 (62)	32	42
	0%	0%	0%	24%	16%	24%	8%	13%	21%	1%	3%	0%	-	-	-
Total	3	0	0	153	21	17	42	8	11	5	3	0	726 (229)	147	108
	0%	0%	0%	21%	14%	16%	6%	5%	10%	1%	2%	0%	-	-	-

(6%), but increase to 10% in PI-2. The full sentence violations increased slightly in PI-1 to 2% (was: 1%), but disappeared in PI-2 (0%).

From both perspectives (quality score and violations per type), Team 1 presents a continuous improvement from baseline to PI-1 to PI-2. The same is true for Team 3, but here we can only make observations regarding the difference between the baseline and PI-1. Team 4 shows some improvement, but in some cases performs worse after the intervention. The same can be said for team 2, but in less severe terms.

4.2 Qualitative Results

We report the results gathered in the semi-structured interviews. We discuss each interview question (see Sect. 3.4) and include additional feedback from the interviewees at the end. For each finding, we specify which team representatives support it by listing their IDs. For instance (T1/T4), means that the POs/SMs of teams 1 and 4 mentioned the finding. When relevant, observations from Sect. 4.1 are included to triangulate the findings.

1. Did You Use the Guidelines? All four teams stated that they used the guidelines for writing their USs during PI-1. Two teams specified that they kept the guidelines at hand while writing USs, but did not check the USs on the guidelines specifically after writing was finished (T1/T4). One of these teams discussed the guidelines with the entire team beforehand (T4), while the other adapted their template; specifically including the benefit of the US (T1). One team summarized the guidelines, keeping only what they 'needed' (T3).

2. Were You Able to Understand the Guidelines? All four teams understood the guidelines just by reading them and had no need to clarify. Two teams were able to recognize many aspects in the guidelines from their own way of working (T1/T4) and one specified that they appreciated this as a validation of what they were already doing (T1).

3. What Was the Most Useful Guideline? *P3* is considered one of the most useful guidelines by Teams 3 and 4. Specifying a need for only one functionality is still a challenge for Team 3, but they noticed that they split USs [7] into smaller parts more often than before. This is also reflected in the quantitative results: Team 3 went from 20% atomic violations to 3% and Team 4 from 24% to 16% (baseline to PI-1). Team 1 also shows an improvement here, from 26% in the baseline to 10% in PI-2.

Three teams (T1/T2/T4) tried to refrain from including unnecessary information (*N3*), for instance by evaluating the US after it was written to check if all information included was truly necessary, if not, it was left out (T1). Team 1 was successful in reducing the share of minimal violations (from 3% to 0%), as was team 3 (from 9% to 0%). Both Teams 2 and 4 had an increase percentage-wise, from 3% to 9% and 8% to 13%, respectively. Two teams (T2/T4) mentioned the avoidance of negations (*N2*). No requirements by negation were observed in the PI-1 and PI-2 phases for Teams 2 and 4.

Team 1 tried to avoid specifying a technical solution (*N1*), because they discuss solutions among the team and may have different opinions on what the solutions should be. To keep all team members in the know, they include implementation hints in the documents and try to keep USs as functional and problem-oriented as possible. This is especially challenging when the stakeholder requesting the feature already includes solutions in their request (T1).

Team 3 mostly prefers the 'positive' guidelines and mentioned *P7* as an important one. At first, they used to include themselves or the system as the role, since they wrote the USs for improvement of that system. Now they choose someone from the business to include in the role and this person is asked to accept the US too (T3). After the intervention, the system was used as a role only once. They also try to write in one language now (*P6*). No USs were written using more than one language after the intervention (jargon excepted). *N4* was mentioned by only one team (T2). After the intervention, all teams still recorded maintenance tasks in a US template, such as: "*I want to update [system] to [version]*".

4. What Was the Least Useful Guideline? Teams 2, 3 and 4 considered *N1* the least useful. Technical solutions are included in the US to ensure all team members are on the same page (T3/T4). They had to start this practice, because in the past some USs were so poorly written that the solution did not meet the requirement (T4). Working with third-party team members is also mentioned as a reason, since they sometimes have to work asynchronously. So, in order to work more efficiently, they include the solution rather than having to schedule another meeting; every feedback cycle and meeting costs time (T4). Team 3 explained it is "pointless" to write 'good' USs (meaning without violations), if you need to have a bunch of conversations about them to make sure everyone understands what they mean (T3). Another motivation for including solutions is the lack of experience of team members (T2). All teams continued to specify (technical) solutions after the intervention. Examples are specifying which modules and APIs to use or specific fields to filter on, e.g.: "*As a [role], I want [module] to use [API] to support [event]*" and "*As a [role], I want [object ID] to be available on [specific page]*".

Including specific stakeholders as a role can be difficult (*P7/N7*), when the team mostly focuses on the back-end of a system (T4) or when the team recognizes it is something that "just needs to be done" (T2). In some cases, they need to search for a user and at that point, they include the system, because it is easier for the team members to understand the need that way (T4).

Bugs are often issues encountered by the business, so in order to relate their planning to their stakeholders' needs, teams write bug fixes (*N4*) in US format (T4). If possible, they would like to see a different template for different topics, such as a bug fix and performance template (T4). Team 2 somewhat agrees, describing that they understand that bug fixes do not belong in USs, but they think maintenance tasks do belong, since they are part of the US lifecycle management (T2). Non-functional requirements (NFRs) (*N5*) are included in USs if team members lack experience and are at risk of not considering them while fulfilling the USs or simply because NFRs can constrain USs (T2). T3 takes a more practical approach: if not in the USs, where do you document maintenance tasks and NFRs? They consider these artifacts necessary building blocks for a US. A solution for them could be an NFR template (T3). Teams 1, 3 and 4 included NFRs in US templates after the intervention, for instance: *"As a [role], I want the status of [module] to be clearer, so that it is easier to interpret."*

Not referring to other USs (*N6*) seems counterintuitive to the teams, as this can often save them time (T1/T2). Other USs can sometimes include information they need for their own work or their USs are dependent on those of other teams (T1/T2). In some cases, there is a 'big' US that various teams divide into USs they can work on, but most information, such as objectives, are included in the 'big' US (T1). Both teams still employ this practice after the intervention.

5. Was Any Information New to You? Two teams (T3/T4) were unaware that NFRs should not be formulated as USs. Team 4 asked when non-functional becomes functional and how to address this. Team 3 did not know technical solutions should not be included.

6. Would You Recommend the Guidelines to Anyone Else? All four teams stated they would recommend the guidelines to others, and one team had already shared them with a team not included in this study (T2). Two teams explained that a standard across the organization would be beneficial, since they sometimes need to collaborate or are dependent on other teams; *"it would be nice to work with USs that you did not write, but that are still well written"* (T1/T3). Notably, both of these teams showed improvement in all four criteria, while the other two did not.

7. Additional Feedback. Team 1 considers the *do's* more useful for beginners and *don'ts* more useful if you already have experience with writing USs. They can help to identify and change 'bad habits' (T1). Additional guidelines were also requested, for instance for test cases (T4) and acceptance criteria (T3/T4). How can you describe acceptance criteria well and make them 'SMART' (T3)? Team 4 thinks LLMs can save time and effort in requirements refinement, for instance by using these guidelines as restrictions for prompts and assessing the USs on the QUS criteria.

5   Discussion

We discuss the threats to validity using the five quality criteria for CAR as recommended by SIGSOFT: reflexivity, credibility, resonance, usefulness and transferability [1].

Reflexivity. The four included criteria were evaluated by one researcher, discussing unclear cases with a second researcher. However, guidelines and instructions were created beforehand and applied to all USs and the selected criteria are mostly objective. Previous work has shown that well-formed and atomic violations can be reliably assessed [27] and the researchers have been familiar with QUS since its publication, with the second author being a co-author of QUS.

Credibility. The guidelines served a particular goal, so it is not unreasonable to assume the participating teams predicted what they would be assessed on in this study. To get better results, they may have put in extra effort beyond what they would do in a non-study related setting or used external sources and support. However, this seems unlikely, as the interviewees did not mention using anything but their experience and the guidelines. Furthermore, they were in no way incentivized to perform better, other than their intrinsic motivation, since results were anonymized and there were no rewards. In addition, we also analyzed lasting effects by assessing their USs again, after the intervention phase ended. We triangulated results by using both quantitative and qualitative findings.

Teams may have improved over time regardless of the intervention. POs and SMs might have paid more attention to US quality, since they were made aware of it, but not necessarily due to applying the guidelines. In an attempt to mitigate this threat, we informed the participating teams that certain errors were made by teams within the organization, but did not tell them which teams made which errors. Therefore, they were unable to focus on specific quality criteria. We also held no authority over any of the participating teams and we did not enforce any of the guidelines throughout the study. The participants were also not informed of which guideline related to which criterion, so they were unable to target a specific 'weakness' in their work. In addition, by sheer chance it is easier for teams to improve on quality criteria with many violations in the baseline assessment. Changes among the team members were also not taken into account, however, the POs and SMs remained the same throughout the study.

CAR often prescribes multiple process cycles and while a single cycle is not unsound, it is rare [6]. We decided to perform one cycle for two reasons. First, it would have been difficult to mitigate the maturity effect; the USs contained fewer violations after the intervention phase, in most cases. Second, participants explicitly stated they did not agree with some of the guidelines, so they will not be using them in the future. Arguments include that they think it takes too much time or makes their process more complex than needed. It would be unethical to 'force' them to continue using guidelines they do not perceive as beneficial. Especially when the intervention is aimed at supporting these industry participants (CAR-ii).

Resonance. In order to obtain a genuine account of their experience, we did not share the quantitative results with the teams in the post-intervention interviews. Nevertheless, our revised guidelines (see next section) are based on their feedback.

Usefulness. In our future research directions (Sect. 6.2), we provide recommendations to both researchers and practitioners based on our findings.

Transferability. The participating teams were selected through convenience sampling; only teams that participated in our previous case study were asked to participate in this study. While we cannot be sure whether these results are generalizable to other teams and organizations, the participating teams used popular methods (Scrum) and requirements practices (USs).

6   Conclusion

We draw conclusions on the effectiveness of the intervention per QUS criterion assessed in this study, combining qualitative and quantitative findings. We then present a reformulation of three guidelines based on the feedback provided by the participants, general conclusions, and end with directions for the future.

Well-Formed. One team specifically mentioned focusing on using function titles as roles (*P7*), rather than the system or application they work on (*N7*). After the intervention, the system was used as a role only once, while before this was the rule and using function titles was the exception. The number of violations decreased after the intervention; however, there were few well-formed violations to begin with.

Atomic. Two teams considered *"specify a desire for exactly one functionality"* (*P3*) one of the most useful guidelines and both these teams reduced their number of atomic violations during the use of the intervention. In general, it seems that the intervention was effective in reducing these violations, as the share of atomic violations decreased by seven percent points during the intervention and by five percent points after the intervention.

Minimal. Three teams found not including unnecessary information (*N3*) one of the most useful guidelines, but only one of them was successful in reducing their minimal violations. The number of minimal violations dropped by one percent point during the use of the intervention, but increased after. A possible explanation is that the participants disagreed with the guidelines that stated not to specify technical solutions and refer to other USs or documents. During the interviews, the interviewees said that the former ensures all the team members are on the same page, especially when working with external team members that may work asynchronously. The latter is counterintuitive for them, since referring to other USs makes dependencies explicit. In other words, they may have a different view of what is 'unnecessary'.

Full Sentence. This criterion was rarely violated, but the share of full sentence violations increased during the use of the intervention and decreased afterward. It is unsure how effective the guidelines were in this case. During the interviews, one team stated that they worked on writing in one language (*P6*) and were successful in this endeavor.

Expressing maintenance tasks, (technical) solutions and non-functional requirements in USs are points of contention between research and industry. First, the practitioners argue that maintenance tasks are part of the product's lifecycle and should therefore be included in fn USs, as they express functional requirements. Second, including (technical) solutions is meant to save time, as this ensures all team members know what to do at any time. Third, non-functional requirements are mentioned in USs, because they should be considered while fulfilling other USs (e.g., they can constrain other (functional) requirements) and because practitioners are unsure how else they can be specified.

All in all, the participating teams would recommend using the guidelines to other teams. They would also benefit from this, as USs they are dependent on are sometimes of poor quality and difficult to work with.

6.1   Reformulation of Guidelines

The CAR principles [6] recommend reflecting on the results and taking these into account for continuation of the project at hand. Therefore, we propose a reformulation of three guidelines. In summary, participants mainly provided compelling arguments against the formulation of guidelines N1, N4 and N6. Based on their feedback, we have reformulated these guidelines as presented in Table 1 below; to make them less restrictive and more pragmatic (CAR-v). The changes are italicized (note that the guidelines are still concerned with the writing of a single US):

- N1: Specify the (technical) solution *in the user story template*;
- N4: Force tasks (e.g. bug fixes, *administrative work*) in user stories;
- N6: Refer to other user stories, *unless including their IDs*, or documents.

6.2   Future Directions

The participants stated that they believe other teams could benefit from using the intervention, therefore an obvious next step would be to share the guidelines with other Agile teams within the organization as well. However, since participants also criticized some of the guidelines, the intervention could benefit from a second iteration; making improvements based on empirical findings. We have made a first proposal by reformulating the contentious guidelines in Sect. 6.1. During the interviews, participants also stated they would appreciate support regarding the definition of NFRs (possibly through a template), how to document maintenance tasks, as well as guidelines for writing high quality acceptance criteria and test cases.

On more than one occasion, the participants explicitly disagreed with a guideline and did not consider using it beneficial. These guidelines, however, are all based on quality criteria from the QUS framework, which has remained largely unchallenged by industry due to its limited testing in practice. Our study shows that situational guidelines are needed, as QUS (and other frameworks) are not one-size-fits-all solutions. CAR and other empirical studies are important for identifying the needs for such more specific approaches for evolving frameworks like QUS. In short, research would benefit from evaluating new tools, methods and applications with their envisioned end-users in a real-world setting, to ensure they are suitable for use by practitioners.

References

1. ACM SIGSOFT: Empirical standards for action research (Accessed 10 June 2025). https://www2.sigsoft.org/EmpiricalStandards/docs/standards?standard=ActionResearch#
2. Berends, J., Dalpiaz, F.: Refining user stories via example mapping: an empirical investigation. In: 2021 IEEE 29th International Requirements Engineering Conference (RE), pp. 345–355. IEEE (2021)
3. Cohn, M.: User stories applied: For agile software development. Addison-Wesley Professional (2004)
4. Curcio, K., Navarro, T., Malucelli, A., Reinehr, S.: Requirements engineering: a systematic mapping study in agile software development. J. Syst. Softw. **139**, 32–50 (2018)
5. Davis, A.M.: Software Requirements: Objects, Functions, and States. Prentice-Hall, Inc (1993)
6. Davison, R., Martinsons, M.G., Kock, N.: Principles of canonical action research. Inf. Syst. J. **14**(1), 65–86 (2004)
7. Dellsén, E., Westgårdh, K., Horkoff, J.: Invest in splitting: user story splitting within the software industry. In: International Working Conference on Requirements Engineering: Foundation for Software Quality, pp. 115–130. Springer (2022)
8. Dikert, K., Paasivaara, M., Lassenius, C.: Challenges and success factors for large-scale agile transformations: a systematic literature review. J. Syst. Softw. **119**, 87–108 (2016)
9. Fucci, D., et al.: A longitudinal cohort study on the retainment of test-driven development. In: Proceedings of the 12th ACM/IEEE International Symposium on Empirical Software Engineering and Measurement, pp. 1–10 (2018)
10. Heck, P., Zaidman, A.: A systematic literature review on quality criteria for agile requirements specifications. Software Qual. J. **26**, 127–160 (2018)
11. Hess, A., Diebold, P., Seyff, N.: Understanding information needs of agile teams to improve requirements communication. J. Ind. Inf. Integr. **14**, 3–15 (2019)
12. Hoda, R., Salleh, N., Grundy, J., Tee, H.M.: Systematic literature reviews in agile software development: A tertiary study. Inf. Softw. Technol. **85**, 60–70 (2017)
13. Hruschka, P., Lauenroth, K., Meuten, M., Rogers, G., Gärtner, S., Steffe, H.J.: RE@Agile Handbook. Handbook, International Requirements Engineering Board (2024)
14. Inayat, I., Salim, S.S., Marczak, S., Daneva, M., Shamshirband, S.: A systematic literature review on agile requirements engineering practices and challenges. Comput. Hum. Behav. **51**, 915–929 (2015)
15. Kasauli, R., Knauss, E., Horkoff, J., Liebel, G., de Oliveira Neto, F.G.: Requirements engineering challenges and practices in large-scale agile system development. J. Syst. Softw. **172**, 110851 (2021)
16. Lucassen, G., Dalpiaz, F., van der Werf, J.M.E., Brinkkemper, S.: Improving agile requirements: the quality user story framework and tool. Requirements Eng. **21**, 383–403 (2016)

17. Lucassen, G., Dalpiaz, F., van der Werf, J.M.E., Brinkkemper, S.: Improving user story practice with the Grimm method: a multiple case study in the software industry. In: International Working Conference on Requirements Engineering: Foundation for Software Quality, pp. 235–252. Springer (2017)
18. Medeiros, J., Vasconcelos, A., Goulão, M., Silva, C., Araújo, J.: An approach based on design practices to specify requirements in agile projects. In: Proceedings of the Symposium on Applied Computing, pp. 1114–1121 (2017)
19. Medeiros, J., Vasconcelos, A., Silva, C., Goulão, M.: Requirements specification for developers in agile projects: Evaluation by two industrial case studies. Inform. Softw. Technol. **117** (2020)
20. Molenaar, S., Dalpiaz, F.: The impact of requirements artifacts on efficiency in agile development: a case study. In: Accepted for Published at the IEEE International Requirements Engineering conference (2025)
21. Rocha Silva, T., Winckler, M., Bach, C.: Evaluating the usage of predefined interactive behaviors for writing user stories: an empirical study with potential product owners. Cogn., Technol. Work **22**(3), 437–457 (2020)
22. Scott, E., Tõemets, T., Pfahl, D.: An empirical study of user story quality and its impact on open source project performance. In: International Conference on Software Quality, pp. 119–138. Springer (2021)
23. Verwijs, C., Russo, D.: A theory of scrum team effectiveness. ACM Trans. Softw. Eng. Methodol. **32**(3), 1–51 (2023)
24. Wake, B.: INVEST in Good Stories, and SMART Tasks. http://xp123.com/articles/invest-in-good-stories-and-smart-tasks/. Accessed 12 Mar 2025 (2003)
25. Wang, X., Zhao, L., Wang, Y., Sun, J.: The role of requirements engineering practices in agile development: an empirical study. In: Requirements Engineering: First Asia Pacific Requirements Engineering Symposium, APRES 2014, Auckland, New Zealand, April 28-29, 2014. Proceedings, pp. 195–209. Springer (2014)
26. Wohlin, C.: Empirical software engineering research with industry: Top 10 challenges. In: 2013 1st International Workshop on Conducting Empirical Studies in Industry (CESI), pp. 43–46. IEEE (2013)
27. Wouters, J., Menkveld, A., Brinkkemper, S., Dalpiaz, F.: Crowd-based requirements elicitation via pull feedback: method and case studies. Requirements Eng. **27**(4), 429–455 (2022)

From Machine Learning Documentation to Requirements: Bridging Processes with Requirements Languages

Yi Peng[1,2]([✉]) [iD], Hans-Martin Heyn[1,2] [iD], and Jennifer Horkoff[1,2] [iD]

[1] University of Gothenburg, Gothenburg, Sweden
[2] Chalmers University of Technology, Gothenburg, Sweden
`{yi.peng,hans-martin.heyn,jennifer.horkoff}@gu.se`

Abstract. In software engineering processes for machine learning (ML)-enabled systems, integrating and verifying ML components is a major challenge. A prerequisite is the specification of ML component requirements, including models and data, an area where traditional requirements engineering (RE) processes face new obstacles. An underexplored source of RE-relevant information in this context is ML documentation such as ModelCards and DataSheets. However, it is uncertain to what extent RE-relevant information can be extracted from these documents. This study first investigates the amount and nature of RE-relevant information in 20 publicly available ModelCards and DataSheets. We show that these documents contain a significant amount of potentially RE-relevant information. Next, we evaluate how effectively three established RE representations (EARS, Rupp's template, and Volere) can structure this knowledge into requirements. Our results demonstrate that there is a pathway to transform ML-specific knowledge into structured requirements, incorporating ML documentation in software engineering processes for ML systems.

Keywords: AI Engineering · Software Processes · Data Sheets · Machine Learning · Model Cards · Requirements Engineering

1 Introduction

Machine learning (ML)-enabled systems are increasingly used across a wide variety of domains, including healthcare, automotive, and manufacturing [18]. However, their non-deterministic behavior and heavy reliance on data complicates software engineering (SE) processes, especially in managing customer expectations, data quality, and ensuring transparency in system design [3]. Requirements Engineering (RE) plays a central role in addressing these challenges by translating stakeholder needs through clear and actionable requirements [16]. With ML components as part of complex software systems, there is a need to re-consider where requirements-related information comes from, and what types of new artifacts or boundary objects we should be considering as part of SE processes for

G. Scanniello et al. (Eds.): PROFES 2025, LNCS 16361, pp. 119–136, 2026.
https://doi.org/10.1007/978-3-032-12089-2_8

ML systems [20]. Defining and integrating processes to capture model and data requirements, which cover aspects such as robustness, interpretability, fairness, and data quality [29], remains a challenge in SE for ML systems [21].

In parallel, the ML community has introduced documentation artifacts such as ModelCards [26] and DataSheets [10] to document component-level information. These artifacts are particularly popular in open-source platforms such as Hugging Face (https://huggingface.co/models), yet they remain loosely structured and inconsistently adopted which limits their integration into software development processes [7]. Nonetheless, we argue that these artifacts could be a potential source of information for RE because they document information about intended use, performance limitations, and biases, which directly relate to requirements, including functional requirements (FRs), non-functional requirements (NFRs), and constraints. Structuring this information through RE languages may be a key step towards integrating these informal artifacts into SE for ML systems processes.

The overall goal of this study is to assess the potential of ModelCards and DataSheets to serve as a bridge between informal ML component descriptions and more structured SE processes. To determine if these artifacts can serve this role, we must first validate that they contain valuable requirements-relevant information in practice. This step is addressed by research question (RQ) 1:

RQ1 How much requirements-relevant information is contained in ModelCards and DataSheets?

    RQ1.1 What are the issues in how this information is documented from an RE perspective?

If the presence of this information is confirmed, the next step is to evaluate whether existing RE languages are suitable for structuring it. RQ2 is formulated to investigate this:

RQ2 How effective are existing requirements representation languages (e.g., EARS, Rupp's Template, Volere) in capturing requirements-relevant information from ModelCards and DataSheets?

    RQ2.1 What types of requirements-relevant information are not well captured by these techniques in the context of ModelCards and DataSheets?

We investigated these questions in two steps: First, we analyze a sample of 20 diverse ModelCards and DataSheet, revealing that these artifacts contain significant RE-relevant information. However, they also exhibit redundancies and inconsistent levels of detail, which may stem from the varied adoption of these documentation practices. Second, we evaluate how well three well-known RE languages – EARS [24], Rupp's Template [33], and Volere [31] – capture this RE-relevant content, finding that while EARS and Rupp's Template can extract much of the RE-relevant information, only Volere captures implementation-level details relevant for integrating ML models and data into broader system specifications. Overall, our findings contribute to the integration of ML documentation artifacts into the software engineering life cycle, aiming to improve communication between ML and SE teams and enhance the engineering of successful ML-systems.

The paper is organized as follows: Sect. 2 presents background and related work, with methodology in Sect. 3. We report the results in Sect. 4 and discuss implications, future work, and threats in Sect. 5. Section 6 concludes this paper.

2 Background and Related Work

2.1 RE Languages and Templates

Structured RE languages and templates enhance clarity, traceability, and consistency in requirements documentation. Among them, EARS, Rupp's template, and Volere are widely adopted [11,13]. Figure 1 shows the core structures of EARS, Rupp's Template and Volere.

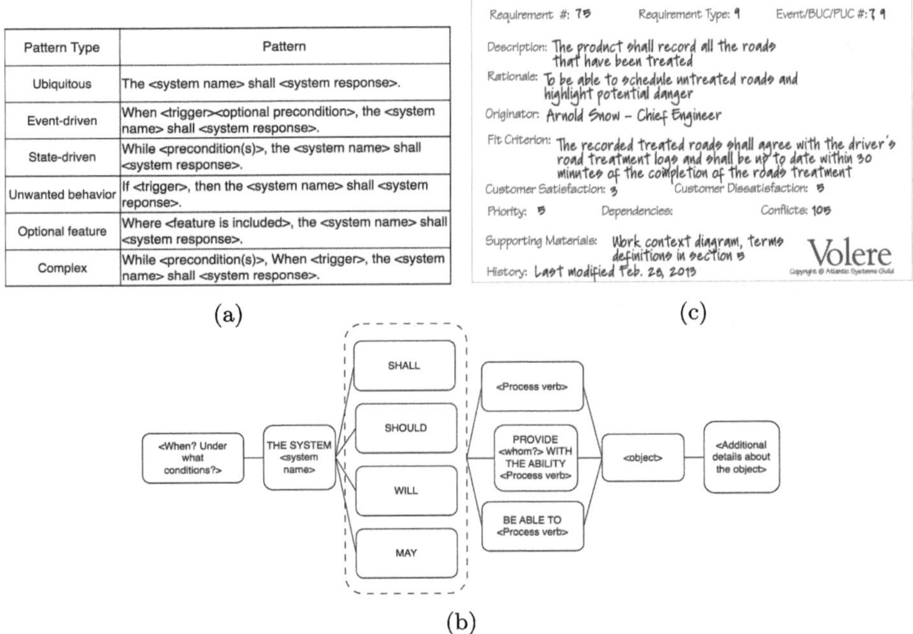

Pattern Type	Pattern
Ubiquitous	The <system name> shall <system response>.
Event-driven	When <trigger><optional precondition>, the <system name> shall <system response>.
State-driven	While <precondition(s)>, the <system name> shall <system response>.
Unwanted behavior	If <trigger>, then the <system name> shall <system reponse>.
Optional feature	Where <feature is included>, the <system name> shall <system response>.
Complex	While <precondition(s)>, When <trigger>, the <system name> shall <system response>.

(a)

(c)

(b)

Fig. 1. (a) EARS [23], (b) Rupp's template [25] and (c) Volere [32].

EARS is a lightweight, structured natural language format, applied successfully in industry [24]. It uses patterns such as ubiquitous, event-driven, state-driven, optional feature, and unwanted behavior to reduce ambiguity and improve readability [12].

Rupp's Template [33], established by the International Requirements Engineering Institute (IREB) as a de facto standard for the syntactic specification of system requirements [25], specifies nine patterns: three for FRs, three for NFRs, and three for conditional clauses. FRs are grouped under FunctionMASTER, classified by activity type: system, user interaction, and interface. NFRs are expressed using PropertyMASTER, EnvironmentMASTER, and ProcessMASTER. Conditional logic is supported by LogicMASTER ("if"), EventMASTER ("as soon as"), and TimeMASTER ("as long as"). The template encourages fine-grained specification using modal verbs and optional details [13].

Volere [30] focuses on traceability of requirements and structured metadata (e.g., rationale, acceptance criteria). It categorizes NFRs (33 types) and constraints (8 types), and includes sections on external factors (e.g., assumptions, risks). With over 20,000 downloads of its online template materials reported on its official website, the Volere template demonstrates significant practical use.

These three RE languages were selected for their popularity and distinct strengths: EARS provides a lightweight, structured syntax for atomic requirements; Rupp's template offers a systematic approach for capturing variability and fine-grained system behavior, and Volere ensures traceability and completeness. Together, they offer a comprehensive lens to assess how information in ML documentation can be utilized as a source of requirements.

2.2   RE for ML Systems

Vogelsang and Borg [36] were among the first to define characteristics and challenges unique to RE for ML-based systems by interviewing data scientists, observing that the development paradigm for ML requires rethinking of RE. Since then, frameworks such as RE for human-centered AI [1], perspective-driven RE [35], as well as extensions of goal-orientated RE [6] have emerged. While these approaches guide requirement elicitation and modeling, they tend to remain high-level and lack concrete guidance for specifying ML requirements. A recent review by Habiba et al. [14] highlights remaining difficulties in concretely specifying low-level requirements, insufficient documentation guidelines, and the need to adapt existing RE practices for ML-based systems.

Several proposed RE for ML frameworks have utilized RE representation such as EARS, and UML to capture FRs for ML systems [2,37]. Dedicated templates [5] and Volere [15] have been applied to specify NFRs. While these approaches provide valuable frameworks for documenting ML system requirements, they focus on specific types of requirements such as FRs, NFRs or quality requirements, and limited dimensions of data requirements, which may not fully capture the breadth of information needed for ML system development. We argue that ML-specific documentation artifacts like ModelCards and DataSheets, which are created during the actual development of ML models and datasets, are a potential source of such information. They offer broad information spanning use cases (FRs), fairness considerations (NFRs), environmental assumptions, and hardware constraints. While related work has mined less structured sources like GitHub README files for requirements [28], we focus on ModelCards and DataSheets for ML-specific requirements, against which we evaluate the applicability and coverage of existing RE languages.

2.3   ModelCards and DataSheets

ML documentation artifacts, including ModelCards [26] and DataSheets [10], exemplified in Fig. 2, aim to support transparency, accountability, and ethical considerations in ML development. ModelCards document a model's performance, intended use, and limitations. DataSheets aim to ease assessment of a dataset's suitability by describing properties such as motivation, composition, collection processes, and potential biases. Their popularity is evidenced by high citation counts (2,000+ each) and ModelCard adoption in the open-source platform Hugging Face.

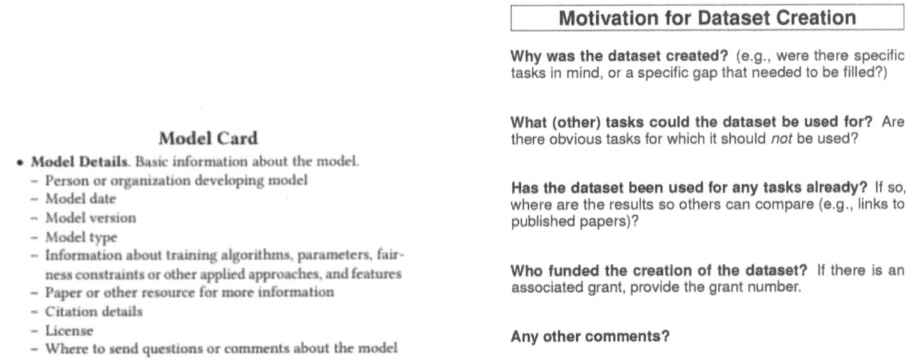

(a) ModelCards template excerpt.

(b) Datasheet template excerpt.

Fig. 2. Examples of template excerpts from ModelCards [26] and DataSheet [10].

Despite their popularity, recent studies show that ML documentation artifacts are often inconsistent [7], incomplete [17], and lack clear purpose or organizational incentives [9]. As such, it can be difficult to integrate these artifacts into established SE processes. However, they describe functionality, quality, assumptions, and constraints – all potentially requirements-relevant information. To the best of our knowledge, this is the first study analyzing and utilizing these ML documentation from a RE perspective in SE for ML systems processes.

3   Methodology

This section describes the selection of data, the evaluation of requirements-relevant content, the extraction of structured requirements, and the validation procedures. All raw and processed data are available in our online repository[1].

[1] https://doi.org/10.6084/m9.figshare.28564058.v1.

3.1 Data Selection

We selected ten ModelCards and ten DataSheets, as listed in Table 1, with sources referenced using a "D" and citations included in our online material. Because our purpose was to evaluate the potential presence of RE-relevant information in ModelCards and DataSheets, we aimed to find high-quality examples of each. We found these documents using Google Scholar by searching for studies that cited the original papers on ModelCards and DataSheets [10,26]. This method assumes that authors citing these papers are more likely to create ML documentation that follow the original intended purpose and structure.

Our selection aimed to ensure: 1) *diversity*, by including examples which can be used in different fields like healthcare, security, and commerce; 2) *variety*, by sourcing documents from both academic projects and industry work; and 3) *paired documents*, including both ModelCard and a DataSheet for the same ML system when available (e.g., MC2,DS2 and MC3,DS3) in order to see how they document an ML artifact together. The final dataset includes over 1,200 analyzed sentences. While publicly accessible repositories of ModelCards and DataSheets exist (e.g., downloadable via API from the Hugging Face website, and in curated research datasets [27,38]), we did not sample directly from these repositories because they are often compiled for specific analytical goals (e.g., criminal justice [38] and transformer models only [27]) that does not align with our desire for diversity across various contexts.

3.2 Identification of Requirements-Relevant Information

We followed a *deductive thematic analysis* approach described by Braun and Clarke [8]. Our coding scheme is based on ISO/IEC/IEEE 29148:2018 [19]. The aim of the chosen coding scheme is to identify information within ModelCards and DataSheets that aligns with what the standard considers to be requirement-relevant or essential supporting information for requirements. We therefore derived deductive codes from these sections of the ISO standard:

Clause 3.1: Terms and definitions: the definition of a "requirement" itself.

Clause 5.2: Requirements fundamentals: how requirements should be formed, what qualities they should possess, and what associated information gives them context.

Clause 9: Information item content: details general content for business, system and software requirements specification.

Annex A: defines system operational concept, providing guidance on user-oriented descriptions of system characteristics and operational scenarios.

We excluded clauses focusing on the RE process itself (e.g., Clause 6) or on conformance to the standard (e.g., Clause 4). Table 2 presents the deductive coding criteria, with a more detailed version showing examples from the chosen ML documents, available in the supplementary material.

Table 1. List of ModelCards and DataSheets (Citations in supplementary material)

Identifier	ModelCard	Description	Source
MC1	FaceDetect-IR	The model detects one or more faces in the given image/ video.	[D10]
MC2	SAM	Model for any prompt-based image segmentation task.	[D6]
MC3	DynaSent	Sentiment analysis of the texts of product and service reviews.	[D12]
MC4	LLAMA 2	Collection of pretrained and fine-tuned large language models.	[D14]
MC5	Summariza-tion model	Model for summarizing text.	[D13]
MC6	InstructGPT	A GPT-style language model fine tuned to follow instructions from human feedback.	[D11]
MC7	RoentGen	A model pre-trained on pairs of natural images and text descriptors to generate synthetic chest X-ray images.	[D2]
MC8	Seamless-M4T	Multilingual and multimodal translation models.	[D1]
MC9	StoryDALL-E	A model trained for the task of Story Visualization.	[D7]
MC10	BRAVE-NET	Model for arterial brain vessel segmentation.	[D3]
Identifier	DataSheet	Description	Source
DS1	CheXpert	Public dataset for chest radiograph interpretation.	[D4]
DS2	SA-1B	Dataset of images for image segmentation.	[D6]
DS3	DynaSent	English-language benchmark task for ternary (positive/negative/neutral) sentiment analysis	[D12]
DS4	Movie review polarity	Movie reviews extracted from newsgroup postings together with a sentiment polarity rating.	[10]
DS5	Meta-album	Multi-domain meta-dataset for few-shot image classification	[D15]
DS6	SVIB	Test-bed to evaluate the systematic generalization ability of visual imagination models.	[D5]
DS7	Youtube ASL	Training data for ASL to English machine translation.	[D16]
DS8	Change Event Dataset	Dataset for developing systems that can automatically detect change events in satellite imagery.	[D8]
DS9	SituatedQA	Information seeking questions that is annotated for its temporal or geographical dependence.	[D17]
DS10	Egoschema	Diagnostic benchmark for assessing long-form video-language understanding capabilities.	[D9]

Table 2. Requirements-relevant Info Deductive Codes Criterion

Requirements-relevant Info.	Requirements-irrelevant Info.
Explicitly states or clearly implies a need, purpose, goal, or intended use of the model/dataset.	Is purely descriptive of the ML model's architecture or dataset creation process *without* direct implications for its use, performance, capabilities, or constraints.
Describes a specific capability, function, or task the model/dataset performs or supports.	Provides general ML or domain knowledge not specific to *this* model/dataset's behavior or characteristics.
Specifies performance characteristics or quality attributes, especially if quantitative or verifiable.	Consists of aspirational statements, highly speculative "future work," or desired features not currently implemented or guaranteed.
Defines operational conditions, constraints, or limitations and negative impacts (e.g., ethical concerns like bias, safety considerations, security vulnerabilities) for the model/dataset's use.	Is purely bibliographic, author names, funding acknowledgments, unless imposing a usage constraint.
Describes assumptions or dependencies crucial for the model/dataset's correct or intended functioning.	Is raw data within a dataset (e.g., pixel values) as opposed to metadata *about* the dataset or statements regarding its use, quality, or format.
Specifies interface details for interaction with the model/dataset.	
Provides information related to user characteristics or the intended operational environment/context of use.	
Details evaluation methods, or metrics used, implying how the model/dataset should be assessed or what constitutes acceptable performance.	

3.3   Requirements Extraction Process

Once requirements-relevant information was identified, we manually extracted structured requirements using the three selected representation languages EARS, Rupp's Template, and Volere. Although we followed central tenants of thematic analysis from Braun and Clarke [8], this process was more-so extraction than qualitative coding, similar to previous work in RE [13].

The first author read the text from the ML documentation artifact, then selected the best-fitting structure from a given template for each requirement-relevant sentence (e.g., one of the five EARS types), and finally mapped the information into structural components. This mapping step involved identifying the subject, formulating the primary assertion (e.g., `<system response>` in EARS, or 'Description' in Volere), and populating the template's specific slots or attributes (e.g., EARS preconditions/triggers, Rupp's template conditional clauses) with corresponding contextual details. Information for some of Volere's meta fields (e.g., 'Originator', 'Customer Satisfaction') was often missing and therefore excluded. External factors (e.g., 'Goals of Project', 'Risks') in Volere were linked using the 'Dependencies' field. Examples of extracted requirements appear in Sect. 4. During this process, we also documented recurring patterns of documentation issues from an RE perspective.

3.4   Validation

We iteratively validated the data for each requirements representation language. After extraction by the first author, the other authors independently reviewed a 10% random sample, following the guidance by Lombard et al. [22]. A total of two iterations were conducted. The initial iteration stopped after extraction issues were found with EARS and Rupp's template, finding inconsistency in judging what information was requirements-relevant (author #2: 19 disagreements out of 325 requirements extracted from the 10% sample, author #3: 35/317). To resolve this, we developed our deductive coding criteria (Table 2) to create a shared standard. In the second iteration, we reviewed a different 10% sample of all three representations and disagreements shifted to how to best represent certain types of information, particularly contextual details and limitations, within the formats of our chosen RE languages (author #2: 10/331 requirements extracted from the new 10% sample, author #3: 17/331). All disagreements were resolved through team discussions with the help of the deductive coding criteria and guidelines for the specific RE language. The first author then adjusted the entire dataset based on the results of the discussions.

3.5   Quantitative Data Analysis

To answer RQ1, we counted all sentences identified as requirements-relevant. Partially relevant sentences were counted as 0.5. For example in DS3: "[Is there an erratum] Not at present, but we will create one as necessary and update this section at that time." The first half of the sentence describes an operational limitation that is relevant according to our criterion, but the latter half is a desired feature not guaranteed, and considered irrelevant from our criterion. For RQ2, we evaluated how well each RE language captured the identified requirement-relevant information. The requirements representations were assessed by computing the percentage of relevant sentences they captured, using the same 0.5 point rule for partially relevant sentences. Volere was also evaluated by computing the percentages of relevant sentences it captured as external factor statements.

4   Evaluation Results

4.1   RQ1: Requirements Relevant Information in ModelCards and DataSheets

The total number of sentences per documentation artifact, the number of requirements relevant sentences, and the corresponding percentage of requirements relevant information is shown in Table 3.

Table 3. Statistics for Information Considered Requirements-relevant

	MC1	MC2	MC3	MC4	MC5	MC6	MC7	MC8	MC9	MC10
# of sentences (S)	69	41	23	30	61	50	25	42	27	32
# of relevant sentences (RS)	53	37	16	25	58	45	18	37	24.5	24
% of relevant information (RS/S)	0.77	0.90	0.70	0.83	0.95	0.90	0.72	0.88	0.91	0.75

	DS1	DS2	DS3	DS4	DS5	DS6	DS7	DS8	DS9	DS10
# of sentences (S)	206	89	129	74	75	70	67	108	69	99
# of relevant sentences (RS)	178.5	79	109.5	63	69	61	56.5	99.5	63	96
% of relevant information (RS/S)	0.87	0.89	0.85	0.85	0.92	0.87	0.84	0.92	0.91	0.87

On average, 83% of ModelCard sentences and 88% of DataSheet sentences were found to be potentially relevant. ModelCards ranged from 70% to 95%, while DataSheets were more consistent, between 84% and 92%.

RQ1.1: Issues with ML documentation. We observed several issues with how information is documented as part of ML Documentation. First, redundancy: the same information was often expressed multiple times in different phrasings or sections. For example, DS1 repeatedly describes the need for radiologist-labeled data using overlapping statements: *"The dataset shall have validation and test sets labeled by multiple board-certified radiologists providing a strong ground truth to evaluate models"*, *"The dataset labels shall have been evaluated against labels manually extracted by board-certified radiologists"*, and *"The dataset shall have strong radiologist-annotated ground truth"*. Second, variation in granularity: Some sections offer high-level, abstract descriptions, while others contain low-level implementation details that are more design decisions than requirements.

Answer to RQ1.1: From an RE perspective, the primary issues with how information is documented in the chosen ModelCards and DataSheets are the redundancy of information and inconsistent level of granularity.

Answer to RQ1: Within our chosen samples, both ModelCards and Data-Sheets are dense with requirements-relevant information (averaging over 80% of sentences), making them a rich source for RE. However, the quality of these documentation may be hampered by redundancy and inconsistent granularity.

4.2   RQ2: Capturing Requirements Relevant Information using Three RE Languages

Table 4 summarizes to what degree the chosen RE languages EARS, Rupp's template, and Volere capture the identified requirements-relevant information from ML documentation artifacts.

EARS captured 37% (MC6) to 79% (MC1) of the sentences of relevant ML documentation, while Rupp's template captured 41% (MC6) to 80% (DS6). For ModelCards, both EARS and Rupp's template worked well in capturing input-output specifications, training algorithms, integration interfaces, usage license

Table 4. Statistics for Information Captured Using RE Templates(E = EARS, R = Rupp's tmp., V = Volere)

	MC1	MC2	MC3	MC4	MC5	MC6	MC7	MC8	MC9	MC10
% information captured in E	0.79	0.64	0.66	0.76	0.44	0.37	0.58	0.64	0.51	0.58
% information captured in R	0.79	0.72	0.69	0.76	0.53	0.41	0.58	0.66	0.53	0.63
% info. captured as V reqs.	0.5	0.73	0.66	0.64	0.23	0.36	0.5	0.41	0.43	0.38
% info. captured as V ext. factors	0.5	0.27	0.34	0.36	0.77	0.64	0.5	0.59	0.57	0.62

	DS1	DS2	DS3	DS4	DS5	DS6	DS7	DS8	DS9	DS10
% information captured in E	0.49	0.71	0.55	0.63	0.75	0.76	0.58	0.71	0.48	0.64
% of information captured in R	0.53	0.76	0.63	0.71	0.78	0.80	0.54	0.70	0.60	0.65
% info. captured as V reqs.	0.59	0.64	0.49	0.62	0.74	0.65	0.43	0.61	0.52	0.67
% info. captured as V ext. factors	0.41	0.36	0.51	0.38	0.26	0.35	0.57	0.39	0.48	0.33

constraints, primary intended users and use cases, as well as for defining metrics for model evaluation. For DataSheets, both templates captured motivation, composition, collection, distribution, and maintenance. Examples of requirements captured by EARS and Rupp's template are shown in Table 5. Rupp's template outperformed EARS in capturing requirements from ML documentation in seven out of ten ModelCards and in eight out of ten DataSheets, with a difference of up to 12%(DS9).

Unlike EARS and Rupp's template, Volere also captures supplementary information from ML documentation that, while not strictly requirements, can be considered as external factors relevant to RE. As such, we judge that Volere is able to capture all the requirements relevant information contained in the chosen sample of ML documentation artifacts. This can be seen in Table 4 where for each document, the sum of percentages of Volere requirements and external factors is 100%. The percentage of external factors is quite substantial, and Volere's capability of documenting external factors is particularly useful for capturing information affecting the design implementation and constraints that may influence the ML specification such as license dependencies. For example, MC1 includes a legal requirement (license compliance) linked to a supporting fact (user agreement), which can be captured using Volere's "Dependencies" field.

Volere also allows capturing "open issues" of the models and datasets and to associate them with "actions" or "resolutions" as illustrated in Fig. 3. Similarly, Volere is able to document constraints over out-of-scope usage, variables that influence model performance, and limitations from ModelCards. From DataSheets, Volere can document limitations in the collection and preprocessing steps, unintended uses of the dataset, and potential risks in the dataset composition.

RQ2.1: Limitations of the RE templates. Rupp's template captured more nuanced content than EARS due to its broader modal vocabulary. For example, DS2 states that the dataset is "believed to be more representative". This uncer-

Table 5. Examples of requirements captured in EARS and Rupp's template.

EARS Examples		Rupp's Template Examples	
Pattern	**Captured requirement and original text**	**Pattern**	**Captured requirement and original text**
Ubiquitous	*The model shall be a 1.3B parameter Transformer model trained with human feedback.* MC5(primary use): This model card details the 1.3 billion parameter Transformer model trained with human feedback.	Function-MASTER (in. sys. act.)	*The model shall accelerate and facilitate inspection of brain vessels in clinical practice...* MC10(motivation): ...accelerating and facilitating inspection of brain vessels in clinical practice for diagnosis of vessel...
Event-driven	*When the pruned model is selected, the model shall accept 384x240x3 dimension input tensors...* MC1 (input/output specification): The pruned model... accepts 384x240x3 dimension input tensors and output...	Function-MASTER (user intera.)	*The model shall provide users who may not have AI development experience with the ability to build and explore language modeling systems...* MC10(integration interfaces): Through the OpenAI API, the model can be used by those who may not have AI development experience...
State-driven	*While training, the model shall be trained and fine-tuned against a cross-entropy loss function.* MC3(training algorithm): The model parameters are trained/fine-tuned against a cross-entropy loss.	Logic-MASTER, property-MASTER	*If an image is with protected health information of any type, the image shall be excluded from the dataset.* DS1(collection): Images that had protected health information (PHI) of any type were excluded from the dataset.
Unwanted behavior	*If Yelp removes data..., the dataset shall remain intact and self-contained.* DS3(composition): ...cannot guarantee that the Yelp Academic Dataset will always be available... Our dataset would remain intact even if this did happen.	Property-MASTER	*The license for model use shall be CC-BY-NC 4.0 b* MC8(license constraint): Model details: – License: CC-BY-NC 4.0 b

tainty is lost in EARS as it only allows "shall" as a modal verb, while Rupp's template allows "should", or "may", which both capture this uncertainty.

A broader challenge for both EARS and Rupp's template is that they cannot intuitively express known limitations and constraints which are requirements relevant, such as, for example, MC4's testing being limited to English, or DS8's change detection algorithm being not 100% accurate. Although this information could be very relevant to a requirement such as "the model shall be tested in multiple languages" and "the change detection algorithm should be 100% accurate", such requirements do not accurately reflect the content of the ModelCard or DataSheet, and therefore is not easily captured by EARS and Rupp's template.

Volere's main limitation is its lack of ML-specific requirement types, forcing the conflation of distinct concepts into its generic categories. For example, a constraint on training data sources and a constraint on evaluation metrics were both categorized simply as a "solution constraint" (MC3). Similarly, a data quality requirement concerning author diversity (DS4) was also classified as a "solution constraint" due to the absence of a dedicated data quality category.

<table>
<tr><td colspan="2">
DS2:
Does the dataset contain data that [...] might be offensive [...] ?
We have two safety measures to prevent objectionable content: (1) Photos are licensed from a photo provider and had to meet the terms of service of the photo provider. We requested that all objectionable content be filtered from the images we licensed. (2) If a user observes objectionable image(s) in the dataset, we invite them to report the image(s) at segmentanything@meta.com for removal. Despite the measures taken, we observe that a small portion of images contains scenes of protests or other gatherings that focus on a diverse spectrum of religious beliefs or political opinions that may be offensive. We were not able to produce a filtering strategy that removes all such images and rely on users to report this type of content.
</td></tr>
<tr>
<td rowspan="3">
Req ID: 27; Req type: open issue;
Description: a small portion of images in the dataset shall contain scenes of protests or other gatherings that focus on a diverse spectrum of religious beliefs or political opinions that may be offensive.
</td>
<td>
Req ID: 28; Req type: action to open issue # 27;
Description: Photos are licensed from a photo provider and had to meet the terms of service of the photo provider. the dataset creators requested that all objectionable content be filtered from the images we licensed.
</td>
</tr>
<tr>
<td>
Req ID: 29; Req type: action to open issue # 27;
Description: If a user observes objectionable image(s) in the dataset, the dataset creators shall invite them to report the image
</td>
</tr>
<tr>
<td>
Req ID: 30; Req type: resolution to open issue #27;
Description: the dataset creators were not able to produce a filtering strategy that removes all such images and rely on users to report this type of content.
</td>
</tr>
</table>

Fig. 3. Example of Volere capturing open issues.

Answer to RQ2.1: EARS fails to capture uncertainty due to its rigid vocabulary. Both EARS and Rupp's template struggle to document contextual information such as limitations and constraints. Volere's generic categories conflate ML-specific concepts.

Answer to RQ2: EARS and Rupp's template can capture a majority of the requirements-relevant information while Volere proves more comprehensive: capturing all relevant information by structuring requirements alongside supplementary "external factors" such as dependencies, limitations and open issues. EARS is limited in its ability to capture uncertainty, while both EARS and Rupp's template struggle to document contextual information. Volere's effectiveness is limited by a generic typology that conflates ML-specific concepts.

5   Discussion

Our study shows that ML documentation artifacts such as ModelCards and DataSheets could contain substantial requirements-relevant information, meaning that they should be considered as key sources of requirements-relevant information as part of SE processes for ML systems. This validates their potential to serve as key boundary objects as part of communication and coordination in SE processes for ML systems [20]. However, although abundant, we found that RE-relevant information is often redundant and inconsistently documented in this format. This inconsistency complicates reuse and traceability, which was also identified by Chang et al.'s [9] investigation of implementation challenges in ML documentation.

To understand the potential of current requirements representations in capturing this information we evaluated three RE templates and found each format had limitations: EARS lacks expressiveness for uncertainty, EARS and Rupp's template both struggle with documenting rationale and limitations; and Volere, though more expressive, uses requirements types too generic for ML-specific content. However, despite these limitations, these representations were reasonably successful in capturing RE-relevant information, particularly Volere, with it's capability to capture external factors.

Our main contribution is a systematic, bottom-up analysis of requirements information drawn from exemplary ML documentation. To our knowledge, this is the first study to examine ModelCards and DataSheets from an RE process perspective. Unlike prior work that proposes high-level frameworks [1,35] or targets specific requirement types [2,5,15], our work quantified the potential presence of relevant information and evaluates how well established RE templates can capture real-world ML documentation content. Our evaluation identifies key obstacles in bridging informal ML documentation artifacts and formal RE processes. Our results can help in supporting traceability: by establishing RE-guided processes for structuring component-level details from ML documentation artifacts, stakeholders can verify if a model or dataset meets broader system-level requirements, such as if a model's performance metrics align with system needs.

Future Work *For Practitioners:* Our findings provide guidance for requirements engineers working with ML components. Our deductive criterion (Table 2) can serve as a checklist to identify requirements relevant information in ML documentation for the RE process in ML systems development. Our evaluation also informs the selection of an appropriate RE language when writing requirements for ML components: EARS and Rupp's template are sufficient for capturing core functionality, while Volere is best suited for documenting context, limitations and dependencies. *For researchers:* Volere's hierarchical structure suggests its potential as a template to mitigate the inconsistent levels of detail found in current ML documentation and reduce information redundancy. However, these established RE languages could also require adaptation for ML. Volere needs a more granular, ML-specific typology to distinguish concepts like data source constraints, evaluation metric requirements and data quality attributes (work on NFRs for ML [15] might be a starting point for such additional concept distinctions), and EARS could be extended with flexible model keywords from Rupp's template (e.g., "should", "may") to better capture uncertainty. Our extraction method could be applied to other ML documentation types like Nutritional Labels [34] and FactSheets [4] to generalize our findings. Our manually created dataset now provides a baseline to develop and evaluate tools that may automate requirement extraction from ML documentation using natural language processing or Large Language Models (LLMs).

5.1 Threats to Validity

Internal Threats. Although all data and analysis procedures are made available, some degree of subjectivity remains in interpreting whether documentation content qualifies as a requirement. The use of templates demands a learning curve and understanding of the underlying semantics. While we applied a clear coding scheme and cross-checked 10% of all decisions among authors, interpretive bias cannot be fully eliminated.

External Threats. Our document sample was selected using Google Scholar and sorted by default relevance, which may bias toward more cited or visible works. Our dataset could be seen as optimistic in terms of content and clarity due to extraction from highly-cited work, but our aim is only to evaluate the feasibility of requirements extraction from ML documentation, not to show that it will always work well in all cases. Though we aimed for domain diversity in this dataset, some sectors may be underrepresented. Our choice of requirements representation templates–EARS, Rupp's template, and Volere–was based on their prominence within the RE community [13]. Other formats such as user stories or use cases could be evaluated in future similar studies.

6 Conclusion

This study first showed that while ModelCards and DataSheets can be rich in requirements-relevant information, they are often descriptive, redundant, and inconsistently documented. We showed further that three established RE process templates – EARS, Rupp's template, and Volere – are able to capture much of this information. However, constrained templates like EARS and Rupp fail to capture necessary ML-specific details like model limitations. Conversely, the Volere framework can capture this information but lacks domain-specific categories to classify it effectively. By identifying these gaps, our work lays a foundation for improving both RE and ML documentation processes.

Acknowledgments. We received support from the Swedish Research Council (VR) iNFoRM Project and the Wallenberg AI, Autonomous Systems and Software Program (WASP).

References

1. Ahmad, K., Abdelrazek, M., Arora, C., Baniya, A.A., Bano, M., Grundy, J.: Requirements engineering framework for human-centered artificial intelligence software systems. Appl. Soft Comput. **143**, 110455 (2023)
2. Al Islam, M.N., Ma, Y., Alarcon, P., Chawla, N., Cleland-Huang, J.: Resam: Requirements elicitation and specification for deep-learning anomaly models with applications to UAV flight controllers. In: 2022 IEEE 30th International Requirements Engineering Conference (RE), pp. 153–165. IEEE (2022)

3. Alves, A.P.S., et al.: Status quo and problems of requirements engineering for machine learning: Results from an international survey. In: International Conference on Product-Focused Software Process Improvement, pp. 159–174. Springer (2023)

4. Arnold, M., et al.: Factsheets: increasing trust in AI services through supplier's declarations of conformity. IBM J. Res. Develop. **63**(4/5), 1–6 (2019)

5. Bajraktari, E., Krause, T., Kücherer, C.: Documentation of non-functional requirements for systems with machine learning components. In: REFSQ Wkshp.s (2024). https://api.semanticscholar.org/CorpusID:269447618

6. Barrera, J.M., Reina-Reina, A., Lavalle, A., Maté, A., Trujillo, J.: An extension of istar for machine learning requirements by following the Dprise methodology. Comput. Stand. Interfaces **88**, 103806 (2024)

7. Bhat, A., et al.: Aspirations and practice of ml model documentation: moving the needle with nudging and traceability. In: 2023 CHI Conference on Human Factors in Computing Systems, pp. 1–17 (2023)

8. Braun, V., Clarke, V.: Thematic Analysis: A Practical Guide. SAGE Publications Ltd, London (2021)

9. Chang, J., Custis, C.: Understanding implementation challenges in machine learning documentation. In: 2nd ACM Conference on Equity and Access in Algorithms, Mechanisms, and Optimization, pp. 1–8 (2022)

10. Gebru, T., et al.: Datasheets for datasets. Commun. ACM **64**(12), 86–92 (Nov 2021). https://doi.org/10.1145/3458723

11. Giménez, P., Llop, M., Gonzalez-Usach, R., Llorente, M.A.: Inter-Iot requirements. Interoperability of Heterogeneous IoT Platforms: A Layered Approach, pp. 27–47 (2021)

12. Gregory, S.C.: Easy EARS : Rapid application of the easy approach to requirements syntax (2011). https://api.semanticscholar.org/CorpusID:2783631

13. Großer, K., Ahmadian, A.S., Rukavitsyna, M., Ramadan, Q., Jürjens, J.: Benchmarking requirement template systems: comparing appropriateness, usability, and expressiveness. Requirements Engineering, pp. 1–42 (2024)

14. Habiba, U.e., Haug, M., Bogner, J., Wagner, S.: How mature is requirements engineering for AI-based systems? a systematic mapping study on practices, challenges, and future research directions. Requirements Engineering, pp. 1–34 (2024)

15. Habibullah, K.M., Gay, G., Horkoff, J.: A framework for managing quality requirements for machine learning-based software systems. In: International Conference on the Quality of Information and Communications Technology, pp. 3–20. Springer (2024)

16. Habibullah, K.M., Horkoff, J.: Non-functional requirements for machine learning: Understanding current use and challenges in industry. In :2021 IEEE 29th International Requirements Engineering Conference (RE), pp. 13–23 (2021). https://api.semanticscholar.org/CorpusID:237386723

17. Heger, A.K., Marquis, L.B., Vorvoreanu, M., Wallach, H., Wortman Vaughan, J.: Understanding machine learning practitioners' data documentation perceptions, needs, challenges, and desiderata. ACM Human-Comput. Interact. **6**(CSCW2), 1–29 (2022)

18. Iqbal, Z.: Assurance of machine learning/tinyml in safety-critical domains. In: IEEE Symposium on Visual Languages / Human-Centric Computing Languages and Environments (2022). https://api.semanticscholar.org/CorpusID:251656076

19. ISO/IEC/IEEE: ISO/IEC/IEEE Int. Standard - Systems and software engineering – Life cycle processes – Requirements engineering (November 2018). https://doi.org/10.1109/IEEESTD.2018.8559686, published on 30 Nov. 2018

20. Kasauli, R., Wohlrab, R., Knauss, E., Steghöfer, J.P., Horkoff, J., Maro, S.: Charting coordination needs in large-scale agile organisations with boundary objects and methodological islands. In: Proceedings of the International Conference on Software and System Processes (PROFES), pp. 51–60 (2020)
21. Letier, E., Van Lamsweerde, A.: Obstacle analysis in requirements engineering: Retrospective and emerging challenges. IEEE Transactions on Software Engineering (2025)
22. Lombard, M., Snyder-Duch, J., Bracken, C.C.: Content analysis in mass communication: assessment and reporting of intercoder reliability. Hum. Commun. Res. **28**(4), 587–604 (2002)
23. Mavin, A.: EARS - the easy approach to requirements syntax (2019). https://alistairmavin.com/ears/. Accessed 04 Jan 2025
24. Mavin, A., Wilkinson, P., Harwood, A., Novak, M.: Easy approach to requirements syntax (EARS). In: 17th IEEE International Requirements Engineering Conference, pp. 317–322 (2009). https://doi.org/10.1109/RE.2009.9, https://doi.org/10.1109/RE.2009.9
25. Mazo, R., Jaramillo, C.A., Vallejo, P., Medina, J.H.: Towards a new template for the specification of requirements in semi-structured natural language. J. Softw. Eng. Res. Develop. **8**, 3 (2020)
26. Mitchell, M., et al.: Model cards for model reporting. In: Conf. on fairness, accountability, and transparency, pp. 220–229 (2019)
27. Pepe, F., Nardone, V., Mastropaolo, A., Bavota, G., Canfora, G., Di Penta, M.: How do hugging face models document datasets, bias, and licenses? an empirical study. In: 32nd IEEE/ACM International Conference on Program Comprehension, pp. 370–381 (2024)
28. Portugal, R.L.Q., Casanova, M.A., Li, T., do Prado Leite, J.C.S.: Gh4re: repository recommendation on github for requirements elicitation reuse. In: CAiSE-Forum-DC, pp. 113–120 (2017)
29. Pradhan, S.K., Heyn, H.M., Knauss, E.: Identifying and managing data quality requirements: a design science study in the field of automated driving. Softw. Qual. J. **32**(2), 313–360 (2024)
30. Robertson, J., Robertson, S.: Volere requirements specification template (2019). https://www.volere.org/templates/volere-requirements-specification-template/. Accessed May 10 2023
31. Robertson, S., Robertson, J.: Mastering the Requirements Process. Addison-Wesley, 1st edn. (1999)
32. Robertson, S., Robertson, J.: Mastering the requirements process: Getting requirements right. Addison-wesley (2012)
33. Rupp, C.: Requirements-Engineering und -Management: Professionelle, iterative Anforderungsanalyse für die Praxis. Hanser Verlag, 4th edn. (2007)
34. Stoyanovich, J., Howe, B.: Nutritional labels for data and models. A Quart. Bull. Comput. Society IEEE Tech. Comm. Data Eng. **42**(3) (2019)
35. Villamizar, H., Kalinowski, M., Lopes, H., Mendez, D.: Identifying concerns when specifying machine learning-enabled systems: a perspective-based approach. J. Syst. Softw. **213**, 112053 (2024)
36. Vogelsang, A., Borg, M.: Requirements engineering for machine learning: perspectives from data scientists. In: 2019 IEEE 27th International Requirements Engineering Conference Wkshps (REW), pp. 245–251. IEEE (2019)
37. Yang, Y., Zeng, B., Gao, J.: Rm4ml: requirements model for machine learning-enabled software systems. Require. Eng. 1–33 (2024)

38. Zilka, M., Butcher, B., Weller, A.: A survey and datasheet repository of publicly available us criminal justice datasets. Adv. Neural. Inf. Process. Syst. **35**, 28008–28022 (2022)

Enhancing Python Code Maintainability Through Large Language Model-Based Approaches

Karthik Shivashankar[(✉)] and Antonio Martini

Department of Informatics, University of Oslo, Oslo, Norway
Karths@ifi.uio.no

Abstract. While Large Language Models (LLMs) increasingly assist in code generation, concerns persist regarding the maintainability of the code they produce–an aspect often overshadowed by functional correctness. Overlooking maintainability can contribute to technical debt and inflate long-term software costs.

This research investigates whether targeted fine-tuning can enhance an LLM's ability to generate more maintainable Python code. We developed a approach involving the curation of custom datasets (from COMMITPACKFT and Code Alpaca Python subsets) specifically annotated for maintainability using metrics like Source Lines of Code (SLOC), Halstead Effort, and Maintainability Index (MI). A weak-to-strong generalization strategy was employed, using a smaller model (Phi 4 14B) to generate maintainability-focused examples for fine-tuning a larger model (QwenCoder2.5 32B Instruct) with parameter-efficient techniques.

Evaluations revealed the fine-tuned model significantly reduced code complexity (Halstead Effort) and length (SLOC) compared to the original code samples. While the model preserved high functional similarity (verified by CodeBERTScore), results for the Maintainability Index metric were inconclusive in this evaluation. Performance on standard functional correctness benchmarks (HumanEval+, MBPP+) was largely comparable to the base model. Nevertheless, expert user feedback confirmed the fine-tuned model's utility as a practical AI companion for code refactoring to improve maintainability.

Keywords: LLM · NLP · Maintainability · Software Quality

1 Introduction

The advent of Code Large Language Models (LLMs) started a new era in automated programming, offering unparalleled assistance in generating syntactically correct and functionally robust code. Despite their increasing adoption as coding assistants [14], concerns regarding the maintainability of the code produced by these models persist [8]. Sustainable software development hinges on quality aspects like maintainability, which is crucial for the long-term success of software

G. Scanniello et al. (Eds.): PROFES 2025, LNCS 16361, pp. 137–152, 2026.
https://doi.org/10.1007/978-3-032-12089-2_9

projects, affecting factors such as technical debt and the cost of future modifications [10]. While existing research has extensively explored LLM-generated code's functional accuracy and testing efficacy, maintainability has often been overlooked [38]. This gap highlights a pressing need to re-evaluate and enhance how code is generated, emphasising its long-term sustainability and adherence to best coding practices [8].

The significance of code quality becomes evident when considering the concept of technical debt, which draws an analogy to financial debt. It characterises the eventual expenses incurred when opting for code that is easy to implement in the short term rather than choosing the best overall solution [12]. Within the realm of Code LLMs, creating code lacking maintainability or conformity to established standards contributes to the accumulation of technical debt [2]. This, in turn, results in higher long-term costs associated with maintenance and scalability [5].

In response to this challenge, our study seeks to explore the potential of fine-tuning Code LLMs to prioritise code maintainability, specifically within the context of Python programming. By focusing on attributes such as code readability, complexity reduction, and overall maintainability, we aim to build an AI-assisted software development towards generating code that is not only functional but also easy to understand, modify, and extend.

Central to our investigation is the inquiry into the extent to which fine-tuning LLMs can enhance their capacity to assess and improve the maintainability of Python code.

RQ1: "How does fine-tuning augment LLMs' capability to generate Python code with higher maintainability, and can the improvements be measured?"

This question underpins our broader objective of setting new benchmarks for Code LLM development, ensuring that the output meets functional requirements and adheres to high standards of code quality and maintainability.

The motivation for exploring RQ1 stems from a recognised gap in the current literature concerning the maintainability of LLM-generated code [38] [8]. High-quality, maintainable code significantly facilitates updates, debugging, and scalability, thus minimising long-term maintenance costs and fostering ongoing innovation [28,32]. As Code LLMs continue to gain traction for their efficiency in streamlining coding tasks, it becomes imperative to ensure that their outputs are operationally effective and maintainable in the long run. This study addresses this critical need by fine-tuning LLMs with a specific emphasis on maintainability and conducting rigorous performance evaluations.

Our contributions are two fold:

Development of a Custom Dataset: Addressing the gap identified in RQ1, we have curated a dataset focusing on the maintainability of Python code, emphasising readability, less complexity and modifiability or ease of refactoring the code. This dataset is engineered for developing and fine-tuning LLMs, ensuring that generated code aligns with maintainability best practices. By making this dataset publicly available, we facilitate broader research and development efforts to embed maintainability principles directly within Code LLM outputs.

Empirical Evaluation of Fine-tuned Model: We introduce an experimental method leveraging our extended custom dataset to evaluate fine-tuned LLMs on maintainability. This method extends conventional functional testing by scrutinising the maintainability of the code generated, thereby offering a comprehensive assessment of the model's output. This approach lays the groundwork for future evaluations of Code LLMs, promoting a balanced consideration of functionality and code maintainability.

Our fine-tuned maintainability model shifts focus from general practice in AI-assisted code, which may require significant adjustments post-code generation, to a proactive approach where code quality and maintainability are prioritised early in the development cycle.

2   Background

2.1   Maintainability

Maintainability is a crucial quality attribute determining the ease of understanding, modifying, and extending software [10]. It is crucial for controlling costs and ensuring the adaptability of software systems over time. Misra et al. have highlighted the importance of evaluating how design and coding practices influence software maintainability, which can lead to significant reductions in maintenance costs and improvements in quality [17].

Adherence to maintainable coding standards promotes code readability and consistency, which are fundamental for collaborative development efforts and the long-term viability of software projects [28,32]. However, there is a gap in research regarding the compliance of Code LLMs with such standards, calling into question their practicality in actual software development scenarios. Addressing this gap is essential for integrating Code LLMs into the industry, ensuring that the code they generate is functional, maintainable, and aligned with professional coding practices. Our research contributes to understanding and improving code maintainability through LLMs, but it does not encompass all dimensions or metrics associated with maintainability. This acknowledgement underscores the complexity of code maintainability and the ongoing need for research in this area.

3   Related Works

Large Language Models (LLMs) for code continue to grow, with limited studies focusing on code maintainability. Building upon the notion of code quality, Zhuo [41] introduces a framework that assesses the quality of LLM-generated code. This framework works by ensuring the code aligns with human standards, In the context of code testing, Xiong, Guo, and Chen ([36]) explore how LLMs can assist in program synthesis by generating test cases. This ability to produce not only functional code but also comprehensive tests underscores the potential of LLMs to work on other qualities or attributes. Shirafuji et al. ([27]) investigate the robustness of LLMs in programming problem-solving and reveal the sensitivity of these models to prompt engineering. This insight is integral to standardisation, suggesting that with suitable prompts, LLMs could be steered to produce code that adheres to specific standards, hence promoting consistency and standardisation in coding practices. Lastly, Le et al. ([11]) proposed "CodeRL," integrating a pre-trained model with deep reinforcement learning for program synthesis. While their focus is on functional correctness, the principles underlying CodeRL could be adapted to emphasise the generation of standard-compliant code. Linking these contributions together, it becomes evident that the field of LLMs for code is expanding beyond mere code generation, delving into broader aspects of code quality. However, despite these advances, there appears to be a gap in research explicitly targeting the maintainability of code generated by LLM. To our knowledge, no studies have yet explored this area in depth. Our research fills this gap, offering unique insights and methodologies for enhancing code maintainability, particularly in Python, using LLMs.

4   Methodology

This research employs a systematic methodology to investigate LLMs' generation and evaluation of maintainable Python code. The approach is structured into several vital steps (Fig. 1), each addressing the main RQ1. The methodology combines dataset preparation, model fine-tuning as shown in Fig. 1, and comprehensive evaluation techniques to assess the capability of LLMs in producing code that functions correctly and adheres to high maintainability standards. We use a mixed-method approach that combines practical experimentation with qualitative analysis. This choice is driven by the need to evaluate the multifaceted nature of code maintainability, which encompasses code's syntactic and functional correctness and aspects such as readability, complexity, and adherence to best practices.

Comparative Analysis and Evaluation. The comparative analysis aims to quantify the improvements in code maintainability due to fine-tuning the LLM. This analysis involves comparing the maintainability metrics (SLOC, Halstead effort, and Maintainability Index) of the original code in the dataset and to that code generated by the base models versus the fine-tuned models. The metrics are calculated for each code sample in the test split, providing a basis for statistical analysis to identify significant trends and improvements. The evaluation process, a crucial part of our work, is designed to validate the functional correctness and maintainability of the generated code. This involves using CodeBertScore [40] to compare the similarity and functional correctness of the code generated by the fine-tuned models against the original code samples.

4.1   Selecting Dataset for Maintainability

For finetuning Code LLMs, the initial step typically involves using various original code samples as the primary input. This immerses the models in various

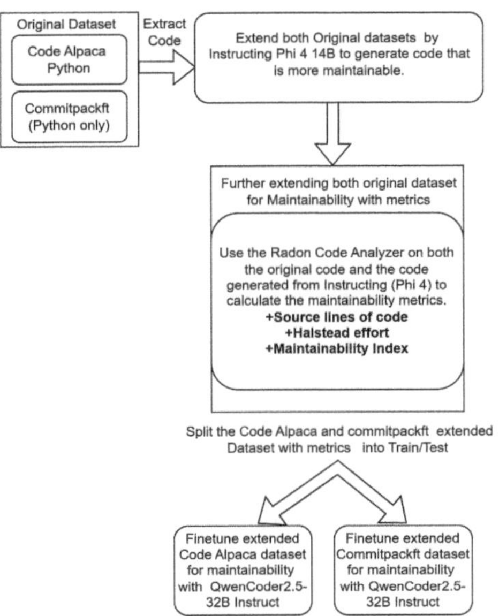

Fig. 1. Steps used for Curating Datasets and Fine-tuning LLM.

authentic coding situations, with the imperfections and inconsistencies they would encounter in the practical coding environment.

COMMITPACKFT(Python subset) [18] offers many real-world programming scenarios and high-quality instructional commit messages. Its critical feature is its focus on high-quality commit messages (that serve as instruction) paired with code. This unique feature makes it particularly suitable for tasks like file-level and repository-level refactoring, which is pivotal for understanding code changes and intentions in software development.

CODEALPACA (Python) [30] provides a diverse set of coding examples and instructional data essential for developing models that can follow instructions in code generation tasks. This dataset stands out due to its variety in code types, including snippets and functions, and its accompanying instructions and inputs. This diversity provides a rich set of coding examples, making it a valuable resource for instruction-following models. The CODEALPACA dataset was inspired by a project aiming to build an instruction-following LLaMA model for code generation based on the Stanford Alpaca model [34].

The distribution of two datasets, COMMITPACKFT Python (total = 17,981) and CODEALPACA Python (total = 16,158), into training and testing sets, which are crucial for fine-tuning and evaluating the model. These datasets are mainly used to fine-tune QwenCoder2.5 32B [9] Instruct model with 80% of the training data, while the remaining 20% for testing, essential for model evaluation and assessing code maintainability improvements.

```
Maintainability_prompt = f"""You are a Python expert ...
    Your main task is to refactor the given Python code ...
    ...
### Input:
{original_code}
### Context:
Objective
- Improve Source Lines of Code (SLOC): ...
- Improve Maintainability Index (MI): Higher scores are desired.
- Reduce Effort: Lower numbers are preferred.
Original Metrics
- Source Lines of Code (SLOC): {original_SLOC}
- Maintainability Index (MI): {original_maintainability_index}
- Effort: {original_effort}
Provide only the refactored version of the code ...
### Response:
{refactored_code_optimised_maintainability}*
"""
```

Fig. 2. Maintainability prompt

4.2   Generating Maintainable Code

To enhance the code maintainability of the code samples from the chosen dataset, we employ the Phi 4 14B model from Microsoft. Our approach draws inspiration from the concept of weak-to-strong generalization, which investigates whether using weak models to supervise strong models [3].

The underlying hypothesis, supported by findings in the weak-to-strong paper [3], is that strong pretrained models finetuned on labels generated by weaker models often generalize beyond their supervisors. Our goal is not necessarily to teach QwenCoder2.5 32B [9] entirely new concepts of maintainability from scratch, but rather to use the structured, synthetic data from Phi-4 to elicit and refine the latent knowledge about code quality and maintainability potentially already present within the larger QwenCoder2.5 32B model.

To structure this process, we utilize instruction tuning, adapting the Alpaca style [24] to our maintainability context. This technique integrates instructions with the input-output pairs (original code to maintainable code generated by Phi-4), aiming to enhance the QwenCoder model's [9] ability to specifically generate more maintainable code based on the patterns learned from the Phi-4 dataset. Our use of instruction tuning on this synthetically generated dataset represents our chosen strategy to bridge the gap and effectively transfer the "maintainability" focus from the weaker Phi-4 model to the stronger QwenCoder2.5 32B model. Given the sensitivity of prompting strategies, we offer our prompt as a starting recipe, encouraging further research into optimizing prompting for this weak-to-strong transfer in improving the code maintainability as shown in Fig. 2.

Rationale for Synthetic Training Data. Instruction tuning with synthetically generated data is a proven method for specializing Large Language Models (LLMs) for specific tasks [33,39]. This strategy's effectiveness is validated by projects like Stanford Alpaca and WizardLM [34,37] and is widely adopted

[25,26]. Following this approach, we fine-tuned the QwenCoder2.5 32B model on a custom, synthetically generated dataset to improve its ability to produce maintainable Python code. The prompt used for this data curation and subsequent fine-tuning is shown in Fig. 2.

4.3   Enhancing the Dataset with a Maintainability Metric

For each piece of code in the original dataset, we compute maintainability metrics–namely, Maintainability Index (MI), Halstead Effort (HE), and Source Lines of Code (SLOC). These metrics are calculated for both the original code samples and those generated by instructing Phi 4, with the resultant maintainability metrics subsequently incorporated into the new fields within the dataset. This augmentation process is meticulously applied to all code samples, ensuring the dataset is comprehensively enhanced with these critical metrics for further evaluation and testing. To obtain these metrics, we utilised the Radon Python package, which provides an extensive suite for assessing the complexity and maintainability of Python code [23]. We selected Radon because of its widespread use in industry tools like Codacy, Code Climate, and CodeFactor.

Rationale for Metric Selection. We selected Maintainability Index (MI), Halstead Effort (HE), and Source Lines of Code (SLOC) from the Radon library for their proven ability to provide objective, quantifiable measures of software quality [16,23]. MI, a composite metric used in industry tools like Visual Studio, is valuable for estimating maintenance effort; HE offers insights into cognitive complexity; and SLOC is a key indicator of project size and potential maintainability challenges [29]. These metrics were preferred over others like cohesion and coupling, which are better suited for multi-file architectural analysis and are considered less objective than the chosen quantitative metrics [31,35]. While these metrics do not capture all facets of maintainability, they provide a practical and tangible basis for our evaluation.

4.4   Fine-Tuning Techniques Employed for Maintainability

We chose QwenCoder2.5 32B [9] model for fine-tuning LLMs for generating Python code focuses on improving the maintainability of the generated Python code, because it performs very well across many coding benchmarks like HumanEval and fits our GPU constraints and budget [1].

QwenCoder2.5 32B Instruct Model. The fine-tuning process for QwenCoder2.5 32B Instruct [15] incorporates the Supervised Fine-tuning Trainer (SFT) from Hugging Face [4], coupled with the Parameter-efficient fine-tuning (PEFT) library [6]. The SFT technique is particularly effective in directing the model towards following instructions and aligning the model to generate code that adheres to high standards of maintainability for our case. The PEFT helps adapt pre-trained language models to specific applications with minimal fine-tuning. It fine-tunes only a few extra parameters, reducing computational and storage demands. This approach is cost-effective compared to the full fine-tuning of large-scale models. Recent PEFT techniques deliver performance similar to complete fine-tuning methods [21]. Additionally, incorporating the QLoRA [22] technique alongside PEFT further reduced the memory requirement to run these models. This is achieved using quantization techniques. SFT with PEFT and QLoRA allows us to fine-tune QwenCoder2.5 32B Instruct on an A100 GPU (40 GB). Using SFT, the model is exposed to examples from our extended datasets, which include the input original code, additional contexts, instruction and the desired output (Refactored code) optimised for maintainability. The model's parameters are adjusted to minimize the difference between its outputs and the correct answers [4]. This is achieved using the maintainability prompt from Fig. 2 alongside our extended dataset.

5   Data Availability

To ensure the reproducibility and reliability of our results, a complete replication package is publicly available at Zenodo[1], with all code appropriately seeded. The corresponding resources are also hosted on Hugging Face, including the **datasets, models**.

6   Results

6.1   RQ1. Fine-Tuning LLM to Generate Python Code with Higher Maintainability

The primary aim of this research question is to critically evaluate the impact of fine-tuning LLMs on their capability to produce maintainable Python code. Following the fine-tuning phase, the model enters a crucial testing stage. In this stage, a portion of the dataset, which remained unused during the training phase (Test split), is presented to the model. This testing aims to gauge the model's ability to apply the coding pattern and characteristics it has learned to new and unseen examples of Python code. This evaluation is essential to determine whether the model can generalize its understanding of high code quality, focusing on maintainability. It also tests the model's capacity to handle various coding scenarios and complexities representing real-world programming environments. This stage is vital in assessing how fine-tuning LLMs can enhance their ability to generate Python code for improved maintainability. Table 1 details the impact of fine-tuning on code metrics using the CODEALPACA and COMMIT-PACKFT datasets (Python subset) on generating Maintainable code, comparing the fine-tuned model's output (FT) against the original code (Orig). Focusing on these maintainability indicators, where higher Maintainability Index (MI) scores and lower programming Effort are preferred, the table reveals specific trends.

---

[1] https://doi.org/10.5281/zenodo.15182371.

Notably, the fine-tuned code (FT) exhibits substantially lower mean Effort (e.g., 55.8 vs 76.6 on CODEALPACA; 25.1 vs 43.0 on COMMITPACK) and is generally shorter (lower SLOC) than the original code. The fine-tuned code shows a lower mean MI (e.g., 73.7 vs 79.8 on CODEALPACA; 68.5 vs 75.4 on COMMIT-PACK), in this evaluation. Median MI results were inconsistent across datasets.

Table 1. Comparison of Maintainability Metrics. We report the Mean (M), Standard Deviation (S), and Median (Md) for Source Lines of Code (SLOC), Maintainability Index (MI), and Effort. FT denotes the finetuned model, while Orig refers to the original code.

Source	SLOC			MI			Effort		
	M	S	Md	M	S	Md	M	S	Md
CODEALPACA									
FT	7.8	7.3	6.0	73.7	30.0	78.0	55.8	229.0	2.4
Orig	9.2	6.9	8.0	79.8	17.2	76.2	76.6	345.3	2.4
COMMITPACKFT									
FT	17.5	11.6	17.0	68.5	34.5	70.1	25.1	157.2	0.0
Orig	20.4	10.6	20.0	75.4	26.0	71.1	43.0	349.9	1.0

Fine-tuning code generation models on datasets like CODEALPACA and COMMITPACKFT yields promising improvements in code maintainability. The resulting code is significantly more concise (lower SLOC) and requires substantially less programming Effort compared to the original versions. This streamlining can accelerate development cycles and reduce the initial cognitive load for developers. While the median Maintainability Index (MI) metric is largely the same and inconclusive in this evaluation, the clear gains in brevity and reduced effort highlight the potential of fine-tuning to optimize code generation for faster development and specific coding maintainability and refactoring tasks.

7   Evaluation

7.1   Evaluating the Functional Similarity on the Test Split

The evaluation of fine-tuned models on Test split using CodeBERTScores shows high functional correctness and similarity between the original reference code from the dataset and the generated code from the FT models on both Commitpack and CODEALPACA datasets.

CodeBERTScore [40] is a metric designed to evaluate the similarity between a reference code snippet and a generated code snippet, focusing on both syntactical and functional equivalence. Unlike traditional metrics such as BLEU [20], which mainly rely on exact token matches, CodeBERTScore leverages the contextual embeddings from a model like CodeBERT [7], which is trained on

Table 2. CodeBERT scores for functional similarity between original and fine-tuned (FT) code. We report the mean, median, and standard deviation for Precision (P), Recall (R), F1, and F3 scores.

Dataset	Metric	Mean	Median	Std Dev
CODEALPACA	P	0.849	0.861	0.083
	R	0.889	0.899	0.058
	F1	0.867	0.875	0.064
	F3	0.884	0.892	0.057
COMMITPACK	P	0.903	0.915	0.071
	R	0.924	0.933	0.058
	F1	0.913	0.921	0.061
	F3	0.922	0.930	0.058

both programming languages and natural language. This approach allows Code-BERTScore to understand the underlying semantics of code snippets beyond mere lexical similarities. The key advantage of CodeBERTScore is its ability to recognize functionally equivalent code snippets that may not share a high degree of lexical similarity. For example, it can be understood that `x ** 0.5` and `math.sqrt(x)` performs the same operation (calculating the square root of `x`) despite having different tokens. This is a significant improvement over traditional metrics, ensuring that generated code is evaluated more accurately in terms of what it does rather than just how it is written.

CodeBERTScore represents a sophisticated approach to evaluating code generation. It prioritizes the functional and semantic accuracy of the generated code over mere lexical matching. This makes it especially suitable for applications where understanding the intent and functionality of code is crucial, such as automated code review or code synthesis tasks. The metrics Precision (P), Recall (R), F1 score, and F3 range from 0 to 1, where 1 indicates a perfect match, and 0 indicates no match at all between the generated code and the reference code. Table 2 presents an evaluation of the functional similarity between original and generated code using the CodeBERTScores [40] metric. These scores reflect the nuanced capability of fine-tuned models to produce code that is not only syntactically correct but also semantically aligned and functionally equivalent to the reference code. A mean score close to 1 (e.g., 0.90 or 0.94) suggests that the generated code is very similar to the reference code in terms of functionality and semantics. The standard deviations associated with these scores, such as (0.08), indicate the variability of the scores across different instances in the dataset. A lower standard deviation means that the scores are more consistent across instances.

This means that the generated code is highly effective and comprehensive, with most of its functionalities correctly implemented. The results demonstrate the potential of these models in applications requiring precise and functionally accurate code generation, moving beyond mere syntactic similarity to ensure semantic and functional alignment with original code snippets.

7.2 Evaluating the Code Generation Capabilities and Test Based Evaluation

In addition to the functional similarity calculations, we also have a comprehensive evaluation of the code generation capabilities and functional correctness of both the base models and our fine-tuned models aimed at improving the maintainability of Python code generated by LLMs. We employed two widely recognised metrics to assess the functional correctness of generated code using the EvalPlus framework [13]. EvalPlus significantly enhances code generation evaluation by expanding test coverage in popular code benchmarks like HumanEval+ (pass@1) and MBPP+. The HumanEval+ (pass@1) metric measures the percentage of problems for which the first generated solution is correct, based on an extended set of test cases of Humaneval [1]. The MBPP+ benchmark evaluates the model's performance on the Most Basic Python Programs (MBPP) dataset [19].

Table 3. Benchmark Pass@1 Performance Results

Model	HumanEval+	MBPP+
Original (QwenCoder 2.5)	0.872	0.77
COMMITPACK-FT	0.82	0.775
CODEALPACA-FT	0.835	0.770

Our evaluation encompassed comparing their original versions of Qwen-Coder2.5 32B Instruct against fine-tuned variants optimised for maintainable Python code generation. Table 3 quantifies the impact of fine-tuning for maintainability on the models' core code generation capabilities, specifically functional correctness. It compares the pass@1 scores (proportion of problems solved correctly on the first try) of the original model (QwenCoder 2.5 32B Instruct) against the COMMITPACK-FT and CODEALPACA-FT dataset Fine-tuned variants on the demanding HumanEval+ and MBPP+ benchmarks, evaluated using EvalPlus.

The data reveals that while the fine-tuning process aimed at improving maintainability metrics, it led to a slight decrease in performance on the HumanEval+ benchmark compared to the original model (scores of 0.820 and 0.835 for FT models vs. 0.872 for Original). However, performance on the MBPP+ benchmark remained stable or saw a marginal improvement (scores around 0.770–0.775 for all models), suggesting that the fine-tuning did not significantly degrade, and in one case slightly enhanced, the ability to solve these basic programming tasks.

7.3 Evaluating and Assessing the Usefulness and Utility

Our evaluation method for assessing a fine-tuned AI model as a programming assistant involved a structured session where participants with varying Python expertise from both industry and academia (A total of 11 participants answered all the questions) interacted with the FT model to complete coding tasks reflective of real-world scenarios. The tasks were self-selected by participants to ensure relevance to their actual coding practices. Feedback was gathered through a questionnaire focusing on the model's usefulness and effectiveness as an AI companion, rated on a 1 to 5 scale, with 1 being "not useful at all" and 5 being "extremely useful".

Table 4. Summary Statistics of Survey Responses

Statistic	Usefulness	AI Companion	Python Exp. (yrs)
Mean	3.44	3.60	10.55
Median	4.00	4.00	10.00
Std. Dev.	1.13	1.07	4.87

Table 4 presents summary statistics for three variables from a survey: Usefulness Rating, AI Companion Rating, and Python Experience (Years). These statistics provide insights into the central tendency and variability of the responses for each variable. We had a total response from 11 users in this survey, who answered all the questions.

For "Usefulness Rating" and "AI Companion Rating". Both ratings have a median of 4.0(Very useful), indicating that the central tendency of user opinions is positive, suggesting the model is generally found useful and performs well as an AI companion. The medians being at 4.0 also imply that at least half of the ratings are at or above this value. The assessment is based on feedback from users with varying levels of Python programming experience, which is critical for a comprehensive evaluation of the model's performance across different expertise levels. Table 4 reveals that users with around 10 years of experience form the largest group, suggesting that their insights are particularly valuable given their considerable expertise.

User feedback on our Fine-tuned AI coding tool reveals that it helps write cleaner, more maintainable code, particularly for experienced Python users. Novice programmers benefit from exposure to best coding practices. Yet, some users noted the AI's suggestions occasionally do not align with specific project needs and called for faster response times and better integration with development environments for enhanced customization. Gathering human feedback grounds our evaluation in practical use and provides empirical data on the tool's effectiveness across varied user experience levels, paving the way for further detailed exploration.

8   Discussion

Our fine-tuned model is designed to refine existing functional code and prioritizes suggestions that adhere to established coding standards and best practices rather than generating new code. This tool has proven to be a valuable AI companion for code refactoring, as demonstrated by positive human evaluations.

Integrating this model into continuous integration and deployment pipelines can streamline development workflows, providing immediate feedback to mitigate technical debt accumulation. Moreover, the model serves as an instructional guide for novices, promoting the development of clean and efficient code while standardizing learning through consistent feedback.

For the research community, it offers a platform to assess the effectiveness of automated refactoring tools and explore different refactoring strategies to enhance long-term software maintenance. This exploration of human-AI collaboration in software development could significantly elevate code quality, efficiency, and cost-effectiveness in software engineering.

The discussion of whether fine-tuning is required despite the existence of capable general models such as GPT-4 for code generation is crucial. Our study highlights that these models may not focus on nuanced aspects of code maintainability without targeted training. We have developed a dataset centred on Python programming, incorporating best practices and examples of highly maintainable code. This dataset is essential for fine-tuning other large language models (LLMs) to improve the maintainability of the code they generate. By utilising this dataset, our fine-tuned model demonstrates improved performance in code quality and maintainability. This not only enhances the model's practicality in software development but also enables the use of smaller, more efficient models. These models, potentially less costly in terms of computational resources, can achieve or exceed the capabilities of larger models like GPT-4, and offer additional security benefits for deployment in sensitive environments.

8.1   Threats to Validity

Our study's validity faces several threats. **Internal validity** is challenged by potential model overfitting if our training data does not comprehensively represent the Python ecosystem, and by the sensitivity of results to hyperparameter selection. **External validity** may be limited by the focus on Python, questioning generalizability to other languages and to the scale of complex industrial codebases. **Construct validity** concerns whether our chosen metrics and tools, with their inherent biases, fully encapsulate the concept of maintainability as understood in professional practice. Furthermore, **conclusion validity** hinges on robust statistical analysis to avoid drawing incorrect inferences from the data. Finally, **reliability** can be affected by model performance inconsistencies and dataset shift as real-world code evolves, necessitating continuous evaluation. We acknowledge that our study does not encompass all dimensions of code maintainability, underscoring the complexity of the concept and the need for ongoing research in this area.

9 Conclusion

This study explores the effectiveness of fine-tuning Large Language Models (LLMs) for generating maintainable Python code. Utilizing our custom extended datasets and leveraging models such as QwenCoder2.5 32B Instruct, we have achieved notable improvements in code maintainability metrics, such as Source Lines of Code, Maintainability Index and Halstead Effort. These enhancements highlight LLMs' potential as powerful tools in automating code refactoring processes, with the promise of advancing software development practices. Central to our investigation is a specially curated dataset designed with a focus on Python programming that can be used to fine-tune other LLMs and improve the generated code quality and maintainability. By examining the strengths and weaknesses of LLMs in producing maintainable Python code, this research contributes significantly to the fields of automated code generation and software maintainability.

References

1. Chen, M., et al.: Evaluating large language models trained on code. CoRR abs/2107.03374 (2021). arXiv: 2107.03374
2. Alsolai, H., et al.: A systematic literature review of machine learning techniques for software maintainability prediction. Inf. Software Technol. **119** , 106214 (2020). ISSN: 0950-5849. https://doi.org/10.1016/j.infsof.2019.106214
3. Burns, C., et al.: Weak-to-strong generalization: eliciting strong capabilities with weak supervision. arXiv preprint arXiv:2312.09390 (2023)
4. Hugging Face. Supervised Fine-tuning Trainer Documentation (2023). Accessed 07 Nov 2023
5. Fan, A., et al.: Large Language models for software engineering: survey and open problems. arXiv preprint arXiv:2310.03533 (2023)
6. Feng, T., et al.: PEFT-SER: on the use of parameter efficient transfer learning approaches for speech emotion recognition using pretrained speech models. arXiv preprint arXiv:2306.05350 (2023)
7. Feng, Z., et al.: CodeBERT: a pre-trained model for programming and natural languages. In: Cohn, T., et al. (eds.) Findings of the Association for Computational Linguistics: EMNLP 2020, pp. 1536–1547. Association for Computational Linguistics (2020). https://doi.org/10.18653/v1/2020.findings-emnlp.139.
8. Hou, H., et al.: Large language models for software engineering: a systematic literature review. arXiv: 2308.10620 [cs.SE] (2023)
9. Hui, B., et al.: Qwen2. 5-coder technical report. arXiv preprint arXiv:2409.12186 (2024)
10. The Software Sustainability Institute. Developing Maintainable Software. Year of access
11. Le, H., et al.: CodeRL: mastering code generation through pretrained models and deep reinforcement learning. In: Koyejo, S., et al. (eds.) Advances in Neural Information Processing Systems, pp. 21314–21328. Curran Associates, Inc. (2022)
12. Lenarduzzi, V., et al.: A systematic literature review on Technical Debt prioritization: strategies, processes, factors, and tools. J. Syst. Software **171**, 110827 (2021). https://doi.org/10.1016/j.jss.2020.110827

13. Liu, J., et al.: Is your code generated by ChatGPT really correct? Rigorous evaluation of large language models for code generation. In: Thirty-seventh Conference on Neural Information Processing Systems (2023)
14. Liu, Y., et al.: Summary of ChatGPT-related research and perspective towards the future of large language models. Meta-Radiology **1**(2), 100017 (2023). https://doi.org/10.1016/j.metrad.2023.100017.
15. Luo, Z., et al.: WizardCoder: empowering code large language models with evol-instruct. arXiv:2306.08568 [cs.CL] (2023)
16. mikejo5000. How Code Metrics Help Identify Risks - Visual Studio (Windows) (2023)
17. Misra, S.: Modeling design/coding factors that drive maintainability of software systems. Software Qual. J. **13**, 297–320 (2005). https://doi.org/10.1007/s11219-005-1754-7
18. Muennighoff, N., et al.: OctoPack: instruction tuning code large language models. arXiv preprint arXiv:2308.07124 (2023)
19. Odena, A., et al.: Program synthesis with large language models. In: n/a. n/a. n/a, n/a (2021)
20. Papineni, K., et al.: Bleu: a method for automatic evaluation of machine translation. In: Proceedings of the 40th Annual Meeting of the Association for Computational Linguistics, pp. 311–318 (2002)
21. PEFT: Parameter-Efficient Fine-Tuning. https://huggingface.co/docs/peft/index. Version 0.6.2. Accessed 18 Nov 2023
22. QLoRA Development Team. QLoRA: efficient fine-tuning of large language models (2023). Accessed 07 Nov 2023
23. Radon Contributors. Radon Documentation. Accessed 08 Nov 2023 (2023)
24. Center for Research on Foundation Models. ALPACA (2023). Accessed 07 Nov 2023
25. Rosenbaum, A., et al.: CLASP: few-shot cross-lingual data augmentation for semantic parsing. In: AACL-IJCNLP 2022 (2022)
26. Rosenbaum, A., et al.: LINGUIST: language model instruction tuning to generate annotated utterances for intent classification and slot tagging. In: COLING 2022 (2022)
27. Shirafuji, A., et al.: Exploring the robustness of large language models for solving programming problems. arXiv:abs/2306.14583 (2023)
28. Siy, H., et al.: Does the modern code inspection have value? In: Proceedings IEEE International Conference on Software Maintenance (ICSM 2001), pp. 281–289 (2001). https://doi.org/10.1109/ICSM.2001.972741.
29. Sjøberg, D.I.K., et al.: Questioning software maintenance metrics: a comparative case study. In: Proceedings of the ACM-IEEE International Symposium on Empirical Software Engineering and Measurement, pp. 107– 110 (2012)
30. Tarun, I.: Python Code Instructions 18k Dataset (2021). Accessed 08 No 2023
31. Tiwari, S., et al.: Coupling and cohesion metrics for object-oriented software: a systematic mapping study. In: Proceedings of the 11th Innovations in Software Engineering Conference. ISEC '18. Hyderabad, India: Association for Computing Machinery (2018). isbn: 9781450363983. https://doi.org/10.1145/3172871.3172878.
32. Michael Wahler et al. "Improving Code Maintainability: A Case Study on the Impact of Refactoring". In: 2016 IEEE International Conference on Software Maintenance and Evolution (ICSME). 2016, pp. 493–501. https://doi.org/10.1109/ICSME.2016.52.

33. Wang, Y., et al.: How far can camels go? Exploring the state of instruction tuning on open resources. In: Oh, A., et al. (eds.) Advances in Neural Information Processing Systems, vol. 36, pp. 74764–74786. Curran Associates, Inc. (2023)
34. Wang, Y., et al.: Self-instruct: aligning language models with self- generated instructions. In: Rogers, A., et al. (eds.) Proceedings of the 61st Annual Meeting of the Association for Computational Linguistics (Volume 1: Long Papers). Toronto, Canada, pp. 13484–13508. Association for Computational Linguistics (2023). https://doi.org/10.18653/v1/2023.acllong.754
35. Woodward, M.R.: Difficulties using cohesion and coupling as quality indicators. Software Qual. J. **2**, 109–127 (1993)
36. Xiong, W., et al.: The Program Testing ability of large language models for code. arXiv:abs/2310.05727 (2023)
37. Xu, C., et al.: WizardLM: empowering large language models to follow complex instructions. arXiv preprint arXiv:2304.12244 (2023)
38. Xu, F.F., et al.: A systematic evaluation of large language models of code. arXiv preprint arXiv:2202.13169 (2022)
39. Zhang, S., et al.: Instruction tuning for large language models: a survey. arXiv preprint arXiv:2308.10792 (2023)
40. Zhou, S., et al.: CodeBERTScore: evaluating code generation with pretrained models of code. In: The 2023 Conference on Empirical Methods in Natural Language Processing (2023)
41. Zhuo, T.Y.: Large language models are state-of-the-art evaluators of code generation. arXiv:abs/2304.14317 (2023)

Enhancing Software Maintainability Through LLM-Assisted Code Refactoring

Tommaso Fulcini[1]([✉])(iD), Riccardo Coppola[1](iD), Flavio Giobergia[1](iD),
Amirali Changizi[1], Meelad Dashti[1], Kimia Dorrani[1], Domenico Amalfitano[2](iD),
Damiano Distante[3](iD), and Filippo Ricca[4](iD)

[1] Politecnico di Torino, Turin, Italy
{tommaso.fulcini,riccardo.coppola,flavio.giobergia,amirali.changizi,
meelad.dashti,kimia.dorrani}@polito.it
[2] Università di Napoli Federico II, Naples, Italy
domenico.amalfitano@unina.it
[3] UnitelmaSapienza Università di Roma, Rome, Italy
damiano.distante@unitelmasapienza.it
[4] Università di Genova, Genoa, Italy
filippo.ricca@unige.it

Abstract. High code quality, particularly in terms of maintainability, is crucial for ensuring that software remains efficient and adaptable over time, while minimizing long-term maintenance costs. As artificial intelligence continues to evolve, its application in software development offers new opportunities to improve code quality. This study investigates the use of Large Language Models (LLMs) to enhance software maintainability through code refactoring. The results indicate that LLMs can be effectively utilized for this purpose, with effectiveness varying depending on the model and the evaluation metric used. Although the study is based on a limited set of Python projects and specific prompting strategies, it provides a meaningful step toward understanding the broader applicability of LLMs in this context.

Keywords: LLMs · Code Maintainability · Code Quality · Technical Debt

1 Introduction

Advancements in artificial intelligence (AI) are significantly influencing a wide range of fields, including software development, opening new possibilities for automation and enhancement. Among these innovations, the development of new solutions for source code analysis and quality improvement plays a crucial role in ensuring that the software remains efficient, scalable, and maintainable [1] over time. Poor code quality, indeed, may lead to increased technical debt [2], hinder collaboration, and result in deteriorated performance. Although traditional methods for code quality improvement, such as manual code reviews

© The Author(s), under exclusive license to Springer Nature Switzerland AG 2026
G. Scanniello et al. (Eds.): PROFES 2025, LNCS 16361, pp. 153–168, 2026.
https://doi.org/10.1007/978-3-032-12089-2_10

Table 1. GQM table for the study

Analyze:	Code refactoring with LLMs
For the purpose of:	Analyzing the impact on code quality
With respect to:	Maintainability metrics
From the viewpoint of:	Developers, LLM users
In the context of:	Python open-source codebases

and static analyzers, are effective, they are usually slow, do not scale, and often fail to capture more significant structural enhancements [3].

Large Language Models (LLMs) have demonstrated their effectiveness in analyzing and improving source code, particularly in identifying inefficiencies [4,5] and recommending targeted enhancements. Their capability to identify sophisticated patterns, adhere to best practices, and suggest refactoring techniques [6] makes them a viable option to replace traditional methods.

This study aims to explore the potential of LLMs in enhancing code quality properties, particularly maintainability, seeking to understand their real-world applications in the field of software development. Our analysis leverages lightweight LLMs that can run locally, thereby reducing execution costs and eliminating the overhead associated with remote access to larger LLMs. We selected three open-source medium-sized GitHub Python projects as our experimental objects to ensure that the starting code had room for improvement. We also chose Deepseek, Llama, and Mixtral, three open-source lightweight models widely used in the literature. We defined a fixed prompting strategy to query the different models and statically evaluated the results obtained with the different LLMs in terms of Maintainability Index, Code and Comment Density, comparing the values before and after the models' intervention.

Results indicate that LLMs have the potential to contribute positively to software maintainability and documentation quality, with varying degrees of effectiveness based on the model and the metric used. Although the experimental study involved a limited set of open-source projects and LLMs (three in both cases), and adopted specific prompting strategies, the proposed approach is generalizable, and the results provide a meaningful step toward understanding the broader applicability of LLMs in improving code maintainability.

2   Methodology

The goal of our research was defined using the Goal-Question-Metric (GQM) template [7], and is presented in Table 1. To achieve this goal, we formulated the following main research question (RQ):

RQ: Can Large Language Models effectively refactor code to enhance its maintainability?

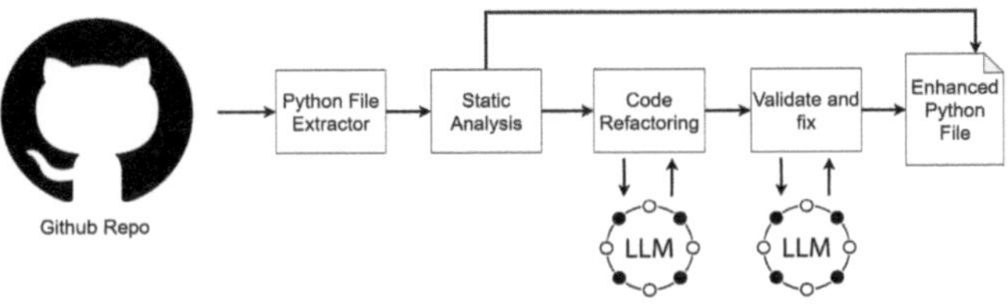

Fig. 1. Overview of the followed process.

In the present section, we discuss the architecture of our prototype solution, the experimental process that we performed, and the selected software artefacts and LLMs used.

2.1 Process Description

A high-level diagram of the followed process is shown in Fig. 1. Once the *Python files are extracted*, the system applies an initial *static code analysis* computation, performed through the use of the Radon tool[1]. Specifically, if the file under analysis has a Maintainability Index MI (described in detail in a following section) below 85, the system queries the selected LLM engine to perform a *refactoring*, otherwise, the code is not modified by the LLM models.

The code in need of refactoring is then inserted in a prompt for the selected LLM model. The refactored code is logged alongside a structured summary of the applied modifications, enabling comparative analysis between the original and improved versions.

Finally, to ensure the structural integrity and correctness of the refactored code, the system incorporates an automated *validation and error fix* mechanism. This phase verifies the syntactic validity of the generated code and applies corrective refinements when inconsistencies are detected. If verification is successful, the code is preserved without modifications. When syntactic inconsistencies are identified, the system dynamically generates a structured error analysis and employs a second prompt to correct such issues.

To allow measurement of the benefits of the application of the LLMs on maintainability, for the files that were modified, we measure the quality metrics also on the version provided as output by the LLM model.

Figure 2 shows the prompt used[2] The prompts were defined with a zero-shot prompting strategy [8] by applying the role assignment, contextualization of variables, multidimensional instruction, and explicit output formatting. These prompting strategies are grounded in prompt-engineering literature and have been proven to increase the predictability and precision of the results and, in

---

[1] https://pypi.org/project/radon/.

[2] All the used prompts, along with the Python scripts for extraction and static code analysis, are available in a replication package at the following link: https://github.com/amiralichangizi/llm-code-quality-analyzer.

```
"""You are an expert Python engineer.
Below is a Python file which is written with python version {python_version}.
File Path: {file_path}

--- CODE ---
{code}
Improve the code for better:
1- Readability: Variable naming conventions, comment quality, and code clarity.
2- Modularity: Function length, coupling, and cohesion.
3- Maintainability: Code duplication, complexity, and  technical debt indicators.

Return your response in the following format:

IMPROVED_CODE:
<your improved code here>
IMPROVEMENTS:
- <improvement 1>
...
CATEGORIES:
- <category 1>
...
"""
```

Fig. 2. Adopted Prompt

addition, they simplify the parsing of the output [9]. We intentionally refrained from guiding the refactoring process through few-shot examples or additional conditioning. This choice was made to evaluate the intrinsic capabilities of each LLM in a zero-shot setting, where no specific examples are embedded in the prompt. Such an approach is consistent with established evaluation practices and enables a clearer assessment of how each model independently interprets and applies general refactoring instructions.

2.2   Code Repositories and LLMs Selection

Object Selection. To prove the ability of different LLMs at code refactoring for maintainability improvement, GitHub was used to search for open-source projects to analyze. Python was selected as the programming language for the project due to its extensive use in contemporary software development. We sought stable repositories that had a limited number of updates, specifically no more than five commits in the past year. Given that the study centers on code refactoring, the aim was to identify small to medium-sized repositories with a codebase that exhibited relatively low maintainability. We conducted an automated search for repositories containing between 5 and 30 Python files, established between the years 2020 and 2025, and with a size ranging from several hundred kilobytes to ten megabytes. From the results of this search, three repositories were chosen at random. The final set of repositories used in the experiment consists of the following three:

- 3DHighlighter[3]: A repository of a project focused on 3D object visualization.

---

[3] https://github.com/threedle/3DHighlighter.

- KRED[4]: A repository of a project based on natural language processing for recommendation systems.
- Auto-Data[5]: A repository of a project that provides tools for easily generating datasets for fine-tuning LLMs.

We used a static parser to extract executable Python scripts with more than 10 lines of code (LOC). From the three repositories, we extracted 27 Python files with a varying number of LOCs (min 10, max 640, mean 112, median 97).

LLMs Selection. The main reasons that guided our selection were: (i) employing open-source models; (ii) selecting lightweight models that could be run locally; (iii) selecting a diverse set of models to enable comparisons between different architectures, training paradigms, and computational footprints. We considered three different LLM models:

- **DeepSeek-r1-distill-llama-70b**[6] (from now on, DeepSeek) is a distilled variant of the 70-billion parameter Llama family, optimized specifically for code tasks. The model was included because it allows for assessing the gains obtainable with a domain-specific fine-tuned model.
- **Llama-3.3-70b-versatile**[7] (from now on, Llama) is a general-purpose LLM, with capabilities spanning across natural language and code. The selection of this model allows for assessing the gains that can be achieved by using an *off-the-shelf* model when applied to code-refactoring tasks.
- **Mixtral-8x7b-32768**[8] (from now on, Mixtral) is a lighter-weight, long-context model designed for efficient and extended sequence handling. The selection of this model allows for assessing the gains that can be achieved in code refactoring by using a smaller-parameter-count model.

2.3   Computed Metrics

To assess the maintainability improvements introduced by the LLMs-based refactoring process, we computed the following software quality metrics: Maintainability Index (MI) [10], Comment Density (ComD), and Code Density (CodD).

Maintainability Index (MI) is a quantitative measure of how easy a program is to maintain. MI is a score between 0 and 100, where higher values indicate better maintainability: a value above 85 indicates ease of maintenance, values

---

[4] https://github.com/danyang-liu/KRED.
[5] https://github.com/Itachi-Uchiha581/Auto-Data.
[6] https://huggingface.co/deepseek-ai/DeepSeek-R1-Distill-Llama-70B.
[7] https://huggingface.co/meta-llama/Llama-3.3-70B-Instruct.
[8] https://huggingface.co/mistralai/Mixtral-8x7B-v0.1.

between 65 and 85 indicate moderate maintainability, and values below 65 are an indicator of difficult maintenance. It is calculated as follows[9]:

$$MI = max(0, (171 - 5.2 \times \ln(V) - 0.23 \times CC$$
$$-16.2 \times ln(SLOC) + 50 \sin \sqrt{2.4ComD}) \times \frac{100}{171}) \,, \tag{1}$$

where:

- V = Halstead Volume [11] (a measure of code complexity based on operators and operands) computed as follows:

$$V = (N_1 + N_2) \cdot \log_2(\eta_1 + \eta_2) \,,$$

where: η_1 is the number of distinct operators, η_2 the number of distinct operands, N_1 the total occurrences of operators, N_2 the total occurrences of operands;
- CC = The total Cyclomatic Complexity (CC), a measure of the number of independent execution paths in a program, indicating its structural complexity [12]. A higher CC value suggests more branching and potential difficulty in understanding or maintaining the code:

$$CC = E - N + 2P \,,$$

where E is the number of edges in the flow graph, N the number of nodes, P the number of connected components (typically, P = 1 for a single program);
- $SLOC$ = The number of Source Lines of Code;
- $ComD$ = The Comment Density (detailed below).

Comment Density (ComD) is used to measure how well-documented the code is. ComD is a value spanning from 0 to 100 as well, with higher values associated with better maintainability, indicating well-documented code. It is calculated as the percentage of comment lines compared to the total lines of code, as follows:

$$ComD = \left(\frac{L_C}{SLOC} \right) \times 100 \,, \tag{2}$$

where L_C is the number of lines of code containing comments.

Code Density (CodD). Code Density is a measure of the ratio of executable code to comments and empty lines. CodD is a percentage value where lower values are associated with better maintainability, indicating a proper balance between comments and code. As CodD increases, ComD decreases, indicating an inverse relationship between these two metrics. It provides an indication of code efficiency by identifying excessive white space or under-commented sections.

$$CodD = \left(\frac{L_E}{SLOC} \right) \times 100 \tag{3}$$

where L_E is the number of lines containing actual executable code.

---

[9] Several definitions are available in the literature for MI. In this study, we use the derivative version computed by Radon as indicated in its official documentation: https://radon.readthedocs.io/en/stable/intro.html.

Table 2. Model Performance Comparison (values in *italic* are referred to files that were not modified by the LLM agents since the original MI was above 85; values in **bold** are the best metrics among the sets, i.e., higher values for MI and ComD, and lower values for CodD)

Project	Filename	Original			DeepSeek			Llama			Mixtral		
		MI	ComD	CodD	MI	ComD	CodD	MI	ComD	CodD	MI	ComD	CodD
KRED	base_data_loader.py	100.00	0.00	60.00	*100.00*	*0.00*	*60.00*	*100.00*	*0.00*	*60.00*	*100.00*	*0.00*	*60.00*
KRED	base_model.py	95.94	0.00	62.50	*95.94*	*0.00*	*62.50*	*95.94*	*0.00*	*62.50*	*95.94*	*0.00*	*62.50*
KRED	base_trainer.py	100.00	0.00	54.17	*100.00*	*0.00*	*54.17*	*100.00*	*0.00*	*54.17*	*100.00*	*0.00*	*54.17*
KRED	KGAT.py	36.30	0.00	87.93	54.54	**9.78**	78.03	**65.71**	0.00	**62.64**	41.15	0.00	78.72
KRED	KRED.py	45.76	0.00	79.49	61.64	13.08	**48.09**	**73.97**	**27.94**	50.36	46.01	0.00	74.70
KRED	logger.py	79.74	**3.70**	69.44	80.11	2.22	**51.81**	**81.91**	2.50	52.63	78.20	3.57	71.79
KRED	main.py	72.62	4.00	66.67	55.67	0.00	64.41	86.54	0.00	**53.33**	**95.03**	**20.00**	**53.33**
KRED	metrics.py	33.27	0.00	96.23	59.70	**10.53**	**43.00**	**64.12**	1.28	47.51	38.66	0.00	86.90
KRED	News_embedding.py	42.38	3.05	78.26	**61.68**	**15.08**	50.52	61.27	4.42	**46.92**	35.20	0.00	82.27
KRED	parse_config.py	**62.62**	11.22	63.19	59.79	7.63	47.79	57.50	**20.56**	**43.96**	62.23	6.25	58.33
KRED	pytorchtools.py	81.86	**6.90**	68.09	75.42	5.71	50.00	69.03	0.00	**44.33**	**82.53**	3.85	50.00
KRED	train_test.py	30.88	0.00	79.80	49.21	5.23	64.00	**65.26**	**25.49**	57.75	33.42	0.00	82.14
KRED	trainer.py	67.53	0.00	68.07	70.43	**27.71**	55.29	66.29	0.00	59.34	**85.69**	0.00	86.09
KRED	User_modeling.py	60.50	0.00	80.00	78.51	**25.71**	**31.19**	**79.31**	5.13	38.89	61.04	0.00	85.00
KRED	**Average**	64.96	2.06	72.42	71.62	**8.76**	54.34	**76.20**	6.24	**52.45**	64.82	2.41	70.42
Auto-Data	base_chat.py	76.09	**2.38**	41.53	72.56	0.00	47.62	**76.85**	0.00	**37.11**	76.17	0.00	53.61
Auto-Data	chat_history.py	100.00	0.00	100.00	*100.00*	*0.00*	*100.00*	*100.00*	*0.00*	*100.00*	*100.00*	*0.00*	*100.00*
Auto-Data	example.py	100.00	0.00	16.67	*100.00*	*0.00*	*16.67*	*100.00*	*0.00*	*16.67*	*100.00*	*0.00*	*16.67*
Auto-Data	loading_bar.py	63.07	0.00	84.62	80.78	5.26	63.89	79.59	**42.86**	46.30	**83.28**	0.00	50.00
Auto-Data	main.py	59.55	0.00	**25.93**	63.24	**5.21**	39.66	**79.33**	0.00	29.70	61.67	1.14	32.35
Auto-Data	native.py	64.80	1.41	39.01	49.38	2.94	**57.80**	70.13	**5.76**	33.80	56.63	1.71	48.53
Auto-Data	text_colour.py	100.00	0.00	100.00	*100.00*	*0.00*	*100.00*	*100.00*	*0.00*	*100.00*	*100.00*	*0.00*	*100.00*
Auto-Data	topic_history.py	100.00	0.00	100.00	*100.00*	*0.00*	*100.00*	*100.00*	*0.00*	*100.00*	*100.00*	*0.00*	*100.00*
Auto-Data	**Average**	82.94	0.47	63.47	83.25	1.68	65.71	**88.24**	6.08	**57.95**	84.72	0.36	62.65
3DHighlighter	main.py	49.86	15.90	64.55	35.45	0.50	72.95	48.94	14.29	70.27	**53.23**	**16.95**	**63.01**
3DHighlighter	mesh.py	44.61	**2.17**	81.42	**61.22**	0.00	55.08	**62.67**	1.01	52.61	34.11	0.00	82.54
3DHighlighter	MeshNormalizer.py	100.00	11.11	69.23	*100.00*	*11.11*	*69.23*	*100.00*	*11.11*	*69.23*	*100.00*	*11.11*	*69.23*
3DHighlighter	neural_highlighter.py	59.63	0.00	90.00	82.18	**46.34**	38.30	77.62	14.81	**28.57**	**85.69**	0.00	57.81
3DHighlighter	Normalizer.py	57.10	0.00	77.78	69.24	0.00	39.56	32.16	0.00	**24.16**	**83.84**	0.00	61.90
3DHighlighter	render.py	48.35	2.50	73.20	**66.12**	14.43	**40.91**	66.90	0.00	50.63	39.01	0.00	68.22
3DHighlighter	utils.py	**72.05**	**20.34**	60.40	68.43	11.11	**38.79**	67.44	13.11	45.45	66.71	0.00	72.73
3DHighlighter	**Average**	61.66	**7.43**	73.80	68.95	11.93	50.69	65.10	7.76	**48.70**	**66.08**	4.01	67.92
	Average	69.12	2.92	70.28	74.18	**7.57**	56.60	**76.84**	6.56	**53.06**	70.61	2.23	67.67
	Median	64.80	0.00	69.44	70.43	**5.23**	54.17	**76.85**	1.01	**50.63**	76.17	0.00	68.22
	Standard dev.	22.93	15.80	20.73	18.83	17.53	19.82	17.61	17.79	20.65	24.89	15.89	19.60

Table 3. Results of statistical tests

Null Hypothesis	p-value	Decision
$H0_{\mathrm{MI}}$: The use of LLMs has no impact on MI for Python source code	0.014	**Reject**
$H0_{\mathrm{ComD}}$: The use of LLMs has no impact on ComD for Python source code	0.126	Accept
$H0_{\mathrm{CodD}}$: The use of LLMs has no impact on CodD for Python source code	<0.001	**Reject**

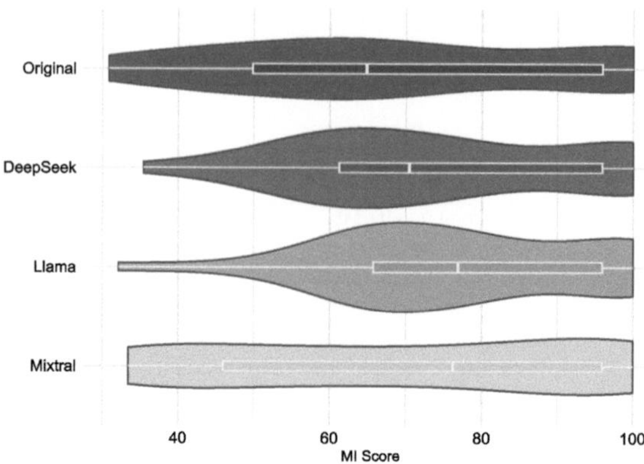

Fig. 3. Distribution of MI.

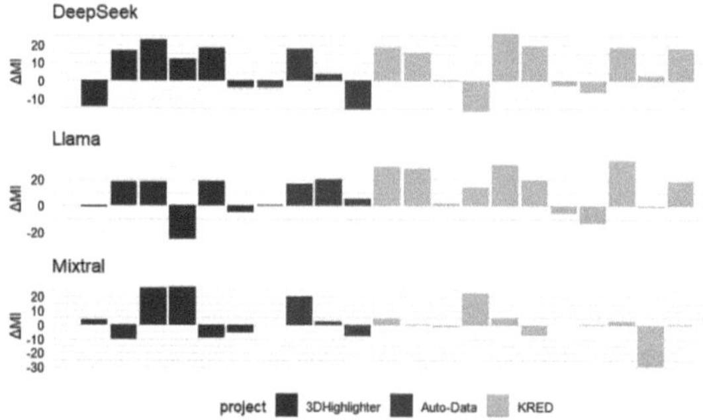

Fig. 4. Differences in MI for modified files.

3 Results

The distributions of MI, ComD, and CodD are reported respectively in the violin plots in Fig. 3, 5, and 7. The plots compare the values computed for the metrics for the original Python scripts and those computed for the set of files after the modifications applied by the LLMs. The distributions include values for the files that were not modified, i.e., those with an original MI value greater than or equal to 95.

The raw data of the metrics for each Python file of the three projects is shown in Table 2, with their values before and after the intervention of the different LLMs. The best value for each metric is highlighted in bold (i.e., higher values for MI and ComD, and lower values for CodD), while the files that remained untouched because they already had an optimal MI are highlighted in italic.

Finally, Table 3 shows the Null Hypotheses that we considered for our statistical tests and the resulting p-value and decision (accept-reject).

Regarding MI (Fig. 3), it can be seen that the metric is improved on average by all LLMs (69.12 for original files, 74.18 for DeepSeek, 76.84 for Llama, 70.61

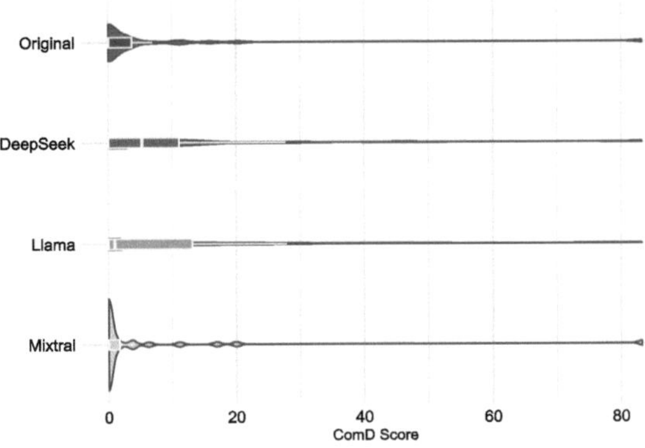

Fig. 5. Distribution of ComD.

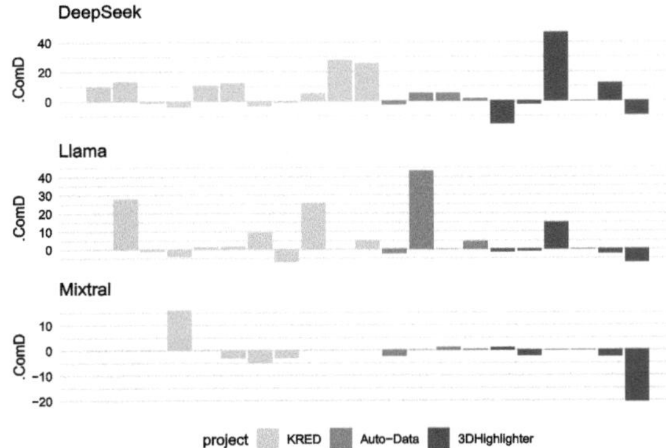

Fig. 6. Differences in ComD for modified files.

for Mixtral). DeepSeek and Llama produced moderate but steady MI improvements in each project. Mixtral achieved the largest MI enhancements for individual files, particularly in the 3DHighlighter project. On the other hand, it failed to increase the average value for the KRED project. As can be seen in Fig. 4, Llama obtained a more consistent increase of MI over the different files that were enhanced, with only six files that witnessed a decrease in MI. On the other hand, Mixtral had a higher number of files where the MI was unchanged or decreased.

3.1 Comment Density (ComD)

As for ComD (Fig. 5), it can be seen that the percentage of comments in the codebase increased on average for all the modified sets of files except those modified with Mixtral, with the highest increase in average obtained with DeepSeek (+4.65%), closely followed by Llama (+3.64%). DeepSeek dramatically increased documentation in previously uncommented files (e.g. from 0% to over 40% in

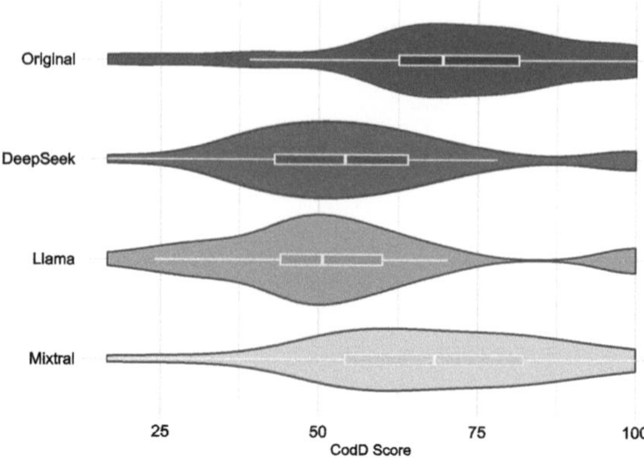

Fig. 7. Distribution of CodD.

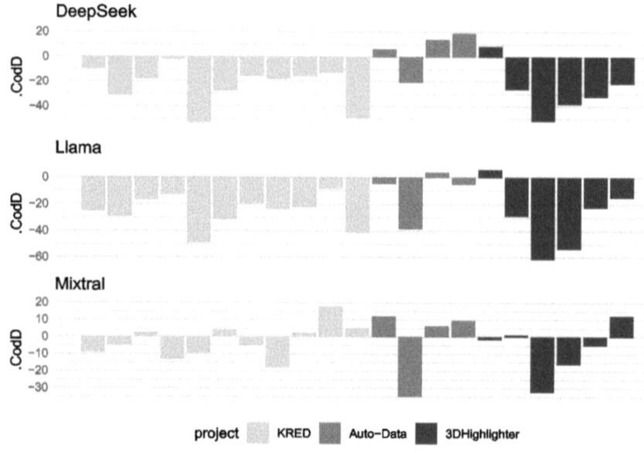

Fig. 8. Differences in CodD for modified files.

some scripts). Shallow results were obtained by using the Llama model. Mixtral made more selective documentation insertions, and many scripts retained very low ComD with the exception of a few sharp spikes. As it can be seen in Fig. 6, DeepSeek and Llama provided a more consistent increase of ComD (only 6 negative cases for DeepSeek and 8 for Llama) whilst Mixtral provided benefits in terms of ComD only in three cases.

3.2 Code Density (CodD)

Regarding CodD (Fig. 7), it can be observed that CodD decreased for all the sets of files provided by the LLMs (-13.68% for DeepSeek, -17.74% for Llama, -2.61% for Mixtral). This result was expected since CodD has by definition an opposite trend with respect to the one for ComD. The largest decrease in CodD was obtained for Llama (-17.22%), followed by DeepSeek (-13.68%) and Mixtral (-2.51%). As it can be seen in Fig. 8, all the models provided a consistent decrease over most of the files for CodD. Exceptions happened especially for the Auto-Data project for all the considered models.

3.3   Answer to Research Question

In order to answer our research question we defined the Null Hypoteses reported in Table 3 and tested them using a *Repeated Measures Analysis of Variance (RM-ANOVA)*. In this context:

- $MI, ComD, CodD$ refer to the metrics computed on the original file.
- $MI_x, ComD_x, CodD_x$ refer to the metrics computed on the resulting file modified by the LLM x, where x varies between DeepSeek, Llama, and Mixtral.

Normality and sphericity were preliminarily verified. Mauchly's test confirmed that the assumption of sphericity was not violated, and inspection of the residuals supported the assumption of normality.

We adopt RM-ANOVA because all measurements were obtained from the same subjects across multiple within-subject conditions, ensuring a paired design and controlling for inter-subject variability. For each of the three metrics under investigation – MI, ComD, CodD – we conducted a separate RM-ANOVA to evaluate whether the means across the four conditions differed significantly. Following a significant RM-ANOVA result, we performed pairwise dependent-sample t-tests with Bonferroni correction to balance the inflation of Type I error due to multiple comparisons. All statistical analyses were conducted using the R environment.

Concerning MI, the RM-ANOVA test revealed a statistically significant result on the analyzed metric (p = 0.014). However, subsequent Bonferroni-adjusted pairwise t-tests did not reveal statistically significant differences between any specific pairs of conditions (p > 0.17 in all cases), except for the comparison between MI and MI_{Llama}, which showed a marginally significant unadjusted p-value of 0.032, but this did not survive correction (p = 0.096).

Regarding $ComD$, the RM-ANOVA test did not reveal a statistically significant effect of condition (p = 0.126). Pairwise comparisons using Bonferroni-adjusted paired t-tests also failed to detect statistically significant differences between any specific pairs of conditions (p ≥ 0.075 in all cases), despite uncorrected p-values suggesting a possible difference between $ComD$ and $ComD_{\text{Llama}}$ (p = 0.037), which did not survive adjustment.

Finally, regarding $CodD$, the RM-ANOVA test revealed a statistically significant difference (p < 0.001). Bonferroni-adjusted pairwise t-tests revealed several statistically significant differences between conditions. In particular, $CodD$ differed significantly from $CodD_{\text{DeepSeek}}$ (p = 0.00022), and $CodD_{\text{Llama}}$ (p < 0.00001). Additional differences were observed between all the observable pairs. These results lead to the following answer to our research question:

```
def forward(self, predictions, targets):
"""Compute combined Softmax and BCE loss.
Args:
    predictions (torch.Tensor): Model predictions, targets (torch.
        Tensor): Ground truth values

Returns:torch.Tensor: Computed loss value
"""
predictions = self.config['trainer']['smooth_lamda'] * predictions
predictions = self.softmax(predictions)
return self.bce_loss(predictions, targets)
```

Fig. 9. Sample of generated comments.

```
def forward(self, predict, truth):
    predict = self.config['trainer']['smooth_lamda'] * predict
    predict = self.softmax(predict)
    loss = self.bceloss(predict, truth)
    return loss

def forward(self, predictions, targets):
    predictions = self.config['trainer']['smooth_lamda'] *
        predictions
    predictions = self.softmax(predictions)
    return self.bce_loss(predictions, targets)
```

Fig. 10. Sample of MI-related improvement of a source file.

> **Answer to Research Question:** Statistical analysis shows a significant effect of the application of LLM-based refactorings on MI ($p = 0.014$), and CodD ($p < 0.001$) metrics, while we don't observe statistically significance in the improvement of ComD. These results support the viability of LLMs as effective tools for automating software maintainability improvement.

4   Discussion

Our research shows that LLM-based code refactoring can improve software maintainability and documentation quality, though effectiveness varies by model and metric. Across all models, improvements were most consistent in MI, suggesting that LLMs help enhance readability, organization, or reduce complexity, aligning with evidence of their role as intelligent refactoring agents with minimal human oversight.

These results highlight both the promise and limits of current LLMs as maintainability enhancers. While measurable gains–especially in MI–are possible, consistency, generalizability, and the true interpretability of changes remain open issues. Higher metric scores may not always reflect long-term maintainability. The weaker statistical support in pairwise comparisons suggests the need for complementary evaluations, such as developer surveys or qualitative analyses. To this end, one author reviewed generated samples, confirming that LLM-introduced comments were generally readable and aligned with function behavior. An example of a generated comment is reported in Fig. 9.

As an example for MI improvement, in Fig. 10 we compare the `forward` function (in KRED.py file of the KRED project) before and after application of the DeepSeek model. As reported by the model itself in its comments for the modifications, the main changes for improved maintainability were a change in the return value formatting and changes in the names of variables for better readability. We sampled code generated by the models, and we were unable to find functions that were functionally not working after the modifications introduced by the LLMs, therefore, in all analyzed cases, the LLMs applied changes that did not go against code functional requirements.

From the described results, we can speculate that each model utilized embodies a distinct refactoring strategy: DeepSeek maximizes readability through comments, Llama balances incremental improvements, and Mixtral optimizes structural quality with minimal code expansion. The optimal choice depends on prioritizing MI, ComD, or CodD according to project goals.

5   Threats to Validity

To discuss the possible threats related to our study, we refer to the categorization of threats to validity in Software Engineering provided by Feldt et al. [13].

Threats to construct validity are related to wrong operational measures for the studied concepts. In the case of our study, this threat is principally associated with the selection of the metrics used to measure maintainability and readability of Python code. Although the related literature has several lower-level metrics measuring each a single facet of code quality, we sought to use MI, a metric widely used in the literature that combines the Halstead volume, measuring complexity in terms of operators and operands, with the CC, which addresses the execution flow graph, and with the source and comment lines of code. Thus, MI allows a proper comparison of the different aspects characterizing code quality. Moreover, to avoid calculation errors, we relied on a reliable tool that automatically computes the metrics. However, while the Maintainability Index offers a practical measure, its original design for languages such as C++ and Smalltalk raises questions about its direct applicability to Python, suggesting that results should be interpreted with care.

Threats to external validity are related to the limited generalization of the results of the study. The discussed results are computed on a limited sample of source files, on three open-source projects written in Python, and with three specific LLMs. Therefore, our results are not generalizable to projects of different nature and sizes, written in different languages, and may not reflect the output of different LLM engines. Although we used well-grounded prompt engineering techniques, we acknowledge the possibility of obtaining varying results by changing the prompts.

Threats to conclusion validity are related to the confidence in the results of the study based on the conducted test. All the measures were automatically collected using pre-validated tools. Additionally, for the statistical analysis, we opted for RM-ANOVA. The experimental design involves repeated measurements of the same variables for each Python program under four conditions:

the original version and the three refactored variants. This setup aligns well with the use of RM-ANOVA, which is specifically designed to compare multiple conditions applied to the same subjects or units – in this case, the programs. Given the unpredictability of the output of LLM engines, it is possible that the conclusions of this study could not be fully reproduced by replications.

Threats to internal validity are related to potential bias that may interfere with the logical link between independent and dependent variables. One potential internal validity threat in our experiment is the initial variability among the programs, as differences in size, complexity, or structure may influence the used metrics, independently of the refactoring applied. Additionally, biases inherent in the refactoring models could affect outcomes, as each model may prioritize different aspects of code quality, leading to inconsistent improvements. Additionally, the refactoring process was not guided by a few-shot examples or demonstrations. While this strengthens the neutrality of the evaluation by avoiding model-specific tuning, it also introduces a threat related to the unpredictability and variability of the output, as models may interpret high-level instructions differently depending on their training and internal representations. The refactorings performed by the LLMs were not functionally evaluated; we simply performed a high-level code review on the produced code. Although the refactorings never created functional mutations, we cannot generalize this result, therefore, future assessments shall consider to functionally validating the code with tests. Furthermore, while the MI metric is widely used to assess maintainability, it may not fully capture all dimensions of maintainability, such as code readability or developer familiarity.

6 Related Work

Given the importance of the topic, several studies in the literature aim to estimate maintainability and improve it using LLMs [5,6,14,15].

The paper by Dillmann et al. [14] investigates whether LLMs can assess code maintainability by measuring how "surprising" code is to the model, using cross-entropy. The idea is that LLMs, trained on large codebases, may implicitly recognize good coding practices, so code that deviates from these patterns (i.e., has higher cross-entropy) might be less maintainable. Using a dataset of 304 Java classes rated by experts on maintainability aspects, the authors calculate cross-entropy scores with ten pre-trained LLMs. They compare these scores with expert ratings and evaluate whether cross-entropy, alone or with lines of code, predicts maintainability. Initially, high cross-entropy correlated with higher maintainability, but when controlling for LLOC, the relationship reversed. LLOC alone was a stronger predictor, and adding cross-entropy offered little improvement. In conclusion, while cross-entropy shows some promise when LLOC is accounted for, it is not yet a reliable standalone metric for maintainability. In contrast, our paper focuses not on assessing code maintainability with LLMs, but on enhancing it through LLM-driven refactoring.

Another relevant study on code quality evaluation using LLMs is the one introduced in [5]. The authors investigate how Large Language Models can be used as static analysis tools to assess code quality – covering aspects like complexity, readability, testability, reusability, and coding practices. They compare the performance of two LLMs (GPT-3.5 Turbo and GPT-4o) with Sonar-Qube's Maintainability metric, analyzing 1,641 classes from two open-source Java projects. The results show that GPT-3.5 Turbo aligns well with Sonar-Qube's assessments, indicating that LLMs can provide meaningful insights into code quality. However, GPT-4o delivered less consistent results, sometimes rating lower-quality code more favorably, suggesting differences in how models interpret quality. In this case as well, the objective differs from ours, the tool used for metric calculation varies (SonarQube vs. Radon), and the programming languages of the analyzed projects are different.

Zhang et al. [15] analyzed code smells in Python code generated by GitHub Copilot and evaluated Copilot Chat's ability to fix them. Using a dataset of 102 smells, they found that 8 of 10 types were present–Multiply-Nested Container being the most common–and Copilot Chat fixed up to 87.1% of issues, performing better with more detailed prompts. Similarly, our work also demonstrates the potential of LLMs to improve Python code quality, even without relying on Copilot Chat, by using simpler prompts and standalone models capable of performing effective code refactoring.

Another study that highlights the potential of LLMs in aiding code refactoring and simplifying the complexity of Python code is the work by Shirafuji et al. [6]. Unlike their approach, which relies on few-shot examples and tailored prompts to steer the refactoring process, our work adopts a zero-shot strategy. This choice allows us to directly evaluate the intrinsic capabilities of LLMs in performing refactoring tasks without external guidance. While Shirafuji et al. report strong quantitative results–95.68% of programs successfully refactored, with an average 17.35% reduction in CC and a 25.84% decrease in lines of code (for semantically correct outputs)–our approach complements this by providing insights into the models' inherent ability to generalize refactoring behavior without handcrafted examples.

7   Conclusion and Future Work

In this study, we investigate the potential of LLMs to improve code maintainability through automated refactoring. We examined 29 Python scripts sourced from three open-source projects, using three different open-source LLMs. Our results show a statistically significant improvement in maintainability, particularly in terms of the Maintainability Index and Code Density metrics, thereby supporting the viability of LLMs as effective tools for software quality improvement, particularly in terms of maintainability.

As future work, we envision extending the starting set of source files by considering a more diverse range of open-source projects, exploring different prompt engineering strategies, and evaluating the applicability of different LLMs. In particular, experimenting with specialized CodeLLMs such as CodeQwen and DeepseekCoder could provide further insights into how domain-optimized models compare with general-purpose LLMs in the context of code refactoring and maintainability. In addition to the qualitative evaluation of the results, we plan to assess the functional correctness of the generated code using automated test suites and evaluate the accuracy of the generated comments by comparing them to a ground truth of correct comments written by human developers. Finally, we plan to supplement the quantitative results with a qualitative human evaluation, such as a developer survey, to assess whether the observed metric improvements translate into tangible, human-centric benefits in real development contexts.

References

1. Nikolić, D., Stefanović, D., Dakić, D., Sladojević, S., Ristić, S.: Analysis of the tools for static code analysis. In: 2021 20th International Symposium INFOTEH-JAHORINA (INFOTEH), pp. 1–6 (2021)
2. Tom, E., Aurum, A., Vidgen, R.: An exploration of technical debt. J. Syst. Softw. **86**(6), 1498–1516 (2013)
3. Al Dallal, J., Abdin, A.: Empirical evaluation of the impact of object-oriented code refactoring on quality attributes: a systematic literature review. IEEE Trans. Softw. Eng. **44**(1), 44–69 (2018)
4. Wadhwa, N., et al.: Core: resolving code quality issues using LLMs, New York, NY, USA (2024)
5. da Silva Simões, I.R., Venson, E.: Evaluating source code quality with large language models: a comparative study (2024). https://arxiv.org/abs/2408.07082
6. Shirafuji, A., Oda, Y., Suzuki, J., Morishita, M., Watanobe, Y.: Refactoring programs using large language models with few-shot examples. In: 2023 30th Asia-Pacific Software Engineering Conference (APSEC), pp. 151–160. IEEE (2023)
7. Van Solingen, R., Basili, V., Caldiera, G., Rombach, H.D.: Goal question metric (GQM) approach. Encyclopedia of Software Engineering (2002)
8. Brown, T.B., et al.: Language models are few-shot learners (2020). https://arxiv.org/abs/2005.14165
9. Sahoo, P., Singh, A.K., Saha, S., Jain, V., Mondal, S., Chadha, A.: A systematic survey of prompt engineering in large language models: techniques and applications, arXiv preprint arXiv:2402.07927
10. Chidamber, S., Kemerer, C.: A metrics suite for object oriented design. IEEE Trans. Software Eng. **20**(6), 476–493 (1994)
11. Halstead, M.H.: Elements of Software Science (Operating and programming systems series). Elsevier Science Inc., USA (1977)
12. McCabe, T.: A complexity measure. IEEE Trans. Softw. Eng. SE **2**(4), 308–320 (1976)
13. Feldt, R., Magazinius, A.: Validity threats in empirical software engineering research-an initial survey. In: International Conference on Software Engineering and Knowledge Engineering (SEKE), pp. 374–379 (2010)
14. Dillmann, M., Siebert, J., Trendowicz, A.: Evaluation of large language models for assessing code maintainability (2024). https://arxiv.org/abs/2401.12714
15. Zhang, B., Liang, P., Feng, Q., Fu, Y., Li, Z.: Copilot-in-the-loop: fixing code smells in copilot-generated python code using copilot. In: Proceedings of the 39th IEEE/ACM International Conference on Automated Software Engineering, ASE 2024, pp. 2230–2234. ACM, New York (2024)

An Investigation of Low-Code Development Adoption in a Finnish IT Consulting Firm

Dongmei Gao$^{(\boxtimes)}$ ⓘ and Fabian Fagerholm ⓘ

Aalto University, Espoo, Finland
`{dongmei.gao,fabian.fagerholm}@aalto.fi`

Abstract. Given the growing popularity and productivity promises of low-code development (LCD), it seems natural that software consulting firms are increasingly offering low-code solutions. This paper explores how a Finnish consulting firm has adopted two LCD platforms and how they impact internal workflows and client relationships. We interviewed 11 members of the firm's LCD team to understand their experience and how clients perceive low-code solutions. While LCD has not fundamentally changed the overall development process or collaboration style, it has enabled faster development and adjustments to the workflow. Clients were generally satisfied, though concerns remain. Participants were positive about LCD and its future potential. The study outlines both benefits and challenges of LCD adoption and highlights key considerations for clients, such as feature limitations, vendor lock-in, cost, and the distribution of responsibilities between consulting firms and platform vendors.

Keywords: low-code development · consulting firm · technology adoption · developer experience

1 Introduction

Over the past few decades, new technologies have continuously emerged and seamlessly integrated into private and business life. To stay competitive, companies are increasingly prioritising business model innovation [28] and embracing digital transformation [17]. Finland's information and communication technology (ICT) industry has experienced major structural changes in the early 2000s [18]. With the rapid downfall of Nokia, once the world's largest mobile phone manufacturer, nearly 10% of ICT manufacturing firms shifted to ICT services between 2007 and 2012, reflecting a broader industry transformation. This shift also indicates significant growth in consulting firms within this sector.

Like their clients, consulting firms face a digital transformation process to enhance service delivery and leverage digital consulting assets [4]. This transformation involves adapting organisational structures, evolving digital business models, and building new forms of client interaction, digital offerings, and ecosystem partnerships [20]. Low-code solutions have emerged in consulting firms as

G. Scanniello et al. (Eds.): PROFES 2025, LNCS 16361, pp. 169–185, 2026.
https://doi.org/10.1007/978-3-032-12089-2_11

a pivotal enabler in this shift. Consulting firms increasingly partner with leading low-code development platform (LCDP) vendors to strengthen their service capabilities and extend their solution offerings.

Although many consulting firms have adopted LCDPs, there is limited research on how these platforms are integrated into consulting practices, how consultants navigate their limitations, or how they influence client relationships. This study investigates the adoption of two different LCDPs within a Finnish consulting firm to deliver low-code solutions to clients. The aim is to explore both the organisational and individual dimensions of adoption, focusing on the initiation process, impacts on team workflows, client perspectives, and consultants' personal experience, as reflected in the following research questions:

RQ1: How are low-code solutions initiated in consulting-client cooperation?
RQ2: How does LCD impact the workflow in software development teams?
RQ3: What are clients' perspectives regarding LCD?
RQ4: What are LCD team members' personal experience with LCD in a consulting context?

This research makes three major contributions:

- It provides insights into the motivations and challenges of adopting LCDPs in consulting firms, with a particular focus on the Finnish market.
- It supports researchers and platform vendors in refining their focus on the broader adoption and untapped opportunities of LCD.
- It develops evidence-based points regarding LCD for client companies when considering more efficient and cost-effective solutions for their business needs.

The rest of this paper is structured as follows: Sect. 2 discusses the background of this study. Section 3 outlines the research methodology. Section 4 reports the results. Section 5 discusses the key findings and threats to validity, while Sect. 6 concludes the study and suggests directions for future work.

2   Background

Low-code development (LCD) can be characterised as "a development approach that enhances rapid, flexible, and iterative software development by enabling quick business requirements translation through visual programming with a graphical interface, visual abstraction, and minimal hand-coding; and involving practitioners with various backgrounds and software development experience" [25]. In practice, LCD refers to the process of creating software applications using LCDPs as the primary environment. These platforms support various techniques [13] which might affect the actual development process. In this paper, we make a distinction between LCD as an approach to software development, and LCDPs as the development environments and tools used to carry out LCD.

2.1   Current Research on LCD Adoption

LCDPs are seeing growing adoption across organisations. Gartner predicts that by 2028, 60% of software development organisations will use enterprise LCDPs as their main internal developer platform, up from 10% in 2024 [22]. Academic research also reflects this trend. Alamin et al. [1] found increased community discussion around LCD adoption. Käss et al. examined adoption drivers and inhibitors through a literature review [14] and a Delphi study with industry experts [15]. Both researchers and industry experts cited improved development efficiency, reduced entry barriers, and lower knowledge requirements as top drivers. However, inhibitor rankings differed: lack of governance dominated the literature, while industry experts emphasised cultural resistance and reluctance to change.

LCDPs reportedly attract small and medium-sized companies (SMEs), helping accelerate company growth [2,5]. One significant advantage is the reduced application development time compared to traditional methods [5], which is especially valuable for startups prioritising innovation and market responsiveness [9,24]. SMEs often face limited resources, and LCDPs help by lowering development costs and technical barriers [3,6]. However, challenges remain. Some platforms lack flexibility or advanced features, limiting their suitability for specific business needs [5,12]. As an emerging technology, LCDPs may also raise concerns about long-term scalability and sustainability [2,24]. Still, LCDP adoption can enhance a startup's cognitive legitimacy, improving investor confidence [27].

2.2   IT Consulting in Finland and Its Relationship to LCD

The consulting industry dates back to the late 19th century [19], when the first modern consulting firms were established. Consulting involves providing specialized expertise in the processing of business-related issues, while a consultant is a professional who offers expert advice in a specific field of science or business to organisations or individuals [10,21]. As digitalisation intensifies, the consulting industry has been compelled to adapt, requiring new business models, expanded service areas, and innovative products. Consequently, IT consulting firms have become major global employers, significantly contributing to economic growth and social well-being [16]. The growing demand for digital transformation drives this expansion, as companies strive to stay competitive with the latest technologies. However, resource constraints, especially in SMEs, lead many to outsource IT expertise rather than maintain in-house teams [23].

Nokia's decline has fuelled the growth of consulting services in Finland [18]. By 2018, Finland had 1,818 computer hardware and software consultancy firms, making it the country's second-largest sub-industry [8]. Within IT services, computer programming accounted for 23.5% of turnover, while computer-related consultancy services made up 14.1% [26]. While academic research on LCD adoption in consulting is limited, firms like KPMG, Luxoft, Solita, and FPT Software publicly promote low-code solutions to their clients. They position LCD as a complement to traditional development, enabling everything from internal process digitalisation to large end-user applications. This study explores this emerging trend from the perspective of the Finnish IT consulting industry.

3   Research Method

To explore the role and impact of LCD in IT consulting, we conducted a case study with a Finnish consulting firm. While focused on one company, the participants work on diverse projects with various clients across multiple domains, providing a wide range of insights. We conducted semi-structured interviews and analysed the data using thematic analysis [7].

3.1   Context

Solita[1] is a 25-year-old Finnish consulting firm with ca. 2 200 employees in 10 European countries specializing in IT services, e-commerce, and knowledge management solutions for businesses and public sector organisations. Since 2020, it has offered low-code solutions to help digitalise clients' operations. Solita partners with two leading LCDPs: Microsoft Power Platform[2] and OutSystems[3]. Power Platform targets business users, enabling rapid app creation, workflow automation, and data analysis, with strong integration into Microsoft services, though it is less suited outside the Microsoft ecosystem. OutSystems is a professional-grade platform designed for complex, large-scale projects. It requires technical knowledge but simplifies coding and offers extensive customization, making it ideal for tailored solutions.

3.2   Participants

Eleven LCD team members from the company participated in the study. Except for the team lead, who oversees members working across platforms, all primarily work with a single platform. The group includes six developers, along with designers, architects, and project managers. Four participants have multiple roles, but only their primary roles are considered here. Participant details are shown in Table 1.

Six participants transferred internally to the LCD team from traditional development roles, with little prior LCD experience. Others had prior LCD experience before joining the company. Among them, two had limited traditional software development backgrounds, coming from the fields of business and art.

---

[1] https://www.solita.fi/.
[2] https://www.microsoft.com/en-us/power-platform.
[3] https://www.outsystems.com/.

Table 1. Participant demographics.

ID	Role	Platform	Duration of general low-code experience
P1	team lead	both	4 years
P2	developer	Power Platform	4 years
P3	developer	Power Platform	2 years
P4	designer	OutSystems	6 months
P5	developer	OutSystems	4 years
P6	developer	Power Platform	6 years
P7	developer	OutSystems	3 years
P8	architect	OutSystems	4 years
P9	designer	Power Platform	1.5 years
P10	project manager	OutSystems	1 years
P11	developer	Power Platform	7 years

3.3   Procedure

Interviews lasted one hour each and were conducted online via Microsoft Teams from 26th September to 28th November 2024. Questions covered four aspects: (i) background,(ii) work mode, (iii) customer collaboration and communication, (iv) overall perception of LCD. Transcriptions were auto-generated by Teams and manually corrected, then pseudonymized and imported into ATLAS.ti for coding. We employed thematic analysis [7] for data analysis, starting with organising transcripts by predefined themes, extracting key insights, and grouping them into broader themes. Finally, we examined the relationships within each theme to understand how individual perspectives collectively formed a cohesive overall narrative. The analysis proceeded in two rounds: the first summarised main ideas and was shared with all participants; two of them provided feedback that was incorporated into a more comprehensive second-round analysis, enhancing validity. The interview protocol and codebook are in the supplementary materials [11].

4   Results

Our analysis is structured around our four research questions. Themes that emerged during analysis are italicized, and key findings are highlighted in bold.

4.1   Initiating Low-Code Solutions in the Consulting Firm (RQ1)

Motivation. According to the LCD team lead (P1), Solita's main motivation for offering low-code solutions is a commitment to **continuous innovation and providing the best client experience**. This aligns with the company's culture of curiosity and exploring new ways of working. Another key driver is the

market pressure to stay competitive, with Solita viewing low-code solutions as essential to keeping ahead in the industry. Although Solita specializes in professional coding, traditional methods can be too costly for some cases, making it hard to win public tenders. Low-code solutions therefore **open new opportunities**, particularly in projects focused on internal process development and digitalisation. They offer an attractive, more affordable alternative for clients who are cost-conscious regarding internal projects.

LCD Adoption Decision. Clients adopt low-code solutions at Solita in two main ways: The first is that **clients directly request low-code solutions** (P1,5,10). In such cases, clients already have LCD practices in place but lack the necessary resources, leading them to turn to a consulting firm (P5). However, LCD is still not popularized among the general public, and many clients are unaware of it. More commonly, **Solita proposes low-code solutions after assessing client needs**. Both traditional and low-code solutions are evaluated to determine the best fit for each case (P1,2,8,10). A multidisciplinary sales team, with technical experts involved, plays a key role in the review process (P1). To further decide whether a low-code solution is a good idea, an early minimum viable product (MVP) might be created in the tendering process, offering clients an initial idea about what LCD is and how they can benefit from it (P2,6).

> **Answer to RQ1:** The consulting firm's motivation to adopt low-code solutions is driven by a commitment to continuous innovation, delivering exceptional client experiences, staying competitive, and pursuing new opportunities. Some clients are aware of LCD and request it directly, or it is recommended by the consulting firm, with each decision tailored to the client's specific needs and preferences.

4.2 Impact of LCD in Development Teams (RQ2)

Most participants viewed **LCDPs as just another development tool**, with no particular impact on their workflow or collaboration. The overall development lifecycle remains largely unchanged, continuing to rely on standard tools (e.g., Teams, Jira, etc.) and routines (e.g., daily and weekly meetings) at work. However, we did observe some differences compared to traditional development.

Preparation. LCD is quite flexible and straightforward to use, so most low-code projects have relatively **small teams**. One participant said his current project team only has two developers because they could do everything, unlike in traditional projects, which usually require front-end and back-end developers, architects, and other roles to be involved (P4). Moreover, the **team structure can be adjusted in low-code projects**. A participant highlighted the importance of thinking about service design and using platform tools effectively (P8). With this change in mindset and reduced development effort, they suggested having fewer developers or more architects in the team.

Before development starts, a preparation phase typically establishes a high-level backlog to estimate time and cost. The **speed and simplicity of LCD**

enables quick prototyping and idea testing (P11), often through the creation of MVPs. MVP specifications define the application's core functionality, primary goals, essential requirements, and key features needed to meet client needs (P3,6). Beyond validating LCDP suitability, **MVPs also serve as the foundation for functional software systems** that future development can build upon (P6,8,9). While MVPs are also used in traditional development, they are notably faster and easier to create with LCDPs. Unlike traditional development, **low-code solutions often require more upfront specification planning** due to their fast pace, which can outpace backlog preparation (P1,2,7). However, LCDPs' flexibility allows developers to adjust if the additional work is not what the clients need. As a result, sometimes they "preferred to do the development first and ask the client if this is right" (P7).

> "There have been situations where they planned something for us to do for the next couple of months, and then we have it done in a couple of weeks, and then we were wondering what to do next. And this has also sometimes led to situations where [...] the development goes ahead of specifications, which is not necessary." (P7)

Effective collaboration requires every team member to understand how LCD works. Initially, many employees knew only marketing claims rather than the platforms' actual functionality (P6). For example, LCDP is more than dragging and dropping; each component has unique properties that control dynamic adjustments and formula dependencies (P6). Developers often explain these details to ensure **a shared understanding of the platform within the team** (P10).

Implementation. Many emphasised the **easy and fast development with an LCDP** after the preparation work is ready. This fosters a **rapid feedback loop** (P1,7,8,9,11). Getting something visible done quickly allows for early input from clients and timely adjustments and improved alignment with client needs (P10). **LCDPs enable quick adaptation to changes**, not only through fast development but also due to their flexibility in allowing changes to applications (P5,8). When processes or methods are too rigid, adapting to changes becomes difficult. LCD significantly improves agility in this regard (P8). Moreover, the lightweight nature of Power Platform allows development directly from a web browser without setting up a complex development environment (P2).

Developers can focus more on business logic thanks to LCDPs' **pre-built functionality**, which ensures quality and reduces coding effort. For example, OutSystems offers well-structured patterns for building robust, adaptable architectures (P8), while Power Platform integrates seamlessly with other Microsoft products through a shared environment (P9). Additionally, the **visual interfaces of LCDPs improve flexibility and transparency** in development. It allows developers to easily review programs together via screen sharing, helping to trace the flow and efficiently pinpoint issues (P5,7).

> "It gives you a lot of flexibility and you don't have thousands of lines to scroll through to find something, but you can see it in a diagram. We

tried to break down the functionality so that we had these understandable chunks and implemented the functionality one by one." (P5)

To fully leverage LCDPs, participants stressed the importance of **following platform conventions** (P2,3,5). Developers often spend significant time adapting to new workflows required by the platform (P5,6). While these conventions streamline development, technical skills remain crucial to **overcome platform limitations** and tailor solutions to client needs (P7,9). For example, integrating external services can be difficult if unsupported, demanding creative workarounds (P5). Each platform comes with its limitations. Power Platform struggles with large data volumes affecting performance (P6), limited support for simultaneous multi-developer editing (P2,3,6), and outdated or sparse documentation (P2). OutSystems faces integration difficulties (P10) and limited customization due to restricted source code access (P7).

A common challenge for both platforms is **the lack of branching and version control features**. However, participants stated that this has not caused major issues, as the platform prevents publishing broken code and identifies errors quickly (P7). Developers can also revert to previous versions if needed (P1,2). A drawback is the difficulty in separating functionalities within releases (P5). To manage changes in existing features, developers often use feature flags to toggle alternative code paths. One participant stated that Microsoft is working to resolve this issue in Power Platform, with steady improvements (P6).

LCD differs slightly from traditional coding in design processes. UI designers are typically involved early on, but once the project is underway, **designers are not needed for each change** (P5). Supported by predefined design systems and platforms' UI components, developers can sketch simple UIs directly within the platform, often faster than using dedicated design tools like Figma (P7).

"If we need new types of views, I often design them myself. If something is unclear, I send sketches or, in OutSystems, screenshots of the implementation to the UI designer for feedback. I ask if they think it looks good, and they may provide input or approve it as is." (P7)

A business designer (P4) shared his first experience joining an OutSystems low-code project, focusing on business logic design. He highlighted the small team size and fast pace of LCD, which called for a rougher, more exploratory design approach to quickly test ideas. He also found design easier, as he did not need to create detailed UX layouts constantly; he could simply describe what was needed and see the design come to life the next day.

Testing and Deployment. OutSystems offers dedicated testing tools, whereas Power Platform lacks the comprehensive testing features expected by professional developers, resulting in a **reliance on manual testing** via the app's user interface (P1). However, because low-code projects are typically small in scope, internal testing and client acceptance testing are usually sufficient. Crucially, both platforms are considered robust enough that developers **do not need to test the underlying code**, which significantly reduces testing effort compared to traditional development (P2,8). Regarding deployment, Power Platform apps are entirely confined within the Microsoft ecosystem, while OutSystems supports more flexibility, allowing deployment both on-premise and in the cloud (P5).

Maintenance. Not all participants had reached the maintenance phase, defined here as the period following the initial delivery of an application, and involving tasks such as monitoring and ongoing improvement. However, most agreed that, in general, **maintenance is less demanding** in low-code projects compared to traditional development (P1,8). That said, **the level of required maintenance can vary based on project complexity**. For instance, using external databases instead of the default internal Microsoft database can significantly increase maintenance effort (P6). A recurring concern was the impact of vendor-controlled platform updates (P3,4,6,11). These updates can introduce changes that affect application functionality, meaning developers **must closely monitor platform updates to ensure continued performance and stability**.

> "We don't have much visibility to those Microsoft updates. If they're changing something, it is very hard [to be] proactive and see that it's coming. There's a schedule of some updates and big features that they're going to be updating in this platform, but sometimes they're fixing something and we don't get any information of that." (P11)

Platform updates can be managed in several ways, such as regularly monitoring apps, adding error visibility, and reviewing logs to track issues. However, in practice, problems often surface through user reports, after which the responsible party is identified (P11). If an issue stems from the platform itself and cannot be fixed, it must be escalated to the vendor (P1). Less ongoing maintenance can also pose challenges for clients. They often expect a service-level agreement and a clear contact for support. However, low-code projects typically involve minimal continuous development and fewer incidents, making it harder for Solita to justify dedicated resources. Compared to traditional projects, low-code initiatives are smaller and shorter, leading Solita to consider **establishing a central client service team** to support multiple projects (P1).

Answer to RQ2: Compared to traditional development, LCDPs are seen as development tools that do not fundamentally change the development life cycle or team collaboration. They simplify and speed up development, enabling rapid prototyping and quick adjustments. Visual interfaces and fast feedback enhance teamwork. The studied platforms are robust, with straightforward testing and maintenance, but each has limitations. Understanding and overcoming limitations requires technical skills and extra effort. Common challenges include the need for more upfront preparation, adherence to platform conventions, the lack of version control, and monitoring platform updates.

4.3   Clients' Perspectives on LCD Adoption (RQ3)

The collaboration model between the consulting firm and client companies typically varies case by case. Similar to its impact on internal team dynamics, LCD adoption has minimal direct effect on consultantâĂŞclient collaboration. However, introducing new technology often brings a mix of confusion, concerns, and expectations. As participants noted, most client-side employees are non-technical, requiring issues to be communicated in layman's terms.

Most participants noted that **clients were generally positive and excited about low-code solutions**, often drawn in by marketing claims about rapid productivity (P5). However, some initial doubts emerged, particularly around the speed of early project phases. Clients sometimes expected immediate results and grew concerned when preparation work (e.g., planning, design, architecture) took longer than anticipated (P7,8,10). In response to this, participants clarified that while these phases still require time, once development begins, the pace accelerates significantly, typically resulting in client satisfaction (P7,10).

Some clients have little or no knowledge of LCD or software development in general. Instead of focusing on specific tools, they **prioritise the people they work with** and **trust Solita to choose the best technologies for them** (P4). Trust plays a central role in the consulting-client relationship. Solita aims to build this trust early, which helps clients feel confident in granting access and recognising the value provided. As a result, collaboration tends to be smooth, with clients open to dialogue and eager to support joint efforts (P1).

> "They trust us more than OutSystems or low code in general, but we trust low code, so we are selling low code for them, and they are buying what we recommend them to buy. So it's kind of a trust chain." (P4)

Moreover, communication plays a crucial role in the consulting-client relationship. As noted earlier, LCD enables **shorter feedback cycles and greater flexibility during development**. Developers use LCDPs to quickly create a mockup and gather feedback by asking clients if it reflects their needs. If changes are required, developers can adjust the design on the spot and immediately show the results, avoiding lengthy exchanges of screenshots and interpretations (P7).

Most participants emphasised the importance of **communicating the features, strengths, and limitations of LCD to clients**. The LCD team takes responsibility for guiding clients through the decision-making process, offering clear explanations to support informed decisions (P8). We categorised the key considerations for clients into three groups:

Applicability of Low-Code Solutions. The first issue to address with clients is tool suitability. Despite market claims, **low-code solutions may not be ideal for all use cases**, particularly those that are critical or complex. Unexpected application crashes can occur due to platform updates (P11). **Vendor lock-in is another concern**. If a client later chooses to migrate to another LCDP from the current one, it can be difficult. For instance, P4 recalled a negative experience manually migrating away from OutSystems after a major update. Power

Platform, tightly integrated with the Microsoft ecosystem, also poses challenges. Although it is technically possible to export code (e.g., in C# or JavaScript), graphical representations and visual workflows created within the platform are lost and hard to restore (P8). Finally, **managing client expectations is crucial when needs conflict with platform conventions**. Some requirements may not be fully supported by the LCDP or may work differently than expected. While workarounds are possible, they can be time-consuming and costly. Developers usually present the trade-offs to clients and guide them to choose between their original vision and a more efficient platform-aligned solution (P5).

Practical Considerations. **The division of responsibilities between the consultancy and the platform vendor should be recognised**. Licensing and cybersecurity are typically vendor-managed (P4), but contacting vendors can be slow and affect efficiency. While having a vendor representative involved in the project could streamline support, it is not always guaranteed (P4). More importantly, platform updates can occasionally break applications (P11), leaving clients unsure who to contact, often reaching out to the consultancy first.

Additionally, **platforms use varying pricing models, complicating cost comparisons**. Projects typically involve multiple development environments: test, development, and production. Power Platform includes all environments in its license, whereas OutSystems' default package covers only two (P1). License fees also depend on the number of features and users, which can be hard to estimate early in the project (P4). Moreover, LCDPs are constantly evolving, with frequent licensing changes that can confuse clients. **Staying informed and communicating any changes promptly to clients** is crucial (P4,11).

> "License is always a pain in the negotiation stage for everyone because nobody can understand it. Even though [you ask] Microsoft, they can't give you a straight answer." (P9)

The costs of the low-code solution include the platform's license fee and the consulting firm's service fee. Considering the cost and perceived value, **comparing costs between LCD and traditional development is very difficult**. It is "not even an apples-to-oranges comparison, but rather apples to hammers" (P8).

> "It could be said that they pay us for 100 development cases and then they pay the same for OutSystems just to run the software. And that can feel like a lot, especially since they might not have a strong background in software development. But they don't realise [with the same budget], we can only produce three or four development cases for them with the traditional method. It seems like they expect [development with both methods to cost the same], and now with OutSystems, they have to pay the license fee on top of the development cost." (P4)

Finally, developers expect **more upfront planning** to match LCD's fast pace (P7). Though preparation phases may take time, development speeds up quickly once the groundwork is laid, often faster than specifications can keep up.

Knowledge and Openness. Solita tries to provide good services for its clients, so it is responsible for understanding clients' needs, picking the right tool, and achieving the business goal. In general, **clients do not need to have any prior knowledge about the technical part of LCD** (P2,3,4). Some clients had already heard about the capabilities and limitations of LCD when they were purchasing licenses for the platform (P5). However, some clients accept what salespeople tell them without fully understanding the implications. When development starts, they might struggle to grasp what LCD truly entails. They may believe it is entirely out-of-the-box and that applications will run instantly, which is not the case (P8). Participants suggested that **clients would benefit from at least a basic, high-level understanding of LCD**, such as recognising Microsoft as an ecosystem and knowing about Dataverse within the Power Platform (P9). It is also important for clients to be aware of LCD limitations (P6) and to understand that while development may be faster and easier, areas like design, testing, and architecture still require significant time and effort (P2,7,10). Having a shared understanding promotes clearer communication and reduces frustration. It is recommended that **clients have someone in their organisation with some LCD experience to facilitate this process** (P9).

Clients' Knowledge About LCD Varies. Some overestimate LCD capabilities, while others underestimate its potential. Most recognise its fast development, but lack awareness of the technical limits, and some even assume it can do everything (P3). One (P6) shared a case where a client expected LCD apps to be unattractive or inflexible because they were "out-of-the-box" with limited customisability. They further emphasised that LCD can achieve much more than expected, as long as its limitations are understood and carefully worked around.

Moreover, **being open-minded** is crucial for successful collaboration in both LCD and traditional projects (P1,8,9). This openness means clients trust Solita enough to grant access and actively engage in discussions. In fast-paced low-code projects, involving business stakeholders enhances communication, as their business knowledge helps articulate requirements more effectively.

> **Answer to RQ3:** Participants noted that clients generally respond positively to LCD, showing trust in consultants. Smooth client-consultancy cooperation depends on four factors: (i) fast feedback cycles and flexibility provided by LCDPs, (ii) clear communication about features, (iii) basic understanding of LCDPs, and (iv) openness.

4.4 Low-Code Developers' Experience and Reflections (RQ4)

Personal Experience. Most participants were **enthusiastic** about LCD, **appreciating its creative and straightforward approach**. They enjoyed using diverse tools like PowerPoint and Power Apps, often integrating them for reporting (P3). LCDP's simplicity allows building solutions without deep technical skills, appealing to those who prefer to avoid complex coding (P4,5,8,9). Participants valued focusing on core tasks like system design and business logic while the platform handled routine work. They also expressed a desire to deepen their

LCD expertise int he future. Five participants **enjoyed the continuous learning** that LCD demands. P5 highlighted gaining valuable knowledge by solving complex problems as the project evolved. The need for ongoing learning is crucial due to the constant evolution of platforms (P3,6), although this adaptability can sometimes be frustrating (P3).

Three participants noted the **career opportunities** that LCD offers. One (P5) said it advanced his career faster than traditional development. Another (P11) said client satisfaction with quick, visible results boosted his motivation and career. Designers also seek opportunities with LCD. One designer (P4) appreciated the business-driven approach and aimed to bridge LCD and design, ensuring that design remains a key consideration when selling low-code solutions. When asked about the future career preference between traditional development and LCD, all participants were positive about the future of LCD and therefore would like to **stay in the LCD space to see what happens**.

Although participants had not yet used AI features in LCDPs in their work, they reflected on the **uncertain role of AI in the future of LCD**, envisioning scenarios from seamless integration to the complete replacement of LCD by AI. They expressed an intention to closely follow developments in this area.

Tips for Newcomers Entering the LCD Field. We asked participants if they had any tips for newcomers in the LCD field. They emphasised skills in four areas:(i) communication (5 participants),(ii) continuous learning (3),(iii) problem-solving (4), and (iv) technical skills (9). Technical skills were considered essential, but success in LCD also depends greatly on strong communication, adaptability, and the ability to collaborate effectively with different roles.

> **Answer to RQ4:** Participants appreciate LCD for its creativity, learning potential, and career growth. Key skills for newcomers include communication, continuous learning, problem-solving, and technical know-how. Participants expect LCD to keep advancing, with clients increasingly building apps independently while consultants provide support. Some participants discussed the relationship between LCD and AI, and considered the latter to be crucial for LCD's future, but containing much uncertainty.

5   Discussion

5.1   Client-Consulting-Platform Vendor Relationship

Client-Consulting: Trust and communication are vital in client-consultant relationships. Trust ensures clients believe the firm acts in their best interest, even when challenges arise. Clear communication enables accurate requirements and smooth collaboration. As LCDPs remain unfamiliar to many, their capabilities and limits must be clearly explained to avoid frustration from unmet expectations. Honest, timely dialogue, along with LCDPs' visual tools and fast feedback loops, improves understanding and satisfaction.

Consulting-Platform Vendor. Offering low-code solutions presents both risks and opportunities for consulting firms. Relying on third-party platforms can pose challenges in security and quality control, especially when technical issues arise beyond the firm's control. However, LCDPs also enable simpler internal solutions for clients, expanding business opportunities. Promoting LCD increases visibility for platform vendors, making partner selection critical. To stay competitive, consulting firms must effectively communicate platform capabilities to clients and maintain strong vendor partnerships, staying informed as platforms evolve.

Client-Platform Vendor. Some clients were already familiar with low-code and requested it, while others had no prior exposure. Consulting firms act as intermediaries, but issues like security must often be addressed directly by platform vendors. Involving a vendor representative or a client stakeholder with LCD experience can support smoother adoption. Clients frequently research LCD online, underscoring the value of a strong user community for support and idea sharing. License fees are a common concern, often seen as added costs beyond service fees. However, they fund platform development and support diverse client needs. Transparent pricing models and helping clients understand the long-term value of licensing can reduce resistance. Despite initial cost concerns, LCD often delivers benefits that outweigh traditional development methods.

5.2   LCD's Impact on Individuals

Many participants viewed LCDPs as just development tools that do not fundamentally change the project life cycle or collaboration. While offering unique benefits and challenges, tool choice depends on project needs. Excitement around new technology partly explains why some shifted from traditional development to LCD. In this study, LCDPs had minimal impact on UI/UX designers, who keep using familiar tools but must adapt to faster development. Developers benefit by focusing more on business logic than low-level code. Testing is easier thanks to built-in quality controls. Communication and overcoming platform limitations remain challenges, but as familiarity and platform evolution progress, these improve. Overall, participants are optimistic about LCD's future.

Most transitioned to LCD through online learning and practice, but found mentorship useful to avoid inefficient early solutions. LCD supports diverse problem-solving approaches and emphasises soft skills like communication. Strong technical skills remain essential to handle platform limits. LCD fosters professional growth by blending technical expertise with adaptability.

Our findings point towards a general LCD adoption in consulting firms, with professional developers leading the transition and integrating LCD into existing workflows. On the client side, non-technical staff may initially struggle but can be supported by external developers or trained internal business professionals.

5.3   Threats to Validity

Construct Validity. This study does not compare Power Platform and OutSystems in detail due to uneven role distribution across projects (e.g., only OutSystems projects involved project managers) and the absence of participants with hands-on experience in both platforms. While platforms differ in features, several common challenges are observed. Consequently, we focus on general insights into LCD adoption rather than platform-specific or quantitative comparisons. Cost and time estimates were also excluded, as they vary significantly by project. Instead, we highlight how LCDPs affect collaboration and workflows.

Interval Validity. This study relies on self-reported data, which may be affected by recall and social desirability biases. As all participants came from the same company, there is also a risk of organisational bias. To mitigate these effects, we emphasised anonymity and voluntary participation before each interview.

External Validity. This study examines a single Finnish consulting firm, which may limit the generalisability of the findings, particularly to other markets. A broader sample across firms would offer a more comprehensive view of LCD adoption in Finland. Solita was selected for its industry leadership and long-standing experience with LCD. Having transitioned from traditional development, teams initially applied conventional methods, gradually adapting to platform-specific challenges. Today, Solita uses LCDPs to accelerate proof-of-concept work and improve customer engagement. Its journey illustrates how traditional and LCD practices can be effectively combined, offering insights beyond this case.

6   Conclusions

Adopting LCD in consulting firms brings both opportunities and challenges. Success with LCD depends on strong internal collaboration and clear communication with both platform vendors and clients. This interview-based case study of Solitan's LCD team explores how LCDPs influence daily work, key challenges, and practitioner perspectives. While LCD does not radically change the development life cycle, it reshapes workflows and roles. Consulting firms play a critical role in managing expectations and bridging gaps between clients and vendors. Future research should explore broader adoption across consulting firms and investigate client perspectives in more detail, as well as compare practices and impacts across different platforms. Independent LCD adoption within client companies also warrants further investigation. Our ongoing work aims to identify effective LCD practices across diverse settings.

Acknowledgments. We would like to express our sincere gratitude to Solita for their collaboration and support throughout this study, and particularly to the LCD team members who generously shared their experiences and insights during the interviews.

References

1. Alamin, M.A.A., Uddin, G., Malakar, S., Afroz, S., Haider, T., Iqbal, A.: Developer discussion topics on the adoption and barriers of low code software development platforms. Empir. Softw. Eng. **28**(1), 4 (2023)
2. Bhattacharyya, S.S., Kumar, S.: Study of deployment of "low code no code" applications toward improving digitization of supply chain management. J. Sci. Technol. Policy Manag. **14**(2), 271–287 (2023)
3. Bies, L., Weber, M., Greff, T., Werth, D.: A mixed-methods study of low-code development platforms: drivers of digital innovation in SMEs. In: 2022 International Conference on Electrical, Computer, Communications and Mechatronics Engineering (ICECCME), pp. 1–6. IEEE (2022)
4. Bode, M., Deneva, M., van Sinderen, M.J.: Requirements for digital IT consulting services and their provision through digital consulting platforms-results from a focus group study. In: 2021 IEEE 23rd Conference on Business Informatics (CBI), vol. 1, pp. 111–120. IEEE (2021)
5. Brühl, S., Bernsteiner, R., Ploder, C., Dilger, T., Spiess, T.: The use of no-code platforms in startups. In: International Conference on Knowledge Management in Organizations, pp. 289–301. Springer (2023)
6. Cai, F.Z., Huang, S.Y., Kessler, T.S., Fottner, F.J.: A case study: digitalization of business processes of SMEs with low-code method. IFAC-PapersOnLine **55**(10), 1840–1845 (2022)
7. Clarke, V., Braun, V.: Thematic analysis. J. Posit. Psychol. **12**(3), 297–298 (2017)
8. Ek, J.: Sector report for the software sector for 2020. Technical report, Ministry of Economic Affairs and Employment of Finland (2020)
9. Elshan, E., Dickhaut, E., Ebel, P.A.: An investigation of why low code platforms provide answers and new challenges. In: Proceedings of the 56th Hawaii International Conference on System Sciences, pp. 6159–6168 (2023)
10. Fowler, K.: What is a consultant? IEEE Instrum. Measur. Mag. **8**(5), 56–57 (2005)
11. Gao, D., Fagerholm, F.: Supplementary materials for the paper "An Investigation of Low-Code Development Adoption in a Finnish IT Consulting Firm" (2025). https://doi.org/10.5281/zenodo.15282220
12. Guthardt, T., Kosiol, J., Hohlfeld, O.: Low-code vs. the developer: an empirical study on the developer experience and efficiency of a no-code platform. In: Proceedings of the ACM/IEEE 27th International Conference on Model Driven Engineering Languages and Systems, pp. 856–865 (2024)
13. Hirzel, M.: Low-code programming models. Commun. ACM **66**(10), 76–85 (2023)
14. Käss, S., Strahringer, S., Westner, M.: Drivers and inhibitors of low code development platform adoption. In: 2022 IEEE 24th Conference on Business Informatics (CBI), vol. 1, pp. 196–205. IEEE (2022)
15. Käss, S., Strahringer, S., Westner, M.: Practitioners' perceptions on the adoption of low code development platforms. IEEE Access **11**, 29009–29034 (2023)
16. Krasavina, V.: Current trends in the IT services market. In: E3S Web of Conferences, vol. 135, p. 04039. EDP Sciences (2019)
17. Kraus, S., Jones, P., Kailer, N., Weinmann, A., Chaparro-Banegas, N., Roig-Tierno, N.: Digital transformation: an overview of the current state of the art of research. SAGE Open **11**(3), 21582440211047576 (2021)
18. Kuosmanen, N., Kuosmanen, T.: Inter-industry and intra-industry switching as sources of productivity growth: structural change of Finland's ICT industries. J. Prod. Anal. **61**(2), 107–120 (2024)

19. McKenna, C.D.: The origins of modern management consulting. Business and Economic History, pp. 51–58 (1995)
20. Nissen, V.: Digital transformation of the consulting industry—introduction and overview. In: Digital Transformation of the Consulting Industry: Extending the Traditional Delivery Model, pp. 1–58. Springer (2017)
21. Nissen, V.: Consulting research: a scientific perspective on consulting. In: Advances in Consulting Research: Recent Findings and Practical Cases, pp. 1–27 (2019)
22. Matvitskyy, O., Davis, K., et al.: Magic Quadrant for Enterprise Low-Code Application Platforms. Technical Report G00804341, Gartner, Stamford, CT, USA (2024)
23. Piumelli, F.: Consulting in the age of digital transformation. In: Advances in Consulting Research: Recent Findings and Practical Cases, pp. 359–370 (2019)
24. Rafiq, U., Filippo, C., Wang, X.: Understanding low-code or no-code adoption in software startups: preliminary results from a comparative case study. In: International Conference on Product-Focused Software Process Improvement, pp. 390–398. Springer (2022)
25. Rokis, K., Kirikova, M.: Exploring low-code development: a comprehensive literature review. Complex Systems Informatics and Modeling Quart, pp. 68–86 (2023)
26. Statistics Finland: Statistics on service industry commodities. Reference period: 2023. https://stat.fi/en/publication/clmrmgre05f7s0avy9xl2rht9. Accessed 20 Mar 2025
27. Sun, Y., Lim, S.Y., Goh, K.Y.: Legitimacy tradeoffs: use of low-code/no-code tools and digital start-ups' funding. In: ICIS 2024 Proceedings (2024)
28. Witschel, D., Baumann, D., Voigt, K.I.: How manufacturing firms navigate through stormy waters of digitalization: the role of dynamic capabilities, organizational factors and environmental turbulence for business model innovation. J. Manag. Organ. **28**(3), 681–714 (2022)

Serverless Adoption in Practice: A Socio-Technical Investigation of Motivations, Challenges, and Strategies

Muhammad Hamza[1]([envelope])[iD], Wardah Naeem Awan[1][iD],
and Muhammad Waheed Sabir[2][iD]

[1] Software Engineering Department, LUT University, Lappeenranta, Finland
`{muhammad.hamza,wardah.awan}@lut.fi`
[2] Louisiana State University, Baton Rouge, LA, USA
`msabir2@lsu.edu`

Abstract. Serverless computing allows developers to concentrate on application logic while delegating infrastructure provisioning, scaling, and maintenance to cloud providers. This architecture reduces operational overhead, enables automatic scalability, and shortens time-to-market, making it attractive for both greenfield development and legacy system migration. While existing research has examined technical aspects such as performance and orchestration, there remains limited empirical understanding of the motivations behind serverless adoption, the practical challenges it introduces, and how these challenges are managed in real-world settings. To bridge this gap, we applied Socio-Technical Grounded Theory (STGT) to analyze 37 practitioner-authored blog posts and 18 semi-structured interviews conducted with serverless professionals from diverse roles and industry domains. Our findings reveal five key motivations for adopting serverless computing (e.g., operational efficiency, developer productivity), seven categories of challenges (e.g., architectural constraints, testing complexity, and organizational skill gaps), and a comprehensive set of mitigation strategies across architecture, DevOps practices, cost management, and developer training. These insights provide practical guidance for organizations adopting serverless architectures and contribute to a deeper understanding of the socio-technical dynamics involved in cloud-native software development.

Keywords: Serverless computing · Motivations · Challenges · Best practices · Empirical study

1 Introduction

Serverless computing has fundamentally reshaped application development in the cloud by allowing developers to focus solely on implementing the application logic, while the cloud provider takes the full responsibility for provisioning, scaling, and maintaining the underlying infrastructure [18]. This reflects a paradigm

© The Author(s), under exclusive license to Springer Nature Switzerland AG 2026
G. Scanniello et al. (Eds.): PROFES 2025, LNCS 16361, pp. 186–202, 2026.
https://doi.org/10.1007/978-3-032-12089-2_12

shift in software engineering as organizations rely on serverless computing to facilitate the design, development, testing, and maintenance of complex software systems [9]. While some organizations adopt serverless computing to build greenfield projects, a more common scenario involves re-architecting existing systems to run on serverless platforms such as AWS Lambda or Google Cloud Functions [12]. Leading companies, such as Capital One [23], iRobot [16], and Airbnb [1], have fully migrated their systems to serverless architecture or leveraged it to power various backend processes, thereby improving operational efficiency. This trend reflects growing interest in adopting serverless computing due to its potential to support scalable, modular architectures, with its market value projected to exceed \$44.7 billion by 2029 [21].

Despite these advantages, developing applications with serverless architecture can be challenging due to its inherent limitations, such as cold start latency and state management [14]. These constraints can complicate the development of latency-sensitive or stateful applications. On the other hand, organizations migrating legacy systems to serverless platforms face additional organizational challenges, such as a shortage of skilled serverless practitioners and a cultural shift in development and operational mindset [13]. While existing research has explored various technical facets of serverless computing, such as performance modeling [31], multi-cloud orchestration [26], application migration [11], and state management [4], identifying serverless patterns [27], assessing its suitability for edge [2], less attention has been paid to understanding the motivations, practical challenges, and mitigation strategies associated with serverless adoption in real-world contexts.

To bridge this gap, it is essential to investigate the key motivations driving organizations to adopt serverless computing, the technical and organizational challenges they encounter along the way, and the best practices practitioners adopt to overcome these challenges. Therefore, a deeper understanding of these factors is crucial for informing and supporting future organizations considering or implementing serverless architectures.

To this end, this study seeks to address this research gap by empirically examining the motivations behind adopting serverless, the challenges organizations encounter, and the best practices they employ to overcome them. We began by analyzing 37 blog posts that discussed the motivations, challenges, and best practices related to serverless adoption using the Socio-Technical Grounded Theory (STGT) approach. Building on these insights, we conducted an in-depth qualitative interview study with 18 practitioners from around the world to gain a more comprehensive understanding. While this study does not aim to construct a theory, it adopts the analytical techniques of Socio-Technical Grounded Theory (STGT) to systematically code and categorize empirical data from blog posts and interviews.

We address the following research questions to achieve the objective of this study:

RQ1: What motivates organizations to adopt serverless computing?

Rationale: To explore the main motivations that lead organizations to adopt serverless computing for application development.

RQ2: What challenges do practitioners encounter when developing serverless applications?

Rationale: To identify and discuss the key challenges that organizations face when developing serverless applications.

RQ3: What are the best practices to effectively mitigate the challenges of serverless?

Rationale: To critically analyze the best practices to overcome the key challenges identified in RQ2.

The findings of this study expand the current body of knowledge by identifying how organizations benefit from serverless computing and deal with its challenges. They also help better understand the social and technical factors involved in adopting serverless computing. Finally, the findings provide practical guidance for organizations planning to adopt serverless for greenfield project development or migrating legacy applications and offer a foundation for future research on organizational readiness, decision-making, and technology adoption in cloud-native software development.

2   Methodology

Adopting serverless computing is not solely a technical decision; it also entails significant organizational and human considerations. According to Bostrom and Heinen's socio-technical perspective [5], technology adoption results from the interaction between technical subsystems (e.g., tools, platforms) and social subsystems (e.g., roles, practices, and mindsets). Thus, to address both the technical and social dimensions of serverless adoption, we adopted Socio-Technical Grounded Theory(**STGT**) as our analytical lens [15]. Although we adopted core procedures from STGT–such as open coding, constant comparison, and axial coding–our goal was not to develop a formal theory. Instead, we employed STGT to systematically analyze practitioner experiences and uncover patterns across real-world serverless adoption contexts. The whole process is depicted in the Fig. 1.

2.1   Data Collection

Blog posts: We began the data collection by reviewing practitioner-authored blog posts in which professionals shared their experiences and insights related to serverless adoption [24]. These blogs, often classified as gray literature [8], offer practical insights into software development practices and help to connect academic research with industry practice [25]. Following the guidelines proposed by Garousi et al. [8], we aimed to capture a broad range of practitioner perspectives from diverse sources.

Therefore, we executed a Google search using the query *("serverless adoption" OR "serverless") AND ("motivations" OR "challenges" OR "strategies")* to

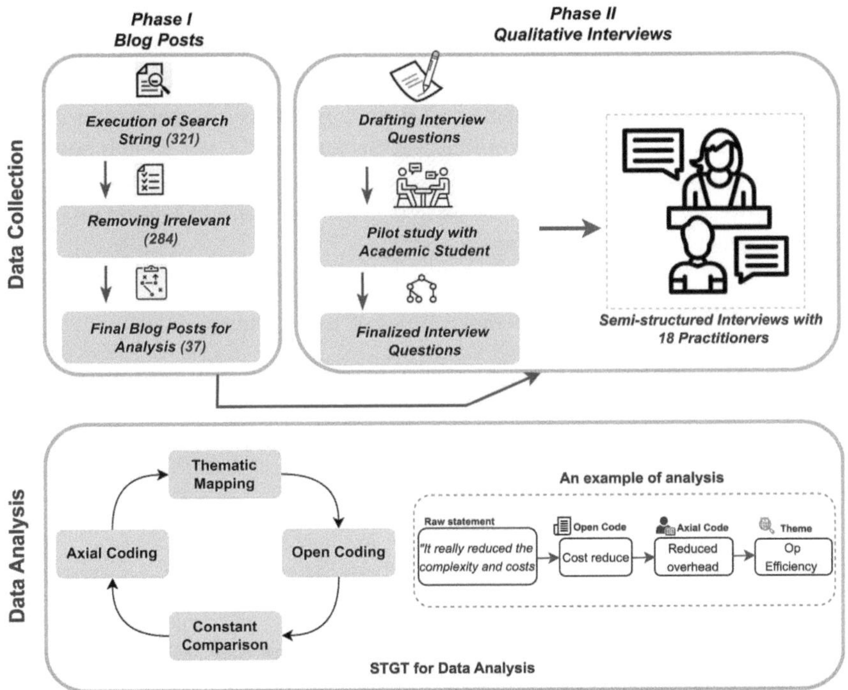

Fig. 1. Research method.

identify the relevant blog posts. This search returned 321 results, which were then exported to a CSV file using the SEOQuake tool[1]. Finally, non-blog content (e.g., videos, job listings, book pages) was manually filtered out to retain only practitioner-driven narratives.

In the next phase, we used a large language model such as ChatGPT to generate abstracts for the blog posts. However, only posts describing real-world experiences in software development contexts rather than general commentary or opinion pieces were included. This multi-step selection process resulted in a final dataset of 37 blog posts for in-depth analysis. This criterion yielded 37 blog posts for further analysis. However, we included only the URLs of the blog posts in our replication package due to potential licensing constraints [22].

Interviews: After analyzing the blog posts, we conducted in-depth interviews with 18 serverless practitioners to gain a more comprehensive understanding of the motivations, challenges, and practices in serverless adoption. We recruited serverless practitioners with diverse backgrounds in terms of experience, age, roles, and domains. However, participants were recruited using purposive sampling [3], primarily through our professional networks, including colleagues, collaborators from previous and ongoing projects, and other industry contacts, as

---

[1] https://www.seoquake.com/.

well as from LinkedIn for outreach. Finally, we employed snowball sampling, asking interviewees to refer additional suitable participants to extend our participant pool [6]. We continued to recruit new practitioners for the interview until no new insights were identified. All the interviews were conducted using a semi-structured protocol (see replication package [22]), with each session lasting between 60 and 90 min and was conducted remotely via Microsoft Teams or Zoom. All interviews were audio-recorded with participants' informed consent and later transcribed for analysis.

Table 1. Demographics of participants.

Organization	Domain	Employee	P. Role	Experience	(Serverless Exp)
O1	Logistics services	37365	Architect	18	5
O2	Financial Services	17500	Lead Engineer	13	4
O3	Security Services	15800	Engineer	8	5
O4	Financial Services	15000	Tech Architect	21	8
O5	E-commerce	15000	Architect	16	5
O6	Web Services	14500	Architect	9	3
O7	E-commerce	12000	Software Engineer	12	4
O8	Cloud Solution Provider	12000	Principal Engineer	17	8
O9	Logistics services	8000	Architect	19	7
O10	Digital marketing	5000	Principal Engineer	17	8
O11	Automotive services	5000	Senior Solution Architect	23	8
O12	Financial Services	536	Lead Engineer	12	4.5
O13	Aviation	300	Solution Architect	17	7
O14	AI & Security Services	300	Architect	10	4
O15	Financial Services	280	Team Manager	5	2
O16	Marketing & Fundraising	200	Principal Engineer	21	5
O17	Web services	50	Full stack Engineer	13	5
O18	Consultancy	20	Lead Engineer	5	2

2.2 Data Analysis

Both datasets, i.e., blog posts and interviews, were analyzed using the principles of Socio-Technical Grounded Theory (STGT), as proposed by Hoda et al. [15]. The analysis began with open coding, where we examined each line of blog posts and interview transcripts to assign a descriptive code. These codes captured motivations, technical challenges (e.g., "cold start latency", "state management", "Testing and Debugging"), organizational challenges (e.g.,"developer mindset shift", "skills gap"), and practitioner-reported best practices. Moreover, codes were iteratively refined by examining patterns across data sources and identifying similarities and differences through constant comparison. This process enabled the identification of recurring motivations, challenges, and strategies related to serverless adoption. Once open coding was completed, we proceeded to axial coding, grouping related codes into broader themes aligned with our research questions. However, we maintained analytic memos to document interpretations, emerging insights, and coding decisions throughout the analysis. These memos supported reflexivity and contributed to the rigor and depth of the analytical process. We used NVivo software to manage the data and streamline the organization and refinement of codes and categories. The first author conducted the initial coding, with the second and third authors contributing to axial coding. All the authors collaboratively reviewed the final themes.

Although core grounded theory techniques such as open coding and constant comparison were applied, the goal was not to develop a formal theory. Rather, we employed STGT to help us structure our analysis and explore the social and technical dimensions of serverless adoption.

3   Results

This section presents the findings derived from our analysis. Figure 2 provides an overview of the key results across all research questions.

3.1   What Motivates Organizations to Adopt Serverless Computing?

We identified five overarching themes that capture the key motivations behind the adoption of serverless computing based on an in-depth analysis of the dataset. These themes reflect not only technical benefits but also strategic goals and developer-centered values. Each theme encompasses a set of sub-motivations that illustrate the multifaceted reasons organizations are adopting serverless for their application development.

Operational Efficiency:A prominent motivation for adopting serverless computing is the pursuit of greater operational efficiency. Serverless platforms allow teams to minimize infrastructure management by abstracting away provisioning, patching, and scaling tasks. This reduction in operational overhead is particularly appealing to organizations with limited DevOps resources. Additionally, the pay-as-you-go pricing model and the ability to allocate resources on demand contribute to cost optimization. This theme includes sub-motivations such as cost efficiency, reduced operational overhead, on-demand resource allocation, and operational simplicity via managed services. One of the interview practitioners stated that:

"We observed that serverless is more appealing for small to medium applications where the setup and operational overhead can be minimized. Also, for developers working with platforms that have large communities (like AWS), serverless can offer better support and problem-solving resources."

Scalability and Reliability: Serverless computing naturally supports automatic scaling, making it a strong fit for workloads with fluctuating demand. The ability to scale granularly, at the function level, ensures that applications remain responsive without manual intervention. Furthermore, built-in features such as fault tolerance and multi-region support enhance system resilience and uptime. This theme encompasses motivations related to scalability, fault tolerance, resilience, and high availability. One of the practitioners stated that they adopted serverless because they were facing seasonal workload. One of the interview practitioners stated that:

"And I say on average, because for example, we don't deliver on Sundays and in the November, December period, it's way busier."

Developer Productivity: Serverless enables developers to focus more on solving business problems rather than managing infrastructure or deployment pipelines. By simplifying DevOps processes and providing built-in monitoring and multi-language support, serverless platforms streamline development workflows and reduce ramp-up time for new team members. This theme encompasses sub-motivations including focus on core logic, improved developer productivity, simplified DevOps, shorter learning curve, polyglot language support, and built-in monitoring and observability. As one of the practitioners stated:

"With serverless, I just wrote code and shipped it. No worrying about how or where it runs."

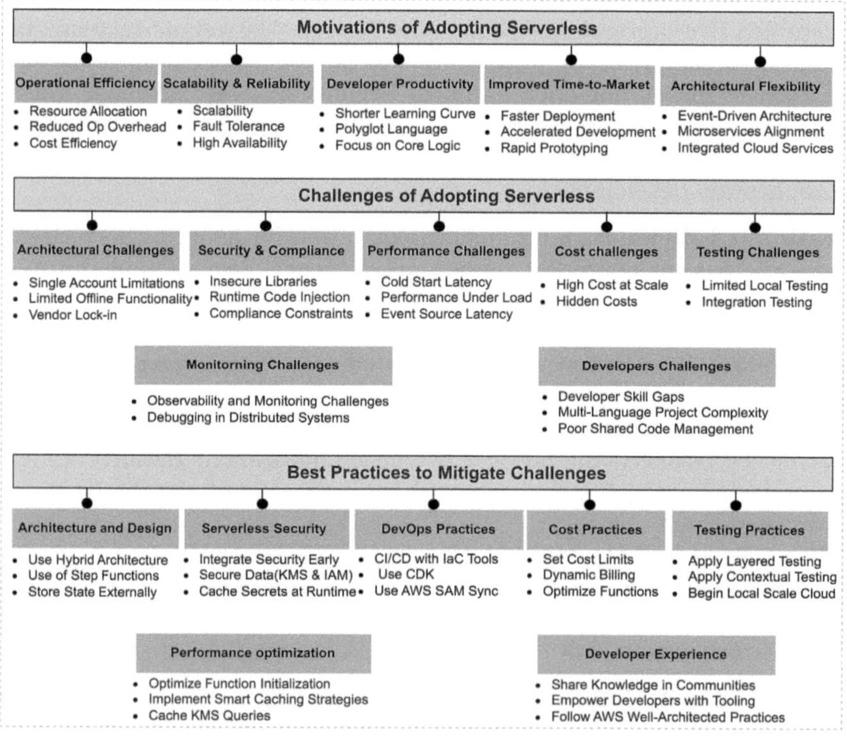

Fig. 2. Findings of Analysis.

Improved Time-to-Market: Another strong motivator for organizations adopting serverless is the ability to release software more quickly. Serverless computing reduces setup and configuration time, allowing teams to prototype, test, and deploy features at a much faster pace. This accelerated cycle is especially valuable in competitive environments where responsiveness to market needs is critical. This theme encompasses sub-motivations including faster deployment, accelerated development, and rapid prototyping. One of the interview practitioners stated that:

"For like what I look at is if you're looking for rapid prototyping, serverless architecture would do."

Architectural Flexibility: Serverless aligns with contemporary architectural patterns like event-driven and microservices-based design. It encourages modularity and loose coupling, while providing seamless integration with other managed cloud services. This architectural flexibility enables organizations to experiment, scale components independently, and adapt systems incrementally. This theme encompasses sub-motivations including event-driven architecture, microservices alignment, and integrated cloud services. One of the interview practitioners stated that:

"We broke our monolith into event-driven components with serverless, and it became easier to iterate without touching everything at once."

3.2 What Challenges Do Practitioners Encounter When Developing Serverless Applications?

We identified seven major categories of challenges that organizations face when adopting serverless computing to address the RQ2. These span technical, operational, and organizational domains and were frequently reported as challenges to efficient, scalable, and secure serverless applications development.

Architectural Challenges: Architectural challenges emerged as a dominant theme in the dataset. Serverless platforms impose constraints on execution time, memory, and deployment models, which can lead to architectural misfits. Similarly, statelessness complicates application design where persistent state is essential, while infrastructure abstraction limits fine-grained control [28]. Teams also face difficulties with orchestrating functions, managing event-driven workflows, and aligning serverless capabilities with their intended use cases. This theme includes sub-challenges such as execution time and payload limits, memory and compute constraints, complexity of state management, lack of fine-grained infrastructure control, vendor lock-in, orchestration overhead, and architectural misalignment with use cases. One of the interview practitioners mentioned that:

"We hit Lambda's timeout ceiling constantly. Chaining functions didn't help– it just made things harder to debug. Also, if it exceeds 5 min, the Lambda instance will crash."

Security and Compliance: Despite being managed by cloud providers, serverless systems are not immune to security risks. Developers often import insecure third-party libraries, face runtime-level code injection risks, and struggle with ensuring compliance with regional data regulations. The distributed nature of serverless functions also increases the attack surface and introduces ambiguity about responsibility boundaries. This theme includes sub-challenges such as insecure third-party libraries, runtime code injection risks, regulatory and compliance constraints, and a high surface area for failures. One of the practitioners stated that:

"After that, security becomes a key point. Obviously, the more expensive services offer higher levels of security. For example, AWS provides VPC (Virtual Private Cloud)."

Performance Challenges: Performance unpredictability is another common concern when deploying applications to serverless platforms such as AWS Lambda, Google Cloud Functions [17]. Cold start latency, especially in low-traffic scenarios, can delay response times, while increased concurrency can lead to throttling or degraded performance. Additionally, maintaining database connections across ephemeral function instances often results in overloaded connection pools. This theme includes sub-challenges such as cold start latency, performance degradation under load, event source latency, database connection overload, and concurrency management limits. One of the interview practitioners stated that:

"With API gateway and Lambda, there's the additional concern you have to think about in terms of a cold start performance."

Cost Challenges: Although serverless promises cost-efficiency, several teams reported rising costs at scale and difficulties forecasting expenses. Hidden costs, such as those for monitoring, debugging, and third-party services, often emerge after adopting serverless [10]. The lack of cost visibility and tooling further complicates budgeting. This theme includes sub-challenges such as high cost at scale, cost unpredictability, and hidden costs related to observability and tooling. One of our practitioners stated that:

"Many companies face high costs due to the combined use of CloudWatch and third-party monitoring tools, often without fully leveraging CloudWatch's capabilities, leading to redundant expenses."

Testing Challenges: Testing serverless applications poses unique difficulties. Local replication of cloud environments is limited, making it hard to debug issues before deployment [20]. Integration testing becomes cumbersome due to the distributed and asynchronous nature of serverless systems. Ensuring idempotency and cross-region consistency further complicates test scenarios. This theme includes sub-challenges such as limited local testing support, integration testing complexity, and resilience challenges across regions. One of the practitioners states that:

"Testing step functions can be tricky, especially with local testing tools like Step Functions Local."

Monitoring Challenges: Observability in serverless systems remains a significant hurdle. Traditional logging and monitoring tools often fall short in tracking distributed executions. Debugging becomes more difficult due to the lack of persistent environments, transient logs, and asynchronous invocation chains. This theme includes sub-challenges such as observability issues, debugging difficulties in distributed systems, and limited traceability across function invocations.

"We were dealing with ghost errors. Event-driven architectures are powerful for building large-scale systems, but challenging to test and monitor in production."

Developer Challenges: Several practitioners pointed out that serverless adoption requires a shift in mindset and skills. Developers unfamiliar with event-driven paradigms or cloud-native patterns struggle to build and maintain serverless applications. Multi-language deployments, poor shared code practices, documentation gaps, and inconsistent tooling further inhibit smooth adoption. This theme includes sub-challenges such as steep learning curves, lack of serverless understanding, multi-language complexity, poor shared code management, platform usability inconsistencies, documentation gaps, and resistance to organizational change. One of the practitioners stated that:

"There's a mindset shift into exactly what you're controlling... you're no longer writing code that is deployed in a governed way."

3.3 What Are the Best Practices to Effectively Mitigate the Challenges of Serverless?

To address the wide array of challenges associated with serverless computing, practitioners have developed a rich set of best practices. These cover everything from how systems are designed and run to how developers are supported. We organized them into seven key themes that reflect the main areas where these practices can help make serverless adoption more successful.

Architecture and Design: Successful serverless adoption starts with careful architectural decisions. Practitioners recommend decomposing workflows into loosely coupled components, using queues to manage flow, and adopting event-driven designs to enable scalability and flexibility. Other practices include storing state externally, planning for fallback during peak loads, and applying hierarchical structures to manage multi-Lambda systems. Teams are also advised to analyze architectural trade-offs early and to adopt single-responsibility principles in function design. This theme includes practices such as using hybrid architectures, provisioned concurrency, API gateways, DynamoDB atomic writes, Lambda layers, centralized API management, and open-source frameworks. One of the interview practitioners stated that:

"What saved us was thinking about architecture upfront, queues for workflow decoupling, step functions for orchestration, and small Lambdas that did one thing well."

Serverless Security: Security in serverless demands a proactive and layered approach. Experts emphasize enforcing least-privilege access using IAM roles, isolating functions within VPCs, and securely managing secrets with services like AWS Secrets Manager and KMS. Similarly, integrating security early in the SDLC and applying secure coding practices with static and dynamic analysis tools helps mitigate vulnerabilities before deployment. This theme includes practices like managing secrets securely, leveraging infrastructure-as-code to avoid misconfigurations, applying DoS mitigation controls, understanding the shared responsibility model, and caching secrets at runtime. One of the practitioners stated that:

"We learned the hard way that treating security as an afterthought in serverless is a recipe for risk. Now, every Lambda gets reviewed for privilege and isolation."

DevOps Practices: Practitioners consistently advocate for integrating DevOps principles into serverless workflows. Infrastructure-as-Code (IaC) tools such as AWS CDK and Terraform are used to manage configurations, while CI/CD pipelines help automate deployments and enable version control. Teams often adopt a multi-account strategy to separate environments and improve governance. This theme includes practices like using Git for rollback, deploying with AWS SAM sync, and enabling cross-language deployment with CDK. One of the interview practitioners stated that:

"We are running three flavors of AWS resource creation (SAM, CDK, Cloud-Formation) through the same pipeline."

Cost Management: While serverless promises lower costs, proactive strategies are needed to manage them effectively. To manage the hidden cost of serverless, teams need to set usage-based billing alerts, optimize function configurations to avoid runaway costs, and monitor hidden expenses like observability tools and third-party services. This theme includes practices such as setting cost limits, requesting dynamic billing models, and fine-tuning functions to balance performance with pricing. One of the practitioners stated that:

"Well, scalability is kind of like the third, but I would also tie it somehow into cost because in itself, scalability is an Aspect coming from the you know monolithic and especially data center world, scalability is not that much of an issue because you always like to scale way more."

Performance Optimization: Optimizing serverless performance involves both design and runtime considerations. However, organizations mitigate the cold starts through function initialization strategies and provisioned concurrency. Similarly, Latency issues can be reduced by using asynchronous processing, batching tasks, and adding caching layers like Redis. Practitioners also recommend offloading large data to S3 and using lightweight languages such as Go or Python for performance-sensitive workloads. This theme includes practices like leveraging Cloudflare Workers, handling dependencies via Lambda layers or EFS, and applying caching techniques such as KMS result caching. One of the practitioners stated that:

"But I think historically .NET and Java have suffered more than the other runtimes with cold starts in Lambda and they've both got better over the years."

Testing Strategies: Testing serverless applications requires adapting traditional practices to a distributed, ephemeral context. We found that many organizations prefer contract and component testing over full end-to-end tests, often using mocks and schema validation to simulate external services. Tools like Vegeta or Artillery help them test how well their systems handle load. They also use a layered testing approach–combining unit, integration, and contextual tests ensures confidence before production deployments. This theme includes practices such as testing locally before scaling to the cloud, managing retries with FIFO queues, and validating schemas during deployment. One of the practitioners stated that:

"We use local responses for testing, but are exploring end-to-end tests that trigger events and check various payload responses."

Developer Experience: A smooth developer experience is critical for adoption. Organizations invest in documentation, community knowledge sharing, and developer training to close the skill gap. Starting with low-risk internal tools allows developers to build confidence. Practitioners warn against overengineering and advocate focusing on essential tasks, supported by frameworks with strong community and vendor support. This theme includes practices such as following AWS Well-Architected practices, using supported frameworks, and enabling developers through tooling and internal knowledge sharing. One of the practitioners stated that:

"In my previous companies, we focused on identifying skill gaps within the team and hiring people with complementary specialities. Also, we have teams that own services, which allows knowledge to be shared easily."

4   Discussion

The analysis revealed that organizations particularly adopt serverless architecture to improve scalability and reduce operational overhead. However, they face technical challenges such as cold start latency, state management, and debugging distributed event-driven applications, and organizational challenges such as skill gap and lack of in-house expertise. They adopt different strategies, such as provisioned concurrency, to address these challenges. These findings show that adopting serverless is more than just a technical change, as it is a shift that also affects people and processes. To succeed, organizations must tackle both technical issues and human factors. Based on this, we provide the implications for researchers, practitioners, and educators.

Implications for Researchers: Based on the findings of this study, (i) researchers can explore the long-term impact of adopting serverless. This includes how serverless systems and teams evolve after adoption, and whether new challenges or unexpected benefits emerge. Similarly, (ii) they can explore how different contexts, such as startups versus large enterprises, influence the success and outcomes of serverless adoption. Furthermore, our study highlights that while serverless can improve developer productivity by offloading infrastructure management, the inherent limitations of this architecture may affect the developer experience. Therefore, (iii) researchers should explore how developer experience (DevX) is transformed in serverless computing. Another critical implication is the need for (iv) research on testing and debugging of serverless applications, as traditional testing approaches may not be effective. Thus, researchers should develop automated frameworks that can simulate cloud environments.

Implications for Practitioners: The findings suggest that adopting serverless architecture improved the scalability and resilience while significantly accelerating time-to-market for new features. This encourages companies (i) to adopt serverless architecture, particularly for greenfield projects. However, practitioners should be aware that adopting serverless is not a silver bullet, as it has several inherent limitations, such as cold start latency and timeout. This suggests that practitioners (ii) should evaluate the serverless over traditional cloud before adopting it. For example, they can run high computing tasks on a container such as Fargate while others on Lambda.ÂăSimilarly, testing can be cumbersome due to the distributed event-driven nature of a serverless application. Thus, organizations (iii) should invest in new testing strategies such as writing comprehensive unit tests for function logic, and then using cloud-based integration tests or staging environments to ensure those functions work together as expected. Similarly, embracing a layered testing approach (from local unit tests to end-to-end tests in the cloud) can maintain quality in a serverless system. On the other hand, adopting serverless requires a mindset change as it requires developers to embrace new design principles such as stateless functions and asynchronous workflows. Therefore, organizations (iv) should invest in training programs and gradually expose teams to serverless through pilot projects.

4.1   Threats to Validity

This section identifies the potential threats to the validity of our study and how we mitigated them. We used Wohlin et al.'s [30] guidelines to analyze threats to external validity, internal validity, construct validity, and reliability.

External validity:reflects how broadly the findings can be applied beyond the specific cases analyzed. We recruited most participants through LinkedIn by inviting connections to join the study. This helped reach a diverse group but may have caused selection bias. To mitigate this, we included practitioners with varied roles and expertise. We also continued data collection until we reached saturation, which helped make our findings more reliable and applicable to other settings.

Internal validity:refers to how accurately our findings reflect the relationships between factors without being affected by other variables. We used constant comparison by combining data from blog posts and interviews to mitigate the potential threat. We further validated interview insights by cross-referencing them with blog posts to strengthen reliability and minimize potential bias.

Construct validity: refers to how accurately the identified constructs capture the concepts the study intended to measure. One possible threat in our study is that we used blog posts written by people we couldn't contact directly. To mitigate this risk, we cross-checked multiple blog posts and confirmed their content with interview data. This triangulation reduces the risk of misinterpretation, although the subjective nature of blogs remains a limitation.

Reliability: refers to the fact that the results of the study remain consistent no matter who conducts the study. We documented the raw data, analysis steps, and research materials to maintain transparency and rigor by following Hoda's guidelines. We aligned our interpretations with new data throughout the process using constant comparison [14]. While these practices support reliability, we recognize that qualitative analysis involves subjective judgment. Therefore, we prioritized transparency and reproducibility to reduce potential bias.

5   Related Work

Since the advent of serverless computing, researchers have explored its different aspects, including how to address technical challenges and evaluate its adoption in industry. For instance, Leitner et al. [19] investigated how companies utilize Function-as-a-Service in real-world projects and identified challenges in testing, deployment, and reusing functions. Hamza et al. [12] found that teams adopt serverless for scalability and efficiency but face challenges with testing, legacy systems, mindset shifts, and hiring skilled developers. Similarly, Eskandani and Salvaneschi [7] explored 2,000 serverless applications. They reported issues with reusing components, working across platforms, and fixing problems during development. Wen et al. [29] explored 619 Stack Overflow posts about serverless. They found common issues with setup and resources caused by missing or unclear guidance. Hamza et al. [13] analyzed 141 job ads in seven countries to understand what companies look for in serverless roles. They mapped 19 key responsibilities and 60 skills that reflect industry needs. Hamza et al. [10] interviewed 15 practitioners from 8 companies to study the cost and workload fit in serverless computing. They created a taxonomy to compare costs and highlighted ways to optimize spending and choose suitable workloads. Similarly, Hamza et al. [14] analyzed 3,550 issues from 12 open-source serverless frameworks. They identified 263 issue types and 158 causes that developers face when developing applications with serverless frameworks.

While technical challenges related to serverless computing are well-documented, there is limited exploration of why companies choose serverless, what challenges they face, and how they mitigate them. To address this gap, the study highlights how both social and technical factors shape serverless application development.

6   Conclusion

In this study, we identified a comprehensive set of motivations for adopting serverless, challenges, and best practices to overcome these challenges by analyzing 37 blog posts and conducting 18 interviews with serverless practitioners.

We identified five key motivations, such as scalability and operational efficiency, that drive organizations to adopt serverless architecture for developing greenfield projects or migrating legacy systems. We further identified the seven major themes of challenges, such as performance unpredictability and testing complexities. To navigate these challenges, practitioners employ a wide range of best practices across architectural planning, DevOps automation, cost optimization, and developer training. Finally, we provide the implications for researchers and practitioners based on the findings.

This study offers a deeper understanding of serverless computing as not just a technical innovation, but a socio-technical shift that changes how modern software systems are designed, developed, and run. Future research should continue to examine these dynamics across varied organizational settings and explore how evolving tools and practices further influence the adoption journey.

7   Declaration

We used Grammarly and ChatGPT to improve the language of the manuscript. However, a replication package is provided for transparency.

References

1. Airbnb: Airbnb's migration to AWS and serverless computing: Optimizing scalability and performance (2023). https://www.bacancytechnology.com/blog/airbnbs-aws-migration
2. Aslanpour, M.S., et al.: Serverless edge computing: vision and challenges. In: Proceedings of the 2021 Australasian computer science week multiconference (2021)
3. Baltes, S., Ralph, P.: Sampling in software engineering research: a critical review and guidelines. CoRR (2020). https://arxiv.org/abs/2002.07764
4. Barcelona-Pons, D., Sutra, P., Sánchez-Artigas, M., París, G., García-López, P.: Stateful serverless computing with crucial. ACM Trans. Softw. Eng. Meth. (2022)
5. Bostrom, R.P., Heinen, J.S.: Mis problems and failures: a socio-technical perspective. part i: The causes. MIS Quarterly (1977). https://doi.org/10.2307/248710
6. Charmaz, K.: Constructing grounded theory. SAGE Publications (2014)
7. Eskandani, N., Salvaneschi, G.: The uphill journey of FAAS in the open-source community. Journal of Systems and Software (2023)
8. Garousi, V., Felderer, M., Mäntylä, M.V.: Guidelines for including grey literature and conducting multivocal literature reviews in software engineering. Inf. Softw. Technol. (2019). https://doi.org/10.1016/j.infsof.2018.09.006
9. Hamza, M.: Software architecture design of a serverless system. In: Proceedings of the 27th International Conference on Evaluation and Assessment in Software Engineering (2023)
10. Hamza, M., Akbar, M.A., Capilla, R.: Understanding cost dynamics of serverless computing: an empirical study. In: Proceeding of 14th International Conference on Software Business (2023)
11. Hamza, M., Akbar, M.A., Smolader, K.: Navigating decision-making in serverless migration: a socio-technical grounded theory approach (2025). https://doi.org/10.2139/ssrn.5161731

12. Hamza, M., Akbar, M.A., Smolander, K.: The journey to serverless migration: an empirical analysis of intentions, strategies, and challenges. In: International Conference on Product-Focused Software Process Improvement (2023)

13. Hamza, M., Kauppinen, V., Akbar, M.A., Awan, W.N., Smolander, K.: Unveiling the skills and responsibilities of serverless practitioners: an empirical investigation. In: Proceedings of the International Conference on Software Business (ICSOB) (2024)

14. Hamza, M., Waseem, M., Akbar, M.A., Smolander, K., Mikkonen, T.: Navigating open-source serverless frameworks: an empirical analysis of issues and their underlying causes. Preprint submitted to Journal of System and Software (2024). https://papers.ssrn.com/sol3/papers.cfm?abstract_id=5023362

15. Hoda, R.: Socio-technical grounded theory for software engineering. IEEE Trans. Software Eng. (2021). https://doi.org/10.1109/TSE.2021.3106280

16. iRobot: irobot's serverless architecture on AWS: managing connected robot fleets with serverless operations (2017). https://www.slideshare.net/slideshow/serverless-operations-for-the-irobot-fleet/80695527

17. Jia, Z., Witchel, E.: Nightcore: Efficient and scalable serverless computing for latency-sensitive, interactive microservices. In: Proceedings of the 26th ACM International Conference on Architectural Support for Programming Languages and Operating Systems (ASPLOS) (2021)

18. Jonas, E., et al.: Cloud programming simplified: a berkeley view on serverless computing. arXiv preprint arXiv:1902.03383 (2019)

19. Leitner, P., Wittern, E., Spillner, J., Hummer, W.: A mixed-method empirical study of function-as-a-service software development in industrial practice. J. Syst. Softw. (2019)

20. Lenarduzzi, V., Panichella, A.: Serverless testing: tool vendors' and experts' points of view. IEEE Software (2020)

21. MarketsandMarkets: serverless computing market worth $44.7 billion by 2029 (2024). https://www.marketsandmarkets.com/PressReleases/serverless-computing.asp

22. Muhammad, H.: Serverless in practice: Understanding motivations, challenges, and strategies through a socio-technical lens (2025). https://doi.org/10.5281/zenodo.15586025

23. One, C.: Serverless technology at capital one: leveraging serverless architecture for scalability and innovation (2024). https://www.capitalone.com/tech/serverless/

24. Rainer, A.: Using argumentation theory to analyse software practitioners' defeasible evidence, inference and belief. Inf. Softw. Technol. (2017). https://doi.org/10.1016/j.infsof.2017.01.011

25. Rainer, A., Williams, A.: Using blog-like documents to investigate software practice: benefits, challenges, and research directions. J. Softw. Evol. Proc. (2019). https://doi.org/10.1002/smr.2197

26. Sampé, J., Garcia-Lopez, P., Sanchez-Artigas, M., Vernik, G., Roca-Llaberia, P., Arjona, A.: Toward multicloud access transparency in serverless computing. IEEE Software (2020)

27. Taibi, D., El Ioini, N., Pahl, C., Niederkofler, J.R.S.: Patterns for serverless functions (function-as-a-service): a multivocal literature review. In: International Conference on Cloud Computing and Services Science (2020)

28. Taibi, D., Kehoe, B., Poccia, D.: Serverless: from bad practices to good solutions. In: 2022 IEEE International Conference on Service-Oriented System Engineering (SOSE) (2022)

29. Wen, J., Chen, Z., Liu, Y., Lou, Y., Ma, Y., Huang, G., Jin, X., Liu, X.: An empirical study on challenges of application development in serverless computing. In: Proceedings of the 29th ACM Joint Meeting on European Software Engineering Conference and Symposium on the Foundations of Software Engineering (2021)
30. Wohlin, C., Runeson, P., Höst, M., Ohlsson, M.C., Regnell, B., Wesslén, A.: Planning. In: Experimentation in Software Engineering. Springer Berlin Heidelberg (2012). https://doi.org/10.1007/978-3-642-29044-2_8
31. Yussupov, V., Soldani, J., Breitenbücher, U., Leymann, F.: Standards-based modeling and deployment of serverless function orchestrations using bpmn and tosca. Practice and Experience, Software (2022)

Generative AI in Simulation-Based Test Environments for Large-Scale Cyber-Physical Systems: An Industrial Study

Masoud Sadrnezhaad[1]([✉]) [ID], José Antonio Hernández López[2] [ID],
Torvald Mårtensson[1] [ID], and Dániel Varró[1] [ID]

[1] Linköping University, Linköping, Sweden
{masoud.sadrnezhaad,torvald.martensson,daniel.varro}@liu.se
[2] University of Murcia, Murcia, Spain
joseantonio.hernandez6@um.es

Abstract. Quality assurance for large-scale cyber-physical systems relies on sophisticated test activities using complex test environments investigated with the help of numerous types of simulators. As these systems grow, extensive resources are required to develop and maintain simulation models of hardware and software components, as well as physical environments. Meanwhile, recent advances in generative AI have led to tools that can produce executable test cases for software systems, offering potential benefits such as reducing manual efforts or increasing test coverage. However, the application of generative AI techniques to simulation-based testing of large-scale cyber-physical systems remains underexplored. To better understand this gap, this study captures practitioners' perspectives on leveraging generative AI, based on a cross-company workshop with six organizations. Our contribution is twofold: (1) detailed, experience-based insights into challenges faced by engineers, and (2) a research agenda comprising three high-priority directions: (a) AI-generated scenarios and environment models, (b) simulators and AI in CI/CD pipelines, and (c) trustworthiness in generative AI for simulation. While participants acknowledged substantial potential, they also highlighted unresolved challenges. By detailing these issues, the paper aims to guide future academia-industry collaboration towards the responsible adoption of generative AI in simulation-based testing.

Keywords: Generative AI · Cyber-physical system · Simulation · Test environment

1 Introduction

Background. Quality assurance for large-scale cyber-physical systems (CPSs), such as aircraft or road vehicles, requires various test environments at different

G. Scanniello et al. (Eds.): PROFES 2025, LNCS 16361, pp. 203–219, 2026.
https://doi.org/10.1007/978-3-032-12089-2_13

levels of granularity and integration [21]. Based on detailed models of hardware components (e.g., a model of fuel injector in a car), software components (e.g., a model of fuel injection controller) and the physical environment (e.g., a model of fuel viscosity), such test environments investigate the system's behavior using a multitude of simulation tools [21].

In previous work, we have repeatedly touched upon problems and challenges related to test environments. In a study of continuous integration impediments, "reliability of test environments" was identified as one of twelve factors that could enable more frequent integration of software [13]. In another study, industry practitioners described how better models of physical systems (e.g., a simulator model of the fuel system in a car) were increasingly important, as testing with real hardware is too expensive [12]. Some interviewees described constructing good models of physical systems as an additional challenge (e.g., simulating how a liquid flows through the pipes). As systems become larger and more complex, the implementation and maintenance costs of simulator models increase over time, necessitating new solutions to reduce costs and save time.

Research question. Thanks to recent advances in generative AI techniques, frameworks based on large language models, such as ChatGPT or Copilot, are capable of writing software that solves complex problems [16,22], generating test cases [2], and evaluating test results [9]. Generative AI techniques can be applied to simulations in test environments for large-scale cyber-physical systems, potentially reducing costs and saving time. In the companies the authors have worked with as researchers, practitioners have begun exploring AI simulation techniques. However, these efforts often lack a structured and holistic approach. To address this gap, the paper aims to answer the following question: *What is the potential of generative AI techniques in simulation-based test environments for large-scale cyber-physical systems according to industry practitioners?*

Contribution. We conducted an in-depth workshop with six companies working on large-scale CPSs, followed by a thematic coding analysis of all the material. Based on this evidence, our contribution consists of two main parts. (1) We provide *industry-grounded insights* into the challenges practitioners face in simulation-based testing. Concrete obstacles include large-scale data handling and scenario evaluation and selection, which offer an up-to-date, experience-based understanding of barriers that limit scalable simulation-based testing. (2) We propose an *actionable research agenda* that outlines three priority directions for the use of generative AI in this context, namely, (a) AI-generated scenarios and environment models, (b) integration of simulators and AI into CI/CD pipelines, and (c) ensuring trustworthiness in generative AI for simulation.

Relevance and novelty. In this paper, we provide researchers with clear, high-impact directions for future work and support practitioners in making informed decisions about adoption, thereby guiding the responsible and effective use of generative AI in large-scale simulation-based testing.

To the best of our knowledge, this is the first paper that investigates the *industrial practitioners' viewpoint* on the use of *generative AI* for *simulation-*

based test environments in *large-scale cyber-physical systems.* Existing studies on using AI in a CPS context [4,11,14] do not specifically target simulation environments, while the authors of [3] assess simulation and generative AI, but not in a CPS context.

Organization. Section 2 explains the research method. Section 3 reviews recent literature and establishes the background for generative AI in simulation-based testing of CPSs. Section 4 summarizes the workshop, detailing the individual presentations and group discussions of the participating companies. Section 5 provides a thematic coding analysis of companies' input. Threats to validity are discussed in Sect. 6, and the paper is concluded in Sect. 7.

2   Research Method

This study has adopted a three-phase methodology shown in Fig. 1. **Phase 1** involved a preliminary study to ground the research on existing literature and present highlights from the literature to participants as a foundation for discussion in the subsequent workshop. In **Phase 2**, we explored practitioners' perspectives in a workshop with company presentations and group discussions. These sessions provided insights into current practices, challenges, and expectations. Finally, in **Phase 3**, we thematically analyzed the workshop data to identify key themes and patterns across practitioners' viewpoints with respect to the role of generative AI in simulation-based test environments for CPS.

2.1   Phase 1: Preliminary Study

Following Wohlin's guidelines for snowballing in literature studies [19], we began by establishing the research goal and scope, focusing on the application of generative AI in modeling and simulation workflows for cyber-physical systems. We then constructed a starting set by performing structured keyword searches in databases such as IEEE Xplore. Search terms included combinations of keywords such as "generative AI," "large language models," "digital twins," "simulation," and "cyber-physical systems." Candidate papers were selected based on relevance to the research focus, publication quality, and citation impact.

We conducted both backward and forward snowballing from the start set by reviewing reference lists for earlier works and using citation indices to identify

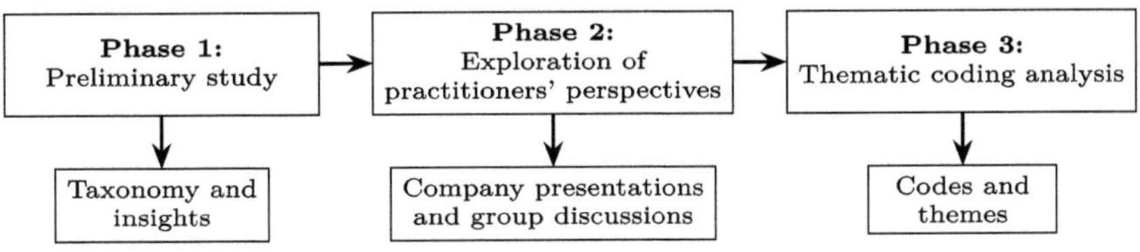

Fig. 1. Research process overview with step labels and outcomes.

newer studies. At each iteration, papers were reviewed and filtered to remove duplicates, non-peer-reviewed sources, and those not aligned with the research focus. This iterative process continued until saturation was reached, that is, no new relevant studies were identified in subsequent snowballing rounds.

The final corpus was classified based on a taxonomy (see Table 1), and these insights were shared with participants as a foundation for discussion.

2.2 Phase 2: Exploration of Practitioners' Perspectives

To collect industry perspectives, we held a one-day, in-person workshop with 33 participants, including university representatives and software engineers, data scientists, and product managers involved in testing from six companies headquartered in Sweden with global presence. Companies were purposefully selected to represent diverse industry domains where generative AI adoption intersects with the complexities of large-scale systems and domain-specific constraints.

Particularly, Companies 1, 2, and 6 represented the *automotive* sector, Company 3 works in *communications*, Company 4 operates in *aerospace*, and Company 5 specializes in *cybersecurity*. The companies range in size from small (around 60 employees) to large enterprises with up to 95,000 employees.

After an initial presentation of research highlights from our preliminary study (results from Phase 1), the workshop was structured into two sessions: company presentations and group discussions. The workshop design was grounded in Kitzinger's principles on leveraging group dynamics in qualitative research [10], fostering dialogic exchange rather than isolated commentary.

Company presentations. The workshop included eight presentations from six companies. Companies 2 and 4 gave two presentations, while the others presented once. Each company's representatives were invited to respond to one or more guiding questions: (P1) What has your *experience* been using generative AI in your test environments? (P2) What *challenges* have you encountered in adopting generative AI techniques? and (P3) What are your *hopes* for using generative AI to address these challenges?

Cross-company group discussions. Participants were divided into five groups with cross-company representatives, each comprising 6–7 members. Each group was asked to answer the following questions: (G1) What are the priority research problems for industrial generative AI adoption? (G2) How should academia-industry collaborations be structured? (G3) What are the first steps for a small team of researchers working on this? Finally, each group shared key discussion points with all attendees and submitted a summary to the authors. Note that the current paper provides an in-depth analysis only for the first question, while industry-academia collaboration aspects are considered out of scope.

2.3 Phase 3: Thematic Coding Analysis

The data analyzed from the workshop consisted of two primary sources: (1) detailed notes taken during company presentations by all researchers, and (2) written summaries submitted by participants following group discussions. These materials from the workshop were analyzed using thematic coding analysis as described by Robson [17], with two researchers conducting the coding and the other two reviewing and refining the results, using the following five steps:

1. **Familiarization with data:** The process began with repeatedly reading the collected notes to identify key patterns and noting initial ideas.
2. **Generating initial codes:** Initial codes were developed by interacting inductively with the data to categorize recurring features. Similar extracts across the dataset were assigned the same codes.
3. **Identifying and refining themes:** Codes were applied consistently to identical or closely related phenomena across different companies' presentations or group discussions. These codes were iteratively refined and collated into broader themes, with continuous comparison across the dataset.
4. **Constructing thematic networks:** Emerging themes were grouped to form main or global themes.
5. **Integration and interpretation:** The themes were compared with existing literature to identify gaps in academic knowledge regarding industrial needs.

3 Preliminary Study

Based on the methodology for the preliminary study described in Sect. 2.1, we reviewed research published after 2023 on how generative AI is utilized to test and simulate CPSs. To categorize and present this work, we used a hierarchical framework that captures levels of abstraction, tool categories, roles of large language models (LLMs), and associated techniques (see Table 1). Testing activities are often discussed according to test levels, including *component*, *integration*, and *system* levels. Software tools used in engineering safety-critical CPS are categorized in tool qualification standards (like DO-330 [18] used in civil avionics) as *development* tools and *verification* tools. In generative AI applications, LLMs can act in different roles depending on the task they are used for, such as *reviewer*, *documenter*, *creator*, or *translator*. Techniques used in this context include *prompt engineering*, *retrieval-augmented generation (RAG)*, *LLM agents*, and *fine-tuning*.

Considering existing approaches applied at the *integration* and *component* levels using *development* tools, Chen et al. focused on deriving UML domain models from textual descriptions using different prompt strategies [5]. These approaches leveraged LLMs as *creator*. Other studies emphasize the *system*-level with *verification* tools. Xia et al. investigated the use of LLM-based multi-agent systems in digital twin environments to automatically adjust simulation parameters. Another example is Jackson et al., who worked on automating simulation scenarios and code generation from descriptions of systems and processes [8,20]. Both studies leverage LLMs as *translator* for high-level descriptions into executable simulations. Another example is Mühlburger and Wotawa, who utilized *RAG* to detect faults in complex integrated systems [15]. Additionally, Deng et al. relied on natural language specifications of traffic rules and domain-specific languages for test scenarios and environments, along with prompting, to generate test scenarios and environment specifications [7]. Ali et al. studied the use of prompting to create digital twins for CPSs [1]. Across these efforts, LLMs are used mainly as *creators* or *reviewers*. Their results demonstrate how generative AI can help users better connect digital models with real-world systems.

Table 1. A classification hierarchy illustrating examples from existing research.

| Reference | Tool Category | | Test Level | | | Role(s) of LLM | | | | LLM Technique | | | |
	Development	Verification	Component	Integration	System	Creator	Translator	Reviewer	Documenter	Prompting	RAG	LLM agents	Fine-tuning
[1]		✓			✓	✓			✓	✓			
[7]		✓			✓			✓		✓			
[8]		✓			✓	✓						✓	
[15]		✓			✓			✓				✓	✓
[20]		✓			✓	✓						✓	
[5]	✓		✓			✓				✓			

In summary, recent studies predominantly focus on *verification* tools used at the *system* level, with fewer addressing *development* tools or targeting the *component* and *integration* levels. Most approaches rely on *prompting* or are implemented via *LLM agent* frameworks, while techniques like *fine-tuning* are less frequently used. LLMs typically serve as *creators* or *translators*, with less emphasis on *reviewer* or *documenter* roles.

4   Cross-Company Presentations and Discussions

This section summarizes the individual presentations delivered by each participating company, along with insights from cross-company group discussions held during the workshop. The cases span a range of industries, including automotive, communications, aerospace, and cybersecurity, and collectively, they offer a glimpse into how generative AI is transforming industrial test practices.

4.1   Company Presentations

Below are summaries of the individual presentations delivered by company representatives during the workshop. These presentations were guided by the questions outlined in Sect. 2.2. For anonymity, companies are labeled C1 to C6.

C1 Representatives from Company 1 reported their *experience* in logging and interpreting real-time signals from truck components for autonomous vehicle development. The ten thousands of signals in modern vehicles require scalable data processing, which earlier state-machine-based approaches were unable to support. They also described efforts to automate build processes and testing to speed up feedback between customers and developers. Scaling to many signals presents *challenges*, such as ensuring accuracy, organizing large log volumes, and adapting to unforeseen sensor needs. Transitioning to autonomous vehicles adds uncertainty in sensor placement and performance metrics due to varied driving patterns and specialized vehicle architectures. Looking ahead, Company 1 *hopes* to leverage AI to utilize the vast amount of available data better, thereby shortening feedback loops and enhancing scalability in their products.

C2 Engineers from Company 2 shared their *experience* with simulation-based testing and large-scale data generation, highlighting its value as autonomous systems continue to evolve. Diverse teams use software-in-the-loop pipelines for validation and experiment with generative AI to build automatic driving controllers. Despite progress, Company 2 reports *challenges* in maintaining model accuracy as simulations increase in scale and complexity. They face issues with reusing AI across environments, and language models show precision limits in complex simulations. Engineers express *hope* for using AI to identify novel test scenarios, accelerate regression testing, and improve quality metrics. They see potential for AI to enhance realism in randomized simulations, support diverse scenario generation, and reduce the number of unproductive runs. Looking ahead, they aim to utilize AI to balance speed, quality, and resources in response to evolving industry demands.

C3 A team from Company 3 did not report direct *experience* with generative AI in simulators. However, other teams have developed simulation frameworks for emulating end users and network interactions. Notably, they shared experiences using generative AI for large-scale telecommunications testing, particularly in writing test cases, documentation, code refactoring, unit test generation, and vulnerability detection. They used retrieval-augmented generation to improve context awareness across codebases and align outputs with internal standards. They noted *challenges* such as potential over-reliance on AI-generated code, which may lack quality or introduce vulnerabilities. Other concerns include intellectual property, security regulations, and difficulties integrating AI tools into existing CI pipelines. Standardizing prompt engineering across teams is also a barrier. They expressed *hope* for more robust, developer-focused AI tools that complement human judgment. These tools could help meet data and security needs while improving efficiency in large-scale testing workflows.

C4 Experts at Company 4 described their *experience* in modeling and simulating complex subsystems using both physics-based and machine learning methods. They compared flight-derived data with simulated outputs to improve model fidelity and detect discrepancies between predictions and real-world behavior. They also used environmental simulation frameworks to advance sensor solutions, including neural model training for water dynamics and sea clutter. Simulated datasets feed into mathematical models, and internally developed architectures help distribute data to enhance simulations and create dynamic environments. Key *challenges* include managing the vast volume of flight test data and converting it into coherent system-level metrics. Capturing subtle, high-level phenomena and modeling complex system-of-systems interactions remains difficult, especially as many simulator components are optimized for standalone rather than integrated performance. Still, they express *hope* in AI-enabled "digital twin" techniques to align simulations with real flight behavior for more holistic system insights. They believe AI can enhance aircraft modeling, training realism, environmental understanding, and system interoperability.

C5 Representatives from Company 5 did not report any *experience* with generative AI in testing. They briefly described work on network segmentation and secure data diode installations. Their smaller size motivates more agile R&D practices. The team identifies a *challenge* in directing testing and quality assurance due to restricted data access and protected production environments. As their customers are security authorities, they must provide high levels of trust and proof of correctness, which increases the need for AI automation. These constraints necessitate innovative strategies that balance security with improved testing. They express a *hope* that automated, accurate modeling of realistic customer environments using AI and digital twins will improve testing and build customer trust to share real-world data. They also see potential in AI-driven, scenario-based simulations for creating cost-effective and adaptable test environments. Combining customer data, simulation, and modeling is seen as invaluable.

C6 Representatives from Company 6 have *experience* in developing autonomous vehicle systems and applying AI-based testing. Their work included large-scale data logging from autonomous trucks and AI-based classification using a taxonomy that defines interests such as roundabouts, highways, or traffic density. This is a guided data-selection tool that sends chosen data for annotation to train AI models and create ground truth for validation. They also experimented with AI to generate challenging near-accident scenarios and build maps from logged data. Their main *challenge* is managing massive data volumes and transitioning from rule-based simulations to dynamic generative AI environments. They face challenges in identifying critical data points, modeling near-accident scenarios, and scaling AI model training within a rigorous MLOps framework, necessitating ongoing refinement of simulation methods for safe and predictive autonomy. They express *hope* in generative AI to create high-fidelity simulations. They anticipate that AI-generated maps, synthetic environments, and expanded MLOps capabilities will improve training and validation of autonomous systems.

4.2 Cross-Company Group Discussions

This section summarizes the key points discussed by each group in response to the guiding question outlined in Sect. 2.2, as collected according to the methodology described previously. The content is summarized but unfiltered, preserving the group-specific perspectives for later thematic coding analysis.

Group 1. discussed the importance of applying generative AI to specific disciplines, noting that the value of results depends on context. They highlighted the challenge of detecting differences between simulations and reality, as well as handling hallucinations. The need for sensor input in test cases, especially in safety-critical testing, was also identified, as was the importance of using declassified, anonymized, and more representative synthetic data.

Group 2. emphasized quality issues, including applicability, suitability, and scalability of generative AI solutions. They discussed both the solution domain (such as effective prompting, tracing, and distilling information) and the problem domain (development, testing, requirements, code, and test strategies). They questioned the extent to which these methods are applicable and suitable for their specific problems and applications. The group also explored the need for effective prompting techniques and noted that tracing information to artifacts is costly, suggesting that generative AI could help address this.

Group 3. questioned whether AI-generated data and models can be trusted and how to prove their trustworthiness, especially when distributed AI systems are involved in handling process parts. They discussed creating machine learning models for agent (user) decision-making, such as those used in training or driving simulators. The group also mentioned the potential for generative AI to bridge the technical gap from requirements to code and its application in scheduling communication in simulators and degradation modeling. They reiterated the importance of ensuring that generated models are representative and relevant.

Group 4. focused on modeling the surrounding environment for sensor simulations and using AI to select scenarios for best coverage or value, including edge cases. Given limited running resources, they discussed the need to evaluate scenario quality to choose among them. The group also raised the question of which metrics are most critical for evaluating or measuring simulation outcomes, and they mentioned the challenge of modeling environments with fidelity higher than current game engines.

Group 5. addressed organizational set-up, specifically the need to bring together experts with domain knowledge and AI/ML experts. They raised the challenge of onboarding both groups effectively, noting that specialists understand the problem domain while technical experts may lack this context.

5   Thematic Coding Analysis

This section presents the results of the thematic coding analysis, organized into themes and sub-themes derived from recurring codes identified in the workshop data. Such themes and sub-themes, with traceability to individual workshop presentations and group discussions, are presented in Table 2. To contextualize the analysis, the table also includes a column referencing companies with reported experiences and related literature for each sub-theme. Note that our thematic coding analysis excludes aspects related to motivation and collaboration.

Next, each theme is discussed with direct references to corresponding statements or paraphrased excerpts that reflect the perspectives of industrial partners.

5.1 AI-Generated Scenarios and Environment Models

Practitioners are exploring the use of generative AI to create scenarios and environment models. The following sub-themes have been identified:

Novel Scenario Generation. involves using AI to generate new, diverse, or rare test scenarios that are challenging to capture with traditional, rule-based methods. The goal is to improve coverage in testing. Both automotive and aerospace companies emphasized the need to move beyond rigid frameworks and utilize AI to generate challenging or near-accident scenarios. For example, Company 2 aims to utilize AI to identify novel test scenarios and expedite regression testing, and Company 6 is experimenting with AI to create more challenging variations of near-accident scenarios. These efforts are echoed in group discussions, where the need for more representative and diverse synthetic data has been highlighted. The alignment across these reports shows a shared motivation to use generative AI for scenario creation.

Table 2. Summary of workshop themes and their mapping with literature

Theme	Sub-theme	Hope/Challenge		Experience	
		Presentation	Group	Literature	Company
AI-generated scenarios and environment models	Novel scenario generation	C2, C3, C4 C5, C6	G1, G4	[1], [7], [8], [15], [20]	C4, C6
	Environment model generation	C4, C6	G1, G3, G4	[1], [5], [7], [20] [20]	C4, C6
	Test scenario evaluation and selection	C6	G4	[15]	C6
Simulators and AI in CI/CD pipelines	Large-scale data handling	C1, C4, C6	-	[15]	C1, C4, C6
	Continuous integration	C1, C3, C6	-	-	C1
	Simulators interoperability	C2, C4	G3	-	C4
Trustworthiness in generative AI for simulation	Model/Simulation fidelity	C2, C4	G1, G3, G4	[1], [20]	C4
	Over-reliance	C3	G1	-	-
	Standardization and regulation	C3, C5	G2	-	C3
	Traceability	-	G2, G4	-	-

Environment Model Generation. involves using AI to build high-fidelity digital representations of real environments, such as flight conditions or customer networks. The aim is to bridge the gap between laboratory simulations and real-world testing. Companies 4 and 5 are working on creating robust virtual models, such as digital twins, to replicate real environments. Company 4 aims to utilize AI-enabled digital twin techniques to align real flight patterns with simulator outputs, while Company 5 recognizes the value in automated, accurate modeling of customer environments using AI and digital twins. Group 1 also mentioned the need for synthetic data generation. These examples demonstrate a consistent trend toward more realistic and adaptable simulation environments utilizing generative AI.

Test Scenario Evaluation and Selection. highlights the need for automated scenario evaluation methods and systems that can dynamically adapt the prompts fed into generative AI models, or even retrain the models themselves, in response to performance feedback. More importantly, we lack well-defined metrics to assess the quality of generated scenarios automatically. This is important for companies because they need it to select the most critical scenarios for running, given limited resources. For instance, Group 4 discussed the importance of evaluating scenario quality and choosing among them due to resource constraints. Company 6 uses AI-based classification to select test data and scenarios for annotation and model training. Current approaches reported in the literature [7,8,15,20] often rely on manual validation of generated scenarios, which is not scalable given the industry's need to use large, complex datasets.

5.2   Simulators and AI in CI/CD Pipelines

This theme addresses the technical challenges of integrating AI-based approaches into existing development and testing pipelines, especially at scale.

Large-scale Data Handling. refers to the need for scalable data processing and management as data volumes and complexity grow, particularly in autonomous systems. Companies 1, 4, and 6 all report handling large amounts of data from real-world operations, such as autonomous trucks or flight tests. Company 1 highlights the need for scalable data processing to handle tens of thousands of signals, while Company 4 focuses on converting vast test data into actionable metrics. Company 6 logs large-scale data from autonomous vehicles. These experiences highlight a common challenge in managing and analyzing complex, high-volume data streams, underlining the need for robust data pipelines.

Continuous Integration (CI). focuses on integrating AI-driven solutions into CI and automated workflows, including regular model retraining and dataset updates. Companies 1 and 3, and Company 6, all emphasize the importance of integrating AI into CI pipelines. Company 1 invests in automated build and testing cycles to speed up feedback, while Company 3 faces challenges adapting AI tools to established CI processes. Company 6 is scaling AI model training within a rigorous MLOps framework. These reports highlight the need for seamless integration of AI into existing development cycles.

Simulators Interoperability. covers the challenge of integrating multiple simulators or subsystems, often designed to operate independently, into a cohesive system for end-to-end validation. Company 4 reports difficulties in connecting separate simulation frameworks for system-of-systems validation, noting that complex interactions between subsystems are challenging to model. Their internal solutions aim to make data accessible across the organization. This aligns with the need for better communication and data sharing between simulators, as discussed in group sessions.

5.3 Trustworthiness in Generative AI for Simulation

This theme focuses on ensuring that AI-generated data, models, and simulations are reliable, accurate, and compliant with standards and regulations.

Model/Simulation Fidelity. is about ensuring that simulations and models accurately reflect real-world behavior, especially in complex or safety-critical systems. Companies 2, 4, and 6, along with several groups, highlighted the challenge of maintaining model fidelity as complexity increases. Company 2 faces difficulties maintaining accuracy as simulation complexity grows, while Company 4 reported their experience in comparing real flight data with simulations to set credibility benchmarks. Group 1 discussed the challenge of distinguishing between simulated and real-world scenarios. These aligned reports show that simulation fidelity is a concern across domains.

Over-reliance. refers to the risk of depending too much on AI-generated outputs, which may be of uncertain quality or introduce errors. Company 3 warns of potential over-reliance on AI-suggested code, while Group 1 raises concerns about handling hallucinations in AI-generated test cases, especially in safety-critical contexts. Both point to the need for careful oversight.

Standardization and Regulation. addresses the need for internal standards and regulatory compliance when using AI-generated artifacts, particularly in terms of intellectual property and data security. Companies 3 and 5 express concerns about intellectual property, data security, and regulatory restrictions when using AI-generated code or test artifacts. Company 3 also notes the challenge of standardizing prompt engineering across teams. Group 2 discussed the need for effective prompting. These reports show a shared need for clear standards and regulatory guidance.

Traceability. aims to link information to artifacts or find relevant requirements. Group 2 suggested that generative AI could assist with such costly tasks.

5.4 Summary and Analysis

The thematic coding analysis presented here in Sect. 5 resulted in three major themes, representing the three areas where generative AI techniques have the most potential for simulations in test environments for large-scale cyber-physical systems, according to the practitioners at the cross-company workshop. Those three areas are AI-generated scenarios and environment models, Simulators and AI in CI/CD pipelines, and Trustworthiness in generative AI for simulation.

Participants from several companies at the cross-company workshop described the need to increase efficiency and effectiveness in their test activities, exemplified by reducing manual work, improving test coverage, shortening feedback loops, and implementing automated testing. For example, one participant described how the company aims to "exploit techniques to harness the vast amount of data already generated", potentially shortening the feedback loop. A participant from another company described how their company sees advanced AI techniques as a means to enhance realism and maintain simulation ecosystems in alignment with rapidly evolving industry demands. In analyzing the results from the cross-company workshop, we found that companies see potential in generative AI for simulation, but do not appear to have a clear agenda going forward, suggesting a need for continued industry-academia collaboration.

6   Threats to Validity

Construct validity. One must always consider that a different set of questions and context for the cross-company workshop can lead to a different focus for the participants. To address threats to construct validity, the questions for the presentations and breakout sessions were designed with open-ended questions. In this paper, we also present background material for both workshop participants and the companies in the study, providing as much information as possible about the context to enable the reproducibility of the study.

Another threat to construct validity is researcher bias while interpreting the results from the cross-company workshop. To mitigate this threat, two researchers analyzed the data separately, and the other two reviewed the results to ensure quality and correctness. The process was conducted iteratively to enhance the quality of the analysis, achieving consensus through discussions and visualizations in diagrams, tables, and text.

External validity. The cross-company workshop included participants from six companies. Due to this, it is conceivable that the findings from this study are only valid for these companies or companies operating in the same industry segments (presented in Sect. 2.2). The diverse nature of these six companies ensures that our study covers a variety of industrial CPSs. As such, it is reasonable to expect that the study's results are also relevant to a large segment of the CPS industry (analytic generalization). However, we consider external validation in other companies (preferably in different industry segments) as future work.

Internal validity. Of the 12 threats to internal validity listed by Cook, Campbell, and Day [6], we consider selection, ambiguity about causal direction, and compensatory rivalry relevant to this work:

- *Selection*: All workshop participants were purposively sampled (selected as good informants with appropriate roles in the companies) according to the guidelines for qualitative data appropriateness provided by Robson [17]. Based on the rationale of these samplings and supported by Robson, who considers this type of sampling superior for this type of study to ensure appropriateness, we consider this threat to be mitigated.

- *Ambiguity about causal direction*: While this study discusses relationships in some cases, we are cautious about making statements regarding causation. Statements that include cause and effect are collected from the presentations and break-out sessions at the cross-company workshop and not introduced in the interpretation of the data.
- *Compensatory rivalry*: In qualitative research, the threat of compensatory rivalry must always be considered. The questions for the presentations and breakout sessions were deliberately designed to be value-neutral for the participants, avoiding judgment of their performance or skills. Generally, the questions were also designed to be open-ended, preventing bias and ensuring open and accurate answers. However, our experiences from previous work indicate that participants are more prone to self-criticism than to self-praise.

7   Conclusions and Future Work

Our cross-company study reveals that while the industry sees potential in generative AI for more scalable and efficient simulation and testing, several key areas require further research for its effective adoption in simulation-based testing. According to practitioners, the three areas where generative AI techniques have the most potential for simulations in test environments for large-scale CPSs are:

- **AI-generated scenarios and environment models:** This line of work applies generative AI to create and enhance simulation scenarios and environment models, and to define clear metrics to assess these artifacts by novelty and realism. Achieving this demands strong domain-specific insight and a deep understanding of the operational context.
- **Simulators and AI in CI/CD pipelines:** This research direction investigates how generative AI and simulation tools can be integrated into CI/CD pipelines to enable scalable data processing, automated model retraining, and orchestrated validation across multi-disciplinary systems or simulators.
- **Trustworthiness in generative AI for simulation:** Research in this direction is about ensuring that AI-generated simulations and models are trustworthy enough for safety-critical systems or production use. It verifies that simulations accurately reflect real-world behavior, establishes systematic oversight and traceability, and aligns outputs with internal standards and external regulations.

While companies seem to lack a clear, actionable agenda for realizing the potential of generative AI in the context of CPSs, our identified areas faithfully capture various opportunities and challenges that participating companies face.

These areas can also serve as a starting point for strengthened industry-academia collaboration, primarily as companies strive to transform large-scale, complex operational data into actionable insights, as mentioned by multiple companies. Participants repeatedly emphasized the value of such collaborations and the importance of tangible outputs to sustain engagement, highlighting the need to deliver visible results and proofs of concept to demonstrate concrete feasibility and value and secure managerial buy-in.

Overall, current generative AI solutions appear more suited for one-off or exploratory use cases rather than integration into production environments, where higher levels of automation and trustworthiness are essential. This was reflected in two key concerns raised by practitioners: the lack of reliable evaluation mechanisms to ensure trustworthy outputs, and the difficulty of integrating generative components into continuous integration and deployment pipelines. When revisiting the literature from the preliminary study phase, we found that these concerns were largely unaddressed, and many approaches relied on manual evaluation and expert-driven prompt or parameter tuning, making them inadequate for scalable, automated deployment. These persistent limitations in both practice and research highlight the need for further development of robust evaluation methods and seamless pipeline integration. Moreover, the anticipated applications of generative AI outlined here remain future work, and structured discussions with experts in the field of generative AI will be essential to assess their feasibility.

Acknowledgment. We sincerely appreciate Software Center for organizing the workshop and the participating companies for generously sharing their experiences and insights. The first author was partially supported by the Vinnova competence center on Continuous Digitalization (CoDiG), while the last author was partially supported by the Wallenberg AI, Autonomous Systems and Software Program (WASP) funded by the Knut and Alice Wallenberg Foundation. The authors grateful to Willem Meijer for his feedback on the manuscript draft.

References

1. Ali, S., Arcaini, P., Arrieta, A.: Foundation models for the digital twins creation of cyber-physical systems. In: Leveraging Applications of Formal Methods, Verification and Validation. Application Areas - 12th Int. Symposium, ISoLA 2024 Part V. LNCS, vol. 15223, pp. 9–26. Springer (2024). https://doi.org/10.1007/978-3-031-75390-9_2
2. Alshahwan, N., et al.: Automated unit test improvement using large language models at meta. In: Companion Proceedings of the 32nd ACM International Conference on the Foundations of Software Engineering, pp. 185–196 (2024)
3. Balog, K., Zhai, C.: User simulation in the era of generative AI: user modeling, synthetic data generation, and system evaluation. CoRR **abs/2501.04410** (2025). https://doi.org/10.48550/ARXIV.2501.04410
4. Cederbladh, J., Eramo, R., Muttillo, V., Strandberg, P.E.: Experiences and challenges from developing cyber-physical systems in industry-academia collaboration. Softw. Pract. Exp. **54**(6), 1193–1212 (2024). https://doi.org/10.1002/SPE.3312
5. Chen, K., Yang, Y., Chen, B., López, J.A.H., Mussbacher, G., Varró, D.: Automated domain modeling with large language models: A comparative study. In: 26th ACM/IEEE International Conference on Model Driven Engineering Languages and Systems, MODELS 2023, Västerås, Sweden, October 1-6, 2023. pp. 162–172. IEEE (2023). https://doi.org/10.1109/MODELS58315.2023.00037

6. Cook, T.D., Campbell, D.T., Day, A.: Quasi-experimentation: design and analysis issues for field settings, vol. 351. Houghton Mifflin Boston (1979)

7. Deng, Y., Yao, J., Tu, Z., Zheng, X., Zhang, M., Zhang, T.: TARGET: automated scenario generation from traffic rules for testing autonomous vehicles. https://doi.org/10.48550/arXiv.2305.06018

8. Jackson, I., Sáenz, M.J., Ivanov, D.A.: From natural language to simulations: applying AI to automate simulation modelling of logistics systems. Int. J. Prod. Res. **62**(4), 1434–1457 (2024). https://doi.org/10.1080/00207543.2023.2276811

9. Karlsson, A., Lindmaa, E., Sun, S., Staron, M.: AI-based automotive test case generation: an action research study on integration of generative AI into test automation frameworks. In: Product-Focused Software Process Improvement. Industry-, Workshop-, and Doctoral Symposium Papers - 25th Int. Conf., PROFES 2024, Tartu, Estonia, December 2-4, 2024. LNCS, vol. 15453, pp. 50–66. Springer (2024). https://doi.org/10.1007/978-3-031-78392-0_4

10. Kitzinger, J.: Qualitative research: introducing focus groups. BMJ **311**(7000), 299–302 (1995)

11. Lee, S., et al.: Cyber-physical AI: systematic research domain for integrating AI and cyber-physical systems. ACM Trans. Cyber Phys. Syst. **9**(2), 19:1–19:33 (2025). https://doi.org/10.1145/3721437

12. Mårtensson, T., Ancher, G., Ståhl, D.: Test environments for large-scale software systems - an industrial study of intrinsic and extrinsic success factors. Softw. Test. Verification Reliab. **33**(3) (2023). https://doi.org/10.1002/STVR.1839

13. Mårtensson, T., Ståhl, D., Bosch, J.: Continuous integration impediments in large-scale industry projects. In: 2017 IEEE International Conference on Software Architecture, ICSA 2017, Gothenburg, Sweden, April 3-7, 2017, pp. 169–178. IEEE Computer Society (2017). https://doi.org/10.1109/ICSA.2017.11

14. Muhammad, K., David, T., Nassisid, G., Farus, T.: Integrating generative AI with network digital twins for enhanced network operations. CoRR **abs/2406.17112** (2024). https://doi.org/10.48550/ARXIV.2406.17112

15. Mühlburger, H., Wotawa, F.: Faultlines - evaluating the efficacy of open-source large language models for fault detection in cyber-physical systems. In: IEEE International Conference on Artificial Intelligence Testing, AITest 2024, pp. 47–54. IEEE (2024). https://doi.org/10.1109/AITEST62860.2024.00014

16. Patil, M.S., Ung, G., Nyberg, M.: Towards specification-driven LLM-based generation of embedded automotive software. In: Bridging the Gap Between AI and Reality - Second International Conference AISoLA 2024, Crete, Greece, October 30 - November 3, 2024. Lecture Notes in Computer Science, vol. 15217, pp. 125–144. Springer (2024). https://doi.org/10.1007/978-3-031-75434-0_9

17. Robson, C.: Real world research. John Wiley and Sons, 5 edn. (2024)

18. RTCA: DO-330 software tool qualification considerations (2011). https://my.rtca.org/productdetails?id=a1B36000001IcfkEAC

19. Wohlin, C.: Guidelines for snowballing in systematic literature studies and a replication in software engineering. In: 18th International Conference on Evaluation and Assessment in Software Engineering, EASE '14, London, England, United Kingdom, May 13-14, 2014, pp. 38:1–38:10. ACM (2014). https://doi.org/10.1145/2601248.2601268

20. Xia, Y., Dittler, D., Jazdi, N., Chen, H., Weyrich, M.: LLM experiments with simulation: large language model multi-agent system for simulation model parametrization in digital twins. In: 29th IEEE Int. Conf. on Emerging Technologies and Factory Automation, ETFA 2024, pp. 1–4. IEEE (2024). https://doi.org/10.1109/ETFA61755.2024.10710900

21. Zhou, X., Gou, X., Huang, T., Yang, S.: Review on testing of cyber physical systems: methods and testbeds. IEEE Access **6**, 52179–52194 (2018). https://doi.org/10.1109/ACCESS.2018.2869834
22. Zhuo, T.Y., et al.: Bigcodebench: benchmarking code generation with diverse function calls and complex instructions. arXiv preprint arXiv:2406.15877 (2024)

Pipelines Under Pressure: An Empirical Study of Security Misconfigurations of GitHub Workflows

Edoardo Riggio[(✉)] [ID] and Cesare Pautasso [ID]

Software Institute, Università della Svizzera italiana (USI), Lugano, Switzerland
`edoardo.riggio@usi.ch`, `c.pautasso@ieee.org`

Abstract. Continuous Integration and Continuous Deployment (CI/CD) pipelines have grown in popularity in recent years and are essential in streamlining the process of development and deployment of high quality software. However, developers often overlook security concerns in CI/CD pipelines, opening the door to many vulnerabilities. This paper presents an empirical investigation of nine security misconfigurations sourced from a comprehensive review of security guidelines, developer blogs, GitHub documentation, and prior research. To study the presence, co-occurrence and yearly trends of these security misconfigurations within current CI/CD practices, we analyzed a large dataset containing the most recent version of over 200 000 GitHub workflow specification files, taken from open source repositories. To aid us in this study, we developed *Soteria*, a static analysis tool equipped with custom detectors that can systematically identify security misconfigurations. Given that less than 1% of the analyzed workflows do not include any misconfiguration, our detection tool makes a contribution to raise awareness about widespread security misconfigurations. Our findings challenge conventional practices and motivate the need for an urgent shift in how security principles are systematically applied in the development and operation of CI/CD pipelines with more robust and finer-grained security controls.

Keywords: DevOps · Security · Misconfigurations · Workflows · CI/CD Build Pipeline · GitHub Actions

1 Introduction

In recent years, DevSecOps [1] has emerged as a transformative approach that fosters a culture of collaboration between developers, operations teams, and other stakeholders involved in the software lifecycle. DevSecOps leverages automation, replicability, continuous integration (CI), and continuous deployment (CD) to streamline and enhance the efficiency of software delivery, all while maintaining high-quality and high-security standards. The increased adoption of CI/CD practices [2] has brought security concerns to the forefront [3]. For example, a

G. Scanniello et al. (Eds.): PROFES 2025, LNCS 16361, pp. 220–236, 2026.
https://doi.org/10.1007/978-3-032-12089-2_14

CI/CD pipeline could be misconfigured to run injected malicious code in privileged environments, which in turn could lead to losses in both the integrity and confidentiality of the software being packaged for release.

Many software repository hosting platforms offer CI/CD functionalities: developers can easily describe custom-made build pipelines as workflows. As developers focus on quickly setting up their CI/CD pipelines, they sometime fall into traps which are reflected by the smells [4] and security misconfigurations introduced in their workflows. As a consequence, there have been many incidents reported due to attacks exploiting vulnerable pipelines [5]. This has led to a growing body of literature collecting security guidelines and sharing experience on how to mitigate and control known vulnerabilities [6–11].

In this empirical study we statically analyze an existing large dataset of GitHub workflow specifications mined from open source repositories [12] looking for nine types of misconfigurations that lead to potential security vulnerabilities in the CI/CD pipeline. Our goal is to answer the following research question:

What are the most frequent and trending types of security misconfigurations found in GitHub CI/CD workflows?

Approach To introduce detectors for 9 types of misconfigurations in GitHub CI/CD workflows that could lead to security vulnerabilities [6], we used a two-step methodology. First, we surveyed the grey literature (GitHub documentation, security guidelines, DevSecOps expert blogs) looking for supply chain attacks caused by misconfigured GitHub workflows. After collecting 9 security misconfiguration types, we searched the academic literature for empirical studies and existing detection and correction tools, finding related work on six. To efficiently detect the miconfigurations, we have built *Soteria*, a static analyzer for GitHub workflow files, available as a VSCode extension[1]. Its source code can be found in the replication package[2] and on GitHub[3].

Main Findings. Our findings highlight how security best practices are widely neglected. The most frequent type of misconfiguration affecting 94.1% of the workflows concerns the use of regular version pins when invoking external actions, which opens the door to supply chain attacks. While half of the misconfiguration types have been detected in less than 2% of the workflows, only 1 641 (0.81%) workflows did not present any misconfiguration at all. We also report an inverse relationship between severity and frequency, where critical misconfigurations can be found, but only rarely.

2   Related Work

Ongoing and recent research contributes to DevSecOps by detecting and mitigating vulnerabilities in the workflow before they can be exploited [6, 13–22]. The

---

[1] https://marketplace.visualstudio.com/items?itemName=aegis-forge.soteria.
[2] https://figshare.com/s/fdaeb40937fbe0af8a13.
[3] https://github.com/aegis-forge/soteria.

position paper by Delicheh and Mens [6] inspired our work by pointing out many security risks associated with workflow misconfigurations. Also Paule et al. [19] identified the pressing need to detect vulnerabilities in CI/CD pipelines. Pecka et al. [13,14] studied vulnerabilities in CI/CD pipelines that use K8 clusters; Benedetti et al. [15] developed the GitHub Action Security Tester (GHAST) tool that performs some automatic security checks on GitHub workflow files; Kushwaha et al. [16] analyzed some misconfigurations in CI/CD pipelines in the context of financial systems; Pan et al. [17] performed attack surface analysis on GitHub workflow files; Li et al. [18] built a tool to detect malicious crypto-mining jobs in GitHub CI/CD workflow files; The ARGUS [21] tool uses static taint analysis to identify code injection vulnerabilities in GitHub Actions. Koishybayev et al. [20] show a detailed comparison of the security properties of GitHub CI/CD with other platforms as well as a large-scale empirical study on over 447 238 workflows used in 213 854 repositories focused on a subset of the misconfigurations we collected in this paper.

3   Security Misconfigurations

Table 1 lists the nine security misconfigurations studied in this paper, together with their short definitions, severity, and literature sources. We marked with a ⋆ the ones which have never been mentioned in previous empirical studies. The security misconfigurations have been divided into five different categories based on OWASP Top 10 CI/CD Security Risks [23].

To collect the security misconfigurations, we have also surveyed CI/CD blogs maintained by cybersecurity companies [7–9], open source security-focused organizations [24], or by GitHub itself [10,11]. In addition, there are also some security researchers that write articles about specific attacks performed on software systems by exploiting CI/CD workflows [25,26].

Blog posts [7,24] and GitHub workflows documentation [11] were the main sources from which we extracted most of the security misconfigurations used in this study. We also consulted research done by security researchers [25,26] to identify three less-known types of security misconfigurations which have not yet been covered by existing empirical studies [15,20,21]. After collecting the misconfigurations, we searched the academic literature for empirical studies and existing detection and correction tools, finding related work on 6 misconfigurations. The used sources all: 1) explicitly discuss the misconfiguration as a security risk; 2) show how to exploit the misconfiguration with proof of concepts or actual attacks; 3) present how to mitigate the misconfiguration impact.

3.1   Dependency Chain Abuse (CICD-SEC-3)

In Dependency Chain Abuse, the software supply chain on which the workflow relies on is compromised. This could enable malicious actors to push tainted version of packages which are then downloaded and executed by workflows with the following misconfiguration:

Table 1. Security Misconfigurations: Definitions, Severity and Sources

Group	ID	Misconfiguration	Severity	Literature
CICD-SEC-3	1	`no-hash-version-pin`	Low	[15, 17, 20, 22, 27, 28]
CICD-SEC-4	2	`unconditional-injection`	High	[6, 10, 15, 21]
	3	`conditional-injection`	Medium	[6, 10, 15, 21]
	4⋆	`pwn-request`	High	[7, 29, 30]
CICD-SEC-5	5	`coarse-permission`	Medium	[6, 15, 20, 22, 31]
	6	`global-secret`	Medium	[6, 15, 20, 32]
CICD-SEC-7	7	`self-hosted-runner`	Medium	[8, 9, 20, 25]
CICD-SEC-9	8⋆	`caching-in-release`	Critical	[26, 33, 34]
	9⋆	`unsafe-artifact-download`	Critical	[35, 36]

no-hash-version-pin. Using regular version pins (such as `@main`, `@v1`, `@v2.1.1`) when calling external GitHub Actions opens the door to supply chain attacks in the pipeline. Being regular version pins mutable, malicious actors could gain access to the repository of the external third-party Action, change its source code, and publish a new release under the same major, minor, or branch tag (via tag-renaming attacks [24]). To avoid this vulnerability, one would have to use a hash version pin when referring to external GitHub Actions [7, 11, 35] – i.e. `actions/checkout@1a...53`.

3.2 Poisoned Pipeline Execution (CICD-SEC-4)

With Poisoned Pipeline Execution, an attacker may manipulate in some way the pipeline process without having direct access to its workflow definition suffering from one of the following misconfigurations:

unconditional-injection. In workflow files, developers can refer to environment variables present in GitHub's context [10], for example, to read the name of the issue that triggered the pipeline, the name of the commit, etc. As we can see on line 9 in Fig. 1, a step runs a bash script. The bash script will run what seems like an innocuous `echo` command. The problem is that the `issue.title` variable is not under the control of the maintainer of the repository, and can be set by anyone. Attackers may create an issue to the repository with the following title: `title" && ls / && echo "`. This will cause GitHub workflow's runner to replace `${{ ... }}` in the `run` section with the tainted issue title. The runner will execute the commands `echo "title" && ls / && echo ""`, thus also running a `ls` command on the root directory of the runner [6, 10, 15, 21]. This becomes especially dangerous when it is paired with a trigger on the creation or modification of an issue. To avoid this, maintainers should save the data in environment variables, so that it will be treated as a string.

conditional-injection This misconfiguration combines the previous misconfiguration with a condition – the `if` section of the workflow – which controls when to run the job containing the problematic GitHub context variable [6,10,15,21].

pwn-request. When a workflow uses the `pull_request_target` trigger, it runs in the context of the target repository – the one under the control of the repository maintainer. Thus, if the workflow also checks out the forked repository, it opens the workflow to possible remote code execution [7,29,30]. To avoid this, never checkout the repository when using a `pull_request_target` trigger.

```
1  on:
2    issues:
3      types: [opened]
4  jobs:
5    print_issue_title:
6      runs-on: ubuntu-latest
7      name: Print issue title
8      steps:
9        - run: echo "${{ github.event.issue.title }}"
```

Fig. 1. An example of workflow vulnerable to a code injection attack.

3.3 Insufficient Pipeline-Based Access Controls (CICD-SEC-5)

Insufficient Pipeline-Based Access Controls (PBAC) represents security misconfigurations that deal with permission-granting and access to sensitive data such as secrets.

coarse-permission. A permission is said to be coarse when the principle of least privilege is not followed – thus ending up with a workflow or job that is too permissive. For example, setting the permissions to be `read-all`, `write-all`, or not setting them at all, are all instances of `coarse-permission` [7]. It is good practice to always set all the permissions to `none` at a workflow level (with the `permissions: {}` syntax) so that at job level only the strictly necessary permissions are granted.

global-secret. Secrets are environment variables containing very sensitive information such as keys, tokens, and passwords. Such variables can be defined at any point in the pipeline. If defined at workflow- or job-levels, there is a risk that the secret is exposed to steps or containers that do not need them. This could allow potentially tainted external GitHub Actions to gain access to such secrets [7].

3.4 Insecure System Configuration (CICD-SEC-7)

Insecure System Configuration concerns flaws in the hardening of external systems used by the pipeline. Such vulnerable systems can facilitate an attacker's process to expand its foothold in the workflow environment.

self-hosted-runner. Workflow jobs can be executed by a GitHub runner or a self-hosted runner [33]. While the former is by default configured to be ephemeral and isolated, the latter must be secured by the workflow developers themselves. Using non-ephemeral self-hosted runners can open the door to runner poisoning attacks. Moreover, if permissions are not set properly, a user can fork the repository and trigger workflow runs without the owner's approval – which could happen especially when a "contributor" badge is assigned to the user after making their first contribution to the repository. After running the payload on the runner, an attacker could get a web shell on the target runner, thus performing a successful runner poisoning attack [8,9,25]. For this reason, self-hosted runners should be avoided in public repositories.

3.5 Improper Artifact Integrity Validation (CICD-SEC-9)

The following misconfigurations allow attackers to modify the artifacts generated by the pipeline by inserting some malicious payload.

caching-in-release. Caching in the CI/CD pipeline [33] can be done in GitHub through the `actions/cache` Action. This Action, if not used correctly, can lead to caching sensitive data or, in worst cases, to cache poisoning attacks [26,34,37]. To conduct a cache poisoning attack, an attacker would need to exfiltrate both the `CacheServerUrl` and the `AccessToken` from a workflow – which can be done through a poisoned pipeline execution (CICD-SEC-4) security misconfiguration or through a compromised dependency. Next, the attacker creates the payload and inserts it in the cache. To do so, the attacker could restore or anticipate the cache keys, or could start blasting the cache such that the oldest cache entries are evicted and the poisoned ones are inserted [26]. In addition, the use of caching in release workflows is especially dangerous. As stated in the SLSA (Supply-chain Levels for Software Artifacts) L3 requirements, "It MUST NOT be possible for one build to inject false entries into a build cache used by another build, also known as 'cache poisoning'. In other words, the output of the build MUST be identical whether or not the cache is used" [38].

unsafe-artifact-download. There is a specific third-party Action used for downloading artifacts that, if not configured correctly, can lead to file overriding. The Action is `dawidd6/action-download-artifact`, which has three parameters `path`, `commit`, and `run_id`. The `path` parameter must be passed to avoid files to be overwritten by tainted ones, while both the `commit` and `run_id` parameters are used to verify that the artifact comes from a known and trusted source. If used without setting these parameters, the Action will extract the downloaded artifact into the default directory, overriding any file with the same name. This means that files to be executed can be replaced with malicious ones [35,36].

4 Dataset

Table 2. Structural Characteristics in Workflows and Repositories

Element	Workflows				Repositories				Total
	Mean	Median	Min	Max	Mean	Median	Min	Max	
Repositories	—	—	—	—	—	—	—	—	40 584
Workflows	—	—	—	—	4.9	3	1	288	200 758
Jobs	1.4	1	0	250	7.0	4	1	750	285 818
Steps	6.8	3	0	681	33.5	16	1	2 992	1 363 134
Containers	0.05	0	0	111	0.24	0	0	201	9 787
Permissions	1.5	0	0	367	1.5	0	0	367	61 070
Env. Variables	12.2	2	0	13 531	12.2	2	0	13 531	495 151
Ext. Workflows	0.08	0	0	175	0.4	0	0	13 531	16 582
Actions	3.6	3	0	681	17.7	9	0	13 531	718 611

The dataset used in this work was taken from Cardoen et al. [12], in particular the latest version of the dataset from October 2024 [39]. In their work, they extracted 2 367 030 workflow files from 43 342 different GitHub repositories thanks to *gigawork*, which iterates through the `.github/workflows` directory for every given GitHub repository, and extracts all the pushed versions of those workflow files. In addition to a ZIP file containing all of the actual workflow files, the authors provided some CSV files containing provenance metadata.

From this huge dataset, we have selected the most recent version of each workflow as we assume them to be the most improved ones and we are not interested (in this study) in performing a historical comparison of different versions of the same workflows. To carry out our study, we performed some data cleaning steps on the CSV file containing the workflows' metadata. In the data cleaning process, we used the `committed_date` column to retrieve the most recent workflow version per history. After retrieving the most recent, we used the `valid_workflow` column to discard all those workflows that were not valid.

From the CSV file provided by Cardoen et al., we created our own CSV file containing all the data and metadata of the workflows. In particular, we have taken the `repository`, `commit_hash`, `file_path`, and `committed_date` columns. In addition to these columns, we've added our own, namely `workflow_id` and `content`. In the `content` column, we have a base64 encoding of the actual content of the workflow, which was taken from the TAR.GZ archive provided by the authors of the dataset. This encoding was done so as to have the necessary information – i.e. data, metadata, and provenance – all in the same place.

After all the data cleaning and preprocessing steps mentioned above – which included discarding 469 non-existent workflows – we are left with 200 759 unique workflows from 40 584 repositories, which have been analyzed in this study.

Table 2 shows statistics on the main structural elements of the dataset's workflows and repositories.

5   Methodology

To detect the security misconfigurations present in GitHub workflows we developed *Soteria*. This tool statically analyzes Y(A)ML files containing GitHub workflows based on detectors which can be customized and defined by developers. It also measures and computes statistics on the structure of the workflows and the misconfigurations detected within a repository.

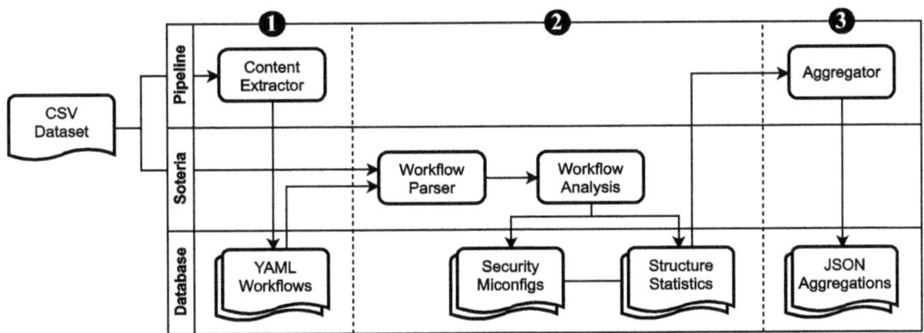

Fig. 2. Analysis pipeline

In this study, we used the analysis pipeline described in Fig. 2. The YAML files extracted from the dataset ❶ are fed to *Soteria* to both detect the security misconfigurations present in the workflows, and to compute workflows' structure statistics ❷. To detect the security misconfigurations, *Soteria* uses pattern matching rules derived from or even provided by the authors of the literature sources identifying the misconfigurations. The tool returns structural metrics together with a collection of detected security misconfigurations. The collections returned by *Soteria* are aggregated ❸ by workflow and by repository and classified by severity. For replicability and transparency purposes, all intermediate data returned by each step of the pipeline is saved to a database. Each file (with the exception of the "YAML Workflows" collection) is structured in a JSON format and contain the frequencies and actual occurrences (i.e. the line of code) of either misconfigurations or structures.

6   Results: Trends and Frequencies

After running the detection and analysis pipeline described in Sect. 5, we obtained the results described in Table 3, presenting statistics on the number of misconfigurations detected in each workflow and in each repository. We also aggregated the results by severity and reported the very low number and percentage of workflows and repositories in which no misconfiguration was detected.

The top two misconfigurations affecting 93% of workflows and found in almost all repositories are `no-hash-version-pin` and `coarse-permission`. All other misconfigurations have a median of 0, indicating that the majority of workflows (and repositories) do not include them. Finally, the `caching-in-release` statistics refer to the best-case scenario, where we consider our heuristics to detect a release workflow to work 100% of the time.

Table 3. Statistics on the number of detected misconfigurations, and number of affected workflows and repositories

ID	Workflows				Repositories				Total
	Mean	Max	Affected		Mean	Max	Affected		
1	3.4	681	188 782	(94.0%)	16.8	2992	40 375	(99.5%)	681 682
low	3.4	681	188 782	(94.0%)	16.8	2992	40 375	(99.5%)	681 682
3	0.0	1	43	(0.0%)	0.0	4	37	(0.1%)	43
5	0.93	7	186 711	(93.0%)	4.61	286	39 836	(98.2%)	186 996
6	0.6	285	48 440	(24.1%)	2.98	1700	18 464	(45.5%)	120 860
7	0.03	113	3 423	(1.7%)	0.15	227	869	(2.1%)	6 029
medium	1.56	286	190 742	(95.0%)	7.74	1988	40 006	(98.6%)	313 928
2	0.0	1	14	(0.0%)	0.0	1	14	(0.0%)	14
4	0.0	1	502	(0.3%)	0.01	107	295	(0.7%)	502
high	0.0	1	516	0.3%	0.01	107	309	(0.8%)	516
8	0.01	1	2 209	(1.1%)	0.05	33	1 436	(3.5%)	2 209
9	0.0	1	387	(0.2%)	0.01	9	266	(0.7%)	387
critical	0.01	2	2 590	(1.3%)	0.06	33	1 670	(4.1%)	2 596
None	—	—	1 641	(0.81%)	—	—	35	(0.08%)	—

6.1   Misconfigurations Trends

GitHub Actions was announced in 2018 and released in 2019, as reflected in the workflow commit dates, spread between the 4th of August 2019 to the 10th of October 2024. Table 4 shows the yearly number of occurrences of each misconfiguration – also grouped by severity. We did not include 2019 since there are only 5 months of data, and only the first 10 months of 2024 are covered.

By looking at Table 4, we can see that the absolute number of misconfigurations tend to vary over the years. However, if we also include the normalized values (the percentage in parenthesis), we can actually see that these values stay more or less the same throughout the 5 years. As reported in the last line of the table, the number of workflows constantly increases over the years. In the case of the single misconfigurations, the most prevalent ones are `no-hash-version-pin` (ID 1), `coarse-permission` (ID 5), and `global-secret` (ID 6).

Table 4. Yearly count of detected misconfigurations and misconfigured workflows

ID	2020		2021		2022		2023		2024	
1	114 697	(69.5%)	151 511	(69.2%)	156 008	(67.8%)	154 087	(67.6%)	91 355	(67.2%)
2	1	(0.001%)	4	(0.002%)	2	(0.001%)	4	(0.002%)	3	(0.002%)
3	2	(0.001%)	10	(0.005%)	10	(0.004%)	12	(0.005%)	9	(0.007%)
4	22	(0.01%)	90	(0.04%)	212	(0.09%)	118	(0.05%)	60	(0.04%)
5	32 550	(19.7%)	41 791	(19.1%)	42 656	(18.5%)	40 841	(17.9%)	24 038	(17.6%)
6	17 003	(10.3%)	23 770	(10.8%)	28 771	(12.5%)	29 795	(13.0%)	19 026	(14.0%)
7	290	(0.1%)	904	(0.4%)	1477	(0.6%)	2214	(0.9%)	1130	(0.8%)
8	370	(0.2%)	597	(0.2%)	560	(0.2%)	451	(0.1%)	205	(0.1%)
9	13	(0.008%)	86	(0.03%)	114	(0.05%)	127	(0.05%)	47	(0.03%)
low	114 697	(69.5%)	151 511	(69.2%)	156 008	(67.8%)	154 087	(67.6%)	91 355	(67.2%)
medium	49 845	(30.2%)	66 474	(30.3%)	72 914	(31.7%)	72 862	(32.0%)	44 203	(32.5%)
high	23	(0.01%)	94	(0.04%)	214	(0.09%)	122	(0.05%)	63	(0.05%)
critical	383	(0.2%)	683	(0.3%)	674	(0.2%)	578	(0.2%)	252	(0.1%)
Total	164 934		218 762		229 806		227 642		135 864	
Workflows	32 563	(99%)	42 149	(99%)	45 541	(99%)	47 039	(99%)	28 346	(97%)
None	13		34		249		754		591	
Repositories	12 452	(100%)	11 022	(99%)	6 955	(99%)	5 283	(99%)	1 993	(99%)

6.2 Misconfigurations Co-occurrence

Figure 3 shows how many distinct security misconfigurations types co-occur in a workflow and a repository. From this figure, we can evince that most of the times (in 69% of workflows and 51.7% of repositories) there is a co-occurrence of two different misconfigurations. The pairwise Jaccard similarity scores (Intersection over Union, IoU) for each co-occurring pairs of misconfigurations can be found in Fig. 4. In this figure, the lower triangular matrix represents the Jaccard scores for the workflow-grouped data, while the upper triangular matrix represents the Jaccard scores for the repository-grouped data. There is a very frequent co-occurrence of `no-hash-version-pin` and `coarse-permission` both in workflow-grouped data (IoU = 0.89) and in repository-grouped data (IoU = 0.98).

6.3 Actions and Version Tag Types

Our analysis pipeline identified 494 265 first-party Actions, 207 577 third-party Actions (Fig. 5). In both, the *major version* tagging method is the most used – respectively 91.4% and 60.7% of the cases. Only 2.4% of first-party Actions and 6.3% of third-party Actions use the full commit hash. Based on the latest

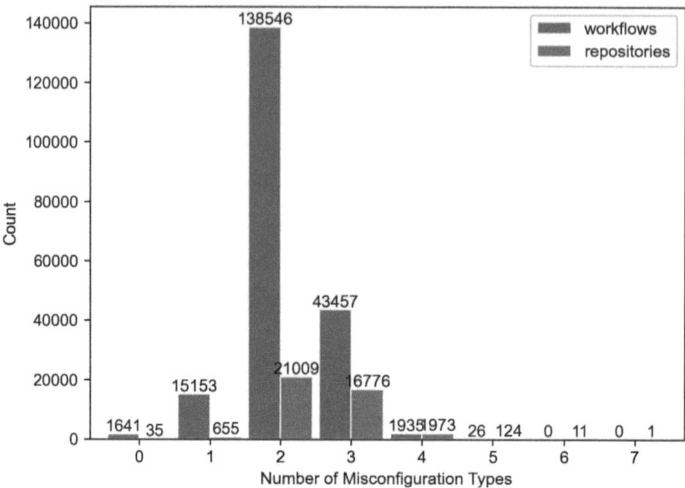

Fig. 3. Co-occurrence of multiple misconfiguration types in the same workflow (in brown) and in the same repository (in blue) (Color figure online)

Fig. 4. Jaccard similarity for pairs of misconfiguration types detected in the same workflow (lower-triangular) or repository (upper-triangular)

security advisories[4], 4 897 actions are vulnerable. Of these, 875 actions (18%) were referenced from 597 workflows using a version for which a security advisory

---

[4] https://docs.github.com/en/code-security/security-advisories/working-with-global-security-advisories-from-the-github-advisory-database/about-the-github-advisory-database.

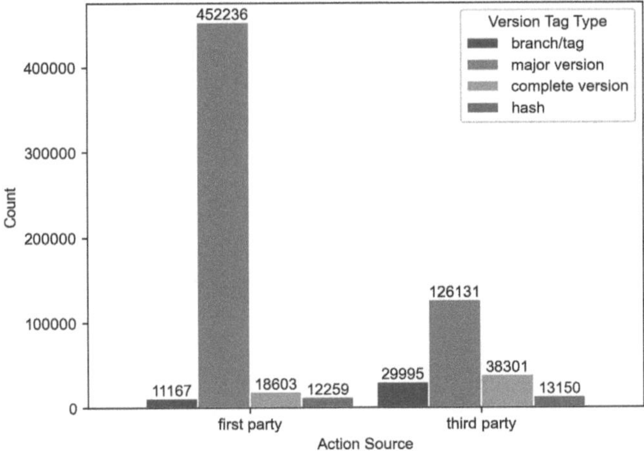

Fig. 5. Number of Action invocations by version tag type

was published before the commit date of the workflow. This is not the case for the remaining 2 569 workflows referencing 4 022 actions.

7   Discussion

The empirical analysis of the most recent version of more than 200 000 GitHub CI/CD workflow specifications carried out in this study shows how security misconfigurations are nearly ubiquitous. Only less than 1% of workflows are free from the security misconfigurations *Soteria* can detect. The pervasive presence of such misconfigurations highlights a shortfall in the adoption of security best practices, raising concerns about the integrity of the open source software supply chain based on GitHub.

The trend analysis of the nine security misconfigurations reveals that while the low severity `no-hash-version-pin` represents between 67% and 70% of all detected misconfigurations every year, the more critical ones such as `pwn-request` fluctuate between 0.013% in 2020 to a small peak of 0.092% in 2022, or become more prevalent – like `global-secret` growing from 10% to 14% in 2024.

In general, there is an inverse relationship between the prevalence and the severity of a misconfiguration: on average, every year we classified 68.32% low and 31.37% medium severity misconfigurations, leaving only 0.3% of highly severe or critical ones. The overall stability of the trend suggests that some developers still need to raise their awareness and remediation efforts as they still rely on build pipelines that are inadequate for the current threat landscape.

Our analysis also indicates that the most common security misconfigurations – `no-hash-version-pin` and `coarse-permission` – are present in more than 93% of the 200 758 workflows in our dataset. This may be due to developers being unaware that version pins are mutable and thus relying on them for external actions exposes the pipeline to potential supply chain attacks. Also, the use of overly permissive token settings violates the principle of least privilege. These results confirm similar "disturbing observations" published in previous studies [15]. If we consider insufficient access control, 10 826 workflows (62%) with no permissions declared – thus using the default permissions defined by `GITHUB_TOKEN` – have been detected in [15], while a very small number of workflows overriding default permission setting was counted at 900 (0.2%) in [20]. In our dataset, this number grows to 14 053 (7%). Regarding self-hosted runners, we detected 3 423 workflows in 227 public repositories affected by this misconfiguration. A lower bound of this metric was set at 565 public repositories in [20]. Immutable references to third-party actions are used only in 6% of the workflows in our dataset across 209 (0.5%) repositories. This is comparable to the observation by [20], where only 1.7% (3 248) of repositories do not incur in the `no_hash_version_pin` misconfiguration. Using ARGUS [21], Muralee et al. used taint analysis to discover code injection vulnerabilities in 4 307 workflows (0.16% of their sample), while our approach detected 57 (0.03%) workflows.

Overall, we present a large-scale, reproducible, exploratory empirical study of 9 security misconfigurations which can be detected using the same tool. Existing studies focus on the detection of individual (or a few) security misconfigurations, mostly on smaller datasets (which have not always been published). Our findings not only cover detecting the presence but also measure the frequency and the co-occurrence. The high correlation between the total number of detected misconfigurations of the two most widespread ones is an example of a surprising observation, which can lead to hypothesis formation and more in-depth studies to provide explanations, which could range from fundamental design issues of the automation platform to developer errors.

8   Threats to Validity

Dataset Limitations—Our dataset of 200 758 workflows provides a large sample size. However, only the most recent versions of the workflows have been selected to be analyzed. By doing so, we are omitting a possible understanding of the historical progression – or regression – of workflow configurations over time. In addition to this, despite the filtering done by the original authors of the dataset, some toy projects might still be present. We also performed the same analysis on an older dataset of 580 187 workflows from [20], also present in the replication package. Due to space restrictions, we could not include the detailed results, which show a similar relative frequency and ranking of the misconfigurations.

Construct Validity—Both types and definitions of the misconfigurations could also represent a threat to validity. The misconfigurations used in this study were chosen based on common CI/CD security guidelines and known vulnerabilities. However, there is a risk that the decision both of the types and the definition of the misconfiguration itself could be limited, and others could exist.

External Validity—This study focuses only on workflows written for GitHub's CI/CD engine, which might not represent also the workflows written for other CI/CD engines – such as GitLab's – or enterprise-level engines. In addition, the workflows in our dataset have been taken only from publicly available GitHub repositories, thus these misconfigurations might not apply to CI/CD workflow files used in private repositories. For example, it is considered safer to use self-hosted runners in private repositories than in public ones [11].

9   Conclusion

This paper presents an extensive empirical investigation into the detection of security misconfigurations within a large collection of GitHub workflow specifications. Aided by *Soteria* we managed to uncover nine different types of misconfigurations, some of which affecting almost all sampled workflow specifications. These misconfiguration types have been gathered by surveying previous literature, including blogs from top cybersecurity firms and researchers.

From our analysis, we were able to find the most recurring security misconfigurations, and report their trends across a five-year time span. We found that the most common security misconfiguration are the ones that use mutable version pins, overly permissive token settings, and secrets at a global scope. We also observed that these nine security misconfigurations often co-occur, broadening the attack surface.

Our main contributions lie in providing a detailed and large scale empirical analysis of these nine security misconfigurations, three of which have not been yet empirically studied. By developing a static analysis tool we automatically detected and characterized these misconfigurations at scale. These results should raise awareness on the current weak state of security practices in DevSecOps. Educators can use this result to raise awareness so that practitioners avoid introducing such security misconfigurations, thus preventing supply chain attacks. In our view, developers should prioritize the removal of critical misconfigurations, especially those affecting workflows used to build releases. Our study also indicates that a complete removal of all misconfigurations would require a large effort as they affect most repositories. The study results justify investing in linters for GitHub workflows, which should not only integrate security misconfiguration detectors but also provide auto-correction recommendations. Designers of future CI/CD automation tools should ensure that workflow languages are improved to reduce exposure and prevent introducing such misconfigurations.

The development of *Soteria* demonstrates the feasibility of using static analysis for automatic detection of many different security misconfigurations in CI/CD workflow specifications. Looking forward, we would like to perform a more detailed research to refine and extend the detection techniques towards the definition of security smells and anti-patterns, possibly extending the analysis to other CI/CD platforms.

References

1. Carter, K.: Francois Raynaud on DevSecOps. IEEE Softw. **34**(5), 93–96 (2017)
2. Humble, J., Farley, D.: Continuous delivery: reliable software releases through build, test, and deployment automation. Pearson (2010)
3. Rajapakse, R.N., Zahedi, M., Babar, M.A., Shen, H.: Challenges and solutions when adopting DevSecOps: a systematic review. Inf. Softw. Technol. **141**, 106700 (2022)
4. Vassallo, C., Proksch, S., Jancso, A., Gall, H.C., Di Penta, M.: Configuration smells in continuous delivery pipelines: a linter and a six-month study on GitLab. In: Proceedings of the 28th ACM Joint Meeting on European Software Engineering Conference and Symposium on the Foundations of Software Engineering (ESEC/FSE), pp. 327–337. ACM (2020)
5. Hsu, T.H.-C.: Hands-On Security in DevOps: Ensure Continuous Security, Deployment, and Delivery with DevSecOps. Packt Publishing Ltd. (2018)
6. Delicheh, H.O., Mens, T.: Mitigating security issues in github actions. In: Proceedings of the 4th International Workshop on Engineering and Cybersecurity of Critical Systems (EnCyCriS) and 2nd International Workshop on Software Vulnerability (SVM), pp. 6–11. ACM/IEEE (2024)
7. Segura, T.: GitHub Actions Security Best Practices. https://blog.gitguardian.com/github-actions-security-cheat-sheet/
8. Vincent, H.: GitHub Actions exploitation: self hosted runners. https://www.synacktiv.com/en/publications/github-actions-exploitation-self-hosted-runners
9. Blit, R.: GitHub, PyTorch and More Organizations Found Vulnerable to Self-Hosted Runner Attacks. https://www.legitsecurity.com/blog/github-pytorch-and-more-organizations-found-vulnerable-to-self-hosted-runner-attacks
10. Lobacevski, J.: Keeping your GitHub Actions and workflows secure Part 2: Untrusted input. https://securitylab.github.com/resources/github-actions-untrusted-input/
11. GitHub. Security hardening for GitHub Actions. https://docs.github.com/en/actions/security-for-github-actions/security-guides/security-hardening-for-github-actions
12. Cardoen, G., Mens, T., Decan, A.: A dataset of GitHub Actions workflow histories. In: Proceedings of the 21st International Conference on Mining Software Repositories (MSR), pp. 677–681. ACM (2024)
13. Pecka, N., Othmane, L., Valani, A.: Making Secure Software Insecure without Changing Its Code: The Possibilities and Impacts of Attacks on the DevOps Pipeline (2022). http://arxiv.org/abs/2201.12879
14. Pecka, N., Ben Othmane, L., Valani, A.: Privilege escalation attack scenarios on the DevOps pipeline within a kubernetes environment. In: Proceedings of the International Conference on Software and System Processes and International Conference on Global Software Engineering (ICSSP), pp. 45–49. ACM (2022)
15. Benedetti, G., Verderame, L., Merlo, A.: Automatic security assessment of github actions workflows. In: Proceedings Workshop on Software Supply Chain Offensive Research and Ecosystem Defenses (SCORED), pp. 37–45. ACM (2022)
16. Kushwaha, M.K., David, P., Suseela, G.: Automation and DevSecOps: streamlining security measures in financial system. In: Proceedings of the International Conference on Electronics, Computing and Communication Technologies (CONECCT), pp. 1–6 (2024)

17. Pan, Z., et al.: Ambush from all sides: understanding security threats in open-source software CI/CD pipelines. IEEE Trans. Dependable Secure Comput. **21**(1), 403–418 (2024)
18. Li, Z., et al.: Robbery on DevOps: understanding and mitigating illicit crypto-mining on continuous integration service platforms. In: 2022 IEEE Symposium on Security and Privacy (SP), pp. 2397–2412 (2022)
19. Paule, C., Düllmann, T.F., Van Hoorn, A.: Vulnerabilities in continuous delivery pipelines? A case study. In: 2019 IEEE International Conference on Software Architecture Companion (ICSA-C), pp. 102–108 (2019)
20. Koishybayev, I., et al.: Characterizing the security of github CI workflows. In: 31st USENIX Security Symposium (USENIX Security 2022), pp. 2747–2763 (2022)
21. Muralee, S., et al.: ARGUS: a framework for staged static taint analysis of github workflows and actions. In: Proceedings of the 32nd USENIX Security Symposium (USENIX Security 2023), pp. 6983–7000 (2023)
22. Khatami, A., Willekens, C., Zaidman, A.: Catching smells in the act: a github actions workflow investigation. In: 2024 IEEE International Conference on Source Code Analysis and Manipulation (SCAM), pp. 47–58 (2024)
23. Daniel, K., Omer, G.: OWASP Top 10 CI/CD Security Risks. https://owasp.org/www-project-top-10-ci-cd-security-risks
24. OpenSSF. Mitigating Attack Vectors in GitHub Workflows. https://openssf.org/blog/2024/08/12/mitigating-attack-vectors-in-github-workflows/
25. Khan, A.: One Supply Chain Attack to Rule Them All – Poisoning GitHub's Runner Images. https://adnanthekhan.com/2023/12/20/one-supply-chain-attack-to-rule-them-all/
26. Khan, A.: The Monsters in Your Build Cache – GitHub Actions Cache Poisoning. https://adnanthekhan.com/2024/05/06/the-monsters-in-your-build-cache-github-actions-cache-poisoning
27. Renaux, J.: Use GitHub actions at your own risk. https://julienrenaux.fr/2019/12/20/github-actions-security-risk/
28. Decan, A., Mens, T., Mazrae, P.R., Golzadeh, M.: On the use of github actions in software development repositories. In: 2022 IEEE International Conference on Software Maintenance and Evolution (ICSME), pp. 235–245 (2022)
29. Lobacevski, J.: Producing artifacts. https://securitylab.github.com/resources/github-actions-preventing-pwn-requests/
30. Khan, A.: Long Live the Pwn Request. https://www.praetorian.com/blog/pwn-request-hacking-microsoft-github-repositories-and-more/
31. Heap, M.: The ultimate guide to GitHub Actions authentication. https://michaelheap.com/ultimate-guide-github-actions-authentication/
32. Mackenzie. Biggest security takeaway of 2020 - Don't leak secrets on GitHub. https://dev.to/advocatemack/biggest-security-takeaway-of-2020-don-t-leak-secrets-on-github-44k2
33. McIntosh, S.: Mining our way back to incremental builds for DevOps pipelines. In: Proceedings of the 21st International Conference on Mining Software Repositories (MSR), pp. 48–49. ACM (2024)
34. Brudo, B.: GitHub Cache Poisoning. https://scribesecurity.com/blog/github-cache-poisoning
35. Noam, D.: GitHub Actions That Open the Door to CI/CD Pipeline Attacks. https://www.legitsecurity.com/blog/github-actions-that-open-the-door-to-cicd-pipeline-attacks

36. Noam, D.: Novel Pipeline Vulnerability Discovered; Rust Found Vulnerable. https://www.legitsecurity.com/blog/artifact-poisoning-vulnerability-discovered-in-rust
37. Khan, A.: Cacheract: The Monster in your Build Cache. https://adnanthekhan.com/2024/12/21/cacheract-the-monster-in-your-build-cache/
38. Lobacevski, J.: Producing artifacts. https://slsa.dev/spec/v1.0/requirements#isolated
39. Cardoen, G.: A dataset of GitHub Actions workflow histories (2024), version Number: 2024-10-25. https://doi.org/10.5281/zenodo.13985548

Towards Effective Automation of Issue–Commit Link Recovery: An Empirical Investigation

Risha Parveen, Zheying Zhang(✉), Kari Systä, Terhi Kilamo, and Ali Mehraj

Tampere University, Tampere, Finland
`{risha.parveen,zheying.zhang,kari.systa,`
`terhi.kilamo,ali.mehraj}@tuni.fi`

Abstract. Traceability between requirements and code changes is critical in software projects, yet links between issue reports and source code are often missing. This paper investigates the use of a machine learning approach to discovering undocumented issue-commit links and explores factors of its effectiveness. Building on earlier work, we extend our evaluation to eleven GitHub repositories and validate the recovered links through developer interviews, link categorization, and analysis of distribution and correlation. Results indicate that the semantic clarity, rather than the length of textual description, significantly affects model prediction accuracy. Fixed confidence thresholds are insufficient, particularly as project size and complexity increase.

Keywords: issue-commit link · requirements traceability · link recovery · T-BERT

1 Introduction

Maintaining traceability between development artifacts, such as issues and commits, is a critical but often labor-intensive task in software engineering. Automating issuecommit link recovery helps teams better understand change rationale, supports impact analysis, and facilitates project evolution. Recent advances in machine learning, especially transformer-based models such as T-BERT [14], have shown promising performance in automating this recovery process [4,9,14].

Despite technical improvements, the success of automated link recovery varies significantly between software projects. The existing work tends to measure the performance by comparing discovered links with documented ones, while undocumented links are not considered in the assessment. In addition, projects differ in size, structure, artifact clarity, and development practices, all of which may influence how well automated tools perform.

In our previous research [17], we presented our initial findings with T-BERT. In this paper, we continue and add more experiments with evaluations. Especially, we interviewed developers to understand whether the discovered links are

© The Author(s), under exclusive license to Springer Nature Switzerland AG 2026
G. Scanniello et al. (Eds.): PROFES 2025, LNCS 16361, pp. 237–252, 2026.
https://doi.org/10.1007/978-3-032-12089-2_15

real. In addition, we conducted an empirical investigation of the project-level factors that shape the effectiveness of automated link recovery. Our aim is to understand how characteristics such as project size, artifact consistency, and description quality interact with the underlying model behavior. In doing so, we seek to identify the conditions under which recovery tools succeed or struggle.

We address the following research questions:

- RQ1: To what extent can an ML-based system effectively recover undocumented issuecommit links in software repositories?
- RQ2: What factors influence the accuracy and reliability of automated issuecommit link recovery?

By examining multiple open-source projects with varying characteristics, we aim to provide insights that are both empirically grounded and practically useful for researchers and practitioners working on software traceability.

The rest of the paper is structured as follows: in Sect. 2 we cover related work. In Sect. 3 we present our research method. Section 4 gives the results and Sect. 5 discusses our findings. Finally, Sect. 6 concludes the paper.

2   Related Work

Automated recovery of traceability links between artifacts, such as issues and commits, have been studied from multiple perspectives. Empirical studies have consistently shown that developers struggle to maintain consistent traceability between issues, commits, and other software artifacts. This inconsistency stems from various practical challenges, including time constraints, lack of tool support, and the perception of traceability as an overhead rather than a value-adding task [1,5]. Rath et al. also highlight that traceability in open-source projects frequently relies on ad hoc linking conventions rather than systematic methods, leading to fragmented or missing connections between related artifacts [18]. Even in platforms like GitHub, where linking mechanisms such as issue references in commit messages are supported, their usage is highly inconsistent and largely dependent on individual developer habits [11].

To address the limitations of manual linking, numerous automated approaches have been proposed. Traditional methods often relied on information retrieval (IR) techniques such as the Vector Space Model (VSM), Latent Semantic Indexing (LSI), or Latent Dirichlet Allocation (LDA), which compare the textual similarity of artifacts to recover missing links [3,6,15].

These approaches were later augmented by ML models that leveraged both textual and non-textual features. For example, RCLinker [13] and FRLink [20] used supervised learning to recover links based on commit messages and surrounding context, while Hybrid-linker [16] incorporated process metadata such as commit timestamps. Semi-supervised learning was also introduced, with models like PULink [19] leveraging unlabelled data to improve generalization.

Recently, transformer-based models have achieved good results. T-BERT [14] applies a pre-trained language model to align issue descriptions and commit texts, outperforming traditional and deep learning baselines. BTLink [12] further refines this idea by using a dual-encoder architecture and separate pre-training for the issues and commits. DSSLink [21] introduces semi-supervised learning over T-BERT to enhance performance under limited supervision, while MTLink [7] uses multi-task learning to model-related traceability objectives jointly.

Despite technical advancements, majority of existing studies benchmark traceability models on curated, well-labelled datasets derived from mature open-source projects. While useful for controlled evaluation, these datasets often fail to reflect the noise, incompleteness, and inconsistency found in real-world repositories. As a result, the robustness of these models under realistic conditions remains largely untested [12,14,21]. Moreover, evaluations often assume documented links as complete and correct and undocumented links as invalid. This simplification can distort precision and recall metrics, especially when evaluating undocumented but semantically valid links. Discovered links are typically not validated with actual developers.

An unexplored area in traceability research is the effect of project-specific characteristics on the performance of automated recovery methods. Factors such as project size, programming language, artifact quality, development workflow, and documentation practices can all potentially influence model effectiveness. However, the existing literature has rarely examined these dimensions systematically. Most models are evaluated in isolation without assessing how changes in data structure or context affect performance. This creates a gap in understanding how traceability tools can be tuned or adapted to different environments.

In our previous study [17], we identified four distinct types of issuecommit links based on their documentation patterns and semantic characteristics.

- Type 1 - Direct References: Links documented by developers when an issue is directly tagged in a commit message, e.g., via keywords like fixes *#123*.
- Type 2 Pull Request References: Implicit links where an issue is linked to a pull request which, in turn, is associated with multiple commits.
- Type 3 Chained Issue References: Links emerging from issue-to-issue associations via e.g. comments or cross-references, which connect a chained issue to commits originally linked to the referenced issue.
- Type 4 Other References: Links potentially representing latent semantic relationships but not explicitly derived by developer actions.

This implies the multifaceted nature of traceability in repositories and reveals that automated methods can recover not only documented but also issue-commit links developers forgot to document. This emphasizes the importance of validating automatically recovered links, particularly in real project settings where documentation practices vary widely.

3   Research Settings

This study investigates the effectiveness of T-BERT [14,17] in recovering undocumented issuecommit traceability links across a variety of software projects. Our goal is to evaluate the performance of the model under realistic conditions, i.e. in projects with incomplete or missing trace links, ambiguous issue descriptions, or unclear commit summary. We examine how project characteristics influence prediction outcomes and identify the practical challenges of deploying such models in real-world development environments. To systematically evaluate the behavior and outputs of the T-BERT model across projects, we analyzed its predictions using a defined set of factors selected to capture different dimensions of model behavior, including prediction correctness, structural link types, distribution patterns, and textual characteristics. To analyze the relationship between artifact characteristics and prediction strength, factors included in the analysis along with how they were obtained are:

- Confusion Matrix Metrics: To evaluate prediction correctness, we computed true positives (TP), false positives (FP), false negatives (FN), and true negatives (TN) after applying fixed classification thresholds (0.01 for Python, 0.998 for JavaScript).
- Link Categorization: Each predicted link was assigned to one of four types presented in Sect. 2 and in [17].
- Distribution Patterns: We recorded the number of predicted commits per issue and issues per commit to assess how predictions were distributed across artifacts within each project.
- Textual and Structural Correlation Analysis: Spearman's rank correlation was computed between model confidence scores and the following features:
  - Jaccard Similarity: token overlap between issue and commit text.
  - BERT Semantic Similarity: cosine similarity of sentence embeddings.
  - Issue/Commit Word Count: total number of words in each text.

The research setup includes model training and selection, threshold selection, repository selection, data preprocessing, and validation of recovered links. We trained language-specific T-BERT variants, applied them to generate predictions for all possible issuecommit pairs, and validated the results through developer interviews and self-review.

3.1   Model Training and Selection

We followed the T-BERT training methodology proposed by Lin et al. [14], which consists of three stages: pre-training, intermediate training, and fine-tuning. In the pre-training stage, we started with MS-CodeBERT [8], a publicly available model pre-trained on the CodeSearchNet dataset [10] to learn general-purpose representations of both code and natural language.

The intermediate training aimed to improve the model's ability to align code with its descriptive text. To do this, we used aligned functiondocstring pairs from the CodeSearchNet dataset, training the model to predict matching code-text pairs This step was performed separately for Python and JavaScript, resulting in two intermediate models adapted to the linguistic and structural characteristics of each language.

In the final fine-tuning stage, the intermediate models were trained on real-world traceability data consisting of issuecommit pairs mined from open-source GitHub repositories. For Python, we used three repositories: Flask, Keras, and Pgcli. For JavaScript, we selected two: Marked and Webpack. Data was collected using GitHub's REST API for issues and pull requests, and GitPython for commits. We extracted only those issuecommit pairs where commits explicitly referenced issues using standard GitHub keywords (e.g., "closes #45", "fixes #12"). These references were identified using regular expressions. Only artifacts involved in at least one valid link were included in the final training sets.

Following data collection, the dataset was preprocessed to fit within the model's context window constraints. This involved removing markdown blocks, HTML comments, and stack traces from issue descriptions. Commit summaries were cleaned and code diffs were simplified to plain-text line-level content. Each training example consisted of two plain-text fields: the issue text (title and description) and the commit text (summary and code diff).

Fine-tuning was performed separately for Python and JavaScript. For Python, we trained three models by fine-tuning the intermediate model independently on each of the three project datasets (Flask, Keras, and Pgcli). For JavaScript, we trained four models: one fine-tuned on the Marked dataset, one on Webpack, one where the model was first fine-tuned on Webpack and then further fine-tuned on Marked, and one trained on a combined dataset where issuecommit pairs from both Marked and Webpack were merged and used together during training.

Each candidate model was evaluated on a 10% test split from its corresponding dataset using ranking metrics such as Mean Average Precision (MAP) and Mean Reciprocal Rank (MRR), as well as classification metrics computed using the optimal F1 threshold. Cross-project evaluations were also conducted to assess how well the models generalized to previously unseen repositories.

For Python, the model trained on the Flask dataset performed consistently well across all test sets and achieved the highest or second highest MAP scores in every evaluation. It was also trained on the largest dataset, which likely contributed to its robustness. This model was selected as the final Python variant. For JavaScript, the model trained using the combined dataset from both Marked and Webpack outperformed all other approaches, including those trained on individual projects or in sequence.

3.2 Threshold Selection

The T-BERT models assign each issue-commit pair a confidence score between 0 and 1, indicating how likely the model believes that a link exists. This must be binarized by setting a threshold: scores above it are treated as links, and all those below are not. In controlled settings where labeled data is available, it is common to select a threshold that maximizes a metric such as F1 score, based on precision-recall curves. However, real-world projects rarely have complete or verified traceability annotations. The true links are unknown or only partially documented, making it impossible to compute validation metrics or dynamically adjust the threshold based on feedback.

To ensure consistent and practical evaluations across all projects, we adopted a fixed threshold approach. This means that the same cut-off value was applied uniformly to all predictions during evaluation, regardless of the dataset. This approach avoids relying on incomplete or inconsistent labels and enables fair comparison of results across different projects.

The fixed threshold values were selected based on the behavior of the models during the training phase. Each fine-tuned model was evaluated on a 10% held-out test split from its corresponding dataset. For each test set, we computed the threshold that maximized the F1 score—referred to as the F1-optimal threshold. These thresholds revealed consistent patterns. For the Python model fine-tuned on Flask, the optimal thresholds across different test sets ranged from approximately 0.0002 to 0.0134. In contrast, the JavaScript model trained on the combined dataset from Marked and Webpack consistently produced much higher thresholds, around 0.998.

These differences reflect the internal score distribution of the models, which vary depending on the training data characteristics, language-specific patterns, and model calibration. To identify stable and reasonable cut-off points, we experimented with candidate thresholds from these ranges on controlled evaluation projects where ground-truth links were known. We observed how different thresholds affected the number and quality of recovered links, including whether relevant links were retained or if the model over-predicted.

3.3 Projects Selection

We investigated the links recovered by T-BERT models on eleven GitHub repositories, each involving 1–6 developers, comprising seven Python-based and four JavaScript-based projects. Nine of these are student projects or research prototypes familiar to the authors. This also allows us to consult with the developers to validate links potentially omitted from documentation. The repositories vary in issues, pull requests, and commits, as well as in issue verbosity and commit frequency. This reflects the variability and noise typical of real-world software development, where trace links are often sparse or incomplete, and the issue description and commit summary may lack clarity.

To provide a controlled baseline, we also created two test repositories, i.e., test-project in Python and test-project-js in JavaScript. They share identical issue descriptions, commit messages, repository structure, and artifact counts across issues, and pull requests and commits. The only difference is the programming language. All traceability links in these test repositories were manually created and verified. They serve as a reliable ground truth for evaluating and comparing links recovered by models trained by Python and JavaScript.

By combining nine diverse projects with two test repositories, we can assess model performance under realistic conditions and understand whether language-related differences affect the recovery of undocumented issuecommit links. Table 1 lists the programming language of each repository alongside its issue and commit counts, with projects within each language sorted by commit count.

Table 1. Overview of Selected Repositories

Project Name (# developers)	Language	Issue count	Commit count	Project Description
test-project (1)	Python	5	9	Testing project with clearly documented issue-commit links
icwe-demo (2)	Python	8	45	Research project on WasmIoT demonstration
Components (3)	Python	4	111	Research project on components for creating an electric vehicle charging simulation based on SimCES platform
intelligent-machine-engine(3)	Python	49	26	Research project on an LLM-based agent system
Autonomous-AI-Agent-Team-Coding (2)	Python	38	123	Research project on using LLMs for code generation
wasmiot-supervisor (6)	Python	16	244	Research project on Prototype implementation of self-adaptive supervisor for IoT devices
postgresql-for-novices (3)	Python	61	261	Student project at Tampere University
test-project-js (1)	JavaScript	5	9	Testing project with clearly documented issue-commit links
GUI (2)	JavaScript	7	83	Research project on GUI for an electric vehicle charging simulation based on SimCES platform
g21-adhd-kinesthetic-game (6)	JavaScript	48	105	Student project of a web-based therapeutic game designed for children with ADHD
wasmiot-orchestrator (6)	JavaScript	48	553	Research on managing package and orchestrating logic for WebAssembly-based microservices

3.4 Project Data Preparation

We adapted GitRepoCollector [14] for project data collection. The tool was adapted to meet the requirements of real-world evaluation by capturing richer and more connected data across artifacts. It integrated two data sources: the GitHub GraphQL API and a local clone of each repository. The GraphQL API facilitates the retrieval of metadata, including issue and pull request descriptions, comments, and timeline events. These timeline events were important for identifying indirect or implicit traceability links. The local repository clone provides full access to the commit history, file-level changes, and code diffs. Commit messages and code diffs underwent similar cleaning as in the training phase, with Git diff markers removed, and only the plain text of code changes retained. However, fine-grained structural elements, such as change order and direction of code changes were not preserved. In this way, we maintain consistency with the training input format.

In contrast to the model training, where issues and pull requests were treated as a single artifact type, the evaluation phase maintained a clear distinction between them to better reflect their distinct roles in modern development workflows. Issues typically describe bugs, features, or tasks, while pull requests represent sets of code changes and reviews. After the pre-processing, the inputs to T-BERT models are formed in plain text. They include the issue title and description, and the commit message along with its cleaned code diff. No contextual data, such as pull request IDs, file names, or existing traceability links, was made available during inference, so that we can ensure a fair evaluation. The known and inferred links were retained separately and used to verify whether the model's predictions matched any known or inferred links.

Table 2. Summary of Validation Setup

Project Name	Validation Type	Validation Mode
intelligent-machine-engine	Developer (2)	Live interview
Autonomous-AI-Agent-Team-Coding-System	Developer (2)	Live interview
Components	Developer (1)	Excel sheet
wasmiot-supervisor	Developer (1)	Excel sheet
test-project	Self-review	Author-reviewed
test-project-js	Self-review	Author-reviewed
g21-adhd-kinesthetic-game	Self-review	Author-reviewed

3.5   Validation Setup

To evaluate the quality and relevance of the links recovered by the T-BERT models, we applied two complementary validation strategies, chosen based on developer availability and the first author's involvement in the respective projects. For each repository, we collected T-BERT predicted issuecommit links along with their prediction scores, as well as manually extracted documented links among issues, pull requests, and commits.

Developer validation was conducted for four Python-based repositories where knowledgeable contributors were available. A total of six developers participated, each with sufficient familiarity with the codebases and workflows of their respective projects. The participants were presented with issuecommit links predicted by T-BERT and requested to classify each as valid, partially valid, unclear, or invalid link. A valid link indicates that the issue and commit are correctly associated. A partially valid link reflects some contextual alignment between the issue and commit, but the link is not fully correct. An unclear link is one for which the developer cannot determine the correctness due to insufficient information. An invalid link means an incorrect association between the issue and commit.

Two developers participated in face-to-face interviews, two in online Teams meetings, and the remaining two completed the validation using a shared Excel sheet with link evaluation instructions[1]. Live interview sessions lasted about 30 to 45 min and also included open-ended questions about the tool's usability and their views on automated traceability recovery.

In projects where the first author had direct development involvement, a self-review was applied. These included the controlled test repositories and one student-led project. In these cases, link validation was based on first-hand knowledge of development activities and the relationships between artifacts.

Table 2 summarizes the validation setup.

4   Results

Based on analysis on how different thresholds affected the number and quality of recovered, we selected 0.01 as the fixed threshold for the Python model and

---

[1] https://doi.org/10.6084/m9.figshare.29949266.v1.

0.998 for the JavaScript model. These values balanced recall and precision, i.e. recovering meaningful links while minimizing false positives in the absence of labeled data. Using a fixed threshold across all evaluations ensured consistency and reproducibility in interpreting the model's predictions.

4.1   Practical Reliability of T-BERT Models

We analyzed model performance across all 11 repositories. Figure 1 shows two key aspects for each project: (1) the proportion of documented links of all links the model recovered (left bar), and (2) Link Categorization, i.e. the percentage distribution of each link type as predicted by the model (right bar). In the left bar for each project, the black segment shows the percentage of documented links that were correctly recovered by the model. The gray segment shows the percentage of documented links that were missed. This gives a project-level view of how well the model recovers known issuecommit links. Some projects have no left bar at all because they had no documented links in the dataset, so the proportion has no value. The right bar shows the percentage breakdown of the link types among the model's recovered links. These are grouped into four categories: Type 1 (direct references), Type 2 (pull requestmediated), Type 3 (indirect links via related issues), and Type 4 (newly discovered links). From the earlier validation study, we found that Type 1 and Type 2 links were generally reliable, while Type 4 links were much less often confirmed. For this reason, a high percentage of Type 4 links is taken as a potential sign of speculative or uncertain model behaviour.

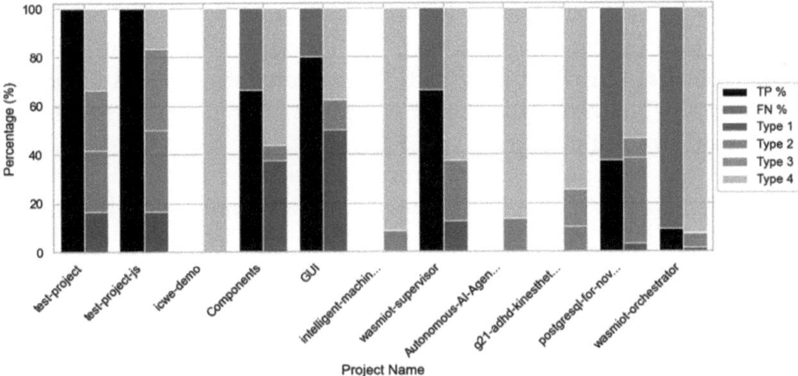

Fig. 1. Link type distribution across projects. Left bars show the proportion of documented links detected. Right bars show the proportion of each link type among recovered links. Projects are sorted in ascending order by total link count.

Validation with Developers: To evaluate the practical reliability of the link recovery we asked developer feedback across seven python projects following the setup described in Sect. 3.5. Figure 2 summarizes the classification. Each recovered link was labelled as valid, partially valid, invalid, or unclear.

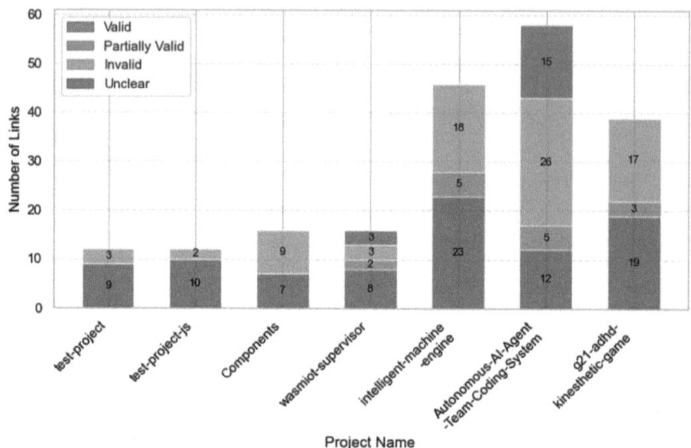

Fig. 2. Classification of recovered links per project based on developer validation.

In the two controlled test repositories, i.e. test-project-js and test-project, the majority of link discoveries were correct. Specifically, test-project-js had 10 valid and 2 invalid links, while the Python-based test-project had 9 valid and 3 invalid link discoveries. The invalid links in both repositories were associated with a single issue titled "Implement Unit Tests for Fibonacci Series Function", which, despite its technical phrasing, provided limited semantic cues. Additionally, the issue included a deliberately misleading comment referencing an unrelated issue, which may lead to false positive Type 3 links.

Results in the real projects were more varied. For example, in intelligent-machine-engine, 23 of 46 links were assessed by developers as valid, but 18 were invalid and 5 partially valid. Autonomous-AI-Agent-Team-Coding-System presented the most challenging assessment scenario, with 26 invalid links, 15 unclear ones, and only 12 valid ones. This outcome highlights the model's limitations in handling vague issue descriptions or inconsistent commit messages.

Interestingly, the student project g21-adhd-kinesthetic-game showed relatively strong results: with 19 of 39 links assessed as valid. The research project Components yielded 9 invalid links and 7 valid links, with no partial or unclear links, while wasmiot-supervisor showed a more balanced outcome with 8 valid links, 2 partially valid, 3 invalid, and 3 unclear. This suggests some structural inconsistencies, but not to the degree observed in larger or more chaotic projects.

To better understand the reliability of different types of recovered links, we grouped the validated predictions by link type. Table 3 aggregates the number and validity of links of each type across the seven projects.

Table 3. Developer validation outcomes by link type

Link Type	Valid	Partially Valid	Invalid	Unclear	Total	Valid %
Type 1	12	0	0	0	12	100.0%
Type 2	27	0	1	0	28	96.4%
Type 3	5	0	6	0	11	45.5%
Type 4	44	12	71	18	145	30.3%

As the table shows, type 1 and type 2 links are highly reliable, with nearly all predictions confirmed by the developers. Type 3 links show mixed results, while Type 4 links, which lack supporting documentation, have the lowest validation rate at just over 30%. Based on this, we interpret the link type as a proxy for the prediction quality, with type 1 being the most reliable, followed by Type 2, then Type 3, and finally Type 4 as the least reliable. This assumption helps our interpretation in the next section, where we examine link type distributions across projects. A high share of type 4 links, in particular, will be considered an indicator of speculative or less reliable model behavior.

4.2   Factors Influencing Model Prediction

Previous research has shown that the characteristics of input artifacts significantly influence the effectiveness of traceability recovery techniques. Ali et al. [2], for instance, addressed that several factors impact the accuracy of information retrieval models. On the basis of this, we further investigate whether features such as textual similarity, word count, and the distribution patterns of predicted links correlate with T-BERT's prediction scores. This analysis helps us better understand how artifact-level attributes influence the model's certainty and prediction correctness in realistic projects settings.

Distribution of Issues and Commits. To investigate variation in model behavior across projects, we analyzed the distribution pattern of recovered links by measuring how they are spread across issues and commits. Specifically, we measured (1) the number of commits linked to each issue and (2) the number of issues linked to each commit. These distributions are visualized in Fig. 3 using grouped violin plots.

The results show clear differences between the controlled and real-world projects. In test repositories such as test-project and test-project-js, both distributions are narrow and centered, implying balanced linking recovery. In contrast, several other projects display heavy-tailed distributions. In wasmiot-orchestrator some issues are linked to 20 commits, while in intelligent-machine-engine and wasmiot-supervisor, individual commits are associated with five or more issues.

Examining specific outliers reinforces this. In wasmiot-orchestrator, the issue "Add tests" was linked to 20 commits. In g21-adhd-kinesthetic-game, "Implement the gameplay settings page" was linked to 11. These issues had no descriptions—just short, vague titles. Despite this, the model linked them

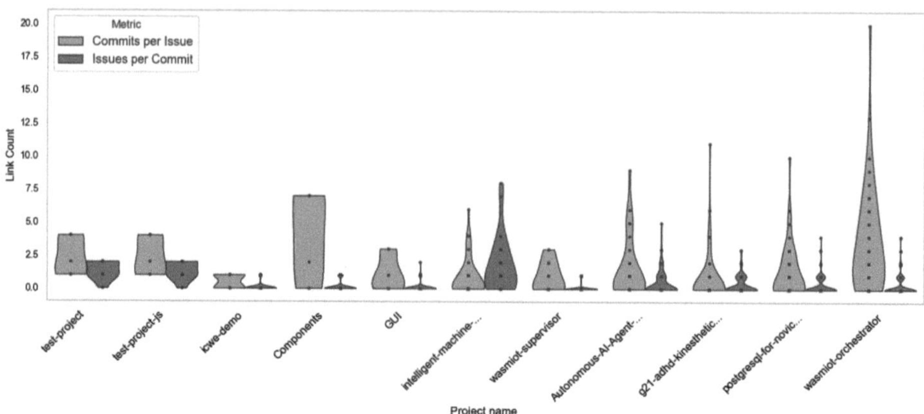

Fig. 3. Distribution of the number of commits per issue (blue) and the number of issues per commit (orange) across projects. (Color figure online)

broadly, likely due to superficial term overlap. This suggests that when context is lacking, the model tends to over-predict.

Correlation Analysis. To explore the influence of artifact-level characteristics on the model's prediction behavior, we conducted a correlation analysis between T-BERT's confidence scores and four measurable features derived from issuecommit pairs: word count of an issue description, word count of a commit description, Jaccard similarity between issue and commit descriptions, and semantic similarity between issue and commit descriptions using cosine similarity of BERT embeddings. These features capture both basic textual properties and semantic relationships, allowing us to assess which aspects align most with the model's confidence. Spearman rank correlation coefficients were computed across all eleven repositories to account for potential non-linear relationships between prediction scores and the selected features.

Table 4 presents the correlation coefficients at both individual project and language group levels. The results reveal several patterns. Firstly, semantic similarity shows a strong positive correlation with prediction scores across most repositories, particularly in test-project and test-project-js, where correlations exceed 0.65. These results indicate that the model effectively leverages semantic alignment in controlled settings. Secondly, Jaccard similarity shows a moderate positive correlation with prediction score in several projects, such as test-project-js, GUI, and intelligent-machine-engineer. This indicates that token-level overlap still influences the model's prediction, although the underlying architecture is based on contextual embeddings.

In contrast, correlations with word count are weak and inconsistent. Issue word count shows modest correlation in some Python projects, but negative or near-zero values in most JavaScript repositories. Commit word count exhibits similarly low or negative correlation in several cases. These findings support the

Table 4. Spearman correlation between artifact features and prediction score

Project	Issue word count	Commit word count	Jaccard similarity	Semantic similarity
test-project	0.1803	-0.0463	0.4346	0.6884
icwe-demo	0.2192	0.2527	0.3166	0.3831
Components	0.2388	0.0841	0.3082	0.5504
intelligent-machine-engine	0.3096	0.2281	0.3928	0.4011
Autonomous-AI-Agent-Team-Coding-System	0.2844	-0.0002	0.2619	0.1952
wasmiot-supervisor	0.2446	0.2451	0.3215	0.2492
postgresql-for-novices1	0.0623	0.1620	0.2294	0.2532
test-project-js	-0.0411	-0.1857	0.6072	0.6597
GUI	0.0001	0.0966	0.3962	0.2280
g21-adhd-kinesthetic-game	-0.1431	-0.1131	0.1910	0.2978
wasmiot-orchestrator	-0.1020	-0.1933	0.1662	0.2956

earlier observation that the textual length alone is not indicative of traceability strength. Instead, clarity and semantic focus appear to matter more.

5   Discussion

The approach gives promising results in helping software teams to understand project evolution. The current version of the tool can detect undocumented links, but the output should not be accepted without a review. Nonetheless, this kind of tool can be beneficial for many purposes such as in investigation of possible impacts of the change made when refactoring or rewriting code as there manual reasoning is needed anyway.

Traceability between requirements and code changes is often needed in regulated software development. For these purposes, traceability information should be as reliable as possible, and an automatic tool should not be trusted alone. In the study, in the two controlled projects, test-project and test-project-js, the model performed well recovering nearly all known links, and most predictions fell into the more reliable Type 13 categories. This suggests that in clean and well-structured environments, the model is both accurate and trustworthy. In larger and more complex projects, however, performance drops. The model misses many known links and generates a higher percentage of Type 4 links. This combination of low recall and high uncertainty points to a deeper problem: the model is failing to recover the links it should, and replacing them with predictions that are harder to justify. The results illustrate how semantic ambiguity and inaccurate cross-references can cause the model to assign high confidence to incorrect associations. It also indicates that the model performs well when working with clearly specified, well-structured artifacts.

Thresholding strategies must become more adaptive. The distributional skew of similarity scores reveals a limitation in commonly used fixed-threshold or top-k link recovery approaches. In our evaluation, vague issue descriptions such as "Add tests" frequently received high confidence scores, which led to incorrect link predictions that crowded out links with lower confidence scores. This implies that current thresholding mechanisms may overlook semantically relevant links. To mitigate this, future tools should adopt adaptive thresholding strategies that take into account artifact clarity and project context. Furthermore, models should also be more cautious when handling vague or under-specified issue or commit descriptions, to avoid concentrating predictions around generic artifacts.

The correlation analysis results indicate that semantic richness is more influential than raw textual length in prediction performance. This observation aligns with developer validation feedback and the distributional skew, both of which highlight the model's improved performance with clear, semantically rich artifacts. In contrast, vague or overly verbose descriptions tend to confuse the model or lead to over-prediction. These findings imply the importance of integrating artifact quality assessment into traceability recovery pipelines. They also provide further motivation for adaptive thresholding strategies, where prediction acceptance is determined by artifact-level context rather than fixed global thresholds.

The characteristics of the project and the size impact the effectiveness. The study confirms a natural expectation that the clarity, consistency, structure influence recovery success. Fixed threshold fails on large or complex projects; adaptive tuning is needed. The length of the textual descriptions has very little impact on accuracy, but semantic clarity seems to help the recovery. Traceability tools could benefit from incorporating artifact quality checks or confidence-based filters. Workflow and linking practices also need more attention. Further research is needed on this topic.

Threats to Validity. The number of projects tested is still rather small. This may limit the reliability of the results. This is a real threat, as the analysis presented in Sect. 4 already indicates that the results are worse in case of large and complex projects.

The projects were also rather small and not the results of professional development. This may skew the results, since student and research projects have different time spans, different requirement management practices and less experienced developer. In addition, the lifetimes of the project were rather short, while this kind of tool might most benefit from long-lasting projects.

The way how the data was preprocessed can be improved. For example, diff representation discarded the original line order and whether the lines were added or removed. This might affect the efficiency of the approach.

The interviews assumed that the interviewed developers remembered details of the projects. We reached only parts of the developers and sometimes interviewed persons who needed to answer on behalf of those who had left.

Directions for Future Research. The used ML model is rather old and new and bigger models might give better results. We have already started testing of other models and may decide to use some of them later. One factor in such selection are the hardware requirements. T-BERT can be used on a laptop computer but stronger models typically require more powerful computational resources.

There is still a considerable amount of work to be done in the pre-processing of the commit data. We assume that inclusion of all relevant information and the exclusion of irrelevant information can improve the performance.

Software development processes vary widely among projects and organizations. That effects how issues, commits, and pull-requests are used in practice. We assume that tools utilizing targetted process as a context should work better.

6   Conclusion

In this paper, we tested the T-BERT model presented in our earlier study [17] with eleven projects, and validated the discovered but undocumented links with project developers. The validation revealed that the tool can indeed discover non-documented links, but the accuracy varies between the projects.

We analyzed the possible reasons affecting the accuracy. The most important factors seem to be the size of the project and the semantic clarity of the textual descriptions. It seems that the challenges imposed by size can be managed by adapting the threshold positive decision in the model.

There is still a significant amount of work required to create truly useful tools. The use of properly pre-processed data should improve the results. Realistic context of the software development process should also improve the tool. In addition, the use of state-of-the-art ML models is another important factor.

Acknowledgements. This work has been supported by Business Finland (project 6GSoft, 8548/31/2022).

References

1. Akman, S., Özmut, M., Aydın, B., Göktürk, S.: Experience report: implementing requirement traceability throughout the software development life cycle. J. Softw. Evolut. Proc. **28**(11), 950–954 (2016)
2. Ali, N., Guéhéneuc, Y.G., Antoniol, G.: Factors impacting the inputs of traceability recovery approaches. In: Software and Systems Traceability, pp. 99–127. Springer (2011)
3. Antoniol, G., Canfora, G., Casazza, G., De Lucia, A., Merlo, E.: Recovering traceability links between code and documentation. IEEE Trans. Software Eng. **28**(10), 970–983 (2002)
4. Borg, M., Englund, C., Duran, B.: Traceability and deep learning-safety-critical systems with traces ending in deep neural networks. In: Proc. of the Grand Challenges of Traceability: The Next Ten Years, pp. 48–49 (2017)
5. Cleland-Huang, J., Gotel, O.C., Huffman Hayes, J., Mäder, P., Zisman, A.: Software traceability: trends and future directions. In: Future of Software Engineering Proceedings, pp. 55–69 (2014)
6. De Lucia, A., Fasano, F., Oliveto, R., Tortora, G.: Can information retrieval techniques effectively support traceability link recovery? In: 14Th IEEE International Conference on Program Comprehension (ICPC'06), pp. 307–316. IEEE (2006)
7. Deng, Y., Wang, B., Zhu, Q., Liu, J., Kuang, J., Li, X.: MTLink: adaptive multi-task learning based pre-trained language model for traceability link recovery between issues and commits. J. King Saud Univ. Comput. . Sci. **36**(2), 101958 (2024)

8. Feng, Z., et al.: CodeBERT: a pre-trained model for programming and natural languages. arXiv preprint arXiv:2002.08155 (2020)

9. Guo, J., Cheng, J., Cleland-Huang, J.: Semantically enhanced software traceability using deep learning techniques. In: 2017 IEEE/ACM 39th International Conference on Software Engineering (ICSE), pp. 3–14. IEEE (2017)

10. Husain, H., Wu, H.H., Gazit, T., Allamanis, M., Brockschmidt, M.: CodeSearch-Net challenge: evaluating the state of semantic code search. arXiv preprint arXiv:1909.09436 (2019)

11. Kalliamvakou, E., Gousios, G., Blincoe, K., Singer, L., German, D.M., Damian, D.: An in-depth study of the promises and perils of mining GitHub. Empir. Softw. Eng. **21**, 2035–2071 (2016)

12. Lan, J., Gong, L., Zhang, J., Zhang, H.: BTLink: automatic link recovery between issues and commits based on pre-trained BERT model. Empir. Softw. Eng. **28**(4), 103 (2023)

13. Le, T.D.B., Linares-Vásquez, M., Lo, D., Poshyvanyk, D.: RCLinker: automated linking of issue reports and commits leveraging rich contextual information. In: 2015 IEEE 23rd International Conference on Program Comprehension, pp. 36–47. IEEE (2015)

14. Lin, J., Liu, Y., Zeng, Q., et al.: Traceability transformed: generating more accurate links with pre-trained BERT models. In: 2021 IEEE/ACM 43rd International Conference on Software Engineering (ICSE), pp. 324–335. IEEE (2021)

15. Marcus, A., Maletic, J.I.: Recovering documentation-to-source-code traceability links using latent semantic indexing. In: 25th International Conference on Software Engineering, 2003. Proceedings, pp. 125–135. IEEE (2003)

16. Mazrae, P.R., Izadi, M., Heydarnoori, A.: Automated recovery of issue-commit links leveraging both textual and non-textual data. In: 2021 IEEE International Conference on Software Maintenance and Evolution (ICSME), pp. 263–273. IEEE (2021)

17. Parveen, R., Mehraj, A., Zhang, Z., Systä, K., Kilamo, T.: Towards automated recovery of links between code commits and requirements–initial results. In: International Conference on Product-Focused Software Process Improvement, pp. 386–394. Springer (2024)

18. Rath, M., Rendall, J., Guo, J.L., Cleland-Huang, J., Mäder, P.: Traceability in the wild: automatically augmenting incomplete trace links. In: Proceedings of the 40th International Conference on Software Engineering, pp. 834–845 (2018)

19. Sun, Y., Chen, C., Wang, Q., Boehm, B.: Improving missing issue-commit link recovery using positive and unlabeled data. In: 2017 32nd IEEE/ACM International Conference on Automated Software Engineering (ASE), pp. 147–152. IEEE (2017)

20. Sun, Y., Wang, Q., Yang, Y.: FRLink: improving the recovery of missing issue-commit links by revisiting file relevance. Inf. Softw. Technol. **84**, 33–47 (2017)

21. Zhu, J., Xiao, G., Zheng, Z., Sui, Y.: Deep semi-supervised learning for recovering traceability links between issues and commits. J. Syst. Softw. **216**, 112109 (2024)

Policy-Driven Software Bill of Materials on GitHub: An Empirical Study

Oleksii Novikov[(✉)], Davide Fucci, Oleksandr Adamov, and Daniel Mendez

Blekinge Institute of Technology, Karlskrona, Sweden
{oleksii.novikov,davide.fucci,oleksandr.adamov,
daniel.mendez}@bth.se

Abstract. *Background.* The Software Bill of Materials (SBOM) is a machine-readable list of all the software dependencies included in a software. SBOM emerged as way to assist securing the software supply chain. However, despite mandates from governments to use SBOM, research on this artifact is still in its early stages. *Aims.* We want to understand the current state of SBOM in open-source projects, focusing specifically on *policy-driven* SBOMs—i.e., SBOM created to achieve security goals, such as enhancing project transparency and ensuring compliance, rather than being used as fixtures for tools or artificially generated for benchmarking or academic research purposes. *Method.* We performed a mining software repository study to collect and carefully select 620 SBOM files hosted on GitHub. We analyzed the information reported in policy-driven SBOMs and the vulnerabilities associated with the declared dependencies by means of descriptive statistics. *Results.* We show that only 0.56% of popular GitHub repositories contain policy-driven SBOM. The declared dependencies contain 2,202 unique vulnerabilities, while 22% of them do not report licensing information. *Conclusion.* Our findings provide insights for SBOM usage to support security assessment and licensing.

Keywords: Supply chain attacks · SBOM · software security · vulnerabilities · dependencies · open-source

1 Introduction

A Software Bill of Materials (SBOM) lists all components that go into a piece of software, making its supply chains more transparent for those who use, make, buy, or regulate it. Creating and maintaining an SBOM is a security practice offering a mechanism to quickly check if software and its dependencies are affected once vulnerabilities are disclosed. The Log4J incident [1] demonstrated the importance of an SBOM. When the Log4Shell vulnerability (CVE-2021-44228) was discovered in the Apache Log4J library, organizations with an SBOM could quickly analyze their dependency tree and identify whether their software included the vulnerable dependency version. A comprehensive SBOM would have allowed them to take immediate action to mitigate risk, patch the vulnerability,

G. Scanniello et al. (Eds.): PROFES 2025, LNCS 16361, pp. 253–268, 2026.
https://doi.org/10.1007/978-3-032-12089-2_16

or apply the necessary workarounds. The rapid increase in software supply chain attacks in the last few years (e.g., SolarWind [2], event-stream [3], Log4J [4]) resulted in the US Government mandating the use of SBOM for their suppliers and with similar actions being taken in the context of the European Union Cyber Resilience Act (EU CRA)[1]. Regarding licensing, SBOM helps organizations comply with open-source license requirements, identify risks due to restrictive licensing (e.g., AGPLv3.0), and support auditing automation (e.g., verifying that software components meet corporate licensing policies). Although SBOMs are crucial for managing dependencies, vulnerabilities, risks, and licenses [5]—and despite a growing interest [6]—industrial adoption is limited [7,8].

At the same time, scientific research on SBOM is still in its infancy. One significant barrier is that their generation varies across the software development lifecycle, without a standard approach to when and how to create and update them [9]. The value of SBOMs is further questioned by the tooling used to generate them, lack of interoperability among formats (e.g., SPDX, CycloneDX, SWID) [5], and the varying quality, accuracy, and completeness of their contents [10,11]. In this respect, *most investigations rely on synthetic ad-hoc SBOMs*—i.e., generated by the researchers themselves from a source code repository or other sources (i.e., a Docker image)—rather than created by practitioners for a practical purpose [12]. This reliance on artificial SBOM limits the ability to draw realistic conclusions about their effectiveness as they often fail to capture the context of real-world software projects, resulting in studies that may not reflect practical issues. On the other hand, SBOMs created intentionally by practitioners as part of a policy are needed to understand their utility, better address issues, and develop best practices for their creation, consumption, and maintenance. In this work, we specifically focus on such type of SBOM files, which we call *policy-driven SBOM*. Although several policies can drive the creation of SBOM, in this work we focus on polices related to security risk assessment, supply-chain transparency, and compliance. Accordingly, our study is driven by the following overarching goal.

> Understand the characteristics of policy-driven SBOM files found in open-source projects.

To that end, we carefully collect and analyze SBOM files mined from GitHub repositories. Moreover, we associate known vulnerabilities to the dependencies specified in the SBOM files we collected. We show how SBOM is currently used in open-source projects and can inform further work supporting vulnerability and license management. The contribution of this paper is threefold:

- It defines a simple taxonomy to identify policy-driven SBOM instead of synthetic ones.
- It proposes a methodology to mine policy-driven SBOM files from open-source software repositories.
- It provides a dataset[2] including 620 policy-driven SBOM files and an analysis of the listed 25,430 dependencies.

---

[1] http://data.europa.eu/eli/reg/2024/2847/oj.
[2] https://github.com/AleX04Nov/sbom_scanning.

This paper is organized as follows. Section 2 introduces the main terminology and ideas behind our work and reviews related literature investigating SBOM, whereas Sect. 3 presents the research question driving this work and the methodology we followed to gather policy-oriented SBOMs, their quality, and associated vulnerabilities. Section 4 provides an overview of the results while Sect. 5 discusses their implication. Section 6 concludes the paper.

2 Background and Related Work

This section establishes relevant concepts and surveys the related literature.

2.1 Background

Following the work of Torres-Arias et al. [10], SBOM files can be categorized into two types, *In-the-Lab* and *In-the-Wild*. In-the-Lab SBOMs are usually generated for research purposes, typically to compare SBOM generation tools. For example, Balliu et al. [13] created SBOM files to highlight the issues with Java-related tools for SBOM generation. SBOM files can be artificially created for comparing vulnerability detection approaches or tools [13–15]. Moreover, researchers compare SBOM by generating them using the same tool but in different formats, such as SPDX and CycloneDX [11].

In-the-Wild SBOMs are *not* generated for research purposes but rather intending to support the following use cases: dependency management, security scanning, licensing, testing of tools, and tracking 3rd party dependencies.

Dependency management supports developers and other stakeholders to understand the components that are eventually included in a software. *Security scanning* supports developers in finding vulnerabilities in their dependencies, usually providing SBOM as input to automated vulnerability scanning tools. *Licensing* supports developers and other stakeholders in dealing with issues relating to, for example, conflicting usage terms between dependencies included in a software. However, in the wild, some SBOM files report licensing information for the project itself rather than for its dependencies. We refer to these as *Self-License* SBOM files. These SBOMs substitute LICENSE.md files commonly found in open-source repositories [16] and do not report any components or dependencies information. SBOM files can also be used as *Test Data* (e.g., test data) for tools that need, for example, to parse SBOM and for testing such tools.

Finally, *3rd party SBOM files* are generated by dependency management tools based on external packages—i.e., they represent transitive dependencies. The SBOM of a project should only include its direct dependencies (e.g., as required by the EU CRA). Transitive dependencies from third parties should be accessed by traversing the dependency tree formed by each individual SBOM.

In our research, we focus on the practical uses of SBOM files. Therefore, we do not consider *In-the-Lab* as well as *Test Data*, *3rd party SBOM*, and *Self-License* SBOM. Our focus remains on use cases that have a direct impact on a project in terms of security and compliance—i.e., *Dependency Management*,

Security scan, and *Licensing*—independently of the nomenclature suggested by
the Cybersecurity and Infrastructure Security Agency [17]. In other words, we
do not distinguish between the different software lifecycle phases (i.e., Design,
Source, Build, Analyzed, Deployed) during which an SBOM can be created or
utilized. The top part of Fig. 1 shows our taxonomy of SBOM files, highlighting
in green the types we study in this work. We refer to these files as *policy-driven
SBOM*—i.e., SBOM created to fulfill a security or legal policy. The bottom part
of Fig. 1 shows an example of each type of SBOM what we consider (on the
right) and that we *do not* consider in this study (e.g., test data on the left).

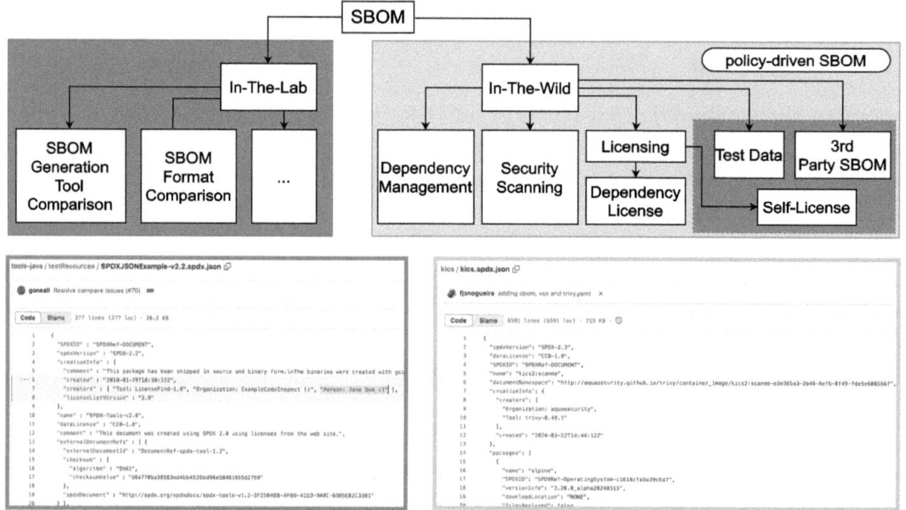

Fig. 1. Taxonomy of SBOM types (green considered in our study, red excluded) with
examples. (Color figure online)

2.2   Related Work

To the best of our knowledge, only a few studies focus, entirely or partially,
on policy-driven SBOMs. Torres-Arias et al. [10] studied SBOMs obtained from
two sources, "In-The-Wild"—i.e., from open-source repositories and "In-The-
Lab"—i.e., which they created ad-hoc from a repository or a Docker image. As
in this study, also Torres-Arias et al. used SourceGraph to collect their In-The-
Wild dataset, resulting in 53 SBOM of this type. The authors used their dataset
to benchmark two tools to assess the quality of SBOMs. They also present a
research agenda about SBOM quality aspects not captured by automated solutions, such as coverage.

Nocera et al. [18] studies the adoption of SBOM in open-source projects
hosted on GitHub. Conversely to our approach, the authors identified repositories containing SBOM files by searching a repository dependency graph for

known tools or libraries used to generate SBOM. They identified 186 repositories providing SBOM and studied their evolution.

Interlynk[3] commercial organization—provides tools for automated SBOM compliance, including `sbomqs` used to calculate the SBOM quality rating in this study. They also maintain a public database of SBOM files found In-The-Wild[4]. However, these datasets include limited information—e.g., project name/URL, the tool used to generate them, format, and provenance. Our study expanded the collected information to facilitate further studies (e.g., related to licenses or vulnerability management).

Recently, Soeiro et al. [19] extracted 78,612 unique SBOMs by mining the Software Heritage Archive, which spans over 1,782 software forges[5]. The authors provide information about SBOM quality, measured using the `sbomqs` tool, and track their evolution over time. However, they do not provide information related to vulnerabilities and licensing.

Similarly to our study, O'Donoghue et al. [12] assess the vulnerabilities associated with SBOM files. To that end, they use a synthetic dataset—i.e., obtained from Interlynk—and two tools, Trivy and Grype, to obtain data related to the vulnerabilities of the dependencies declared in the SBOM (e.g., CVE, CVSS score). They found approximately 350,000 vulnerabilities, of which approximately 10,000 were critical. Besides basing our analysis on policy-driven SBOMs only, we use a different tool, osv-scanner, to obtain vulnerabilities.

3 Methodology

Based on our goal, we devised the following Research Questions (RQ) to understand the current status of policy-driven SBOM.

RQ1. *What is currently the prevalence of policy-driven SBOM in open-source projects?* Our aim is to determine how often SBOMs are created as part of a policy (e.g., for risk assessment) compared to other purposes (e.g., providing test fixtures). We provide a snapshot of the current state of practice in the light of upcoming legislation, such as EU CRA.

RQ2. *What are the structural properties of policy-driven SBOM?* We investigate the formats used to create SBOMs, their quality, and components.

RQ3. *What is the current state of policy-driven SBOM regarding vulnerability management and licensing?* Policy-driven SBOM support policies related to vulnerability management and licensing obligations. This RQ focuses on information relevant to these policies, such as classes and severity of vulnerabilities and types of licenses.

To answer the RQs, we performed an *explorative* mining software repository study [20]. We collect and analyze the contents and quality of 620 SBOM files

---

[3] https://www.interlynk.io
[4] https://github.com/interlynk-io/sbomdb.
[5] https://www.softwareheritage.org.

mined from GitHub. We associate known vulnerabilities from 28 databases with the dependencies listed in the SBOM to provide insights into the risks these dependencies pose. Figure 2 summarizes the steps we followed in our research.

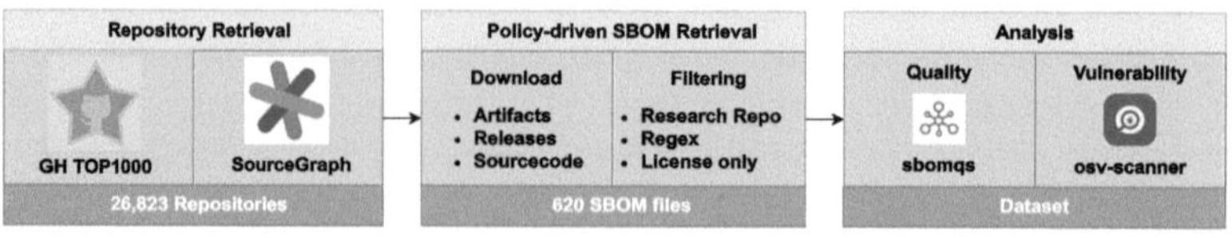

Fig. 2. Overview of the steps for gathering and analyzing SBOM files.

3.1 Repository Retrieval

We retrieved repositories in two steps. First, we retrieve the most starred repositories from GitHub for each of the most popular programming languages as reported by TIOBE[6] and GitHub Advanced Search[7], as per April, 2025.

For this search, we set an initial threshold of 100 stars. If we could not retrieve at least 1000 repositories for a given language, we lowered the threshold until we reached the lowest threshold of 35 stars. Accordingly, we retrieved 26,625 repositories from GitHub and searched them for policy-driven SBOM files.

For the second phase of the search, we leveraged the SourceGraph[8] (version 6.2.0) code search engine, looking for SBOM across all of the indexed repositories (>1 million). To that end, we created regexes specific to the two most popular SBOM formats (i.e., SPDX and CycloneDX) based on their required attributes (i.e., containing the string `SPDXID` for SPDX and `bomFormat` for CycloneDX) and file extensions (e.g., `.yaml`, `.spdx`, `.xml`, and `.json`). We applied 19 regex patterns[9] retrieving 26,823 repositories—26,625 directly obtained from GitHub and additional 198 from SourceGraph after removing duplicates.

To retrieve policy-driven SBOM, we download data from the GitHub Releases, Artifact pages, and source code. Specifically, considering the latest release, we downloaded (and extracted) every archive and file available and later applied the same regex described above. From a repository release, we downloaded all artifacts archives smaller than 100MB (due to API limitation). However, in cases where any of the archives did not meet the threshold (i.e., > 100MB), we only downloaded the largest among them instead. Then, we checked that these archives related to the latest available commit in the repository's main branch and searched for SBOM files within them using the same regex. Moreover, we searched workflow artifacts (e.g., GitHub Actions) in every repository but were not able to retrieve any additional SBOM files.

3.2   Policy-Driven SBOM Retrieval

We are interested in studying SBOM files used to implement risk management or legal policies (e.g., vulnerability management or license compliance). We started by manually analyzing repositories containing SBOMs to identify—based on their description and *README* instructions—the ones belonging to research projects (i.e., *In-the-Lab*), such as BOM shelter [10]. In this step, we filtered out 25 repositories. We then manually analyze the fully-qualified name (FQN) of SBOM files in each of the remaining repositories, looking for strings that could identify irrelevant categories—such as *Test Data*, *3rd Party*, and *Self-License*—and adding such strings to our regex. We continued this process iteratively until we could not find any more SBOM files to exclude. To that end, we applied 29 additional regex rules. Table 1 reports the strings used to exclude repositories containing SBOM files. To verify that these are *policy-driven*—i.e., none belonged to the excluded categories, we manually checked a representative sample. Given that there is a small variability across files, and for a 95% confidence level and 5% margin of error, a representative sample is at least $n=96$ [21]. Therefore, from the remaining 620 files, we randomly sampled 100 SBOM. In total, we retained 620 policy-driven SBOMs. Table 2 reports descriptive statistics for repositories containing SBOMs.

Table 1. Exclusion criteria for repositories with SBOM. For *Test Data* and *3rd Party* regex applied to filename, for *Self-License* applied to SBOM content.

Exclusion criteria	Regex	Example excluded repository
Test Data	example, expect, test, demo, sample, results	CycloneDX/cyclonedx-dotnet-library, cybeats/sbomgen
3rd Party	bundled, fixture, contrib*, dependenc*, lib*, modules, package*	apache/airflow-site, mercedes-benz/sechub
Self-License	*contains a reference to a license but has empty dependencies*	allusive-dev/compfy

3.3   Analysis

We use the **sbomqs** tool[10] (version 1.0.4) to calculate the quality score of each policy-driven SBOM file. The tool calculates the quality score, between 0 and 10, based on the completeness of the SBOM structural properties (e.g., elements used based on the format specifications), its semantics (e.g., proper versioning for licenses), and the recommendations from the National Telecommunications and

---

[10] https://github.com/interlynk-io/sbomqs.

Table 2. Summary statistics for repositories containing policy-driven SBOMs.

	Stars	Contributors	Commits
Median	303	29	1304
Mean	4822.21	212.93	12369.28
Std. dev.	11235.29	884.06	83572.10
Min	6	0	2
Max	95443	13551	1133064

Information Administration agency of the USA government (NTIA)—i.e., inclusion of information regarding supplier name, component name, component version, other identifiers for the same component, dependency relationship, author, and timestamp. We selected this tool as it incorporates several SBOM quality guidelines and supports customizable quality checklists [11].

We scan the SBOM files for vulnerabilities reported in the Google Open-Source Vulnerabilities Database using its associated tool `osv-scanner`[11] (version v2.0.1). The tool uses 28 advisory databases (e.g., GitHub Advisory Database, PyPi Advisory Database) covering 21 software ecosystems (e.g., Maven, crates.io) to identify known vulnerabilities in the dependencies reported in the SBOM files. The scan results include the Common Vulnerabilities and Exposures (CVE) identifier, the Common Weakness Enumeration (CWE) identifier, the Common Vulnerability Scoring System (CVSS) score, and the severity of the vulnerability, as well as a natural language description. Despite other tools reported in the literature (e.g., [12,14]), such as Trivy or Grype, use the same databases, we selected osv-scanner as it provides a standardized format—called osv-schema—which simplifies parsing and analyzing its results. We created a dataset including information from SBOMs, their quality, and associated vulnerabilities.

4   Results

This section presents the results of applying our methodology to identify policy-driven SBOMs and analyzing their contents through descriptive statistics.

4.1   Prevalence of Policy-Driven SBOM (RQ1)

Of the 26,823 processed repositories, 152 repositories contained policy-driven SBOM files—i.e., 0.56%. The most used format is SPDX, with 336 files, whereas 284 are in CycloneDX format. For CycloneDX, the majority uses the latest version 1.6. Conversely, most SBOM in SPDX format use version 2.3—i.e., the second most recent version as per April 2025. For SPDX, its latest version, 3.0,

---

[11] https://osv.dev.

is not used by any policy-driven SBOM. Regarding representation, CycloneDX uses JSON and XML, whereas SPDX uses JSON, YAML and their own tag-value format (i.e., `.spdx`). In particular, across formats, 542 SBOM use JSON, 23 use XML, 2 YAML, and 53 the SPDX tag-value. Table 3 shows a breakdown of SBOM formats according to their versions. Moreover, we found that most SBOM files, 313, belong to repositories using the Go language. SBOM were found in repositories using popular languages, such as Java, with 41, C with 37, Rust with 25, and Python with 21 files.

Table 3. Format and version of retrieved SBOM files.

Format	Version	No. SBOM	Format	Version	No. SBOM
	1.6	97		3.0	0
	1.5	51	SPDX	2.3	278
	1.4	71		2.2	54
CycloneDX	1.3	59		2.1	4
	1.2	5			
	1.1	0			
	1.0	1			

Answer to RQ1

Only 0.56% of top open-source repositories use *policy-driven* SBOM. The majority of SBOM do not use the latest version available for their format (SPDX or CycloneDX). The Go community is the most aware regarding the use of SBOM.

4.2 Properties of Policy-Driven SBOM (RQ2)

In this section, we focus on properties of policy-driven SBOM. In total, the SBOMs we collected report 181,283 dependencies, of which 25,430 are unique. On average, a policy-driven SBOM of an open-source project contains 291.86 dependencies, with a median of 93 and a standard deviation of 1131.23. Such variation (see Fig. 3) is due to large projects, such as `jaegertracing/jaeger` reporting 17,825 dependencies whereas several projects report only a single one.

The average quality of the SBOMs in our dataset is 7.07 (median = 7.32) with some variation (standard deviation = 0.88) across them. Specifically, both CycloneDX and SPDX SBOM have an average quality of 7, although the former has a slightly higher standard deviation than the latter (1.00 vs 0.76). The best score, 9.42, is achieved by the `intel/cve-bin-tool` project, whereas the project with the lowest SBOM quality of 3.04 is `scanoss/engine`. Table 4 reports the quality score breakdown according to SBOM formats and their representations.

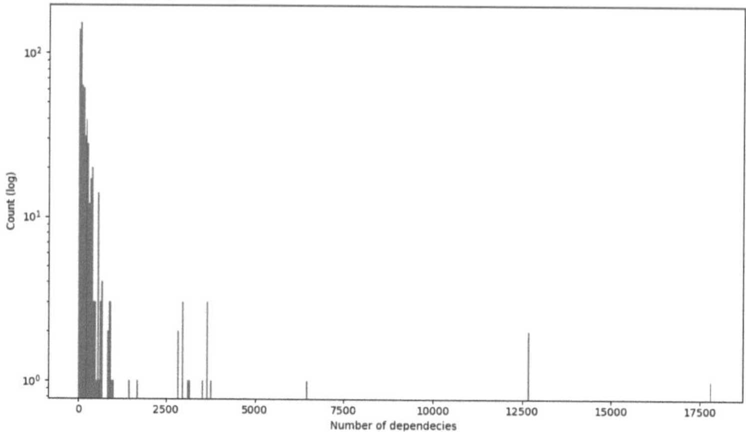

Fig. 3. Distribution of dependencies declared in SBOM.

Table 4. Summary of SBOM quality score according to their formats.

	CDX (JSON)	CDX (XML)	SPDX (JSON)	SPDX (tag)	SPDX (YAML)	Total
Median	6.95	8.17	7.36	6.09	8.17	7.32
Mean	6.99	7.61	7.16	6.65	8.17	7.07
Std	0.96	1.33	0.54	1.38	0.00	0.88
Min	3.04	4.35	4.13	4.35	8.17	3.04
Max	9.38	8.68	8.18	9.42	8.17	9.42

Answer to RQ2

Although used to document a large number of dependencies, on average, the quality of policy-driven SBOM is good (i.e., 7 on a 0–10 scale).

4.3 Current State of Policy-Driven SBOM (RQ3)

We analyze SBOMs from the perspective of the main policies they serve—i.e., vulnerability management and licensing.

Vulnerability Management. A large part (i.e., 39.15%) of the dependencies reported in SBOMs did not contain any vulnerabilities. On average, we observed 7.61 vulnerabilities per SBOM (standard deviation = 39.83). Projects, such as `aboutcode-org/dejacode`, show a large number of vulnerabilities (n = 564), explaining the observed variability. On average, there are more *high* and *medium* severity vulnerabilities than *critical*, while *low* ones appear less often. Table 5 reports vulnerabilities information related to SBOM files.

In total, we identified 19,225 CVEs, of which 2,202 tracking unique vulnerabilities. The most common vulnerability is tracked as CVE-2025-22872, which impacts 824 dependencies. The oldest vulnerabilities is from 2012, and is tracked

Table 5. Summary of vulnerabilities found in dependencies declared in SBOM files according to their severity.

	Critical	High	Medium	Low	Total
Mean	0.55	2.65	3.89	0.51	7.61
Std	3.17	14.64	20.45	2.34	39.83
Min	0	0	0	0	0
Max	56	232	296	37	296

as CVE-2012-0805. All the Top-10 most common vulnerabilities (see Table 6) were published between 2020 and 2025. Regarding categories, the vulnerabilities found in the dependencies of the collected SBOM files cover 223 unique CWE (8,726 in total). On average, the vulnerabilities are associated with three CWE categories (standard deviation = 4.85, median = 2, max = 56). The most vulnerabilities fall under CWE-20 related to weak input validation which can lead to other attack vectors, such as different types of injections. Furthermore, denial of service (e.g., through computing resource consumption), such as CWE-400, CWE-1333, and CWE-770 are the second most common types of vulnerability affecting the dependencies declared in policy-driven SBOMs. Figure 4a reports the CWE of with vulnerabilities observed in policy-driven SBOMs.

Licensing. The collected SBOMs report a total of 384 unique licenses. Each SBOM file reports, on average, 107 licenses (median = 1) per project, with a standard deviation of 370. This is due to projects containing a high number of licenses, such as **apache/camel-quarkus** reporting 3757 licenses. Interestingly, 139 SBOMs (22.41%) do not report any license (83 in CycloneDX and 56 in SPDX format). Apache and MIT are the most utilized licenses, representing approximately 70% of the total. Figure 4b reports the occurrences of different licenses in policy-driven SBOMs.

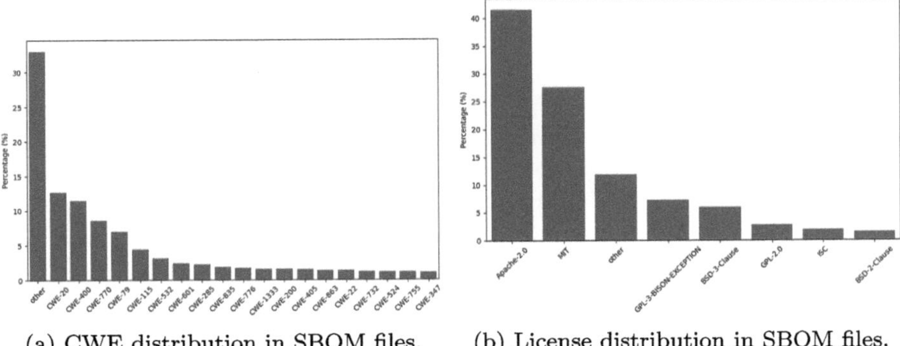

(a) CWE distribution in SBOM files.   (b) License distribution in SBOM files.

Fig. 4. SBOM vulnerability and licensing information.

Answer to RQ3

Although the majority of dependencies reported in SBOM do not contain vulnerabilities, medium to high-severity ones are still common and unpatched. Moreover, there are hundreds license reported, although 22% of policy-driven SBOM do not report any licensing information. Permissive licenses (e.g., Apache 2.0 and MIT) are the most common.

Table 6. Top-5 CVEs by occurrence found in dependencies declared in SBOMs.

CVE ID	Deps. impacted	Percentage
CVE-2025-22872	824	4.28
CVE-2025-22870	766	3.98
CVE-2025-22869	510	2.65
CVE-2024-45337	370	1.92
CVE-2025-22871	363	1.88

5   Discussion

This section shows the limitations of our results and discusses their implications.

5.1   Limitations

Although we followed similar existing studies in the area of SBOM and supply chain security (e.g., [14,15,18,22]), our limitation is that we used GitHub as the only source for SBOM.

SourceGraph only searches within the contents of files smaller than 1MB. Other limitations that could impact our results deal with the SourceGraph indexing strategy, which limits our search to the main branch of a repository. Moreover, we could not search repositories larger than 10GB as they are not indexed. Our results are based on the top-1000 repositories for each language. Accordingly, we acknowledge that the results could differ for SBOM files belonging to projects utilizing less popular programming languages or simply less popular projects. However, our results are based on an initial set of 26,823 repositories which we believe to be representative.

Another limitation of our study is the regex used to search for policy-driven SBOM files. There is a chance that our regexes filtered out actual policy-driven SBOM (i.e., false negatives). Moreover, we could have included irrelevant SBOM files due to their non-standard template, such as mis-using keywords used in our regexes (i.e., false positives). However, through manual analysis, we detected non-policy-driven SBOMs and iteratively improved the regex used for filtering them out. A manual inspection of a significant sample of the final dataset showed no false positives. We limited our search to SPDX and CycloneDX, as these are the two most widespread formats [10,13,18].

Finally, we acknowledge a limitation due to the SBOM tools we used. To calculate the SBOM scores, we have used a single tool, although we acknowledge that using different tools (e.g., OWASP SCVS, Ebay's SBOM scorecard) could yield different results [11]. The tool could not parse 66% of SBOM files in SPDX `tag-value` format across versions due to missing fields and invalid relationship type. We tried to address this by converting the tag-value format to JSON, using the official tool provided by SPDX, to no avail. The `osv-scanner` tool failed to obtain information from the advisory databases for 22% of the SBOMs in our dataset. Similar issues are reported in previous research (e.g., [11]) showing that SBOM tooling is currently immature.

5.2 Implications

As reported in this paper and previous studies (e.g., [10]), there are very few publicly available SBOMs compared to the number of open-source projects. Further, the results of RQ1 show that only a small percentage of repositories contain SBOM created and shared as part of a policy. By empirically investigating the current state of policy-driven SBOM and their contents, we aim to improve SBOM research, specifically the study of SBOM usage by software providers.

> **Takeaway 1**: Researchers investigating SBOM mined from GitHub should consider whether the SBOM they are investigating are *policy-driven* or not, or at least consider whether they are analyzing In-the-Wild or In-the-Lab SBOM.

For researchers, further analysis of our dataset will serve as the first step towards answering fundamental questions, such as *"What is actually documented in an SBOM?"* and *"How does SBOM support risk assessment in practice?"*

Also in RQ1, we show that only 34% of CycloneDX SBOM are using the latest standard version, whereas 20% are still using a version from January 2022. For SPDX, although the latest major version of the standard is not in use yet In-The-Wild at the time of this study, we show that 16% of SBOM use a version (v2.2) from May 2020.

> **Takeaway 2**: Software vendors should consider updating their SBOM to the latest available version of the most popular formats to avoid compatibility issues in the future. Software integrators operating down the supply chain should be aware of older SBOM format version limitations, such as lack of attestation.

The results of RQ2 show that the policy-driven SBOM are of good quality and can be used as an initial benchmark for In-the-Wild evaluation of tools that use SBOM as part of their input, such as vulnerability scanners (e.g., [23,24]). Such evaluation can inform practitioners in selecting an appropriate tool for downstream tasks (e.g., scanning for licenses). Similarly to previous work (i.e., [10]), we contribute to the research area of SBOM quality. The analysis of policy-driven SBOMs can guide the development of an empirically-based definition of what is an SBOM of high quality and what is not in different contexts (e.g., at different stages of a software supply chain) and for different use cases [11].

Given the current legislation in the US and the upcoming one in Europe, SBOM will be integrated into the development lifecycle to help identify known vulnerabilities in the listed dependencies. In our study (RQ3), we show that high-severity vulnerabilities affecting dependencies are left unpatched for several months. Connecting vulnerability information to an SBOM can support suppliers and integrators to quickly assess the security posture of a software product, leading to better risk mitigation strategies for the users and downstream actors in the supply chain. The security community is moving in this direction by developing the Vulnerability Exploitability eXchange (VEX) format [8].

> **Takeaway 3**: Open source project maintainers as well as software vendors using open source should be aware that upcoming regulations, such as EU CRA, will enforce strict time limits for patching vulnerabilities and updating vulnerable dependencies.

Further research needs to deal with how to use the information contained in SBOMs, aligning them with vulnerability databases, and communicating these vulnerabilities to development teams so they can act upon them and make informed decision when using a third-party library. When investing RQ3, we show that there are several unique licenses (107 on average) appearing in the supply chain of an open-source project. Managing such variety can cause issues, from a legal standpoint, for detecting and resolving conflicts between licenses. Tools developed for analyzing licenses (e.g., [25]) can use the dataset provided in this research to created benchmarks of the current state of open-source licenses for components documented in SBOM files. The large number of licenses in dependencies should be a warning sign for software vendors.

> **Takeaway 4**: Researchers should investigate how SBOMs are explicitly used to support licensing of software dependencies (e.g., resolving incompatibility issues). Software vendors should be aware that SBOM can help them review possible licensing issues related to the software they provide.

Our analysis of both vulnerabilities and licenses contained in policy-driven SBOM can guide researchers to develop approaches for automatic recommendation of dependency replacements—e.g., when a dependency declared in an SBOM contains vulnerabilities above a certain risk threshold or the dependency is incompatible with the product licensing scheme.

6   Conclusion

This study analyzed 620 policy-driven SBOM files mined from open-source projects. The results show that only 0.56% of repositories contain SBOM that serve a policy, such as vulnerability risk assessment or licenses management. Structural properties of policy-driven SBOMs show a good level of quality. We show that policy-driven SBOM in GitHub still contain high-severity unpatched CVEs, which could result in a violation of the upcoming EU CRA. The large number of licenses of dependencies we found can cause issues when these are not properly managed (e.g., license conflicts). We emphasize the importance of investigating policy-driven SBOMs to improve supply chain security.

Future research will focus on the time-related aspects of *policy-driven* SBOMs. This includes understanding the time frame for their inclusion in a project and determining whether specific formats and versions become prevalent over time. Moreover, we will investigate the motivation for the low adoption of SBOM, repository maintainers policy to create and maintain them.

Acknowledgments. We would like to acknowledge that this work was supported by the KKS foundation through the S.E.R.T. Research Profile and the SESAM research project at Blekinge Institute of Technology.

References

1. Feng, S., Lubis, M.: Defense-in-depth security strategy in LOG4J vulnerability analysis. In: 2022 International Conference Advancement in Data Science, E-learning and Information Systems (ICADEIS), pp. 01–04. IEEE (2022)
2. Wolff, E.D., GroWlEy, K.M., Lerner, M.O., Welling, M.B., Gruden, M.G., et al.: Navigating the SolarWinds supply chain attack. Procurement Lawyer **56**(2), 3 (2021)
3. Arvanitis, I., Ntousakis, G., Ioannidis, S., Vasilakis, N.: A systematic analysis of the event-stream incident. In: Proceedings of the 15th European Workshop on Systems Security, pp. 22–28 (2022)
4. Everson, D., Cheng, L., Zhang, Z.: Log4shell: redefining the web attack surface. In: Workshop on Measurements, Attacks, and Defenses for the Web (MADWeb) 2022 (2022)
5. Zahan, N., Lin, E., Tamanna, M., Enck, W., Williams, L.: Software bills of materials are required. Are we there yet? IEEE Secur. Priv. **21**(2), 82–88 (2023)
6. Hendrick, S., Zemlin, J.: The state of software bill of materials (SBOM) and cybersecurity readiness. Tech. Rep, The Linux Foundation (2022)
7. Kloeg, B., Ding, A.Y., Pellegrom, S., Zhauniarovich, Y.: Charting the path to SBOM adoption: a business stakeholder-centric approach. In: Proceedings of the 19th ACM Asia Conference on Computer and Communications Security, pp. 1770–1783 (2024)
8. Stalnaker, T., Wintersgill, N., Chaparro, O., Di Penta, M., German, D.M., Poshyvanyk, D.: Boms away! inside the minds of stakeholders: a comprehensive study of bills of materials for software systems. In: Proceedings of the 46th IEEE/ACM International Conference on Software Engineering, pp. 1–13 (2024)

9. Xia, B., Bi, T., Xing, Z., Lu, Q., Zhu, L.: An empirical study on software bill of materials: where we stand and the road ahead arXiv (2023)
10. Torres-Arias, S., Geer, D., Meyers, J.S.: A viewpoint on knowing software: bill of materials quality when you see it. IEEE Secur. Priv. **21**(6), 50–54 (2023)
11. Mirakhorli, M., et al.: A landscape study of open source and proprietary tools for software bill of materials (SBOM). arXiv preprint arXiv:2402.11151 (2024)
12. O'Donoghue, E., Reinhold, A.M., Izurieta, C.: Assessing security risks of software supply chains using software bill of materials. In: 2nd International Workshop on Mining Software Repositories for Privacy and Security, MSR4P&S,(SANER 2024), Rovaniemi, Finland (2024)
13. Balliu, M., et al.: Challenges of producing software bill of materials for Java. IEEE Secur. Priv. **21**, 12–23 (2023)
14. Yu, S., Song, W., Hu, X., Yin, H.: On the correctness of metadata-based SBOM generation: a differential analysis approach. In: 2024 54th Annual IEEE/IFIP International Conference on Dependable Systems and Networks (DSN), pp. 29–36. IEEE (2024)
15. Rabbi, M.F., Champa, A.I., Nachuma, C., Zibran, M.F.: SBOM generation tools under microscope: a focus on the NPM ecosystem. In: Proceedings of the 39th ACM/SIGAPP Symposium on Applied Computing, pp. 1233–1241 (2024)
16. Vendome, C., Bavota, G., Penta, M.D., Linares-Vásquez, M., German, D., Poshyvanyk, D.: License usage and changes: a large-scale study on GitHub. Empir. Softw. Eng. **22**, 1537–1577 (2017)
17. Stewart, K., Rhodes, M.: Types of software bill of materials (SBOM). https:// web.archive.org/web/20240907164647/https://www.cisa.gov/sites/default/files/ 2023-04/sbom-types-document-508c.pdf
18. Nocera, S., Romano, S., Di Penta, M., Francese, R., Scanniello, G.: Software bill of materials adoption: a mining study from Github. In: 2023 IEEE International Conference on Software Maintenance and Evolution (ICSME), pp. 39–49. IEEE (2023)
19. Soeiro, L., Robert, T., Zacchiroli, S.: Wild SBOMS: a large-scale dataset of software bills of materials from public code (2025). https://arxiv.org/abs/2503.15021
20. Hassan, A.E.: Mining software repositories to assist developers and support managers. In: 2006 22nd IEEE International Conference on Software Maintenance, pp. 339–342. IEEE (2006)
21. Taherdoost, H.: Determining sample size; how to calculate survey sample size. Int. J. Econ. Manage. Syst. **2** (2017)
22. Bi, T., Xia, B., Xing, Z., Lu, Q., Zhu, L.: On the way to SBOMs: investigating design issues and solutions in practice. ACM Trans. Softw. Eng. Methodol. **33**, 1–25 (2024)
23. Imtiaz, N., Williams, L.: Memory error detection in security testing (2021)
24. Cruz, D.B., Almeida, J.R., Oliveira, J.L.: Open source solutions for vulnerability assessment: a comparative analysis. IEEE Access **11**, 100234–100255 (2023)
25. Xu, S., Gao, Y., Fan, L., Liu, Z., Liu, Y., Ji, H.: LIDetector: license incompatibility detection for open source software. ACM Trans. Softw. Eng. Methodol. **32**(1), 1–28 (2023)

Generating Business Process Models with Open Source Large Language Models Using Instruction Tuning

Gökberk Çelikmasat[1]([envelope]) [ORCID], Atay Özgövde[1], and Fatma Başak Aydemir[2] [ORCID]

[1] Boğaziçi University, İstanbul, Turkey
`gokberk.celikmasat@std.bogazici.edu.tr`, `ozgovde@bogazici.edu.tr`
[2] Utrecht University, Utrecht, The Netherlands
`f.b.aydemir@uu.nl`

Abstract. Domain models play a central role in software development. They support communication, foster collaboration, and serve as references throughout the process. They also allow for automated analysis and can be used for code generation in model-driven development. Despite these benefits, software practitioners often neglect building domain models because they demand significant time, deep subject-matter expertise, and advanced modeling skills. To address these challenges and automatically generate domain models from text, we leverage generative large language models and apply instruction tuning to further enhance their performance. We demonstrate the applicability of our approach by tuning an open-source large language model to generate dynamic domain models as business process models and comparing its performance with off-the-shelf models. The results show that the instruction-tuned model outperforms off-the-shelf models in not only the key text-similarity metrics, BLEU, ROUGE, and METEOR, but also in Graph Edit Distance that captures structural correctness. Our qualitative assessment confirms that industry experts find the outputs accurate and useful. These experts demonstrate a willingness to integrate the system into their workflow. Our study demonstrates the first application of instruction tuning to business process model generation and highlights the potential for domain-specific adaptation of large language models.

Keywords: automated software engineering · model generation · generative AI · large language models · instruction tuning

1 Introduction

Domain models are conceptual representations of entities, relationships, and business logic within a specific domain [12]. They establish a shared vocabulary among stakeholders, facilitating collaboration and supporting model-driven development practices [10,30].

Although domain models capture both static and dynamic aspects of a system [38], they are often underused due to the time and expertise required

G. Scanniello et al. (Eds.): PROFES 2025, LNCS 16361, pp. 269–284, 2026.
https://doi.org/10.1007/978-3-032-12089-2_17

to create them [35]. Traditional automation approaches offer limited support [3,7,31], and often lack generalizability. Motivated by the needs of our industry collaborator—an international bank with over 1,700 IT professionals—and the opportunity offered by large language models (LLMs), we aim to improve software engineering practices through generative AI.

To support the initial modeling phase, we apply instruction tuning, which fine-tunes an LLM using supervised input-output pairs tailored to a domain. This process enables the model to internalize modeling syntax, structure, and conventions, making it more suitable for structured tasks such as model generation. Prior work has explored rule-based systems and classical machine learning, but these struggle with semantic ambiguity and poor generalization [1,17,33]. More recent generative approaches also have key limitations. Prompt engineering cannot change model weights and thus fails to teach deeper structural patterns, while retrieval-augmented generation (RAG) requires additional infrastructure and is not optimized for graph-structured outputs [21,26].

We address this gap by instruction-tuning an open-weight LLM to directly embed Business Process Model and Notation (BPMN) knowledge and generate consistent Business Process Models (BPMs) under on-prem constraints. Specifically, we use Gemma-2 9B [34] for its strong performance-cost balance and license compatibility, and apply parameter-efficient fine-tuning (PEFT) [16] to support 4-bit quantization and low-resource training. We train on the MaD dataset [22], which offers clean, paired process descriptions and BPMN-DOT models across diverse domains, which is well-suited for instruction tuning.

We investigate the following research questions:

RQ1: What is the impact of instruction tuning on BPMN model generation in a zero-shot setting?

RQ2: How do users perceive the accuracy and usefulness of BPMN models generated by the instruction-tuned LLM?

To answer RQ1, we develop an instruction tuning pipeline and compare the tuned Gemma-2 9B model against several off-the-shelf LLMs using textual and structural metrics. For RQ2, we conduct a qualitative study with domain experts to assess the usability and accuracy of the generated models. Our findings show that the outputs are accurate and useful for early modeling. The tuned model and dataset are available in our replication package [15].

The rest of the paper is organized as follows: Sect. 2 introduces relevant concepts. Section 3 presents our framework. Section 4 details our evaluation methodology, and Sect. 5 discusses our findings. We explore implications in Sect. 6, review related work in Sect. 7, and conclude in Sect. 8.

2   Background

This section explains business process modeling using BPMN and instruction tuning. The former is the output of our approach, while the latter is the method we use to fine-tune LLMs.

In software engineering, BPMN 2.0 [20] is a widely adopted international standard (ISO/IEC 19510) that provides a graphical representation for modeling business processes. It facilitates clear communication among stakeholders by visually capturing workflows, tasks, events, and decision points within a process. Specifically, BPMN defines key constructs such as tasks (atomic activities), events (start and end points of processes), gateways (decision nodes controlling process flows), and sequence flows (edges defining execution order).

Instruction tuning is a supervised fine-tuning technique where a pre-trained LLM is adapted using instruction-output pairs specific to a downstream task. This allows the model to generalize more effectively to unseen instructions by learning patterns that align with task-specific requirements. Instruction tuning can be viewed as a structured variant of traditional fine-tuning, where instruction-output pairs guide the model toward generalizable reasoning patterns rather than narrow task adaptation. This formulation enables the model to learn not just surface-level input-output mappings, but also the intent and structure behind task formulations.

Compared to prompt engineering, which modifies only the input without changing model weights, instruction tuning alters internal parameters to embed domain-relevant behaviors. This is especially beneficial for tasks requiring structural consistency, such as generating formal diagrams.

Prior studies show the efficacy of instruction tuning in boosting zero-shot performance. Sanh *et al.* [32] and Wei *et al.* [37] report notable improvements across general NLP tasks, with Wei *et al.* observing over 10% gains on Super-GLUE [36] benchmarks compared to untuned models.

However, tuning all model parameters is resource-intensive, especially for models with billions of parameters. PEFT [16] addresses this by updating only a fraction of the weights, thereby lowering memory and compute requirements. PEFT techniques such as Low-Rank Adaptation (LoRA) [18], and prefix-tuning enable practical fine-tuning on limited hardware while preserving model quality.

Zhang *et al.* [41] emphasize that PEFT, when combined with instruction tuning, allows for rapid adaptation to specialized domains with minimal retraining. This makes it particularly suitable for tasks like BPMN model generation, where domain-specific syntax and structure must be captured accurately without incurring the overhead of full-model fine-tuning.

3   The **BPMG-IT** Framework

This section describes our BPMG-IT framework, which consists of two stages:

1. Data preparation: Cleaning, filtering, and formatting the dataset for instruction tuning (Sect. 3.1).
2. Instruction tuning: Fine-tuning a pre-trained LLM on task-specific instruction-output pairs (Sect. 3.2).

3.1 Dataset Construction

We base our instruction tuning pipeline on the MaD dataset [22], which provides 30,000 paired examples of textual business process descriptions and corresponding BPMN models in DOT format[1]. Covering 15 domains such as loan processing and onboarding, it offers structured samples suitable for supervised fine-tuning.

To improve training quality and robustness, we applied several preprocessing steps. We removed samples with malformed DOT syntax (using the `pydot` library), duplicates, samples with typos in textual descriptions, and instances that exceeded our 2048-token input limit. After filtering, we retained 27,000 valid pairs. On average, models contained 12.25 nodes, 13.44 edges, and 4.18 gateways, while input descriptions averaged 132 words across 7.8 sentences. We then use this filtered data to create our instruction-output pairs for our instruction-tuning pipeline, which is described in Sect. 3.2.

3.2 Instruction Tuning Pipeline

We instruction-tuned an open-source LLM using the filtered instruction-output pairs to teach domain structure and modeling conventions for zero-shot BPMN generation. An overview of the pipeline is shown in Fig. 1.

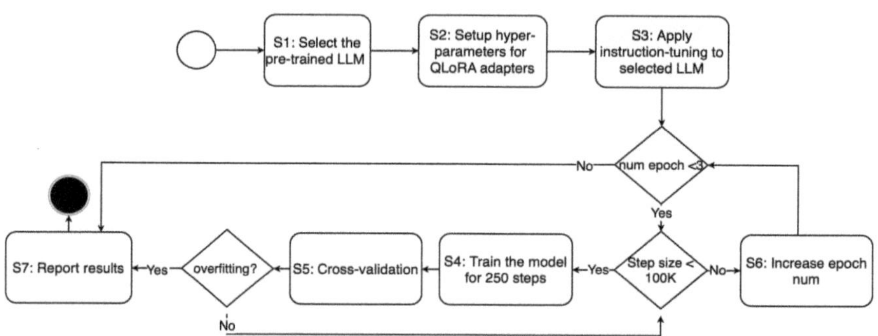

Fig. 1. Instruction tuning pipeline.

We selected Gemma-2 9B [34] for its strong performance-to-size ratio, permissive open licensing, and compatibility with on-prem deployment. The model was pre-trained on high-quality English text and code using knowledge distillation, offering a strong base for instruction tuning (S1).

To reduce training cost while maintaining output quality, we adopted QLoRA [9], which applies 4-bit quantization to LoRA adapter weights while freezing

---

[1] https://graphviz.org/doc/info/lang.html

the base model. This compression scheme reduces memory usage significantly compared to conventional fp16 or fp32 precision, while preserving generation quality. Training was conducted on a single NVIDIA L40S GPU (48 GB) and we used a rank of 32, alpha of 64, and a dropout rate of 0.05 (S2). The process completed in approximately 10 h, and inference per BPMN model averaged under 5 s on the same hardware.

For each sample (natural language description and corresponding business process model) in our filtered dataset, we dynamically created an instruction by combining the instruction template presented in Fig. 2a and the natural language description of the business process from the sample. We paired this instruction with the output from the dataset (business process model in DOT as presented in Fig. 2b). Data was split into training (80%), validation (10%), and test (10%) sets and is available in our replication package [15].

The model was instruction-tuned on these instruction-output pairs for 3 epochs, totaling 100,000 steps (S3). We used a per-device batch size of 8, gradient accumulation of 16, and a learning rate of 3e-5, which we found to balance convergence speed and generalization. To ensure efficient preprocessing, tokenization, and formatting were parallelized using 16 workers. Validation was conducted every 250 steps using held-out samples (S4), and early stopping was applied based on loss plateauing to prevent overfitting (S5). Training was terminated either when the validation loss stabilized or the final epoch was completed (S6), then we proceeded with reporting the results (S7).

Following training, the instruction-tuned model was used to generate BPMN models from the instances in the test set. Outputs were rendered using Graphviz[2] (see Fig. 2c for an example) to enable visual inspection by the domain experts, as described in Sect. 4. The final model and training artifacts are publicly available on HuggingFace[3] as part of our replication package [15].

4   Quantitative and Qualitative Evaluation

To answer RQ1 and RQ2, we adopt a dual evaluation strategy that measures both the technical accuracy and practical usability of the generated BPMN models. This section outlines our methods for measuring model performance using quantitative metrics and expert assessments.

4.1   Quantitative Evaluation

We evaluate our model using two metric types: textual similarity and graph-based structural metrics. This dual approach helps us comprehensively assess the generated BPMN models against their ground truth counterparts.

Textual Similarity Metrics. Since our task involves generating BPMN diagrams as DOT code, we use three widely accepted metrics from the text/code generation literature:

---

[2] https://graphviz.org/.
[3] https://huggingface.co/gcelikmasat-work/gemma-2-9b-it-BPMN.

> You are an expert in BPMN modeling and DOT language. Your task
> is to convert detailed textual descriptions of business processes
> into accurate BPMN model codes written in DOT language. Label all
> nodes with their activity names. Represent all connections between
> nodes without labeling the connections. Represent each node and
> its connections accurately, ensuring all decision points and flows
> are included and connected. Now, generate BPMN business process
> model code in DOT language for the following textual description
> of a business process: <BUSINESS PROCESS DESCRIPTION>

(a) Instruction template given during instruction tuning

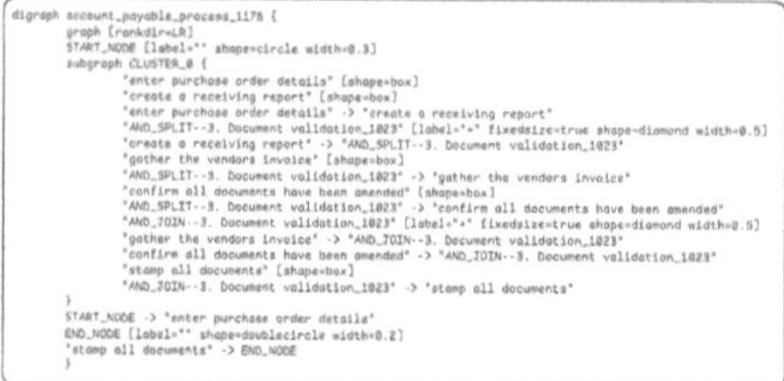

(b) Output BPMN Diagram in DOT

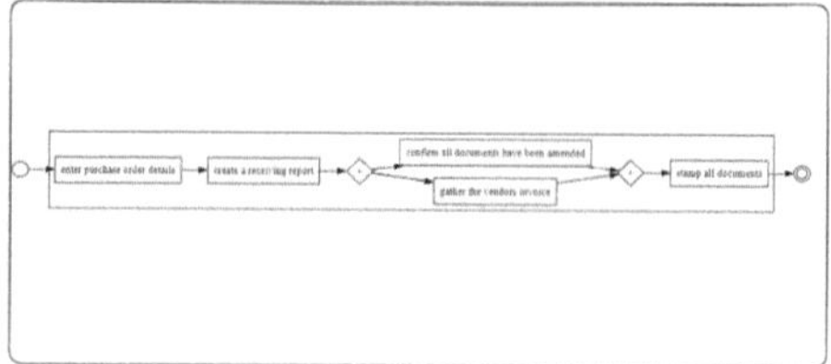

(c) Rendered Output

Fig. 2. Instruction Template (2a), DOT Output (2b), and Output Visualization 2c

BLEU: Measures precision-based overlap of n-grams between generated and reference outputs [29].

ROUGE-L: Captures the longest common subsequence, reflecting fluency and structural overlap [24].

METEOR: Considers synonym matching and word order, offering a more semantic-level evaluation [4].

While not structure-aware, these metrics remain standard in generative tasks and support consistent benchmarking across future studies. They serve as a first-order approximation of output fidelity before deeper structural validation.

Graph-Based Structural Metrics. NLP metrics mentioned in the prior section mostly rely on the similarity between the original text (business process model in DOT) and the generated text (business process model in DOT). This may cause models to appear similar in code form while still differing structurally, potentially masking errors in model content. Since BPMN models have an inherent graph structure, we implemented Graph Edit Distance to further assess the structural accuracy of our generated models.

Graph Edit Distance (GED): Measures the minimum number of graph modifications (node and edge insertions, deletions, substitutions) required to transform the generated graph into the ground truth graph [13]. We calculated GED using the NetworkX[4] library in Python and compared the generated graph with

---

[4] https://networkx.org.

the target graph, considering all the package's default parameters. Some outputs yielded a GED of 0, indicating a perfect structural match. This typically occurred when the model reproduced canonical BPMN patterns or process structures seen during training.

All models were evaluated on a fixed set of 45 randomly sampled instances from the test set of the MaD dataset. These instances were evenly distributed across 15 business domains to ensure diversity. The subset size was chosen to balance diversity with the practical cost of generating and evaluating outputs across multiple LLMs. Then the evaluation metrics were averaged over these samples for comparability.

4.2 Qualitative Evaluation

To complement our quantitative analysis, we conducted a structured qualitative study to assess real-world usability, clarity, and correctness. While automated metrics provide an objective assessment of accuracy, they cannot fully capture the usability or correctness of the models, especially in business settings where human stakeholders interact with BPMN diagrams. Therefore, we designed a qualitative evaluation protocol grounded in expert feedback.

We interviewed four domain experts from private and public sector organizations, including a major international bank. All participants had hands-on experience with BPM tools and modeling tasks, ranging from 2 to 10 years. The demographic of the experts who attended our interviews is displayed in Table 1.

Table 1. Demographics of Experts

ID	Current Role	Years of BPM Experience
E1	System Analyst	2
E2	Business Analyst	4
E3	Workflow Automation Engineer	6
E4	Lead Business Analyst	10

The study followed a semi-structured format. Experts evaluated four generated diagrams spanning different complexities. We define simple models as those with nodes less than 10 and no parallel gateways, medium as 10 to 20 nodes with light branching, and complex as anything beyond. They also compared outputs from GPT-4o, Gemma-2-9B-IT (base), Gemma-2-27B-IT, and our tuned model. Finally, each participant submitted a custom prompt and reviewed the generated result in a live session to simulate real-world usage.

We adapted the evaluation rubric from Ferrari *et al.* [11], asking experts to rate models across four dimensions:

- Accuracy: Does the model correctly reflect the textual description?

- Structural Correctness: Are all control flow elements, nodes, and gateways logically valid and properly connected?
- Usability and Practicality: Can the model be used as-is or with minimal edits in the actual context?
- Understandability: Is the model clear, readable, and easy to follow for business stakeholders?

The collected feedback from the experts were monitored and analyzed to identify recurring insights and areas of consensus. Results and aggregated insights are presented in Sect. 5.

5   Results

This section presents our experimental findings in response to the research questions outlined in Sect. 1. We analyze the quantitative performance of our instruction-tuned model across standard metrics and compare it with open-source and proprietary LLMs (RQ1). We also report qualitative insights gathered from expert evaluations to better understand the perceived usefulness and structural quality of the generated BPMN models (RQ2).

5.1   RQ1: What Is the Impact of Instruction Tuning on BPMN Model Generation In a Zero-Shot Setting?

To evaluate the effect of instruction tuning, we compared our tuned Gemma-2 9B model against its untuned counterpart, the larger Gemma-2 27B variant, and several open and proprietary LLMs. The Qwen 2.5 series [40] was included due to its strong baseline performance and scalable architecture (7B–32B). GPT-4o [19], DeepSeek v3 [25], R1 [14], Claude Haiku and Sonnet [2], and Gemini 2.5 Flash and Pro [8] were included as proprietary baselines to benchmark against high-performance general-purpose models. These models represent the current state-of-the-art in commercial LLMs and provide a strong reference point for assessing the effect of instruction tuning on BPMN generation.

To ensure fairness, untuned baselines were prompted using a strong zero-shot prompt with syntax hints and a single example. Without this prompt engineering, their scores fell to roughly half the reported values, underscoring the difficulty of raw zero-shot BPMN generation. In contrast, our tuned model was evaluated using the instruction format it was trained on.

As shown in Table 2, the instruction-tuned model achieved the highest scores across all textual similarity metrics and recorded a GED of 0.00. Although GED is 0 in some cases—indicating perfect structural alignment—the corresponding textual similarity scores remained below 100 due to variations in node ordering, formatting, and syntactic choices that do not affect the underlying graph structure. Untuned open-weight models showed significantly weaker performance despite prompt engineering, highlighting their limited understanding of BPMN's structural conventions. Proprietary models produced moderately better results

Table 2. BPMN Model Generation Textual Similarity Evaluation Results

Models	BLEU	ROUGE-L	METEOR	GED
Open-Weight LLMs				
Gemma2-9b-BPMG-IT (Ours)	**75.72**	**87.63**	**85.57**	**0.00**
Gemma2-9b-IT	4.32	25.70	31.80	13.26
Gemma2-27b-IT	1.89	35.97	34.35	14.60
Qwen2.5-7B-Instruct	5.34	41.77	43.01	**7.08**
Qwen2.5-14B-Instruct	4.77	41.15	37.99	22.84
Qwen2.5-32B-Instruct	6.65	43.58	43.95	23.57
Proprietary LLMs				
GPT-4o	6.87	45.19	46.50	23.26
Deepseek-v3	10.85	42.03	48.68	24.86
Deepseek-R1	13.06	43.76	53.16	23.15
Claude-3-Haiku	6.84	43.15	45.91	21.28
Claude-3.7-Sonnet	7.96	45.42	53.80	25.31
Gemini-2.5-Flash	22.07	44.23	54.35	**20.80**
Gemini-2.5-Pro	**23.03**	**46.53**	**61.11**	21.11

than open-weight baselines but still fell short of the tuned model. Notably, Gemini 2.5 Pro achieved the highest proprietary BLEU and METEOR scores, yet these results remained considerably below those of our tuned model. This highlights the advantage of domain-specific instruction tuning, which enables smaller open models to outperform larger, general-purpose commercial LLMs on structured generation tasks.

These findings demonstrate that domain-specific instruction tuning empowers smaller open-source models to surpass both untuned open models and commercial LLMs in structured tasks like BPMN modeling.

5.2 RQ2: How Do Users Perceive the Accuracy and Usefulness of BPMN Models generated by the Instruction-Tuned LLM?

We used the four evaluation dimensions introduced in Sect. 4: accuracy, structural correctness, usability, and understandability. Across these dimensions, experts consistently rated the instruction-tuned model as producing clear and coherent BPMN diagrams. Labels were appropriately descriptive, control flow was logical, and most models were usable with minimal post-editing.

In particular, participants praised the instruction-tuned model's ability to correctly capture the key steps of a process, even in moderately complex cases. However, they also identified areas for improvement:

- BPMG-IT occasionally included redundant or overly generic node labels when textual inputs were vague.

- BPMG-IT needs to improve gateway logic handling, particularly to avoid unnecessary chaining or ambiguous loop creation.
- Experts expressed interest in an iterative interaction loop, where they could refine BPMG-IT's output by either adjusting the initial prompt or engaging in a conversational exchange with the model to clarify vague process steps and improve output incrementally.
- BPMG-IT does not currently support languages other than English. Experts highlighted the need for multilingual support to better integrate the tool into their localized workflows.

Despite these limitations, the consensus was that BPMG-IT can significantly accelerate early-stage modeling. Experts reported that the models were particularly effective for simple to medium processes. For example, E1 emphasized that the tool could rapidly produce first drafts for approval workflows, significantly reducing manual modeling time. E2 observed that the system handled sequential tasks reliably but occasionally misused gateways. E3 stressed that while missing labels remained an issue, the overall structure was clear enough to refine quickly. E4 highlighted potential for onboarding and training, where automatically generated diagrams could serve as a starting point for newcomers. They also noted its potential to standardize modeling practices by reducing individual variation, especially when used as a practical assistant with iterative refinement but not as a full automation solution.

These results align partially with the findings of Ferrari *et al.* [11], who observed strong readability but structural inconsistencies in UML generation. In contrast, our instruction-tuned model maintained both readability and structural soundness more reliably, underscoring the value of domain-specific adaptation.

Importantly, the experts' organization—an international bank—has expressed interest in piloting BPMG-IT to automate internal documentation processes. While promising, all experts agreed that fully replacing manual modeling is premature. The tool is best suited for augmenting expert workflows, not automating them end-to-end.

6 Discussion

This section reflects on our findings, discusses how our findings can inform both academic research and real-world BPM practice, and outlines potential limitations and threats to validity.

Finding 1: Instruction tuning significantly improves LLM performance on BPMN generation tasks. Our experiments consistently showed that an instruction-tuned Gemma-2-9b LLM can surpass not only its pre-trained counterpart and larger alternatives but also other proprietary models, especially in generating accurate and structurally correct BPMN models. Instruction tuning significantly enhanced the model's capacity to represent business processes accurately and reduced typical errors seen in zero-shot outputs, particularly in edge-node connections and control flow.

Finding 2: Combining textual and structural evaluations reveals hidden performance gaps. Our dual evaluation strategy using both textual similarity metrics and the GED metric uncovered insights that would have been missed if only one category were used. Some models showed acceptable BLEU or ROUGE scores but high GED, revealing logical inconsistencies. This reinforced the need to go beyond text-level evaluation in tasks involving structured outputs, highlighting that textual similarity alone may be insufficient for assessing correctness in diagram generation tasks.

Finding 3: Expert involvement remains crucial for BPMN validation and model refinement. While our instruction-tuned model demonstrated substantial accuracy, expert evaluations underscored the need for human oversight in result evaluation. Even though our quantitative results may suggest our generated models are accurate, experts unanimously agreed that there are redundancies and issues present in our outputs. This suggests that human-in-the-loop validation remains necessary for deployment in complex workflows.

Finding 4: Parameter-efficient instruction tuning is crucial for scalability and practical adoption. Adopting parameter-efficient tuning techniques allowed us to significantly reduce computational resource requirements without compromising performance. This enabled us to fit additional domain-specific information into our LLM without expanding memory usage. This shows that domain-specific adaptation is achievable at low computational cost, making advanced, tailored AI solutions accessible even to smaller organizations or research groups without extensive GPU resources.

6.1 Implications for Research and Practice

The results of this study support instruction tuning as an efficient and cost-effective method for adapting LLMs to specialized structured generation tasks. Unlike RAG, which requires a supporting retrieval infrastructure or prompt engineering, which leaves model weights unchanged, instruction tuning integrates domain knowledge directly into the model. This approach offers better alignment for structured outputs like diagrams and process models, especially in constrained, on-premise environments.

Practically, this enables smaller open-source LLMs to be deployed privately and effectively in modeling workflows. For organizations with data privacy constraints or limited cloud access, our approach offers a viable GenAI solution for prototyping business process models. Additionally, it demonstrates that domain-specific tuning can make compact models outperform much larger general-purpose ones in targeted tasks.

The early industry interest we mentioned in Sect. 5, regarding the use of instruction tuning for generating workflow diagrams from textual descriptions, highlights the practical feasibility and relevance of our method for large-scale deployments.

6.2 Threats to Validity and Limitations

Following Wohlin *et al.* [39], we outline threats across four categories:

Construct Validity. Construct validity is ensured by explicitly structuring our instruction-response pairs using clearly defined BPMN modeling standards. Nevertheless, the complexity in natural language descriptions and their BPMN representation introduces potential ambiguity. We mitigated this via iterative data validation and preprocessing to align descriptions and BPMN models.

Internal Validity. Our filtering of malformed and long sequences may have skewed the dataset toward cleaner examples. We addressed this risk by explicitly documenting preprocessing steps, allowing replication, and a clear understanding of dataset limitations. Additionally, our qualitative evaluation was conducted independently by domain experts who were uninvolved in the training and instruction tuning process, further mitigating internal validity concerns.

Conclusion Validity. Although a GED of 0 suggests perfect structural matches, the average GED score of 0 for our instruction-tuned model suggests that graph-based operations may underrepresent true model quality in some cases. Pairing structural metrics with expert judgment helped triangulate our findings and avoid overconfidence in numerical scores.

External Validity. Our tuning process and evaluations were limited to English-language BPMN descriptions from the MaD dataset. Diversity across languages, notations, or workflows may challenge generalization. Multilingual instruction tuning and broader domain datasets are directions for future work.

Limitations. The dataset used for instruction tuning is synthetically enhanced and may not capture the full variability of real-world modeling data, potentially limiting the model's generality and applicability in practical settings. We briefly explored synthetic augmentation to increase the variability of the dataset, but observed quality degradation, so we excluded it to preserve fidelity.

7   Related Work

In this section, we take a closer look at studies related to our work in automated model generation. We divided this section into two parts: the first part groups studies that utilize rule-based and NLP/ML-based techniques; the second part focuses more on recent studies that propose generative AI-based approaches.

7.1 Rule-Based and NLP/ML-Based BPMN Model Generation

Early work focused on rule-based and NLP pipelines for translating textual process descriptions into BPMN models. Sonbol *et al.* [33] approached this as a machine translation task, using syntactic and semantic parsing to generate structured BPMN diagrams, achieving up to 81% model similarity. Similar to our evaluation approach, they used similarity-based metrics such as Graph Edit

Distance to compare the extracted and ground truth models. As well as an expert evaluation to evaluate their results from an expert point of view.

Similarly, Van der Aa *et al.* [1] outlined the challenges in NLP-based process extraction, such as coreference resolution and syntactic ambiguity, highlighting a clear need for techniques capable of capturing a deeper semantic understanding.

Despite partial success, these methods struggled with structural consistency and required heavy manual post-processing. Honkisz *et al.* [17], for instance, proposed spreadsheet-based intermediate representations, which reduced ambiguity but introduced new manual steps. Despite simplifying the extraction process, their methodology still introduced additional manual steps, posing challenges for fully automated workflow generation.

7.2   Generative AI and LLM-Based BPMN Model Generation

More recent work explores the use of LLMs to automate BPMN generation. Beheshti *et al.* [5] introduced ProcessGPT, an LLM-based system for process understanding and augmentation. Although not focused on diagram generation, it highlights the potential of LLMs in process-centric reasoning.

Licardo *et al.* [23] proposed combining GPT-4 with a fine-tuned BERT pipeline to extract models from structured documents. They reported notable improvements in accuracy, achieving around 96% relative graph edit distance accuracy scores. However, their approach requires manual component pipelines and offers limited flexibility in generation. Our method bypasses such pipelines by utilizing a single, instruction-following LLM, enabling more scalable generation with less engineering effort.

Nivon and Salaün [27] used a fine-tuned GPT-3.5 to map textual requirements to formal grammars and ASTs. Their method allows precise control but limits generalization to new phrasing. They later extended this to include BPMN optimization [28], refining models for execution time. In contrast, our instruction-tuned LLM learns to generate complete BPMN representations directly from free-form descriptions, without relying on grammar engineering or AST synthesis. Our framework also introduces flexible prompting techniques and supports quantized models with parameter-efficient tuning.

Ferrari *et al.* [11] evaluated ChatGPT for UML sequence diagram generation. Their qualitative study uncovered structural inaccuracies and semantic gaps, concluding that LLM outputs require expert validation. Their study highlights the importance of qualitative analysis and human feedback when using generative AI methods, which inspired us to conduct a similar evaluation approach. While we share this emphasis on qualitative evaluation, our findings show that instruction-tuned models yield higher structural fidelity, particularly for simpler workflows, compared to few-shot prompting alone.

Kourani *et al.* [21] explored prompt engineering strategies—such as role prompting, knowledge injection, and multi-step verification—to generate BPMN and Petri net models using LLMs. While their method effectively avoids structural errors via layered prompting, it relies heavily on carefully crafted prompts and does not adapt the model weights. Our approach, by contrast, learns structured generation patterns from instruction-output pairs, minimizing reliance on prompt complexity.

Mansouri *et al.* [6] introduced BPLLM, a framework for business process-aware LLMs using a RAG setup. The system dynamically retrieves context from a process repository to guide LLM reasoning in process-related conversations. While effective in task support and question-answering, its reliance on external retrieval components limits control over structured diagram generation. In contrast, our method embeds domain knowledge into the model itself, enabling fully offline generation suitable for on-premise deployments.

While these generative methods show promise, many rely on proprietary APIs, handcrafted pipelines, or external data retrieval. Our framework instruction tunes an open-source model with quantized adapters, offering a scalable, efficient, and privacy-preserving alternative for BPMN generation from scratch.

8   Conclusions and Future Work

In this study, we presented BPMG-IT, an instruction-tuned LLM capable of generating BPMN process models directly from natural language descriptions. Using a curated dataset of instruction-response pairs, we instruction-tuned an open-source model via QLoRA with 4-bit quantization, enabling efficient domain adaptation under resource constraints. Our evaluation spanning textual similarity metrics, graph edit distance, and expert assessment demonstrated that the instruction-tuned model significantly outperforms both untuned open-source and proprietary models like GPT-4o in terms of accuracy and structural correctness. To the best of our knowledge, BPMG-IT is the first approach to apply instruction tuning to BPMN generation from text.

Future work could extend this to other modeling domains, such as UML sequence or class diagrams, to support broader software modeling tasks. Incorporating multilingual capabilities, especially for low-resource languages, also represents a promising direction. Additionally, expanding the training dataset with new or synthetically generated examples may improve robustness and generalization, facilitating broader adoption in real-world business environments.

Acknowledgments. The authors have no competing interests to declare that are relevant to the content of this article.

References

1. Van der Aa, H., Carmona Vargas, J., Leopold, H., Mendling, J., Padró, L.: Challenges and opportunities of applying natural language processing in business process management. In: COLING 2018, pp. 2791–2801. Association for Computational Linguistics (2018)
2. Anthropic: Claude models overview (2025). https://docs.anthropic.com/en/docs/about-claude/models/overview. Accessed 17 Aug 2025

3. Arora, C., Sabetzadeh, M., Nejati, S., Briand, L.: An active learning approach for improving the accuracy of automated domain model extraction. ACM TOSEM **28**(1), 1–34 (2019)
4. Banerjee, S., Lavie, A.: Meteor: an automatic metric for MT evaluation with improved correlation with human judgments. In: Proceedings of the ACL Workshop on Intrinsic and Extrinsic Evaluation Measures for Machine Translation and/or Summarization, pp. 65–72 (2005)
5. Beheshti, A., et al.: Processgpt: transforming business process management with generative artificial intelligence. In: 2023 IEEE ICWS, pp. 731–739. IEEE (2023)
6. Bernardi, M.L., Casciani, A., Cimitile, M., Marrella, A.: Conversing with business process-aware large language models: the BPLLM framework. J. Intell. Inf. Syst. **62**(6), 1607–1629 (2024)
7. Chen, K., Yang, Y., Chen, B., López, J.A.H., Mussbacher, G., Varró, D.: Automated domain modeling with large language models: a comparative study. In: MODELS 2023, pp. 162–172. IEEE (2023)
8. DeepMind, G.: Gemini API: Available models (2025). https://ai.google.dev/gemini-api/docs/models. Accessed 17 Aug 2025
9. Dettmers, T., Pagnoni, A., Holtzman, A., Zettlemoyer, L.: QLoRA: efficient fine-tuning of quantized LLMs. Adv. Neural. Inf. Process. Syst. **36**, 10088–10115 (2023)
10. Evans, E.: Domain-driven design: tackling complexity in the heart of software. Addison-Wesley Professional (2004)
11. Ferrari, A., Abualhaija, S., Arora, C.: Model generation with LLMs: from requirements to UML sequence diagrams. In: MODRE, pp. 291–300. IEEE (2024)
12. Fowler, M.: Patterns of enterprise application architecture. Addison-Wesley (2012)
13. Gao, X., Xiao, B., Tao, D., Li, X.: A survey of graph edit distance. Pattern Anal. Appl. **13**, 113–129 (2010)
14. Guo, D., et al.: Deepseek-r1: incentivizing reasoning capability in LLMs via reinforcement learning. arXiv preprint arXiv:2501.12948 (2025)
15. Gökberk, C., Aydemir, F.B., Ozgovde, A.: BPMN Model Generation with Instruction Tuned LLM. Zenodo (2025). https://doi.org/10.5281/zenodo.15133252
16. Han, Z., Gao, C., Liu, J., Zhang, J., Zhang, S.Q.: Parameter-efficient fine-tuning for large models: a comprehensive survey. arXiv preprint arXiv:2403.14608 (2024)
17. Honkisz, K., Kluza, K., Wiśniewski, P.: A concept for generating business process models from natural language description. In: International Conference on Knowledge Science, Engineering and Management, pp. 91–103. Springer (2018)
18. Hu, E.J., et al.: Lora: low-rank adaptation of large language models. ICLR **1**(2), 3 (2022)
19. Hurst, A., et al.: GPT-4o system card. arXiv preprint arXiv:2410.21276 (2024)
20. ISO/IEC.: Information technology — Object Management Group Business Process Model and Notation (2013)
21. Kourani, H., Berti, A., Schuster, D., van der Aalst, W.M.: Process modeling with large language models. In: BPMDS, pp. 229–244. Springer (2024)
22. Li, X., Ni, L., Li, R., Liu, J., Zhang, M.: Mad: a dataset for interview-based bpm in business process management. In: 2023 IJCNN, pp. 1–8. IEEE (2023)
23. Licardo, J.T., Tanković, N., Etinger, D.: A method for extracting BPMN models from textual descriptions using natural language processing. Procedia Comput. Sci. **239**, 483–490 (2024)
24. Lin, C.Y.: Rouge: a package for automatic evaluation of summaries. In: Text Summarization Branches Out, pp. 74–81 (2004)
25. Liu, A., et al.: Deepseek-v3 technical report. arXiv preprint arXiv:2412.19437 (2024)

26. Minor, M., Kaucher, E.: Retrieval augmented generation with LLMs for explaining business process models. In: International Conference on Case-Based Reasoning, pp. 175–190. Springer (2024)
27. Nivon, Q., Salaün, G.: Automated generation of BPMN processes from textual requirements. In: ICSOC, pp. 185–201. Springer (2024)
28. Nivon, Q., Salaün, G.: Semi-automated refactoring of BPMN processes. In: 2024 IEEE 24th International Conference on Software QRS, pp. 677–688. IEEE (2024)
29. Papineni, K., Roukos, S., Ward, T., Zhu, W.J.: Bleu: a method for automatic evaluation of machine translation. In: Proceedings of the 40th Annual Meeting of the Association for Computational Linguistics, pp. 311–318 (2002)
30. Pastor, O., España, S., Panach, J.I., Aquino, N.: Model-driven development. Informatik-Spektrum **31**, 394–407 (2008)
31. Saini, R., Mussbacher, G., Guo, J.L., Kienzle, J.: Domobot: a bot for automated and interactive domain modelling. In: Proceedings of the 23rd ACM/IEEE International Conference on Model Driven Engineering Languages and Systems: Companion Proceedings, pp. 1–10 (2020)
32. Sanh, V., et al.: Multitask prompted training enables zero-shot task generalization. In: International Conference on Learning Representations (2022)
33. Sonbol, R., Rebdawi, G., Ghneim, N.: A machine translation like approach to generate business process model from textual description. SN Comput. Sci. **4**(3), 291 (2023)
34. Team, G., et al.: Gemma 2: improving open language models at a practical size. arXiv preprint arXiv:2408.00118 (2024)
35. Tolvanen, J.P., Kelly, S.: Model-driven development challenges and solutions: experiences with domain-specific modelling in industry. In: MODELSWARD, pp. 711–719. IEEE (2016)
36. Wang, A., et al.: Superglue: a stickier benchmark for general-purpose language understanding systems. In: Advances in Neural Information Processing Systems, vol. 32 (2019)
37. Wei, J., et al.: Finetuned language models are zero-shot learners. arXiv preprint arXiv:2109.01652 (2021)
38. van der Weide, T., Tulinayo, F.P., van Bommel, P.: Static and dynamic aspects of application domains: an inductively defined modeling technique that allows decomposition. Complex Syst. Inf. Model. Q. **7**, 25–50 (2016)
39. Wohlin, C., et al.: Experimentation in software engineering, vol. 236. Springer (2012)
40. Yang, A., et al.: Qwen2.5 technical report. arXiv preprint arXiv:2412.15115 (2024)
41. Zhang, S., et al.: Instruction tuning for large language models: a survey. arXiv preprint arXiv:2308.10792 (2023)

Temporal Evolution of Architectural Complexity and Technical Debt in Microservices: An Exploratory Case Study

Bhuwan Paudel[1]($\boxtimes$) , Javier Gonzalez-Huerta[1] , and Ehsan Zabardast[1,2]

[1] Software Engineering Research Lab SERL, Blekinge Institute of Technology, Karlskrona, Sweden
{bhuwan.paudel,javier.gonzalez.huerta,ehsan.zabardast}@bth.se
[2] Gaetir, Karlskrona, Sweden

Abstract. Over the last decade, software organizations have increasingly adopted microservices to effectively deal with evolving software systems, frequent demands for new features, and changing technologies. However, microservices are not a silver bullet; their success depends on the specific context and needs of each organization. Therefore, tracking the evolution of architectural complexity indicators is crucial for effective architectural governance and decision-making. In this paper, we explore the relationship between architectural complexity indicators and their evolution, specifically declared dependencies, API endpoints, inter-service communications, size, and technical debt. We used the static source code analysis methods along with SonarQube to measure architectural complexity, collecting data on all indicators over the past two and a half years. Our findings indicate that architectural complexity consistently grows, even within microservices. Most importantly, these indicators co-evolve, making the overall architecture more complicated than expected. Additionally, all complexity indicators grow rapidly when services are small and still evolving. The insights gained from this study can assist organizations in effectively managing their microservices, highlighting when they might be most prone to architectural degradation.

Keywords: Microservices Architecture · Architectural Complexity · Complexity Evolution · Technical Debt · Industrial Case Study

1 Introduction

Software systems are evolving at an unprecedented pace, driven by rapidly changing technologies, competitive markets, continuous delivery expectations, and the growing pressure to release features more frequently. Consequently, these rapid changes and growth inevitably lead to an increased complexity [16]. In order to manage such evolving complexity, microservices have become highly popular

G. Scanniello et al. (Eds.): PROFES 2025, LNCS 16361, pp. 285–302, 2026.
https://doi.org/10.1007/978-3-032-12089-2_18

in recent years as an effective way to develop scalable and more maintainable software systems [12,32]. Further, organizations are adopting microservices due to their support for modularity, independent deployability, decentralized ownership and governance of services, and evolutionary design [8,19,25]. Nonetheless, real-world implementations often fall short of these ideals due to several reasons, such as limited architectural tool support for architecture evaluation, lack of consistent design principles [1,7], challenges in managing shared code [36], and other organizational challenges [15,33], such as managing decentralized teams.

As microservices evolve, architectural complexity and challenges increase in measurable ways [1,7,30], leading to erosion of well-known architecture principles. This includes issues such as cyclic dependencies, broken hierarchies [9], violation of modular boundaries, and degradation of structural clarity, i.e., finding the right service granularity without harmful dependencies [7,36,38]. The rise in inter-service communication and architectural coupling diminishes the independence of individual services, thereby hindering their isolation and independent deployment [3,33,39]. Likewise, as the services grow in size, they take on more functionalities, and often deviate from bounded-context principles [8], which reduces the cohesion and maintainability. Moreover, the expansion of API surfaces introduces fragile contracts and compatibility issues [18]. Addressing breaking API changes [7,36] and versioning of APIs [30,33] are yet other major challenges. As all of these challenges evolve, they often contribute to the architectural erosion [20] and hence lead to the quality degradation, architectural defect, and accumulation of architectural debt gradually [20,34].

Despite widespread adoption by the industry and increasing interest from academia, only a handful of studies have empirically investigated the evolution of architectural complexity in microservices within a real-world setting [7] across multiple dimensions. However, most existing research (e.g., [2,3,13,18,26,39]) focus on isolated aspects (e.g., API changes, coupling metrics, or architectural smells) or uses synthetic datasets and open-source repositories, which often lack industrial relevance [7], where architectural decisions are shaped by evolving technical constraints, sustained delivery demands, and deployment complexities.

In this study, we develop and implement a lightweight static source code analysis method and perform a longitudinal analysis of the evolution of architectural complexity and code technical debt of a real-world microservice system from one of our industry collaborators. We measure five key architectural complexity dimensions: (1) declared dependencies, (2) inter-service communications, (3) API Endpoint exposure, (4) service size, and (5) technical debt. The dataset contains 15 services with lines of code ranging from 979 to 15,798, collected over 2.5 years of continuous development. By investigating how these dimensions evolve together, we identify complexity growth patterns, co-evolution trends, and early indicators of architectural degradation. The findings are intended to support practitioners and architects in anticipating complexity-related risks, improving system maintainability, and governance strategies in microservice-based systems.

Paper Structure: Sect. 2 provides background on technical debt and architectural complexity indicators. Section 3 reviews the related works, and Sect. 4

outlines the case study design and our method for identifying architectural complexity. Section 5 presents and discusses the results, while Sect. 6 addresses the threats to validity. Finally, Sect. 7 concludes with future work.

2 Background

2.1 Technical Debt (TD)

Technical debt is a metaphor coined by Cunningham [11] to describe how shortcuts in software development can lead to faster delivery in the short term, but may result in higher maintenance costs in the long run if not properly addressed. Over time, the concept of TD has evolved and refers to sub-optimal design decisions or implementation choices that may seem beneficial initially but ultimately make future changes more costly or even impossible, leading to lasting impacts on maintainability and evolvability of the software [4,21].

SonarQube[1] is one of the most widely used static code analysis tools for measuring TD in practice [5] despite some criticism from practitioners regarding its accuracy of the remediation time to resolve issues [6]. Nevertheless, it has been used by several other microservices and TD-oriented studies (e.g., [17,23,35]). In our study, we used SonarQube to measure the code TD due to its convenience, as the case company uses it. The detailed explanation of how SonarQube calculates TD is provided in Sect. 4.3.

2.2 Architectural Complexity Indicators

SonarQube does not always capture the architectural debt effectively. Therefore, we measured architectural complexity through some of the key measurable indicators: 'declared dependencies', 'inter-service communications', 'API endpoint exposure', and the 'evolving size' of microservices, along with 'code technical debt'. We selected these indicators based on discussions held during the early stages of research with key contacts: a development manager and a senior product owner, both with over 20 years of professional experience in software development and around 5 years of experience with the case company. Additionally, we based this choice on our prior research experience in the field. These specific indicators have also been explored in literature (e.g. [3,13,18,39] independently.

Declared Dependencies refer to explicit references to external software modules or libraries that a service requires to compile or run. In our case, these dependencies are typically defined in build or configuration files, such as pom.xml, since the microservices we analyze are built on Apache Maven. The uncontrolled growth of such dependencies can increase coupling, reduce service independence, and lead to architectural degradation and technical debt.

Inter-service Communications describe service-to-service communication patterns across the system, implemented via HTTP-based clients (e.g.,

---

[1] https://www.sonarsource.com/products/sonarqube/.

`axios.get()`, `RestTemplate.getForObject()`), RPC protocols (e.g., gRPC), or messaging queues. These interactions are foundational to microservice coordination, but their proliferation can introduce architectural risks, such as reduced independence and maintainability of services due to excessive service coupling [39].

API Endpoint Exposure quantifies the number and structure of externally exposed HTTP endpoints a service offers. They are generally declared using routing annotations or framework-specific handlers (e.g., `@GetMapping()`, `app.post()`) in source code. A broader API surface increases integration flexibility but also raises risk for backward incompatibility and maintainability [18].

3   Related Work

To the best of our knowledge, no single study has explored the evolution of all of these complexity indicators within a real industrial setting. However, several studies have examined architectural evolution, focusing on specific aspects. Studies (e.g., [3,7,13,39]) emphasize that microservices rarely evolve in isolation. Instead, they often undergo co-evolution and structural drift, leading to hidden coupling, architectural smells, and degradation. Assunção et al. [3] conducted a longitudinal study of 11 open-source systems and found recurring co-evolution patterns like "shotgun surgery," where multiple microservices are modified in a single commit [3]. This indicates significant dependencies across services, challenging the core microservice principle of loose coupling. Bogner et al. [7] investigate the industry practices, such as guidelines, patterns, and tools, as well as challenges like service decomposition to ensure the evolvability of microservice architecture. Zhong et al. [39] analyzed 15 open source projects consisting of 113 microservices. They proposed and measured the Microservice Coupling Index (MCI), a metric based on relative measurement theory to assess inter-service dependencies and coupling more rigorously than traditional absolute metrics.

Apolinário and de França [2] proposed a method to monitor service-level coupling evolution by mining repositories and tracking dependency graphs. However, their approach mainly relies on runtime behavior, unlike our method, which focuses on declared, configuration-bound dependencies. Lercher et al. [18] analyzed microservices API evolution through interviews with 17 practitioners. The study identified six evolution strategies (e.g., API versioning) and six common challenges. While strategies like API versioning and collaboration among teams are intended to facilitate evolution, they often result in tight organizational coupling and consumer lock-in, leading to the accumulation of TD. Genefer and Zdun [13] conducted a static source code analysis to track and assess the evolution of microservice architecture through repository mining and architectural reconstructions. By analyzing API interactions and computing various architectural metrics over time, their results revealed that the system initially showed a growing trend in inter-service dependencies. However, this trend was later reversed as developers redesigned the architecture, as evidenced by a decrease in couplings, a reduced length of API calls, and improved cyclic dependencies.

Capilla et al. [9] conducted an empirical study using Archan and Designite to identify architectural smells. They found that cyclic and hub-like dependencies are particularly common in large systems. Likewise, Soares de Toledo et al. [34] listed some other architectural debt issues, including an excessive number of point-to-point connections among services, the absence of a communication standard, and a knowledge gap. Zhong et al. [38] investigate architectural smells in microservice systems and analyze their causes. The study shows that these smells increase coordination effort and change failure rates, which degrade the system's maintainability. However, there remains a lack of proactive tools for identifying architectural debt in evolving systems [7,30].

4   Case Study Design

This study investigates the evolution of architectural complexity indicators of 15 microservices from a large-scale software development company. The case study is designed based on the guidelines established by Runeson and Höst (2009) [27].

4.1   Research Goal and Questions

Research indicates that as software systems grow in size over time, their complexity evolves. Therefore, it becomes crucial to track the evolution of the architectural complexity of microservices for better and informed architectural decisions. Hence, this paper investigates how architectural complexity indicators of microservices characterized by declared dependencies, API endpoint exposure, inter-service communications, and size evolve together with TD. This investigation will allow software organizations to understand their architectural evolution over time, pinpointing specific periods when the architecture may be more prone to vulnerabilities, such as higher architectural and code TD. Based on the research goal, this case study investigates the following research questions:

> **RQ$_1$:** How are architectural complexity indicators and technical debt correlated?
>
> **RQ$_2$:** How do architectural complexity indicators evolve in microservice architecture?
>
> **RQ$_3$:** How do architectural complexity indicators behave with evolving size of microservices?

RQ$_1$ investigates the relationship among architectural indicators, specifically, exploring how complexity indicators relate to one another. Our primary focus is to understand how declared dependencies, API endpoints, inter-service communications, and size correlate with code TD. We further aim to assess the extent to which these four architectural indicators can explain the variation in TD using the `Generalized Additive Model (GAM)` [14] and `adjusted R-squared` value.

RQ_2 explores the evolution of architectural complexity indicators, including TD and size, over time. This analysis enables organizations to understand how their architecture is performing regarding these complexity indicators, whether there are improvements, or if further maintenance activities are necessary. While RQ_3 identifies thresholds at complexity indicators that exhibit different behaviors with the growing size of the microservice. For example, at what point does the size of microservices cause these four variables to increase significantly, and when do they begin to decrease or stabilize? This extended visualization will provide valuable insights for organizations, guiding them to decide when to prioritize refactoring and maintenance of microservices based on their size evolution.

4.2   Context

This case study is based on the proprietary code base from one of our industrial collaborators, a Swedish Fintech company. The company has an extensive code base consisting of over 2.5 MLOC, comprising over 250 services. Most of these services are microservices, but there are also a few larger services with multiple responsibilities, and one monolith with more than 410k lines of code. The company has around 63 teams with hundreds of developers. For this analysis, we selected 15 Java-based microservices based on their size and responsibilities variability (ranging from less than 1k up to 15k on average). Furthermore, most of the selected services are dedicated to specific business responsibilities such as authentication, user rights, payment processing, and licenses. The collected data for all variables spans from August 2022 to March 2025 on a weekly basis.

Table 1 displays the detailed statistics of all 15 selected microservices. The company was initially interested in exploring the evolution of its architecture, the various indicators of architectural complexity, and determining the microservices that require prioritization for architectural refactoring or maintenance. The collected TD and size measurements were gathered from SonarQube. This tool was selected for convenience, as the company has been using it for several years to monitor its TD and other quality-related metrics.

4.3   Data Collection

Measuring Technical Debt (TD) and Size: In this study, we measure TD using SonarQube (SQ), a static code analysis tool used by the case company for several years. SQ is one of the most popular and commonly used static code analysis tools [5,17] with several built-in rules. SQ generates issues whenever predefined coding rules or quality gates are violated [6]. These issues are categorized into three different types: 'code smell' (related to maintainability), 'bugs' (related to reliability), and 'vulnerability' (related to security). Furthermore, SQ classifies issues by their severity into categories such as info, minor, major, critical, or blocker [6]. Afterwards, the tool estimates the remediation effort for each issue, which is the estimated development time required to address and refactor those issues. This remediation time is the metric for TD for this study.

We gathered all the Sonar Issues for 15 microservices from August 2022 to March 2025. The collected TD datasets contain information about the microservices, violated rules, severity, issue status and types, and remediation effort (i.e., TD). In addition, it also provides the issue creation, update, and fix timestamps. As SonarQube sometimes can report false positive issues, we systematically excluded issues marked as 'false-positive' and issues marked as 'safe' and 'wontfix' by developers. Subsequently, to calculate the weekly TD, we first converted the timestamps into dates. Next, we accumulated TD for each sonar issue from the time it was created until it was fixed. For issues that remained open until our data collection period, we used the latest date as the resolution date.

Furthermore, we collected the lines of code for each microservice from SonarQube, which serves as the metric for microservice size in this study. SonarQube calculates lines of code (LOC) by counting all non-commented and non-blank lines in source files. Details about how SQ counts lines of code can be found in their documentation[2]. Table 1 presents the average number of weekly architectural indicators, including size and TD, for each microservice. It shows that the microservice's weekly average size varies from approximately 979 lines of code to 15798. Meanwhile, the TD ranges from around 77 to 2477 min.

Extraction of Architectural Complexity: In this study, we analyzed the evolution of architectural complexity indicators of 15 Java-based microservices from a proprietary codebase over a two and a half year period. We developed and implemented a lightweight static source code analysis tool[3] that basically inspects the source code and configuration files of software repositories without actually building them locally or executing them. We mainly investigated important architectural indicators such as declared dependencies, API endpoint exposure, inter-service communications, and size. Our method traverses the Git history of each microservice using a time-based snapshotting strategy, selecting commits at weekly intervals. However, due to the proprietary restrictions and NDA agreement, the dataset cannot be made publicly available.

To calculate the declared dependencies, the tool first parses the root `pom.xml` file to identify the sub-modules for focused analysis. After extracting the sub-modules, the tool parses all the available `pom.xml` files from each sub-module and identifies dependencies using structured XML extraction, which includes both default (compile) and explicitly declared runtime dependencies. However, we excluded the dependencies declared as `test`, `provided`, `system`, or `import` because they do not end up in the project's built artifact. This ensures we count only actual declared dependencies. Additionally, dependencies declared in `<dependencyManagement>` without being re-declared in the module are also excluded. Although all selected 15 microservices are Java-based, our tool can also recognize other dependency files such as `package.json` (Node.js), `requirement.txt` (Python), `go.mod` (Go), `build.gradle` (Gradle),

---

[2] https://docs.sonarsource.com/sonarqube-server/9.9/instance-administration/lines-of-code/.

[3] https://doi.org/10.5281/zenodo.16906941.

Table 1. Weekly average number of architectural indicators for all 15 microservices. Microservice names are obfuscated for anonymity.

Microservice	Endpoints #	Dependencies #	Inter-service Communications#	TD (minutes)	Size (nloc)
M1	28.00	28.20	5.00	1391.01	15798.07
M2	8.30	36.12	2.30	1041.22	5316.99
M3	76.63	30.38	17.90	814.65	11793.30
M4	14.64	18.29	3.41	786.03	2640.11
M5	5.69	11.76	0.00	574.37	1475.27
M6	17.45	17.45	3.11	239.32	2243.85
M7	59.38	30.65	13.39	1070.70	7241.48
M8	34.38	20.33	4.00	2476.78	13393.13
M9	46.27	21.12	14.46	1174.92	8838.40
M10	4.01	15.40	1.00	76.91	979.42
M11	15.48	30.09	12.91	1313.68	5247.58
M12	19.74	18.09	8.00	304.10	3825.49
M13	50.69	29.64	15.41	1319.22	14446.29
M14	35.88	21.00	0.00	308.04	3989.24
M15	44.84	26.93	5.71	1763.47	7704.85

and `composer.json` (PHP) to support other architectures for reproducibility. All the dependencies across modules are aggregated and deduplicated into a single set of unique identifiers per snapshot to avoid overcounting the same library declared across multiple modules. Furthermore, our method does not include the transitive dependencies[4] as it only focuses on explicitly declared dependencies in the build configuration files to ensure stability and reproducibility without requiring dependency resolution or building services locally.

Likewise, in order to detect the `API endpoint` exposures, the tool scans the source code files using regular expressions via common annotations and routing functions, which include `@GetMapping()`, `@Path()`, and `app.post()` in Java, Python, and JavaScript frameworks. It then deduplicates so that repeated definitions count only once. The API endpoints extracted are represented as combinations of HTTP method and path, giving a reliable picture of each snapshot's exposed interface. The tool identifies `inter-service` communications by scanning for specific invocation patterns in HTTP and RPC calls, such as `fetch()`, `axios.get()`, `requests.get()`, `RestTemplate.getForObject()`, and `Grpc.newBlockingStub()`. It also detects references to internal endpoints (e.g., `/api/..`) and full service URLs. To ensure clarity, all call expressions are deduplicated, reflecting the number of unique service integration points rather than their frequency in the code.

4.4 Data Analysis

The dataset spans from August 2022 to March 2025, incorporating various TD and other indicators of architectural complexity. A detailed explanation of the

---

[4] https://maven.apache.org/guides/introduction/introduction-to-dependency-mechanism.html.

preprocessing for both TD and architectural data can be found in Sect. 4.3. The preprocessing and analysis were conducted using `Jupyter Notebook` with `Python version 3.11.0` and the necessary libraries.

Initially, we assessed the distribution of variables through histograms and the Shapiro-Wilk test [29]. Both methods conclusively indicated that all variables are non-normally distributed with a very low *p-value* of $4.13e^{-23}$, $7.80e^{-30}$, $1.19e^{-31}$, $3.59e^{-34}$ and $3.27e^{-30}$ for dependencies, API endpoints, size, inter-service communications, and TD respectively. Therefore, to answer RQ_1, we opted for a non-parametric test, called `Spearman correlation` [31], to investigate the relationships between TD and the architectural complexity indicators. However, given the multiple variables involved in our analysis, we computed a comprehensive Spearman correlation matrix to systematically explore pairwise correlations among all variables. Spearman correlation provides insights into both the strength and direction of monotonic associations between two variables. The interpretation of the correlation coefficient follows widely accepted conventions reported in the study [28], where correlation ranges from -1 to $+1$. A correlation of ± 0.00 to ± 0.10 is considered `negligible`, ± 0.10 to ± 0.39 `weak`, ± 0.40 to ± 0.69 `moderate`, ± 0.70 to ± 0.89 `strong`, and ± 0.90 to ± 1.00 `very strong`.

We then applied a nonlinear multiple regression model using `Generalized Additive Model (GAM)` [14] to explore the potential relationship between architectural complexity and TD. The key assumptions of GAM are that the effects of each predictor (in our case, architectural complexity indicators) contribute additively to the response (TD), and that the relationship between each architectural complexity indicator and TD is a smooth, potentially nonlinear function rather than strictly linear. GAM extends traditional linear models by allowing each predictor to have its own smooth, non-parametric function, typically implemented using spline-based functions [14,37]. The adjusted `R-squared` value was used to quantify the variation in TD that other dependent variables can explain.

In order to answer RQ_2, we visualized the temporal evolution of all indicators across 15 microservices, as illustrated in Fig. 2. For each indicator, we plotted the mean and median trajectories over time, with ± 1 standard deviation(σ), which captures the variability around the mean. We overlay the mean trend line by applying `LOWESS smoothing` [10] to highlight the directional tendency of each indicator. It effectively captures nonlinear trends without assuming the functional form of data, making it ideal for providing the average behavior of a specific complexity indicator across all microservices at each time point.

To answer RQ_3, which investigates how various microservice indicators respond to changes in microservice size, we applied piecewise linear regression (also known as segmented regression) [24] using Python `pwlf` library. This method effectively detects structural changes or trend shifts by introducing one or more breakpoints, also known as change-points or thresholds [22]. The main assumption is that the relationship between the predictor and responses is linear within each segment, reflecting the expectation that microservices complexity generally increases with size, albeit the slope may vary across segments. We configured with three segments (i.e., two breakpoints) because these segments can be interpreted as small, medium, and large services, making the model intuitive and easy to interpret. As a result, it helps us understand how the behavior of microservices, measured by various architectural complexity indicators, changes at different stages of size evolution. For each fitted model, we report the coefficient of determination (R^2) to evaluate the model's explanatory power.

5   Results and Discussions

In this section, we present findings, answer research questions, and interpret them in relation to existing literature and insights from company contacts—a development manager and a senior product owner, each with over 20 years of experience in software development and around 5 years with the case company.

5.1   RQ$_1$: Relationship Between Architecture Complexity and TD

The Spearman correlation matrix (Fig. 1) shows the correlation coefficients across all complexity indicators, revealing that they are moderately to strongly correlated and tend to vary together. It indicates a moderate positive correlation between architectural complexity indicators (API endpoint exposure, declared dependencies, and inter-service communications) and code TD, with correlation coefficient values of 0.37, 0.51, 0.41, respectively. Moreover, the size of microservices is strongly correlated with TD, with a correlation coefficient of 0.70.

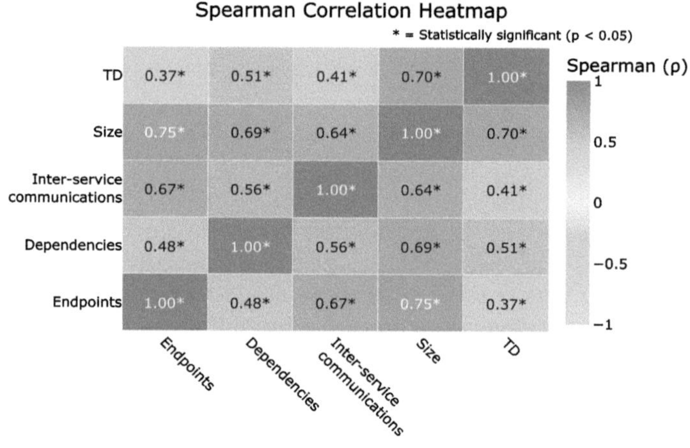

Fig. 1. Spearman-correlation matrix across all complexity indicators.

The Generalized Additive Model (GAM) demonstrates a good fit for the data, evidenced by an RMSE of 357.66 (with the average weekly TD across all microservices being approximately 1000 min) and an adjusted R-squared of 0.77. This indicates that about 77% of the variation in TD can be explained by architectural indicators, including size. All indicators' smooth terms are highly significant ($p < 1e^{-16}$), and the model's effective degrees of freedom (DoF) of about 49.1 suggest considerable flexibility in capturing these complex effects.

> **As the first takeaway**, complexity indicators of microservices are correlated and often follow similar trends. In practice, an increase in one indicator is statistically associated with increases in others. Consequently, leaving some indicators unaddressed, assuming they have no negative impact, may still be linked to increases in other forms of complexity. Furthermore, complexity indicators additively explain a substantial variation in TD.

5.2 RQ$_2$: Evolution of Architectural Complexity in Microservices

The temporal evolution of complexity indicators in Fig. 2 reveals a persistent upward trend across all 15 microservices. All of these trends are consistent with the longitudinal observations from Assunção et al. [3], which noted a sustained co-evolution of microservice systems over time. Overall, the median trend consistently falls below the mean across all five indicators. This indicates right-skewed distributions, where a small subset of particularly complex services inflates the overall behavior. This skewness aligns with observations from another study by Capilla et al. [9], which reported that most smells can be concentrated in a few services, and that smell density can differ widely between systems of similar size.

The LOWESS curve further shows that these indicators not only continue to rise but also become significantly steeper as they approach 2025. This demonstrates that the complexity indicators are growing at a faster rate lately. These irregular evolution trends to some extent align with findings from other studies (e.g., [3,9,13]). For example, studies like [3,7] observe that microservice evolution dynamically varies over time. Genfer and Zdun [13] noted an initial increase in API invocation that drops after architectural refactoring. Moreover, we observed a rapid growth in code TD during the early stages, as seen in previous studies [17,23], followed by a linear trend, and recent rapid increases. During our regular meeting with key contacts after the data analysis, we discussed these trends. They indicated that this could be partly attributed to the introduction of new sonar rules and recent changes in the codebase, such as a version upgrade. Overall, these patterns show a continuous evolution in architectural complexity, as well as the growing structural inconsistency within the system. These trends also highlight the temporal effects of targeted interventions, such as refactorings, the addition of new rules, or changes made to the codebase.

> **As the second takeaway**, microservice complexity indicators consistently evolve as the services evolve. Furthermore, a high complexity in a small number of complex services can disproportionately affect the overall architecture's complexity. We therefore recommend that practitioners prioritize such highly

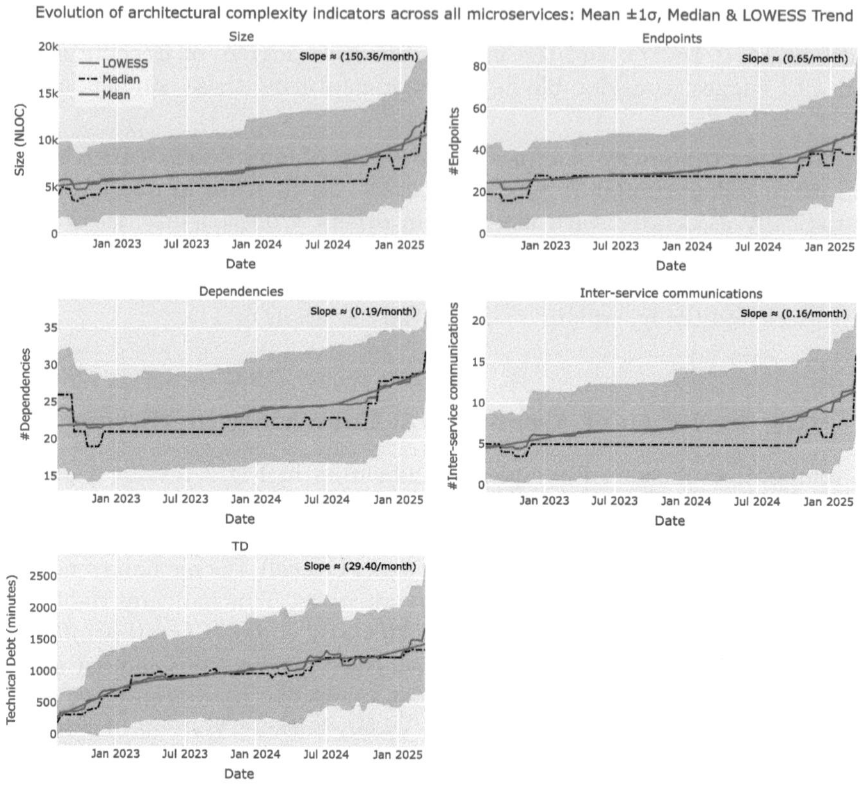

Fig. 2. Weekly evolution of complexity indicators across all microservices. The Legends in the top left plot are applicable to all plots.

complex services and regularly refactor them, as doing so may help mitigate complexity growth across the microservice architecture as a whole.

5.3   RQ₃: Architectural Complexity with Evolving Size of Services

Figure 3 shows that architectural complexity indicators generally increase with size, although the rate of growth (slopes) varies across the different size segments of microservices. The growth of API endpoints in smaller microservices is rapid, indicating that smaller services quickly expand their public interfaces. This growth is followed by a drop during the mid-size phase, after which comparatively larger services experience an increase again. Lercher et al. [18] suggest that API exposures often escalate during service expansion due to frequent breaking changes and extensions. Over time, the growing trend stabilizes due to several strategies applied, such as API versioning, adopting better governance practices. However, it may increase again when services grow larger with broader roles.

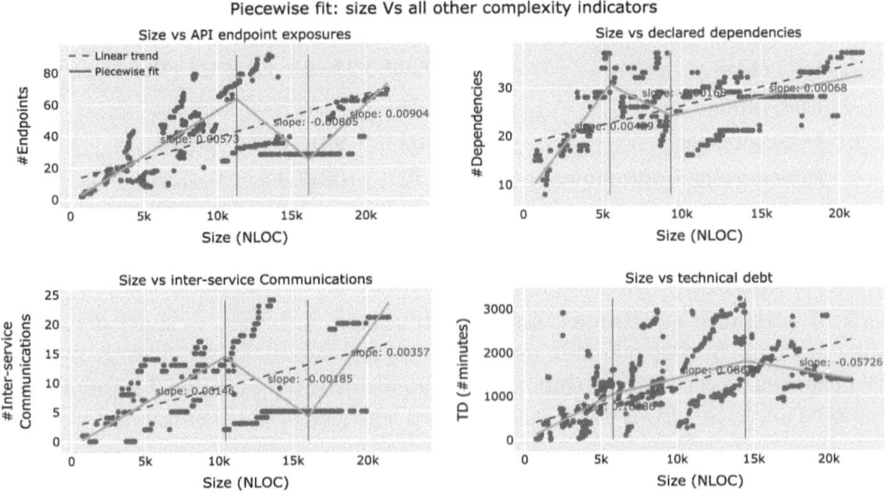

Fig. 3. Behavior of complexity indicators across all 15 microservices with size (NLOC), using piecewise fit regression. The legends in the top left plot apply to all plots.

Likewise, in the early expansion phase of services, declared dependencies and inter-service communications also tend to increase rapidly. This reflects a period of rushed development with new features added without adequate governance and clearly defined service boundaries, as mentioned by company contacts during the discussion. Subsequently, as services grow to a mid-size, there is a decline in declared dependencies and inter-service communications. This reduction may be due to the modular restructuring and refactoring efforts that enhance maintainability. However, in large services, these indicators begin to rise again as services take on more functionalities, often deviating from the bounded-context principle [8]. Moreover, TD in general grows with size, albeit at different rates across distinct segments. It tends to accumulate rapidly in small services, stabilizes or increases at a slower pace in mid-sized services. Counterintuitively, TD declines in large services as its pain reaches a point where teams start refactoring. Additionally, maintaining the quality of these services is vital since many of them are critical to the overall architecture, as noted by practitioners during discussions. The observed thresholds for all indicators range approximately from 5k to 16k NLOC (see Table 2), indicating the size at which these indicators change their growth behavior. Additionally, the R^2 values in Table 2 show that size explains 43.73% to 65.31% variation in these complexity indicators.

As the third takeaway, architectural complexity does not necessarily grow consistently with service size. Instead, it evolves in phases of escalations, stabilization, and re-accumulations, influenced by factors such as architectural maturity, governance, team strategies, and planned refactorings. Complexity often rises rapidly in small services due to continuous feature addition and

Table 2. Thresholds of architectural complexity indicators by service size (NLOC).

Indicators	Threshold 1	Threshold 2	R^2 (Piecewise)
Endpoints	11335.04	16153.58	0.6292
Dependencies	5480.00	9314.04	0.6531
Inter-service Communications	10462.77	16037.47	0.4739
Technical Debt (min)	5799.29	14448.00	0.4373

lack of adequate governance and maintenance, stabilizes or even declines as they become mid-sized, and usually increases again as services grow large. We therefore recommend that practitioners initiate small yet frequent maintenance activities from early stages, when services are still small and evolving.

6   Threats to Validity

Construct validity: We detected declared dependencies, API exposure, and inter-service communications using our static method. However, we acknowledge that our approach may overlook dynamic or reflective routes/calls, such as those constructed at runtime, as well as transitive dependencies. To minimize risk, we carefully adhered to the `Apache Maven` documentation while designing our tool, as services are built on Maven. We gathered TD and size from SonarQube, a widely used tool that, despite criticisms on its accuracy, has been used in several other studies (e.g., [17,23]). To enhance TD measurement accuracy, we excluded issues marked as `false-positive`, `wontfix`, and `safe`. Further, the company frequently updates its sonar rules and actively addresses issues identified.

Internal Validity: The evolution of complexity indicators over time, and their behavior with the increasing size of services, may be affected by confounding variables. These variables may include factors such as planned refactoring, domain complexity, and various organizational and human aspects like ownership, team experience, and turnover. To mitigate risk, we implemented robust statistical methods such as `LOWESS curves`, `GAM`, and `Piecewise fit regression` to capture such fluctuations and discussed the observed pattern with key contacts.

External Validity: The specific industrial context of a fintech company limits the generalizability of findings in a broader context. However, to mitigate this risk, we carefully chose services with various sizes and business functionalities. Additionally, the use of well-established tools like SonarQube enhances the comparability of findings. In any case, the goal of an exploratory case study is not to reach statistical generalizability but rather to start building a theory.

Reliability: We can rely on SonarQube, as it is still one of the most widely used tools [5]. However, adjusting our regex pattern or modifying exclusions could alter the count of measured indicators. To mitigate this risk, we archived the source code of our static analysis along with clear guidelines on how to use it. Besides, we utilize well-established statistical methods using `Python 3.11` to analyze and visualize data. These methods include `histograms`, the `Shapiro-Wilk` test, `Spearman Correlations`, `GAM`, and `piecewise regression`, all of which further reinforce the reliability of our results.

7 Conclusions and Future Work

In this study, we analyzed the evolution of architectural complexity indicators, including declared dependencies, API endpoint exposures, inter-service communications, code TD, and the size of 15 microservices, all developed in Java and built with Apache Maven. We also implemented our own static approach to measure such architectural complexity indicators together with SonarQube. Our findings have outlined many interesting insights for practitioners and the research community. RQ_1 reveals that complexity indicators are moderately to strongly correlated with each other and often follow similar growth patterns. RQ_2 found that the complexity indicators tend to grow consistently, with occasional short-term declines due to the intended refactorings. Moreover, it is also found that certain complex services often influence the average behavior of complexity indicators. Furthermore, as service grows in size, complexity initially escalates, then stabilizes or even decreases through targeted interventions, and again reaccumulates as services grow larger. We also identified different thresholds in service size when they usually change their behavior, confirming complexity growth is neither uniform nor static, but governed by strategic shifts throughout the service evolution.

This study can be further enhanced by refining our static method for detecting architectural complexity indicators. For example, we suggest including transitive dependencies and reflective calls that occur during runtime. Additionally, future research could investigate the impact of these complexity indicators on other aspects of the software development process, such as lead time.

Acknowledgments. This research was supported by the KKS Foundation through the KKS SERT Research Profile project (Ref. 2018010), Blekinge Institute of Technology.

References

1. Adams, L., S. et al.: Evolution and anti-patterns visualized: microprospect in microservice architecture. In: Software Architecture. ECSA 2023, pp. 309–325. Springer, Istanbul Turkey (2024). https://doi.org/10.1007/978-3-031-66326-0_19
2. Apolinário, D.R.F., de França, B.B.N.: A method for monitoring the coupling evolution of microservice-based architectures. J. Braz. Comput. Soc. **27**(1), 1–35 (2021). https://doi.org/10.1186/s13173-021-00120-y
3. Assunção, W.K., Krüger, J., Mosser, S., Selaoui, S.: How do microservices evolve? an empirical analysis of changes in open-source microservice repositories. J. Syst. Softw. **204**, 111788 (2023). https://doi.org/10.1016/j.jss.2023.111788

4. Avgeriou, P., Kruchten, P., Ozkaya, I., Seaman, C.: Managing Technical Debt in Software Engineering (Dagstuhl Seminar 16162). Dagstuhl Reports **6**(4), 110–138 (2016). https://doi.org/10.4230/DagRep.6.4.110

5. Avgeriou, P.C., et al.: An overview and comparison of technical debt measurement tools. IEEE Softw. **38**(3), 61–71 (2021). https://doi.org/10.1109/MS.2020.3024958

6. Baldassarre, M.T., Lenarduzzi, V., Romano, S., Saarimäki, N.: On the diffuseness of technical debt items and accuracy of remediation time when using sonarqube. Inf. Softw. Technol. **128**, 106377 (2020). https://doi.org/10.1016/j.infsof.2020.106377

7. Bogner, J., Fritzsch, J., Wagner, S., Zimmermann, A.: Industry practices and challenges for the evolvability assurance of microservices. Empir. Softw. Eng. **26**(5), 1–39 (2021). https://doi.org/10.1007/s10664-021-09999-9

8. Bogner, J., Wagner, S., Zimmermann, A.: Using architectural modifiability tactics to examine evolution qualities of service- and microservice-based systems. SICS Softw.-Intensive Cyber-Phys. **Systems 34**(2–3), 141–149 (2019). https://doi.org/10.1007/s00450-019-00402-z

9. Capilla, R., Fontana, F.A., Mikkonen, T., Bacchiega, P., Salamanca, V.: Detecting architecture debt in micro-service open-source projects. In: 2023 49th Euromicro Conference on Software Engineering and Advanced Applications (SEAA), pp. 394–401 (2023). https://doi.org/10.1109/SEAA60479.2023.00066

10. Cleveland, W.S.: Robust locally weighted regression and smoothing scatterplots. J. Am. Stat. Assoc. **74**(368), 829–836 (1979). https://doi.org/10.1080/01621459.1979.10481038

11. Cunningham, W.: The WyCash portfolio management system. ACM Sigplan Oops Messenger **4**(2), 29–30 (1992)

12. Dragoni, N., et al.: Microservices: Yesterday, today, and tomorrow. In: Mazzara, M., Meyer, B. (eds.) Present and Ulterior Software Engineering, pp. 195–216. Springer International Publishing, Cham (2017). https://doi.org/10.1007/978-3-319-67425-4_12

13. Genfer, P., Zdun, U.: Exploring architectural evolution in microservice systems using repository mining techniques and static code analysis. In: Galster, M., Scandurra, P., Mikkonen, T., Oliveira Antonino, P., Nakagawa, E.Y., Navarro, E. (eds.) Software Architecture, pp. 157–173. Springer Nature Switzerland, Cham (2024)

14. Hastie, T., and, R.T.: Generalized additive models: some applications. J. Am. Stat. Assoc. **82**(398), 371–386 (1987). https://doi.org/10.1080/01621459.1987.10478440

15. Kalske, M., Mäkitalo, N., Mikkonen, T.: Challenges when moving from monolith to microservice architecture. In: Garrigós, I., Wimmer, M. (eds.) Current Trends in Web Engineering. pp. 32–47. Springer International Publishing, Cham (2018). https://doi.org/10.1007/978-3-319-74433-9_3

16. Lehman, M.M.: Laws of software evolution revisited. In: Montangero, C. (ed.) EWSPT 1996. LNCS, vol. 1149, pp. 108–124. Springer, Heidelberg (1996). https://doi.org/10.1007/BFb0017737

17. Lenarduzzi, V., Lomio, F., Saarimäki, N., Taibi, D.: Does migrating a monolithic system to microservices decrease the technical debt? J. Syst. Softw. **169**, 110710 (Nov2020). https://doi.org/10.1016/j.jss.2020.110710

18. Lercher, A., Glock, J., Macho, C., Pinzger, M.: Microservice API evolution in practice: A study on strategies and challenges. J. Syst. Softw. **215**, 112110 (2024). https://doi.org/10.1016/j.jss.2024.112110

19. Lewis, J., Fowler, M.: Microservices: a definition of this new architectural term. MartinFowler. com **25**(14–26), 12 (2014)

20. Li, R., Liang, P., Soliman, M., Avgeriou, P.: Understanding software architecture erosion: a systematic mapping study. J. Softw.: Evol. Process **34**(3), e2423 (2022). https://doi.org/10.1002/smr.2423
21. Li, Z., Avgeriou, P., Liang, P.: A systematic mapping study on technical debt and its management. J. Syst. Softw. **101**, 193–220 (2015). https://doi.org/10.1016/j.jss.2014.12.027
22. Lu, K.P., Chang, S.T.: An advanced segmentation approach to piecewise regression models. Mathematics **11**(24) (2023). https://doi.org/10.3390/math11244959
23. Maggi, K., Verdecchia, R., Scommegna, L., Vicario, E.: Evolution of code technical debt in microservices architectures. J. Syst. Softw. **222**, 112301 (2025). https://doi.org/10.1016/j.jss.2024.112301
24. Muggeo, V.M.R.: Estimating regression models with unknown break-points. Stat. Med. **22**(19), 3055–3071 (2003). https://doi.org/10.1002/sim.1545
25. Newman, S.: Building Microservices: Designing Fine-Grained Systems. O'Reilly, second edn. (2021)
26. Pigazzini, I., Fontana, F.A., Lenarduzzi, V., Taibi, D.: Towards microservice smells detection. In: Proceedings of the 3rd International Conference on Technical Debt. p. 92–97. TechDebt '20, Association for Computing Machinery (2020). https://doi.org/10.1145/3387906.3388625
27. Runeson, P., Höst, M.: Guidelines for conducting and reporting case study research in software engineering. Empir. Softw. Eng. **14**(2), 131–164 (Apr2009)
28. Schober, P., Boer, C., Schwarte, L.A.: Correlation coefficients: appropriate use and interpretation. Anesthesia Analgesia **126**(5), 1763–1768 (2018). https://doi.org/10.1213/ANE.0000000000002864
29. Shapiro, S.S., Wilk, M.B.: An analysis of variance test for normality (complete samples). Biometrika **52**(3–4), 591–611 (Dec1965). https://doi.org/10.1093/biomet/52.3-4.591
30. Soldani, J., Tamburri, D.A., Van Den Heuvel, W.J.: The pains and gains of microservices: A Systematic grey literature review. J. Syst. Softw. **146**, 215–232 (Dec2018). https://doi.org/10.1016/j.jss.2018.09.082
31. Spearman, C.: The proof and measurement of association between two things. Am. J. Psychol. **100**(3/4), 441–471 (1987)
32. Taibi, D., Lenarduzzi, V., Pahl, C.: Processes, motivations, and issues for migrating to microservices architectures: an empirical investigation. IEEE Cloud Comput. **4**(5), 22–32 (2017). https://doi.org/10.1109/MCC.2017.4250931
33. Taibi, D., Lenarduzzi, V., Pahl, C.: Microservices anti-patterns: a taxonomy. In: Bucchiarone, A., Dragoni, N., Dustdar, S., Lago, P., Mazzara, M., Rivera, V., Sadovykh, A. (eds.) Microservices: Science and Engineering, pp. 111–128. Springer, Cham (2020). https://doi.org/10.1007/978-3-030-31646-4_5
34. Soares de Toledo, S., Martini, A., Przybyszewska, A., Sjøberg, D.I.: Architectural technical debt in microservices: A case study in a large company. In: 2019 IEEE/ACM International Conference on Technical Debt (TechDebt), pp. 78–87 (2019). https://doi.org/10.1109/TechDebt.2019.00026
35. Verdecchia, R., Maggi, K., Scommegna, L., Vicario, E.: Technical debt in microservices: a mixed-method case study. In: Tekinerdoğan, B., Spalazzese, R., Sözer, H., Bonfanti, S., Weyns, D. (eds.) Software Architecture. ECSA 2023 Tracks, Workshops, and Doctoral Symposium, pp. 217–236. Springer Nature Switzerland, Cham (2024). https://doi.org/10.1007/978-3-031-66326-0_14
36. Wang, Y., Kadiyala, H., Rubin, J.: Promises and challenges of microservices: an exploratory study. Empir. Softw. Eng. **26**(4), 1–44 (2021). https://doi.org/10.1007/s10664-020-09910-y

37. Wood, S.N.: Generalized Additive Models: An Introduction with R, 2nd edn. Chapman and Hall/CRC, Boca Raton, FL (2017)
38. Zhong, C., Huang, H., Zhang, H., Li, S.: Impacts, causes, and solutions of architectural smells in microservices: An industrial investigation. Softw.: Pract. Exper. **52**(12), 2574–2597 (2022). https://doi.org/10.1002/spe.3138
39. Zhong, C., Zhang, H., Li, C., Huang, H., Feitosa, D.: On measuring coupling between microservices. J. Syst. Softw. **200**, 111670 (2023). https://doi.org/10.1016/j.jss.2023.111670

Improving Behavior-Driven Development Scenarios: Empirical Evaluation of a Quality Assessment Framework

Dillan Wyatt Sears[1], Konstantinos Tsilionis[2]([envelope]) [ORCID], and Yves Wautelet[1] [ORCID]

[1] KU Leuven, Brussels, Belgium
{dillan.sears,yves.wautelet}@kuleuven.be
[2] Eindhoven University of Technology, Eindhoven, The Netherlands
k.tsilionis@tue.nl

Abstract. Behavior-Driven Development (BDD) is an agile practice used to specify expected system behavior for validating a feature. BDD utilizes scenarios written in structured natural language which, when combined with a user story, express a functional requirement more concisely. However, BDD scenarios often suffer from ambiguity, redundancy, and lack of focus, which limits their effectiveness in validating intended requirements. A recently introduced evaluation framework called *Quality Attributes-Based Guidelines for Evaluation* (QABAGE), defines seven key attributes, namely *Uniqueness, Integrity, Essentiality, Singularity, Completeness, Clarity,* and *Focus*, to improve the quality of BDD scenarios. Although QABAGE has undergone preliminary ex-ante evaluation with software engineering experts, establishing its acceptance and practical utility is still an ongoing process. Effective design and implementation of such frameworks aiming to enhance software engineering practices require both ex-ante and iterative ex-post evaluations to assess their impact across different contexts and conditions. Building on prior research, we empirically evaluate QABAGE by analyzing scenarios first without and then with the framework, combined with semi-structured interviews to assess its perceived structure and utility. The findings suggest that using QABAGE as a guiding framework enhances the *Essentiality* and *Completeness* of BDD scenarios, with participants reporting clearer, more readable scenarios and reduced ambiguity during the scenario-writing process. However, challenges emerged in applying *Singularity*, particularly in decomposing complex functionalities into distinct, manageable elements within a single scenario. This paper provides insights for improving BDD practices and highlights the need for techniques that bridge technical and non-technical stakeholder communication.

Keywords: Behavior Driven Development · BDD Scenarios · BDD Quality Attributes · Agility · Agile Software Development

1 Introduction

Behavior-Driven Development (BDD) is a widely adopted practice in agile software engineering, offering a test-driven approach that encourages the definition of acceptance criteria for system requirements before any code is written [9]. BDD aims to enhance communication between technical and non-technical stakeholders by using natural language constructs, known as BDD scenarios, to describe system behavior in an executable format. This approach ensures that all team members have a shared understanding of the system's requirements and expected outcomes [22]. These scenarios are typically written in the Gherkin[1] language, which structures them around three primary dimensions: GIVEN, WHEN, and THEN. This structure provides a clear, concise, and non-technical way to describe user actions and system responses, conveying that, *given* a specific context, *when* an event is triggered by a user or the system, *then* an expected system behavior should manifest. Ideally, these BDD scenarios are developed alongside their corresponding user stories to ensure alignment between user needs and system behavior, supporting both requirement validation and test automation [5]. The benefit of this approach is its simplicity and clarity, making it accessible to all stakeholders, regardless of technical expertise [15]. The result is improved collaboration and a streamlined process for translating requirements into automated acceptance tests.

Despite its simplicity, BDD is often seen as practice-oriented, with experience in creating acceptance tests being crucial for drafting and structuring BDD scenarios effectively [15]. This reliance on experience poses challenges, as many agile and BDD practitioners lack structured frameworks and guidelines to enhance their scenarios' quality [21,23]. In this context, quality in BDD scenarios refers to defining a set of attributes that make them clear and effective for specifying requirements and guiding development and testing [11]. Without such attributes, scenarios risk being ambiguous, redundant, or misinterpreted, ultimately undermining software development efficiency and stakeholder satisfaction. Ensuring that BDD scenarios meet formalized specifications —such as focus, integrity, and the ability to test singular, complete, and clearly defined functionalities— is crucial for achieving the communication and alignment benefits that BDD promotes [12]. To address these challenges, prior research has explored various strategies to enhance the quality of BDD scenarios. For example, Oliveira et al. [11] conducted a literature review on quality characteristics in agile requirements, identifying essential attributes for BDD scenarios. They found that high-quality scenarios are concise, testable, clear, unambiguous, and valuable. Building on the latter, Binamungu [2] proposed four principles for assessing BDD test suite quality at the feature level: (1) keep scenario steps concise, (2) use consistent domain terms, (3) favor general over technical terms, and (4) maintain consistent abstraction levels. These principles aim to improve the coherence and effectiveness of BDD scenarios, enhancing alignment and communication across development teams.

---

[1] More information can be found on: https://cucumber.io/docs/gherkin/.

While such studies have provided reference quality attributes and guiding principles to assist practitioners before starting to write BDD scenarios, to the best of the authors' knowledge, there is a lack of frameworks applicable throughout the entire writing process (i.e., both before and during BDD scenario development). To address this gap, the *Quality Attributes-Based Guidelines for Evaluation* framework (QABAGE), described by Wautelet et al. [24], formalizes a comprehensive set of quality attributes that practitioners can continuously use as guidelines while writing BDD scenarios. The framework builds on the fact that well-defined system requirements start at the user story level. Since user stories and BDD scenarios both use structured natural language and are often developed in parallel, it is logical to assess how quality attributes of user stories align with those of BDD scenarios. Thus, QABAGE aims to improve consistency and clarity in BDD documentation by aligning BDD scenario quality attributes with those of user stories, consolidating them into a formalized set practitioners can consistently apply throughout the scenario-writing process.

Although the design of QABAGE, as outlined in [24], includes a preliminary evaluation through an ex-ante demonstration with two software engineering experts, we contend the evaluation process for framework acceptance remains incomplete. The process of designing and releasing software engineering artifacts, such as QABAGE, which helps practitioners evaluate and improve BDD scenario quality, requires combining ex-ante and iterative ex post evaluations [16]. These evaluations assess how well the artifact performs under different conditions and situational contexts. In this regard, the present study aims to continue the research strand initiated by Wautelet et al. [24] by further evaluating QABAGE. Accordingly, the research question guiding this study is: *How does the application of QABAGE, with its structured quality attributes, impact the quality of BDD scenarios based on expert feedback and experiences?*

Presently, we adopt a more empiricist approach to evaluating QABAGE by collecting qualitative data through a multi-modal survey that combines BDD scenario-writing analyses and semi-structured interviews. This approach allows us to assess the framework's impact on scenario quality and stakeholder understanding. As such, the contribution of this paper is twofold: (i) conduct an empirical evaluation of QABAGE, highlighting its benefits and limitations, and (ii) derive insights into the challenges practitioners face when applying structured quality guidelines to BDD scenarios.

The paper is organized as: Sect. 2 reviews related work and introduces QABAGE. Section 3 outlines the methodology. Sections 4 and 5 present the results and address threats to validity, while Sect. 6 concludes the paper.

2   Background

2.1   Related Work

Several studies have aimed to address quality issues in BDD scenario writing. For example, Lucassen et al. [8] developed a framework for evaluating user story quality, emphasizing attributes such as clarity, completeness, and consistency.

While designed for user stories rather than BDD scenarios, these attributes have influenced subsequent research in improving quality in agile requirements engineering artifacts. The study of Silva [14] introduces an approach to automate the testing process for the iterative development of various software releases. Rather than writing test scenarios for each artifact individually, the approach investigates the use of ontologies to define the test once and then apply it to all artifacts that share the same ontological concepts. Even though the provided approach simplifies the connection between user stories and tested system behaviors, it does not evaluate the quality of the generated testing scenarios. Hotomski et al. [7] introduce a three-step approach to synchronize changes in software requirements with acceptance tests. The process identifies change patterns, generates natural language suggestions for handling these changes, and disseminates relevant information to stakeholders. This ensures that updates in requirements are accurately reflected in acceptance tests, enhancing traceability and alignment throughout the software's evolution. Tsilionis et al. [20,21] introduce an ontology that visually connects the dimensions of user stories with their corresponding BDD scenarios. Their work provides a unified template, outlining a set of concepts with semantic descriptions to assist agile practitioners in crafting more precise and structured BDD scenarios.

While the majority of the aforementioned studies enhance the rigor of the BDD scenario-writing process, they do not explicitly address potential quality issues within the generated scenarios. This study helps address this gap by empirically evaluating the BDD quality framework described in an earlier study. It offers insights into its effectiveness in improving BDD practices and identifies areas where the framework could be enhanced.

2.2 A Generic Overview of QABAGE

QABAGE provides a structured approach to evaluating BDD scenario quality. A detailed explanation of the framwork is available in [24] and will not be provided here. However, we do offer a brief overview of the framework's formalization of key quality attributes for clarity. In general, a BDD scenario μ, contains three elements represented as triples $\mu = \langle\ c,\ e,\ o\ \rangle$, where c denotes the *context*, e the *event*, and o the set of *outcomes*. A set of scenarios in a feature file is denoted by $S = \{\ \mu_1,\ \mu_2,...,\ \mu_n\ \}$. The framework introduces seven key attributes to guide the writing of high-quality BDD scenarios. According to the framework, a BDD scenario μ is considered:

1) **Unique** if it lacks any complete duplicate or semantically identical scenario within a specific feature file. The logical negation of this criterion stipulates that, within a feature file, there are 2 scenarios can either be full-duplicates or semantic duplicates. In other words, a BDD scenario μ_1 is considered a full-duplicate of scenario μ_2 when μ_1 and μ_2 are completely identical. Contrastingly, a BDD scenario μ_1 is deemed a semantic duplicate of scenario μ_2 when μ_2 employs a different event e or context c to achieve a similar outcome o as μ_1. In this case, the outcomes $o1$ and $o2$ are either identical or semantically equivalent.

2) ***Integrous*** when containing a *context*, an *event*, and an *outcome*. This means that each tuple of the set $\mu = \langle\ c,\ e,\ o\ \rangle$ must be non-empty.

3) ***Essential*** when each tuple of the set $\mu = \langle\ c,\ e,\ o\ \rangle$ contains a single-element. To comply with this, additional explanations or details (i.e., comments, references, descriptions of expected behavior, steps, or testing hints) should be moved to other sections of the feature file.

4) ***Singular*** when each element of the tuple $\langle\ c,\ e,\ o\ \rangle$ is associated with the same purpose ρ and they are consumed to describe that purpose. In that aspect, consolidating or aggregating scenarios into larger and more complex ones reduces the accuracy of the scenario's intended purpose.

5) ***Complete*** *at the feature level* when two conditions are met: With F representing the set of features in the application, and for each feature f belonging to the set F, a set of scenarios $(\mu_1, \mu_2, ..., \mu_n)$ is defined as *complete* for a feature f when: 1) the feature file generated from the scenarios $(\mu_1, \mu_2, ..., \mu_n)$ covers all the necessary scenarios required for feature f, and 2) the feature file generated from the scenarios $(\mu_1, \mu_2, ..., \mu_n)$ includes all the essential scenarios for the implementation and functionality of feature f. Contrastingly, a BDD scenario μ can be defined as *complete at the scenario level* if and only if all the information needed to understand and follow the steps consecutively within μ is available.

6) ***Clear*** when written in a non-ambiguous manner. Since ambiguity is inherent in structured natural language, QABAGE does not offer a formal rule-based definition for clarity. Instead, it recommends using this attribute alongside Focus. Therefore, a BDD scenario μ is ***Clear*** and ***Focused*** when it specifies what the scenario should accomplish and the requirement it aims to validate. Details on *how* to solve the problem should be excluded to avoid jargon that could undermine clarity.

3   Methodology

3.1   Research Design

Our study intends to further understand the contribution of QABAGE in influencing the quality of scenarios produced by agile software engineers and BDD practitioners. This study aims to evaluate the framework's efficacy and identify previously undefined challenges practitioners face when applying it in complex cases. Consequently, an exploratory research design was adopted, as it is well-suited for examining complex, context-dependent practices in real-world settings [10]. Since we were interested in capturing rich in-content data through practitioners' experiences and expertise, a qualitative research methodology [6] was adopted via the conduct of semi-structured interviews. Indeed, the setting of our study began with the identification of agile software engineers and practitioners that are knowledgeable of testing practices in the context of their work. Given that QABAGE is being considered as *a-priory* (published) framework in the content of our present study, we follow thus a deductive logic described in the study of Gilgun [4], which inscribes to: (i) first look at the theory (i.e., by considering QABAGE as described in [24]), (ii) produce hypotheses from the theory (i.e., by considering that QABAGE improves the BDD scenario-writing process as supported in [24]), (iii) and then proceed to assess such hypotheses (i.e., by using expert assessments and interviews to evaluate such claims).

3.2 Sampling and Data Collection Techniques

Given our study's focus on practitioners with specific educational and work-related training, we chose a non-probability sampling technique. We used purposive sampling [13] to target individuals academically trained and professionally skilled in requirements engineering, software engineering, agile methodologies, and feature-driven testing practices. These individuals should primarily possess a technical perspective on agile framework implementation. However, technically-oriented professionals who have transitioned into broader managerial roles within software engineering project implementation are also considered suitable participants for our survey. No industry limitations were set, as we aimed to capture diverse viewpoints from various sectors. Initial candidates were selected from the professional network (using LinkedIn) of one research team member, with consent from the others. A snowball sampling technique [13] was then used to identify additional candidates meeting the selection criteria. At the end, a total number of 7 candidates expressed interest in participating in the survey. Our final sample comprised software engineers, testers, developers, product owners, and managers with prior experience in BDD through their professional practice (see Table 1). While the sample may appear heterogeneous in terms of roles, we do not regard this as a limitation. On the contrary, this diversity aligns with a core principle of BDD which is to facilitate communication and collaboration among a wide range of stakeholders engaged in agile software engineering.

Table 1. Participant Profiles and Experience Levels

Participant	Role	Experience Level
P1	Software Engineer	5 years in BDD practices
P2	Product Owner	8 years in agile practices
P3	Quality Assurance Tester	3 years in testing practices
P4	Developer	6 years in software development
P5	Project Manager	10 years in software project management
P6	Business Analyst	4 years in requirements analysis practices
P7	Senior Developer	12 years in software development

The seven candidates were invited via email to attend a 90-min individual evaluation session, which included scenario analyses with and without the use of QABAGE, and semi-structured interviews, conducted at a designated location.

The semi-structured interview format enabled in-depth discussions on the perceived utility of the framework, guided by a set of key questions. Indeed, given the relatively small sample size, our goal was to reach a state of information saturation. To minimize bias, we carefully worded and sequenced the semi-structured interview questions to avoid leading prompts and enhance clarity. The details of the entire evaluation protocol are outlined below.

3.3 Evaluation Protocol

The protocol that was followed for the evaluation of QABAGE was the same for the seven participants and was structured into three main phases. Each phase was designed to focus on distinct aspects of experience-capturing and evaluation for the framework. Below are detailed descriptions of these phases.

1. **Background Information and BDD Knowledge Testing**: The initial phase of the protocol gathered background information on practitioners' expertise, their experience with BDD, and their understanding of writing BDD scenarios. Example questions asked during this phase included: *"What are your main challenges when writing BDD scenarios?"*, and *"How do you ensure the capture of unique functionalities when writing BDD scenarios?"*. Most important, in this phase, participants drafted BDD scenarios based on their existing knowledge, without exposure to QABAGE. This approach aimed to capture their natural methods and identify common challenges in their scenario-writing process. The case descriptions to support scenario drafting were sourced from GitHub and incorporated applications spanning diverse use cases including an email client application, an open-source social media platform, a food ordering system, and an ATM banking system. A total of 17 scenarios were produced during this phase across participants (see Appendix A), with each scenario differing in the complexity of its requirements and the depth of its background information.

2. **Introducing QABAGE with Guided Scenario-Writing**: In this phase, a team member introduced QABAGE, covering its key quality attributes: *Uniqueness, Integrity, Essentiality, Singularity, Completeness, Clarity,* and *Focus*. Each attribute was explained with practical examples to illustrate its application in scenario writing (see Appendix B). To avoid bias, the team member ensured that the case descriptions and scenarios from the GitHub repository, which were used as examples to illustrate the applicability of the framework, were **not** to be used by the participants. After this demonstration, participants created new BDD scenarios using the framework as a guide. To ensure result comparability, participants were instructed to use the same cases and examples from the first phase of the evaluation protocol. These cases served as the basis for writing new scenarios with the guidance of QABAGE, maintaining consistency and facilitating the evaluation of the framework's impact. It is important to note that during this phase, the interviewer did not assist participants in writing their scenarios; they had to rely solely on the assistance of QABAGE to write their scenarios.

3. **Qualitative Audit of QABAGE via Semi-Structured Interviews**: After engaging with QABAGE, participants took part in a second round of semi-structured interviews. This phase included 18 open-ended questions designed to capture their experiences and perceptions following their interaction with the framework. Given the scarcity of formal frameworks for assessing quality attributes in BDD, the interview questions were based on Oliveira et al. [12] and adapted as needed. That study introduces 12 heuristics-based questions to assess BDD scenarios post-development, addressing aspects such as the evaluation level (e.g., feature files versus individual scenarios) and the impact of specific quality attributes. We expanded this question set to enable a more comprehensive evaluation of the formal representation of quality attributes as defined in QABAGE. In particular, we focused on areas that emerged as candidates for refinement during the design and ex-ante evaluation of QABAGE, such as *Uniqueness, Clarity, Singularity,* and *Completeness,* to better capture the practical challenges participants encountered when applying the framework for quality assessment. Sample questions used in this phase included: "*Do you understand the Uniqueness quality attribute? If yes, how do you understand the Uniqueness quality attribute?*" and "*How do you perceive its effect when drafting scenarios?*". Subsequent questions and follow-up questions were designed to explore the type of support each quality attribute is intended to provide during the scenario writing process. For example, "*Did the use of the Clarity attribute, as prescribed in QABAGE, help improve your scenarios? If yes, in what way(s)?*" and "*Were there any challenges that you faced when applying the Singularity attribute as prescribed in QABAGE? If yes, what were those?*". A final set of questions aimed to explore the framework's perceived capacity to support learning and adaptation in facilitating collaboration between IT and non-IT stakeholders across the organization.

4   Data Analysis and Results

With the participants' consent, the evaluation and interview sessions were recorded and transcribed for analysis. The data were systematically organized and coded to assess the framework. Given the three-phase evaluation protocol, we applied three corresponding data analysis techniques to capture insights specific to each phase, as detailed below.

4.1   BDD Knowledge Testing Results

For the data analysis of this phase, the research team reviewed the BDD scenarios participants created prior to being introduced to QABAGE. These will be hereafter referred to as first-phase scenarios. The analysis was empirical, with each team member, an expert in BDD, independently reviewing each scenario to determine whether they comply with the quality requirements *Uniqueness, Essentiality, Singularity, Integrity, Completeness, Clarity,* and *Focus.* Each team member evaluated whether the first-phase scenarios satisfied the specified quality attributes and identified any scenarios that failed to meet these requirements.

They also documented the rationale behind their assessments, providing clear explanations for their evaluations. The team convened to review their assessments and agreed on the scenarios that most members identified as not meeting the aforementioned quality requirements. The first-phase scenario-writing exercise revealed key challenges participants faced when crafting BDD scenarios. The ones consistently identified by the research team included the *use of ambiguous language*, *redundant steps*, and the tendency to write scenarios that *combined multiple functionalities without a clear focus*. These challenges emerged across participants, regardless of their experience level. To illustrate these issues, we provide an example scenario written by P1, a software engineer with 5 years of experience in BDD, who noted difficulties in maintaining clarity and a clear focus of the main functionality that should be tested in a singular BDD scenario. The case that required the drafting of scenarios referred to the required functionalities of an open-sourced social media platform when users interact with this platform (see Appendix A). To test the achievement of one of the functionalities for this platform, the survey participant wrote the following:

- **Scenario:** "GIVEN a user logs into the platform, WHEN they create a new post and share it, THEN the post should be visible on their profile and notify followers."

According to the guidelines provided by QABAGE, the scenario in the example above should be decomposed into smaller, functional chunks that each serve a single, clear purpose. By failing to do so, it violates the *Singularity* quality attribute by combining multiple complex steps in the WHEN and THEN clauses. To adhere to this attribute, each step in the WHEN and THEN dimensions should be separated into distinct individual scenarios, ensuring that each scenario remains focused and specific. Due to space limitations, examples of participants' first-phase scenarios are provided in Appendix A.

4.2   Guided Scenario-Writing Results

To analyze the data from the 2nd phase of our evaluation protocol, we conducted a pre- and post-framework-explanation scenario analysis to assess whether the introduction of QABAGE led to improvements in scenario quality on the part of the survey participants. The evaluation process for the second-phase scenarios (those written after the introduction of the framework) closely mirrored that of the first-phase scenarios. Specifically, the research team reviewed both the first- and second-phase scenarios and compared the results using QABAGE and the BDD evaluation checklist provided by Oliveira et al. [12] to assess discrepancies between the two phases submitted by the respondents. We also utilized a Computer-Aided Software Engineering (CASE) tool to assess the conformance of quality attributes of the second-phase BDD scenarios. Due to space limitations, we will not provide a detailed description of the CASE tool here, as it is fully outlined in [24]. We just note here that the tool assists practitioners in evaluating the quality of scenarios by automating the assessment of key quality attributes defined in QABAGE.

As mentioned earlier, prior to the introduction of the framework, the scenarios written by participants often contained ambiguous language, redundant steps, and lacked clear focus. However, after the framework was introduced, a noticeable shift in the quality of their scenario-writing process emerged: their scenarios became more structured, concise, and better aligned with the intended business requirements outlined in the case descriptions. To illustrate this, we provide an example from the second participant (P2), who was asked to draft BDD scenarios for an ATM banking application. This case required the description of the user flow for logging into an ATM system and performing cash withdrawals.

- **P2 Scenario Prior to the Introduction of the Framework:**
  "GIVEN the user logs in and navigates to the dashboard, WHEN they try to withdraw money, THEN the ATM processes the transaction."

- **P2 Scenarios After the Introduction of the Framework:**
  Scenario 1: "GIVEN the user is logged into the ATM system, WHEN they navigate to the withdrawal section, THEN the withdrawal options are displayed."
  Scenario 2: "GIVEN the user has selected a withdrawal option, WHEN they confirm the amount, THEN the ATM processes the transaction."

We observe that the participant's first-phase scenario for the ATM banking application violates several quality attributes such as *Singularity*, *Essentiality*, *Completeness* and *Focus*. However, with the use of QABAGE, P2 was able to streamline the structure of the second-phase scenarios, resulting in clearer structure and more explicitly defined expected outcomes. Overall, the CASE tool analysis showed that, aside from a consistent violation of the *Singularity* attribute, most quality attributes were generally satisfied in the second-phase scenarios for the majority of participants. The exercise revealed that applying the *Singularity* attribute can be challenging, especially when multiple related actions need to be captured in a single scenario.

4.3   Qualitative Audit Results

To analyze the interview data collected during the 3rd phase of our evaluation protocol, we employed qualitative content analysis [1]. The latter supports both a deductive analysis approach, using a predefined coding framework based on the quality attributes identified in QABAGE, and an inductive approach, allowing additional codes to emerge organically from the participants' responses. In this context, excerpts from interviewees' answers were annotated with codes that captured specific opinions and observations. Given the relatively small number of participants, we applied the principles of analytic generalization [3] to interpret the findings. This means that, rather than seeking statistical generalizability, we treated each interview as a rich source of empirical insight, contributing to the broader evaluation of the framework's quality attributes.

Table 2. Qualitative Content Analysis of Interview Data

Quality Attribute	Theme	Code	Participant Statement
Uniqueness	Effort to Maintain Scenario Uniqueness	Difficulty in Differentiating Similar Scenarios	*I understand this attribute well, but in practice, I catch myself writing steps that are similar because they seem more fitting in the context of a new scenario (P1).*
		Avoidance of Feature Duplication	*I understand the importance of making each scenario unique, but it can be difficult to differentiate between features in a large project (P3).*
		Need for Precision in Feature Separation	*It is sometimes challenging to maintain uniqueness across all scenarios. It requires careful attention to detail (P4).*
			I tried to make each scenario unique, but I recognize that in a few cases, the scenarios could have been further differentiated to avoid any overlap (P5).
			I initially struggled with understanding uniqueness, but after clarification, it improved my understanding (P6).
Singularity	Tension Between Understanding and Applying Singularity	Challenging to Apply in Practice	*I understand this quality attribute, but I do not agree with its logic (P2).*
			I get the idea of keeping scenarios focused on a single functionality but it is challenging to apply this in practice (P3).
		Need for Singular Scenarios	*I understand the need for a single functionality and I already try to balance this in my activities (P4).*
			I aimed to keep each scenario focused on a single functionality, but there were a couple of instances where multiple actions or outcomes were combined. These could have been indeed split to improve clarity (P5).
Completeness	Exploring Boundaries of Completeness	Challenge in Ensuring Scenario Completeness	*Writing complete scenarios is challenging due to the complexity of capturing complete requirements. My focus has primarily been on design and functionality rather than on certain aspects of robust testing examples (P1).*
		Thoroughness in Step Coverage	*It helped me to make sure to cover all necessary steps and conditions in each scenario to ensure they were thorough and complete and nothing important was left out (P5).*
Essentiality	Ensuring Scenario Relevance and Brevity	Emphasis on Essential Information	*It made important that we need to focus on the core aspects of the functionality without getting bogged down by unnecessary details. I find this attribute to align well with how I approach scenario writing (P3).*
		Intent to Keep Scenarios Brief and Clear	*I focused on the key actions and outcomes in each scenario, keeping them concise and avoiding any unnecessary details. This made the scenarios straightforward and to the point (P5).*

Table 2 provides the results of this analysis, illustrating how identified themes relate to their corresponding codes and supporting interview data. Due to space constraints, the table highlights key positive and negative issues for selected quality attributes, rather than presenting the full set. The first column lists the quality attributes under examination. The second column summarizes the themes derived from participant feedback, helping clarify their contextual meaning. The third column presents the codes that group similar sentiments across participant responses. The fourth column includes verbatim excerpts from participants, offering raw data to support the codes and themes. To minimize bias and uncover potential blind spots, the coding and content analyses were conducted collaboratively, with all members of the research team independently reviewing the data and engaging in joint discussions to reach consensus on each coding decision.

The interview data reveals positive aspects of QABAGE, particularly in guiding practitioners to produce scenarios that are unique, complete, and essential. Participants generally appreciated the role of quality attributes in improving the structure and contextual brevity of BDD scenarios. *Essentiality* and *Completeness* received near-unanimous support, with participants like P3 and P5 emphasizing the role of the corresponding quality attributes in helping them cognitively retain that scenarios have to be concise yet thorough. The underlying logic for formally defining *Uniqueness* as it is in QABAGE was also well comprehended, as illustrated by P1, P3, P5 and P6's recognition of the need for a guiding principle to help BDD practitioners effectively distinguish between semantically distinct scenarios; nevertheless, participants recognized the difficulty of operationalizing this principle in practice. Furthermore, participants reflected positively on how *Completeness* prompted them to consider testing and verification steps early in the requirements gathering process. This suggests that attributes incorporated in the framework foster a more holistic mindset in agile requirements engineering processes: one that not only ensures the capture of system functionality and attention to design, but also bridges the requirements modeling phase with testing processes, which, although typically addressed later in the software development life cycle, are critical to ensuring quality.

At the same time, participants noted practical challenges in applying certain quality attributes within real-world project settings. *Uniqueness* and *Singularity* were seen as conceptually valuable but difficult to implement in environments with overlapping or complex functionalities. P3, P4, and P5 acknowledged the intent to focus on single functionalities per scenario but pointed to the difficulty of maintaining that focus in practice. Notably, P2 rejected the logic behind *Singularity* altogether, emphasizing the need for a more robust rationale in the design of this attribute. When prompted further, the participant argued that focusing on single-ended functionalities can hinder stakeholder alignment, since different users often need similar but not identical features, making the creation of singular scenarios unsustainable. Finally, while participants did not extensively comment on attributes such as *Clarity*, *Focus*, and *Integrity*, their effective implementation in the second-phase scenarios suggests a solid understanding of these elements and their role in ensuring scenario comprehensibility within QABAGE.

5   Threats to Validity

Some threats to validity are considered according to the prescriptions of Wohlin et al. [25]. Threats to **construct validity** arise when there is a potential mismatch between the quality attributes as defined in the framework and participants' understanding of these concepts. To address this risk, the interviewer took deliberate steps in the 2nd phase of the interview protocol to clarify the definition of each QABAGE quality attribute. Detailed explanations were provided, with the interviewer presenting three distinct examples for each attribute to demonstrate how the framework could be practically applied to enhance the scenario-writing process.

Threats to the **internal validity** stem from potential errors in the knowledge acquisition process, particularly during the design and implementation of the evaluation protocol. This effect may be amplified in this study, as the interviews in the 3rd phase focus on participants' perceptions of QABAGE, potentially emphasizing the framework over the experimental object, which is the effect of the framework on the BDD scenarios from the 1st and 2nd phases. As a result, the findings may capture practitioners' subjective perceptions rather than accurately reflecting the framework's impact on the quality of the scenarios. To reduce the impact of such threats, we took several steps before conducting the interviews. First, we performed baseline assessments by comparing scenarios written before applying QABAGE with those written afterward. This helped us evaluate how the framework influenced the specific set of BDD scenarios under study. The use of an extended scenario output (17 scenarios) was implemented to mitigate potential bias stemming from participants' prior exposure to these scenarios during the 1st scenario-writing phase. This approach ensured a diverse set of scenarios when participants were asked to draft them again in the 2nd scenario-writing phase, with the assistance of QABAGE. To further minimize potential bias toward favoring QABAGE during the design of the entire evaluation process, we involved a new research member in the data collection, analysis, and scenario-review process, who was not part of the framework's development (as reported in [24]). This person was tasked with developing the interview questionnaire, which was carefully designed to avoid leading questions and included control questions to minimize bias.

Finally, threats to **external validity** limit the generalizability of the study's findings to other contexts. We acknowledge that our sampling technique, which combined purposive and snowball sampling, may have been suboptimal in providing a comprehensive sample, potentially affecting the accuracy of our understanding of how QABAGE influences the cognitive capacities of experts in recognizing the quality attributes meant to be incorporated into BDD scenarios. So, despite the limited sample size posing an additional threat to the generalizability of our results, we align with Saunders et al. [13] who argue that purposive sampling techniques can effectively capture highly informative cases. This was considered particularly important in our study, as QABAGE is a relatively new framework. The use of the specific sampling technique was deemed fit to capture survey participants with particular traits, namely those who had accumulated significant experience in development and testing practices.

6   Discussion and Conclusion

To answer our question *"How does the application of QABAGE, with its structured quality attributes, impact the quality of BDD scenarios based on expert feedback and experiences?"*, we implemented a methodological approach that collects qualitative data from experts actively engaged in development and testing practices, capturing their experiences with the framework. The findings indicate that the application of the framework results in enhanced scenario quality, especially with regard to *Essentiality*, *Completeness* and *Focus*. However, challenges emerged in the understanding and application of attributes such as *Uniqueness* and *Singularity*. Difficulties with *Singularity*, in particular, were consistently reported during the 2nd and 3rd phases of the evaluation protocol, as participants struggled to decompose complex functionalities into simple, single-purpose scenarios. This suggests that the framework may need refinement or additional training to facilitate the evaluation of complex requirements. While the framework's structured approach supports practitioners in consistently adhering to key constraints that must be upheld when drafting scenarios, its rigidity in its incorporated definitions can create a steep learning curve which may not align with the need for flexibility in agile environments where rapid iteration and adaptability are essential [19]. Therefore, balancing the framework's rigor with the adaptability needed for agile practices is crucial for its broader adoption in dynamic software development projects. A key insight from the study is that participants working in structured agile environments (e.g., P1, P3) found certain attributes within the framework that align well with their existing practices. In contrast, those operating in hybrid or less formalized agile settings (e.g., P4, P7), often relying on loosely defined requirements specification templates, emphasized the framework's value in formalizing their scenario writing processes and reducing redundancies, particularly during the early stages of requirements definition. However, this does not take out a commonly reported challenge which was the framework's current lack of built-in mechanisms for learning and adaptation, which posed difficulties for teams operating with flexible or evolving requirements-gathering procedures. While certain quality attributes were seen as helpful in maintaining focus and direction during scenario development, participants noted that their practical application often required contextual adaptation to align with each team's specific workflows and operational norms. As the next step, we will conduct a controlled experiment building on the approach in [17, 18], in which novice testers develop BDD scenarios based on a given set of user stories. One group will apply QABAGE, while a second group will complete the same task without it. This design will allow us to compare the outcomes of both groups and evaluate QABAGE's acceptance dimensions, such as its understandability and ease of use. The experiment will likely also incorporate a cost-benefit assessment by examining authoring time, cognitive load, and rework reduction, in order to determine whether the quality improvements delivered by QABAGE justify the additional effort it requires across different agile contexts.

References

1. Bihu, R.: Qualitative Data Analysis: Novelty in Deductive and Inductive Coding. Authorea Preprints (2024)
2. Binamungu, L.P., Embury, S.M., Konstantinou, N.: Characterising the quality of behaviour driven development specifications. In: 21st International Conference on Agile Software Development, pp. 87–102. Springer (2020)
3. Evers, C.W., Wu, E.H.: On generalising from single case studies: epistemological reflections. J. Philos. Educ. **40**(4), 511–526 (2006)
4. Gilgun, J.F.: Deductive qualitative analysis and grounded theory: sensitizing concepts and hypothesis-testing. In: The SAGE Handbook of Current Developments in Grounded Theory, pp. 107–122 (2019)
5. Heng, S., Tsilionis, K., Wautelet, Y.: Building user stories and behavior driven development scenarios with a strict set of concepts: ontology, benefits and primary validation. In: Proceedings of the 38th ACM/SIGAPP Symposium on Applied Computing, pp. 1422–1429 (2023)
6. Hennink, M., Hutter, I., Bailey, A.: Qualitative Research Methods. Sage (2020)
7. Hotomski, S., Ben Charrada, E., Glinz, M.: Keeping evolving requirements and acceptance tests aligned with automatically generated guidance. In: Kamsties, E., Horkoff, J., Dalpiaz, F. (eds.) REFSQ 2018. LNCS, vol. 10753, pp. 247–264. Springer, Cham (2018). https://doi.org/10.1007/978-3-319-77243-1_15
8. Lucassen, G., Dalpiaz, F., Werf, J.M.E.M., Brinkkemper, S.: The use and effectiveness of user stories in practice. In: Daneva, M., Pastor, O. (eds.) REFSQ 2016. LNCS, vol. 9619, pp. 205–222. Springer, Cham (2016). https://doi.org/10.1007/978-3-319-30282-9_14
9. North, D., et al.: Introducing BDD. Better Softw. **12** (2006)
10. Olawale, S.R., Chinagozi, O.G., Joe, O.N.: Exploratory research design in management science: a review of literature on conduct and application. Int. J. Res. Innov. Soc. Sci. **7**(4), 1384–1395 (2023)
11. Oliveira, G., Marczak, S.: On the empirical evaluation of BDD scenarios quality: preliminary findings of an empirical study. In: 25th International Requirements Engineering Conference Workshops (REW), pp. 299–302. IEEE (2017)
12. Oliveira, G., Marczak, S., Moralles, C.: How to evaluate BDD scenarios' quality? In: Proceedings of the XXXIII Brazilian Symposium on Software Engineering, pp. 481–490 (2019)
13. Saunders, M.: Research Methods for Business Students. Person Educ. Ltd. (2009)
14. Silva, T.R.: Definition of a behavior-driven model for requirements specification and testing of interactive systems. In: 24th International Requirements Engineering Conference (RE), pp. 444–449. IEEE (2016)
15. Smart, J.F., Molak, J.: BDD in Action: Behavior-Driven Development for the Whole Software Lifecycle. Simon and Schuster (2023)
16. Sonnenberg, C., Vom Brocke, J.: Evaluation patterns for design science research artefacts. In: Practical Aspects of Design Science: European Design Science Symposium 2011, pp. 71–83. Springer (2012)
17. Tsilionis, K., Maene, J., Heng, S., Wautelet, Y., Poelmans, S.: Evaluating the software problem representation on the basis of rationale trees and user story maps: premises of an experiment. In: International Conference on Software Business, pp. 219–227. Springer (2020)
18. Tsilionis, K., Maene, J., Heng, S., Wautelet, Y., Poelmans, S.: Conceptual modeling versus user story mapping: which is the best approach to agile requirements engineering? In: RCIS 2021, Proceedings 15, pp. 356–373. Springer (2021)

19. Tsilionis, K., Sassenus, S., Wautelet, Y.: Determining the benefits and drawbacks of agile (Scrum) and DevOps in addressing the development challenges of cloud applications. In: The International Research & Innovation Forum, pp. 109–123. Springer (2021)
20. Tsilionis, K., Wautelet, Y., Faut, C., Heng, S.: Unifying behavior driven development templates. In: 29th International Requirements Engineering Conference (RE), pp. 454–455. IEEE (2021)
21. Tsilionis, K., Wautelet, Y., Heng, S.: Building a unified ontology for behavior driven development scenarios. In: International Conference on Product-Focused Software Process Improvement, pp. 518–524. Springer (2022)
22. Wake, B.: INVEST in Good Stories, and SMART Tasks (2003)
23. Wautelet, Y., Heng, S., Kolp, M., Mirbel, I.: Unifying and extending user story models. In: International Conference on Advanced Information Systems Engineering, pp. 211–225. Springer (2014)
24. Wautelet, Y., Nassiri, A.K., Tsilionis, K.: Investigating quality attributes in behavior-driven development scenarios: an evaluation framework and an experimental supporting tool. In: IFIP Working Conference on The Practice of Enterprise Modeling, pp. 125–142. Springer (2023)
25. Wohlin, C., Runeson, P., Höst, M., Ohlsson, M.C., Regnell, B., Wesslén, A.: Experimentation in Software Engineering. Springer (2012)

Application of Large Language Models in Product Management: A Systematic Literature Review

Vitor Mori Serra[1]([✉]) [iD], Jan Bosch[2] [iD], and Helena Holmström Olsson[3] [iD]

[1] Department of Mathematics and Computer Science, Eindhoven University of Technology, Eindhoven, Netherlands
`v.serra.mori@tue.nl`
[2] Department of Computer Science and Engineering, Chalmers University of Technology, Gothenburg, Sweden
[3] Department of Computer Science and Media Technology, Malmö University, Malmö, Sweden

Abstract. This systematic literature review analyzes how Generative AI (GenAI), specifically Large Language Models (LLMs), impacts Software Product Management (SPM). Based on recent studies, our analysis reveals that current research is in a nascent, experimental phase, focusing on task-level applications like requirements engineering and user persona generation, which show potential for efficiency gains. However, the field suffers from critical limitations, including a lack of methodological standardization, an over-reliance on a narrow range of LLMs like ChatGPT, and a focus on superficial efficiency metrics over measures of product success. We conclude that while LLMs show promise for discrete PM tasks, their true transformative potential lies in integrated, workflow-centric systems. This paper provides a baseline of the current research and calls for a more rigorous, impact-focused agenda for future studies.

Keywords: Generative Artificial Intelligence · Product Management · Systematic Literature Review · Software Engineering

1 Introduction

The rapid rise of Generative AI (GenAI) is profoundly transforming various sectors and activities [1], offering immense potential to revolutionize Software Product Management (SPM). From ideation to market launch, this powerful technology can augment team capabilities, uncover hidden insights, and dramatically accelerate the innovation process [2].

While the fluency and apparent sophistication of GenAI can be impressive, this initial 'wow factor' can lead to over-reliance and blind trust. This is a critical risk, as technology still faces challenges like hallucinations and factual inaccuracies [3]. If product managers accept its output without critical validation, this unmitigated trust can severely compromise or restrict GenAI's effective application in Product Management

© The Author(s), under exclusive license to Springer Nature Switzerland AG 2026
G. Scanniello et al. (Eds.): PROFES 2025, LNCS 16361, pp. 319–333, 2026.
https://doi.org/10.1007/978-3-032-12089-2_20

(PM). Consequently, a significant gap emerges between the perceived potential of GenAI and its reliable, practical implementation.

To address this critical gap, this systematic literature review (SLR) examines how GenAI, particularly Large Language Models (LLMs), can be leveraged in PM. To this end, the review offers three key contributions. First, it analyzes the primary in-depth experiments being explored by researchers on GenAI in PM. Second, it synthesizes insights from these experiments to provide a comprehensive understanding of the challenges, strategic considerations for its adoption, and readiness for continuous and scaled deployment. Finally, it envisions how advanced AI will reshape the strategic focus, operational execution, and overall value proposition of PM.

2 Background

SPM focuses on managing software products throughout their lifecycle to achieve economic success [4]. Core activities include defining and evolving a product's strategy and planning its development and evolution.

Artificial Intelligence (AI) is a technology that enables computers and machines to simulate human capabilities such as learning, comprehension, problem-solving, decision-making and creativity [5]. By this definition, it is evident that AI has a substantial impact on PM.

The emergence of GenAI, especially LLMs like ChatGPT, has accelerated this impact [6]. GenAI can create diverse content, and while LLMs focus on text, other forms, including multimodal systems, are developing rapidly. It has become a key driver in the evolving landscape of SPM practices through two interrelated areas: externally, by requiring new skills to manage AI-embedded products, and internally, by changing how products are managed [7]. It has become a key driver in the evolving landscape of SPM practices both externally, by requiring new skills to manage AI-embedded products, and internally, by changing how products are managed [7]. The former has received significantly more attention than the latter, focusing on defining the 'AI Product Manager' and the changes required to manage an AI product [8]. This latter area, known as AI-driven PM, leverages data for numerous applications that drive efficiency, innovation, and value—a key example of which is improved decision-making [9]. This approach enables faster development and more relevant products by enhancing human capabilities and is the focus of this research [10, 11].

Prior systematic literature reviews have examined the broader application of AI in PM contexts. [12] conducted a comprehensive review of AI's impact on PM, identifying key areas where AI technologies show promise for improving product outcomes. Similarly, [13] specifically investigated GenAI applications in SPM, revealing potential benefits in idea generation, market research, and customer insights.

While existing reviews either focus on AI broadly, without specific attention to LLMs, or examine GenAI at a high level, our work contributes to this growing body of literature by providing the first systematic literature review specifically focused on LLMs in PM. This more targeted analysis of a rapidly evolving subset of AI technologies allows us to present the opportunities alongside the challenges and limitations, which were identified during a review of highly cited articles on GenAI [3] and are outlined in Table 1.

Table 1. Challenges and limitations of LLMs and GenAI found in the literature

Hallucinations and Factuality Issues [3]	Bias and Fairness Issues [14]
Interpretability and Explainability [15]	Reliability and Robustness [16]
Ethical and Social Challenges [15]	Technical and Implementation Limitations [15]

The continuous development of more powerful GenAI, Agentic AI [17], and the pursuit of Artificial General Intelligence (AGI) [18] underscore the need for ongoing research to help product leaders adapt their strategies and leverage GenAI's full potential.

3   Methodology

This systematic literature review, following the PRISMA protocol [19] and associated guidelines [20], employs a methodology summarized in Fig. 1 to examine the application of GenAI in PM by addressing three key research questions:

- RQ1: What are the dominant use cases for LLMs in current Product Management research?
- RQ2: What are the key challenges and limitations identified in these applications?
- RQ3: How could advanced AI reshape the future of PM if current limitations are overcome?

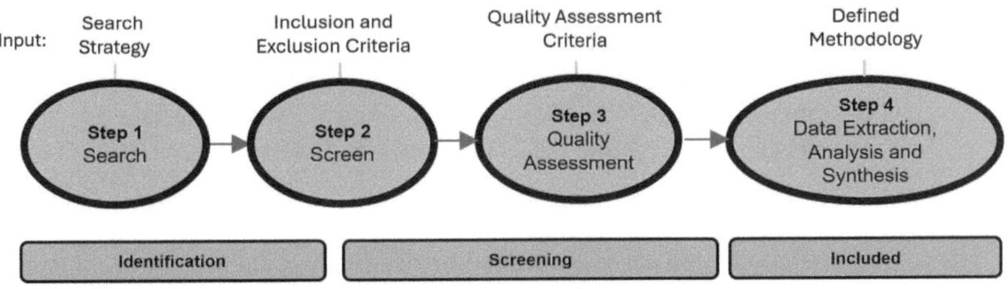

Fig. 1. Research Methodology

3.1 Step 1 - Search

This review identifies and selects studies that (1) utilize GenAI as the primary AI technique, (2) assist in the execution of professional activities, and (3) are situated within or applicable to the context of SPM.

Search Query: A comprehensive search query was constructed using keywords organized into four segments, as detailed in Table 2.

Table 2. Keywords Segments

AI Technique	"Generative Artificial Intelligence", "Generative AI", "Gen AI", "GenAI", "Large Language Model", "Large Language Models", "LLM"
Aspect: Role	"product manager"
Aspect: Practice	"Product Management", "Product Innovation", "Product Discovery", "Market Analysis", "Product Analysis", "Product Strategy", "User Experience", "Product Vision", "Product Positioning", "Delivery Model", "Service Strategy", "Ecosystem Management", "Sourcing", "Pricing", "Financial Management", "Performance Management", "Risk Management", "New product development", "Business Model", "Product performance", "Product usage", "Product Planning", "Customer Insight", "Life Cycle Management" OR "Life-cycle" OR "Lifecycle Management", "Roadmapping", "Release planning", "Requirements management", "Requirements elicitation", "Feature elicitation", "User Research", "Design Thinking", "Modeling", "Prototyping"
Aspect: Artifact	"Product Definition", "Product Scope", "Customer insight", "Customer Journey", "Customer feedback", "Voice of the Customer", "Persona", "User Behavior", "Issue tracking", "Knowledge base" OR "knowledgebase" OR "knowledgebase", "UX design", "User Story", "Requirements specification", "Roadmap", "Backlog", "Release Plan"

The search was conducted across four leading academic databases relevant to SPM: SpringerLink, IEEE Xplore, ScienceDirect, and the ACM Digital Library, covering the period between January 2023 and March 2025.

3.2 Step 2 - Screen

The principal researcher first screened titles and abstracts to exclude irrelevant studies, remove duplicates, and filter by language. This yielded a list of candidate studies for full-text review based on the eligibility criteria in Table 3 inspired by [21]. During this initial screen, criteria #1–#5 were strictly applied, while #6 and #7 were assessed on a preliminary basis.

Table 3. Inclusion and Exclusion Criteria Codes

	Criteria		
#1	Publication date within the defined time frame.	I1	E1
#2	A primary study, not a secondary or a tertiary study	I2	E2
#3	Published in a peer-reviewed journal, conference proceeding, or book chapter	I3	E3
#4	Published in English	I4	E4
#5	Not a duplicate or a version of another included study	I5	E5
#6	Applies GenAI to software product management activities.	I6	E6
#7	Evaluates GenAI via a vision, experiment, or case study.	I7	E7

To establish a verifiable baseline of academic research, this review excludes gray literature. While acknowledging this may omit some practitioner-driven use cases, it ensures methodological rigor and traceability.

3.3 Step 3 – Quality Assessment

The full text of candidate papers was retrieved to finalize inclusion based on criteria #6 and #7. Each included study was then assessed for quality using the QualSyst tool [22] with a 3-point Likert scale (Table 4). Studies scoring below 60% were excluded. The final list of studies was confirmed by all researchers.

Table 4. Quality Assessment Criteria

QC1	Objective sufficiently described?	QC2	Study design evident and appropriate?
QC3	Data sources described and appropriate?	QC4	Subject characteristics sufficiently described?
QC5	Data size appropriate?	QC6	Means of outcome assessment reported?
QC7	Results reported in sufficient detail?		

324 V. Mori Serra et al.

Table 5. Summary of Studies.

| | | Research | | | | | | | | Challenges | | | | | |
Application Area	Specific Application & Pertinent Study	Experiment(E), Case Study (C) or Vision (V)	Research Methodology	Improve Efficiency?	Improve Effectiveness?	Requires Human Validation?	LLMs Used	Justified LLM choice?	Results	Hallucinations and Factuality Issues	Bias and Fairness Issues	Interpretability and Explainability	Reliability and Robustness	Ethical and Social Challenges	Technical and Implementation Limitations
Customer Insights	Customer Insight - VoC analysis [23] (2024)	E	Qualitative	Time savings	Utility, Applicability	Y	ChatGPT-3.5 Turbo	No	Not Entirely Satisfactory	Y	Y	NA	Y	Y	Y
Requirements Engineering, Roadmapping, Release Planning	Prototyping, Ideas Generation, Initial Plans, Plan Review [24] (2024)	E	Qualitative	Time savings	Not evaluated	Y	ChatGPT-4o	Yes	Satisfatory	Y	Y	Y	NA	Y	Y
Requirements Engineering	Active Personas (APs) [25] (2024)	V	N/A	N/A	N/A	Y	ChatGPT	N/A	N/A	-	-	-	-	-	-
Requirements Engineering	User Stories Creation [26] (2024)	E	Quantitative	Time savings	Quality	Y	ChatGPT-3.5	No	Satisfatory	Y	NA	NA	Y	NA	NA
Requirements Engineering	Problem-Driven GenAI Requirements Elicitation Process [27] (2024)	E	Qualitative	Time savings	Not evaluated	Y	ChatGPT-4	No	Satisfatory	Y	NA	NA	NA	NA	Y
Requirements Engineering	User Personas from Live Activity [28] (2024)	E	Qualitative	Not evaluated	Transparency	N/A	ChatGPT-4o	No	Satisfatory	N	NA	Y	NA	Y	Y
Requirements Engineering, Roadmapping, Release Planning	Requirements Elicitation and Analysis [29] (2024)	E	Mixed	Time savings	Accuracy	Y	ChatGPT-3.5, ChatGPT-4o, LLaMA3-70, Mixtral-8B	No	Not Entirely Satisfactory	Y	NA	NA	Y	NA	Y
Requirements Engineering	Creating functional prototypes [30] (2023)	E	Mixed	Time savings, Faster Delivery	Effectiveness, Risk Reduction	N/A	LaMDA	No	Satisfatory	Y	NA	NA	Y	NA	Y
Market Analysis, Roadmapping, Release Planning	Feature competitor analysis [31] (2024)	E	Mixed	Time savings	Relevancy	Y	ChatGPT-4	Yes	Not Entirely Satisfactory	Y	NA	Y	Y	Y	Y
Requirements Engineering	Users' behavior tendencies, pain points, and other attributes, from LogData [32] (2024)	E	Mixed	Not evaluated	Concreteness, realism, and utility	Y	ChatGPT	No	Not Entirely Satisfactory	Y	NA	Y	Y	NA	Y
Release Planning	Decision-making Support for Release Plan [33] (2025)	E	Quantitative	Time savings, Manual interventions	Accuracy, Reliability	Y	ChatGPT-3.5 Turbo	Yes	Satisfatory	Y	NA	Y	Y	NA	Y
Requirements Engineering	Improve Requirements Quality [34] (2024)	C	Quantitative	Time savings	Precision, Relevancy, Faithfulness	Y	Mixtral 8x7B, LLaMA-2, Claude 3-opus, ChatGPT	Yes	Not Entirely Satisfactory	Y	Y	NA	NA	NA	Y
Requirements Engineering	Enhancing persona consistency for role-playing [35] (2024)	E	Quantitative	Time savings	Consistency	Y	Qwen-7B, Baichuan2-7B, CharacterGLM-6B, GPT-3.5 Turbo, GPT-4	Yes	Satisfatory	Y	NA	NA	Y	NA	Y
Customer Insights	Customer behavior simulation [36] (2024)	E	Mixed	Time savings	Accuracy	Y	ChatGPT-4	No	Not Entirely Satisfactory	NA	Y	N	Y	Y	Y
Requirements Engineering	User Stories Quality Evaluation [37] (2023)	E	Mixed	Not evaluated	Benchmarking	Y	ChatGPT-3.5	Yes	Not Entirely Satisfactory	Y	Y	Y	Y	Y	Y
Use Case Analysis															

3.4   Step 4 – Data Extraction, Analysis and Synthesis

This study used a two-phase qualitative analysis to synthesize findings from the selected papers.

3.5   Step 4.1 – Data Extraction

Following software engineering SLR guidelines [20], we extracted key metadata and relevant text segments from each study into a master spreadsheet. The extracted data was then subjected to a two-phase analysis: a descriptive analysis to summarize the literature, followed by an in-depth thematic analysis using deductive and inductive coding to identify key patterns and gaps.

3.6   Step 4.2 – Data Analysis

The data analysis and synthesis process were guided by established frameworks [19, 20] and were conducted in two stages:

Descriptive Analysis: First, a matrix was populated for each study to capture key characteristics, including its use case, methodology, benefits, limitations, tools and identified challenges. This provided a high-level overview of literature.

Thematic Analysis: An in-depth thematic analysis was conducted, beginning with an inductive coding approach to identify use cases and application areas, which were subsequently segmented according to an established PM framework [4]. Following this, a deductive approach was employed to determine the specific capabilities associated with each use case. Finally, a hybrid methodology was utilized to analyze challenges and limitations; this process used the themes defined in Table 1 as an initial coding framework while also allowing for the emergence of new concepts from the data.

4   Results

4.1   Literature Search and Study Selection

The study selection process is detailed in the PRISMA flow diagram presented in Fig. 1. An initial search across all databases identified 8,378 records. Following the screening process, 15 studies were selected for this review.

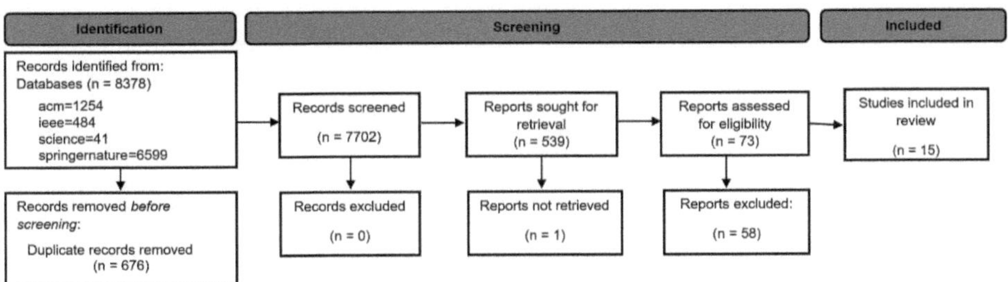

Fig. 2. PRISMA flow diagram for study selection

4.2 Descriptive Synthesis

The selected studies, as shown in Table 5, include papers on applying GenAI to diverse PM activities, such as customer insight analysis, prototyping, user story creation, and customer behavior simulation. Although all studies included an evaluation of their work, no common framework was employed. Sixty percent of the papers assessed both efficiency and effectiveness. The primary reported benefit was improved efficiency, demonstrated by time savings, faster delivery, and potential cost reductions. Effectiveness was measured using various metrics, such as insight quality, accuracy, and relevance. Costs reduction were mentioned in some cases, but no formal estimation or evaluation was provided.

Most experiments utilized versions of OpenAI's ChatGPT, yet only 40% of these studies provided justification for their model choice. Three studies conducted a comparative analysis of multiple models. The most frequently cited challenges were technical and implementation issues (93%), hallucinations and factuality (86%), and reliability and robustness (71%). In contrast, challenges related to bias and fairness, interpretability and explainability, and ethical and social implications were each evaluated in less than 43% of the studies.

4.3 Thematic Synthesis

The synthesis is structured around the primary use cases identified in the literature. For each use case, we detail its implementation, broader implications, and identified gaps and limitations, extending beyond the common challenges associated with LLMs, such as extrinsic hallucinations and inherent model biases.

Market Analysis

Established Capabilities. The literature demonstrates the application of LLMs for competitive feature analysis, as exemplified in the context of mobile apps [31]. By processing app descriptions, user feedback in app stores, and potential functionalities, LLMs can identify popular features, market trends, and unmet user needs. This capability suggests significant potential for automating and scaling competitive intelligence gathering.

Identified Gaps and Limitations. A comprehensive market understanding requires human analysts to filter and validate the insights, particularly in assessing the feasibility and market presence of novel features [31].

Customer Insights

Established Capabilities. Research has focused on transforming customer data into actionable assets. This process includes proactive customer insight extraction, the use of log data to identify user behavior and pain points, and the generation of user personas from live application activity. A potential advancement is the concept of "Active Personas," which are dynamic and evolve as new user data becomes available, moving beyond traditional static personas. Furthermore, research has provided robust methods to ensure persona consistency. A more advanced application involves using LLMs for simulation in addition to analysis. For instance, one study explored using ChatGPT as a simulation tool for the customer discovery process by generating synthetic customer personas and modeling their willingness to pay for a new service.

Identified Gaps and Limitations. The performance of LLMs in analyzing customer feedback is constrained by several significant challenges stemming from both interpretive and operational limitations. The models' reliance on training data, which often lacks contemporary slang and specific cultural nuances, can lead to the misinterpretation of user input. Furthermore, inherent difficulties in discerning tone, overcoming language barriers, and compensating for the absence of non-verbal cues may introduce bias into the analysis. Moreover, customer privacy concerns can deter open information sharing within these systems, limiting the richness and effectiveness of the data gathered.

Product Requirements Engineering

Established Capabilities. There is strong evidence of GenAI's potential to automate and enhance requirements engineering. Specific applications include generating initial drafts of user stories, supporting requirements elicitation through systematic questionnaires, and identifying critical questions to ensure comprehensive data gathering.

Furthermore, GenAI can be used for quality assurance by evaluating existing user stories against predefined criteria. Other use cases include idea generation and initial planning. One study even demonstrated using an LLM as a direct backend for a user interface, bringing mockups to life and enabling the rapid creation of interactive prototypes for immediate user feedback.

Identified Gaps and Limitations. Research indicates that these models are ineffective at comprehending non-functional requirements, a weakness attributed to their difficulties with ambiguity and a lack of contextual sensitivity. This accuracy issue is compounded by hallucinations, which can generate plausible yet incorrect responses, underscoring the need to equip it with more comprehensive domain knowledge. Furthermore, this deficiency is evidenced by studies where an LLM failed to recognize critical dependencies during user story creation, resulting in structurally flawed output. Consequently, these combined shortcomings affirm the ongoing necessity for human oversight to validate and revise GenAI-generated content, ensuring its practical viability and correctness.

Roadmapping and Release Planning

Established Capabilities. Directly assisting software release decisions by automating the analysis of complex, test data that generates concise reports to support go/no-go decisions, thereby enhancing the reliability of gatekeeping in the development cycle. Beyond this case, it's important to note that it mentions how other capabilities inform this one including the formulation of initial plans [24], the systematic prioritization of user stories [29], and the analysis of crowdsourced insights from app reviews [31].

Identified Gaps and Limitations. Human expertise remains critical for strategic decision-making, as processes like roadmapping and release planning can be compromised if they rely on AI-assisted outputs derived from flawed premises, such as market misreadings. This initial strategic instability inevitably cascades down to release planning, which inherits the flaws. The problem can be further amplified by a lack of transparency and traceability, particularly in the case of AI-driven prioritization recommendations.

5 Discussion

5.1 Discussion of Research Questions

In this discussion, we explore areas where GenAI can have the most significant impact on SPM.

RQ1: Which Cases and Themes Have Emerged as the Primary Focus of Recent Research on LLMs in Product Management?

The reviewed literature demonstrates a primary concentration on Strategic Management, particularly Market Analysis, and on Product Planning, specifically Customer Insights and Product Requirements Engineering. These domains encompass key outputs for Roadmapping and Release Planning that were highlighted, plus case explicitly covering Release Planning. Such a focus indicates that the scientific community perceives these areas as the most viable for exploration, thereby establishing them as the forefront of academic inquiry into the application of GenAI within PM.

RQ2: What Crucial Challenges and Considerations Emerged for Maximizing GenAI's Potential?

Maximizing the potential of GenAI requires addressing several crucial challenges. A significant hurdle involves enhancing the accuracy and consistency of LLMs, which necessitates embedding domain-specific knowledge to improve contextual understanding and develop the models' capacity to evaluate their own output quality. This is compounded by the difficulty of processing contemporary customer content, including evolving slang and cultural nuances, while navigating privacy constraints and confronting the ethical dimension of bias and misrepresentation due to stereotypes in the training data. Furthermore, the practical application of LLMs is constrained by their limited ability to assess the technological, risk, and regulatory feasibility of generated proposals or to manage the complexity of real-world data, and they may be unsuitable for handling non-functional requirements. Consequently, as a consistent finding across all explored use cases is the indispensable need for human oversight, determining the proper extent and nature of that involvement remains a central question for responsible implementation. This is compounded by the observed instability of LLM outputs, where repeated queries can yield different results, making reliability a significant challenge that requires mitigation strategies.

A systematic review of the literature reveals that prevailing research treats GenAI as a tool for augmenting or automating discrete PM tasks, with studies typically isolating a single activity, such as persona generation or requirements elicitation, for LLM application. Although this approach demonstrates clear efficiency gains at the task level, a significant finding is the lack of studies exploring the integration of these activities into a cohesive, end-to-end workflow. This gap highlights a disconnect between the current experimental phase and the potential for systemic transformation within the PM field. Consequently, the most promising future research direction lies not in the continued optimization of isolated tasks but in investigating how to interconnect these GenAI-powered functions.

RQ3: How will Advanced AI Capabilities Reshape PM?

As its technical capabilities mature and expertise in its application grows, GenAI is poised to reshape the field of PM by driving significant gains in efficiency, quality, and scope across the entire value delivery chain. In market analysis, GenAI can enhance competitive intelligence by synthesizing vast amounts of information, such as competitor strategies, and leveraging powerful algorithms to predict customer sentiment, thereby enabling broader, more rapid analysis and even the forecasting of competitive actions. It can also transform customer insight generation from a reactive, often biased endeavor into a continuous and predictive process by analyzing large quantities of unstructured feedback to identify latent needs and systematically structure them into actionable assets, such as user personas. Furthermore, GenAI can streamline requirements engineering by automating laborious tasks like drafting user stories, enabling the rapid creation of interactive prototypes, and providing analytical support to improve requirement quality. This analytical support can extend to release planning, where GenAI can assist in prioritizing features and refining iterative decision-making, ultimately allowing PM professionals to focus on more strategic initiatives and accelerate product lifecycles.

5.2 Methodological Observations

The literature reveals significant methodological limitations, including an overwhelming reliance on OpenAI's models and a lack of comparative analysis between different LLMs in most studies. Furthermore, a common evaluation framework is absent, as concepts such as 'efficiency' and 'effectiveness' are often not properly structured or covered. Reliability, for example, could be considered a critical aspect for evaluation exemplified by [37] which found inconsistent outputs when testing the same task multiple times, indicating that demonstrating the reliability of achieved results would be highly beneficial for all studies. Additionally, while some studies argue for benefits such as cost savings, they provide no evaluation rationale, rendering such claims implicit and unsubstantiated.

Consequently, the current body of research is more characteristic of preliminary experiments with specific models than a mature exploration of GenAI's systemic impact on PM. While studies report positive outcomes, such as time savings and enhanced insights, these findings are intrinsically tied to specific models. This renders claims of effectiveness subjective and incomparable, raising substantial questions about their generalizability. In contrast, [29, 34, 35] provides examples of more robust methodological practices for evaluating and comparing the performance of multiple LLMs.

5.3 Underexplored Research Areas

To enrich our findings, incorporating practitioner literature from industry blogs, talks, and surveys is essential to capture real-world AI use cases in PM. This practical approach provides a comprehensive overview of key activities often missing from academic work, helps measure AI's impact on generic tasks (e.g., using GenAI for strategy definition and review), and allows for the extrapolation of findings.

Further analysis is needed to determine how well GenAI is suited for PM activities and the level of difficulty in implementing the necessary tools. For instance, an out-of-the-box GenAI can provide a superficial market analysis—limited by its training data and propensity for hallucinations—that may be sufficient for a quick overview. However, achieving more focused and up-to-date results through advanced solutions, such as pulling relevant market data and implementing a Retrieval-Augmented Generation

(RAG) system requires a substantial upfront investment. A key question is whether the benefits of using GenAI for in-depth analysis justify this cost, as the incremental value may be limited once the data is curated.

Current research tends to overlook integrated systems, focusing excessively on isolated tasks. Future studies should therefore address how AI alters collaboration and teamwork dynamics. Finally, the resulting impact on performance and efficiency requires further investigation. A standardized evaluation methodology is crucial for consistently assessing GenAI's impact on PM, enabling more rapid and replicable studies across different models to project the evolution of GenAI's influence.

5.4 Future Directions

Future research should explore the extent to which AI will dominate the creation and evolution of product management artifacts and, consequently, define the essential, evolving purpose of human oversight. As reliance on AI-driven insights from vast datasets increases, it is imperative to investigate how to prevent the erosion of genuine customer empathy and to assess whether an algorithm can truly capture the nuance of human need. Further inquiry is needed to determine if the quest for optimized team flow and predictable velocity comes at the cost of the creative friction necessary for breakthrough innovation. Ultimately, future studies should investigate whether the endgame of AI in product management is simply to reduce failures and alter lifecycles, or if it is to fundamentally redefine the very meaning of product success.

5.5 Threats to Validity

We acknowledge several threats to this review's validity. *Internal validity* may be affected by selection bias, as our search was limited to four databases and could have missed relevant studies. Subjective judgment was also a factor in quality assessment and data synthesis, which relates to *construct validity*. For *external validity*, excluding gray literature and using specific keywords may limit the generalizability of our findings to practitioner contexts and related concepts. Finally, *temporal validity* is a limitation, as our conclusions are contingent on the literature available at the time of the review and may be superseded by future work.

6 Conclusion

Early applications of GenAI in PM indicate a nascent but rapidly advancing field, demonstrating results primarily in efficiency and, to a lesser extent, efficacy. While many use cases remain experimental and focused on accessible tasks such as user story generation, recent research demonstrates an expansion into more complex, high-stakes operational domains like release management support. This trend confirms the significant potential of GenAI to enhance effectiveness and drive innovation in core PM activities, although this potential requires further exploration.

The absence of standardized evaluation frameworks prevents meaningful comparisons across studies, while a predominant focus on a narrow range of LLMs limits technological breadth and complicates the assessment of broader evolutionary trends. Consequently, research findings are often transient, risking rapid obsolescence with the emergence of new models. Furthermore, the current emphasis on intermediate metrics focuses on output, and should be expanded for crucial outcome metrics such as product delivery speed and user satisfaction.

A promising future application of GenAI in PM involves creating an integrated, intelligent workflow that spans the entire product lifecycle. This approach entails moving from automating discrete tasks toward developing integrated systems, a vision exemplified by [33]. Rather than generating a user story in isolation, the system connects data analysis directly to the release management workflow, bridging the gap between raw data and actionable insights. This represents a tangible step toward an intelligent, interconnected product lifecycle where LLMs augment key decision points, allowing product managers to focus on strategic initiatives. This integrated vision, extending beyond discrete task automation, represents the next frontier for research and practice.

In summary, while valuable LLM use cases are emerging in PM, the research community must overcome significant methodological and conceptual gaps. This requires a shift from a model-centric perspective to a holistic, problem-oriented view that leverages a suite of advanced AI techniques to solve core PM challenges with greater rigor. This review establishes a baseline and calls for more rigorous and impactful future investigations into the applications of GenAI in PM.

References

1. Kanbach, D.K., Heiduk, L., Blueher, G., et al.: The GenAI is out of the bottle: generative artificial intelligence from a business model innovation perspective. RMS **18**, 1189–1220 (2024). https://doi.org/10.1007/s11846-023-00696-z
2. Bouzid, A., Narciso, P., Ma, W.: Harnessing Generative AI for Product Innovation. In: Generative AI For Executives, pp. 87–103. Apress, Berkeley, CA (2024)
3. Farquhar, S., Kossen, J., Kuhn, L., Gal, Y.: Detecting hallucinations in large language models using semantic entropy. Nature **630**, 625–630 (2024). https://doi.org/10.1038/s41586-024-07421-0
4. Kittlaus, H.-B.: Software Product Management –The ISPMA-Compliant Study Guide and Handbook, 2nd edn., p. 2022. Springer-Verlag, New York / Berlin / Heidelberg (2022)
5. Xu, Y., Liu, X., Cao, X., et al.: Artificial intelligence: a powerful paradigm for scientific research. Innov. **2**, 100179 (2021). https://doi.org/10.1016/j.xinn.2021.100179
6. Huang, G., Huang, K.: ChatGPT in Product Management, pp 97–127 (2023)
7. Cagan M.: AI Product Management 2 Years In (2024)
8. Bratsis I.: AI Product Manager's Handbook: Build, Integrate, Scale, and Optimize Products to Grow as an AI Product Manager. Packt Publishing Ltd (2024)
9. Olsson, H.H., Bosch, J.: Strategic digital product management in the age of AI. In: Lecture Notes in Business Information Processing (2024)
10. Ogundipe, D.O., Babatunde, S.O., Abaku, E.A.: AI and product management: a theoretical overview from idea to market. Int. J. Manag. Entrep. Res. **6**, 950–969 (2024). https://doi.org/10.51594/ijmer.v6i3.965
11. Mahajan P (2024) Artificial Intelligence in Product Management. International Journal of Computer Trends and Technology 72:84–93. https://doi.org/10.14445/22312803/IJCTT-V72 I6P112

12. Khare, P., Srivastava, S.: The impact of AI on product management: a systematic review and future trends. Int. J. Res. Anal. Rev. **9**, 736–741 (2022)
13. Parikh, N.A.: Managing AI-first products: roles, skills, challenges, and strategies of AI product managers IEEE Eng. Manage. Rev., 1–11 (2025). https://doi.org/10.1109/EMR.2025.3530942
14. Gallegos, I.O., Rossi, R.A., Barrow, J., et al.: Bias and fairness in large language models: a survey. Comput. Linguist. **50**, 1097–1179 (2024). https://doi.org/10.1162/coli_a_00524
15. Bilal A, Ebert D, Lin B.: LLMs for explainable AI: a comprehensive survey (2025)
16. Laskar, M.T.R., Alqahtani, S., Bari, M.S., et al.: A systematic survey and critical review on evaluating large language models: challenges, limitations, and recommendations. In: Proceedings of the 2024 Conference on Empirical Methods in Natural Language Processing. Association for Computational Linguistics, Stroudsburg, PA, USA, pp 13785–13816 (2024)
17. Sapkota, R., Roumeliotis, K.I., Karkee, M.: AI agents vs. agentic AI: a conceptual taxonomy, applications and challenges (2025)
18. Bikkasani, D.C.: Navigating artificial general intelligence (AGI): societal implications, ethical considerations, and governance strategies. AI Ethics **5**, 2021–2036 (2025). https://doi.org/10.1007/s43681-024-00642-z
19. Page, M.J., McKenzie, J.E., Bossuyt, P.M., et al.: The PRISMA 2020 statement: an updated guideline for reporting systematic reviews. BMJ **372** (2021)
20. Kitchenham B (2007) Guidelines for performing systematic literature reviews in software engineering. Technical report, Ver 23 EBSE Technical Report EBSE
21. Hegazy, S., Elsner, C., Bosch, J., Olsson, H.H.: Analytics and data-driven methods and practices in platform ecosystems: a systematic literature review. In: 2023 49th Euromicro Conference on Software Engineering and Advanced Applications (SEAA). IEEE, pp 61–69 (2023)
22. Kmet, L.M., Cook, L.S., Lee, R.C.: Standard quality assessment criteria for evaluating primary research papers from a variety of fields (2004)
23. Shahin, M., Chen, F.F., Maghanaki, M., Hosseinzadeh, A.: Adapting the GPT engine for proactive customer insight extraction in product development. Manuf Lett **41**, 1376–1385 (2024). https://doi.org/10.1016/J.MFGLET.2024.09.164
24. Paliwal G, Donvir A, Gujar P, Panyam S.: Accelerating time-to-market: the role of generative AI in product development. In: 2024 IEEE Colombian Conference on Communications and Computing (COLCOM). IEEE, pp 1–9 (2024)
25. Simaremare, M., Edison, H.: Accelerating new product development: a vision on active personas, pp 461–466 (2025)
26. Brockenbrough, A., Salinas, D.: Using generative AI to create user stories in the software engineering classroom. In: 2024 36th International Conference on Software Engineering Education and Training (CSEE&T). IEEE, pp 1–5 (2024)
27. Rauer, J., Pham, T.K.B., Supakkul, S., et al.: Service-oriented requirements elicitation through systematic questionnaire design: a problem-driven GenAI approach, pp 236–252 (2025)
28. Kronhardt, K., Hoffmann, S., Adelt, F., Gerken, J.: PERSONÆR - Transparency Enhancing Tool for LLM-Generated User Personas from Live Website Visits. In: Proceedings of the International Conference on Mobile and Ubiquitous Multimedia. ACM, New York, NY, USA, pp 527–531 (2024)
29. Sami, M.A., Waseem, M., Zhang, Z., et al.: AI based Multiagent Approach for Requirements Elicitation and Analysis (2024)
30. Petridis, S., Terry, M., Cai, C.J.: PromptInfuser: Bringing User Interface Mock-ups to Life with Large Language Models. In: Extended Abstracts of the 2023 CHI Conference on Human Factors in Computing Systems, pp. 1–6. ACM, New York, NY, USA (2023)

31. Wei, J., Courbis, A-L., Lambolais, T., et al.: Getting inspiration for feature elicitation: app store- vs. LLM-based approach. In: Proceedings of the 39th IEEE/ACM International Conference on Automated Software Engineering. ACM, New York, NY, USA, pp 857–869 (2024)

32. Sera, R., Washizaki, H., Chen, J., et al.: Development of data-driven persona including user behavior and pain point through clustering with user log of B2B software. In: Proceedings of the 2024 IEEE/ACM 17th International Conference on Cooperative and Human Aspects of Software Engineering. ACM, New York, NY, USA, pp 85–90 (2024)

33. Khoee AG, Yu Y, Feldt R, et al (2025) GoNoGo: An Efficient LLM-Based Multi-agent System for Streamlining Automotive Software Release Decision-Making. pp 30–45

34. Biswas, C., Das, S.: ARIA-QA: AI-agent based requirements inspection and analysis through question answering. Innov. Syst. Softw. Eng. **21**, 1009–1024 (2025). https://doi.org/10.1007/s11334-024-00589-8

35. Shi, H., Niu, K.: Enhancing persona consistency with large language models. In: Proceedings of the 2024 5th International Conference on Computing, Networks and Internet of Things. ACM, New York, NY, USA, pp 210–215 (2024)

36. Ilagan, J.B., Alabastro, Z.M., Basallo, C.L., Ilagan, J.R.: Exploratory customer discovery through simulation using ChatGPT and prompt engineering, pp 51–60 (2024)

37. Ronanki, K., Cabrero-Daniel, B., Berger, C.: ChatGPT as a tool for user story quality evaluation: trustworthy out of the box? pp 173–181 (2024)

Detecting Technical Debt in Source Code Changes Using Large Language Models

Merve Astekin[(✉)], Arda Goknil, Sagar Sen, Simeon Tverdal, and Phu Nguyen

SINTEF, Oslo, Norway
{merve.astekin,arda.goknil,sagar.sen,
simeon.tverdal,phu.nguyen}@sintef.no

Abstract. Technical Debt (TD) remains a critical challenge in software engineering, degrading maintainability and long-term quality. While traditional TD detection methods rely heavily on static analysis and manual inspection, recent advances in Large Language Models (LLMs) offer a compelling new approach for automating and scaling this process. In this paper, we present DebtGuardian, the first open-source LLM-based framework for detecting TD directly from source code changes. DebtGuardian combines zero-shot and few-shot prompting strategies, supports both granular and batch-level detection, and employs GuardrailsAI for validating and standardizing model outputs. To enhance robustness, it enables majority voting across multiple LLMs. We evaluate DebtGuardian using the MLCQ dataset, applying a variety of state-of-the-art open-source LLMs specialized for code understanding, as well as generalpurpose LLMs. The results demonstrate that granular prompting, codespecialized models, and larger context windows significantly improve TD detection performance. Majority voting boosts recall by 8.17%, showing clear benefits in model ensemble strategies. We also conduct a detailed evaluation of line-level metrics and find that using a 10-line threshold achieves the best balance between precision and tolerance for small discrepancies in predicted TD locations. DebtGuardian advances the field by offering a flexible, extensible, and empirically validated LLM-based solution for TD detection. Our framework paves the way for integrating AI-driven analysis into continuous integration pipelines, making TD management more scalable and accurate in modern software development workflows.

Keywords: Software quality · Technical debt detection · Large language models

1 Introduction

In fast-paced software development, technical debt (TD) is inevitable. Introduced by Cunningham [11], TD refers to future costs from quick, suboptimal solutions. As systems grow more complex, effective TD detection and management becomes essential for sustaining software quality, efficiency, and long-term

G. Scanniello et al. (Eds.): PROFES 2025, LNCS 16361, pp. 334–352, 2026.
https://doi.org/10.1007/978-3-032-12089-2_21

maintainability [6,7]. A closely related notion is that of code smells, symptoms in source code that suggest deeper design or maintainability issues [13]. Code smells often act as observable indicators of underlying code-related TD, since they often increase maintenance effort and reduce evolvability if left unaddressed. We scope our study to this code-related dimension of TD, operationalized through code smells.

Detecting TD in source code changes requires a nuanced understanding of programming constructs, design principles, and component interactions [1]. While static analysis tools like SonarQube [8], CAST [12], and Squore [5] have advanced debt detection, they rely on predefined rules and often miss semantic issues, such as misuse of inheritance instead of composition, architectural drift like introducing cross-layer dependencies, or maintainability issues from adding duplicated logic across modules. Large Language Models (LLMs) offer a flexible alternative, capable of analyzing both code and unstructured artifacts like code comments. Unlike static analyzers, LLMs are language-agnostic, easy to deploy, require minimal setup, and can detect TD without relying on heavy rule engineering, making them especially promising for early prototyping and evolving systems where adaptability and broad coverage are critical. Despite their promise, LLM-based TD detection faces key challenges. Output varies with prompt and model choice [22,24,30,33], causing inconsistencies. False positives are common, and probabilistic behavior complicates evaluation [9,22]. Potential data leakage raises concerns about inflated performance metrics. High costs, latency, and opacity in proprietary models like ChatGPT limit CI/CD integration [10,26].

To address these challenges, we propose and assess DebtGuardian, an LLM-powered tool for automated technical debt detection in source code changes. DebtGuardian leverages open-source language models and combines zero-shot and few-shot prompting strategies to improve detection accuracy. To mitigate output inconsistencies, it employs majority voting by querying multiple LLMs and aggregating their responses. DebtGuardian is evaluated using two metrics: exact matches between predicted and ground truth line ranges, and a more lenient overlap-based criterion to capture near-miss detections. Central to DebtGuardian is its integration with Guardrails-AI [16], an open-source Python framework used to validate and structure LLM outputs. We chose Guardrails-AI over tools like Instructor [17] and Marvin [25] due to its flexible validation logic, support for complex rules, and extensible custom validators. DebtGuardian follows a three-step process: it first extracts and analyzes source code changes, then generates targeted prompts aligned with a TD schema using Guardrails-AI, and finally validates LLM responses. When outputs fail validation, Guardrails-AI appends corrective instructions (e.g., "Fix the JSON formatting") to the original prompt and resubmits it to the LLM while preserving conversational context, allowing the model to iteratively "learn" from its previous error. Once validated, outputs are classified by TD type and stored for developer action.

To evaluate DebtGuardian, we conduct an extensive study using the MLCQ dataset [23], a curated benchmark that annotates code smells as proxies for code TD in specific code fragments from real-world open-source Java projects.

Each instance is linked to its TD type, severity, and precise location within the codebase. Unlike outputs from static analysis tools like SonarQube, the MLCQ annotations are created by human experts who assess subjective design issues such as Blob, Data Class, and Feature Envy. These code smells often depend on contextual factors like developer intent and system architecture, which rule-based tools struggle to infer. As a result, MLCQ offers a richer and more nuanced ground truth for evaluating LLM-based detection. We benchmark six state-of-the-art open-source LLMs on this dataset, analyzing the effects of prompting strategies, model size, context length, and domain specialization.

Results show that code-specialized models outperform general-purpose ones by up to 115.8% in average recall. Larger context windows improve recall by 26–43%, and granular prompting outperforms batch prompting by 8–10%. The best-performing model, Qwen2.5-Coder:7b, achieves 77% average recall. Majority voting boosts recall by 8.17%, especially for hard-to-detect TD types. Since missed technical debt poses greater long-term risk than occasional false positives, recall is prioritized over precision—capturing more potential debt enables proactive review and mitigation. While LLMs detect debt presence effectively using file- and line-level metrics, precisely locating TD remains challenging. These findings demonstrate the value of open-source LLMs, structured prompting, and ensemble techniques in advancing automated TD detection. Our key contributions include:

- **DebtGuardian Framework**: An open-source LLM-based system for TD detection in code changes, integrating Guardrails-AI, prompting strategies, and majority voting to enhance reliability.
- **Prompting Strategy Design**: Evaluation of zero-shot and few-shot prompts, and comparison between batch and granular detection strategies.
- **Systematic Evaluation**: Extensive analysis using the MLCQ dataset adapted for commit- and file-level TD assessment.
- **Cross-Model Benchmarking**: Performance comparison of six state-of-the-art open-source LLMs across TD types, analyzing model size, context length, and domain specialization.
- **Majority Voting Integration**: Demonstrated recall gains from aggregating outputs across models, especially for context-sensitive debt.
- **Evaluation Metrics**: Two-level evaluation—file and line-level with thresholding—balancing detection coverage and localization precision.
- **Open-Source and Reproducibility**: Full release of DebtGuardian and its experiments using open models, ensuring transparency and reproducibility[1].

The paper is structured as follows. In Sect. 2, we present DebtGuardian. Section 3 reports on the evaluation. In Sect. 4, we provide insights into our evaluation. We give related work in Sect. 5. Section 6 concludes the paper.

---

[1] https://doi.org/10.5281/zenodo.16947426.

2 DebtGuardian Approach

Our approach (Fig. 1) introduces DebtGuardian, a multistage pipeline that identifies and validates technical debt (TD) in source code repositories using large language models (LLMs) and schema-based validation. The pipeline consists of three main steps: (1) source code loading and commit analysis, (2) debt identification, and (3) LLM output validation. The process enables structured, interpretable detection of TD types, even those not easily captured by traditional static analysis tools.

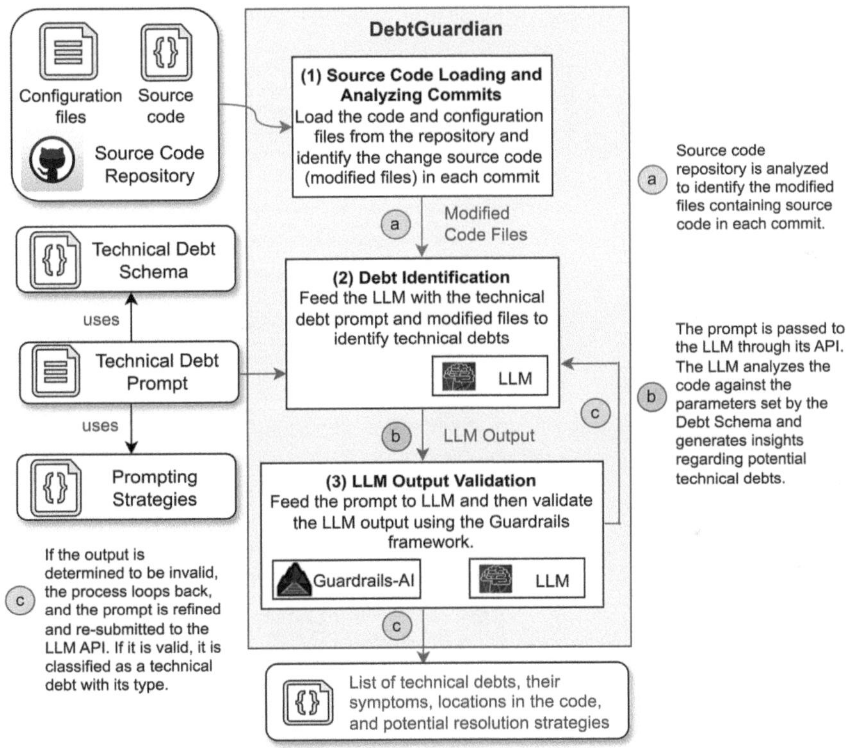

Fig. 1. Overview of DebtGuardian.

In Step 1 (Fig. 1, box 1), DebtGuardian connects to a source code repository and retrieves commits along with associated configuration and source files. It analyzes commit histories to detect modified files—typically indicative of evolving or problematic code regions. These modified files (Fig. 1, arrow a) serve as the basis for TD detection and are passed to the next stage.

In Step 2 (Fig. 1, box 2), DebtGuardian constructs LLM prompts that combine the modified code files with a structured technical debt schema. This schema—defined using Pydantic—captures core properties of TD such as the debt type, symptom, location, and suggested remediation (see Fig. 2, box 4). By embedding this schema into the prompt alongside the code snippet (entire Fig. 2),

DebtGuardian ensures that the LLM response is both syntactically and semantically aligned with the intended output format. The use of prompting strategies further enhances accuracy, generalization, and interpretability.

In Step 3 (Fig. 1, box 3), DebtGuardian validates the LLM-generated output using Guardrails-AI [16]. The technical debt schema is encoded in a RAIL (Reliable AI Markup Language) specification, which defines the output structure and allowed values. Guardrails enforces this specification by validating the JSON-formatted LLM response (Fig. 1, arrow c). When violations are detected, such as incorrect types or malformed fields, Guardrails issues automatic reasks with corrective instructions and preserves conversational context to guide the LLM to compliance. The result is a validated and structured list of technical debt instances, each annotated with its type, symptoms, location in the code, and potential resolution strategy (Fig. 1, bottom output node). By combining LLM

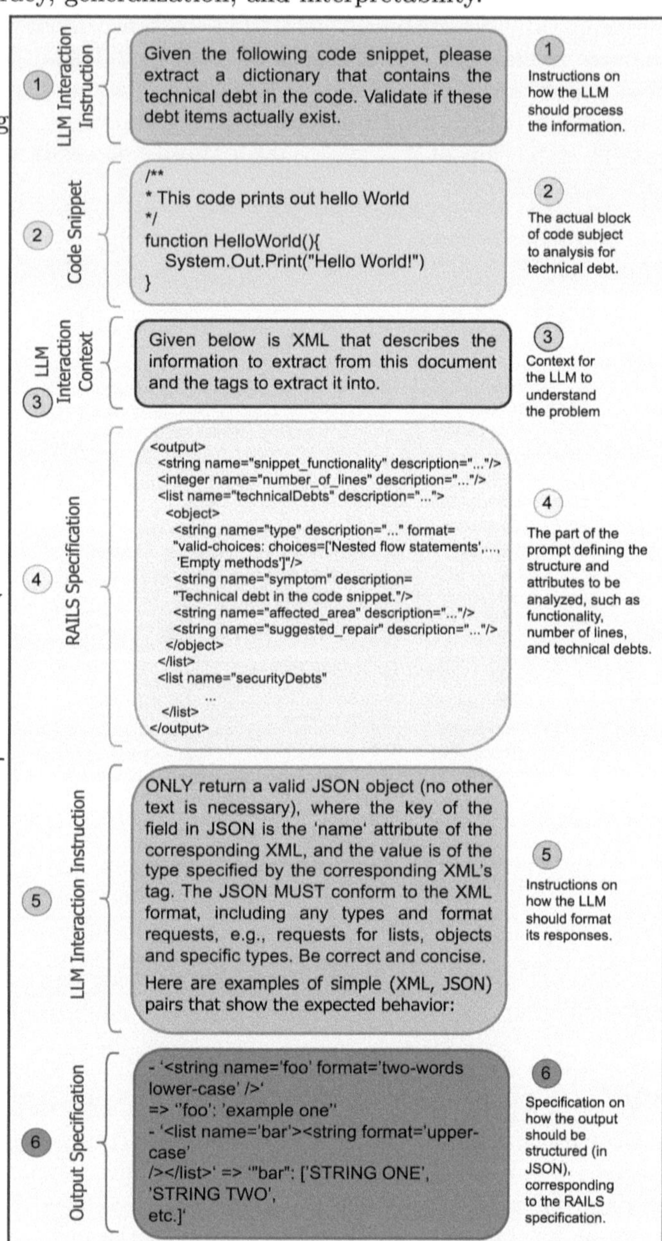

Fig. 2. Example prompt in DebtGuardian.

reasoning with structured prompts and schema-based validation, DebtGuardian offers a scalable, interpretable, and project-adaptive framework for TD detection that extends beyond the limitations of rule-based static analysis tools.

DebtGuardian employs multiple prompting strategies to enhance the accuracy and reliability of TD detection in source code modifications. The main strategies are:

- **Zero-shot prompting:** Prompts are issued to the LLM without examples, relying entirely on the model's pretrained understanding of technical debt concepts.
- **Few-shot prompting:** Prompts include illustrative examples of annotated technical debt instances, enabling the LLM to generalize more effectively across similar patterns in the input.
- **Batch prompting:** A single prompt includes instructions for detecting multiple debt types at once, improving efficiency and enabling the model to reason over interrelated patterns.
- **Granular prompting:** Prompts are narrowly focused on one debt type per request, allowing for fine-tuned and high-precision analysis in targeted scenarios.
- **Majority voting:** Results from multiple LLM runs are aggregated, and only the most frequently reported debt instances are retained to increase robustness and reduce stochastic variance.
- **Strategy combination:** Strategies such as few-shot learning and batch prompting can be combined with majority voting to maximize both precision and recall in TD detection.

3 Evaluation

In our evaluation, we address three Research Questions:

- ***RQ1.*** *How do different LLMs and prompting strategies impact the performance and reliability of technical debt detection in source code modifications?*
- ***RQ2.*** *How does majority voting across multiple LLMs influence the performance of technical debt identification?*
- ***RQ3.*** *How do different evaluation metrics affect the assessment of technical debt detection, and which metric provides the most reliable insights?*

3.1 Experiment Design

Dataset: Identifying a suitable dataset for evaluating technical debt (TD) detection in code changes was challenging, as few provide detailed, versioned annotations reflecting real-world practices. After reviewing available options, we selected the MLCQ (Madeyski Lewowski Code Quest) dataset [23], which uniquely offers expert-validated TD instances linked to source code modifications. Our choice prioritized professional annotations, version history, and project diversity. Alternative datasets were found inadequate. The Landfill dataset [27], despite its influence, lacked working repository links, limiting reproducibility. *The Technical Debt Dataset* [18] relied on tool-generated labels without expert input, reducing reliability. MLCQ provides over 15,000 annotated TD instances from open-source Java projects, covering multiple debt types (blob, long method, feature envy, data class) and severity levels (none, minor, major, critical). Unlike isolated samples, it captures TD in the context of actual code changes. To support our change-based analysis in DebtGuardian, we updated commit hashes to recover original modifications, enabling a realistic evaluation of both file-level detection and TD localization.

Preprocessing: We refined the dataset by correcting commit hashes to access original modified files and converting the format from CSV to JSON, keeping key fields: commit hash, repository, file path, TD type, and line ranges. We retained only 'major' and 'critical' TD items, discarding entries from inaccessible repositories, missing files, and hidden or outdated content. The final dataset (Table 1) includes 201 repositories, 375 commits, and 438 files across four TD categories.

An important characteristic of MLCQ is that each record represents an evaluation of

Artifact	Count
Repositories	201
Commits	375
Files	438
Blob TD items	155
Long method TD items	93
Feature envy TD items	82
Data class TD items	191

Table 1. Overview of preprocessed MLCQ dataset.

a specific (sample, code smell type) pair. A 'none' severity value indicates the absence of that particular smell, but not necessarily the absence of all smells. Consequently, the dataset does not directly provide true negative examples at the snippet level. To approximate such cases, we manually inspected a subset of records annotated with 'none' and verified whether the corresponding code snippets were free from all four smell types. This process yielded 47 manually validated negative samples, which we then used in experiments to complement the recall-based evaluation with an assessment of true negative handling.

Models: To evaluate DebtGuardian, we selected recent state-of-the-art LLMs based on availability, size, context window, and code-task suitability. The set includes both code-specialized and general-purpose models. Table 2 lists their versions, sizes, and context limits. Our selection includes Qwen2.5-Coder and CodeGemma (code-specialized), their base models Qwen2.5 and Gemma, and high-capacity models DeepSeek-Coder-V2 and Codestral. Most were released within six months of the experiments. Instruct versions were chosen for their prompt-handling capabilities.

Setup: We ran experiments using the Ollama Python library on a server with an NVIDIA RTX 6000 Ada (48GB) GPU. For Qwen2.5-Coder (7B), CodeGemma (7B), and DeepSeek-Coder-V2 (16B), evaluations were done at both 2K and maximum context lengths; other models were tested only at their maximum. All runs used a temperature of 0 for reproducibility.

Table 2. Overview of large language models used in the experiments.

Model	Version(s)/Release time	Model size	Context length
Qwen2.5-Coder	qwen2.5-coder:7b-instruct, qwen2.5-coder:14b-instruct/ November, 2024	7B 14B	128K
Qwen2.5	Qwen2.5:7b-instruct/ October, 2024	7B	128K
CodeGemma	codegemma:7b-instruct/ July, 2024	7B	8K
Gemma	gemma:7b-instruct/ February, 2024	7B	8K
DeepSeek-Coder-V2	deepseek-coder-v2:16b/ June, 2024	16B	128K
Codestral	codestral:22b/ September, 2024	22B	32K

3.2 Evaluation Metrics

To assess DebtGuardian's performance, we adopt a two-tiered evaluation: **file-level** and **line-level** metrics. This captures both the ability to detect technical debt (TD) and the precision in locating it.

We primarily report **Recall**, because most MLCQ records are labeled 'none' for the evaluated TD type, making the dataset predominantly negative at the type level. However, 'none' indicates the absence of only a specific TD type and does not guarantee that a code snippet is free of all technical debt. To estimate performance on truly non-smelly code, we manually inspected a subset of 'none' records and verified that the corresponding code snippets were free from all four TD types. This process yielded 47 manually validated negative samples, which we used to compute an exploratory **True Negative Rate (TNR)**. Given the small size of this set relative to the full dataset, TNR results are presented as indicative rather than definitive.

File-Level Evaluation. This evaluates whether DebtGuardian correctly identifies the presence of a specific TD type in a file, regardless of location. A prediction is correct if the model flags a file containing the targeted debt type. We compute standard classification metrics: TP (correctly flagged files), and FN (missed). This reflects how well LLMs highlight files for review.

Line-Level Evaluation. This assesses whether DebtGuardian pinpoints the TD location. Let (s_p, e_p) and (s_g, e_g) denote predicted and ground truth line ranges. A correct prediction must:

1. Identify the correct TD type, and
2. Match or acceptably overlap with the ground truth range.

This fine-grained evaluation measures the model's localization accuracy. Combining both metrics offers a comprehensive view of DebtGuardian's ability

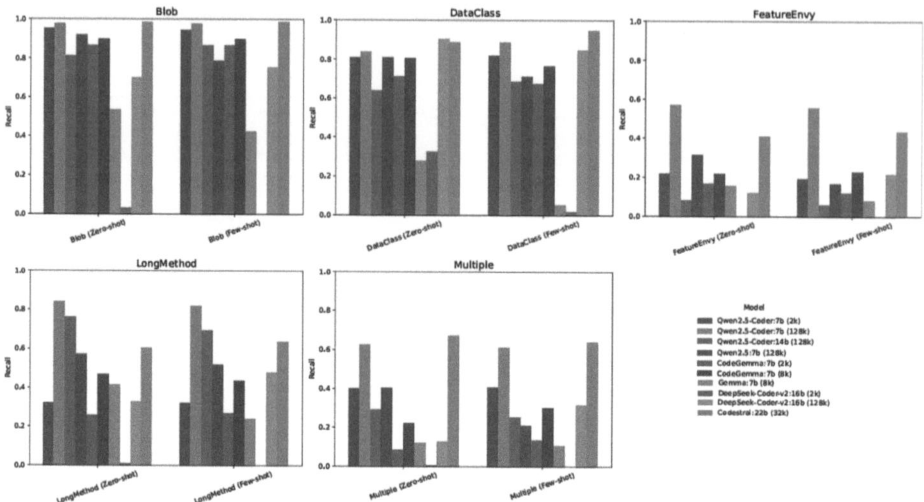

Fig. 3. Recall comparison by prompting strategy and model configuration (Line-level, TH = 10).

to detect and locate TD, clarifying strengths and limitations of different LLM configurations in evolving codebases.

3.3   Results

RQ1: Effectiveness of Models and Prompting Strategies in Detecting Technical Debt. To answer *RQ1*, we evaluated DebtGuardian using six state-of-the-art LLMs across various prompting strategies and TD types. We focused on two factors: (i) **Prompting strategy:** Zero-shot vs. Few-shot, Granular vs. Batch; and (ii) **Model characteristics:** size, context window, and specialization (code-specific vs. general-purpose). In the Granular setting, each prompt targets a single technical debt (TD) type (**Blob, Data Class, Feature Envy**, or **Long Method**), while the Batch setting combines all four types into one comprehensive prompt (called **Multiple**). Each setup is tested with both Zero-shot and Few-shot strategies, resulting in configurations named *[TD Type] ([Prompt Type])* (e.g., *Blob (Zero-shot), Multiple (Few-shot).*

Evaluation Metric. As described in Sect. 3.2, we primarily report **Recall** due to the type-specific nature of MLCQ labels. Precision and F1 may be underestimated, while exploratory **TNR** on 47 manually validated negatives provides a preliminary view of performance on truly non-smelly code.

Zero-Shot vs. Few-Shot Prompts. Figure 3 shows that **Few-shot prompting** does not consistently outperform **Zero-shot**. For instance, Qwen2.5-Coder:14b (128k) and Gemma:7b (8k) achieve higher recall with Zero-shot. Anchoring effects from unrepresentative examples may hinder Few-shot performance.

Granular vs. Batch Prompts. Granular prompts outperform Batch across TD types (e.g., Blob Zero-shot reaches 0.84 recall vs. Multiple Few-shot at 0.35). This indicates that joint queries overload models and dilute focus, whereas single-target prompts lead to better detection, especially for Blob and Data Class. Feature Envy remains challenging across all setups.

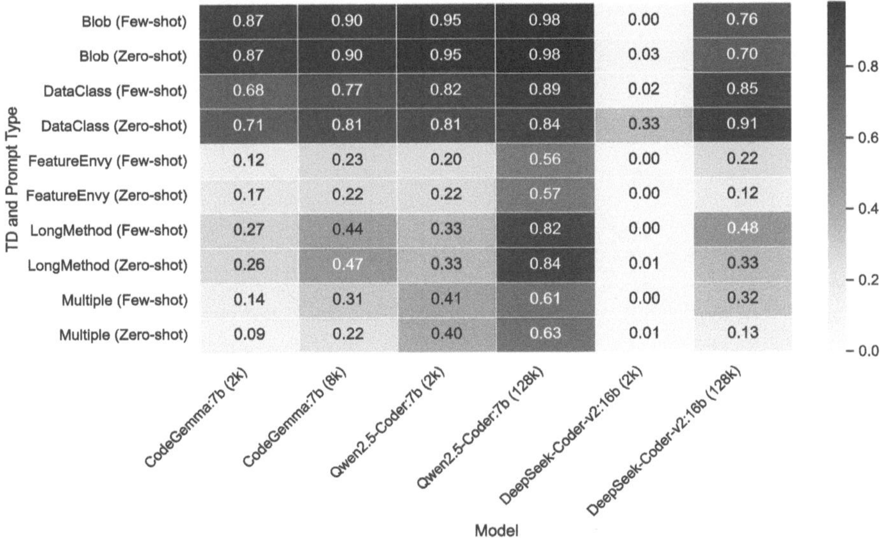

Fig. 4. Recall heatmap across prompts and models at default vs. max context lengths.

Context Window. Figure 4 shows significant recall gains with increased context length. DeepSeek-Coder-v2:16b improves over 1000% from 2k to 128k, while Qwen2.5-Coder:7b and CodeGemma:7b gain 43% and 26%, respectively. Larger windows improve reasoning over extended code.

Model Size. Recall does not consistently improve with model size (Fig. 5). Qwen2.5-Coder:14b underperforms its 7b variant. Codestral:22b performs best for Blob/Data Class but is outmatched by Qwen2.5-Coder:7b on Feature Envy and Long Method. Thus, size alone is not a predictor of TD detection accuracy.

Model Specialization. Figures 6 and 7 compare general and code-specialized variants. Code-specialized LLMs show substantial gains: CodeGemma:7b achieves 115.83% higher recall than Gemma:7b; Qwen2.5-Coder:7b outperforms Qwen2.5:7b by 42.09%. This highlights that domain specialization for code tasks substantially improves debt detection, even among models with identical size and architecture.

Best Models per TD Type. Table 3 lists top performers for each TD type based on average recall values. Codestral:22b excels at class-level TDs (Blob,

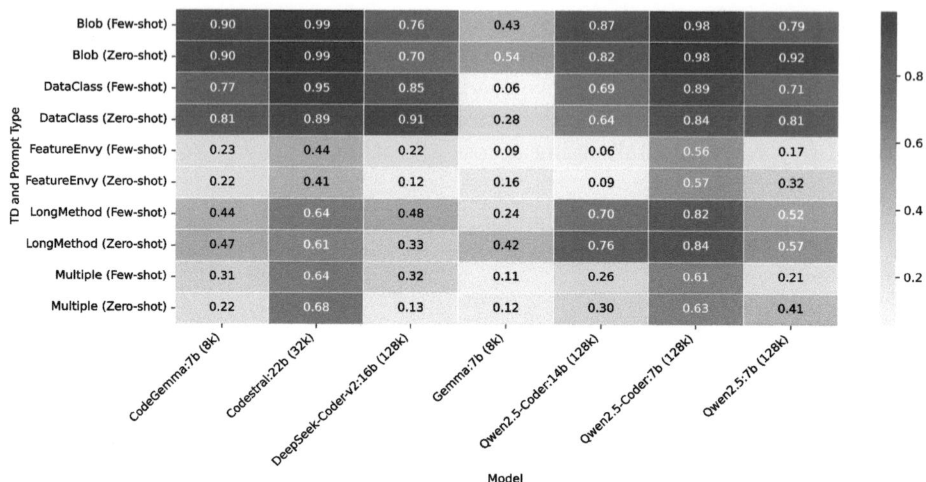

Fig. 5. Recall heatmap at max context lengths (Line-level, TH = 10).

Data Class), while Qwen2.5-Coder:7b leads for method-level TDs (Feature Envy, Long Method) and is the overall best-performing model.

Table 3. Best Models by TD Type (TH = 10)

TD Type	Best Avg. Recall	Model
Blob	0.99	Codestral:22b
Data Class	0.92	Codestral:22b
Feature Envy	0.57	Qwen2.5-Coder:7b
Long Method	0.83	Qwen2.5-Coder:7b
Overall	**0.77**	**Qwen2.5-Coder:7b**

Exploratory True Negative Evaluation. In addition to recall, we performed an exploratory evaluation on the 47 manually validated TN samples using only the two best-performing models from prior experiments: Qwen2.5-Coder:7b and Codestral:22b. Both Zero-shot and Few-shot Batch prompting strategies were tested. Across these configurations, the tool achieved a TNR ranging from 0.59 to 0.84, with Qwen2.5-Coder:7b achieving the highest TNR. While limited in scope, this analysis complements the recall-focused evaluation and provides a first estimate of DebtGuardian's behavior on truly non-smelly code.

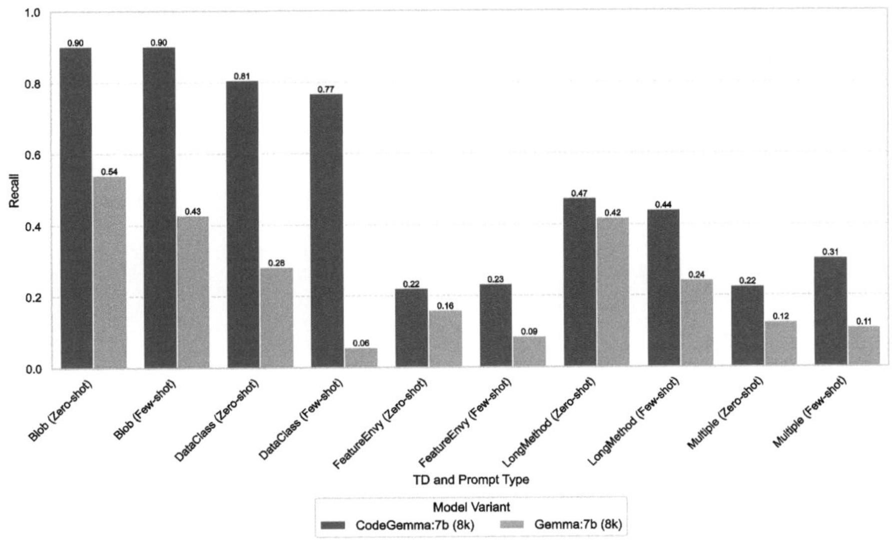

Fig. 6. Gemma Models: Recall comparison (Line-level, TH = 10).

RQ1 Conclusion. Granular prompting consistently yields better recall than Batch. Zero-shot prompts often match or outperform Few-shot due to better generalization. ode-specialized models outperform general-purpose counterparts, and longer context windows lead to higher recall. Qwen2.5-Coder:7b (128k) emerges as the most effective model overall across TD types.

RQ2: Majority Voting Performance Analysis. To answer *RQ2*, we evaluated whether combining top models via majority voting improves performance over individual models. Using the four highest-recall models, we applied majority voting; accepting predictions supported by at least two models. Results in Fig. 8 (Line-level, TH = 10) show recall across TD types and prompts.

Majority voting consistently outperformed individual models, including Qwen2.5-Coder:7b, with an average recall gain of 8.17%. Excluding weak Multiple prompts, the gain remains 7.90%. Recall was especially high for Blob (0.99) and Data Class (0.97), with notable gains for Feature Envy (+13.97%) and Long Method (+6.75%). Despite improved recall, the approach increases API calls and computational cost, raising scalability concerns. Task-specific model selection may offer a more efficient alternative.

RQ2 Conclusion. Majority voting among top-performing LLMs significantly improves debt detection performance, achieving an average recall gain of 8.17%, with notable improvements for challenging debt types such as Feature Envy and Long Method. However, the added computational cost suggests model selection per task as a more efficient alternative.

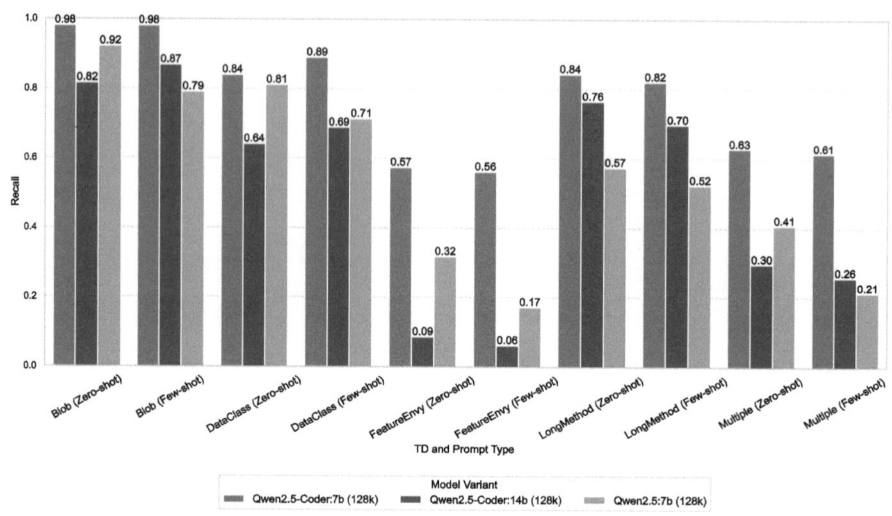

Fig. 7. Qwen2.5 Models: Recall comparison (Line-level, TH = 10).

RQ3: Evaluation Metrics for Technical Debt Detection. To answer *RQ3*, we evaluate LLMs in DebtGuardian using two metrics: file-level for debt presence and line-level for localization accuracy, with thresholds (0, 5, 10, 20) to measure tolerance. Figure 9 shows high file-level recall across models, confirming effective TD detection. However, Fig. 10 reveals sharp drops in line-level recall at strict thresholds, especially TH = 0. Most localization gains occur before TH = 10, making it the optimal baseline metric for further analysis. At TH = 0, Qwen2.5-Coder:7b (128k) outperforms all models in average recall, followed by Codestral:22b (32k). Threshold effects vary by TD type:

- **Class-level TDs** (Blob, Data Class) see negligible gains ($\leq 2.9\%$) with relaxed thresholds—models are already precise.
- **Method-level TDs** (Feature Envy, Long Method) improve up to 35%, especially for Feature Envy at TH = 20. Long Method gains level off after TH = 10.

> **RQ3 Conclusion.** LLMs in DebtGuardian effectively detect TDs at the file level but face localization challenges, especially for method-level TDs. A threshold of 10 strikes the best precision-tolerance tradeoff and is used for further evaluation.

3.4 Threats to Validity

Internal Validity. Our results depend on the design of DebtGuardian and the selected open-source LLMs. While models were chosen for recency and code specialization, detection performance hinges on their ability to generalize TD

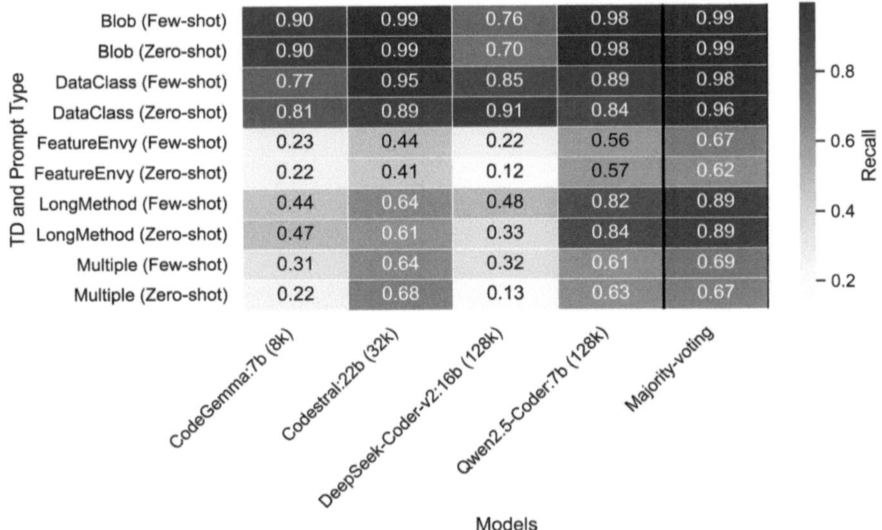

Fig. 8. Model performance comparison against Majority-voting approach by TD Type and Prompt (Line-level, TH = 10).

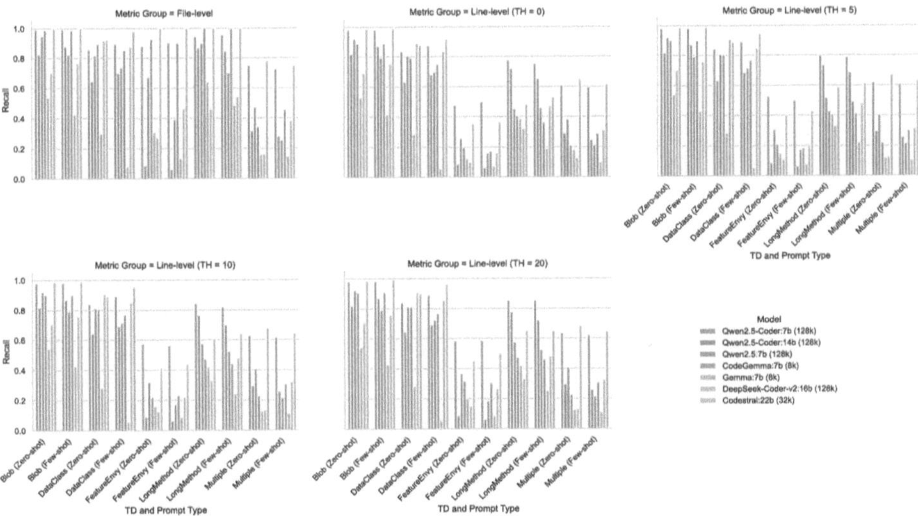

Fig. 9. Recall across prompts and models (at max context length) by metric group.

patterns. Output variability due to prompt and model choice, as well as the probabilistic behavior of LLMs, may introduce inconsistencies. We mitigated these risks by testing multiple prompting strategies (zero-/few-shot, batch, granular), employing majority voting across multiple LLMs, and using Guardrails-AI to validate and iteratively correct structured outputs. Potential data leakage is also

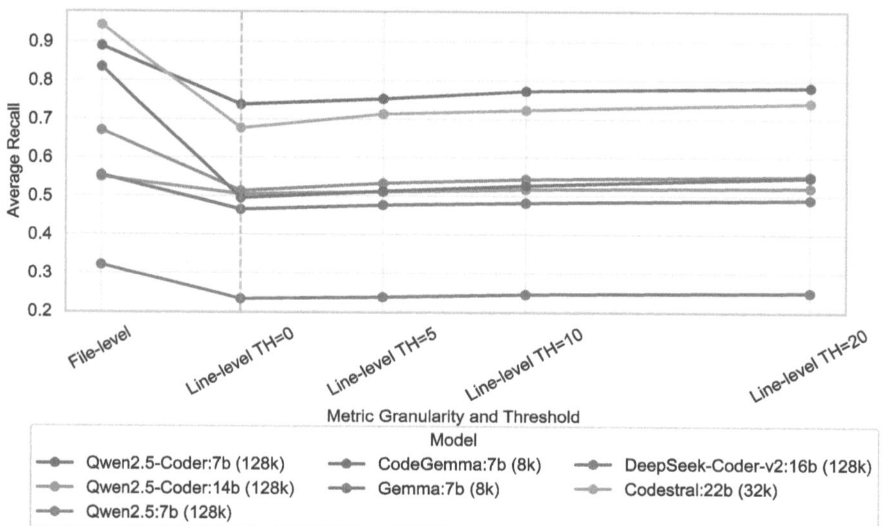

Fig. 10. Average recall trend by metric groups across models.

a concern in LLM evaluation; we minimized this by using open-source models trained on publicly available corpora.

External Validity. Findings are based on the Java-only MLCQ dataset with four TD types. Results may not generalize to other languages, debt types, or industrial code. Broader, multilingual datasets are needed for stronger generalization.

Construct Validity. Recall was prioritized due to MLCQ's type-specific labeling: while 'none' entries serve as negatives for a given smell type, they do not guarantee the absence of all other types. To complement this, we manually verified 47 entries that were free from all four smell types, providing a small set of negatives for exploratory evaluation of true negative handling. Guardrails-AI improved consistency, but subjective judgment of TD may introduce some bias.

Conclusion Validity. Consistent metrics across models, prompts, and strategies support credible findings. However, lack of false positive labels in MLCQ limits F1 and precision reliability. Broader datasets are needed to validate Debt-Guardian in real-world use.

4   Discussion

While code-specialized models consistently outperformed their general-purpose counterparts, the absolute gains were not uniform across all TD types. Models like Qwen2.5-Coder:7b demonstrated strong generalization capabilities, particularly for detecting structural debt types such as Blobs and Long Methods.

However, detecting more semantic and context-dependent debts, such as Feature Envy, remained challenging even for specialized models. This suggests that while specialization improves average performance, addressing nuanced design-level debts still requires deeper code reasoning beyond syntax and structure.

Our results show that increasing the context window significantly improves recall. Models with longer context lengths were better able to reason across larger code modifications, capturing TD patterns that span multiple methods or classes. This highlights that TD often arises from broader structural changes rather than isolated code snippets, and LLMs benefit from seeing the full scope of these modifications.

Prompting strategies played a crucial role. Granular prompting, where each TD type is queried separately, consistently outperformed batch prompting. This confirms that decomposing complex tasks into simpler, focused queries allows LLMs to produce more accurate and precise outputs. Interestingly, few-shot prompting did not always yield better results than zero-shot prompting, suggesting that LLMs' pre-trained knowledge can often generalize effectively without additional examples. In some cases, few-shot examples may even introduce unintended biases if not carefully curated.

Overall, our results suggest that open-source LLMs, when combined with careful prompting and ensemble strategies, can augment CI/CD workflows by providing early, automated insights into potential technical debt.

5   Related Work

Self-Admitted Technical Debt (SATD). TD detection has been widely studied, with a strong focus on self-admitted technical debt (SATD) via developer comments [4, 14, 19–21, 28, 32, 34]. Li et al. [19], for instance, analyzed SATD in issue trackers across two open-source projects, identifying eight TD types. These approaches provide insights into when and how TD is acknowledged. In contrast, DebtGuardian targets code changes rather than static comments, enabling dynamic, evolution-aware TD detection.

Static Analysis Tools. Rule-based static analysis tools systematically flag potential TD [2, 4]. Avgeriou et al. [4] reviewed 26 tools supporting TD detection and repayment. However, their reliance on rigid rules and varying definitions limits adaptability. DebtGuardian instead applies LLMs to interpret code in context, offering flexibility beyond fixed rule sets.

ML-Based TD Detection. ML methods provide adaptive alternatives to static tools. Tsoukalas et al. [31] used metrics-based classification, while Skryseth et al. [29] employed Transformer-based models on 55K+ TD issues mined from GitHub. Aversano et al. [3] used TCNs to forecast TD growth from class-level metrics. Unlike these, DebtGuardian directly analyzes evolving code, enabling real-time, context-aware TD identification.

LLM-Based Industry Tools. Industrial tools like GitHub Copilot [15] assist coding through real-time suggestions. In contrast, DebtGuardian evaluates code changes to detect and localize TD, emphasizing long-term maintainability over immediate productivity. This positions DebtGuardian as a complementary tool focused on sustained code quality.

6 Conclusion

We introduced DebtGuardian, an LLM-based framework for detecting technical debt (TD) in code changes. Unlike traditional static or SATD-based methods, DebtGuardian uses open-source LLMs, Guardrails-AI validation, and flexible prompting to enable precise and adaptable TD detection. Evaluated on the MLCQ dataset, we found that LLM choice and prompting significantly impact recall; code-specialized models, longer contexts, and structured prompts perform best. Majority voting further boosts performance, especially for complex TD types like Feature Envy. We also show that line-level evaluation with a 10-line threshold offers the best balance between precision and tolerance. While promising, challenges remain: scalability, fine-tuning few-shot prompts, and extending beyond Java. Still, DebtGuardian marks a step forward in LLM-enhanced TD detection. Future work includes fine-tuning LLMs for TD, expanding to other quality issues and languages, optimizing efficiency, and exploring multi-agent LLM collaboration.

Acknowledgment. The work has been conducted with funding from the Research Council of Norway's Innovation Project for the Industrial Sector (IPN) Programme under grant agreement No. 340991 (TechDebtOps), and from the European Union's Horizon Europe research and innovation programme under grant agreement No. 101120657 (ENFIELD). The authors would like to thank Prof. Hasan Sözer for his efforts on the manual analysis of data samples.

References

1. Alves, N.S., Mendes, T.S., De Mendonça, M.G., Spínola, R.O., Shull, F., Seaman, C.: Identification and management of technical debt: a systematic mapping study. Inf. Softw. Technol. **70**, 100–121 (2016)
2. Amanatidis, T., Mittas, N., Moschou, A., Chatzigeorgiou, A., Ampatzoglou, A., Angelis, L.: Evaluating the agreement among technical debt measurement tools: building an empirical benchmark of technical debt liabilities. Empir. Softw. Eng. **25**(5), 4161–4204 (2020). https://doi.org/10.1007/s10664-020-09869-w
3. Aversano, L., Bernardi, M.L., Cimitile, M., Iammarino, M.: Technical debt predictive model through temporal convolutional network. In: IJCNN 2021, pp. 1–8. IEEE (2021)
4. Avgeriou, P.C., et al.: An overview and comparison of technical debt measurement tools. IEEE Softw. **38**(3), 61–71 (2020)
5. Baldassari, B.: SQuORE: a new approach to software project assessment. In: SEAPP 2013, vol. 6 (2013)
6. Besker, T., Martini, A., Bosch, J.: Software developer productivity loss due to technical debt–a replication and extension study examining developers' development work. J. Syst. Softw. **156**, 41–61 (2019)

7. Brown, N., et al.: Managing technical debt in software-reliant systems. In: Proceedings of the FSE/SDP Workshop on Future of Software Engineering Research, pp. 47–52 (2010)

8. Campbell, G.A., Papapetrou, P.P.: SonarQube in Action. Manning Publications Co. (2013)

9. Chang, Y., et al.: A survey on evaluation of large language models. ACM Trans. Intell. Syst. Technol. **15**(3), 1–45 (2024)

10. Chen, T.: Challenges and opportunities in integrating LLMs into continuous integration/continuous deployment (CI/CD) pipelines. In: 2024 5th International Seminar on Artificial Intelligence, Networking and Information Technology (AINIT), pp. 364–367. IEEE (2024)

11. Cunningham, W.: The WyCash portfolio management system. ACM SIGPLAN OOPS Messenger **4**(2), 29–30 (1992)

12. Curtis, B., Sappidi, J., Szynkarski, A.: Estimating the principal of an application's technical debt. IEEE Softw. **29**(6), 34–42 (2012)

13. Fowler, M.: Refactoring: Improving the Design of Existing Code. Addison-Wesley Longman Publishing Co., Inc., USA (1999)

14. de Freitas Farias, M.A., de Mendonça Neto, M.G., Kalinowski, M., Spínola, R.O.: Identifying self-admitted technical debt through code comment analysis with a contextualized vocabulary. Inf. Softw. Technol. **121**, 106270 (2020)

15. GitHub Copilot. https://github.com/features/copilot. Accessed 2025

16. Guardrails AI. https://github.com/guardrails-ai/guardrails. Accessed 2024

17. Instructor-AI. https://github.com/instructor-ai/instructor. Accessed 2024

18. Lenarduzzi, V., Saarimäki, N., Taibi, D.: The technical debt dataset. In: PROMISE 2019, pp. 2–11 (2019)

19. Li, Y., Soliman, M., Avgeriou, P.: Identification and remediation of self-admitted technical debt in issue trackers. In: SEAA 2020, pp. 495–503. IEEE (2020)

20. Li, Y., Soliman, M., Avgeriou, P., Van Ittersum, M.: DebtViz: a tool for identifying, measuring, visualizing, and monitoring self-admitted technical debt. In: ICSME 2023, pp. 558–562. IEEE (2023)

21. Li, Z., Avgeriou, P., Liang, P.: A systematic mapping study on technical debt and its management. J. Syst. Softw. **101**, 193–220 (2015)

22. Liu, Y., et al.: Trustworthy LLMs: a survey and guideline for evaluating large language models' alignment. arXiv preprint arXiv:2308.05374 (2023)

23. Madeyski, L., Lewowski, T.: MLCQ: industry-relevant code smell data set. In: Proceedings of the 24th International Conference on Evaluation and Assessment in Software Engineering, EASE 2020, pp. 342–347 (2020)

24. Maia Polo, F., et al.: Efficient multi-prompt evaluation of LLMs. Adv. Neural. Inf. Process. Syst. **37**, 22483–22512 (2024)

25. Marvin. https://github.com/prefecthq/marvin. Accessed 2025

26. Pahune, S., Akhtar, Z.: Transitioning from MLOps to LLMOps: navigating the unique challenges of large language models. Information **16**(2), 87 (2025)

27. Palomba, F., et al.: Landfill: an open dataset of code smells with public evaluation. In: 2015 IEEE/ACM 12th Working Conference on Mining Software Repositories, pp. 482–485 (2015)

28. Sharma, R., Shahbazi, R., Fard, F.H., Codabux, Z., Vidoni, M.: Self-admitted technical debt in R: detection and causes. Autom. Softw. Eng. **29**(2), 53 (2022)

29. Skryseth, D., Shivashankar, K., Pilán, I., Martini, A.: Technical debt classification in issue trackers using natural language processing based on transformers. In: TechDebt 2023, pp. 92–101. IEEE (2023)

30. Stureborg, R., Alikaniotis, D., Suhara, Y.: Large language models are inconsistent and biased evaluators. arXiv preprint arXiv:2405.01724 (2024)
31. Tsoukalas, D., et al.: Machine learning for technical debt identification. IEEE Trans. Softw. Eng. **48**(12), 4892–4906 (2021)
32. Tu, H., Menzies, T.: DebtFree: minimizing labeling cost in self-admitted technical debt identification using semi-supervised learning. Empir. Softw. Eng. **27**(4), 80 (2022)
33. Wang, L., et al.: Prompt engineering in consistency and reliability with the evidence-based guideline for LLMs. npj Digit. Med. **7**(1), 41 (2024)
34. Yu, Z., Fahid, F.M., Tu, H., Menzies, T.: Identifying self-admitted technical debts with Jitterbug: a two-step approach. IEEE Trans. Softw. Eng. **48**(5), 1676–1691 (2020)

Towards Understanding Team Congestion in Large-Scale Software Development

Javier Gonzalez-Huerta[1(✉)] [iD] and Ehsan Zabardast[1,2] [iD]

[1] Software Engineering Research Lab (SERL), Blekinge Institute of Technology,
371 79 Karlskrona, Sweden
{javier.gonzalez.huerta,ehsan.zabardast}@bth.se
[2] Gaetir, Karlskrona, Sweden

Abstract. Background: Software Development organisations tend to organise the development of software-intensive products and services as a constellation of components meant to be developed and maintained by independent, autonomous teams. However, the maintenance and evolution of said products and services require team collaboration and coordination. This collaboration and coordination overhead piles on top of teams' workload, often hindering teams' throughput and lead time.

Objectives: This paper aims to discuss how the use of pull request data can help identify congested teams when the arrival of new tasks exceeds the team's ability to close them. To do so, we have conducted an empirical study in a software development organisation developing a large-scale product, to try to characterise congested teams and the characteristics of the code reviews they are involved in.

Method: We have conducted a case study to start exploring how code review data can help us model team congestion, and understand whether the features of the code-review network, or the team type (platform vs product), can have a major impact on team congestion.

Results: The results show that teams seem to experience varying levels of congestion based on pull request activity, with some indicating potential congestion. However, increased PR accumulation did not consistently lead to longer lead times, as seen in some teams where high PR backlogs did not significantly impact delivery cadence.

Conclusions: Our findings suggest that while PR data can indicate potential congestion, its impact on lead time varies across teams. Both technical factors and unobserved contextual elements shape congestion. Deeper insights require combining repository metrics with qualitative inputs.

Keywords: Team Congestion · Team Coordination · Code-Review Data Analysis · Case Study

1 Introduction

The development of Software Intensive Products and Services (SIPS) has become a collective endeavour that requires software development organisations to organ-

G. Scanniello et al. (Eds.): PROFES 2025, LNCS 16361, pp. 353–368, 2026.
https://doi.org/10.1007/978-3-032-12089-2_22

ise their systems as a constellation of components to be developed by independent, ideally autonomous teams. However, the development of new features or the maintenance of existing ones very often requires altering the behaviour of several of those components, sometimes requiring several teams to cooperate, creating the need for coordination, sometimes unexpectedly, especially when there are no dependencies among the said components [14]. In certain cases, the teams' regular workload, together with these communication and coordination needs, might lead to their throughput being reduced or experiencing delays. Despite the increased use of data-driven metrics in DevOps and agile environments, there is limited empirical evidence on how artefact-based indicators, such as pull request activity, reflect coordination bottlenecks or delivery impacts across teams.

We borrow the congestion concept from networking, although it was already introduced to the software development field in [2]. In networking, a congested node is a node whose rate of incoming requests exceeds the node's capacity to process or forward them, leading to queuing problems, data losses, or delays [13]. In software development, the concept applies to teams whose coordination overhead, or dependencies, makes their throughput decrease and their lead time increase, often becoming a bottleneck in the software delivery pipeline [1]. A congested team is hence a team for which the arrival of new tasks exceeds its ability to close them, due to communication and coordination overhead, and task dependencies.

While prior studies have examined task overload, reviewer workload, and inter-team dependencies, little is known about whether repository-level artefacts, such as pull request balance and network structures, can serve as reliable indicators of team congestion in large-scale software systems. Moreover, conflicting findings on the relationship between workload and delivery performance leave open questions about when and how congestion impacts software delivery.

The objective of this paper is to report an empirical enquiry aiming at understanding whether code review data can help characterise congested teams in large-scale software development organisations developing software-intensive products and services. We have conducted a case study in a software firm developing a large-scale software system in the Fintech domain. Using archival analysis as the main data collection method, we have analysed the evolution of the Pull Request (PRs) that each opens and closes. Understanding how to identify and manage team congestion is crucial for organisations operating large-scale architectures with weak ownership models.

This paper makes the following contributions: (i) an exploratory case study in a large-scale industrial setting analyzing over three years of PR data across multiple teams; (ii) a taxonomy of PR in-flows distinguishing between intra-team, cross-team, bot-generated, and outgoing contributions; (iii) the introduction of $PR_{balance}$ and PR network topology as quantitative indicators for detecting potential team congestion; and (iv) empirical insights on the complex relationship between PR accumulation, inter-team dependencies, and delivery lead time. These contributions advance current knowledge by showing that congestion symptoms do not uniformly translate into increased lead time, highlighting the need for multi-faceted approaches, combining artefact-based metrics with qualitative insights, to understand and mitigate team-level bottlenecks.

By clarifying when and how PR-based metrics might reveal congestion risks, our work lays the foundation for actionable monitoring approaches and future research combining quantitative metrics with qualitative studies to fully understand team coordination challenges.

The remainder of the papers is structured as follows: Sect. 2 summarises related worksteam congestion and team performance; Sect. 3 reports on the research methodology we followed to address our research questions; Sect. 4 reports the main results of the study; Sect. 5 discusses the main findings; finally, Sect. 7 draws the main conclusions and discusses potential further works on the area.

2   Related Work

Task overload and congestion in software development have been studied extensively, given their significant impact on team productivity and individual developer experience.

Cantor et al. [2] introduced congestion as a state where task inflow surpasses a team's processing capacity, drawing parallels between software development and network queuing. They emphasise the importance of actively managing queues and work-in-progress constraints to mitigate congestion. Šmite et al. [12] investigated decentralised decision-making at Spotify, observing that while scaled autonomy can foster team independence, it also increases complexity due to cross-team dependencies and the resulting coordination overhead. Their findings underscore that even autonomous teams face congestion due to the interdependent nature of their tasks, particularly when teams need to modify code owned by others.

The consequences of workload and delivery cadence have been addressed in other studies. Zhang et al. [15] investigate the relationship between reviewer and project workload and pull request (PR) lead time. The study shows that increased load correlates with longer PR delivery times. Their findings reveal that both temporal load (PRs under review simultaneously) and historical project workload significantly predict delays.

Razzaq et al. [10] systematically reviewed developer experience (Dev-X), showing that frequent interruptions, multiple contexts of work, and unclear or fragmented tasks significantly reduce developer productivity. Their analysis aligns closely with the congestion phenomenon, where task overload manifests as reduced focus, efficiency, and satisfaction, negatively impacting overall productivity.

Girardi et al. [5] found a direct correlation between developer emotions and perceived productivity, indicating that negative emotional states, often triggered by congestion, overload, or task interruptions, significantly decrease productivity. They highlight emotional states as vital indicators of overload conditions, suggesting that emotional monitoring could aid in managing task overload.

Greiler et al. [6] introduced an actionable framework for improving developer experience, identifying clear directional clarity, manageable workload, and supportive team culture as critical factors. Their findings align with congestion literature, reinforcing that excessive workload and poor team dynamics can exacerbate team congestion and negatively impact developer satisfaction and productivity.

Michels et al. [8] employed Interpretative Phenomenological Analysis to explore software developer experiences of overwhelm. They found that psychological overwhelm, induced by high task variety, technical complexity, and organisational disturbances, significantly reduced productivity and heightened stress. They note that while overload typically leads to negative outcomes, certain levels of overwhelm might occasionally enhance focus and productivity temporarily.

These studies collectively underscore that team congestion and task overload are multifaceted issues impacting software development at both the team and individual levels. Overload and congestion are consistently associated with reduced productivity, decreased emotional well-being, and increased coordination complexity. Effective management of congestion thus requires comprehensive strategies addressing workflow optimisation, team autonomy balance, emotional monitoring, and improved developer experience. Future research should continue exploring adaptive mechanisms that enable teams to anticipate, detect, and manage congestion proactively.

3   Research Methodology

We have conducted an exploratory case study aiming at understanding whether pull request (PR) data can help organisations identify congested teams, and whether we can observe an impact on the resolution time for pull requests (open to merge), by analysing development artefacts in a FinTech company developing a large-scale software system.

More specifically, in our case study, we address the following research questions:

> – **RQ1:** How can code review data be used to identify potential signs of team congestion in large-scale software development?
> – **RQ1.a:** What insights about team congestion can we extract from analysing the balance of pull requests (opened vs closed) for each team?
> – **RQ1.b:** How do the size and structure of the code review social network differ for teams with varying pull request balances?
> – **RQ2:** In what way does team congestion relate to changes in Lead Time (open to merge) across different teams?

The case study is exploratory, aiming to understand the phenomenon of team congestion, potential factors that can have an influence, and the consequences in the development workflow.

The case study was designed following the guidelines by Runeson et al. [11], adapted for an exploratory, artefact-based study.

3.1 Context and Case Selection

The study is conducted in a Swedish FinTech company developing financial solutions, which has decided to remain anonymous. The selection of the company is by convenience, based on access and availability, since the company is participating in several research projects. In their efforts to improve ways of working and the potential usage of data-driven decision-making techniques, the company was willing to participate in the study [4].

The organisation has a hybrid architecture, combining more traditional services with microservices while maintaining a monolith that holds the original front-end, from which the services and microservices have been extracted from the monolith over the years. Today, the architecture contains more than 200 components (services, microservices and the monolith) developed and maintained by sixty-seven teams, following a weak-ownership model [3]. It is important to note that, although the majority of services and microservices have been extracted from the monolith, the monolith continues growing both in functionality and size, since the majority of the front-end functionality still resides in that module.

The unit of analysis is the development team workflow. This paper focuses on following up and analysing four teams of different characteristics, as captured using pull request data.

The criteria for selecting the teams were:

- To observe active PR activity during the whole period of analysis (January 2022 to May 2025).
- To have a mixture of platform and product teams.
- To include both teams taking care of services and microservices, as well as the team in charge of maintaining the big monolithic component.

Table 1 reports the details of the teams under analysis. We report the number of developers in each team, sampled quarterly, i.e., every three months. Please note that `National Peacock` is not the sole contributor to the Monolith repository, whose size exceeds 2.5 MLOC, including 0.5 MLOC of XML files. There are another 20 teams owning different submodules of the monolith; however, the `National Peacock` is the designated responsible for its architecture, several core submodules, and its overall code quality.

3.2 Data Collection and Data Analysis

We defined the following PRs workflows:

- $PRs_{Intra}(team, month)$: $PRs_{opened} - PRs_{closed}$ created by members of the team under analysis in repositories the team is responsible for.

Table 1. Details of the selected teams. The Number of developers has been sampled every quarter, and then we report Median, Min, and Max.

Team	Type	Num Developers		
		Median	Min	Max
Glorious Finch	Product	7	5	9
National Peacock	Platform	2	1	3
Stripped Magpie	Product	9	7	11
Silent Constrictor	Platform	5,5	4	8

- $PRs_{Inconming}(team, month)$: $PRs_{opened} - PRs_{closed}$ created by developers who do not belong to the team under analysis (at the time of the creation of the PR) in repositories the team under analysis is responsible for.
- $PRs_{Bot}(team, month)$: $PRs_{opened} - PRs_{closed}$ created by automation bots in repositories the team under analysis is responsible for. Although automatically created by the bots, these pull requests need to be revised and approved (or rescoped) by members of the team under analysis. In most cases, these pull requests are for upgrading third-party libraries to their latest version.
- $PRs_{Outgoing}(team, month)$: $PPRs_{opened} - PRs_{closed}$ the team under analysis creates in repositories that other teams are responsible for. In most cases, these pull requests will be reviewed and approved, declined, or rescoped by members of the *owning* team, but this is another flow of work that might affect the potential congestion of the team under analysis.

We calculate $PRs_{Balance}(team, month)$ as the monthly difference between $PRs_{opened} - PRs_{closed}$ in that particular month by that particular team, considering all the PRs workflows described above. This absolute measure captures the raw backlog of pending work, which we consider meaningful in its own right since teams must ultimately review and close each remaining PR regardless of overall throughput. We acknowledge, however, that absolute counts may disadvantage teams with higher activity levels, where a larger backlog might represent a smaller proportion of total work. For this exploratory study, we deliberately chose the absolute metric for its simplicity and interpretability when investigating congestion symptoms. In future work, we plan to complement this measure with normalised variants, e.g., backlog ratios relative to total PR volume, to test whether our observations hold under different scaling assumptions.

The pull request data was downloaded from the company's Bitbucket internal server. The company also accounts for a system that tracks team affiliation over time (each developer is assigned to the team they belong to), as well as historical information about the team that *owns* each particular repository.

With that information, we created a dataset that cannot be made available due to confidentiality concerns. The dataset contains information regarding the repository, its owning team, the team the developer who creates the PR belongs to, and the lead time (open-to-merge) for each PR that has been closed. To remove seasonality in the lead-time data, we calculate the rolling average of the lead time over a period of three months, since the company organises their development in quarters (three months).

For RQ1.b, we constructed code review social networks where each node represents a development team, and a directed edge from team A to team B indicates that members of A opened pull requests in repositories owned by B during that quarter. Edge weights represent the number of such PRs, capturing collaboration intensity. These networks allow us to examine whether higher inter-team collaboration (e.g., larger, denser networks) correlates with greater PR backlog and potential congestion.

Finally, we are aware that we are leaving outside of the analysis PRs that are still open, which might have a high resolution time, but we are applying the same principle to all PRs owned by any team.

4   Results

Table 2 summarises the PRs inflow of the four selected teams. The team `National Peacock` is responsible for the quality control of the monolithic component in the architecture that accounts for more than $410 KLOC$. However, there are around 20 teams *owning* submodules of the Monolith. `National Peacock` is responsible for closely monitoring the changes in the Monolith's main module and its overall code quality.

As can be noted, the `National Peacock` team has received more incoming PRs per month than the average product team, and also has a balance that doubles the average for product teams, which might be a symptom of congestion.

Table 2. PRs opened and closed per team per month per category—**prod.** for product, **plat.** for platform teams, and final balance (average)

Team	type	PRs_{Bot} Opened	PRs_{Bot} Closed	$PRs_{Incoming}$ Opened	$PRs_{Incoming}$ Closed	PRs_{Intra} Opened	PRs_{Intra} Closed	$PRs_{Outgoing}$ Opened	$PRs_{Outgoing}$ Closed	PRs_{Total} Opened	PRs_{Total} Closed	Balance
Glorious Finch	**prod.**	53,2	53,2	10,9	10,4	73,3	71,5	9,9	9,8	147,3	144,8	2,5
National Peacock	**plat.**	21,2	21,2	197,7	179,4	12,5	10,6	2,6	2,4	234,0	213,6	20,3
Stripped Magpie	**prod.**	3,0	2,9	1,2	1,2	24,7	20,8	13,4	12,1	42,3	37,0	5,3
Silent Constrictor	**plat.**	68,3	68,2	24,8	23,2	53,0	45,5	16,4	15,6	162,5	152,6	9,9
Avg	**prod.**	55,9	55,7	69,0	63,1	37,3	33,7	12,6	12,3	174,7	164,7	10,0
Avg	**plat.**	17,5	17,2	11,4	10,9	36,8	35,4	14,2	13,4	79,8	76,8	3,1

Figure 1 shows the temporal evolution of PRs over time (top plot), which might be the indicator of a team being congested, and the evolution of open-to-merge lead time for the `National Peacock` team, responsible for the Monolith component. Although we can see certain parallelism in higher accumulation of PRs (around May 2023 and May 2024, and to a lesser extent in April 2025) that comes in parallel to a rise in the lead time (rolling average), there are other periods in which the PRs are also accumulating, but without a noticeable impact on lead time.

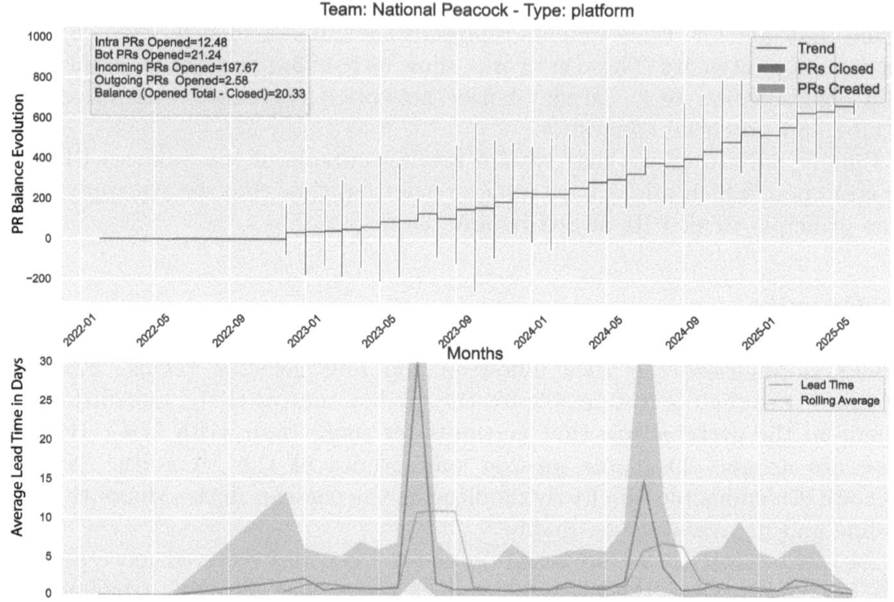

Fig. 1. Evolution of PRs over time (top) and *open-to-merge* lead time (bottom) in the product team responsible for the development in the Monolith.

Figure 2 shows the evolution of PRs over time (top plot), and the evolution of the open-to-merge lead time for the `Glorious Finch` team. In this case, the average monthly balance shows a very slow accumulation of PRs, and therefore, the case of a non-congested team. The fluctuations in lead time are also small in magnitude, ranging from 0.25 days to 1.75 days in the top peak.

Figure 3 shows the evolution of PRs over time (top plot), and the evolution of the open-to-merge lead time for the `Stripped Magpie` team. In this case, the average monthly balance shows a quicker accumulation of PRs, and therefore, a potential case of a congested team. However, the impact on lead time seems negligible, with a decrease in the average lead time, even though the accumulated PRs that remain open consistently grows.

Figure 4 shows the evolution of PRs over time (top plot), and the evolution of the open-to-merge lead time for the `Silent Constrictor` team. In this case, the average monthly balance shows an even quicker accumulation of PRs, and therefore, a potential case of a congested team. However, the impact on lead time again seems negligible, with a decrease in the average lead time, even though the accumulated PRs that remain open consistently grows, on average 9.90 PRs per month.

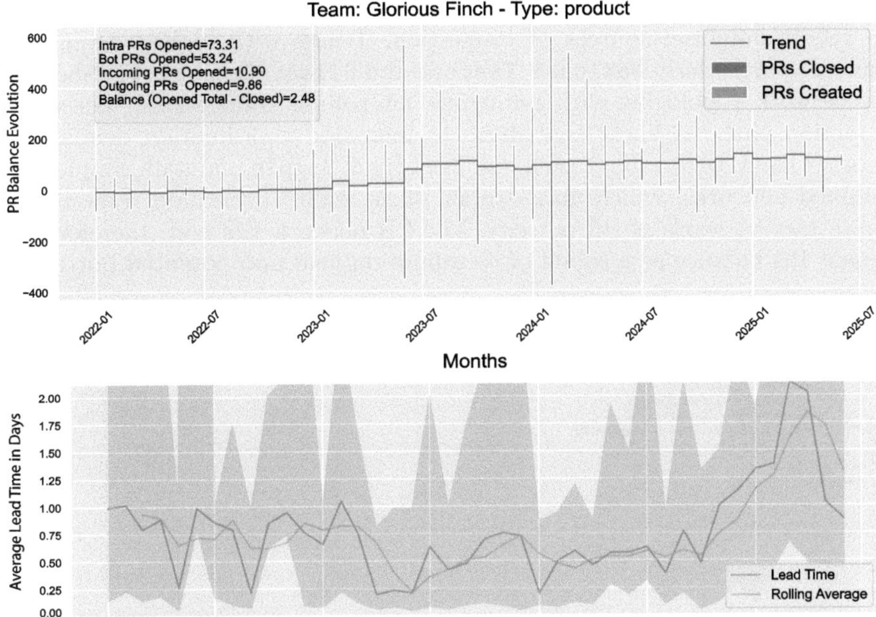

Fig. 2. Evolution of PRs over time (top) and *open-to-merge* lead time (bottom) in a product team responsible for a set of microservices.

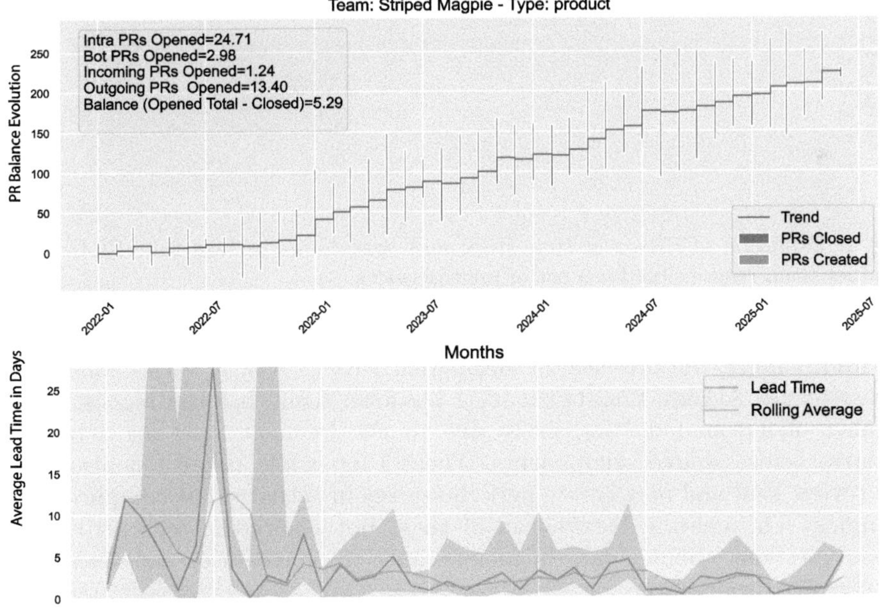

Fig. 3. Evolution of PRs over time (top) and *open-to-merge* lead time (bottom) in a product team responsible for a set of microservices.

The structural characteristics of the PR networks, illustrated in Fig. 5, also reflect potential sources of congestion. Teams with higher incoming PR volumes—particularly `National Peacock` and `Silent Constrictor` show complex network topologies with numerous inter-team connections. These dense interaction patterns likely contribute to increased coordination demands. On the other hand, `Glorious Finch` and `Stripped Magpie` maintain simpler, more contained networks, which may explain their ability to sustain responsiveness despite varying levels of PR activity. The PR network size may, therefore, complement PR balance as a signal of coordination load and potential bottlenecks.

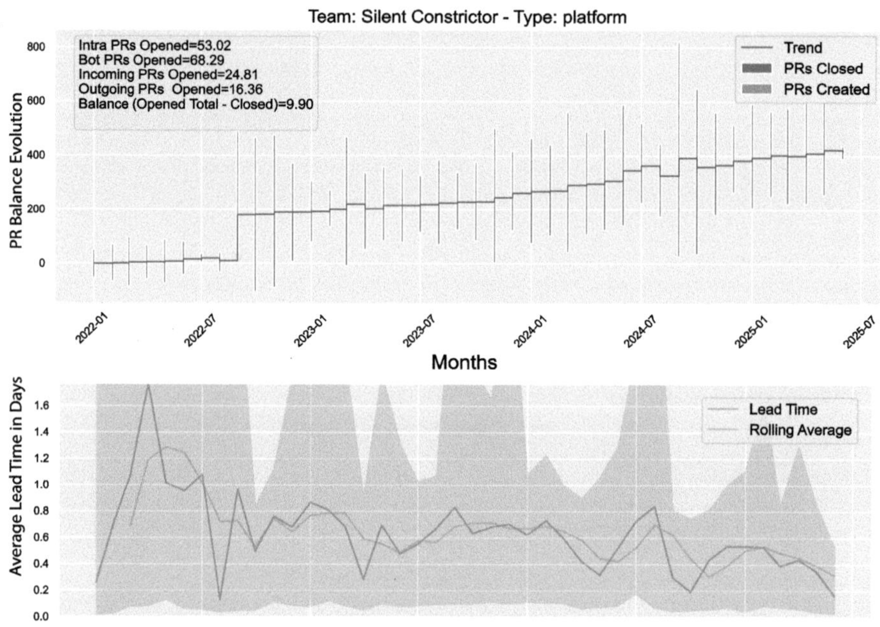

Fig. 4. Evolution of PRs over time (top) and *open-to-merge* lead time (bottom) in a product team responsible for a set of microservices.

Additionally, the presence of automated PRs (PRs_{Bot}) varies considerably across teams. `Silent Constrictor`, a platform team, has the highest average number of automated PRs, likely due to the frequent need for dependency updates across shared components. These PRs, while necessary, also add to the review load and may create periodic spikes in activity that complicate team planning. The uneven distribution of these bot-generated tasks across teams raises questions about equity in maintenance responsibilities and their impact on perceived congestion.

Comparing Figs. 1, 2, 3 and 4, we can see that teams exhibit distinct patterns: `National Peacock` shows partial alignment between PR backlog peaks and lead time increases; `Stripped Magpie` and `Silent Constrictor` accumulate PRs

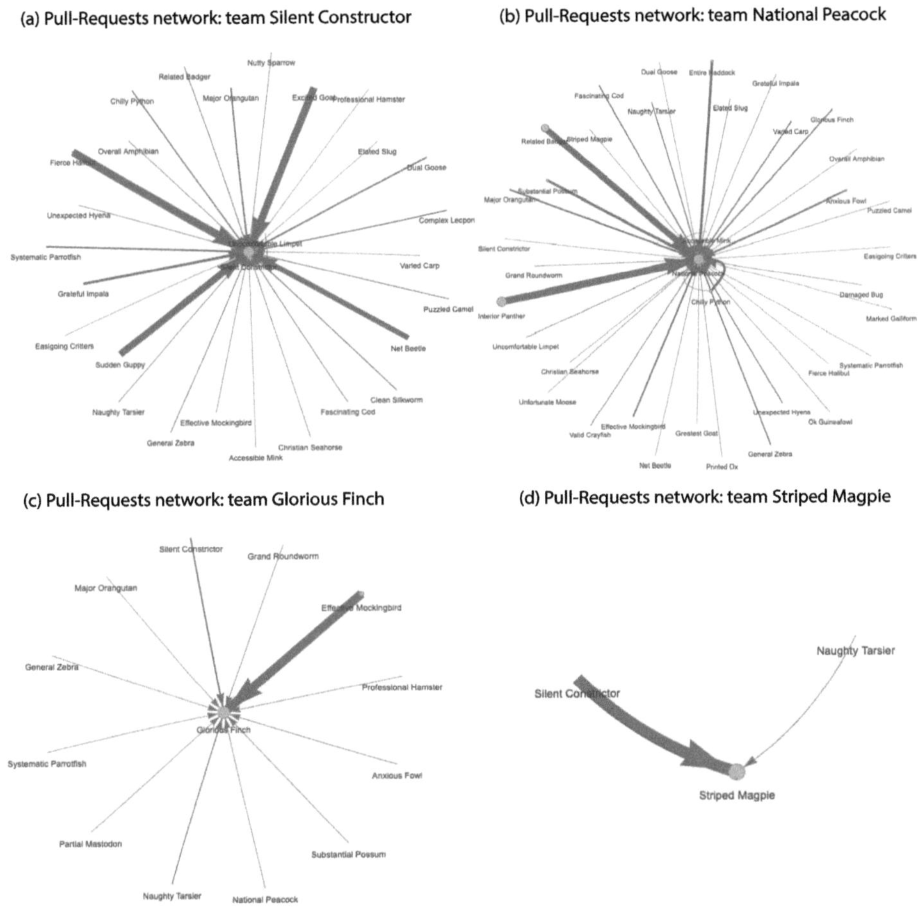

Fig. 5. PR network topology of the four teams under study. The node in the centre represents the team under analysis. Nodes in the perimeter represent teams with which the team under analysis shares PRs.x§Thickens of the arrow indicate the number of PRs opened by the given team in the repositories the team of interest owns $PR_{Incoming}$.

without rising delays; and **Glorious Finch** maintains both low backlogs and stable lead times. This variability suggests that factors beyond PR volume, e.g., review practices or prioritisation, may moderate congestion effects.

Finally, our analysis focused on absolute $PR_{balance}$ values, which highlight teams experiencing growing backlogs over time. Future work could normalise this metric by total PR activity, i.e., as a proportion of all opened and closed PRs, to separate absolute workload from relative efficiency. Such normalisation may reveal whether teams with high raw backlogs, like **Silent Constrictor**, remain outliers when controlling for throughput.

5 Discussion

Our findings both reinforce and nuance prior research on task overload and team congestion in software development. Studies such as Cantor et al. [2] and Šmite et al. [12] emphasise that when task inflow exceeds a team's processing capacity, coordination overhead and inter-team dependencies frequently lead to congestion. Our results partially align with these observations: teams such as National Peacock and Silent Constrictor, which operate in contexts with high incoming PR volumes and dense PR network topologies, exhibit symptoms of congestion consistent with coordination overload. However, contrary to expectations, the lead time for these teams does not always rise proportionally with PR accumulation.

This divergence contrasts with findings by Zhang et al. [15], who reported a link between reviewer and project workload and longer PR lead time. The temporal evolution of the balance of PRs over time in the team seems to impact lead time for the team responsible for the Monolith National Peacock, when the slope is more prominent, which might indicate that the team is congested. However, the impact that a higher balance of PRs over time has on lead time for the other three teams seems negligible. Of course, the teams might get used to the inflow, and the lead time (rolling average) remains stable. This divergence invites further interpretation. One possible explanation lies in adopting implicit or explicit triage mechanisms, where teams consciously defer low-priority PRs without allowing them to affect core workflows. Similarly, asynchronous review practices, high reviewer availability, or internal prioritisation strategies may buffer the impact of congestion symptoms. Though not observable in the artefact data alone, these practices might explain the apparent resilience of specific teams. Such hypotheses align with prior literature on adaptive coordination and workload regulation in agile environments [6, 12], suggesting that congestion is not solely a function of volume but also of team-level process maturity. While our study does not yet include qualitative data, these patterns underscore the need to capture contextual team practices in future work, including surveys and focus group interviews, to enrich our understanding of how perceived and actual congestion manifest differently across teams. This lack of impact on lead-time may suggest team-level mitigation strategies, such as prioritisation mechanisms or asynchronous collaboration, not captured by artefact data alone.

Table 2 shows that each team has a different distribution of PRs inflow. The National Peacock team has a much higher inflow of $PRs_{incoming}$, from developers outside of the team, while all other teams have a lesser inflow of $PRs_{incoming}$. They tend to open more PRs in their owned repositories PRs_{intra}. Stripped Magpie is the team which seems to create more PRs in repositories owned by other teams $PRs_{outgoing}$. Creating PRs in repositories owned by other teams might introduce waiting times, translating into a higher Balance of PRs. In general, we observe a significant number of automatically created PRs, i.e., PRs_{Bot}, that respond to the need to upgrade third-party libraries to their latest version in all products and microservices. This inflow is especially noticeable in Silent Constrictor, which seems to have a significant inflow of this type of PRs, probably due to the platform nature of the team, which might be taking care of platform components where the presence of third-party libraries might be very prominent.

The size of the code review social network seems to be slightly different for those teams that have, on average, a higher balance of PRs over time, and it is especially noticeable in the case of the National Peacock team, responsible for the development on the monolith. While the balance of PRs portrayed in Table 2 and its evolution in Figs. 1, 2, 3, and 4 points to symptoms of congestion, i.e., the accumulation of PRs not closed over time, the networks shown in Fig. 5 seem to be an explanation for this potential congestion. Of course, first, there might be many other explanations on why PRs remain open, like tasks with low priority, task dependencies or simply PRs that are likely to be declined. All these aspects seem especially prominent in the monolith, since more than twenty teams are contributing to its different modules, and many changes need the approval of the owning team.

Our findings partially align with existing literature on task overload and developer congestion. The high PR balance observed in National Peacock team aligns with the notion of coordination overload discussed in [2], where the task queues exceed the team capacity, and this is especially relevant in components with high centrality such as the monolith. Similarly, the complexity of the PR network topology for teams such as National Peacock and Silent Constrictor supports the observation that scaled autonomy and inter-team dependencies can increase coordination overhead, even among autonomous teams [12].

The presence of automatically created PRs (i.e., PRs_{Bot}) also plays a significant role in shaping team workload patterns. In our case, Silent Constrictor has the highest inflow of such PRs, likely due to the platform nature of the team, where dependency updates and security patches occur frequently. Prior work by Greiler et al. [6] highlights the importance of workload clarity and supportive practices to maintain developer productivity under high load. Complementing this, studies on dependency management bots such as Mirhosseini & Parnin [9] and He et al. [7] show that while automated PRs can accelerate maintenance tasks and reduce technical debt, they may also lead to notification fatigue, excessive review overhead, and even mistrust of automated changes if not properly triaged or configured. These findings resonate with our observation that unregulated inflows of automated PRs can contribute to perceived congestion, especially in platform-oriented teams, unless accompanied by deliberate scheduling and ownership strategies.

These findings extend and reinforce existing knowledge while revealing important nuances in the manifestation of team congestion. Although artefact-based measures such as PR balance and lead time offer valuable indicators, they provide only a partial view. Team congestion seems to be a multifaceted phenomenon, and task volume and coordination structures are two aspects. Contextual and human factors that cannot be captured in repository data alone are as crucial as those studied in this paper. First, we need richer data to understand the phenomenon and its consequences further. In this paper, we report the first version of the metrics, but this is part of a bigger study, in which we plan to run company-wide surveys to capture potential teams that feel congested. The survey results and metrics reported in this paper will be used to select teams to conduct focus group interviews. These interviews will help to refine the concept further and evaluate whether we can identify congested teams or teams close to being congested to help frame mitigation strategies.

6   Threats to the Validity

Construct Validity: The study uses PR balance (opened minus closed pull requests) and lead time as proxies for team congestion and the size of the PR social network. While these metrics are meaningful, they might not capture the nuanced causes of congestion, such as developer availability, review quality, or hidden coordination efforts. Moreover, PRs may remain open for various reasons (e.g., task priority, task dependencies, strategic delay), which can misrepresent actual team bottlenecks.

Internal Validity: Due to the exploratory nature of this case study, the causal relationships between PR accumulation and increased lead times are suggested but not confirmed. External variables, e.g., team size, release cycles, or individual productivity, are not controlled for and could confound the results. Additionally, unresolved PRs are excluded from analysis, which could systematically underreport actual congestion effects within teams. We also note that our network analysis remains exploratory: while it visualises inter-team dependencies and potential congestion risks, more sophisticated analyses, e.g., centrality measures or a temporal network model, would be needed to fully establish causal relationships.

External Validity: Findings are based on a single case study within a Swedish FinTech company, potentially limiting generalizability. Organisational context, tooling, and the weak ownership model in a hybrid architecture with a monolith and microservices coexisting may not reflect practices in other contexts. The selection of only four teams, chosen for activity and diversity, may not represent the broader population of teams within or beyond the company. A more exhaustive analysis, involving more teams and replications in other organisations, is planned as further work in the short term, which will help to continue modelling the congestion phenomenon.

Conclusion Validity: While visual trends suggest congestion may affect lead time in some teams, the lack of statistical validation weakens confidence in the conclusions. Contradictory patterns, i.e., teams with growing PR backlogs but stable or reduced lead time, introduce uncertainty. The PR balance, its components, and the networks have been developed in close collaboration with the company and validated in several of our recurring collaboration workshops.

7   Conclusions and Further Work

This exploratory case study investigates whether pull request (PR) data can serve as an indicator for identifying team congestion in large-scale software development. The findings reveal that teams experience different levels of PR accumulation, with some teams showing signs of potential congestion through consistently positive PR balance over time.

However, a key finding is that high PR does not always result in increased lead times. Even in teams with evident PR accumulation for the team, the lead time remained stable or declined, indicating that congestion, as operationalised in this study, does not necessarily impact the delivery cadence.

The topology of the code review social network appeared more complex for teams with higher PR Balance, especially with higher incoming PRs, particularly those working on shared or central components (e.g., the monolith). This network complexity suggests that inter-team dependencies may contribute to team congestion, though their actual effect on delivery performance seems mixed.

Overall, while PR data—especially balance and lead time can indicate workload patterns and potential bottlenecks, they are insufficient to confirm congestion. The study demonstrates the need for multi-faceted indicators, including qualitative data and contextual analysis, when diagnosing team-level delivery issues.

Our immediate goal is to expand the current analysis, incorporating qualitative data, to complete the view of team congestion. Organisation-wide surveys to identify potential congested teams, and focus groups with teams who report themselves as congested and with teams that report a sustainable work inflow, will help us evaluate and refine the metrics discussed in this paper. Finally, developing predictive models or dashboards for congestion detection could have practical value for engineering management.

Finally, replicating the study in other organisational contexts is essential to enhance generalizability. Exploring the impact of team composition, review policies, and task prioritisation practices on congestion would also be valuable.

Acknowledgments. This research is supported through the KKS SERT Research Profile project (Ref. 2018010), Blekinge Institute of Technology.

References

1. Cantor, M.: Software Leadership: A Guide to Successful Software Development. Addison-Wesley Longman Publishing Co., Inc., USA (2001)
2. Cantor, M., MacIsaac, B., Mannan, R.: Steering software development workflow: lessons from the internet. IEEE Softw. **33**(5), 96–102 (2016). https://doi.org/10.1109/MS.2016.105
3. Erl, T.: Service-Oriented Architecture: Concepts, Technology and Design. Pearson Education, Boston, ME, USA (2005)
4. Fowler, M.: Code ownership (2006). https://martinfowler.com/bliki/CodeOwnership.html

5. Girardi, D., Lanubile, F., Novielli, N., Serebrenik, A.: Emotions and perceived productivity of software developers at the workplace. IEEE Trans. Softw. Eng. **48**(9), 3326–3341 (2021)
6. Greiler, M., Storey, M.A., Noda, A.: An actionable framework for understanding and improving developer experience. IEEE Trans. Softw. Eng. **49**(4), 1411–1425 (2022)
7. He, R., He, H., Zhang, Y., Zhou, M.: Automating dependency updates in practice: an exploratory study on GitHub Dependabot. IEEE Trans. Softw. Eng. **49**(8), 4004–4022 (2023). https://doi.org/10.1109/tse.2023.3278129
8. Michels, L.M., Petkova, A., Richter, M., Farley, A., Graziotin, D., Wagner, S.: Overwhelmed software developers. IEEE Softw. **41**, 51–59 (2024)
9. Mirhosseini, S., Parnin, C.: Can automated pull requests encourage software developers to upgrade out-of-date dependencies? (2017)
10. Razzaq, A., Buckley, J., Lai, Q., Yu, T., Botterweck, G.: A systematic literature review on the influence of enhanced developer experience on developers' productivity: factors, practices, and recommendations. ACM Comput. Surv. **57**(1), 1–46 (2024)
11. Runeson, P., Host, M., Rainer, A., Regnell, B.: Case Study Research in Software Engineering: Guidelines and Examples. Wiley (2012)
12. Šmite, D., Moe, N.B., Floryan, M., Gonzalez-Huerta, J., Dorner, M., Sablis, A.: Decentralized decision-making and scaled autonomy at Spotify. J. Syst. Softw. **200**, 111649 (2023). https://doi.org/10.1016/j.jss.2023.111649
13. Tanenbaum, A.S., Feamster, N., Wetherall, D.J.: Computer Networks, 6th edn. Pearson, Harlow (2021)
14. Tanveer, B., Zabardast, E., Gonzalez-Huerta, J.: An approach to align socio-technical dependencies in large-scale software development. In: International Conference on Software Architecture (2023)
15. Tkalich, A., Klotins, E., Sporsem, T., Stray, V., Moe, N.B., Barbala, A.: User feedback in continuous software engineering: revealing the state-of-practice. Empir. Softw. Eng. **30**(3), 79 (2025). https://doi.org/10.1007/s10664-024-10557-2

Influence of LLM Prioritizations on Human Decisions in Requirements Engineering

Amna Pir Muhammad[(✉)], Richard Berntsson Svensson, and Irum Inayat

Department of Computer Science and Engineering, University of Gothenburg and Chalmers University of Technology, Gothenburg, Sweden
`amnap@chalmers.se`, `richard@cse.gu.se`, `irum@chalmers.se`

Abstract. Prioritizing software requirements is a critical yet subjective task in early-stage development. As large language models (LLMs) such as ChatGPT become increasingly integrated into software engineering workflows, it remains unclear how their suggestions influence human decision-making in tasks that require judgment and trade-offs. In particular, little is known about how the reasoning style of LLM-generated justifications, whether intuitive or analytical—affects user trust, confidence, and behavioral responses. This study explores how LLMs shape human prioritization decisions through a controlled survey. Participants ranked requirements for two hypothetical projects, then reviewed LLM-generated prioritizations framed using either intuitive (System 1) or analytical (System 2) reasoning. After exposure, they could revise their rankings and changes in confidence, cognitive effort, and trust in the LLM. Findings show that participants treated the LLM as a cognitive aid rather than an authority: most retained their original decisions, but confidence increased and perceived effort declined. Evaluations of the LLM's accuracy and trustworthiness were generally moderate, with reasoning style having a limited effect. These results suggest that LLMs can support human reasoning in requirements engineering, not by replacing human judgment but by reinforcing it through structured external input.

Keywords: Requirements Engineering · Requirements Prioritization · Large Language Models · System 1 and System 2 Thinking · Cognitive Effort

1 Introduction

Prioritizing software requirements is a foundational task in requirements engineering. It determines which features are implemented first, shaping project scope, resource allocation, and stakeholder satisfaction [1]. Although various structured techniques exist to support this activity, prioritization decisions are often subjective, influenced by intuition, past experience, and contextual judgment rather than formal analysis [2,3]. These challenges make prioritization not only a technical task but also a cognitive one.

G. Scanniello et al. (Eds.): PROFES 2025, LNCS 16361, pp. 369–384, 2026.
https://doi.org/10.1007/978-3-032-12089-2_23

With the increasing integration of Large Language Models (LLMs) like GPT-4 into software engineering workflows, their potential role in supporting requirement prioritization deserves closer examination. LLMs have shown promise in assisting high-level decision-making by generating plausible justifications, simulating reasoning, and providing structured outputs across diverse domains [4,5]. Their applications in software engineering already span code generation, defect prediction, and documentation tasks [6,7]. However, little is known about how LLM-generated suggestions influence human decisions in subjective and comparative tasks such as requirement prioritization.

One potentially important factor is how the LLM presents its reasoning. Drawing on dual-process theory from cognitive psychology [8], we distinguish between two modes of reasoning: System 1 (intuitive and fast) and System 2 (analytical and deliberate). The framing of explanations in these styles may influence how users interpret the output, how much effort they expend, and how much confidence or trust they place in the system. Yet little is known about whether an LLM's reasoning style influences users' confidence, perceived cognitive effort, or trust in its output, factors critical to meaningful AI-human collaboration.

This paper investigates how people engage with LLM-generated requirement prioritizations framed using these two reasoning styles. In a controlled survey involving two hypothetical projects, participants were asked to rank requirements, then review LLM-generated prioritizations, each accompanied by either intuitive or analytical justifications, and decide whether to revise their rankings. We also measured changes in their confidence, perceived cognitive effort, and perceptions of the LLM's trustworthiness and accuracy before and after exposure.

Our findings show that while most participants retained their original decisions, many reported increased confidence and slightly reduced effort after reviewing the LLM suggestions. The reasoning style had limited impact on behavior or trust, though analytical framing was associated with slightly higher confidence gains. Participants treated the LLM not as an authority but as a cognitive aid, supporting their reasoning without overriding it.

These results add to ongoing discussions about the role of LLMs in early-stage software engineering tasks. They suggest that AI-generated justifications can aid human decision-making by reinforcing reflection, even in subjective tasks. They also raise questions about how explanation framing, prior experience, and trust shape human–AI interaction.

The rest of the paper is structured as follows: Sect. 2 reviews background and related work. Section 3 outlines the research design and methodology. Section 4presents and discusses the results in relation to the research questions. Finally, Sect. 5 concludes the paper and outlines directions for future work.

2   Background and Related Work

Requirement prioritization is a critical activity that directly impacts project success. It ensures that resources are allocated efficiently and that essential functionalities are delivered early [9,10]. Given typical constraints in time, budget, or capacity, teams must make difficult decisions about which features to implement first. To support this, a wide range of techniques have been proposed [11], from informal ranking and voting to structured approaches like the Analytic Hierarchy Process (AHP), MoSCoW, and cost-value frameworks [1,12–14].

Despite these tools, prioritization remains largely subjective. Stakeholders often rely on intuition or past experience rather than structured analysis [2,3,15]. Assessments can vary due to incomplete knowledge, conflicting roles, or project context [16,17]. This subjectivity makes requirement prioritization a compelling case for examining the role of AI support.

To better understand this subjectivity, insights from cognitive psychology are useful. Dual-process theory, proposed by Kahneman [8], offers a useful framework. It distinguishes between System 1 thinking—fast, intuitive, and heuristic-driven, and System 2 thinking, which is slower, more deliberate, and analytical.

In software engineering, especially in early design and requirements phases, stakeholders often rely on System 1 thinking due to time pressure or cognitive load. This can lead to biases like anchoring, availability, or overconfidence [17]. Though System 2 thinking may counter these, it requires more effort and is less likely in fast-paced or group settings where quick agreement is favored over individual reflection [18,19].

This psychological perspective highlights the limits of unaided human decision-making in complex software tasks. At the same time, it suggests a potential role for external aids—such as AI-based decision support systems—in improving consistency and reducing bias [20].

Traditionally, AI decision support tools have focused on structured outputs like risk scores or diagnostic predictions [21]. However, recent advances in large language models (LLMs) have shifted attention toward systems capable of generating natural language explanations. This development is particularly relevant in contexts where decisions require not only computation, but also explanation, justification, and negotiation [22].

Recent LLMs, such as GPT-4, have expanded the scope of decision support by generating explanations, trade-offs, and justifications in natural language. In software engineering, LLMs have already been used for tasks like code generation, test creation, and requirements classification [6,23,24]. Some studies suggest they can even produce plausible requirement rankings with human-like justifications [25]. However, the usefulness of these outputs depends on how users evaluate the system's competence, transparency, and fairness [26].

Nevertheless, while LLMs have been applied to various requirements engineering tasks, such as classification, extraction, and generation, their role in shaping human decisions during requirement prioritization remains largely unexamined. In particular, no prior work has systematically investigated how the style of AI-generated reasoning—intuitive versus analytical—affects stakeholder judgments in this context. Given that explanation framing can influence user trust and decision outcomes [27,28], this presents a timely and important research opportunity.

3   Method

The main objective of this study was to investigate how LLMs influence human decision-making in software requirements prioritization, with particular attention to user confidence, cognitive effort, and trust. The study examined how participants interacted with LLM-generated prioritizations framed using different cognitive reasoning styles, inspired by dual-process theory.

In order to address this objective, the following research questions (RQs) were formulated:

- **RQ1:** How does exposure to LLM-generated prioritizations affect participants' initial prioritization of software requirements?
- **RQ2:** How does the LLM's reasoning style influence participants' confidence and perceived cognitive effort?
- **RQ3:** How do participants perceive the accuracy, trustworthiness, and overall confidence in the LLM-generated prioritizations?

To answer the research questions, this study employed a quantitative research design using a survey research approach.

The survey was designed to assess several key aspects of participants' interactions with the LLM-generated prioritizations. Specifically, it measured participants' confidence in their initial requirement rankings, the perceived mental effort involved in the task, and their willingness to revise decisions after viewing the LLM output. It also captured changes in confidence and effort following LLM exposure, as well as participants' evaluations of the LLM's perceived accuracy and trustworthiness. These measures provided both behavioral and perceptual insight into how users engaged with the AI-generated recommendations.

The survey consisted of four main sections: (1) demographic background, (2) Project 1 (Customer Support Chatbot), (3) Project 2 (Event Registration System), and (4) general questions about participants' perceptions of LLM accuracy and trustworthiness. It included a combination of multiple-choice, Likert-scale, and ranking questions to collect structured responses on participants' experiences and perceptions. Each of the two project scenarios was introduced with a short description and a list of ten functional software requirements. Participants were first asked to independently prioritize these requirements. They then reviewed a prioritization generated by GPT-4o, which included brief justifications for each item, and were given the option to revise their original rankings.

The two LLM-generated outputs were crafted to reflect distinct cognitive reasoning styles, drawing on dual-process theory [29]. For the Chatbot scenario, the output followed System 1 reasoning, intuitive, emotionally framed, and user-centered. For the Event System scenario, the output reflected System 2 reasoning, deliberative, structured, and logic based. To avoid priming effects, participants were not informed about the reasoning styles in advance.

Before distributing the main survey, a pilot test was conducted with two domain experts in requirements engineering. Their feedback helped improve the clarity of instructions, refine scenario descriptions, and simplify the wording of some Likert-scale items.

Data Collection: The survey was administered online using the SoSci Survey platform[1], which ensured secure data collection and participant anonymity. Data were collected over an eight-week period in 2025, resulting in 33 complete and valid responses. The survey link is available here.

Informed consent was obtained from all participants prior to beginning the survey, and no personally identifying information was recorded. The target population for the survey consisted of software professionals, including requirements engineers, product managers, developers, and other roles involved in software design and planning. Participants were expected to have some familiarity with requirement analysis or prioritization, though no specific expertise was required.

A combination of convenience and snowball sampling was used to recruit participants. Initial outreach was conducted through personal contacts and professional networks, such as LinkedIn. Participants were encouraged to share the survey with colleagues in similar roles, which helped extend the reach across both industry and academic environments.

Data Analysis: Quantitative data were analyzed using both descriptive and inferential methods. Before analysis, the dataset was reviewed for completeness. Missing values were minimal and were excluded from the analysis where necessary. Descriptive statistics were used to summarize participant demographics and to report percentages for Likert-scale items such as confidence, effort, trust, and perceived accuracy. To evaluate pre- and post-exposure differences in confidence and effort, the Wilcoxon signed-rank test was applied. This non-parametric test is appropriate for paired ordinal data where normality cannot be assumed.

Visualizations, including bar charts, were generated to illustrate response distributions and group-level differences, aiding interpretation of the results.

Threats to Validity: Following established guidelines for evaluating empirical research validity [30], we discuss threats to internal, external, construct, and conclusion validity. *Internal validity* concerns arise from the nature of self-reported measures. Participants' confidence and effort ratings could be influenced by social desirability bias, potentially affecting the accuracy of these subjective responses. *External validity* is another consideration, as the survey focused on hypothetical software projects rather than real-world cases. This may limit the applicability of the findings to practical settings. Additionally, the recruitment of participants primarily through convenience and snowball sampling methods, and mainly from technology sectors, might have constrained the diversity of the sample. *Construct validity* could be threatened by the way LLM-generated prioritizations were presented. Although the outputs were crafted to simulate System 1 and System 2 thinking styles, participants were not informed of this distinction. Their reactions to the justifications might have varied in ways not directly aligned with the intended cognitive framing, impacting how they assessed and trusted the outputs. *Conclusion validity* is limited by the relatively small sample size of 33 participants, which reduces the statistical power of the findings. As a result, broad generalizations should be made cautiously.

---

[1] https://www.soscisurvey.de.

4 Results and Discussions

This section presents and discusses the results corresponding to the three research questions introduced in Sect. 3.

Respondents Demographics: Most participants (73.8%) reported roles in areas such as requirements engineering, development, architecture, testing, or product-related positions. The remaining 26.2% identified their primary role as "researcher." Since institutional affiliation was not collected, this group may include individuals working in either academic or industry research settings.

Participants had varied levels of experience in software development. The largest group (38.1%) reported 6–10 years of experience, followed by 23.8% with 0–2 years, 21.4% with 3–5 years, and 16.7% with over 11 years of experience. Engagement with requirements prioritization also varied: 31.0% reported being "sometimes" involved, 19.0% "rarely," and 14.3% "never." The rest indicated more regular involvement, with 16.7% selecting "often" and 19.0% "always."

A majority (66.7%) of participants had previously used LLM-based tools in their work. However, regular reliance was less common. Only 18.4% reported using them "often," while 34.2% used them "sometimes," 26.3% "rarely," and 21.1% had never used them. No participant reported always relying on LLM suggestions. When asked about general trust in LLM tools for software-related tasks, most participants expressed only moderate trust. Specifically, 40.5% selected "slightly," another 40.5% chose "moderately," while 9.5% indicated "mostly," 2.4% "completely," and 7.1% reported no trust at all.

This diversity in professional background, experience, and exposure to LLMs provides important context for understanding participants' responses and interactions with AI-generated prioritizations.

4.1 Change in Prioritization Behavior (RQ1)

In analyzing RQ 1, this section examines how exposure to LLM-generated suggestions influenced participants' requirement prioritization behavior. Overall, the results point to a moderate and selective openness to LLM input, with most participants retaining their original rankings but some making substantial changes.

In Project 1 (Chatbot), 36.4% of participants revised their prioritization after viewing the LLM-generated suggestions; in Project 2 (Event System), a similar pattern emerged, with 36.7% making changes. The majority in both cases, 63.6% and 63.3%, respectively, retained their original rankings, as shown in Fig. 1.

We further assessed the nature of these changes using a Wilcoxon signed-rank test, which showed no significant difference (W = 1824.50, p = 0.8396). This lack of consistent directional shift suggests that participants did not collectively adopt the LLM's prioritization. Instead, the varied changes across individuals point toward more selective engagement, likely driven by case-by-case judgments.

This result is reinforced by the pattern of individual changes. Among participants who did revise their rankings, adjustments were often substantial. In the Chatbot project, participants changed between 0 and 10 items (mean = 5.9),

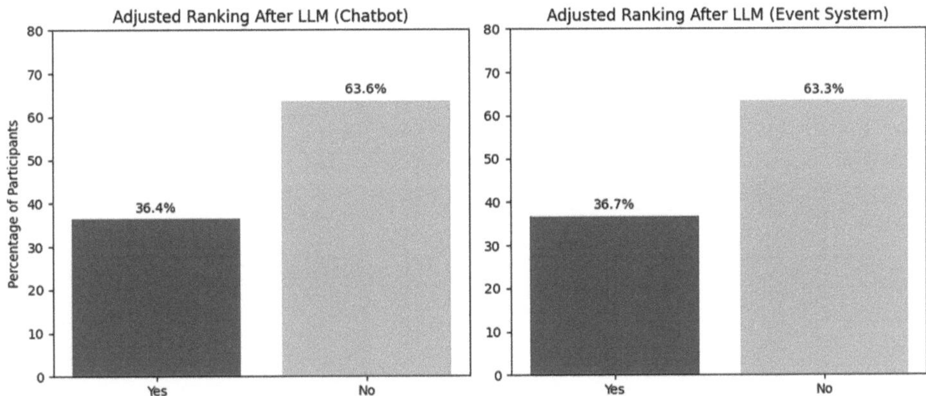

Fig. 1. Adjusted Ranking After Seeing LLM Input.

while in the Event Project, the range was 0 to 8 items (mean = 5.5). Most participants who made changes altered five or more items, suggesting meaningful rethinking rather than token modifications. For example, three participants in the Chatbot project changed nine or ten items, and two participants in the Event project adjusted eight items each.

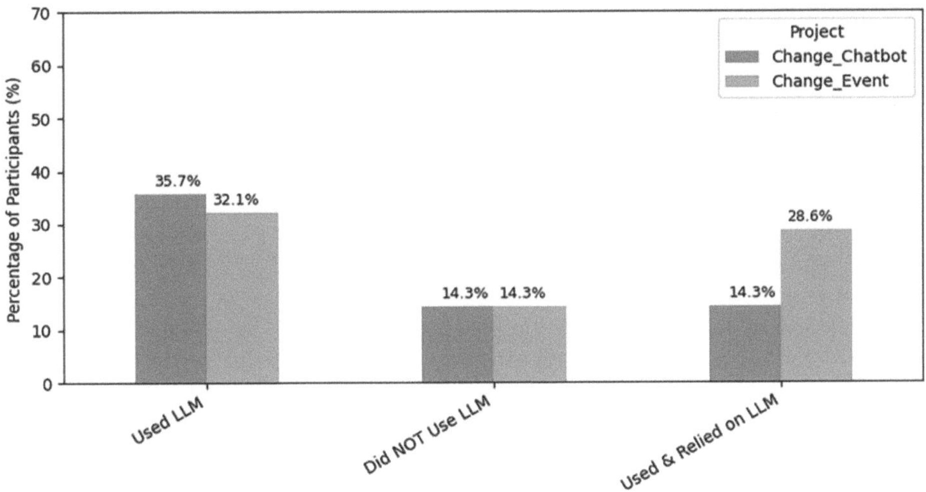

Fig. 2. Change in Prioritization Among Different Groups.

Despite the extent of these changes, the revised rankings rarely mirrored the LLM's suggestions in full. **This implies that even when participants were influenced by the model, they did not adopt its output wholesale. Rather, they integrated elements of it into their own reasoning, confirming or adjusting their views based on perceived fit.**

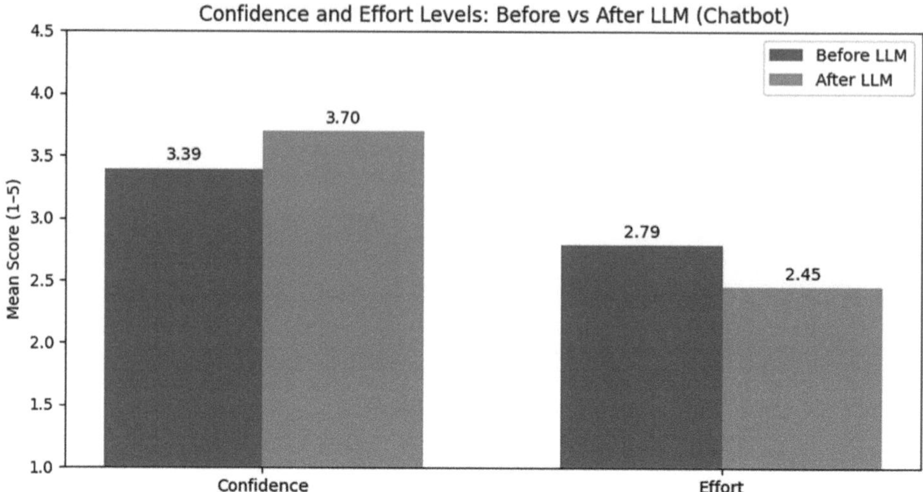

Fig. 3. Confidence and Effort Levels: Before vs After LLM (Chatbot System).

To better understand the nature of prioritization changes, we examined how changes were distributed across different types of participants. Our results, as illustrated in Fig. 2, shows that participants who had previously used LLMs were more likely to revise their prioritizations compared to those who had not. In the Chatbot project, 35.7% of users of LLM made changes, compared to 14.3% of non-users. A similar pattern was observed for perceived effort: in some cases, participants reported reduced effort even when they did not change their decisions, indicating that the LLM may have eased the task cognitively, independent of behavioral change. Interestingly, participants who both used and relied on LLMs showed the highest change rate in the Event project (28.6%), suggesting that reliance, not just familiarity, shaped responsiveness to LLM output. This reinforces the idea that trust and prior experience mediate how AI-generated suggestions are interpreted and acted upon.

Overall, in general, reliance on the LLM, not just usage, appears to influence its impact on both confidence and perceived effort. **These patterns point to the role of perceived trust and familiarity in shaping how participants engage with and benefit from AI-generated suggestions. Taken together, these findings suggest that LLMs were treated not as authoritative decision-makers but as advisory tools. The influence of the model was real but limited, shaped by user judgment and context.** This pattern aligns with existing research on algorithm aversion and selective adherence [31,32]. Rather than outsourcing their decisions, participants appeared to weigh the LLM's input against their own reasoning, selectively integrating suggestions when they seemed helpful.

In subjective domains like requirements prioritization, where trade-offs depend on context and judgment, such selective use is not only expected but desirable. While the framing of justifications (System1 vs. System2) had little effect on revision behavior, the impact of the LLM varied based on trust, perceived utility, and individual disposition.

4.2 Confidence in Own Judgment and Cognitive Effort (RQ2)

This section examines how exposure to LLM suggestions influenced participants' confidence and perceived cognitive effort during requirements prioritization.

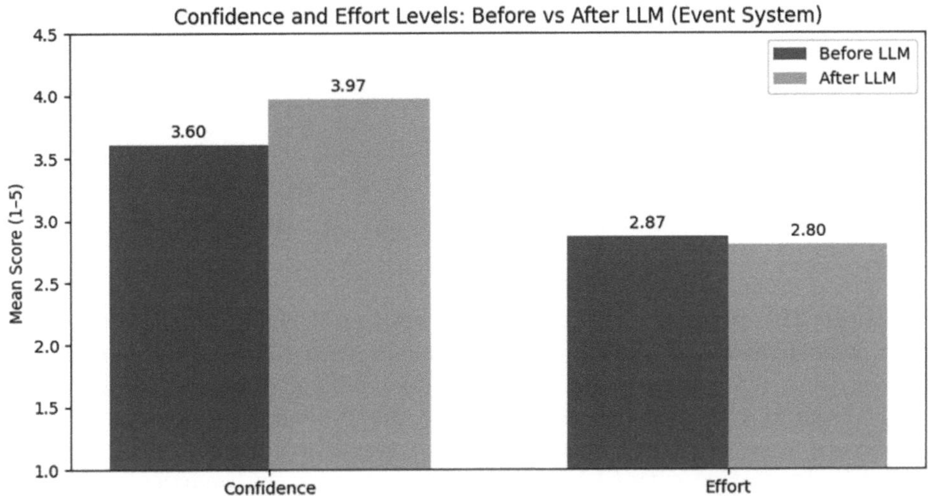

Fig. 4. Confidence and Effort Levels: Before vs After LLM (Event System).

Across both projects, participants generally reported increased confidence in their final decisions after reviewing the LLM output. In the Chatbot task (Project 1), mean confidence rose from 3.39 to 3.70; in the Event System task (Project 2), it increased from 3.60 to 3.97 (Fig. 3 and Fig. 4). At the same time, perceived cognitive effort decreased modestly. In the Chatbot task, effort dropped from 2.79 to 2.45, and in the Event System task, from 2.87 to 2.80. **These results suggest that LLM suggestions (regardless of their reasoning style) acted as a cognitive aid, helping participants feel more assured in their decisions while slightly reducing the mental workload.**

To assess whether these confidence gains were statistically meaningful, we conducted a Wilcoxon signed-rank test. In the Chatbot project (System 1 framing), the increase in confidence approached significance ($W = 18.00$, $p = 0.0389$), while in the Event System task (System 2 framing), it reached statistical significance ($W = 9.50$, $p = 0.0307$). These findings suggest a modest but measurable impact on confidence, particularly under analytical framing. **These results reinforce the idea that LLM-generated justifications functioned as a form of cognitive support. Even when participants did not revise their**

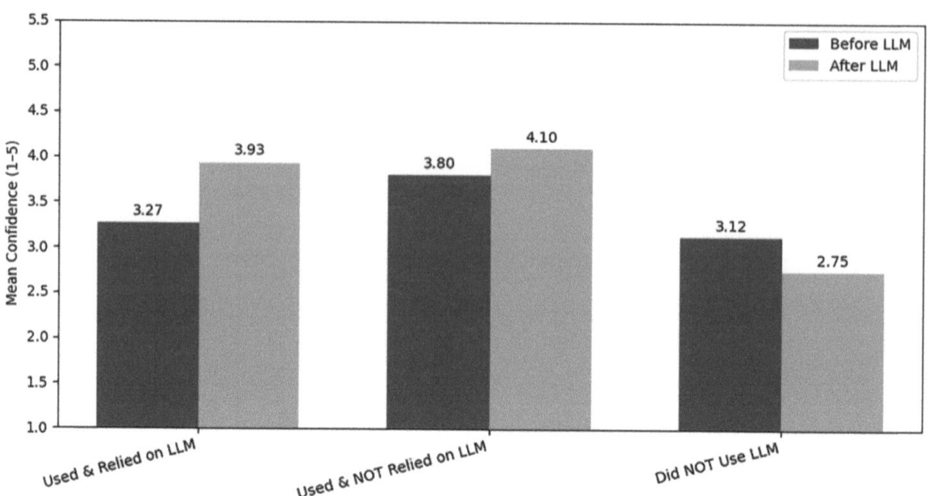

Fig. 5. Confidence Before and After LLM Exposure for Different Groups (Chatbot).

rankings, the presence of structured, external reasoning appeared to offer reassurance or validation. This aligns with findings from prior work showing that decision aids can increase user confidence and reduce perceived cognitive effort even when users do not fully adopt their recommendations [33].

We also analysed how participants' self-reported confidence changed before and after interacting with LLM-generated suggestions, with particular focus on their LLM usage behavior. Participants were categorized into three groups: those who used and relied on the LLM, those who used it but did not rely on it, and those who did not use the LLM.

Figures 5 and 6 show group-wise changes in confidence for the Chatbot and Event system tasks, respectively. Across both tasks, confidence gains were most pronounced among participants who used and relied on the LLM. In the Chatbot task (Fig. 5), participants who used and relied on the LLM reported a mean confidence increase from 3.27 to 3.93. Those who used the LLM but did not rely on it showed a smaller gain, from 3.80 to 4.10. Interestingly, participants who did not use the LLM actually reported a drop in confidence, from 3.12 to 2.75. In the Event system task (Fig. 6), the same pattern emerged but with generally higher baseline confidence. Confidence rose from 3.71 to 4.00 among those who used and relied on the LLM. Among non-reliant LLM users, the increase was larger—from 3.88 to 4.38. Even participants who did not use the LLM reported a moderate increase (3.12 to 3.50), unlike in the Chatbot task.

These results indicate that exposure to LLM suggestions increased confidence, especially when participants perceived the system as trustworthy and useful. The differential outcomes across groups suggest that reliance, not just exposure, played a key role in shaping perceived support. This aligns with earlier findings suggesting that users are more receptive to AI support in tasks

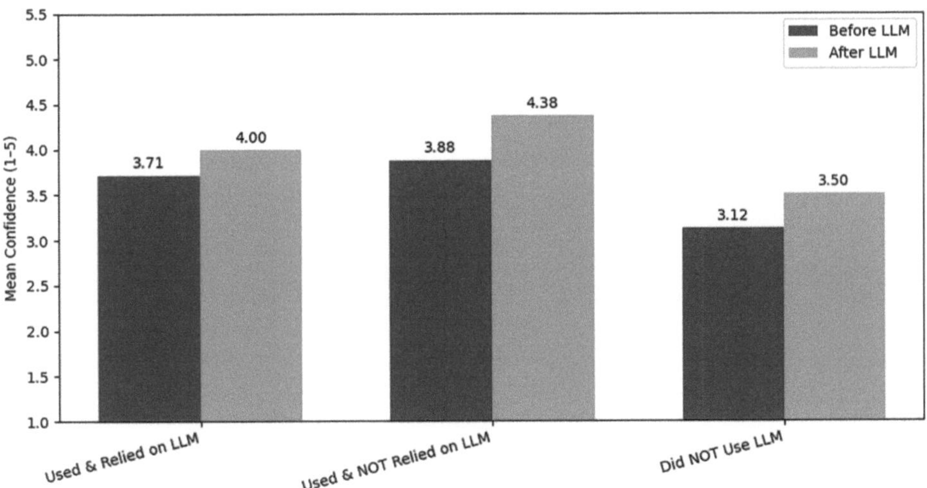

Fig. 6. Confidence Before and After LLM Exposure for Different Groups (Event System).

that appear logic-driven or objective. **Overall, these findings highlight that LLMs are most impactful when users actively engage with them. Trust and reliance mediate the effect on confidence, and this varies depending on task framing.**

One interesting pattern is the disconnect between behavioral and attitudinal change: while most participants did not alter their prioritizations, a sizable portion still reported increased confidence. **This supports the idea that LLMs were not used as decision-makers, but as reflective scaffolds tools that helped users think more clearly about their own decisions.** This finding echoes prior research showing that AI systems can serve as psychological support tools, helping people feel more confident even when the system's output is not directly adopted [8,33].

4.3 Evaluation of LLM Output: Accuracy, Trust, and Confidence in the Model (RQ3)

Participants' perceptions of the LLM's output were assessed using three measures: confidence, perceived accuracy, and trust. These dimensions capture how participants evaluated the model's prioritization, distinct from their confidence in their own judgment.

Participants were first asked how confident they were that the LLM's output reflected the best possible prioritization for both projects. This measure—confidence in the LLM output—is conceptually distinct from confidence in their own decisions. Figure 7 shows that participants' confidence mostly clustered around the middle of the scale (levels 3 and 4). In Project 1 (Chatbot), 36.4% selected level 3 and 24.2% level 4. In Project 2 (Event System), 40.0% selected

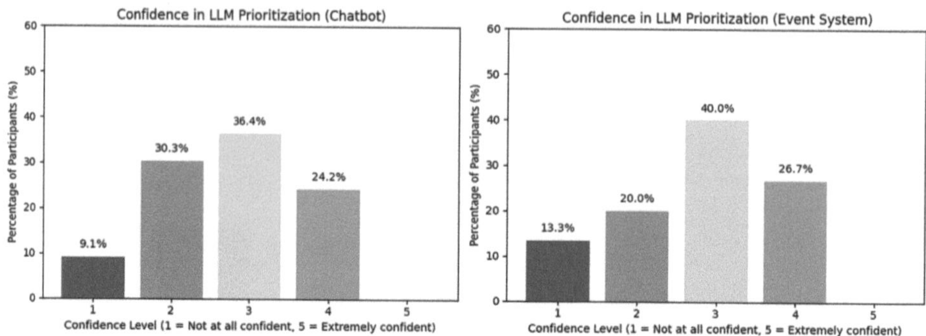

Fig. 7. Confidence in LLM Prioritization.

level 3 and 26.7% level 4. Very few participants reported high confidence (level 5), and only 9.1% and 13.3% chose level 1 for Projects 1 and 2, respectively.

These middle-range confidence ratings suggest that participants generally saw the LLM as a helpful but limited advisor. Interestingly, participants expressed moderate confidence in the LLM's output, even when their ratings of its trustworthiness and accuracy were low (discussed below).**One possible explanation is that the LLM functioned less as a persuasive authority and more as a cognitive reference point—prompting participants to reflect more deeply on their own choices.** This effect has been noted in prior work, where even untrusted systems can support decision-making by promoting critical engagement [33].

In terms of perceived accuracy, most participants rated the LLM output as at least moderately accurate, though strong agreement was uncommon. In the general case, 38% of participants rated the LLM output as "moderately" accurate, 7% selected "mostly," and none chose "completely." A combined 53% expressed low agreement, selecting "not at all" (23%) or "slightly" (30%). For Project 1 (Chatbot), 33% rated the output as "moderately" accurate, with 7% selecting "mostly" and 6% "completely." In Project 2 (Event System), 29% chose "moderately," and 11% "mostly." However, 33% of participants selected "not at all" for Project 2—higher than the 29% who did so in Project 1. These distributions are presented in Fig. 8.

Despite slight variation between projects, **fewer than 15% of participants in either case rated the LLM output as "mostly" or "completely" accurate.** This cautious stance is consistent with previous studies showing that users tend to approach AI-generated outputs with skepticism—particularly in settings that require domain knowledge or contextual reasoning [22,32]. While Project 2 (System 2 framing) used a more analytical justification, the gain in perceived accuracy was minimal. This suggests that structured explanations alone may not be enough to shift user evaluations significantly.

A similar pattern emerged in participants' trust ratings. As shown in Fig. 9, trust levels were generally low to moderate. For Project 1, 44% selected "slight"

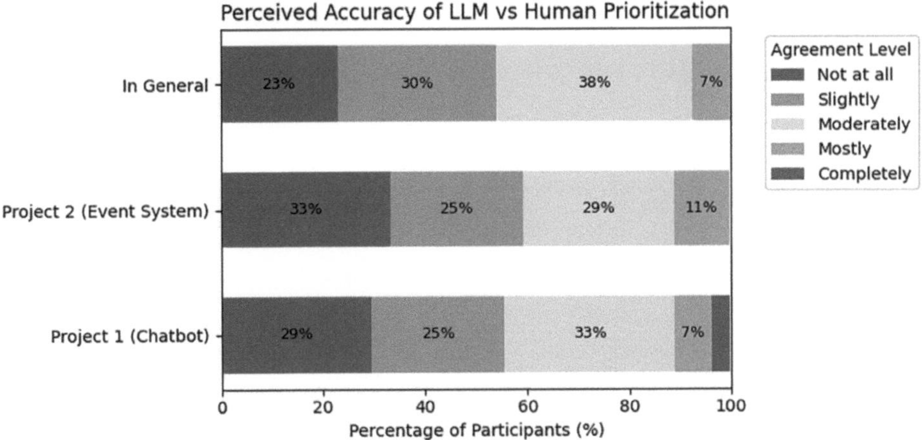

Fig. 8. Perceived Accuracy of LLM.

trust, and 33% chose "moderate." Fewer than 5% selected "mostly" or "completely." In Project 2, 37% indicated "slight" trust, 29% "moderate," and 14% "mostly" or "completely." In the general case, 44% of participants selected "moderate," and fewer than 10% rated the LLM as highly trustworthy.

While slightly higher trust ratings appeared in Project 2, the difference was not large. Still, this may reflect a general preference for structured, logical justifications, as prior research suggests such framing is more likely to be perceived as credible [27,28]. Even so, most participants withheld strong trust in the system. This aligns with broader evidence that user trust in automation depends more on prior attitudes and long-term exposure than on any single interaction [22,32]. Indeed, participants' general trust in LLM tools, captured in the pre-task survey, closely mirrored their post-task ratings, with over 75% expressing only slight or moderate trust before and after the task.

In summary, participants' evaluations of the LLM—across confidence, accuracy, and trust—were mostly moderate. While the LLM was seen as helpful, strong endorsement was rare. **Participants approached the system with caution, and even when they did not fully trust or agree with the LLM, it still played a role in prompting reflection and shaping user confidence in their own decisions.**

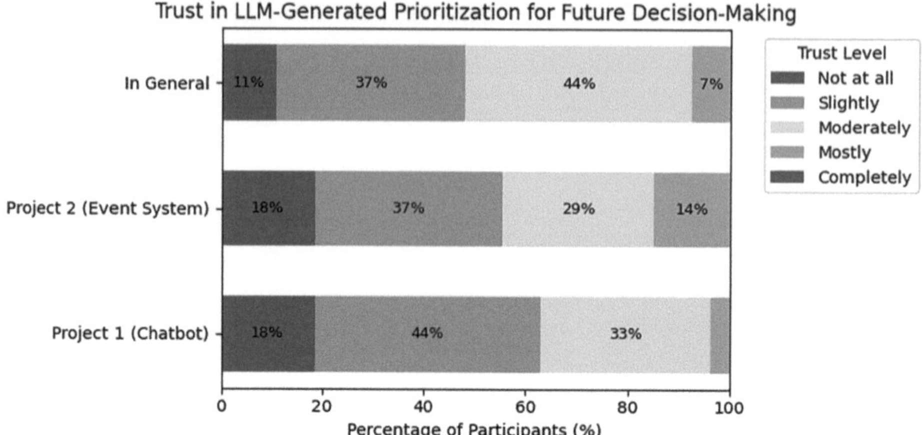

Fig. 9. Perceived Trust in LLM.

5   Conclusion

This study investigated how LLMs influence human decision-making in software requirements prioritization, with a focus on confidence, trust, and reasoning style. By comparing two cognitive styles, intuitive (System 1) and analytical (System 2), we examined how participants engaged with LLM suggestions and whether these shaped their prioritization behavior or perceptions of the model.

Across all three research questions, a consistent pattern emerged: participants engaged selectively with the LLM. While some revised their rankings, most retained their initial decisions, suggesting LLM functioned more as a cognitive reference point than as an authoritative advisor. Confidence in decisions increased and perceived cognitive effort decreased after exposure to LLM output, even when trust and perceived accuracy remained moderate. These effects were stronger among users familiar with LLMs, highlighting the role of prior familiarity in shaping AI influence. The explanation style, intuitive or analytical, had little measurable impact on trust, accuracy ratings, or behavioral change.

Taken together, the findings suggest that LLMs can serve as valuable cognitive aids in early-stage software engineering. Rather than replacing human judgment, they help users reflect, compare, and consolidate their decisions, especially when framed as advisory tools rather than persuasive agents.

Future research should explore how LLMs function in real-world, collaborative RE settings, where task complexity and stakeholder diversity are higher. Qualitative methods such as think-aloud protocols or post-task interviews could offer deeper insight into how users interpret AI-generated justifications and negotiate disagreement. Finally, investigating longitudinal use could help clarify whether trust and influence evolve with continued exposure, and how domain expertise moderates reliance on AI support.

References

1. Wiegers, K.: First things first: prioritizing requirements. Softw. Dev. **7**(9), 48–53 (1999)
2. Achimugu, P., Selamat, A., Ibrahim, R., Mahrin, M.N.: A systematic literature review of software requirements prioritization research. Inf. Softw. Technol. **56**(6), 568–585 (2014)
3. Lehtola, L., Kauppinen, M., Kujala, S.: Requirements prioritization challenges in practice. In: International Conference on Product Focused Software Process Improvement, pp. 497–508. Springer (2004)
4. Open AIP: GPT-4 technical report. arXiv preprint arXiv:2303.08774 (2023)
5. Bubeck, S., et al.: Sparks of artificial general intelligence: early experiments with GPT-4 (2023)
6. Chen, M., et al.: Evaluating large language models trained on code. arXiv preprint arXiv:2107.03374 (2021)
7. Fan, A., et al.: Large language models for software engineering: survey and open problems. In: ICSE-FoSE, pp. 31–53. IEEE (2023)
8. Kahneman, D.: Thinking, Fast and Slow. Macmillan (2011)
9. Karlsson, J., Ryan, K.: A cost-value approach for prioritizing requirements. IEEE Softw. **14**(5), 67–74 (2002)
10. Sommerville, I.: Software Engineering, 10th edn. (2015)
11. Ahmad, K., Abdelrazek, M., Arora, C., Bano, M., Grundy, J.: Requirements engineering for artificial intelligence systems: a systematic mapping study. Inf. Softw. Technol. **158**, 107176 (2023)
12. Saaty, T.L.: The analytic hierarchy process (AHP). J. Oper. Res. Soc. **41**(11), 1073–1076 (1980)
13. Akao, Y.: Quality Function Deployment: Integrating Customer Requirements into Product Design. CRC Press (2024)
14. Clegg, D., Barker, R.: Case Method Fast-Track: A RAD Approach. Addison-Wesley Longman Publishing Co., Inc. (1994)
15. Hidellaarachchi, D., Grundy, J., Hoda, R., Madampe, K.: The effects of human aspects on the requirements engineering process: a systematic literature review. IEEE Trans. Softw. Eng. **48**(6) (2021)
16. Berander, P., Andrews, A.: Requirements prioritization. In: Engineering and Managing Software Requirements, pp. 69–94. Springer (2005)
17. Mohanani, R., Salman, I., Turhan, B., Rodríguez, P., Ralph, P.: Cognitive biases in software engineering: a systematic mapping study. IEEE Trans. Softw. Eng. **46**(12), 1318–1339 (2018)
18. Svenson, O.: Differentiation and consolidation theory of human decision making: a frame of reference for the study of pre-and post-decision processes. Acta Physiol. (OXF) **80**(1–3), 143–168 (1992)
19. Evans, J.S.B.: Dual-processing accounts of reasoning, judgment, and social cognition. Annu. Rev. Psychol. **59**(1), 255–278 (2008)
20. Lim, B.Y., Dey, A.K., Avrahami, D.: Why and why not explanations improve the intelligibility of context-aware intelligent systems. In: Proceedings of the SIGCHI Conference on Human Factors in Computing Systems, pp. 2119–2128 (2009)
21. Topol, E.J.: High-performance medicine: the convergence of human and artificial intelligence. Nat. Med. **25**(1), 44–56 (2019)
22. Binns, R., Van Kleek, M., Veale, M., Lyngs, U., Zhao, J., Shadbolt, N.: 'It's reducing a human being to a percentage' perceptions of justice in algorithmic decisions.

In: Proceedings of the 2018 Chi Conference on Human Factors in Computing Systems, pp. 1–14 (2018)
23. El-Hajjami, A., Fafin, N., Salinesi, C.: Which AI technique is better to classify requirements? An experiment with SVM, LSTM, and ChatGPT. arXiv preprint arXiv:2311.11547 (2023)
24. Allamanis, M., Barr, E.T., Devanbu, P., Sutton, C.: A survey of machine learning for big code and naturalness. ACM Comput. Surv. (CSUR) 51(4), 1–37 (2018)
25. Hemmat, A., Sharbaf, M., Kolahdouz-Rahimi, S., Lano, K., Tehrani, S.Y.: Research directions for using LLM in software requirement engineering: a systematic review. Front. Comput. Sci. 7, 1519437 (2025)
26. Eigner, E., Händler, T.: Determinants of LLM-assisted decision-making. arXiv preprint arXiv:2402.17385 (2024)
27. Hoff, K.A., Bashir, M.: Trust in automation: integrating empirical evidence on factors that influence trust. Hum. Fact. 57(3), 407–434 (2015)
28. Eiband, M., Schneider, H., Bilandzic, M., Fazekas-Con, J., Haug, M., Hussmann, H.: Bringing transparency design into practice. In: Proceedings of the 23rd International Conference on Intelligent User Interfaces, pp. 2105–2127 (2018)
29. Da Silva, S.: System 1 vs. System 2 thinking. Psych 5(4), 1057–1076 (2023)
30. Wohlin, C., Runeson, P., Höst, M., Ohlsson, M.C., Regnell, B., Wesslé n, A.: Experimentation in Software Engineering. Springer (2012)
31. Dietvorst, B.J., Simmons, J.P., Massey, C.: Algorithm aversion: people erroneously avoid algorithms after seeing them err. J. Exp. Psychol. General 144(1), 114 (2015)
32. Logg, J.M., Minson, J.A., Moore, D.A.: Algorithm appreciation: people prefer algorithmic to human judgment. Organ. Behav. Hum. Decis. Process. 151, 90–103 (2019)
33. Buçinca, Z., Malaya, M.B., Gajos, K.Z.: To trust or to think: cognitive forcing functions can reduce overreliance on AI in AI-assisted decision-making. Proc. ACM Hum. Comput. Interact. 5(CSCW1), 1–21 (2021)

Short Research Papers

Lab Package Development as a Means for Educating Software Engineering Students

Eliisabet Kaasik, Faiz Ali Shah$^{\textbf{ID}}$, and Dietmar Pfahl$^{(\boxtimes)}$ $^{\textbf{ID}}$

University of Tartu, Narva mnt 18, 51009 Tartu, Estonia
`{eliisabet.kaasik,faiz.ali.shah,dietmar.pfahl}@ut.ee`

Abstract. The education of future software engineers has been challenging for universities worldwide with regards to both quantity and quality. One way of addressing this challenge is to involve students into the development of teaching materials. In this paper, we describe how bachelor thesis projects can be employed to continuously evolve teaching materials and at the same time acquire new subject matter knowledge and transferable skills. We explain this with the help of a recent example in the context of popular course taught to 2nd year bachelor students at the University of Tartu. The subject matter of the course is software testing and the newly developed teaching material is a lab package on the topic of metamorphic testing. The lab package was developed using a design science approach. The lab package was delivered to more than 150 students and received positive feedback, re-confirming the effectiveness of the idea to use lab package development as an educational tool.

Keywords: Design science · Education · Lab package · Metamorphic testing · Software testing

1 Introduction

Technical courses in computer science bachelor programs often use lab sessions (or practice sessions) and associated homework assignments to help students gain deeper knowledge and skills on a specific topic of the subject matter taught. This attitude is inspired by recommendations of professional organisations like the ACM and IEEE on the design of computer science and related curricula [8].

With high demand by software industry for well-educated graduates from bachelor programs, student numbers of the relevant curricula are growing. In the United States alone, the number of bachelor degree students in the field "Computer and Information Sciences and Support Services" has increased from 64,492 graduates in the academic year 2013–14 to 120,372 graduates in the academic year 2023–24 [2]. But not only growing student numbers, also the fast evolving competencies and skills needed by the industry impose additional demands on the resources available for teaching and developing new teaching materials.

G. Scanniello et al. (Eds.): PROFES 2025, LNCS 16361, pp. 387–396, 2026.
https://doi.org/10.1007/978-3-032-12089-2_24

One way to address this challenge is to employ students not only for teaching tasks, e.g., as teaching assistants that supervise lab sessions and help with homework grading, but to also for the evolution of existing or development of new teaching materials. In this paper, we explain through an example case, how we combine the development and application of new lab packages for a 2nd year bachelor course with the supervision of a bachelor thesis project conducted by a 3rd year bachelor student who has previously taken the course.

The context is the course *Software Testing (LTAT.05.006)*, an important course taken by 150+ 2nd year students enrolled in the Computer Science bachelor program of the University of Tartu, Estonia. More precisely, we describe in detail how a new lab package on the topic *Metamorphic Testing* (MT) has been designed, executed, and evaluated, following a model that has been previously used in the development of eight lab packages. Our contribution is twofold:

- A conceptual model used for the development, application, and evaluation of new lab packages via bachelor thesis projects in the context of a large 2nd year bachelor course taught at the University of Tartu.
- A fully published and re-usable instantiation of the conceptual model as well as its output[1], including a description of the development, application, and evaluation of the newly created lab package *Metamorphic Testing*.

2   Background

2.1   Software Testing Course and Its Practice Sessions (Labs)

Software Testing (LTAT.05.006) [17] is a 2nd year bachelor course offered every year in the spring term by the University of Tartu as a part of the Software Development Specialty Module in the Computer Science curriculum. The purpose of the course is to introduce students to different software testing strategies.

Typically, each lecture is complemented by practice sessions (labs) in the following week. During the labs, students receive a hands-on introduction into one of the topics taught in the previous lecture by getting acquainted with a topic-relevant tool and doing some in-class exercises. After this warm-up, the homework assignment is introduced and students start working on the assignment alone or in pairs. During the past 10 years, several lab packages have been produced by students as BSc thesis project, covering the topics Visual testing, Debugging, Web application testing, Combinatorial testing, Random testing, Scriptless GUI testing, Mutation testing, and Security testing of mobile apps.

2.2   Metamorphic Testing

Traditional testing methods often rely on the presence of a *test oracle*. A test oracle is a mechanism or procedure used to determine whether the output of

---

[1] The BSc thesis by E. Kaasik is available at URL https://thesis.cs.ut.ee/c57f84f3-8349-43b3-81d3-17bade261e54.

a program is correct or incorrect [1]. According to Zheng et al. [19], there are many cases where the oracle is either unknown or impractical to apply, making it challenging to determine whether the output of the system under test (SUT) is correct, leading to what is known as the *oracle problem*.

Metamorphic Testing (MT) was first introduced by Chen et al. in 1998 [3] as a new approach to software testing in cases where a test oracle is unavailable or unreliable. According to Segura et al. [11], metamorphic testing is an effective method for verifying the correctness of so-called "untestable" programs, where errors cannot be easily detected by simply checking the outputs, as there are no test oracles. They explain how the MT strategy differs from other approaches: instead of focusing on individual outputs, MT examines the results of multiple program executions by checking whether the inputs and outputs satisfy certain properties. These properties are called Metamorphic Relations (MRs).

The core of MT lies in exploring the relations between inputs and outputs across multiple executions of the SUT; such relations are known as MRs. Formally, a MR is a property that relates the input and output of the SUT to another set of input and output [6]. Overall, the MT workflow involves five steps:

1. Generation of the initial Test Data (TD).
2. Identification of MRs that the SUT should satisfy.
3. Transformation of the TD by applying selected MR-specified transformations to the initial TD.
4. Execution of corresponding TD and the Transformed Test Data (TTD) pairs.
5. Verification of whether the observed changes in the output during the TD and TTD executions match the changes defined by the used MRs.

The final step requires further analysis to determine the outcome of the MT workflow, as no violations do not guarantee that the SUT is implemented correctly. If an MR is violated, it suggests a fault in the SUT, assuming the MR is correctly defined and is valid for the defined input data space [7].

MT has applications in various fields where traditional testing methods are insufficient. One usage of metamorphic testing lies in verifying scientific computations, where complex calculations make it difficult to determine the correct result [9]. During the last decade, MT has also been used for testing in machine learning (ML) models. Saha and Kanewala [10] described in their research non-testable programs, such as classifier models, whose correctness often cannot be determined using more traditional techniques. According to them, since classifiers are not always perfectly accurate, an incorrect result may not necessarily indicate a program fault, which makes testing machine learning models complex. One of the main challenges in testing ML models, more specifically image classification models, is their non-deterministic behaviour [5].

2.3 Teaching Metamorphic Testing

Although MT is a topic in the list of specification-based test techniques defined by ISO/IEC/IEEE 29119, MT is not frequently taught at universities. For example, a recent study [15] mapping the state of the practice in software testing teaching in four European countries (Portugal, Spain, Italy, Belgium), analyzed 119 courses with regards to its software testing content. The courses, of which only 19 are dedicated software testing courses (most of them taught at Master's level) are offered by 49 randomly selected universities. It turned out that only 9% of the dedicated software testing courses, and none of the other courses with some software testing content, cover the topic MT.

Nevertheless, MT seems to be increasingly appearing in software testing curricula, especially at the Bachelor's level. For example, the Singapore University of Technology and Design's course *Software Testing and Verification* [13] introduces metamorphic testing near the end of the syllabus as part of its advanced testing methodologies. The course covers topics such as testing without oracles and testing ML-based systems, positioning metamorphic testing alongside techniques like fuzzing and differential testing. Similarly, Idaho State University's course *Software Testing and Quality Assurance* [16] highlights metamorphic testing with other advanced techniques such as mutation testing and test automation. The inclusion of MT in university courses reflects its growing relevance in the software testing area. One industry observer, Michael Stahl [14], stated that while MT has previously been absent from most of the materials for basic or advanced software testing, it is now gaining popularity seemingly due to its utility for testing AI-based applications.

Previous teaching experiences, summarized by Chen et al. [4], have shown that students generally understand MT concepts easily and can apply them in practice, which makes MT a suitable topic for higher education in software testing. In particular, the task of identifying MR has been found to increase student engagement and creativity in testing exercises. However, due to the relative novelty of MT, challenges such as the lack of high-quality learning materials remain. At the University of Tartu, MT was previously not covered in the Bachelor's level Software Testing course, which has created the need for suitable lab materials, addressed in this thesis.

3   Conceptual Model of Lab Package Development

In order to fit into the scope of a BSc thesis project at the University of Tartu, which corresponds to a workload of 9 ECTS, the budget for development and evaluation of the lab package, as well as writing the thesis document must not exceed $9 \times 27 = 243$ person-hours. Students usually start working on their thesis project in November and submit the thesis in mid-May of the following year. Figure 1 shows a common timeline with milestones of a lab package development.

Typically, the development of a lab package needs four iterations. The first iteration is needed by the student to familiarize with the topic and the design and implementation of the first set of artifacts. The first frozen version of artifacts is reviewed by the thesis supervisor and, ideally, key persons responsible for conducting the labs. This milestone (M1) is important as here a decision must be made, whether the chances are good enough that the lab package is ready for use in the teaching of the upcoming spring term. After thorough review,

Activity	15.Oct	15.Nov	15.Dec	15.Jan	15.Feb	15.Mar	15.Apr	15.May
Student Instructions V1 dev.	■	■	■					
Student Instructions V2 dev.				■	■			
Student Instructions V3 dev.						■	■	
TA Instructions V1 dev.		■	■					
TA Instructions V2 dev.				■	■			
TA Instructions V3 dev.						■	■	
SUT V1 dev.		■	■					
SUT V2 dev.				■	■			
SUT V3 dev.						■	■	
Lab execution						■		
Feedback collection						■		
Thesis writing				■	■	■	■	■

Iteration 1 — M1 — Iteration 2 — M2 — Iteration 3 — M3 — It. 4 — M4

Fig. 1. Typical schedule of a lab package development project.

the artifacts are improved and frozen in a second version (M2). This version must be mature enough such that it can be used in the dedicated lab session. After the lab session, feedback from the involved TAs is collected. Once the students taking the *Software Testing* course have completed and submitted their homework assignments, they fill in a feedback form. Based on the observations and the feedback received, the artifacts are once again improved and the final version frozen for reuse in the next academic year (M3). Thesis writing typically starts during the second iteration. After analysis of observations and feedback received, the thesis student can complete the evaluation section of the thesis and wrap it up for submission (M4).

As indicated in Fig. 1, three artifacts are iteratively developed for any Lab Package, i.e., Student Instructions, TA Instructions, and Software Under Test (SUT). Often, additional artifacts are included in a Lab Package as needed, e.g., test code, test data, defect lists, issue reports or other auxiliary materials. The Student Instructions describe the tasks to be solved by the students and include information about the required software and the grading rubric. The confidential TA Instructions are typically an extension of the Student Instructions, containing model solutions and hints and tips about the application of the grading scheme as well a set of slides that can be used by the TAs during the lab session.

The conceptual model of lab package development instantiates the design science (or engineering research) approach. Design science entails a rational problem-solving process consisting of the tasks Problem Investigation, Treatment Design, Treatment Validation, Treatment Implementation, and Implementation Evaluation [18].

4   Design of the Lab Package "Metamorphic Testing"

For the development of the lab package on MT (in the following: MT lab), the thesis student followed the conceptual model described in Sect. 3. The purpose of the lab package is to provide learners with a practical understanding of MT and its usefulness by applying it to realistic scenarios relevant for the verification of software used in autonomous vehicles.

4.1 MT Lab Examples and Homework Tasks

The goal of the homework is to have students identify the most reliable software for two critical functions of a self-driving car: emergency braking distance calculation and traffic sign recognition. The tasks were chosen, because they reflect two main application areas of MT, i.e., testing scientific computations and machine learning models. The braking distance calculator represents a system based on physical and mathematical relationships, which can be easily expressed as MRs. It is a suitable introduction to MT since the students can use real-world experience and intuition to check whether the output changes as expected when the input parameters, like speed or slope, are altered. This is a straightforward example of how MT can be applied in scientific computing, where complex formulas make it difficult to know the correct output for a specific input. The traffic sign classification task was selected to introduce students to the application of MT in the verification of AI-based systems, which have non-deterministic behavior and must be treated as a black-box.

Task 1: Braking Distance Calculators. Braking distance refers to the distance a vehicle travels from the moment the braking is started until it comes to a complete stop. It depends on several factors, including vehicle speed, road conditions, and reaction time before pressing the brake.

The calculators used in this lab are implemented as Java classes, sharing a common interface to ensure consistency. There are four calculators in total of which only one is correct, while the others contain defects. To make sure that the testing focuses on finding defects in calculations, and not runtime errors or other similar problems, input validation is implemented. Students have two ways of interacting with the system. They can either use the main file, which provides a command-line interface (CLI) for inputting parameters and viewing results, or they can directly execute test cases through as a JUnit test suite. The CLI allows users to manually explore different input scenarios and get an understanding of the impact of the variables on braking distance. The test suite has to implement the previously identified MRs and tests all calculators automatically.

MT is useful for this task since it allows checking for correctness without requiring previously calculated expected outputs, which are not available. Instead, MRs define how the braking distance changes if an input variable is changed. The expected MRs are based on common sense and general world experience, therefore students are not expected to have deep knowledge of physics to identify these. To get lab students started, one example MR is given out (*If the coefficient of friction decreases, e.g., from dry to wet road surface, the stopping distance should increase.*) With this MR, one can test the calculators by reducing the friction parameter, while leaving the other parameters unchanged, and observe if the output changes accordingly. If the calculated distance decreases, the students should notice this to indicate a defect.

Task 2: Traffic Sign Classifiers. In Task 2, the students evaluate the performance of four convolutional neural network (CNN) models for traffic sign recognition by applying MT. CNNs have shown high performance in image classification tasks [12], including object recognition. For this reason, CNNs were chosen for the traffic sign recognition task. Different to Task 1, MT is not used to check how all the four presented classifiers classify detected traffic signs into 58 categories. Rather, the task is to find out which of the four models is best suited for the specific environmental challenges in Sweden, California, and Kenya, respectively. The underlying idea is that a given model might be more suited to sunny, dry, and dusty conditions than rainy, foggy, and snowy conditions.

All models were trained on an open-source dataset from Kaggle (Traffic Sign Dataset - Classification[2]). This dataset was chosen due to its high usability rating on Kaggle. It contains 58 classes, with an average of 73 images per class. The dataset also includes a "labels.csv" file with labels for each class, allowing categorization of traffic signs. The data is split into training and test datasets. All models underwent the same pre-processing steps, i.e., resizing images to a fixed dimension, normalizing pixel values to a range of 0 to 1, and converting them into arrays for input into neural networks. The models were trained using a CNN architecture built with TensorFlow[3] and Keras[4]. The training process used the Adam optimizer and categorical cross-entropy loss, a common setup for multi-class classification tasks.

While all models follow the same general training process, models better suited for California, Sweden, and Kenya, respectively, have some custom modifications to make them more robust to the specific conditions. The modifications involve adding noise and blur to the training data, as well as darkening and brightening the images, based on which model is meant for which environment. Despite the modifications all four models achieve similar F1 scores of approximately 0.85 when tested on unaltered data. The training dataset is not shared with the students and they have no knowledge upfront which model works best for the three country-specific environmental conditions.

Students must use MT for evaluating the robustness of the traffic sign classifiers by making slight transformations on the test data. For example, in the case of Sweden, with long dark winters, they are expected to darken the test data and observe whether and how the predictions of the models change. They then have to compare the consistency of the classifications on altered and unaltered data. If a model's predicted labels differ too much between original and transformed test data, then that indicates that a model is not suitable for the target country.

4.2 MT Lab Materials

The lab materials[5] consist of two parts: (a) lab and homework instructions and (b) a ZIP file containing the SUT. There are separate instructions for students

---

[2] Traffic Sign Dataset: https://www.kaggle.com/datasets/ahemateja19bec1025/traffic-sign-dataset-classification.

[3] TensorFlow: https://www.tensorflow.org/.

[4] Keras: https://keras.io/.

[5] URL to public lab materials: https://github.com/EliisabetK/MT-Materials.

and lab supervisors (confidential). The instructions for students introduce MT, the contents of the lab, and the homework tasks. There are step-by-step instructions on how to set up both of the programs in the ZIP file and run the first sample tests. The instructions also contain the grading rubric, one MR as a solution example, and helpful tips to assist students in completing the homework.

The two systems that students have to test are contained in a ZIP file. For the first task, there is a folder named "task1" with a JAR file containing the four braking distance calculators to be tested by the students (three are faulty and one is correct). Additionally, there is a test suite "Testing.java", where students must add their own tests throughout the homework. The materials for the second task are in the folder "task2", which contains four traffic sign classification models, testing data (images of traffic signs), and a testing file.

The TA materials enhance the materials provided to students by including additional information about the SUTs, written in red text, as well as model solutions and other details, such as grading instructions. Moreover, they have access to the training files through GitHub for each of the models.

5   Evaluation of the Lab Package "Metamorphic Testing"

The MT lab sessions were conducted on April 8 and 9, 2025, at the University of Tartu's Delta Centre. Each session took 90 min, and students were divided into six lab groups of which four were conducted on April 8 and two on April 9. After the homework deadline for all groups had passed, an anonymous feedback form was sent out to the students the following week. The feedback form[6] consisted of 10 questions. Five questions were written as statements with four response options: *agree, somewhat agree, somewhat disagree,* or *disagree* to avoid neutral answers. In addition, the form included one question about the amount of time it took to complete the homework, one about the difficulty of the lab, and one asking if students believe that testing AI-based applications should be more prominent in the course. The last question is an open-ended question asking for any additional feedback.

Quantitative Feedback. 37 students completed the questionnaire. The responses to all agree/disagree questions are summarized in Fig. 2. They indicate a clear understanding of the lab's objectives and tasks, indicating that the intended learning outcomes were effectively communicated. The balance of perceived difficulty and the distribution of time spent suggest that the lab was appropriately planned. The even split between students who found the lab easier or harder than previous assignments can likely reflect differences in overall course performance or academic ability, rather than a flaw in the task design. The data also reinforces the relevance of the lab's focus area. This feedback confirms that there is interest among students in learning about techniques relevant to AI-based systems, supporting the value of including MT as part of the course.

---

[6] URL to feedback form: https://github.com/EliisabetK/MT-Materials.

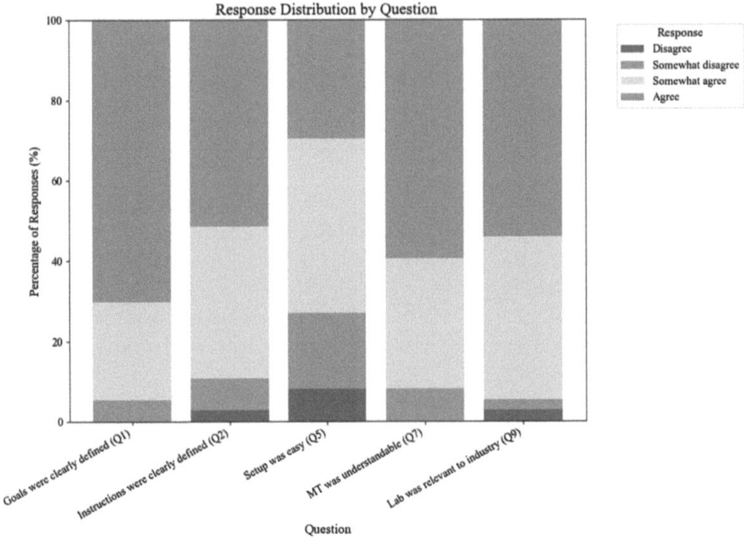

Fig. 2. Responses to agree/somewhat agree/somewhat disagree/disagree questions.

Qualitative Feedback. In addition to scaled responses, students were asked to provide open-ended feedback in two questions. The feedback from the open-ended question was very positive. 13 students explicitly mentioned that the lab should be kept in future versions of the course for different reasons, often pointing out the increasing relevance of learning about testing AI-based systems, as well. Many students mentioned that the instructions were clearer than in the previous labs, and one noted that this lab felt the closest to testing real-world applications instead of toy programs. Several responses stated that the MT lab was more fun and interesting when compared to the previous labs.

6   Conclusion

In summary, the latest instance of the lab package development in the context of a bachelor thesis confirmed that our conceptual model continues to be working for both groups of students, 2nd year bachelor students taking the *Software Testing* course and 3rd year bachelor students producing a new lab package for this course as their thesis project. We will continue this model in the future.

Acknowledgments. We would like to thank all students for their participation in the lab session on MT and the constructive feedback provided.

Disclosure of Interests. The authors have no competing interests to declare that are relevant to the content of this article.

References

1. Barr, E.T., et al.: The oracle problem in software testing: a survey. IEEE Trans. Softw. Eng. **41**(5), 507–525 (2015)
2. National Student Clearinghouse Research Center, Undergraduate degree earners. Acad. Year 2023–24, April 10, 2025 (2025). Accessed 23 Apr 2025
3. Chen, T.Y., Cheung, S.-M., Yiu, S.-C.: Metamorphic testing: a new approach for generating next test cases. CoRR, abs/2002.12543 (2020)
4. Chen, T.Y., et al.: Metamorphic testing: a review of challenges and opportunities. ACM Comput. Surv. **51**(1) (2018)
5. Cooper, A.F., Frankle, J., De Sa, C.: Non-determinism and the lawlessness of machine learning code. In: Proceedings of the 2022 Symposium on Computer Science and Law, CSLAW 2022. ACM (2022)
6. Duque-Torres, A., Pfahl, D., Klammer, C., Fischer, S.: Using source code metrics for predicting metamorphic relations at method level. In: 2022 IEEE International Conference on Software Analysis, Evolution and Reengineering (SANER), Los Alamitos, CA, USA, pp. 1147–1154. IEEE Computer Society, March 2022
7. Duque-Torres, A., Pfahl, D., Klammer, C., Fischer, S.: Bug or not bug? Analysing the reasons behind metamorphic relation violations. In: IEEE International Conference on Software Analysis, Evolution and Reengineering (SANER), pp. 905–912 (2023)
8. CC2020 Task Force: Computing curricula 2020: paradigms for global computing education (2020). Accessed 17 Nov 2024
9. Lin, X., Simon, M., Niu, N., Carver, J., Rouson, D.: Exploratory metamorphic testing for scientific software. Comp. Sci. Eng. **22**(2), 78–87 (2020)
10. Saha, P., Kanewala, U.: Fault detection effectiveness of metamorphic relations developed for testing supervised classifiers. In: 2019 IEEE International Conference on Artificial Intelligence Testing (AITest), pp. 157–164, April 2019
11. Segura, S., Towey, D., Zhou, Z., Chen, T.Y.: Metamorphic testing: testing the untestable. IEEE Softw. **37**(3), 46–53 (2020)
12. Sharma, N., Jain, V., Mishra, A.: An analysis of convolutional neural networks for image classification. Procedia Comput. Sci. **132**, 377–384 (2018). Int. Conf. on Computational Intelligence and Data Science
13. Singapore University of Technology and Design. 50.053 software testing and verification (n.d.). Accessed 12 Apr 2025
14. Stahl, M.: Metamorphic testing (2021). Accessed 06 Mar 2025
15. Tramontana, P., et al.: State of the practice in software testing teaching in four European countries. In: 2024 IEEE Conference on Software Testing, Verification and Validation (ICST), pp. 59–69 (2024)
16. Idaho State University: Computer Science (CS) graduate courses - academic catalog 2024-25 (2024). Accessed 06 Mar 2025
17. Institute of Computer Science, University of Tartu. Sis software testing (6 EAP) LTAT.05.006 course description (2024). Online. Accessed 07 Dec 2024
18. Wieringa, R.J.: The Design Cycle, pp. 27–34. Springer, Heidelberg (2014)
19. Zheng, Z., Ren, D., Liu, H., Chen, T.Y.: Metamorphic fault tolerance: addressing the oracle problem of reliability assurance for contemporary software systems. Computer **57**(7), 77–86 (2024)

A Model-Driven Engineering Method for the Development of Digital Twins

Emilio Carrión[1,2(✉)] [iD], Pedro Valderas[2] [iD], and Óscar Pastor[2] [iD]

[1] Mercadona Tech, Mercadona, Valencia, Spain
emcaryp@gmail.com
[2] PROS – VRAIN, Universitat Politècnica de València, Valencia, Spain

Abstract. Digital Twins (DTs) are consolidating as a transformative technology across various industries. However, the increasing heterogeneity of DT implementations has led to increasing complexity in DT development and integration challenges between conceptual design and technical implementation. This paper presents a model-driven engineering method that faces these challenges by transforming Entity-Relationship Digital Twin conceptual models into platform-specific implementations based on the Web of Things standard. The integration with runtime platforms like Eclipse Ditto also demonstrates how our approach reduces technological complexity and improves its integration. In addition, we validate the proposed contributions through a real-world case study at Mercadona, Spain's largest supermarket chain. Thus, this work contributes to the improvement of DT development by offering a practical solution to the challenge of technological fragmentation and complexity in DT industrial applications.

Keywords: Digital Twins · Model-Driven Development · Modelling

1 Introduction

Digital twins (DTs) have emerged as a transformative technology in manufacturing, urban infrastructure, logistics and healthcare [26]. According to [24], a DT is constructed from five dimensions: physical entities, virtual models, services, data and connections (see Fig. 1). Virtual models synchronize digital representations of physical entities at various fidelities [12,13,16] throughout a connection model-world (M2W). Services such as predictive maintenance, simulation and quality control leverage the virtual models [17] by means of a connection model-services (M2S). Finally, data is persisted and exchanged beneath these layers.

Developing a DT is complex [14], and Model-Driven Engineering (MDE) offers a way to focus on the software infrastructure for virtual models, connections and data management [7]. We introduced the Entity-Relationship Digital Twin (ERDT) model, extending the classic Entity-Relationship model [11] to conceptually define physical entities, the access interface for connection M2S and data flows for connection M2W [10]. Subsequent work provided a Domain-Specific

© The Author(s), under exclusive license to Springer Nature Switzerland AG 2026
G. Scanniello et al. (Eds.): PROFES 2025, LNCS 16361, pp. 397–407, 2026.
https://doi.org/10.1007/978-3-032-12089-2_25

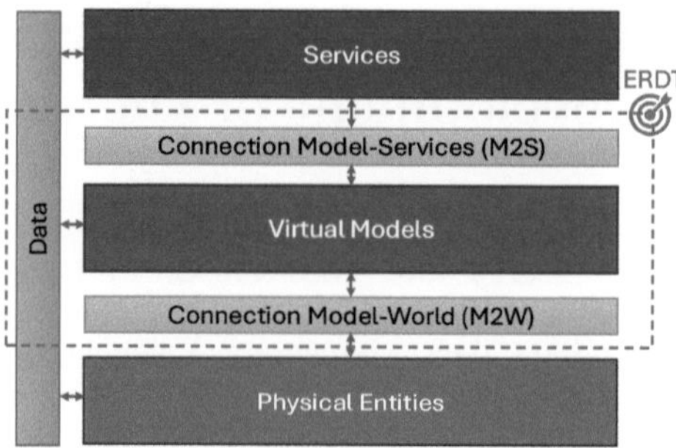

Fig. 1. DT dimensions and contextualization of ERDT.

Language (DSL) that transforms ERDT views into a REST API for connection M2S [8,9]. This paper integrates this previous work with tool-supported model transformations to present a complete MDE method for DTs considering the virtual model, the underlying data, and the two connections introduced above. This method reduces implementation complexity via WoT models and an automatic transformation deriving WoT specifications from ERDT. To validate our approach, we modeled and implemented Mercadona's logistics scenario—over 1000 delivery trucks across 1600 stores—demonstrating feasibility in a large-scale environment.

The remainder of the paper reviews related work (Sect. 2); presents the MDE method (Sect. 3) by giving details about ERDT (Sect. 3.1), its WoT transformation (Sect. 3.2), and the deployment (Sect. 3.3); discusses results (Sect. 4) and concludes (Sect. 5).

2   Related Work

Model-based approaches for developing DTs has been analysed by different surveys such as [7] and [20]. Some of the works more related to ours are: [18], which explored model-driven approaches by introducing a method to describe the software of cyber-physical systems. Similarly, [5] proposed an MDE approach for creating reactive DTs by employing DSLs to define system behaviour. This work was later extended by [12] to include a graphical control interface (cockpit) for monitoring and interacting with physical entities. A method to create DTs for IoT devices based on WoT models was introduced by [21], which demonstrated the potential to abstract and simplify the interactions of this type of system using model-driven approaches. [27] introduced an MDE framework for industrial DTs, validating their approach through an iron ore sintering plant case study.

All these works focus on specific domains and custom software solutions, leaving a gap in comprehensive, domain-independent DT development methods that make use of technologies already established in the industry. An exception to this is [4], which proposes a domain-independent MDE approach to simplify the development of DTs. However, this work is in its early stages of development.

Our work addresses these limitations by proposing an MDE method that uses the ERDT model, which supports a domain-independent DT modelling, and integrates both existing and industry-tested DT software solutions such as the Ditto platform, and standards that are well known and accepted in the DT development community. This allows us to offer a more unified approach to DT creation that reduces development complexity.

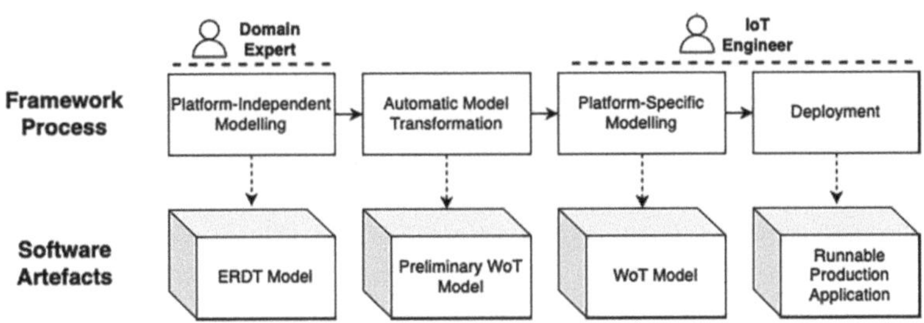

Fig. 2. DT Development Method.

3   An MDE Approach to Develop Digital Twins

The proposed MDE method, grounded in MDA concepts [22], consists of three main steps (see Fig. 2). First, *Platform-Independent Modelling* involves instantiating an ERDT model that captures the DT's conceptual characteristics without reference to any technology; this is performed by domain experts or business analysts familiar with the business requirements. Second, *Platform-Specific Modelling* applies a transformation to translate ERDT instances into preliminary WoT models and then enriches them with implementation details—such as device connection parameters (IP, port, protocol)—a task for IoT engineers. Third, *Deployment* interprets WoT descriptions on a DT platform—here demonstrated via Eclipse Ditto—to produce a fully operational implementation supporting the DT model. Next subsections explain these steps in detail.

3.1   Platform-Independent Modelling: ERDT

The first step of the proposed method is the conceptual modeling of a DT with ERDT. The model uses typical ER entities (with attributes) and relationships to represent the physical objects we are digitizing in the modeled DT (i.e., Truck, Driver, Hive and Picker). One of the main contributions of ERDT models is the definition of historical attributes as DTs often rely on historical data for operational functionalities. For example, a Truck entity may include a Location

History attribute that tracks the past locations of the truck. This property is key for the representation of the temporal aspects of a DT and enables complex queries and analyses over time. Note that these conceptual elements capture the main characteristics of the physical entities that must be represented by the virtual model (see Fig. 1).

Other key concepts introduced by ERDT are interfaces and data flows. Interfaces act as controlled access points to entity attributes (i.e., getters and setters), hiding internal complexity and facilitating interaction with the DT; they're represented in the model as capsule-shaped elements connected to attributes, such as Get Location and Set Speed. Data flows represent bidirectional communications between the DT and the physical components, keeping the virtual model updated with real-time data and providing feedback to the physical entities; they're shown as arrow-like elements connecting the physical world with interfaces. ERDT defines three types of data flows, but this paper focuses on two: incoming events (sent by the physical entities to notify changes in their state, e.g., Driver assigned or Picker telemetry) and outgoing events (sent from the virtual model to the physical entities to execute actions or send commands, e.g., warning that a truck has entered a Low-Emission Zone).

Tool Support. As a contribution of this paper, we present a web-based visual model editor[1] to define ERDT models and automatically generate the equivalent WoT models from them. Figure 3 shows a snapshot of the tool used to create part of the model presented above. The model transformation implemented by this tool is presented in the next section.

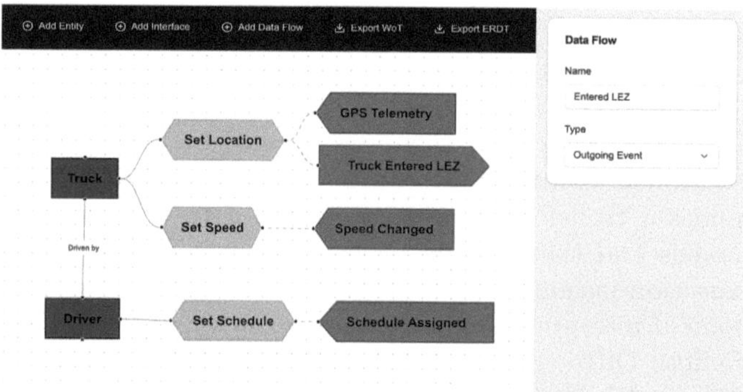

Fig. 3. ERDT Editor and Model of a Delivery Truck Fleet.

3.2 Platform-Specific Modelling: WoT Models

The second step of the proposed method is to transform ERDT models into WoT-based descriptions. To explain this, we first introduce the WoT standard.

---

[1] Available at: https://erdt-builder.vercel.app/.

Next, we present a model transformation to automatically derive s preliminary WoT model from ERDT models. Finally, we explain the data that must be manually introduced to obtain a complete WoT model.

WoT Models. Web of Things (WoT) [15] is a specification proposed by the W3C to act as a Thing's entry point. A Thing is used to abstract a physical entity. There is a growing interest for WoT in the field of DTs, as demonstrated by the increasing number of implementations [21,25], tools [6,19], and interest groups [2]. Also, the W3C identifies DT as one of the cases of use of WoT [3].

WoT proposes to describe a Thing in a specific format, typically JSON-LD. Its basic elements are properties, actions, and events. *Properties* describe the state of a Thing, and they can be complemented with a set of *forms* that define protocol-bound end-points to access or update each property. There are different types of end-points, which are defined by the *op* property. For instance, *readproperty* represents a getter end-point and *writeproperty* a setter. *Actions* represent functions of a Thing that execute physical (and hence time-consuming) processes (e.g. activate a warning led in a Truck or reduce the Truck speed). And *Events* describe asynchronously push communications performed by a Thing to inject some data into a target (e.g., a Truck automatically informs about its speed every time it changes).

Model Transformation: From ERDT to WoT. We have implemented an unidirectional exogenous model transformation [23] to automatically generate WoT models from ERDT models. To do this, we have defined a set of transformation mappings between the ERDT and WoT concepts. They are explained below and are shown in Fig. 4.

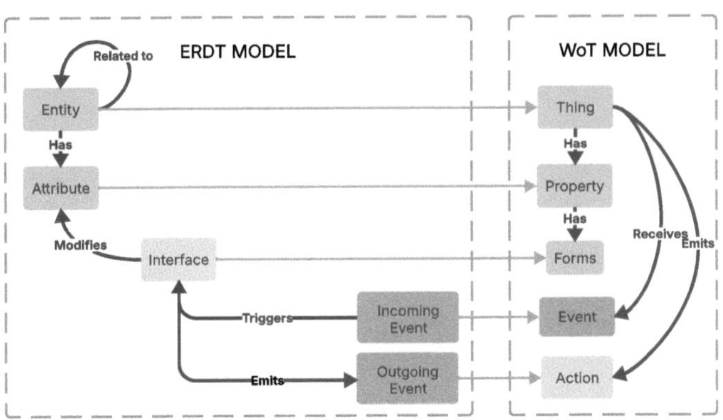

Fig. 4. Mappings between ERDT and WoT concepts.

– *ERDT Entities map to WoT Things.* The *entities* in ERDT represent the physical elements that make up our DT such as, for instance, a truck. This concept directly maps to that of *Thing* in WoT, which refers to an abstraction of a physical thing.

- *ERDT Attributes map to WoT Properties. Attributes* are the different data associated with an entity. They represent internal values such as the coordinates of a truck. In WoT this concept fits well with *properties*, which exposes state of the Thing.
- *Interfaces map to WoT Property Forms.* In ERDT, we use *interfaces* to query or modify entity attributes. In WoT, each property of a Thing can be complemented with a set of *forms* that allow us to define end-points to get or set the values of these properties (i.e., an access interface). Thus, each ERDT attribute interface is mapped to a form in the corresponding WoT property. Each interface that represents a getter is transformed into a *readProperty form* and each that represents a setter into a *writeProperty form*.
- *ERDT Outgoing Events map to WoT Actions.* In ERDT, Outgoing Events are data flows that represent a communication from the digital entity to the physical one. They are sent from the DT to the physical entity in order to request the execution of a physical action (e.g. reduce the speed of a Truck). Thus, the WoT model that describes this physical entity needs to include specific *actions* that support these requests.
- *ERDT Incoming Events map to WoT Events.* In ERDT, Incoming Events are data flows that represent a communication from the physical entity to the digital one. They are sent by physical entities to notify the DT of a change in their state. Thus, ERDT incoming events map with the notion of *event* proposed by WoT.

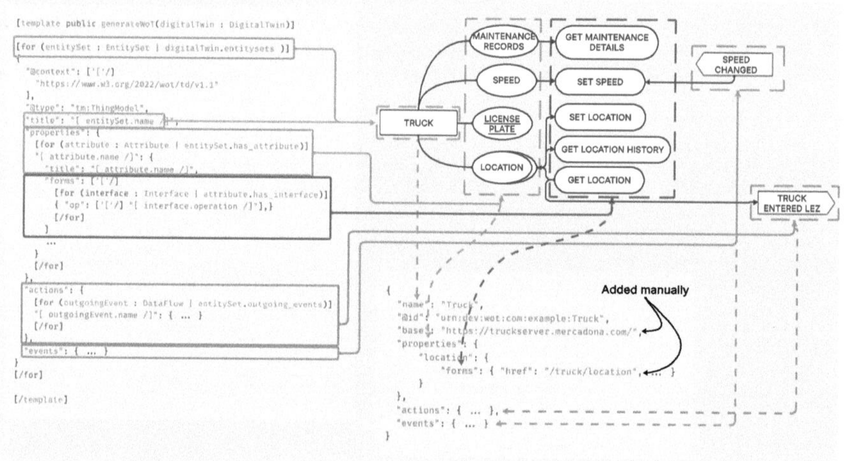

Fig. 5. Code Templates and Transformation to WoT.

Manual Completion. The preliminary WoT model needs to be completed with the device connection data (i.e., IP of the physical device, access protocol, port, etc.). In the WoT standard, this data is defined through: (1) the *base* URI that is used to reference the Thing; and (2) additional elements that complement each *form* to define data such as the target IRI (i.e., *href*) or the HTTP method (i.e. *htv:methodName*), which are required to perform the operation described by the form. This completion is also highlighted in Fig. 5, in which we have manually defined that the location of a truck can be accessed at (*base* + *href*) https:// truckserver.mercadona.com/truck/location.

3.3 Deployment

The final step is to deploy the WoT model to a runtime platform such as Eclipse Ditto [1]. Ditto persists the underlying data for a dashboard-based virtual model and implements connection M2W for two-way synchronization with physical entities via technology-specific access points. For example, the Ditto dashboard shows real-time truck properties (license plate, location, speed) and lets users trigger actions (e.g., "Truck Entered Lez") on the physical entity. The REST API generated from ERDT models in prior work [8,9] interacts with Ditto to implement connection M2S, while developing a higher-fidelity virtual model remains further work (Fig. 6).

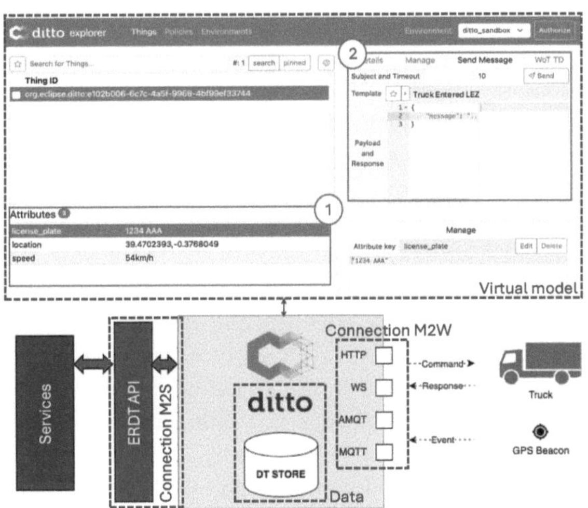

Fig. 6. DT Architecture (bottom) and Ditto UI (Top).

4 Results

The proposed MDE method lets us define a DT at a conceptual level without tying it to specific implementations, then effortlessly generate working software artifacts, reducing complexity. The ERDT model enriches semantic design by incorporating attribute history, access interfaces and data flows (elements that WoT alone does not define) enabling more complete modelling of the virtual model, underlying data, and both synchronization with physical entities and support for DT services. Applied to Mercadona Tech's logistics case study, the MDE solution outperforms the current system, which relies on ad-hoc code for each real-time requirement (for example, the GPS-dependent Truck Viewer) and must be re-implemented whenever data sources or business requirements change. In contrast, our ERDT-based approach handles requirement changes at the conceptual level by redefining the model and regenerating the WoT implementation, centralizes all communication in the DT platform for better scalability and heterogeneous-source integration, and enables bidirectional interaction with physical things rather than simple viewing. Thus, MDE provides robust, technology-agnostic conceptual modelling and an automated transformation to concrete implementations, facilitating rapid iteration and seamless integration with standards like WoT and Eclipse Ditto.

Expert Evaluation Survey. To further support our empirical results, we conducted a preliminary evaluation with Mercadona employees familiar with existing solutions. The experts included a head of engineering (20+ years), two senior engineers (12+ years), a mid engineer (7+ years) and a junior engineer (2+ years), all of whom routinely build similar systems in Mercadona's logistics environment. In a two-hour session (40 min tutorial, 20 min case details, 45 min hands-on, 15 min survey), participants used our tool to build an ERDT model, generate WoT artifacts, validate Ditto compatibility and compare MDE versus their current approach in terms of component count, code complexity (1–5), development effort, maintenance effort (1–5), steps for minor/major changes and change difficulty (1–5). Results show MDE requires fewer components (3 vs. 6), has lower complexity (1.8 vs. 4.2), reduces development from 1–2 weeks to 2 h, lessens maintenance (1.6 vs. 3.8), decreases steps for minor changes (1–2 vs. 3) and cuts major change time to 2 h versus days/weeks, with difficulty dropping from 3.4 to 1. Participants noted benefits like faster setup (only Ditto deployment), easier modeling of major changes, reduced maintenance, higher abstraction, simplified complexity, enhanced testing, fewer errors and better maintainability via automatic artifact generation, while citing drawbacks such as loss of control over implementation details, potential vendor lock-in, harder ad-hoc modifications outside ERDT, challenging debugging of unintended behaviors and limited flexibility for new backends. Despite these, participants valued the benefits and would adopt MDE. To address these issues, we will introduce customization mechanisms such as overrides, plug-ins and modules to integrate external libraries without altering the core, adopt open standards and decoupled architectures to mitigate lock-in and maintain flexibility, and conduct a controlled, subject-based experiment to enhance external validity by involving developers from diverse companies and environments and improve construct validity by gathering objective measures beyond subjective impressions.

5 Conclusions and Further Work

In this work, we have introduced an MDE method for DT development that provides structure on the DT construction, reducing its complexity and bridging technological silos by narrowing the gap between conceptual modelling and specialized technologies. By incorporating established industry technologies such as Ditto, this method adapts to the current state-of-the-art ecosystem without reinventing the wheel. We validated it through a proof-of-concept in Mercadona's logistics (managing a fleet of over 1,000 vehicles) and gathered expert developers' feedback to confirm its applicability to complex real-world scenarios.

As future work, we will address the drawbacks identified by experts and perform more comprehensive validation; refine our conceptual model, transformations, and modelling tool to support high-fidelity virtual models; and enhance security in the reference architecture to control who can do what with the underlying data of the virtual model.

References

1. Eclipse ditto - open source framework for digital twins in the IoT. https://eclipse.dev/ditto/
2. Web-based digital twins for smart cities interest group charter. https://www.w3.org/2024/06/smart-cities/
3. Web of things (WoT): Use cases and requirements (2022). https://www.w3.org/TR/wot-usecases/
4. Barriga, A.: Model-driven software engineering to foster the adoption of digital twins. In: Congresso Ibero-Americano em Engenharia de Software (CIbSE), pp. 280–287. SBC (2025)
5. Bibow, P., et al.: Model-driven development of a digital twin for injection molding. In: Dustdar, S., Yu, E., Salinesi, C., Rieu, D., Pant, V. (eds.) CAiSE 2020. LNCS, vol. 12127, pp. 85–100. Springer, Cham (2020). https://doi.org/10.1007/978-3-030-49435-3_6
6. Blank, M., Lahbaiel, H., Kaebisch, S., Kosch, H.: Role models and lifecycles in IoT and their impact on the W3C wot thing description. In: Proceedings of the 8th International Conference on the Internet of Things, IOT 2018, pp. 1–4. Association for Computing Machinery, New York (2018). https://doi.org/10.1145/3277593.3277908
7. Bordeleau, F., Combemale, B., Eramo, R., van den Brand, M., Wimmer, M.: Towards model-driven digital twin engineering: current opportunities and future challenges. In: Babur, Ö., Denil, J., Vogel-Heuser, B. (eds.) ICSMM 2020. CCIS, vol. 1262, pp. 43–54. Springer, Cham (2020). https://doi.org/10.1007/978-3-030-58167-1_4
8. Carrión, E., Pastor, O., Valderas, P.: Querying digital twin models. In: 20h International Conference on Evaluation of Novel Approaches to Software Engineering (Publication Pending) (2025)
9. Carrión, E., Valderas, P.: Implementing digital twin query views. In: International Conference on Research Challenges in Information Science, pp. 279–294. Springer (2025)

10. Carrión, E., Pastor, Ã., Valderas, P.: Conceptual modelling method for digital twins. In: Maass, W., Han, H., Yasar, H., Multari, N. (eds.) Conceptual Modeling, pp. 417–435. Springer, Cham (2025). https://doi.org/10.1007/978-3-031-75872-0_22

11. Chen, P.P.S.: The entity-relationship model–toward a unified view of data. ACM Trans. Database Syst. **1**(1), 9–36 (1976). https://doi.org/10.1145/320434.320440

12. Dalibor, M., Michael, J., Rumpe, B., Varga, S., Wortmann, A.: Towards a model-driven architecture for interactive digital twin cockpits. In: International Conference on Conceptual Modeling, pp. 377–387. Springer (2020)

13. Digital Twin Consortium: Digital twin definition (2024). https://www.digitaltwinconsortium.org/glossary/glossary/#digital-twin

14. Fuller, A., Fan, Z., Day, C., Barlow, C.: Digital twin: enabling technologies, challenges and open research. IEEE Access **8**, 108952–108971 (2020). https://doi.org/10.1109/ACCESS.2020.2998358

15. Guinard, D., Trifa, V.: (2008). https://webofthings.org/2017/04/08/what-is-the-web-of-things/

16. Hananto, A.L., et al.: Digital twin and 3D digital twin: concepts, applications, and challenges in industry 4.0 for digital twin. Computers **13**(4), 100 (2024)

17. Jones, D., Snider, C., Nassehi, A., Yon, J., Hicks, B.: Characterising the digital twin: a systematic literature review. CIRP J. Manuf. Sci. Technol. **29**, 36–52 (2020)

18. Kirchhof, J.C., Michael, J., Rumpe, B., Varga, S., Wortmann, A.: Model-driven digital twin construction: synthesizing the integration of cyber-physical systems with their information systems. In: 23rd ACM/IEEE International Conference on Model Driven Engineering Languages and Systems, MODELS 2020, New York, NY, USA, pp. 90–101 (2020). https://doi.org/10.1145/3365438.3410941

19. Korkan, E., Kaebisch, S., Kovatsch, M., Steinhorst, S.: Safe interoperability for web of things devices and systems. In: Kazmierski, T.J., Steinhorst, S., Große, D. (eds.) Languages, Design Methods, and Tools for Electronic System Design. LNEE, vol. 611, pp. 47–69. Springer, Cham (2020). https://doi.org/10.1007/978-3-030-31585-6_3

20. Lehner, D., et al.: Model-driven engineering for digital twins: a systematic mapping study. Softw. Syst. Model. 1–39 (2025)

21. Lopez-Arevalo, I., Gonzalez-Compean, J.L., Hinojosa-Tijerina, M., Martinez-Rendon, C., Montella, R., Martinez-Rodriguez, J.L.: A wot-based method for creating digital sentinel twins of IoT devices. Sensors **21**(1616), 5531 (2021). https://doi.org/10.3390/s21165531

22. Mellor, S.J.: MDA distilled: principles of model-driven architecture. Addison-Wesley Professional (2004)

23. Mens, T., Van Gorp, P.: A taxonomy of model transformation. Electron. Notes Theor. Comput. Sci. **152**, 125–142 (2006). https://doi.org/10.1016/j.entcs.2005.10.021

24. Qi, Q., et al.: Enabling technologies and tools for digital twin. J. Manuf. Syst. **58**, 3–21 (2021)

25. Sciullo, L., Trotta, A., Montori, F., Bononi, L., Di Felice, M.: Wotwins: automatic digital twin generator for the web of things, pp. 607–612 (2022). https://doi.org/10.1109/WoWMoM54355.2022.00095

26. Tao, F., Zhang, H., Liu, A., Nee, A.Y.C.: Digital twin in industry: state-of-the-art. IEEE Trans. Industr. Inf. **15**(4), 2405–2415 (2019). https://doi.org/10.1109/TII.2018.2873186

27. Vale, S., et al.: A model-driven approach for knowledge-based engineering of industrial digital twins. In: 2023 ACM/IEEE 26th International Conference on Model Driven Engineering Languages and Systems, pp. 13–23. IEEE (2023)

LLM-Based Multi-agent System
for Intelligent Refactoring of Haskell Code

Shahbaz Siddeeq[1]([⊠]) [iD], Muhammad Waseem[1] [iD], Zeeshan Rasheed[1] [iD],
Md Mahade Hasan[1] [iD], Jussi Rasku[1] [iD], Mika Saari[1] [iD], Henri Terho[2],
Kalle Mäkelä[2], Kai-Kristian Kemell[1] [iD], and Pekka Abrahamsson[1] [iD]

[1] Tampere University, Tampere, Finland
{shahbaz.siddeeq,muhammad.waseem,zeeshan.rasheed,mdmahade.hasan,
jussi.rasku,mika.saari,Kai-Kristian.Kemell,pekka.abrahamsson}@tuni.fi
[2] Eficode Oy, Tampere, Finland
henri.terho@eficode.com, kalle.makela@gmail.com

Abstract. Refactoring is an important part of software development
and maintenance. However, this process is still labor intensive, as it
requires programmers to analyze the codebases in detail to avoid introducing new defects. In this paper, we introduce a Large Language Model
(LLM)-based multi-agent system to automate the refactoring process for
Haskell-based code. The objective of this research is to evaluate the effectiveness of LLM-based agents in performing structured and semantically
accurate refactoring of Haskell code. Our proposed multi-agent system is
based on specialized agents with distinct roles. We conducted evaluations
using different open-source Haskell codebases. The results of the experiments show that the proposed LLM-based multi-agent system achieved
an average reduction of 11.03% in code complexity and a 22.46% improvement in overall code quality. These results highlight the capability of
the LLM-based multi-agent system to manage refactoring tasks targeted
toward functional programming paradigms. Our findings suggest that
integrating LLM-based multi-agent systems into the refactoring of functional programming languages can enhance maintainability and support
automated development workflows. The source code of our proposed system and the metrics results are publicly available on GitHub (https://
github.com/GPT-Laboratory/Intelligent-Haskell-Code-Refactoring).

Keywords: Code Refactor · Large Language Models · Multi-agent
System · Software Engineering · Haskell Programming

1 Introduction

Functional programming languages are known for their higher-order functions
and immutability, which make them suitable for accurate and concurrent processing [9]. This core strength of functional programming is showcased in languages like Haskell [11]. However, these characteristics also make Haskell based
systems challenging to refactor [5]. Traditionally, refactoring efforts in functional

© The Author(s), under exclusive license to Springer Nature Switzerland AG 2026
G. Scanniello et al. (Eds.): PROFES 2025, LNCS 16361, pp. 408–418, 2026.
https://doi.org/10.1007/978-3-032-12089-2_26

languages focus on restructuring code to improve readability and maintainability while ensuring correctness, but the presence of type systems and non-linear evaluation strategies adds difficulty to the process [13].

Researchers have explored the use of multi-agent systems in software engineering for tasks such as automated analysis [20] and distributed processing [1]. These studies have primarily focused on Imperative and Object-Oriented Programming. Similarly, the adoption of Large Language Models (LLMs) for code generation, error detection, and basic refactoring has demonstrated potential, but their application to functional programming languages like Haskell remains explored limited. Tasks like code analysis and code refactoring [14] can be distributed with agents to address the structured manner complexity by applying multi-agent system principles to Haskell code refactoring.

Motivation behind this research is to meet Eficode[1] company needs for automated refactoring system for complex codebases.

The primary **contributions** of this study are: (i) Development of an LLM-based multi-agent system for refactoring Haskell code. (ii) Evaluation of the developed system against code quality metrics, including cyclomatic complexity, runtime efficiency, memory usage, and comparisons with HLint. (iii) Public release of the developed system, which is made available online [16], allowing researchers and practitioners to access, replicate, and validate the system.

2   Related Work

Functional programming languages like Haskell present challenges due to their emphasis on immutability, lazy evaluation, and higher-order functions [4]. Most research on refactoring in functional programming mainly focuses on traditional methods. Mens and Tourwé [13] conducted a comprehensive survey highlighting refactoring patterns applicable across programming paradigms. Recent work [19] has shown that LLMs can not only generate syntactically correct code but also adapt to specific programming paradigms, making them valuable assets for software refactoring.

Using an LLM-based multi-agent system for code refactoring is an approach that has not been extensively explored in existing literature. Recently Baumgartner *et al.* [3] introduced a multi-agent learning system for automatic code refactoring, which demonstrated improvements in handling distributed code modifications. However, their approach was primarily focused on imperative programming languages and did not explore applications in functional programming. Similarly, Huang [10] discussed a multi-agent approach to software maintenance but their work did not consider the challenges associated with functional languages like Haskell.

Our research, unlike prior works that treat refactoring as a static rule-based process [15], introduces a multi-agent system specifically designed for functional

---

[1] https://www.eficode.com/fi.

programming refactoring, enhanced by the contextual analysis and code generation capabilities of LLMs. By assigning each agent a specialized task, our approach simplifies Haskell refactoring [18] in a scalable, autonomous manner.

3   Experiment Design

The experiment design is divided into three phases, as illustrated in Fig. 1.

3.1   Phase I - Determining Research Questions

Considering our research objective, we formulate the following two RQs.

- **RQ1.** How effectively can LLM-based multi-agent systems improve Haskell codebases in terms of cyclomatic complexity, runtime, and memory usage? The **objective** of this RQ is to evaluate the effectiveness of multi-agent systems in automating Haskell code refactoring, specifically focusing on reducing cyclomatic complexity, improving runtime performance, and optimizing memory usage.
- **RQ2.** What is the impact of using multi-agent approaches on refactoring workflows for functional programming languages? The **objective** of this RQ is to assess the flexibility of a multi-agent system in addressing the challenges of refactoring Haskell code, particularly focusing on aspects such as immutability, lazy evaluation, and type safety.

3.2   Phase II - Designing Multi-agent System

In this phase, we focus on the design and management of our multi-agent system and the system is model agnostic in practice (can be implemented with any LLM), but that we have tested it specifically with GPT-4o.

Prompt Strategies: The success of a multi-agent system relies on the precision and adaptability of its prompt engineering. In this work, prompts are designed to ensure role-specific task delegation, facilitate inter-agent collaboration, and follow the principles of functional programming. Each agent operates on structured prompts tailored to its specific role and highlighted the structure on GitHub wiki [16]. The prompt strategies in this study are based on the following: (i) Role-specific Prompting: Tailored prompts enable agents to focus on specific tasks. This approach builds on prior research [6] highlighting task-specific prompt engineering in LLMs. (ii) Dynamic and Iterative Prompt Refinement: Prompts are updated based on intermediate outputs, aligning with strategies employed in adaptive language models.

Multi-agent System: In this phase, we present an LLM-based multi-agent system for automated Haskell refactoring, where specialized agents collaboratively identify issues, apply improvements, and verify results. Each agent operates autonomously with dedicated logic for tasks such as structural analysis,

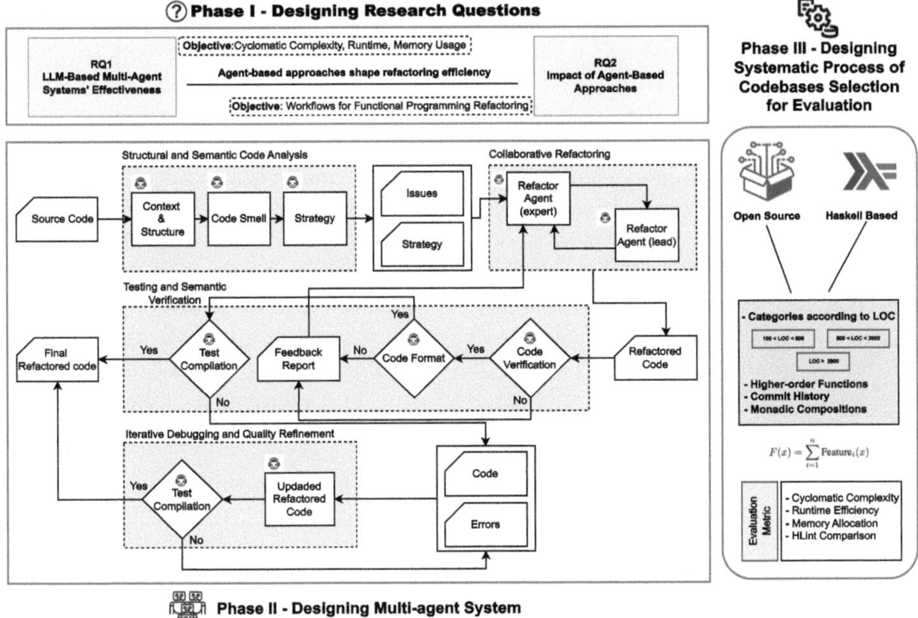

Fig. 1. Overview of the experiment design illustrating the three main phases: (I) Designing research questions; (II) Designing a multi-agent system; and (III) Designing the systematic process of codebases selection for evaluation.

code smell detection, refactoring, testing, and debugging, but they remain coordinated through structured data exchanges and prompt chaining. This workflow ensures that the output of one agent serves as the context for the next, allowing iterative and consistent refinement of the codebase.

The system begins with structural and semantic analysis, detecting inefficiencies such as high complexity, weak modularity, and problematic monadic or higher-order constructs. We grouped the 42 refactoring items into eight high-level categories, then merged them into agent responsibilities, which is available on GitHub wiki [16]. Refactoring agents then execute strategies ranging from simplifying functions and removing redundancies to reorganizing modules and optimizing performance. Verification and testing agents evaluate correctness, stability, and style compliance, while debugging agents resolve residual issues through iterative cycles.

3.3 Phase III - Codebase Selection for Evaluation

This phase evaluates the effectiveness of the multi-agent system using Open Source Projects (OSP). We included OSP to meet the goal of testing the multi-agent system under natural conditions. The OSP was curated through a systematic selection process applied to public Haskell repositories on GitHub. Initially, repositories created before 2023, with more than 500 stars and written in Haskell, were shortlisted (213 total). Additional filters were applied to ensure activeness (updated within 12 months), collaborative development (≥ 3 contributors), and adequate versioning complexity (≥ 2 branches), narrowing the list to 133. A commit history scan then searched for terms such as "refactor," "rewrite," "enhance," and "optimize," indicating meaningful maintenance activity. Repositories also needed basic documentation with keywords like "usage," "install," or "example." This reduced the pool to 112 projects. These were classified by size using LOC: small (<500), medium (500–2000), and large (>2000). Table 1 lists their key attributes: repository popularity, development activity, contributor count, project age, and forks. A stratified sample of 10 projects (4 large, 4 medium, 2 small) was selected for evaluation. The selected codebases in Table 1 were processed through the multi-agent system in a controlled environment.

Table 1. List of Haskell-based OSP evaluated in this study

Project	Stars	Commits	Contributors	Age (years)	Forks
Cryptol	1,200	4,521	58	11	126
Granule	617	3,879	18	8	38
Obelisk	1,000	2,847	51	6.9	107
Fused Effects	656	5,206	28	6.6	53
Nix-tree	854	230	12	4.8	17
Erd	1,830	152	24	11.5	153
Tetris	936	124	4	7.9	41
Greenclip	1,504	168	14	8.3	35
Xdg-inja	2,816	534	170	3	157
Bench	887	71	7	9.1	21
Total	**12,300**	**17,732**	**386**		**748**

3.4 Evaluation

Multi-agent system is evaluated using metrics specific to functional programming and software engineering to assess its effectiveness and performance. This ensures refactoring outputs meet established standards for quality, and performance.

Cyclomatic complexity and structural dependencies are measured before and after refactoring using established software metrics. To measure the complexity, we utilized McCabe's cyclomatic complexity metric [12], which quantifies the number of linearly independent paths through a program. Runtime and memory usage are evaluated using GHC profiling tools. This aligns with prior studies on performance optimization in Haskell [7]. Runtime refers to the execution time of a program, often measured in ticks or seconds. Memory usage refers to the total bytes allocated during execution. HLint is a static code analysis tool for Haskell that suggests stylistic improvements to enhance code readability and maintainability. HLint was used to evaluate these improvements in the refactored codebases.

Table 2. Post-refactoring improvements on open source Haskell codebases

Project	Code Complexity Improvement (%)			Code Quality Improvement (%)			Code Performance Improvement (%)	
	Lines of Code	Cyclomatic Complexity	Branching Depth	Suggestions	Warnings	Errors	Runtime Efficiency	Memory Allocation
Cryptol	5.88	4.28	8.63	11.12	1.15	5.32	8.03	38.7
Granule	8.09	17.99	6.57	22.76	1.04	4.24	3.35	18.9
Obelisk	15.36	0.82	9.38	4.35	5.40	2.05	11.50	19.4
Fused Effects	1.09	3.49	14.29	31.60	37.5	2.10	7.15	18.1
Average (Large)	**7.61**	**6.65**	**9.72**	**17.46**	**11.27**	**3.43**	**7.51**	**23.78**
Nix-tree	7.16	3.02	0	25.00	57.14	5.41	10.76	67.7
Erd	15.74	1.98	12.5	0	0	6.34	3.67	47.1
Tetris	0.43	22.14	0	40.00	21.20	2.56	8.34	0.4
Greenclip	0.95	17.98	0	60.00	100.00	59.38	0	0
Average (Medium)	**6.07**	**11.28**	**3.13**	**31.25**	**44.59**	**18.42**	**5.69**	**28.8**
Xdg-inja	30.72	17.59	42.85	57.14	78.57	32.30	0	0.6
Bench	3.54	8.33	50.00	0	0	0	0	1.8
Average (Small)	**17.13**	**12.96**	**46.42**	**28.57**	**39.28**	**16.15**	**0**	**1.2**
Total Average	**8.90**	**9.76**	**14.42**	**25.20**	**30.2**	**11.97**	**5.28**	**21.27**

4 Results

4.1 RQ1: Effects of LLM-Based Multi-Agent Systems on Haskell Codebases

Cyclomatic Complexity: Through the multi-agent system, reductions in this metric were achieved. An average reduction of 8.90% was observed, demonstrating that the multi-agent system simplified branching and conditional structures within organically written Haskell code. This suggests that the multi-agent system not only handles real-world complexities but also excels in applying targeted simplifications when the structural boundaries are more predictable.

Branching Depth Reduction: System measures branching depth as the maximum number of nested control structures (e.g., if, case, and loops) within a function. Deep nesting increases cognitive load and raises the risk of bugs. Our agents cut the average branch depth by 14.42%. This reduction translates to fewer indentation levels and a clearer logical path in each function. Shallower nesting improves readability, eases future modifications, and reduces error proneness in Haskell code.

Runtime Efficiency Gains: Runtime performance is crucial for any production level software system. Among the OSP projects, runtime efficiency improved by an average of 5.28%, reflecting the multi-agent system's capacity to navigate and optimize complex, often unstructured logic. This showed that multi-agent system-generated transformations led to reductions in execution time.

Memory Allocation Optimization: We measured execution time and memory allocation with GHC profiling. Figure 2 shows a representative function runtime profile before and after refactoring. OSP codebases experienced an average memory usage reduction of 21.27% and improved runtime efficiency by 5.28%. These gains underline the multi-agent system's competence in managing both abstract and concrete data manipulations with precision.

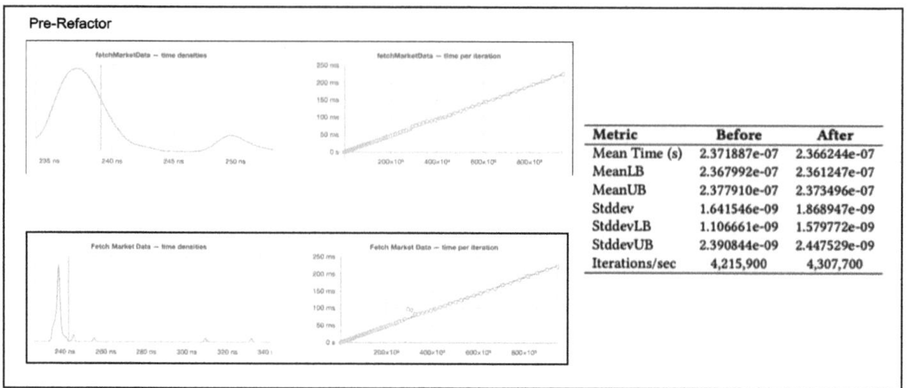

Metric	Before	After
Mean Time (s)	2.371887e-07	2.366244e-07
MeanLB	2.367992e-07	2.361247e-07
MeanUB	2.377910e-07	2.373496e-07
Stddev	1.641546e-09	1.868947e-09
StddevLB	1.106661e-09	1.579772e-09
StddevUB	2.390844e-09	2.447529e-09
Iterations/sec	4,215,900	4,307,700

Fig. 2. Pre-refactor and post-refactor performance comparison of function.

4.2   RQ2: Evaluating the Impact of Multi-agent Approaches on Refactoring Workflows

HLint-Based Code Quality: To assess stylistic and semantic code quality improvements, the refactored code was subjected to HLint, a widely used static analysis tool in the Haskell ecosystem. Post-refactoring assessments revealed that the multi-agent system had successfully removed redundant expressions, enforced consistent naming conventions, and enhanced code readability.

Our multi-agent system targets HLint flags and compiler diagnostics with precise refactorings—adding missing type signatures, pruning unused bindings, swapping partial functions for total ones, and streamlining expressions. Table 2 shows HLint suggestions fell by 25.20%, compiler warnings by 30.20%, and compiler errors by 11.97%. These gains confirm that our agents enforce idiomatic Haskell, eradicate common code smells, and resolve release-blocking issues.

4.3   Consolidated Observations

The results demonstrate that the LLM-based multi-agent system provides reliable and scalable improvements in software quality metrics. Consistently strong performance on real-world OSP codebases confirms the system's adaptability

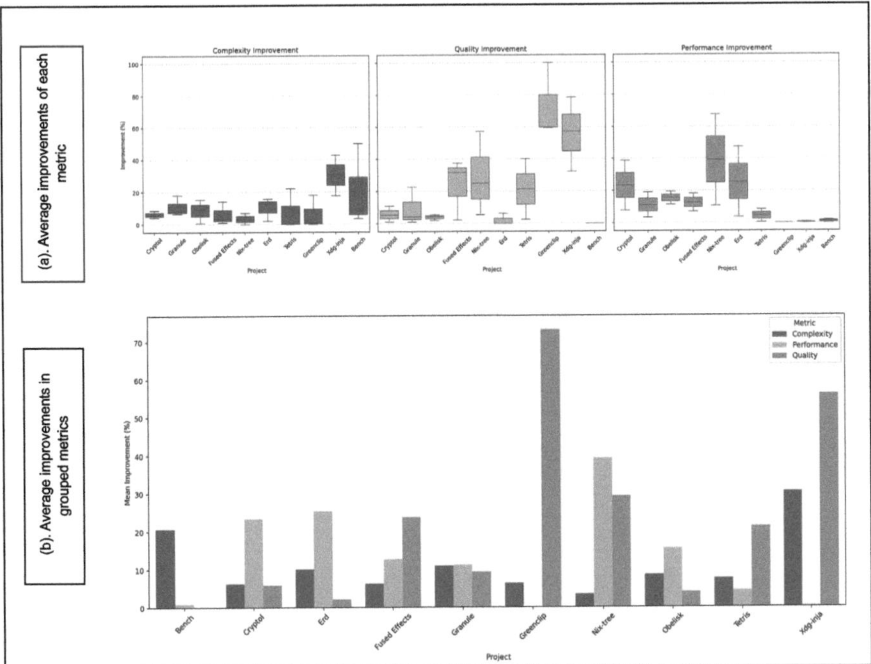

Fig. 3. Overall OSP post-refactor improvements comparison of different metrics.

to codebases shaped by diverse development practices, histories, and conventions. To further illustrate these improvements, we provide a visual summary of the average improvements in individual metrics and grouped metrics (see Fig. 3). Part (a) of the figure highlights gains across metrics. Part (b) emphasizes grouped metric improvements, showing that complexity and quality-related metrics saw notable enhancements, underscoring the overall effectiveness the multi-agent refactoring approach.

5   Discussion

5.1   LLM-Based Refactoring Efficiency (RQ1)

Our study found that the proposed multi-agent system reduced cyclomatic complexity by an average of **8.90%**, improved runtime efficiency by **5.28%**, and optimized memory allocation by **21.27%**. These findings indicate that the system was able to simplify, making the code more readable and maintainable. **Implications:** For researchers, this study provides a proof of concept for applying multi-agent systems in functional programming code refactoring, suggesting that these systems can be adapted to handle domain-specific challenges in functional languages [18]. For practitioners, the findings indicate that LLM-based multi-agent systems can automate refactoring tasks, leading to more maintainable, optimized code with minimal human intervention.

5.2 Multi-agent-Based Refactoring Impact (RQ2)

The multi-agent approach improved the refactoring workflow, leading to a **30.20%** reduction in HLint warnings and **11.97%** reduction in errors. This suggests that the multi-agent system was effective in enhancing code quality by addressing both stylistic and semantic issues. **Implications:** For researchers, these results suggest that multi-agent systems can provide improvements in code quality within functional programming contexts [8], such as Haskell. For practitioners, the findings suggest that incorporating multi-agent-based tools can directly enhance the efficiency of the refactoring process by addressing semantic issues [17], ultimately contributing to software maintenance practices [2].

6 Threats to Validity

Internal validity concerns the accuracy of our design and measurements. We used controlled benchmarking tools, but variations in code quality, developer choices, and system configurations may introduce bias. The automated refactoring process might also alter structures in ways not fully captured by our metrics. **External validity** relates to the generalizability of our findings. Our evaluation focused on a limited set of open-source Haskell projects, which may not represent domain-specific systems. Larger and more diverse codebases should be explored in future work.
Construct validity addresses whether our metrics capture refactoring efficacy. While measures such as cyclomatic complexity and runtime efficiency provide insight, qualitative aspects (e.g., developer experience and code readability) were not considered. Moreover, reliance on GPT-4o constrains outcomes to the model's capabilities and training data.

7 Conclusions

We presented an LLM-based multi-agent system for the intelligent refactoring of Haskell codebases. Through a structured system comprising agents for analysis, transformation, and validation, the system achieves improvements in code quality. The multi-agent system was tested on OSP. The results showed improvements in all the dimensions measured, including 11.03% in code complexity and a 22.46% improvement in overall code quality. These outcomes validate the multi-agent system's capability to support high-impact code maintenance while minimizing manual intervention. In summary, the proposed multi-agent system exemplifies the convergence of LLM and multi-agent coordination for scalable, intelligent code refactoring. Future research should focus on the improvements of context management and long-term memory to overcome the token window limits. This will help agents to process longer code without context loss.

References

1. Abdallah, C., Bouziane, H.: Dynamic maintenance and evolution of critical components-based software using multi agent systems. Comput. Inf. Sci. **4**(5), 78 (2011)
2. AlOmar, E.A., AlRubaye, H., Mkaouer, M.W., Ouni, A., Kessentini, M.: Refactoring practices in the context of modern code review: an industrial case study at xerox. In: 2021 IEEE/ACM 43rd International Conference on Software Engineering: Software Engineering in Practice (ICSE-SEIP), pp. 348–357. IEEE (2021)
3. Baumgartner, N., Iyenghar, P., Schoemaker, T., Pulvermüller, E.: Ai-driven refactoring: a pipeline for identifying and correcting data clumps in git repositories. Electronics **13**(9), 1644 (2024)
4. Bragilevsky, V.: Haskell in Depth. Simon and Schuster (2021)
5. Brown, C., Li, H., Thompson, S.: An expression processor: a case study in refactoring haskell programs. In: Page, R., Horváth, Z., Zsók, V. (eds.) TFP 2010. LNCS, vol. 6546, pp. 31–49. Springer, Heidelberg (2011). https://doi.org/10.1007/978-3-642-22941-1_3
6. Brown, T., et al.: Language models are few-shot learners. Adv. Neural. Inf. Process. Syst. **33**, 1877–1901 (2020)
7. Gill, A., Hutton, G.: The worker/wrapper transformation. J. Funct. Program. **19**(2), 227–251 (2009)
8. Gyori, A., Franklin, L., Dig, D., Lahoda, J.: Crossing the gap from imperative to functional programming through refactoring. In: Proceedings of the 2013 9th Joint Meeting on Foundations of Software Engineering, pp. 543–553 (2013)
9. Hu, Z., Hughes, J., Wang, M.: How functional programming mattered. Natl. Sci. Rev. **2**(3), 349–370 (2015)
10. Huang, Y.: Levels of AI agents: from rules to large language models. arXiv preprint arXiv:2405.06643 (2024)
11. Hudak, P., Fasel, J.H.: A gentle introduction to haskell. ACM Sigplan Not. **27**(5), 1–52 (1992)
12. McCabe, T.J.: A complexity measure. IEEE Trans. Software Eng. **4**, 308–320 (1976)
13. Mens, T., Tourwé, T.: A survey of software refactoring. IEEE Trans. Software Eng. **30**(2), 126–139 (2004)
14. Rajendran, V., Besiahgari, D., Patil, S.C., Chandrashekaraiah, M., Challagulla, V.: A multi-agent LLM environment for software design and refactoring: a conceptual framework. In: SoutheastCon 2025, pp. 488–493. IEEE (2025)
15. dos Santos Neto, B.F., Ribeiro, M., Da Silva, V.T., Braga, C., De Lucena, C.J.P., de Barros Costa, E.: Autorefactoring: a platform to build refactoring agents. Expert Syst. Appl. **42**(3), 1652–1664 (2015)
16. Siddeeq, S.: Intelligent haskell code refactoring using mulit-agent system (2025). https://github.com/GPT-Laboratory/Intelligent-Haskell-Code-Refactoring. Accessed 10 June 2025
17. Tan, I., Poskitt, C.M.: Fixing your own smells: adding a mistake-based familiarisation step when teaching code refactoring. In: Proceedings of the 55th ACM Technical Symposium on Computer Science Education, vol. 1, pp. 1307–1313 (2024)
18. Thompson, S., Li, H.: Refactoring tools for functional languages. J. Funct. Program. **23**(3), 293–350 (2013)

19. White, J., Hays, S., Fu, Q., Spencer-Smith, J., Schmidt, D.C.: Chatgpt prompt patterns for improving code quality, refactoring, requirements elicitation, and software design. In: Generative AI for Effective Software Development, pp. 71–108. Springer (2024)
20. Wooldridge, M., Jennings, N.R.: Intelligent agents: theory and practice. Knowl. Eng. Rev. **10**(2), 115–152 (1995)

Learning Observability Tracing Through Experiential Learning

Anders Sundelin[(✉)][iD]

Blekinge Institute of Technology, Karlskrona, Sweden
`anders.sundelin@bth.se`

Abstract. In a large-scale software development product development organization, we found that most developers, although experienced, were lacking architectural knowledge of the specific developed product.

As a remedy, we evaluated whether we could stimulate learning the product architecture by conducting training in how to use the product's distributed tracing platform, built on the OpenTelemetry standard and the open-source Jaeger Tracing visualization tool.

We planned and participated in a training event, where parts of the organization explored, using experiential learning, how to set up and use tracing to troubleshoot a realistic fault scenario we prepared. Respondents were asked to rate the tool according to the Technology Adoption Model (TAM), and responses were collected on Likert-type scales, analyzed, and summarized using a Bayesian workflow.

Even as tool usage post-training was low, respondents still had a positive attitude toward using the tool, valued the experiential training, and expressed a strong intent to use the tool for program comprehension.

Keywords: Micro-services · Observability · Distributed tracing · Experiential learning

1 Introduction

Even with comprehensive design documentation, becoming fluent in a codebase with millions of lines is difficult. Feature location involves static (source-code-based) and dynamic (logging, tracing) methods [3], but trace-based call-flow visualizations require setup and usage skills. With the advent of distributed microservices, where one request passes through multiple services before returning, the problem of locating features is even more complex, and distributed tracing tools have emerged to facilitate program comprehension and fault localization [2].

Over six months, we conducted a three-cycle action research study in a large-scale software development organization, encompassing around 100 developers (15 teams) on multiple sites in two time zones (Europe and India). As the majority of developers were relatively new to the large code base (more than 12 MLOC Java code), dating back 15 years, we wanted to understand if a distributed tracing tool could be used to help developers understand the program flow. To test

G. Scanniello et al. (Eds.): PROFES 2025, LNCS 16361, pp. 419–428, 2026.
https://doi.org/10.1007/978-3-032-12089-2_27

this theory, we planned and executed a learning session in which 19 developers, on two sites, learned how to set up and use the Jaeger tracing tool in a realistic problem scenario. Throughout the study, we collected feedback via surveys from the whole organization on how they perceived their competence and their experience with the training.

This paper is structured as follows: This section contains the overall problem formulation and the research questions. Section 2 contains background and related work, while Sect. 3 includes the research design, studied context, and methodology. Section 4 presents the results of our action cycles, which are condensed into learnings in Sect. 5, before we end the paper in Sect. 6 with conclusions.

1.1 Problem Statement and Research Questions

In our studied case, even as the product had supported tracing for over six months, few developers used it to learn about the product, which leads us to our problem formulation:

Can we use a tracing tool, like Jaeger, to increase architectural knowledge of a large product in a development organization where most developers lack specific product experience?

To investigate this problem, we formulated the following research questions:

(RQ1): To what extent do developers perceive that tracing tools help them understand the system architecture of a large-scale, multi-service system, most of which has been written by other developers?

(RQ2): How do developers perceive learning Jaeger tracing via experiential learning, using the system where they usually work?

(RQ3): To what extent do developers intend to continue using the tracing tools?

2 Background and Related Work

The Open-Source standard and framework OpenTelemetry[1] was formed to enable practical observability of microservices in an easy, universal, vendor-neutral, loosely coupled, and built-in way. To meet these goals, it provides standards and reference implementations that generate, collect, and export telemetry data in traces, metrics, and logs. Jaeger Tracing[2] is an open-source tool that produces web visualizations of collected OpenTelemetry data.

Gortney et al. [6] conducted a systematic mapping study and found that dynamic tracing, log analysis, and metrics collection were the three main practices used to visualize microservice architectures.

To assess the state of observability tools in industry, Li et al. [8] conducted an interview study, where 25 interviewees from ten companies of different sizes

---

[1] https://opentelemetry.io/.
[2] https://www.jaegertracing.io/.

and in five domains were interviewed about their tracing practices and tools. All but the smallest of the studied companies (≈ 10 services and ≈ 20 kLOC) were employing, or considering using, some trace and log processing pipeline. The trace function was most commonly used for timeline and root cause analyses.

3 Research Design

3.1 Context

The organization consists of 15 cross-functional teams of $6-8$ developers, equally split between Europe and India. The product runs on Kubernetes in the cloud, and includes both in-house and externally sourced services, mostly Java (3.01 MLOC production, 2.22 MLOC unit tests, 6.49 MLOC functional tests), plus smaller Vue.JS (181 kLOC) and TypeScript (817 kLOC) front ends.

Half of the 15-year-old code base is older than five years, and only 30% is written by current employees, with the most experienced team contributing 8.8%, and average team contributions under 1%. A survey (55% response rate) shows both European and Indian developers average over ten years in general software development experience, but those in Europe have more product knowledge (average 4.2, max 15 years) than those in India (average 2.5, max 4 years).

3.2 Summary of Research Cycles

The organization asked us to investigate why OpenTelemetry and Jaeger were not used, even though architects saw them as valuable for exploring product architecture and unfamiliar features.

Cycle 1: Problem identification and formulation assessed the organization's development practices by collecting system statistics and administering a survey[3], asking respondents to rate their skills in six development areas, using a $0-100$ scale with descriptive anchors for five levels.

Cycle 2: Planning and executing the training session involved developing and delivering Jaeger training simultaneously at the European and Indian development centers. The session was one of six optional tracks during an organization-wide training day, with instructor-led, in-office participation to promote skill sharing and cross-team networking, while organizers allocated attendees based on budget and preferences.

Cycle 3: Follow-up of the training examined whether developers used Jaeger after the training by monitoring internal wiki page views. After one month, a follow-up survey was distributed to gather feedback on the training experience.

3.3 Data Collection and Analysis Methods

All our surveys used 7-level symmetric Likert scales with mandatory items and optional qualitative questions to assess agreement with survey statements. We

---

[3] Available in the replication package: https://doi.org/10.5281/zenodo.15678405.

applied Bayesian data analysis [5,9] under the TAM framework to model constructs like usability, ease-of-use, and intent-to-use, comparing our treatment group to two control groups from unrelated training sessions. Models were ranked using PSIS-LOO [11] and built with the brms framework [1], interfacing with the Stan language, with full methodology available in the replication package [4].

We compared training sessions and sites by analyzing distributions, means, and credible intervals of the expected rating (defined as $\mathbb{E} \equiv \sum_{k=1}^{7} p(k) \times k$, where $p(k)$ is the probability of rating k) for the different constructs. We also summarized the qualitative feedback and presented this to the organization.

4   Results and Interpretation

We follow recommendations from Staron [10] and report the results per cycle.

Cycle 1: Problem identification and formulation focused on assessing the current situation, from a tracing and observability perspective. We administered a survey to assess the self-rated competence level in the organization from various development perspectives. While the majority of the 55 respondents, in both Europe and India, are confident in writing and debugging Java code, fewer were confident in Vue.JS, and only four individuals (all based in Europe) reported that they were confident in Jaeger tracing.

We presented these findings, together with the proposed training, to the organization, which agreed to continue the study.

Cycle 2: Planning and executing the training session started with collecting background knowledge and planning an interactive training session. We wanted to involve participants and use a realistic scenario recognizable to developers. The cycle lasted six weeks, with regular follow-up meetings, comprising four phases: (i) planning and scoping the tutorial, (ii) preparing the setup instructions and developing the scenarios the students would face, (iii) validating the instructions (also including fixing issues found in existing documentation), and finally (iv) executing the training sessions, and collecting direct feedback.

Our planning phase focused on how to introduce a condition that would trigger a suitable anomaly (e.g., prolonged response time). We developed one mandatory "seeded" problem and four "overflow" tasks, freely chosen by each team. To aid teams, we developed four hints for our problem, where the first hint indicated the product area, and the last one pointed to a complete functional test case reproducing the problem. Depending on the team's problem-solving progress, teachers distributed hints as text on printed paper. All teams needed the first hint, and one team used all four.

After one experienced developer formulated and implemented the seeded problem, including hints, we used two validation phases. First, one developer on each site independently followed and commented on the instructions. After adjustments and clarifications of instructions and hints, one junior developer performed final validation, including measuring the required time.

The training day comprised five one-day training sessions, from requirements engineering to security analysis. Participants ranked their preferences, and orga-

nizers allocated spots based on these choices and available capacity. All participants in the *Generative AI* and Vue.JS tracks had chosen these as their primary
alternative. All architect and developer teams were represented in the *Jaeger
tracing* track, but only 70% had ranked it as their primary choice.

After the training day, we collected opinions on the training from participants
on both sites via a prepared survey. The tool-centric training sessions shared the
same TAM-based structure of the questions, but had different characteristics:

Generative AI. Participants in this track would learn principles behind
RetrievalAugmented Generation (RAG), use and partially develop a Python-
based RAG solution in an existing Jupyter Notebook. Developers currently
use none of these tools in their daily work.

Jaeger Tracing. This is our treatment group, where we explain how to set
up OpenTelemetry and Jaeger in an experiential learning setting, and use
these tools to solve a realistic, prepared problem in a special product branch.

Vue.JS. Participants in this track would learn how to leverage the (for the
product) new Vue.JS component pattern[4]. They were expected to learn the
pattern and refactor existing views by developing and using common components in their normal development environment.

We asked the participants to rate the tools they used in their training from the
angles of:(i) usability, (ii) ease-of-use, (iii) ease-of-access, and (iv) intent to use
the tool in the future. Overall, the ratings were positive and similar for both
sites, indicating that the training was well received.

Table 1. Respondents per training session, their reported years of professional experience, and the percentage of participants responding to the survey.

	Site	N	Years of prof. experience					Response
			Mean	σ	Median	Min	Max	Rate
GenAI	Europe	3	14.0	14.2	9	3	30	50%
	India	6	13.7	3.6	13	10	20	75%
Jaeger	Europe	10	17.5	8.7	17.5	8	30	83%
	India	9	12.9	3.4	14	5	17	100%
Vue.JS	Europe	5	14.8	10.2	19	0	25	83%
	India	5	7.8	4.0	10	3	12	71%

Table 1 shows the number of respondents per session and site, and summary
statistics on their (self-reported) professional developer experience. All sessions
involved experienced professional developers, with a median experience ranging
between 9 and 19 years. The response rate varied between 50% and 100%.

---

[4] https://vueschool.io/articles/vuejs-tutorials/5-component-design-patterns-
toboost-your-vue-js-applications/.

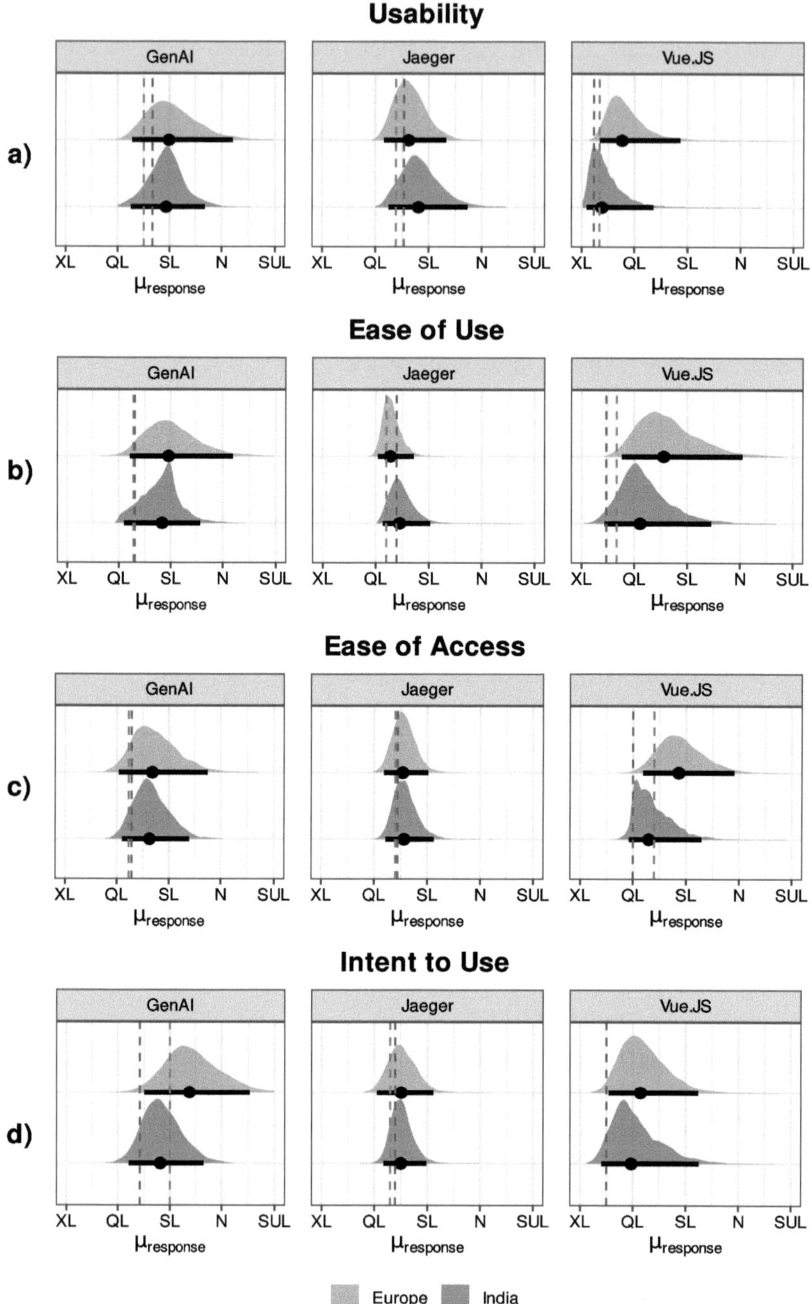

Fig. 1. The distributions, by tool and training site, of the posterior expected rating for the four constructs: usability, ease-of-use, ease-of-access, and intent-to-use. Likert levels on the x-axis represent *Extremely Likely*, *Quite Likely*, *Slightly Likely*, *Neutral*, and *Slightly Unlikely* agreement, omitting the last two levels. The point estimate of the expected rating is shown as a dot, surrounded by the 95% credible interval. Sample (response) means are shown as dashed lines.

Figure 1a) shows the expected average usability rating, distribution, point estimate, and 95% credible interval. The figure shows that Vue.JS participants perceived the strongest usability, especially the Indian cohort. However, the European participants are *Quite Likely* to agree that Vue.JS components are usable. Both cohorts of Generative AI participants agree that the RAG tool is *Slightly Likely* to be usable, though the European cohort also tends towards *Neutral*. The Jaeger participants take the middle ground, rating the tool between *Quite Likely* and *Slightly Likely* to agree on its usability. The Indian cohort leans more towards *Slightly Likely*, though the difference is negligible.

Concerning ease-of-use, Fig. 1b) show that the Vue.JS participants are more skeptical, particularly the European cohort, which rates ease-of-use *Slightly Likely*, while the Indian cohort leans more towards *Quite Likely*. Both the other tracks are very similar between sites. However, the Jaeger distribution is slightly narrower, and estimates, with 95% probability, that the expected value for ease-of-use lies between *Slightly Likely* and *Quite Likely*. Although the point estimate of the Generative AI track is similar, the distribution is wider, meaning there is more uncertainty about where the expected value lies, particularly towards the *Neutral* level.

Figure 1c) shows the perception of how easy the tools are accessed in day-to-day use. All tools rate between *Quite Likely* and *Slightly Likely*, though the European Vue.JS participants lean closer towards *Slightly Likely*, while their Indian counterparts lean more towards *Quite Likely*.

Finally, as shown in Fig. 1d), we measured the intent to use the tool in the future. Not surprisingly, the Vue.JS participants were most certain that they would use Vue components, with the expected value close to *Quite Likely* for both European and Indian cohorts. The Generative AI participants were more skeptical, particularly the European cohort, where the expected rating was estimated to lie between *Slightly Likely* and *Neutral*. The Indian cohort was more positive, though close to *Slightly Likely*. Both Jaeger groups were equally certain that they lean between *Slightly Likely* and *Quite Likely* to continue using the tracing tool in the future.

Fifteen of the 19 participants in the Jaeger training also provided qualitative responses. The thirteen positive responses range from: "Knowing that the tool exists" to the more explicit: "Save significant debugging time when you have visibility on complete code flow across components along with their respective process time." Five respondents found things to improve related to the training (e.g., "Docker logins should be fully working"), and six respondents commented on the Jaeger GUI (e.g., "I found the comparison feature difficult to understand").

We also surveyed the teachers, achieving between 50% and 100% response rates for the tool sessions. The most positive teachers were found in the Jaeger track, where teachers indicated "it went generally well," and "pretty much smooth." The primary Vue.JS track teacher indicated that the session probably had "too much freedom," and that "letting people choose what they want to do can be overwhelming." The teacher indicated that more structure and options would be imposed if the track were held again. The single (out of two) AI teacher respondent indicated that developers requested "more post-practices," indicating that the participants wanted more experience with the tool they partly developed. The Jaeger tracing and Generative AI teachers were *Extremely* or *Quite* agreeing that they had enough time and resources for preparations and that the tasks were adequate for the participants. In contrast, one Vue.JS teacher was only *Slightly* agreeing to those statements. However, all teachers enjoyed being mentors and agreed that participants learned something useful.

Cycle 3: Follow-up of the training investigated Jaeger tool usage after the training by analyzing page views of the setup instructions on the corporate wiki[5]. Due to low page traffic, we conducted a follow-up survey one month later to assess how participants applied their learnings and identify barriers to tool adoption.

The survey had a low response rate, with only 23 replies, including six Jaeger training participants, none of whom reported using the tool. However, they expressed motivation to use tracing for learning program flow, and slightly agree that it would improve their understanding and development speed. All six respondents provide qualitative feedback (e.g., "I will use it when needing to trace something that is hard to track down in some other way").

Conclusion. Related to **RQ1**, respondents have a favorable view of the utility of a tracing toolchain like OpenTelemetry and Jaeger to aid program comprehension. The expected intent to use the tools is close to "*Quite Likely*" and our model is 95% sure that the intent to use is higher than "*Slightly Likely*". This is also confirmed by the qualitative data collected via the survey.

Related to **RQ2**, we find from qualitative survey responses that the respondents view the training session positively, though two respondents indicate they had to overcome troubles with the used environment. No respondents stated that the problem was too complex or that the hints gave away too much. The participants appear engaged, and they seem to appreciate the preparations.

Related to **RQ3**, web access logs indicate that the setup instructions were rarely accessed, and survey responses, although limited, state that no respondent had used the Jaeger tracing tool one month after training. However, all six respondents reported that they were positive and would use it when they needed to learn more about the product architecture. This might indicate that the tool's utility is real, but the need to use it is infrequent. We intend to follow up on how the tool is perceived and how the competence spreads in the organization.

5   Learnings

5.1   Contribution to Theory

Our study indicates that tracing tools, such as OpenTelemetry and Jaeger are valuable for visualizing system architecture and localizing features. However, despite developers recognizing their usefulness, usage remains limited six months after introduction and one month after training, suggesting these tools are used sparingly, mainly when exploring new domains or unfamiliar features.

---

[5] https://www.atlassian.com/software/confluence.

The experiential learning event, featuring one structured track and four "open-ended" problems, was well received, with all respondents providing positive feedback on their learning. Teachers also noted that they enjoyed guiding participants and making new social connections.

5.2   Recommendations to Other Companies

We structure our recommendations according to the study phases:

Prepare problem(s) well in advance, and validate (using "fresh" developers) that the problem is attainable, but still challenging. If possible, frame tasks in the regular code base, not a synthetic toy problem.

Problems can be "open" or "closed", and participants appreciated the "closed path" in the beginning, while enjoying the "open tasks" when they had learned more. To gain confidence in problem complexity, we used a representative developer to solve the "closed" problem, reviewing the number of hints needed and their detail.

Hints should be at different levels of detail, and we used paper slips rather than digital web pages. Teachers need to be prepared to disseminate these among the training groups, according to where they are in the learning journey.

6   Conclusions and Future Work

Our study adds to the findings by Li et al. [8] and Gortney et al. [6] that tracing can be an important tool to discover and learn about the product architecture. However, even as training participants perceived the tool and training positively, we found that these tools appear to be used relatively infrequently, possibly because developers rarely venture into unknown components.

We created a "Goldilocks problem," that was challenging yet attainable to help students focus on learning the tool chain, and used three developers to validate that the instructions were clear and unambiguous. Both students and teachers appreciated the initial structured approach, along with the four open-ended problems that allowed students to explore the tool freely.

Experiential learning [7] relies on attentive, self-directed students, so we provided hints of varying explicitness to participants as needed during the training. Survey responses show students found training tied to their daily work more usable, with higher scores for the Vue.JS component and tracing tool tracks than for Generative AI.

Despite developers expressing positive intent, one month after the training, none of our respondents had used the tracing tool in their daily work. This suggests that longer studies are needed to properly assess its adoption. We plan to continue surveying developers over time to monitor their work practices.

Acknowledgments. This research was supported by the Knowledge Foundation through the KKS Profile project SERT 2018/010 at Blekinge Institute of Technology, Sweden.

Disclosure of Interests. The author declares that he has no competing interests in the methods or tools mentioned in this article.

References

1. Bürkner, P.C.: brms: an r package for bayesian multilevel models using Stan. J. Stat. Softw. **80**(1), 1–28 (2017). https://doi.org/10.18637/jss.v080.i01
2. Cassé, C., Berthou, P., Owezarski, P., Josset, S.: Using distributed tracing to identify inefficient resources composition in cloud applications. In: 2021 IEEE 10th International Conference on Cloud Networking (CloudNet), pp. 40–47 (2021). https://doi.org/10.1109/CloudNet53349.2021.9657140
3. Dit, B., Revelle, M., Gethers, M., Poshyvanyk, D.: Feature location in source code: a taxonomy and survey. J. Softw. Evolution Process **25**(1), 53–95 (2013)
4. Sundelin, A.: epkanol/observability-tracing-experiential-learning: First zenodo release (2025). https://doi.org/10.5281/zenodo.15678406
5. Gelman, A., Hill, J.: Data Analysis Using Regression and Multilevel/Hierarchical Models. Cambridge University Press, Analytical Methods for Social Research (2006)
6. Gortney, M.E., Harris, P.E., Cerny, T., Maruf, A.A., Bures, M., Taibi, D., Tisnovsky, P.: Visualizing microservice architecture in the dynamic perspective: a systematic mapping study. IEEE Access **10**, 119999–120012 (2022). https://doi.org/10.1109/ACCESS.2022.3221130
7. Kolb, D.A.: Experiential learning: experience as the source of learning and development. FT Press (2014)
8. Li, B., et al.: Enjoy your observability: an industrial survey of microservice tracing and analysis. Empir. Softw. Eng. **27**(1), 1–28 (2021). https://doi.org/10.1007/s10664-021-10063-9
9. McElreath, R.: Statistical rethinking: a bayesian course with examples in R and Stan. CRC Press (2020)
10. Staron, M.: Action research in software engineering. Springer Cham (2020). https://doi.org/10.1007/978-3-030-32610-4
11. Vehtari, A., Gelman, A., Gabry, J.: Practical bayesian model evaluation using leave-one-out cross-validation and WAIC. Stat. Comput. (1), 1–20 (2016). https://doi.org/10.1007/s11222-016-9696-4

Privacy-Enhanced Software Design: Purpose-Aware UML Diagrams

Evangelia Vanezi[(✉)], Georgia Kapitsaki, and Anna Philippou

Department of Computer Science, University of Cyprus, Nicosia, Cyprus
{vanezi.evangelia,gkapi,annap}@ucy.ac.cy

Abstract. The General Data Protection Regulation (GDPR) was introduced and applied in the EU to help users protect their personal data. An important principle of the regulation is 'Purpose Limitation', stating that personal data should be processed only in ways (purposes) clearly stated and agreed upon between the system and the user. One major challenge in Software Engineering is the integration of processing purposes into the system design. Aiming to address this challenge, we present a software design methodology allowing to formulate the processing purposes of a system and integrate them with the functional requirements. We present a purpose-aware version of the UML Use Case and Sequence diagrams to assist engineers in visualising the purpose-aware requirements, and a prototype tool to automate this process. We furthermore present an evaluation of the methodology, gathering overall positive results, especially regarding users' confidence, simplicity, and ease of use.

Keywords: GDPR Purpose Limitation · UML Use Case Diagrams · UML Sequence Diagrams · Software Engineering Design Practices

1 Introduction

Tons of personal data of individuals are being stored, processed, and shared by software and web systems worldwide. A significant step towards the protection of users' privacy was the enforcement of several regulations across the globe, one being the European Union (EU) General Data Protection Regulation (GDPR) [11], imposing rights for data owners and liabilities for data processors and data controllers. The principle of *Purpose Limitation*, defined in GDPR Article 5, mandates that personal data should only be processed following clearly defined, specific *processing purposes*. One major challenge is the integration of processing purposes into software system design, and prior works have used Unified Modelling Language (UML) and Data Flow Diagrams (DFDs) for this purpose [14,15].

Aiming to define a design method that integrates purpose, we contribute with the following: (1) we propose a step-by-step methodology for defining and incorporating processing purposes into functional requirements and purpose-aware UML Use Case and Sequence diagrams for visualising them during system design

G. Scanniello et al. (Eds.): PROFES 2025, LNCS 16361, pp. 429–439, 2026.
https://doi.org/10.1007/978-3-032-12089-2_28

(Sect. 3); (2) we automate the process of creating purpose-enhanced sequence diagrams, on top of basic sequence diagrams with a prototype web-based tool (Sect. 3.3); (3) we evaluate our methodology and diagrams with Computer Science students (junior developers), and we discuss the results (Sect. 4). Moreover, Sect. 2 gives a brief overview of the relevant literature, while in Sect. 4.3, we further discuss our findings, and in Sect. 5, we summarize our conclusions.

Data and Tool Availability. All our diagrams and the source code of the presented tool are openly available in the following GitHub repository: https://anonymous.4open.science/r/PA-UML-EC62/[1]

2   Related Work

Following the enactment of the GDPR, *purpose* has been discussed in many research works, such as [16], in which the authors try to rigorously define it through formal methods, or in [6,7] in which the authors try to integrate it into a system technical design via data flow diagrams. UML diagrams and DFDs have been used for defining, verifying and enforcing purpose-specific constraints in several works [2–4,14,15]. UML Use Case diagrams were used in an attempt towards ensuring compliance with GDPR principles relating to the processing of the personal data [13]. Purpose labels are used by Alshareef et al. for tracking and verifying data usage in system design via DFDs [5] . Aiming to design, monitor, and ensure that data processing is only done for intended purposes, collaboration diagrams are used in [12]. On the other hand, unauthorised data access detection is suggested by Tong et al. with the use of class, use case, and activity diagrams [18], while Veseli et al. use DFDs to model the retrieval of data by users, and recognise relevant threats in terms of purpose of using the data [17]. Ahmadian et al. use class and activity diagrams to verify if a piece of personal data is processed for authorised purposes [1]. Sequence diagrams were also used to track the requests for data access in cloud environments [9].

Even though there have been works using diagrams for purpose-based system design, they rely on the representation of purpose as plain textual labels, or on the application of access control. They do not define purpose in detail, and do not examine the actions taking place around the processing of personal data, as done in the current work.

3   Defining and Visualising Purposes in System Design

3.1   Methodology Overview

We present a step-by-step methodology for defining a system's processing purposes, and visually integrating them with its functional requirements during the design stage, using UML diagrams. We demonstrate it via an example of a *simplified online library management system* in which users register, borrow and return books.

---

[1] To be made publicly available in case of acceptance.

1. *Define functional requirements* (e.g., user logs in, user borrows books with their username and book ID stored in the DB, due date notifications sent to the user's email address).
2. *Identify system entities* (e.g., User, Log-in User Interface, Database).
3. *List personal data* (e.g., username, password, email).
4. *Define the processing purposes* for all system entities by defining which personal data each will provide, collect, and process, and how exactly they will be processing them, and if needed define under which conditions (e.g., the User, who owns the username and password provides them to the system to log-in; the Log-in UI receives these data and forwards them to the Authorisation entity (does not read them). The Authorisation entity reads the data to validate the log-in attempt).
5. *Integrate purposes into requirements visually* via the purpose-aware UML Use Case and Sequence diagrams (see Sect. 3.2).

3.2   Purpose-Aware UML Diagrams

Use Case Diagrams. We have chosen to utilize UML Use Case diagrams to demonstrate a high-level overview of purpose-aware requirements including the input of personal data into the system from external actors and the output of personal data from the system to external actors, but not any other flow of personal data between the system use cases. As such, Use Case diagrams cannot replace the textual description of purpose; they can, however, complement it. We extend basic use case diagrams with three additional elements: (i) Personal data to be added on each use case in which they are used; (ii) Personal data stores (containers holding the personal data) to be added next to the actor to which the data belong to, and on the associations between external actors and the system if they are exchanged between them; and (iii) Ownership of personal data defined when a personal data store is placed next to the actor to whom the data belong. Figure 1 demonstrates the Use Case diagram for the previously discussed online library system. The diagram shows that the user actor owns three pieces of personal data: username, password, and email. The username and password are shared between the user actor and the system (input), in specifics the 'Log-in' use case, and the username is shared between the system ('Borrow Books' use case) and the database external actor (output). Furthermore, the diagram shows that all use cases process the username, while 'Log-in' also processes the password, and 'Receive notifications' also processes the email.

Sequence Diagrams. UML Sequence diagrams demonstrate the sequence of the interactions between system entities and the messages exchanged, and as such can capture the detailed flow of personal data. We extend basic Sequence diagrams with three additional elements: (i) Personal data stores (containers holding the personal data that should be passed on to entities that will process the data) to be added next to the actor to which they belong to, and on message exchanges between entities if the data are passed on (an additional different colored edge line should be used in such cases); (ii) Personal data read from the

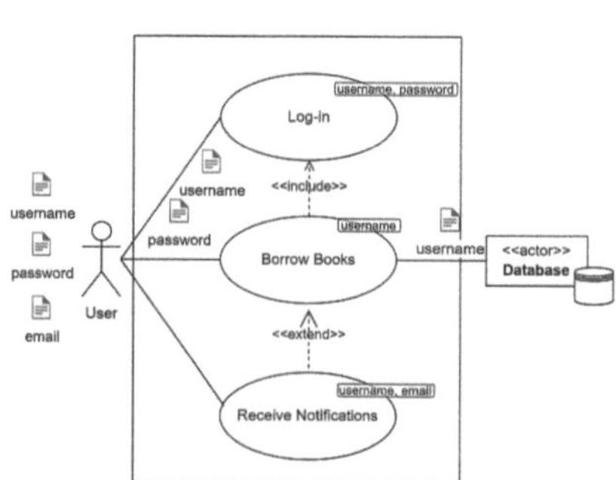

Fig. 1. Purpose-Aware Use Case Diagram Example.

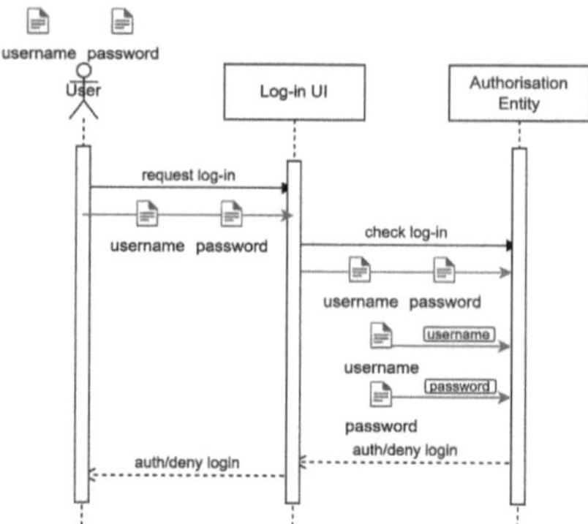

Fig. 2. Purpose-Aware Sequence Diagram Example.

personal data stores (before being used), signified by a colored edge line directed from the store to the entity, or updated by the entity signified by a colored edge line directed from the entity to the store ; (iii) Personal data ownership, defined in a similar manner as in extended Use Case diagrams. The diagrams are closely related with a formal purpose language presented in our prior work [16]. Elements in our diagrams follow the formal language, such as personal data handed over to other entities via passing on the personal data stores. This alignment allows the direct translation between the two.

Figure 2 presents the purpose-aware Sequence diagram for the online library system and specifically the log-in functionality. During this process, the user requests to log in, sending the username and password to the log-in UI. The log-in UI is not responsible for performing the credentials check, and will not be reading the personal data. It will pass the data (i.e., the personal data stores), along with a 'check log-in' request, to the authorisation entity. This entity will read both data from the stores, perform some checks that are omitted for simplification reasons, and pass back a message of authorisation or denial to the UI, which in turn will inform the user.

3.3   A Tool For Purpose-Aware Sequence Diagrams Design

We developed a prototype web-based tool to assist engineers in enhancing their Sequence diagrams with purposes, offering the following functionality:

1. The user imports an XML file with the basic Sequence diagram.
2. The tool parses the file, and recognizes all lifelines, activator boxes, actors, and messages and some important metadata, like their names, their position, or the source and target entities of messages.
3. The system visualises the basic Sequence diagram.
4. The tool provides a sidebar with fields asking the user to provide purpose-relevant information as follows: (i) for every entity or actor recognized, the

user is prompted to define if there are any personal data owned, by adding these data names in the corresponding fields; (ii) for every message recognized, the user is prompted to define if there are personal data passed from the source to the target, by adding these data names in the corresponding fields; (iii) for every passing of personal data on a message, the user is prompted to define if the receiving entity is going to actually use or read these data at some point, and if yes when is this going to happen.

5. The user completes the relevant fields and clicks the 'Apply & Update Diagram' button. The purpose-aware information is added on the diagram, and the visualisation is updated with the personal data ownerships, the personal data exchanges, and the personal data usage.

6. An XML file is prepared representing the purpose-aware Sequence diagram, and is automatically downloaded. The user can import the purpose-aware diagram into a design tool (e.g., draw.io) to continue working on it.

The tool source code, and a screenshot of the single-page UI is available in the work's GitHub repository, and can be executed locally in the browser.

4 User Evaluation

This section presents the evaluation that we conducted for our methodology and purpose-aware UML diagrams. We present the evaluation process, the participants, the questions we asked them, and the quantitative and qualitative results.

4.1 Evaluation Methodology

The evaluation was conducted in two sessions of a software engineering (SE) course at the University of Cyprus in the fall semester of 2024–2025. The SE course is compulsory and attended by third-year bachelor students (in a four-year bachelor's program). All students have followed the same or similar course in their program. The same procedure and evaluation were employed in both sessions. The sessions structure was designed by all authors, while one of the authors guided the participants during the process. The whole duration of each session was 1 h and 15 min, and was unfolded as follows:

1. In the first 20 min, we gave an introduction of the methodology and the purpose-aware diagrams. The students already had basic knowledge of UML.
2. In the following 45 min the students divided into teams of two or three people received handouts with the details for a case study system and of the methodology presented , and were asked to enhance the diagrams with purposes. For the case study they received the requirements, the system entities list, the personal data, the processing purposes, and basic (not purpose-aware) Use Case and Sequence diagrams , as shown in Figs. 3 and 4.
3. Finally, in the last 10 min the participants were asked to evaluate the whole process, methodology, and diagrams individually. For the evaluation questionnaire, we exploited the Technology Acceptance Model (TAM) [10], measuring

perceived usefulness, perceived ease of use, and intention to use, and the System Usability Scale (SUS) [8], measuring the perceived usability of a product. A set of questions from each was selected and adjusted, since some questions were not applicable in our case in their original format. Additionally, a few YY questions were added to recognize the initial students' level of knowledge about the GDPR, the number of members in each team, and the time needed to complete the task. All questions are presented in Table 1. The type of question is also shown in the table (Likert scale 1-5 or short answer open-ended text). In the end, the participants returned to the facilitator the enhanced diagrams with all their additions and notes taken, and the individually completed questionnaires.

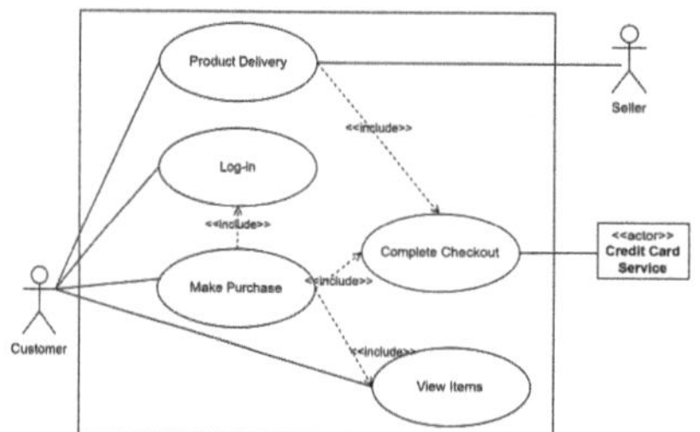

Fig. 3. Basic Use Case Diagram for the Case Study System.

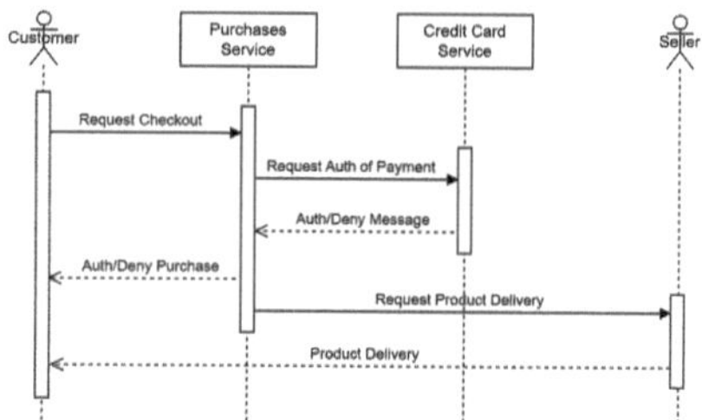

Fig. 4. Basic Sequence Diagram for the Case Study System.

4.2 Results

We had a total number of $n = 63$ participants. 34 students attended the first session, and 29 students attended the second session. Both in the first and second sessions, the students were divided into 12 teams (in total, we had $t = 24$ teams across our evaluation sessions). In the first session, we had 10 teams of 3 students each and 2 teams of 2 students each, while in the second session, we had 5 groups of 3 students each and 7 groups of 2 students each.

A. Prior Knowledge. The majority of students (57.1%, n = 36) responded with 1 (No prior knowledge) and 2 (Little prior knowledge), in Q1 , while 33.3% of the students (n = 21) responded with 3 (Medium level of knowledge), and only a 9.5% stated a level above the middle: n = 5 students (7.9%) responded with 4 (Good knowledge), and n = 1 student (1.6%) with 5 (Fully knowledgeable). Therefore, we studied the rest of the results, bearing in mind that the majority of students were not well acquainted with the GDPR.

Table 1. Evaluation Questions

Part A	
Q1	What was your level of knowledge about the GDPR notion of "Purpose" before this lecture? *Likert scale (1: No prior knowledge, 5: Completely knowledgeable)*
Q2	Would you feel confident in using the methodology suggested to describe your software system's purpose? *Likert scale (1: Not confident at all, 5: Completely confident)*
Q3	Would you feel confident in using the methodology suggested to integrate 'purpose' with the functional requirements using the methodology and the extended diagrams? *Likert scale (1: Not confident at all, 5: Completely confident)*
Q4	Would you use the methodology suggested frequently (to integrate 'purpose' into the software functional requirements) *Likert scale (1: I would never use it, 5: I would use it very frequently)*
Q5	Did you find it unnecessarily complex to adjust the basic diagrams given to you, enhancing them with purpose-aware elements? textitLikert scale (1: Not complex at all, 5: Entirely complex process)
Q6	Do you find this methodology easy to use? *Likert scale (1: Not easy at all, 5: Completely easy)*
Q7	Using this methodology would enable you to integrate 'purpose' into requirements more quickly (in comparison to not using this methodology). textitLikert scale (1: I do not agree at all, 5: I agree completely)
Q8	Using this methodology would make it easier for you to integrate 'purpose' into requirements (in comparison to not using this methodology). *Likert scale (1: I do not agree at all, 5: I agree completely)*
Part B	
Q9	How many students were in your team? *Short answer text (open-ended)*
Q10	How much time was needed to adjust the basic diagrams given, enhancing them with purpose-aware elements? *Short answer text (open-ended)*
Q11	How easy or difficult did you find the process of integrating 'purposes' into the diagrams? *Likert scale (1: Completely Difficult, 5: Entirely easy)*
Q12	How useful do you find this process for integrating 'purposes' into the diagrams? *Likert scale (1: Not useful at all, 5: Completely useful)*

B. Perceived Usability (SUS). Questions Q2-Q5, and Q11, adapted from the SUS, measure perceived usability. Most of the participants responded positively in Q2 and Q3 regarding their confidence in using the methodology to describe purposes and integrate them with functional requirements. Specifically, 52.5% (n = 33) responded with 4 (Very Confident) in both questions, while 7.9% (n = 5) in Q2 and 11.1% (n = 7) in Q3 responded with 5 (Completely Confident). Furthermore, 38.1% (n = 24) in Q2 and 31.7% (n = 20) in Q3 responded with 3 (medium confidence level). Negative results include 1.6% (n = 1) and 4.8% (n = 3) in Q2 and Q3, respectively, which responded with 2 (Low level of Confidence). There was no participant responding with 1 (Not confident at all). In Q4, 47.6% (n = 30) of the participants responded positively, either with 4 (I would use this methodology to integrate purposes with requirements frequently) or with 5 (I would use it very frequently), while 39.7% (n = 25) responded with 3, and a 12.7% (n = 8) responded negatively with 2 (I would not use it so frequently). In Q5 , we received very positive results as 82.5% of the participants (n = 52) stated that they did not find the creation of the purpose-aware diagrams unnecessarily complex responding with 1 and 2. At the same time, 14.3% (n = 9) responded with 3 (neutral), and only 3.2% (n = 2) responded with 4 finding it somehow complex. Finally, in Q11 , studying how easy or difficult the participants have found the integration of purposes into diagrams, most of the participants (84.1%, n = 53) responded with 4 (Very easy) or 5 (Entirely easy), while 12.7% (n = 8) responded with 3 (neutral) and 3.2% (n = 2) with 2 (difficult).

C. Perceived Usefulness, Ease of Use, and Intention (TAM). Q6-Q8 and Q12, adapted from the TAM, measure the perceived usefulness, ease of use and intention to use. By analysing the responses, we get the following results: In Q6, assessing the ease of use of the methodology, there were no negative responses collected. More specifically, 11.1% of the participants (n = 7) responded with 3 (neutral), 65.1% (n = 41) responded with 4 (very easy), and 23.8% (n = 15) responded with 5 (completely easy). The majority of the participants (73% - n = 46) responded positively with 4 (I agree) and 5 (I agree completely) when asked if the methodology would enable them to integrate purpose into requirements more quickly in Q7 . Additionally, 19% (n = 12) of the participants responded with 3 (neutral), and 7.9% (n = 5) responded with 2 (I do not agree). Similarly, 50.8% (n = 32) of the participants responded with 4 (I agree), and 17.5% (n = 11) with 5 (I agree completely) when asked if the methodology would make it easier for them to integrate purpose into requirements in Q8. In this case, 28.6% (n = 18) of the participants responded with 3 (neutral), and 3.2% (n = 2) with 2 (I do not agree). Finally, Q12 , assessing the usefulness of our process for integrating purposes with the requirements through the diagrams, has received positive results, with 49.2% (n = 31) responding with 4 (Useful), 27% (n = 17) responding with 5 (Completely Useful), and 22.2% (n = 14) responding with 3 (neutral). Only a small percentage (1.6%, n = 1) responded with 2 (Not so useful). Overall, we observe positive outcomes in this aspect.

D. Time Spent (Q10). 82.53% of the participants (n = 52) stated that they needed 15 min or less to enhance the diagrams, 12.69% (n = 8) stated that they needed 20 min, while 4.76% (n = 3) needed between 30 and 45 min.

E. Qualitative Results. Use Case Diagrams: (1) Participants added personal data on the edges connecting one use case to another but should only be added on the edges connecting the system with external actors to demonstrate input and output. (2) Participants added the email address and username on the edge connecting the 'Product Delivery' use case with the 'Customer' where no new data will be received. (3) Similarly, participants added the username and password on the edge between the customer and the 'Make purchase' use case, but these data were given as input into the system in the 'Log-in' use case. (4) We also observed non-personal data added on the edges. (5) Participants discussed the fact that the edges on the Use Case diagrams do not have a direction, making it hard to perceive whether the personal data are incoming or outgoing. *Sequence Diagrams.* (1) Some teams incorrectly included non personal data on edges (e.g., the email message sent towards the participant for the delivery of the product). (2) In other cases, some teams incorrectly placed the customer's email address on the edge of the product delivery. (3) Similarly, personal data that were sent from the customer to the system are incorrectly returned on the edges sending the auth/deny message. (4) Unnecessary personal data was passed on in some flows (e.g., the username and password were sent from the purchase service to the credit card service, whose only task is to validate the credit card payment). Sending these data violates the system's processing purposes.

4.3   Discussion

The evaluation provided insights on how purpose can be added to existing UML diagrams by junior developers. Positive results were gathered regarding participants' confidence in using our methodology and diagrams and their assessment of complexity and ease. However, there is room for improvement regarding the intention to use our methodology frequently. Since not all participants had the same level of knowledge of the GDPR, we checked whether this prior knowledge affects the responses to any of the other questions, by running a one-way ANOVA parametric statistical test but no statistically significant differences were found. An important implication is that privacy aspects should be integrated in the system design in an easy way that does not take a long time to complete (in the user evaluation this process took 15 min or less for most participants). Incorrect uses of the purpose-aware diagrams were also observed, and some are related to what is considered personal data in specific interactions (e.g., information sent back to the client), so another wider implication concerning educators is that software engineering and data science courses need to put emphasis on the notion of personal data within the legal frameworks, such as GDPR.

5   Conclusions

In this work, we presented a methodology for defining processing purposes and incorporating them into software requirements. We proposed purpose-aware UML Use Case and Sequence diagrams for visualising the privacy-enhanced system design, and presented the initial evaluation conducted on our methodology and diagrams along with the analysis of the results. Overall, we gathered positive results, especially regarding users' confidence, simplicity, and ease of use. We also presented a web-based tool, automating the generation of purpose-aware diagrams. As future work we aim to evaluate our methodology and tool with software engineers from the industry, and to enhance the tool's features based on gathered feedback, in order to improve the observed shortcomings and evaluate its use in different contexts and more complex systems.

References

1. Ahmadian, A.S., Jürjens, J., Strüber, D.: Extending model-based privacy analysis for the industrial data space by exploiting privacy level agreements. In: Proceedings of the 33rd Annual ACM Symposium on Applied Computing, pp. 1142–1149 (2018)
2. Ahmadian, A.S., Strüber, D., Jürjens, J.: Privacy-enhanced system design modeling based on privacy features. In: Proceedings of the 34th ACM/SIGAPP Symposium on Applied Computing, pp. 1492–1499 (2019)
3. Alshareef, H., Stucki, S., Schneider, G.: Refining privacy-aware data flow diagrams. In: International Conference on Software Engineering and Formal Methods, pp. 121–140. Springer (2021)
4. Alshareef, H., Stucki, S., Schneider, G.: Transforming data flow diagrams for privacy compliance. MODELSWARD **21**, 207–215 (2021)
5. Alshareef, H., Tuma, K., Stucki, S., Schneider, G., Scandariato, R.: Precise analysis of purpose limitation in data flow diagrams. In: Proceedings of ARES 2022. ACM (2022)
6. Antignac, T., Scandariato, R., Schneider, G.: A privacy-aware conceptual model for handling personal data. In: Margaria, T., Steffen, B. (eds.) ISoLA 2016. LNCS, vol. 9952, pp. 942–957. Springer, Cham (2016). https://doi.org/10.1007/978-3-319-47166-2_65
7. Antignac, T., Scandariato, R., Schneider, G.: Privacy compliance via model transformations. In: Proceedings of EuroS&P Workshops 2018, pp. 120–126. IEEE (2018)
8. Brooke, J., et al.: SUS - A quick and dirty usability scale. Usability Evaluation Industr. **189**(194), 4–7 (1996)
9. Cambronero, M.E., Martínez, M.A., Llana, L., Rodríguez, R.J., Russo, A.: Towards a GDPR-compliant cloud architecture with data privacy controlled through sticky policies. PeerJ Comput. Sci. **10**, e1898 (2024)
10. Davis, F.D., Bagozzi, R., Warshaw, P.: Technol. Accept. Model. J. Manag. Sci. **35**(8), 982–1003 (1989)
11. European Parliament and Council of the European Union: General data protection regulation. Off. J. European Union (2015)
12. Kammüller, F., Ogunyanwo, O.O., Probst, C.W.: Designing data protection for GDPR compliance into IoT healthcare systems. arXiv preprint arXiv:1901.02426 (2019)

13. Mougiakou, E., Virvou, M.: Based on GDPR privacy in UML: case of e-learning program. In: 2017 8th International Conference on Information, Intelligence, Systems & Applications (IISA), pp. 1–8. IEEE (2017)
14. Pedroza, G., Muntes-Mulero, V., Martin, Y.S., Mockly, G.: A model-based approach to realize privacy and data protection by design. In: 2021 IEEE European Symposium on Security and Privacy Workshops (EuroS&PW), pp. 332–339. IEEE (2021)
15. Rahman, M.: A petri nets semantics for privacy-aware data flow diagrams (2017)
16. Vanezi, E., Kapitsaki, G.M., Kouzapas, D., Philippou, A., Papadopoulos, G.A.: Diálogop-a language and a graphical tool for formally defining GDPR purposes. In: Research Challenges in Information Science: 14th International Conference, RCIS 2020, Limassol, Cyprus, September 23–25, 2020, Proceedings 14, pp. 569–575. Springer (2020)
17. Veseli, F., Olvera, J.S., Pulls, T., Rannenberg, K.: Engineering privacy by design: lessons from the design and implementation of an identity wallet platform. In: Proceedings of the 34th ACM/SIGAPP Symposium on Applied Computing, pp. 1475–1483 (2019)
18. Ye, T., Zhuang, Y., Qiao, G.: Mbipv: a model-based approach for identifying privacy violations from software requirements. Softw. Syst. Model. **22**(4), 1251–1280 (2023)

Requirements Communication at the Intersection Between RE and UX

Anne Hess[1]([✉]), Gerald Heller[2], Hartmut Schmitt[3], Cornelia Seraphin[4], and Oliver Karras[5]

[1] Technical University of Applied Sciences Würzburg-Schweinfurt, Würzburg, Germany
anne.hess@thws.de
[2] Consultant and Trainer, Stuttgart, Germany
gerald.heller@swq4all.de
[3] HK Business Solutions GmbH, Friedrichsthal, Germany
hartmut.schmitt@hk-bs.de
[4] msg systems ag, Ismaning, Germany
cornelia.seraphin@msg.group
[5] TIB - Leibniz Information Centre for Science and Technology, Hanover, Germany
oliver.karras@tib.eu

Abstract. Although requirements engineering (RE) and user experience (UX) design share similar goals, their processes are typically managed and executed by different roles, often leading to poor requirements communication. To explore communication flows, challenges, and best practices from RE and UX perspectives, we interviewed six experts from four software companies. This article presents our study's design and findings, comprising two communication flows illustrating requirements elicitation and communication processes in two distinct project contexts ("new development" versus "ongoing development"). Additionally, we discuss key insights from our qualitative analysis. The study's results are intended to serve as an impetus for future research and guide practitioners to enhance collaboration between the two disciplines.

Keywords: User experience · communication · industry experience

1 Introduction

Nowadays, a positive user experience (UX) is one of the most important quality attributes that contribute to the success of software products [4,17]. It comprises "a person's perceptions and responses that result from the use and/or anticipated use of a product, system, or service" ([10], p.10). These perceptions and responses, which include, among others, the users' emotions, preferences, physical and psychological responses ([10], p.10), are strongly related to the users' needs, requirements, and expectations [4,9,19]. In particular, a positive UX can only be achieved if users' needs, requirements, and expectations are

G. Scanniello et al. (Eds.): PROFES 2025, LNCS 16361, pp. 440–450, 2026.
https://doi.org/10.1007/978-3-032-12089-2_29

fulfilled – or even exceeded – whereas not meeting them leads to a negative UX [3,5].

This correlation shows that there is a strong synergy between the disciplines of UX and requirements engineering (RE) as the identification, elicitation, and analysis of relevant user groups, including their characteristics, needs, requirements, and expectations, is one of the core objectives and tasks of RE [6,18]. The aforementioned synergy is promoted through human-centered design [10,11] and RE frameworks like Task-oriented Requirements Engineering (TORE) [1,14], which show how techniques of both disciplines (such as observations, surveys, or creativity techniques) are often interlinked in early user research.

Despite this relation, it can be observed that RE and UX activities are often practiced in the industry by different roles [7,15], making efficient and effective collaboration and communication crucial for successful software development [8].

This paper presents an exploratory interview study conducted with six experts from four software development companies. The study investigates requirements elicitation and communication flows, including best practices and challenges, within the early phases of software development processes from the perspective of RE and UX professionals. The presented interview study is a follow-up study to an online survey among 123 UX professionals that revealed challenges and deficits in the communication of requirements within software development processes, especially in the context of agile project development [7,15]. Both the interview study and the online survey have been performed as part of our collaboration within the working group "REUX" associated with the German Informatics Society[1]. The insights gained from our joint research activities are intended to provide impetus for further research. Moreover, we aim to provide practitioners with concrete tips and guidelines to address current practical challenges and foster a stronger integration and more efficient and effective collaboration between the two disciplines RE and UX.

The remaining paper is structured as follows: Sect. 2 provides information about the study design which is followed by the introduction of two communication flows illustrating requirements elicitation and communication processes in two distinct project contexts in Sect. 3. In Sect. 4, we present and discuss key findings before concluding the paper in Sect. 5.

2   Study Design

In the following, we provide insights into the overall design of our interview study, comprising information about the context and background of the participants as well as an overview of our data collection and analysis strategies.

2.1   Study Context and Participants

Motivated by the results of our previously conducted online survey [7,15], we designed a follow-up exploratory interview study to investigate requirements

---

[1] Website Working Group: https://ak-reux.gi.de/, last access: 22/08/2025.

elicitation and communication flows, including best practices and challenges that foster or hinder the collaboration within the early phases of software development from the perspective of RE and UX professionals in industry.

We distributed a call for participation via mailing lists and contacts from our personal network and ultimately recruited a total of six participants from four different companies.

Table 1 summarizes each participant's background information, including their role, company type, company size, as well as key activities and responsibilities. The role abbreviations used in the table are referenced in later sections (Sect. 3 and Sect. 4) when referencing to individual participants respectively when citing participants' statements.

Table 1. Background on Study Participants

ID	Role	Company Type	Company Size	Key Activities and Responsibilities
UX_M	UX Manager	German UX Service Provider (Company 1)	small-medium-sized enterprise	Overseeing and leading the UX strategy and delegation of UX-related tasks.
Sen_UXR	Senior Team Lead UX Research	German UX Service Provider (Company 1)	small-medium-sized enterprise	UX management, account management, UX research, and ensuring the continuous UX process.
Asst_UXR	Assistant Team Lead UX Research	German UX Service Provider (Company 1)	small-medium-sized enterprise	Elicitation of user needs, support of the user research team.
UX_DM	UX Design Manager	US Software Company (Company 2)	large enterprise	Product owner of the design system team that standardizes the user interfaces of the developed products.
CX_R	Customer Experience Researcher	German Financial Services Provider (Company 3)	large enterprise	Optimization of the customer experience and development of new products together with the product teams.
REr	Requirements Engineers	German IT Service Provider (Company 4)	large enterprise	Communication interface between development and business side/customers, RE-related tasks, working closely with the Product Owner on the business side as "Proxy Product Owner" on the supplier side.

2.2 Data Collection

We prepared several documents for data collection: an *informed consent form*, a *preliminary survey*, and an *interview guideline*. All documents were developed collaboratively by all authors through iterative revision cycles and feedback discussions and are available online[2].

Informed Consent and Preliminary Survey.

Prior to the interviews, participants signed a consent form outlining the study's objectives, data protection details, and their rights. They also completed a survey via email with closed and open-ended questions about company background, project organization, development processes, interviewee roles, team organization, and techniques used in requirements elicitation and specification.

This information was helpful for the interviewers during the preparation to get an initial understanding of typical project situations in the companies.

---

[2] Link to study material https://ak-reux.gi.de/mitteilung/materialien-zur-fallstudie, last accessed: 22/08/2025.

Interview Guideline and Sessions.

Each interview was conducted by an author, with another author present to record data. While one interview took place on-site, the other five were held via video conferencing. In addition to notes taken by a designated note-taker, all sessions were recorded, with participants' consent, to aid subsequent analysis. As defined in our interview guideline, the interviews were structured into five parts that are shortly introduced in the following.

At the beginning of each interview, participants described a *reference project* that typified their work in size, team composition, and tasks.

The second part focused on *requirements elicitation*, covering primary and secondary requirements sources, types of requirements, and elicitation techniques collected via the aforementioned preliminary survey, including roles involved. Participants concluded this section by reflecting on elicitation success factors, challenges, and improvements.

The third part addressed *requirements specification*, detailing typical artifacts, responsible roles, and quality assessment, especially when different individuals handle elicitation and documentation. Similarly to the elicitation part, the participants discussed success factors, challenges, and improvements.

The fourth part covered *requirements communication* focusing on channels and physical proximity's effect on collaboration, therby reflecting on best practices, challenges, and improvements.

The last part focused on *RE and UX in agile settings*, addressing RE and UX tasks and collaboration before and during (design) sprints including challenges, effective collaboration practices and improvements in these settings.

2.3 Data Analysis and Process Modeling

Following the transcription of the interviews, we began our data analysis. Initially, we extracted coded snippets from the transcripts, categorizing them into roles, artifacts, process steps, and activities. In the next step, we used the FLOW notation [16] to visualize information flows in the collaborations between RE and UX professionals during the requirements elicitation phase.

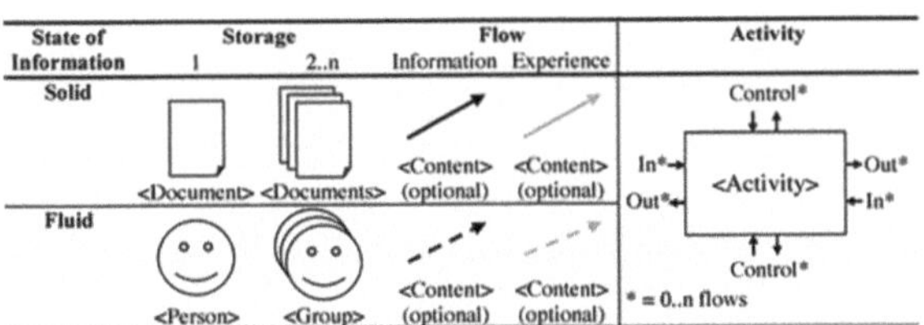

Fig. 1. FLOW Notation [16].

FLOW is a method for documenting and improving information flows. It distinguishes between *solid* information, which is repeatedly retrievable, long-term available as well as comprehensible to third parties (e.g., documents, videos), and *fluid* information, which lacks one or more of the properties persons, knowledge, and experiences. The FLOW notation (see Fig. 1) is straightforward, primarily differentiating solid and fluid information storage (document or smiley) and flows (solid or dashed line), as well as groups (three overlapping entities). FLOW also incorporates activities, noting incoming and outgoing information, along with controlling and supporting elements, though it doesn't detail how output derives from input. Examples include meetings or analysis activities.

Besides modeling in FLOW, insights and notable observations from all six interviews were extracted from recordings and transcripts. These notes were documented on a digital whiteboard, analyzed, coded, and clustered through discussions among the authors, using affinity diagrams for qualitative analysis [13]. The gained and consolidated key findings are discussed in Sect. 4.

3   Insights Into Requirements Elicitation Processes

This section presents two exemplary communication flows, derived from recorded data from two companies and modeled using FLOW notation (see Sect. 2.3). The flows illustrate the requirements elicitation and communication processes in two different project contexts: the development of new products (Sect. 3.1) and the continuous development of products (Sect. 3.2).

3.1   Communication Flow: New Development

The consolidated results discussed in the following are based on three interview sessions conducted with the UX manager (UX_M) as well as two UX researchers (Sen_UXR, Asst_UXR) of Company 1 (see Table 1). Figure 2 illustrates an excerpt of the FLOW model, the full model can be accessed online[3].

The communication flow is initiated by a scoping workshop that is mainly moderated by the UX manager in the leading role as project manager. In addition to representatives from the customer side, several team members from the UX company who are actively involved in the project in the role of user researcher, concept designer or product owner take part in this workshop.

The goal of this scoping workshop is to identify, discuss, negotiate, and agree with the customer on a set of key stakeholders, key as-is scenarios, and an initial set of (still hypothetical) user needs that will be supported, further refined, and addressed within the scope of the project. Typically, the outputs from this workshop include proto-personas representing key stakeholders, detailed descriptions of current as-is scenarios highlighting existing problems from the key stakeholders' perspectives, and the corresponding needs. These artifacts are incorporated into an in-house software tool for further processing and refinement.

---

[3] Access to complete FLOW model *New Development*: https://ak-reux.gi.de/fileadmin/AK/REUX/user_upload/NewProductDevelopment.pdf, last accessed 22/08/2025.

Fig. 2. Communication Flow: *New Development* of Company 1 (Excerpt).

To supplement the initial findings, further user research activities are planned and conducted, headed by UX researchers, to gain a better understanding of stakeholder needs and problems. Techniques include artifact-based elicitation from forums, social media, documents, and competitive systems, alongside interviews and focus groups with key user representatives (proto-personas). Concept designers passively participate as note-takers, gaining insight into user groups and needs for developing solution concepts.

It is important to note that the user needs, identified so far, are still considered as "assumptions". To ultimately validate these hypothetical user needs, further interview sessions are conducted with representatives of key stakeholders. These validated user needs are documented in the form of user stories in the aforementioned in-house developed software tool and then serve as a baseline for subsequent design and concept activities under the lead of the concept designers.

3.2   Communication Flow: Continuous Development

The results presented in this section are based on an interview conducted with a customer experience researcher (CX_R) from Company 3 (see Table 1). Figure 3 illustrates an excerpt of the FLOW model, the full model can be accessed online[4].

The communication flow typically involves the business analyst, the product owner, and the CX team biweeklyreviewing new enhancement requests derived from product usage analyses or executive leadership (CTO/CEO). The requests are documented by a CX team member using a standardized story template, utilized throughout the story's lifecycle. Initially, not all details are required; additional information is integrated as further research is conducted.

---

[4] Access to complete FLOW model *Continuous Development*: https://ak-reux.gi.de/fi leadmin/AK/REUX/user_upload/ProductEvolution.pdf, last accessed 22/08/2025.

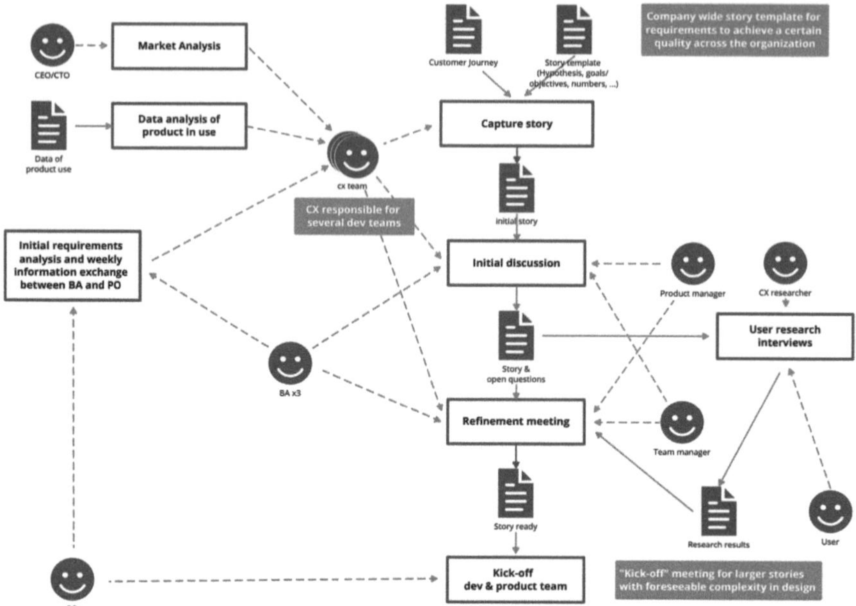

Fig. 3. Communication Flow: *Continuous Development* of Company 3 (Excerpt).

These stories are often framed within the context of a customer journey narrated by a member of the CX team. Following the drafting of an initial story, a discussion is convened with the business analyst, product manager, a CX team representative, and the development team's manager. These conversations may lead to user research tasks, typically executed through interviews by CX team members. The findings from this research are then incorporated into the story template, addressing any raised inquiries.

After updating the story with insights from user research, it is re-evaluated in a refinement meeting attended by the same stakeholders, now including developers. After the meeting, stories classified as "Ready" move to the design phase. For more extensive stories, a kickoff meeting with the entire development team is organized, including sketch sessions where pairs generate preliminary designs, usually about 30% of the final design.

At this point, the CX team is tasked with evolving the design concept to 60% completion, at which point user testing is initiated. Based on real-user feedback, the design is iteratively enhanced to reach a 90% completion. Upon achieving this level of design maturity, the development team takes over, incorporating the solution into their agile Scrum workflow.

4   Key Findings

This section highlights the most intriguing findings from our six expert interviews, as derived from the affinity analysis (Sect. 2.3). These findings, grounded in individual experiences and opinions, offer valuable insights applicable to other project contexts or as thought-provoking ideas. However, due to the limited sample size of six interviews, these insights should not be generalized.

All interview participants described their development processes as agile with artifacts, roles, and ceremonies in the development process loosely aligned with Scrum practices but customized to meet specific organizational needs.

RE activities are often distributed among various roles, each with their own specific objectives. UX/User Research focuses on system users, interactions and flows within a given context beyond the use of the software product. Product management and product owner prioritize goals and epics, and are responsible for decision-making, while RE handles system and product requirements together with their economic viability, holistic view, and interrelationships. Each aspect is crucial for the final product and must be seamlessly integrated. (*"User requirements are prioritized by the product owner, who is kept up-to-date during development."* [CX_R] and *"Here, proactivity is required from all participants, especially regarding the competencies that are more pronounced within the T-shaped skills, e.g., IT security, accessibility, or ethical issues."* [CX_R])

Communication, Trust, and A Shared Language, as Well as Transparency, are The Keys to Success. (*"Lack of trust and respect are often the cause when something is driven against the wall."* [UX_DM]). Transparency can be enhanced through joint meetings, consistent documentation, backlog management, Definition of Ready (DoR), Definition of Done (DoD), acceptance criteria, and user stories with hypotheses and business value.

Understanding the Problem is Essential Before Diving into Solutions. Most user researchers in Germany have a background in psychology[5], a discipline that emphasizes understanding problems rather than immediately focusing on problem-solving prevalent in typical engineering approaches. From a UX perspective, understanding a problem provides the foundation for finding solutions, rather than requiring immediate answers (*"Written requirements, regardless of where they originate, are validated and verified through discussions."* [Asst_UXR]; and *"The aim is to think everything through early on so that technical complexity can be managed."* [CX_R]). However, communicating the significance and value of this approach to customers is crucial, albeit challenging.

User Research Plays A Crucial Role in Providing Insights. Many companies consolidate activities like identifying context information as well as deriving user needs and requirements in a preliminary phase or early in the development project. In hybrid-agile methodologies, this is known as a user requirements sprint [2,12], which extends beyond the Sprint Zero[6] discussed in Scrum literature. It lays the foundational basis to ensure future sprints can efficiently add incremental value.

A Combination of Qualitative And Quantitative User Research Methods Help Clarify the Problem Statement and Assess Relevance.

---

[5] https://germanupa.de/wissen/branchenreport, last access: 22/08/2025.

[6] https://resources.scrumalliance.org/Article/sprint-zero, last access: 22/08/2025.

Quantitative methods like data-driven analysis assess the importance of issues in existing products, while qualitative methods, such as contextual interviews, help understand user perspectives in new product development. UX professionals often analyze product data to integrate user insights for continuous validation and improvement. User research findings must align with product owners, business analysts, and management to iteratively enhance the product. (*"A joint RE and UX team adds value and should be standard practice. The result will be more well-rounded because there is a different focus."* [REr]).

Scoping and Ideation Workshops are Essential to Ensure that All Relevant Aspects, Including user, Business, and Technology, are Addressed and Prioritized. They promote a shared understanding about key personas, scenarios, business cases, as well as the "big picture", and define the problem context - even if solutions are not immediately apparent. Collaborative idea development in kick-off meetings, such as sketching sessions with cross-functional teams, integrate participants' knowledge and deepen understanding, often supported by joint exploration and visible idea boards that foster open communication.

Although it is Generally Considered Beneficial to use Personas for Deriving and Validating Requirements Based on User Needs, Their Potential is Often not Fully Realized. Frequently, personas are created at the beginning of a project but eventually lose relevance as the project progresses (*"We have created personas, but they are not used correctly or consistently."* [CXR]). However, the interviewees emphasized the importance of **consistently maintaining focus on the user's needs and problems throughout the project**. In fact, this focus is crucial, as shifting towards solution-finding can cause team members to lose sight of the original user need. (*"The later you are in the project, the more you lose sight of the actual situation/need."* [UX_M]). Lastly, **continual interaction with customers and users is essential** to understand the changing context of use and the evolving needs of the user *"Finding and accessing suitable users for usability testing is often a challenge."* [Asst_UXR]). Clear criteria for participant selection should be established, and in addition to usability testing, in-app survey evaluations can provide valuable feedback during the initial use of the application.

5   Summary

In this paper, we presented the design and results of an exploratory interview study aimed at understanding requirements communication and collaboration between RE and UX, two closely related disciplines. Through six interviews with four software companies, we developed two FLOW models illustrating requirements elicitation and communication processes in new and continuous development. Key findings indicate that a scoping approach at project start effectively aligns UX and RE activities; similar strategies are beneficial in continuous development, especially for large projects. A centralized UX/RE tool enhances team communication and understanding of user needs, while maintaining the relevance of personas remains challenging. RE processes often don't require a dedicated role and are driven by UX/CX professionals with product managers.

As part of our future work, we aim to validate our findings with literature and further studies, and compile a compendium of best practices. Moreover, we will explore current tools and trends, like AI technology and "user research democratization," where more stakeholders engage in user research. These developments could significantly impact UX professionals, product managers, and requirements engineers by offering automated, data-driven insights into user needs and system requirements, thus influencing roles and interaction between RE and UX.

Acknowledgments. We would like to thank all interview participants for sharing their valuable experience. Parts of this work were performed within the D'accord project, funded by the German Federal Ministry of Education and Research (BMBF, grant number 16KIS1506K).

Disclosure of Interests. The authors have no competing interests to declare that are relevant to the content of this article.

References

1. Adam, S., Riegel, N., Doerr, J.: TORE. a framework for systematic requirements development in information systems, requirements engineering magazine (2014)
2. Anwar, S., Motla, Y., Siddiq, Y., et al.: User-centered design practices in scrum development process: a distinctive advantage? In: 17th IEEE International Multi Topic Conference (2014)
3. Hassenzahl, M.: The thing and i: understanding the relationship between user and product. Funology 2: From Usability to Enjoyment, pp. 301–313 (2018)
4. Hassenzahl, M., Burmester, M., et al.: User experience is all there is: twenty years of designing positive experiences and meaningful technology. i-com **20**(3) (2021)
5. Hassenzahl, M., Wiklund-Engblom, A., et al.: Experience-oriented and product-oriented evaluation: psychological need fulfillment, positive affect, and product perception. Int. J. Hum. Comput. Interaction **31**(8) (2015)
6. Heiskari, J., Kauppinen, M., Runonen, M., et al.: Bridging the gap between usability and requirements engineering. In: 17th IEEE International Requirements Engineering Conference (2009)
7. Heller, G., Schlipf, C., Karras, O., et al.: Wie interagieren UX-professionals mit ihrem Umfeld und ihren Kollegen? In: Mensch und Computer (2019)
8. Hess, A.: Crossing disciplinary borders to improve requirements communication, pp. 115–141. Springer International Publishing (2022)
9. Inan, N., Santoso, B., O. Hadi Putra, P.: The method and metric of user experience evaluation: a systematic literature review. In: 10th International Conference on Software and Computer Applications (2021)
10. ISO/IEC: ISO 9241-210:2019 Ergonomics of Human-System Interaction - Part 210: Human-Centred Design for Interactive Systems (2019)
11. Kropp, E., Koischwitz, K.: Experiences with user-centered design and agile requirements engineering in fixed-price projects. In: Usability- and Accessibility-Focused Requirements Engineering (2016)

12. Kuusinen, K.: Beyond the "one sprint ahead" approach: organizing user experience work in agile software development. In: Nordic Conference on Human-Computer Interaction (2014)
13. Lucero, A.: Using affinity diagrams to evaluate interactive prototypes. In: Abascal, J., Barbosa, S., Fetter, M., Gross, T., Palanque, P., Winckler, M. (eds.) INTER-ACT 2015. LNCS, vol. 9297, pp. 231–248. Springer, Cham (2015). https://doi.org/10.1007/978-3-319-22668-2_19
14. Paech, B., Kohler, K.: Usability engineering integrated with requirements engineering. In: ICSE Workshop on SE-HCI (2003)
15. Schmitt, H., Heller, G., et al.: Ermittlung und kommunikation von anforderungen in etablierten UX-prozessen. In: Softwaretechnik-Trends Band 42-3 (2022)
16. Stapel, K., Schneider, K.: Managing knowledge on communication and information flow in global software projects. Expert Syst. **31**(3) (2014)
17. Sudiana, Chandra, Y.U., Angela, L.: Key success factors for a better user experience in e-commerce website. In: International Conference on Information Management and Technology (2021)
18. Sutcliffe, A., Sawyer, P., Bencomo, N.: The implications of 'soft' requirements. In: 30th IEEE International Requirements Engineering Conference (2022)
19. Zarour, M., Alharbi, M.: User experience framework that combines aspects, dimensions, and measurement methods. Cogent Eng. **4**(1) (2017)

Architecture Degradation at Scale: Challenges and Insights from Practice

Ehsan Zabardast[1,2]([✉]) [iD], Bhuwan Paudel[1] [iD], and Javier Gonzalez-Huerta[1] [iD]

[1] Software Engineering Research Lab SERL, Blekinge Institute of Technology, Karlskrona, Sweden
{ehsan.zabardast,bhuwan.paudel,javier.gonzalez.huerta}@bth.se
[2] Gaetir, Karlskrona, Sweden

Abstract. Large-scale software systems often experience architectural degradation, affecting maintainability, scalability, and quality. To investigate this, we conducted focus groups with senior practitioners across three large organizations. Our analysis revealed four core challenge areas: managing dependencies, ownership and organizational barriers, balancing agility with stability and cost, as well as documentation drift. These findings offer practical insights for mitigating architectural degradation in complex environments.

Keywords: Architecture Degradation · Architecture Erosion · Technical Debt · Challenges · Insights

1 Introduction

Software architecture is key to managing complexity and supporting the sustainable evolution of software-intensive systems. As systems scale, maintaining coherence becomes harder, leading to architectural degradation [11]. This includes drift—unintentional deviation from the intended design—and erosion—violations of architectural rules—both of which undermine maintainability, evolvability, and quality [1,9]. Such degradation often appears as technical debt (TD), where short-term decisions create long-term costs that hinder future modifications and system qualities like maintainability [2,5].

Although well-studied in academia, industry still struggles with architectural degradation. Challenges include outdated documentation, limited resources, unclear responsibilities, and poor communication, all of which complicate maintenance tasks [1,2,10]. Existing TD management strategies, focused mainly on code-level analysis, neglecting socio-technical and architectural aspects, hindering effective management [2]. Empirically grounded insights are therefore needed to capture both technical and organizational factors at scale.

To tackle these challenges, we conducted an empirical study with senior architects and developers from three large-scale software organizations. We first held an exploratory focus group to identify and categorize architectural challenges, producing four main categories. Structured focus groups then validated and

G. Scanniello et al. (Eds.): PROFES 2025, LNCS 16361, pp. 451–460, 2026.
https://doi.org/10.1007/978-3-032-12089-2_30

refined these findings, adding perspectives that strengthened their robustness and practical relevance.

The paper is organized as follows: Sect. 2 discusses related work on architectural technical debt (ATD), degradation, and erosion. Section 3 outlines our research approach, while Sect. 4 presents the findings. Section 5 discusses their implications, Sect. 6 addresses limitations, and Sect. 7 summarizes contributions and future work.

2   Related Work

Prior research has extensively examined architectural degradation and technical debt, stressing their impact on software maintenance and evolution. Li et al. [9] mapped the causes, impacts, and management of architecture erosion, citing factors such as design flaws, poor documentation, and communication issues. Anthony et al. [1] studied architectural drift from developers' perspectives, highlighting challenges like prioritization conflicts, resource limits, and missing documentation.

The management and impact of ATD have been studied through mapping studies, grounded theory, and empirical evaluations. Das et al. [6] mapped TD from architectural degradation and code smells, stressing systematic detection, prioritization, and mitigation. Verdecchia et al. [19] used grounded theory to show that effective management depends on clear documentation, defined responsibilities, and proactive practices. Sutoyo et al. [18] applied dependency metrics, linking architectural dependencies to TD accumulation and repayment.

Research on microservice architectures has focused on architectural challenges and TD. Soldani et al. [15] reviewed the trade-offs of microservices, noting benefits like flexibility and independent deployment alongside complexity and management issues. Sas et al. [14] empirically studied architectural smells, identifying causes, impacts, and solutions ranging from technical refactoring to organizational improvements.

Avgeriou et al. [2] highlighted the socio-technical nature of TD, calling for transparent, context-aware practices involving both technical and non-technical stakeholders. They proposed principles for reframing TD management, including integrated toolchains, comprehensive data, and attention to architectural implications. Building on this, our study offers empirical validation and new insights into architectural challenges in large-scale software development, enriching understanding of degradation at scale.

3   Methodology

We adopted a qualitative empirical methodology involving structured focus group sessions, an established method in software engineering research for capturing practitioner experiences and insights [8,17]. We aimed to answer the following research question:

What are the primary challenges and pain points contributing to architectural degradation in large-scale software development organizations?

The study began with a preparatory phase defining objectives on architectural degradation and related challenges. We then created a structured discussion guide and used purposive sampling to select large-scale software organizations and experienced participants (e.g., head and senior architects, developers), ensuring authentic industry insights [12].

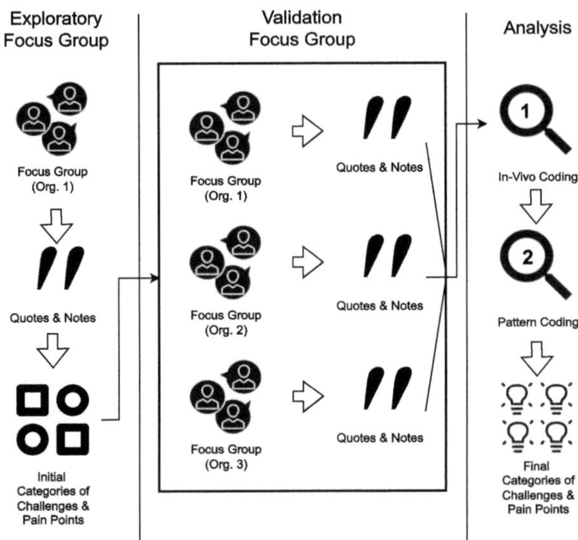

Fig. 1. General overview of the research methodology used in this study.

We conducted a 3-hour exploratory focus group with three senior architects and the head of architecture from a large telecommunication software organization (Org. 1). After being briefed on objectives and format, participants identified and categorized architectural challenges. They documented individual insights, then discussed and grouped them collectively. The research team summarized the results into categories, which served as input for validation focus groups.

To validate and extend the exploratory findings, we held three additional focus groups across the first organization and two new ones. The first, with three senior architects and the head of architecture from Org. 1, elaborated and verified themes. The others involved two senior developers and three architects from a public-sector organization developing large-scale Intelligent Transport Systems (Org. 2) and a development manager and senior product owner from a fintech company (Org. 3), adding diverse perspectives. Participant details are shown in Table 1. The methodology used for this research is illustrated in Fig. 1.

To situate the study, we briefly describe the participating organizations. Org. 1 is a multinational telecom provider building mission-critical systems with mil-

Table 1. Participants' information—role and years of industry experience.

Organization	Role	Experience in Years
Org. 1 - telecommunication	Head of Architecture	22
Org. 1 - telecommunication	Domain Chief Architect	18
Org. 1 - telecommunication	Domain Chief Architect	17
Org. 1 - telecommunication	Domain Chief Architect	27
Org. 2 - public sector	Head of ICT	20
Org. 2 - public sector	Chief Architect	22
Org. 2 - public sector	Solution Architect	15
Org. 2 - public sector	Senior System Developer	14
Org. 2 - public sector	Senior System Developer	13
Org. 2 - public sector	System Developer	8
Org. 3 - fintech	Development Manager	23
Org. 3 - fintech	Senior Product Owner	19

lions of lines of code and thousands of distributed developers. Org. 2 is a public-sector body managing nationwide intelligent transport systems with decades of operational history. Org. 3 is a fintech company focused on high-throughput, compliance-heavy transaction processing, supported by several hundred engineers. All three organizations employed service-oriented or microservices-based architectures, though legacy monolithic components remained in production. Development practices in all cases followed agile approaches (Scrum or scaled frameworks such as SAFe), with continuous integration and deployment pipelines in active use.

3.1   Data Collection and Analysis

Data collection drew on two sources: participant notes and verbatim transcriptions of focus group discussions. Notes captured immediate insights and were organized through affinity grouping [8] to support initial theme identification. Discussions were audio-recorded and transcribed to preserve detail and context, while post-session summaries documented fresh reflections and interpretations.

Data analysis followed two coding phases. First, in vivo coding [13] used participants' own words from notes and transcripts as initial codes, preserving their voice. Next, pattern coding [13] grouped these codes into broader themes and categories, synthesizing the data into key challenges of architectural degradation at scale. This iterative process ensured systematic identification of themes, providing both practical insights and academic rigor.

4   Results

We identified four main categories of challenges:

Challenge No.1: Managing Architectural Dependencies: Participants emphasized the complexities arising from extensive architectural dependencies. Dependencies were not confined to technical aspects—compile-time and run-time dependencies—alone but encompassed testing, packaging, deployment, and planning. For example, one participant highlighted the problem of "high interdependencies across services, particularly affecting test suites during integration," which complicates integration testing and slows down development cycles. The challenges also extended to issues around data stability and consistency: "Data stability and consistency issues are common; verifying data in the automatic test is difficult." Another prominent concern was human factors, such as the dependency on specific people's expertise, leading to bottlenecks and reduced organizational efficiency.

Challenge No.2: Ownership & Organizational Barriers: A lack of clear ownership was consistently noted as a significant impediment to effective architectural management. Quotes such as "Everyone is opinionated but no one is an owner" and "Who is owning the architecture?" illustrate the prevailing confusion around responsibility and accountability. Additionally, organizational structures often exacerbated architectural challenges, reflected in statements like "Organizational barriers are often the most significant challenge within an organization," and the mention of Conway's Law [4,7], where organizational silos mirror architectural silos. Issues such as the "blame game" and "fear-driven design" further highlighted cultural and structural dysfunctions.

Challenge No.3: Scaling Agility, Stability, Cost, & Complexity: Participants identified significant tension between maintaining agility and ensuring system stability. The complexity was further amplified by misaligned financial structures and planning models, limiting the flexibility and autonomy of teams. One participant aptly described the architecture as a "self-eating beast," indicating a continuous cycle of complexity increase with each additional feature. Moreover, participants frequently referenced the "high cost to deploy & manage the system" and expressed concerns regarding the misalignment of budget constraints, highlighting a prevalent practice where "teams are financed based on wrong premises." This misalignment significantly hampered the ability to properly manage TD and complexity.

Challenge No.4: Documentation and Intent Drift: The final major challenge identified was the erosion of architectural clarity through insufficient documentation and the drift between initial architectural intentions and actual implementations. Participants stressed the issue with statements like "Another significant issue is the lack of clear documentation in the organization, as no one takes the time to properly record design decisions," indicating substantial documentation gaps. Furthermore, informal or undocumented decisions exacerbated knowledge gaps, leading to duplicated efforts, captured succinctly by the statement "building the same thing again and again." Participants also noted the permanence of temporary solutions, pointing to this phenomenon as a critical trigger for system decay.

4.1 Mapping the Challenges to Literature

We mapped the identified challenges to key supporting points from the existing literature on architectural degradation, erosion, and TD. The mapping is presented in Table 2.

Li et al. [9] highlight technical and organizational causes of architecture erosion, aligning with our findings on dependencies and organizational barriers. Similarly, Anthony et al. [1] emphasize the human and organizational aspects of drift, such as documentation gaps, unclear ownership, and accountability issues, which our study also observed. Our findings on documentation and intent drift align

Table 2. Mapping of Identified Challenges to Literature on Architectural Degradation, Erosion, and Technical Debt.

Challenge	Key Supporting Points from Literature
No.1 Managing Architectural Dependencies	- Dependencies as a major source of ATD (Sousa et al. [16]). - Difficulty identifying runtime dependency violations (Verdecchia et al. [20]). - Finding appropriate service decomposition is difficult, leading to further challenges like inter-service dependencies (Bogner et al. [3]). - Dependency-related architectural smells contribute to erosion (Das et al. [6]). - Unmanaged inter-module dependencies drive erosion (Li et al. [9]).
No.2 Ownership & Organizational Barriers	- Lack of ownership causes drift and debt (Verdecchia et al. [19]). - Diffusion of responsibility and absence of architectural stewards (Anthony et al. [1]). - Organizational misalignment exacerbates erosion (Li et al. [9]).
No.3 Scaling Agility, Stability, Cost, and Complexity	- Agility vs. architectural soundness tension increases ATD (Sousa et al. [16]). - Overengineering raises Total Cost of Ownership (Verdecchia et al. [20]). - Complexity from conflicting planning paradigms (Das et al. [6]). - Technical complexity (Bogner et al. [3])
No.4 Documentation & Intent Drift	- Poor documentation leads to architectural drift (Verdecchia et al. [19]). - Loss of architectural decision rationale (Anthony et al. [1]). - Gradual divergence due to lack of traceability (Li et al. [9]).

with prior work stressing sustained documentation for architectural integrity [6]. We also echo with another study by Avgeriou et al. [2], which shows that misaligned financial and managerial structures intensify TD and complexity.

The organizational barriers we found align with Conway's Law, confirming prior studies that link organizational structure to system architecture [1]. Participants also stressed human factors, such as knowledge dependencies and skill gaps, as central to understanding degradation. Overall, our insights validate existing perspectives while adding nuance on how organizational structures and practices interact at scale.

5   Discussion

Our findings highlight key factors driving architectural degradation in large-scale software, extending existing perspectives. The main categories—dependencies, organizational barriers, agility versus stability, cost and complexity, and documentation drift–capture the multifaceted nature of these challenges. Among them, managing architectural dependencies stands out as a core issue, with inter-module and behavioral dependencies driving system complexity and degradation [16,20].

Implication 1: Organizations must invest not only in advanced tooling to detect runtime and structural dependencies but also in cultural shifts toward better collaborative practices and shared architectural knowledge to reduce dependency-induced bottlenecks.

The lack of clear ownership and persistent organizational barriers pose serious risks to architectural sustainability. As noted by Anthony et al. [1] and Li et al. [9], such barriers stem from entrenched hierarchies, vague role definitions, and weak accountability.

Implication 2: Practically, these findings suggest organizations need to reevaluate their structural and cultural paradigms, emphasizing clearly defined architectural stewardship roles and collective accountability to mitigate the diffusion of responsibility and promote proactive issue resolution.

Scaling challenges highlight trade-offs between agility, stability, cost, and complexity. Organizations often face tension between rapid delivery and architectural integrity, worsened by misaligned financial and managerial models [16,20].

Implication 3: The findings reveal the critical need for aligning financial planning models with architectural realities, allowing for more accurate forecasting and budgeting processes that consider long-term sustainability and TD management. Furthermore, strategic balancing between agility and architectural soundness must become a prioritized management goal, addressing overengineering and uncontrolled complexity.

Documentation and intent drift undermine system maintainability and evolvability. Gaps between intended and implemented architecture—driven by poor or outdated documentation—reduce clarity and manageability [1,19].

Implication 4: This challenge underscores the critical importance of systematically capturing and maintaining architectural decisions and rationales.

Organizations must prioritize investments in better documentation tools and processes, and foster cultures where documentation tasks are valued, integrated, and consistently maintained.

While many of the challenges confirmed findings from prior studies, our investigation also uncovered novel dimensions:

- **Financial models as an architectural driver:** Participants repeatedly emphasized how budgeting practices constrained architectural sustainability ("teams financed based on wrong premises"), a perspective underexplored in existing research.
- **The "self-eating beast" metaphor:** Practitioners vividly described architectures as consuming themselves under the weight of complexity, providing an original lens into how degradation is perceived in practice.
- **Organizational silos interacting with architectural dependencies:** Whereas prior studies treat silos and dependencies separately, our findings suggest they interact to amplify architectural drift.

6   Limitations and Threats to Validity

We acknowledge that our study is potentially exposed to threats to validity that could impact the reliability and generalizability of the findings. **Internal Validity:** Researcher bias and participant subjectivity may threaten reliability. We mitigated this with a structured guide, audio recordings, two-phase coding (in vivo and pattern), and validation sessions across multiple organizations to enhance objectivity and cross-validate insights. **External Validity:** Our findings may have limited generalizability due to the small number of organizations and specific industry contexts. To mitigate this, we selected experienced participants from varied roles and contexts, though broader studies are needed to confirm applicability. **Construct Validity:** This concerns how accurately our study captures architectural degradation and related challenges. Focus groups risk misinterpretation, which we mitigated by grounding topics in established literature, validating interpretations during sessions, and using transcripts and direct quotes to ensure clarity. **Reliability:** Replicability may be affected by differences in moderation or participant interaction. We improved consistency by standardizing processes, using multiple data sources (notes and transcripts), and applying systematic, well-documented analysis methods.

7   Conclusions

This study empirically examined key challenges driving architectural degradation in large-scale systems through structured focus groups. Our findings reinforce existing literature while extending it with insights on organizational-financial dynamics, practitioner metaphors, and coping strategies. We show that degradation is not purely technical but also shaped by budgeting, cultural silos, and informal practices. Addressing these dynamics requires holistic strategies that combine technical and organizational measures. Future research should assess the long-term impact of such interventions to foster more resilient and maintainable architectures.

Acknowledgments. This research is supported through the KKS SERT Research Profile project (Ref. 2018010), Blekinge Institute of Technology.

References

1. Anthony, E., Berntsson, A., Santilli, T., Wohlrab, R.: We're drifting apart: architectural drift from the developers' perspective. In: 2024 IEEE 21st International Conference on Software Architecture (ICSA), pp. 101–111. IEEE (2024)
2. Avgeriou, P., Ozkaya, I., Koziolek, H., Codabux, Z., Ernst, N.: Reframing technical debt (perspectives workshop 24452). Dagstuhl Reports **14**(11), 16–39 (2025)
3. Bogner, J., Fritzsch, J., Wagner, S., Zimmermann, A.: Industry practices and challenges for the evolvability assurance of microservices: an interview study and systematic grey literature review. Empir. Softw. Eng. **26**(5), 104 (2021)
4. Conway, M.E.: How do committees invent. Datamation **14**(4), 28–31 (1968)
5. Cunningham, W.: The WyCash portfolio management system. ACM Sigplan Oops Messenger **4**(2), 29–30 (1992)
6. Das, D., et al.: Technical debt resulting from architectural degradation and code smells: a systematic mapping study. ACM SIGAPP Appl. Comput. Rev. **21**(4), 20–36 (2022)
7. Herbsleb, J.D., Grinter, R.E.: Architectures, coordination, and distance: Conway's law and beyond. IEEE Softw. **16**(5), 63–70 (1999)
8. Kontio, J., Lehtola, L., Bragge, J.: Using the focus group method in software engineering: obtaining practitioner and user experiences. In: Proceedings. 2004 International Symposium on Empirical Software Engineering, 2004. ISESE'04, pp. 271–280. IEEE (2004)
9. Li, R., Liang, P., Soliman, M., Avgeriou, P.: Understanding software architecture erosion: a systematic mapping study. J. Softw. Evolution Process **34**(3), e2423 (2022)
10. Martini, A., Bosch, J.: The danger of architectural technical debt: contagious debt and vicious circles. In: 2015 12th Working IEEE/IFIP Conference on Software Architecture, pp. 1–10. IEEE (2015)
11. Martini, A., Bosch, J., Chaudron, M.: Investigating architectural technical debt accumulation and refactoring over time: a multiple-case study. Inf. Softw. Technol. **67**, 237–253 (2015)
12. McLafferty, I.: Focus group interviews as a data collecting strategy. J. Adv. Nurs. **48**(2), 187–194 (2004)
13. Saldaña, J.: The coding manual for qualitative researchers (2021)
14. Sas, D., Avgeriou, P., Uyumaz, U.: On the evolution and impact of architectural smells—an industrial case study. Empir. Softw. Eng. **27**(4), 1–45 (2022). https://doi.org/10.1007/s10664-022-10132-7
15. Soldani, J., Tamburri, D.A., Van Den Heuvel, W.J.: The pains and gains of microservices: a systematic grey literature review. J. Syst. Softw. **146**, 215–232 (2018)

16. Sousa, A., Rocha, L., Britto, R.: Architectural technical debt-a systematic mapping study. In: Proceedings of the XXXVII Brazilian Symposium on Software Engineering, pp. 196–205 (2023)
17. Stol, K.J., Fitzgerald, B.: The ABC of software engineering research. ACM Trans. Softw. Eng. Methodol. (TOSEM) **27**(3), 1–51 (2018)
18. Sutoyo, E., Avgeriou, P., Capiluppi, A.: Tracing the lifecycle of architecture technical debt in software systems: a dependency approach. arXiv preprint arXiv:2501.15387 (2025)
19. Verdecchia, R., Kruchten, P., Lago, P.: Architectural Technical Debt: A Grounded Theory. In: Jansen, A., Malavolta, I., Muccini, H., Ozkaya, I., Zimmermann, O. (eds.) ECSA 2020. LNCS, vol. 12292, pp. 202–219. Springer, Cham (2020). https://doi.org/10.1007/978-3-030-58923-3_14
20. Verdecchia, R., Kruchten, P., Lago, P., Malavolta, I.: Building and evaluating a theory of architectural technical debt in software-intensive systems. J. Syst. Softw. **176**, 110925 (2021)

From Scenario Selection to Simulation: Safety Testing of an Automated Driving System

Fauzia Khan[✉][iD], Ali Ihsan Gullu[iD], Hina Anwar[iD], and Dietmar Pfahl[iD]

University of Tartu, Narva mnt 18, 51009 Tartu, Estonia
{fauzia.khan,ali.ihsan.gullu,hina.anwar,dietmar.pfahl}@ut.ee

Abstract. An Automated Driving System (ADS) may encounter infinite scenarios in the real world, making it impossible to test every scenario in simulation. To address this, we previously introduced the Simulation-Based Safety Testing Scenario Selection (SSTSS) process, which prioritizes and selects scenarios for simulation-based safety testing of ADS. In this paper, we select the top-prioritized scenario identified by the SSTSS process to evaluate the safety behavior of UT-ADS, an ADS developed at the University of Tartu. We simulate a *"Follow Lead Vehicle"* scenario to evaluate if UT-ADS maintains a safe following distance as per the Responsibility-Sensitive Safety (RSS) model. Our preliminary simulation results show that UT-ADS maintains safe following distances at lower speeds but violates the RSS minimum safe distances at higher speeds. Our simulation results could provide useful feedback for UT-ADS developers.

Keywords: Automated Driving Systems (ADS) · Simulation-based Testing · Safety Testing · Scenario Prioritization · Follow Lead Vehicle Scenario

1 Introduction

Automated Driving Systems (ADS) have progressed rapidly in recent years, giving rise to innovative business models such as self-driving taxis, autonomous public buses, shuttle services, and robotic last-mile delivery [1,14,16]. Despite the progressive growth of ADS, safety testing remains crucial to ensure its reliability, public acceptance, and trustworthiness. ADS safety testing can be performed through real-world testing, test beds, and simulation-based methods. Among these, simulation-based safety testing is a cost-effective method that accelerates the testing process and significantly reduces the testing effort and resource requirements. Simulation-based safety testing uses a scenario-based approach, where specific driving scenarios are simulated to evaluate the behavior and performance of the ADS. A scenario refers to a specific situation that the ADS under test (typically called an 'ego vehicle') might encounter during its operation.

G. Scanniello et al. (Eds.): PROFES 2025, LNCS 16361, pp. 461–469, 2026.
https://doi.org/10.1007/978-3-032-12089-2_31

Since ADS may encounter infinite real-world scenarios, it becomes impractical to simulate and test every scenario individually. To address this, a few studies [3–5,10,11,13] have proposed different techniques for reducing or prioritizing test case scenarios to focus on the most critical and relevant scenarios. Among these studies, one notable approach is the SSTSS (Simulation-based Safety Testing Scenario Selection) process, introduced in our previous work [10].

The SSTSS process begins by using a publicly available scenario catalog—e.g., the National Highway Traffic Safety Administration (NHTSA)[1] and Euro NCAP[2]. It then filters these scenarios based on the Operational Design Domain (ODD)[3] of the test vehicle and the limitations of the simulator. Next, the SSTSS process prioritizes the filtered scenarios using accident datasets. The final outcome is a sorted and prioritized list of test scenarios suitable for simulation-based safety testing of the ADS.

In our previous study, we applied the SSTSS process to UT-ADS[4] (the ADS developed at the University of Tartu) to generate a ranked list of test scenarios for its safety evaluation. UT-ADS is the autonomous driving system developed at the University of Tartu, within its Autonomous Driving Lab (ADL)[5]. In this paper, we extend our previous work by evaluating the safety behavior of UT-ADS in a scenario selected through the SSTSS process. The following are the contributions of this work:

- We implement the top-priority scenario from the SSTSS process output by modeling the dynamic behavior of other vehicles interacting with the ego vehicle using a Python-based script.
- We set up the simulation environment using CARLA and ScenarioRunner, and integrated the ego vehicle, UT-ADS autonomy stack, via CARLA ROS bridge to enable closed-loop control and execution of the driving behavior within the simulated scenario.
- We run experiments and evaluate the safety of whether the UT-ADS avoids collision and maintains a safe following distance.

The rest of this paper is organized as follows. Section 2 presents the related work. Section 3 presents the methodology. Section 4 presents the experiments. Section 5 presents the preliminary results, and Sect. 6 presents future work.

2   Related Work

Due to space limitations, we present only a few relevant studies related to simulation-based safety testing of ADS. Li et al. [12] proposed AV-FUZZER using genetic algorithms to identify safety violations of Baidu Apollo in urban

---

[1] List of Pre-Crash Scenarios for Crash Avoidance Research.

[2] Test Scenarios – European New Car Assessment Programme.

[3] ODD: The ODD defines the specific conditions under which the ADS is designed to operate, including road types, weather conditions, and traffic patterns.

[4] UT-ADS is based on a Lexus RX450h and is sponsored by BOLT OÜ.

[5] Autonomous Driving Lab – (ADL).

driving environments. Garcia et al. [7] systematically analyzed bugs in Apollo and Autoware, focusing on their GitHub repository commits. Gambi et al. [6] generated virtual roads using procedural road generation and genetic algorithms and evaluated their approach using two different ADSs to generate efficient virtual road networks. Jha et al. [9] introduced Kayotee, a fault injection tool for systematically assessing the ADS's resilience to faults and errors. Matthew et al. [15] proposed a simulation framework using adaptive sampling to test entire ADS, focusing on those utilizing deep-learning perception and control algorithms. Ben et al. [2] presented an approach to test ADS in Simulink. They used multi-objective search and surrogate models based on a neural network to identify critical test cases regarding an ADS behavior. Unlike the above studies, our work focuses on simulating a high-priority driving scenario selected using the SSTSS process. We demonstrate how simulation-based safety testing can be applied to real automated vehicle UT-ADS by modeling, executing, and analyzing a scenario chosen based on its ODD and accident data.

3   Methodology

In this section, we present our methodology for evaluating the safety behavior of UT-ADS using a scenario selected through the SSTSS process. Figure 1 shows the overview of the method.

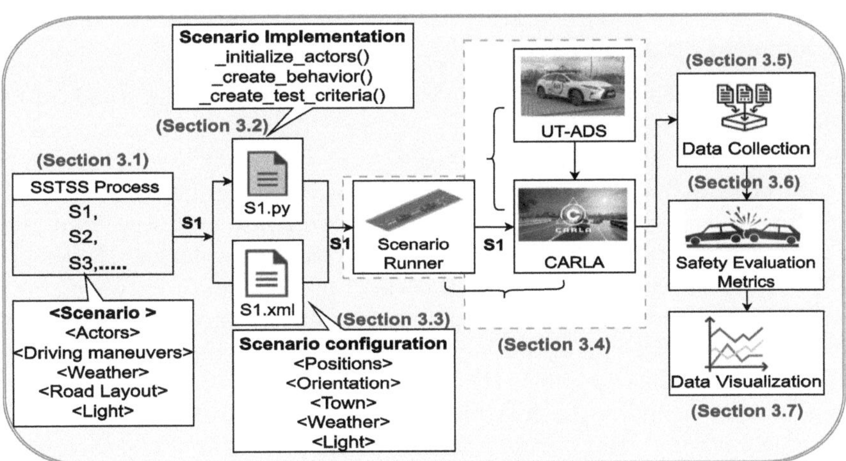

Fig. 1. Methodology Overview.

3.1   Scenario Selection

A scenario is a quantitative description of its components, including the ego vehicle, other actors (e.g., vehicle, pedestrian), static environment (e.g., road layout), dynamic environment (e.g., weather and light conditions), and driving maneuvers [8]. In our previous work [10], we applied the SSTSS process to UT-ADS to get a prioritized list of scenarios for safety testing of ADS. This list is available online[6]. In this study, we select the top-priority scenario from this list and simulate it to evaluate the safety behavior of the ego vehicle UT-ADS. The selected scenario is *"A lead vehicle driving in front of the ego vehicle at a slower speed"*, as shown in Fig. 2. The scenario includes two actors: the ego vehicle with speed v_r and the lead vehicle with speed v_f. The initial distance between the vehicles is denoted d_i. To make the scenario more interesting, we add a variation in which a lead vehicle drives in front of the ego vehicle at a slower speed and stops abruptly. We refer to the selected scenario as the *Follow Lead Vehicle* scenario.

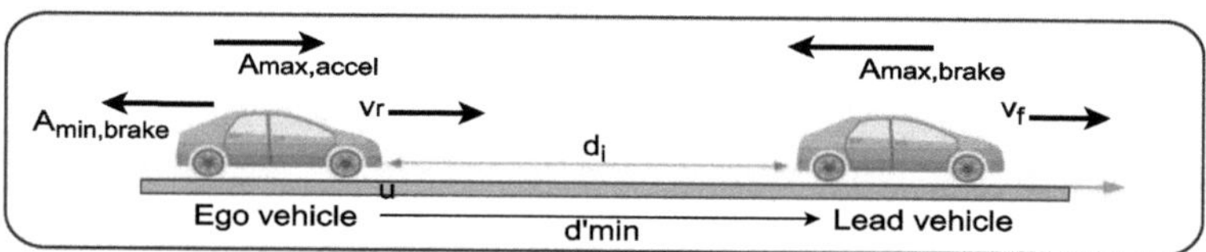

Fig. 2. Follow Lead Vehicle scenario.

3.2   Scenario Implementation

To implement the *Follow Lead Vehicle* scenario, we followed the standard procedure provided in the CARLA `ScenarioRunner`[7] for creating custom scenarios. We developed a Python class that inherits from the `BasicScenario` base class. The base class defines how the lead vehicle behaves, controls the flow of the scenario, and sets up the evaluation criteria. We consider three input parameters that could affect the safety behavior of the ego vehicle: (i) ego vehicle speed v_r, (ii) lead vehicle speed v_f, and (iii) initial distance between the vehicles d_i. We use different combinations of speed and distance to assess how these parameters could affect the ego vehicle's ability to maintain a safe following distance and avoid collisions when the lead vehicle stops suddenly. The scenario implementation includes the following key methods: `_initialize_actors()`, `_create_behavior()` and `_create_test_criteria()`. Details of each method, and a complete Python script are available online in Appendix A[8].

3.3   Scenario Configuration

The scenario configuration file specifies simulation parameters such as the map, vehicle positions, and environmental conditions. We use the CARLA map

---

`Town01`, positioning the ego vehicle on a straight 220-meter road. In addition, we configure the environmental settings for clear skies, no wind, and daylight with sun altitude at 75 degrees. The configuration file in .xml format is available online[9].

3.4   Simulation Setup and Execution

We set up the simulation environment using CARLA[10], ScenarioRunner (see footnote 7), and the ego vehicle (UT-ADS) (see Footnote 4). The ego vehicle uses the Autoware Mini autonomy stack based on ROS 1 Noetic. The integration details of Carla with ScenarioRunner and UT-ADS, including hardware specifications, software versions, and configuration steps, are available online in Appendix A[11].

3.5   Data Collection

During simulation, we record the data for both vehicles at each time frame and save it into a CSV file. The data includes: timestamp (s), the speed of the ego and lead vehicle (km/h and m/s), the longitudinal distance between ego and lead vehicle (m), and the cumulative distance traveled by both vehicles (m).

3.6   Safety Evaluation Metrics

We evaluate two safety metrics: (i) collision detection and (ii) maintaining a safe following distance. Collisions are detected using the `CollisionTest()` method provided by ScenarioRunner. However, for calculating the safe following distance, we use the Responsibility Sensitive Safety (RSS) model to evaluate the minimum required distance that the ego vehicle must maintain from the lead vehicle to avoid a collision.

During the simulation, we calculate the actual longitudinal distance between the ego and lead vehicles at each time step and compare it with the theoretically calculated RSS minimum safe distance to assess whether the ego vehicle remains within a safe distance. Full details on the RSS model, actual longitudinal distance calculation, and formulas are available online in Appendix A[12].

3.7   Data Visualization

We exclude the first 200 frames from the CSV file to mitigate the initialization noise of the simulation. For visualization, we generate a plot that shows the actual distance and the corresponding theoretical RSS minimum safe distance between the ego and lead vehicle. Collisions are marked with a point.

---

[9] See FollowLeadVehicle.xml .
[10] CARLA Simulator.
[11] See Appendix A - (Sect. 3.4).
[12] See Appendix A - (Sect. 3.6).

4   Experimental Setup

We use the CARLA simulator to test the ego vehicle's ability to maintain a safe following distance and avoid collisions in the *Follow Lead Vehicle* scenario. We consider three input parameters: (i) ego vehicle speed (v_r), (ii) lead vehicle speed (v_f), and (iii) initial distance (d_i). To observe their impact systematically, we vary one parameter at a time while keeping the others constant. The lead vehicle's speed and initial distance are configured in ScenarioRunner, while the ego vehicle speed is set through the UT-ADS autonomy stack.

We define ranges for each parameter. Both v_r and v_f range from 10 km/h to 50 km/h, while d_i ranges from 10 m to 80 m. These ranges show the urban conditions: 50 km/h as the speed limit and 10 km/h showing low-speed or congested traffic. Since this work is still in progress, we vary only the ego vehicle speed (v_r) from 10 km/h to 50 km/h in steps of 10 km/h, which results in five test cases. For each test, the lead vehicle speed (v_f) is kept constant at 10 km/h and the initial distance (d_i) is fixed at 80 m.

5   Preliminary Results

Figure 3 shows the preliminary results. The plot shows the ego and lead vehicle speeds, the actual longitudinal distance d between the ego and lead vehicle, and the theoretical RSS safety distance $d'_{\min}$ over time.

In the plot, the x-axis shows time in seconds, the left y-axis indicates the speeds of the ego and lead vehicles in km/h, while the right y-axis shows the actual distance between the vehicles and the RSS safety distance in meters. The blue and yellow solid lines show the speed of the ego and the lead vehicle, respectively. The red dashed line shows the theoretical RSS minimum safe distance $d'_{\min}$ that the ego vehicle should maintain. The red solid line shows the actual longitudinal distance d between the lead vehicle and the ego vehicle. The ego vehicle maintains a safe distance when the solid line stays above the red dashed line; if it drops below, it violates the RSS safe distance.

For the runs at 10, 20, and 30 km/h, UT-ADS maintains the minimum safe distance according to the RSS model (see Figs. 3a–3c). At 40 km/h, the distance comes very close to $d'_{\min}$ but does not go below it, showing that the ego vehicle maintains the required safe distance (see Fig. 3d). However, at 50 km/h, between the 20–25 time frames, the actual distance d goes below $d'_{\min}$ showing that the ego vehicle violates the RSS rule and follows the lead vehicle too closely at higher speeds (see Fig. 3e).

Based on these results, we recommend that UT-ADS developers improve the planning and control modules of the UT-ADS current version to estimate safe distances at higher speeds more accurately.

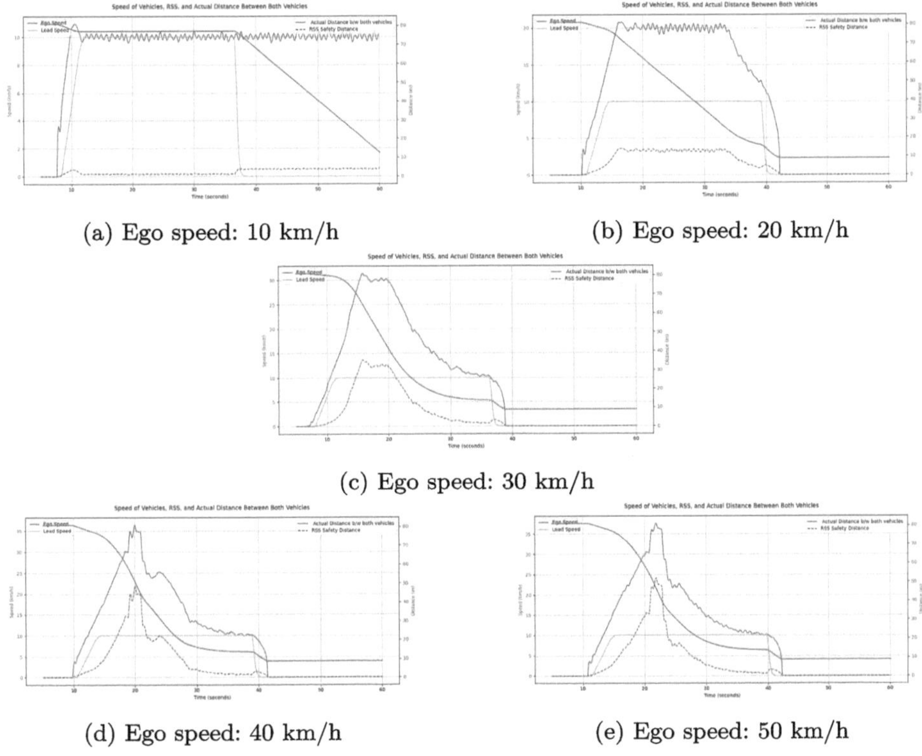

(a) Ego speed: 10 km/h

(b) Ego speed: 20 km/h

(c) Ego speed: 30 km/h

(d) Ego speed: 40 km/h

(e) Ego speed: 50 km/h

Fig. 3. Ego vehicle speed, lead vehicle speed, actual longitudinal distance, and RSS minimum safe distance over time for different ego vehicle speeds.

6   Conclusion and Future Work

This paper presented a preliminary safety evaluation of the UT-ADS using a *Follow Lead Vehicle* scenario based on the (RSS) model. Our initial results show that the UT-ADS maintains a safe following distance under lower speeds but may violate the minimum safe distance at higher speeds. UT-ADS has room for improvement in its current implementation. This work is still in progress. In future work, we aim to investigate and provide feedback to the UT-ADS developers to improve UT-ADS by simulating the remaining combinations of input parameters and environmental conditions (weather & lighting). Finally, we plan to evaluate more complex scenarios with multiple actors interacting with UT-ADS and other autonomous stacks, i.e., Autoware.

Acknowledgements. Thanks to the University of Tartu and its ADL for their support.

References

1. Bellan, R.: Waymo launches robotaxi service in san francisco. In: https://techcrunch.com/2021/08/24/waymo-launches-robotaxi-service-in-san-francisco/ (2021)
2. Abdessalem, B., Nejati, R., Briand, S., Stifter, L.C.T.: Testing advanced driver assistance systems using multi-objective search and neural networks. In: Proceedings of the 31st IEEE/ACM international conference on automated software engineering, pp. 63–74 (2016)
3. Birchler, C., Ganz, N., Khatiri, S., Gambi, A., Panichella, S.: Cost-effective simulation-based test selection in self-driving cars software. Sci. Comput. Program. **226**, 102926 (2023)
4. Birchler, C., Khatiri, S., Derakhshanfar, P., Panichella, S., Panichella, A.: Single and multi-objective test cases prioritization for self-driving cars in virtual environments. ACM Trans Softw. Eng. Methodology **32**(2), 1–30 (2023)
5. Deng, Y., Zheng, X., Zhang, M., Lou, G., Zhang, T.: Scenario-based test reduction and prioritization for multi-module autonomous driving systems. In: Proceedings of the 30th ACM Joint European Software Engineering Conference and Symposium on the Foundations of Software Engineering, pp. 82–93 (2022)
6. Gambi, A., Mueller, M., Fraser, G.: Automatically testing self-driving cars with search-based procedural content generation. In: Proceedings of the 28th ACM SIGSOFT International Symposium on Software Testing and Analysis, pp. 318–328 (2019)
7. Garcia, J., Feng, Y., Shen, J., Almanee, S., Xia, Y., Chen, Q.A.: A comprehensive study of autonomous vehicle bugs. In: Proceedings of the ACM/IEEE 42nd international conference on software engineering, pp. 385–396 (2020)
8. de Gelder, E., den Camp, O.O., de Boer, N.: Scenario categories for the assessment of automated vehicles. CETRAN, Singapore, Version **1** (2020)
9. Jha, S., Tsai, T., Hari, S., Sullivan, M., Kalbarczyk, Z., Keckler, S.W., Iyer, R.K.: Kayotee: a fault injection-based system to assess the safety and reliability of autonomous vehicles to faults and errors. arXiv preprint arXiv:1907.01024 (2019)
10. Khan, F., Anwar, H., Pfahl, D.: A process for scenario prioritization and selection in simulation-based safety testing of automated driving systems. In: International Conference on Product-Focused Software Process Improvement, pp. 89–99. Springer, Austria (2023)
11. Khan, F., Anwar, H., Pfahl, D.: Comparing approaches for prioritizing and selecting scenarios in simulation-based safety testing of automated driving systems. WiPiEC J. Works Prog Embed. Comput. J. **10**(2) (2024)
12. Li, G., et al.: Av-fuzzer: finding safety violations in autonomous driving systems. In: 2020 IEEE 31st international symposium on software reliability engineering (ISSRE), pp. 25–36. IEEE (2020)
13. Lu, C., Zhang, H., Yue, T., Ali, S.: Search-based selection and prioritization of test scenarios for autonomous driving systems. In: International Symposium on Search Based Software Engineering, pp. 41–55. Springer (2021)
14. Ohnsman, A.: Robotruck startup gatik making delivery runs for walmart without humans at the wheel. In: https://www.forbes.com/sites/alanohnsman/2021/11/08/robotruck-startup-gatik-making-walmart-delivery-runs-without-human-drivers/ (2021)

15. O'Kelly, M., Sinha, A., Namkoong, H., Tedrake, R., Duchi, J.C.: Scalable end-to-end autonomous vehicle testing via rare-event simulation. Adv. Neural Inf. Process. Syst. **31** (2018)
16. Tartu: International self-driving shuttle project. In: https://tartu.ee/en/culture-bus (2024)

Prompts as Software Engineering Artifacts: A Research Agenda and Preliminary Findings

Hugo Villamizar[1]([⊠]) [ID], Jannik Fischbach[1,2] [ID], Alexander Korn[3] [ID],
Andreas Vogelsang[3] [ID], and Daniel Mendez[1,4] [ID]

[1] fortiss GmbH, Munich, Germany
guarinvillamizar@fortiss.org
[2] Netlight Consulting, Munich, Germany
jannik.fischbach@netlight.com
[3] University of Duisburg-Essen, Essen, Germany
{alexander.korn,andreas.vogelsang}@uni-due.de
[4] Blekinge Institute of Technology, Karlskrona, Sweden
daniel.mendez@bth.se

Abstract. Developers now routinely interact with large language models (LLMs) to support a range of software engineering (SE) tasks. This prominent role positions prompts as potential SE artifacts that, like other artifacts, may require systematic development, documentation, and maintenance. However, little is known about how prompts are actually used and managed in LLM-integrated workflows, what challenges practitioners face, and whether the benefits of systematic prompt management outweigh the associated effort. To address this gap, we propose a research programme that (a) characterizes current prompt practices, challenges, and influencing factors in SE; (b) analyzes prompts as software artifacts, examining their evolution, traceability, reuse, and the trade-offs of systematic management; and (c) develops and empirically evaluates evidence-based guidelines for managing prompts in LLM-integrated workflows. As a first step, we conducted an exploratory survey with 74 software professionals from six countries to investigate current prompt practices and challenges. The findings reveal that prompt usage in SE is largely ad-hoc: prompts are often refined through trial-and-error, rarely reused, and shaped more by individual heuristics than standardized practices. These insights not only highlight the need for more systematic approaches to prompt management but also provide the empirical foundation for the subsequent stages of our research programme.

Keywords: software engineering · AI engineering · prompt management

1 Introduction

Large language models (LLMs) are now integral to software engineering (SE) tasks, supporting code generation, debugging, testing, and documentation [13].

As prompts serve as the sole mechanism for interfacing with LLMs, their role and importance in SE workflows have expanded, raising the question of how they should be positioned within these workflows. In SE, an artifact is a self-contained work result with a context-specific purpose, comprising a physical representation, syntactic structure, and semantic content [7]. From this definition, prompts arguably fulfill the role of artifacts: they encapsulate developer intent, embody critical design decisions, and evolve iteratively as developers refine them to improve LLM outputs. Moreover, they appear in varied contexts, from embedded in source code to detached environments (*e.g.*, ChatGPT) or context-aware tools (*e.g.*, Copilot).

Over the past few years, research on prompts has gained attention across multiple disciplines. Studies have explored strategies for crafting effective prompts [6,17], developed interactive tools to support their refinement and evaluation [2,4,8], examined how non-expert users approach the task [19], and exploring meta-cognitive demands in LLMs usage [15]. In SE, prompts has been investigated in contexts such as traceability, testing, and pattern use [11,12,16], as well as in terms of its evolution and quality concerns [1,14]. Some work has even framed prompts as "programs," developing an understanding of prompt programming [5].

However, existing research largely addresses isolated aspects without offering a holistic, empirically grounded understanding of how prompts should be systematically managed across LLM-integrated workflows. In particular, little is known about their long-term evolution, traceability, and reuse, as well as the trade-offs between the effort of managing them and the benefits this brings. We also lack empirical insight into how software professionals perceive the process of treating prompts as first-class SE artifacts.

To advance a systematic understanding of prompts as SE artifacts, this work makes two main contributions:

- **A research agenda** for investigating prompts as SE artifacts, focusing on three key aspects: (i) characterizing current prompt practices, challenges, and influencing factors; (ii) analyzing prompts in terms of their evolution, traceability, and reuse; and (iii) developing and empirically evaluating guidelines for their systematic management.
- **Emerging empirical insights from an exploratory survey** with 74 software professionals, offering early evidence on practices and challenges relevant to managing prompts as SE artifacts in LLM-integrated workflows.

In this work, we distinguish two complementary dimensions of working with prompts. *Prompt engineering* is the technical process of designing and refining prompts to achieve desired LLM outputs, covering early stages such as specifying intent, structuring text, and embedding prompts in workflows. *Prompt management*, in contrast, is the broader set of practices to keep prompts effective, maintainable, and reusable over time, including versioning, and tracing links to other artifacts (*e.g.*, requirements, code). Together, they form a *prompt life-cycle* from initial specification to long-term reuse. While both matter, this work focuses on the management dimension and how they can be systematically used in LLM-integrated workflows.

2   Research Agenda

Our long-term objective is to provide a systematic empirical foundation for understanding the role of prompts as SE artifacts and establish evidence-based practices for managing them systematically in LLM-integrated workflows. Figure 1 illustrates the overall structure of the research agenda.

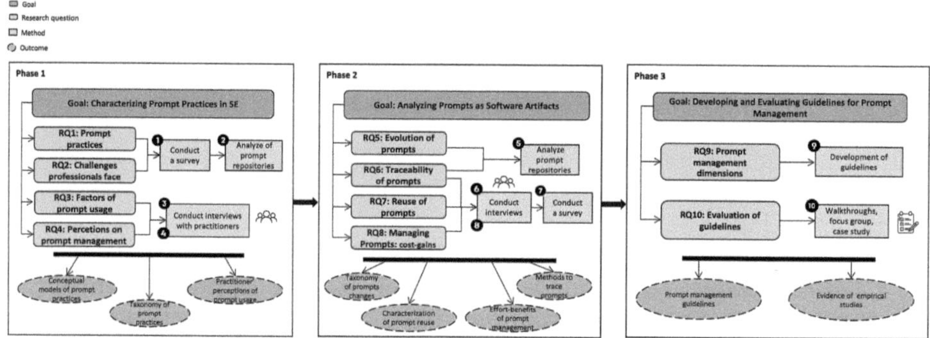

Fig. 1. Overview of our proposed research agenda.

2.1   Characterizing Prompt Practices in SE

Phase 1 of our research agenda focuses on understanding how professionals currently interact with prompts in the context of SE tasks and what challenges and factors shape these practices. The following research questions (RQs) guide this phase:

- **RQ1** What prompt practices are currently followed by software professionals in SE contexts?
- **RQ2** What challenges do software professionals face when using and managing prompts in SE contexts?
- **RQ3** What factors influence the way prompts are created, adapted, and reused in SE workflows?
- **RQ4** How do software professionals perceive the process of managing prompts as software artifacts?

To address these questions, we first conducted an exploratory survey, which enabled us to identify current prompt practices and challenges encountered in SE contexts (*Cf.* Sect. 4). Second, we plan to analyze publicly available prompt repositories and datasets such as PromptBase [10], PromptSet [9] and DevGPT [18] to identify recurring patterns and strategies. Finally, we will conduct semi-structured interviews with practitioners to (i) understand what drives their prompt choices (*e.g.*, task complexity, prior experience with LLMs, team norm) and (ii) whether they see value in treating prompts more systematically.

2.2   Analyzing Prompts as SE Artifacts

Phase 2 builds on the results of Phase 1 to investigate the extent to which prompts exhibit characteristics of SE artifacts and what this implies for their systematic management. We will focus on understanding prompt evolution, traceability, reuse, and the effort-benefit trade-off involved in managing prompts in a structured way. The following RQs guide this phase:

- **RQ5** How do prompts change throughout a software project, and what patterns of evolution can be observed?
- **RQ6** How can we establish traceability between prompts, the LLM-generated artifacts they produce, and downstream software components?
- **RQ7** What mechanisms support effective storage, indexing, and reuse of prompts across projects and teams in SE?
- **RQ8** What are the trade-offs between the effort of managing prompts and the benefits in terms of maintainability, reuse, and confidence in LLM-assisted development?

To address these questions, we will first conduct repository mining to analyze prompt evolution and traceability, examining changes across commits and their links to input and output artifacts. Second, we will perform interviews with practitioners to capture their mental models, strategies, and pain points around prompt change, reuse, and traceability. Third, we will complement these findings with a survey to quantify reuse and storage practices across different SE settings. Finally, we will conduct targeted interviews or focus groups to explore how professionals perceive the effort-benefit trade-off of systematic prompt management.

2.3   Developing and Evaluating Guidelines for Prompt Management

Phase 3 builds on the empirical insights from Phases 1 and 2 to synthesize a set of evidence-based guidelines for the systematic management of prompts in LLM-integrated workflows. The following RQs guide this phase:

- **RQ9** What practices and recommendations support the systematic management of prompts in LLM-integrated workflows?
- **RQ10** How do software professionals perceive the usefulness and applicability of these prompt management guidelines in practice?

To address these questions, we will synthesize findings from Phases 1 and 2 to distill recurring challenges, effective practices, and practitioner needs into a structured set of guidelines. The synthesis will follow established practices for creating empirical SE guidelines, with each recommendation specifying its application context, the core advice, and the rationale supported by evidence. Guidelines will be enriched with illustrative examples from our data (*e.g.*, documenting prompt intent, maintaining version history, modularizing prompts for reuse). The guidelines will then be evaluated through a combination of structured walkthroughs, focus groups, and field-based case studies.

3   Exploratory Survey Design

We conducted an exploratory, questionnaire-based online survey, following established guidelines for survey research in SE [3]. The aim was to obtain early insights into how software professionals use prompts in LLM-assisted SE tasks and the challenges they face. As a pre-study, the results provide an initial empirical basis for the more extensive investigations planned in our research agenda.

The survey targeted professionals with experience using LLMs in SE contexts. Developers, testers, data scientists, architects, managers, and researchers were eligible to participate. The instrument comprised 18 questions organised into three themes: demographic background, prompt practices, and challenges. Questions included multiple-choice, single-choice, five-point Likert scales, and open-ended formats. The latter enabled participants to elaborate on aspects such as the contextual information included in prompts or preferred structuring approaches. The survey was piloted with one developer and two researchers, resulting in refinements to improve clarity and consistency.

Data were collected in May 2025 using the Unipark platform[1] and distributed through professional networks, LinkedIn, and direct contacts. We received 74 valid responses, with no indications of incomplete or unserious participation.

Given the sample size and scope, the analysis focused on descriptive statistics, including frequencies, percentages, and cross-tabulations, complemented by subgroup comparisons to explore potential variations. Open-ended responses were analysed using lightweight thematic coding to identify recurring themes. These qualitative insights enrich the quantitative findings and provide a richer picture of current practices and challenges in prompt use for SE tasks. All material and data are available in https://doi.org/10.5281/zenodo.15464269.

4   Preliminary Results

We collected 74 valid responses from professionals with experience using LLMs in SE contexts, mainly located in Germany (51%), Brazil (26%), and Sweden (12%). Most respondents were developers (59%), followed by researchers (31%), and data scientists (22%). The sample was predominantly mid-career, with 55% reporting 4–10 years of experience, and 43% identifying as practitioners.

---

[1] https://www.unipark.com.

4.1   Prompt Practices

Our results show that software professionals use LLMs frequently, with over 90% of participants reporting daily or weekly use, primarily for code generation (77%), bug fixing (55%), writing documentation (50%), and code explanation (49%). Professionals also reported using prompts to find library functionality, compare approaches, and explore tools, essentially using LLMs as an alternative to search engines. Other reported activities include generating prompts themselves and brainstorming both technical and conceptual solutions to problems.

Prompt structure typically combines elements such as task descriptions (93%), code snippets (57%), and project context (53%). Participants also reported including constraints and examples, most of the time in a single detailed instruction (57%). The amount of context typically added is moderate (50%). Open-ended responses suggest that the level of context provided often depends on the task: for simple functions, a basic prompt may suffice, while test generations typically require more extensive input.

Prompt reuse also remains uncommon: only 11% reuse prompts regularly, while 46% never do. The lack of modular structures renders it difficult to apply prompts across tasks, reinforcing a tendency to start from scratch with each new query. The use of *prompt guidelines in SE contexts* appears rather mixed. While 34 participants reported following no guidelines, others referred to personal practices (26), online resources (20), or organization-wide standards (3). This variation suggests a lack of standardization and a high degree of individual experimentation.

Prompt refinement also emerged as a common part of the practice, with over 85% of participants reporting that they refine prompts at least sometimes. Refinement is typically triggered by issues such as hallucinated output (69%), unmet requirements (65%), or vague responses (57%). This behavior resembles a lightweight validation loop, where prompts are reworked until the output aligns with the user's intent. Participants stopped refining prompts when the output is considered "good-enough" (68%) or when it meets the requirements (58%). While "good-enough" was not explicitly defined, this suggests that many practitioners rely on highly subjective, task-specific thresholds rather than formal correctness criteria.

A closer look at participants with 10 or more years of experience $(N=11)$ reveals some notable deviations from the overall trends. This group prefers using structured templates (6) and step-by-step instructions (4). Additionally, experienced professionals show greater reliance on external resources, with the majority (7) reporting the use of literature or internet-based guidelines. This suggests that more experienced professionals tend to adopt more structured and externally informed prompting approaches, possibly reflecting their preference for systematic and reusable practices.

4.2   Prompt Challenges

Participants reported a range of challenges when formulating prompts for SE tasks. We found that the most frequently cited difficulties include determining the appropriate level of detail (68%) and ensuring that the LLM understands the provided context (47%). These findings reflect the inherent ambiguity of prompt development: too little detail may lead to generic or incorrect outputs, while too much can overwhelm the LLM. Other common challenges included overcoming LLM limitations (42%), translating requirements into clear instructions (36%), and managing large requirements (30%). Collectively, these challenges reveal a tension between the tacit knowledge embedded in SE and the explicit representations required to prompt LLMs effectively.

To navigate these difficulties, participants stated to employ a variety of strategies. The most common ones were making instructions more explicit (80%), adding more contextual information (68%), and breaking tasks into smaller subcomponents (49%). Additional strategies included giving examples, rephrasing prompts, and adding constraints on output style, highlighting a predominantly iterative approach to prompt refinement, often guided by trial-and-error.

5   Conclusions and Discussion

This work sets out a research agenda that positions prompts as SE artifacts. Our vision addresses three key aspects: (i) characterizing current prompt practices and influencing factors, (ii) analyzing prompts in terms of their evolution, traceability, and reuse, and (iii) developing evidence-based guidelines for their management. As a first step, we conducted an exploratory survey with 74 software professionals from six countries. The findings reveal that while LLMs are already embedded in daily SE activities, prompting is highly ad-hoc, shaped by individual experimentation rather than systematic practices. Reuse is rare, guidelines are inconsistently applied, and refinement is largely reactive, driven by issues such as hallucinated output and unmet requirements. These patterns point to a lack of structured support for sustaining prompt quality over time.

The survey also highlights challenges primarily linked to prompt engineering, such as determining the right level of detail, ensuring LLMs understand the provided context, and translating requirements into clear instructions. While these issues are closely tied to the creative and technical aspects of prompt formulation, they also have implications for prompt management since better documentation, reuse, and traceability could help mitigate them.

These results provide empirical grounding for our central premise: that prompts should be treated as first-class SE artifacts. Like other artifacts, they influence system behavior, evolve over time, and incur maintenance overheads. Managing them systematically has the potential to improve maintainability, reproducibility, and trust in LLM-assisted development. However, our findings also make clear that any management approach must balance potential benefits with the perceived effort, addressing practitioners' concerns about over-engineering.

References

1. Chen, Z., et al.: Promptware engineering: software engineering for LLM prompt development. arXiv preprint arXiv:2503.02400 (2025)
2. Cheng, Y., Chen, J., Huang, Q., Xing, Z., Xu, X., Lu, Q.: Prompt sapper: a LLM-empowered production tool for building ai chains. ACM Trans. Softw. Eng. Methodol. **33**(5), 1–24 (2024)
3. Ciolkowski, M., Laitenberger, O., Vegas, S., Biffl, S.: Practical experiences in the design and conduct of surveys in empirical software engineering. In: Conradi, R., Wang, A.I. (eds.) Empirical Methods and Studies in Software Engineering. LNCS, vol. 2765, pp. 104–128. Springer, Heidelberg (2003). https://doi.org/10.1007/978-3-540-45143-3_7
4. Kim, T.S., Lee, Y., Shin, J., Kim, Y.H., Kim, J.: EvalLM: interactive evaluation of large language model prompts on user-defined criteria. In: Proceedings of the CHI Conference on Human Factors in Computing Systems, pp. 1–21 (2024)
5. Liang, J.T., Lin, M., Rao, N., Myers, B.A.: Prompts are programs too! understanding how developers build software containing prompts. Proc. ACM Softw. Eng. **2**(FSE), 1591–1614 (2025)
6. Liu, V., Chilton, L.B.: Design guidelines for prompt engineering text-to-image generative models. In: Proceedings of the 2022 CHI Conference on Human Factors in Computing Systems, pp. 1–23 (2022)
7. Méndez Fernández, D., et al.: Artefacts in software engineering: a fundamental positioning. Softw. Syst. Model. **18**(5), 2777–2786 (2019). https://doi.org/10.1007/s10270-019-00714-3
8. Mishra, A., Soni, U., Arunkumar, A., Huang, J., Kwon, B.C., Bryan, C.: PromptAid: prompt exploration, perturbation, testing and iteration using visual analytics for large language models. arXiv preprint arXiv:2304.01964 (2023)
9. Pister, K., Paul, D.J., Joshi, I., Brophy, P.: PromptSet: a programmer's prompting dataset. In: Proceedings of the 1st International Workshop on Large Language Models for Code, pp. 62–69 (2024)
10. PromptBase: PromptBase: a marketplace for buying and selling prompts (2025). https://promptbase.com. Accessed 22 May 2025
11. Rodriguez, A.D., Dearstyne, K.R., Cleland-Huang, J.: Prompts matter: insights and strategies for prompt engineering in automated software traceability. In: 2023 IEEE 31st International Requirements Engineering Conference Workshops (REW), pp. 455–464. IEEE (2023)
12. Ronanki, K., Cabrero-Daniel, B., Horkoff, J., Berger, C.: Requirements engineering using generative AI: Prompts and prompting patterns. In: Generative AI for Effective Software Development, pp. 109–127. Springer (2024)
13. Stack Overflow: Stack overflow developer survey 2024 (2024). https://survey.stackoverflow.co/2024. Accessed 29 Apr 2025
14. Tafreshipour, M., Imani, A., Huang, E., Almeida, E., Zimmermann, T., Ahmed, I.: Prompting in the wild: an empirical study of prompt evolution in software repositories. arXiv preprint arXiv:2412.17298 (2024)
15. Tankelevitch, L., et al.: The metacognitive demands and opportunities of generative AI. In: Proceedings of the CHI Conference on Human Factors in Computing Systems, pp. 1–24 (2024)
16. Vogelsang, A., Korn, A., Broccia, G., Ferrari, A., Fischbach, J., Arora, C.: On the impact of requirements smells in prompts: the case of automated traceability. In: Proceedings of the International Conference on Software Engineering, pp. 1–24 (2025)

17. White, J., Hays, S., Fu, Q., Spencer-Smith, J., Schmidt, D.C.: ChatGPT prompt patterns for improving code quality, refactoring, requirements elicitation, and software design. In: Generative AI for Effective Software Development, pp. 71–108. Springer (2024)
18. Xiao, T., Treude, C., Hata, H., Matsumoto, K.: DevGPT: studying developer-chatGPT conversations. In: Proceedings of the 21st International Conference on Mining Software Repositories, pp. 227–230 (2024)
19. Zamfirescu-Pereira, J., Wong, R.Y., Hartmann, B., Yang, Q.: Why Johnny can't prompt: how non-AI experts try (and fail) to design LLM prompts. In: Proceedings of the 2023 CHI Conference on Human Factors in Computing Systems, pp. 1–21 (2023)

An Application of Program Mutations for Generating Negative Test Scripts Mimicking Human Errors on Web Applications

Tomoya Yamashita[1], Hirohisa Aman[2(✉)] , Sousuke Amasaki[3] ,
Tomoyuki Yokogawa[4] , and Minoru Kawahara[2]

[1] Graduate School of Science and Engineering, Ehime University, Matsuyama, Japan
[2] Center for Information Technology, Ehime University, Matsuyama, Japan
`{aman,kawahara}@ehime-u.ac.jp`
[3] Faculty of Science and Technology, Nanzan University, Nagoya, Japan
`amasaki@nanzan-u.ac.jp`
[4] Faculty of Computer Science and Engineering, Okayama Prefectural University,
Soja, Japan
`t-yokoga@cse.oka-pu.ac.jp`

Abstract. Web applications have gained widespread use in various contexts, and their increasing popularity has led to growing demands for automated testing. Testing Web applications requires operating Web browsers based on test scenarios, which can be costly work for test engineers. Moreover, there can be various negative test cases corresponding to operational errors caused by human errors, and thorough testing becomes more challenging. This paper proposes a novel method for generating negative test cases from normal test cases by utilizing the mutation technique. Furthermore, the paper proposes categorizing negative test cases by their final screen (i.e., the last Web page) similarity to help check their behaviors efficiently. The paper then examines the usefulness of the proposed method through an experiment.

Keywords: Web application · Negative test · Test case generation · Program mutation · Selenium · Edit distance

1 Introduction

A Web application is a software that uses a Web browser as its user interface. Many companies and organizations offer their services as Web applications due to their beneficial features, such as no installation required and low development and maintenance costs [1]. As Web applications work in diverse contexts, exhaustive testing under various test scenarios has become more crucial [2]. Although positive (normal) tests corresponding to the normal operations of Web applications are significant, negative (abnormal) tests that check the behaviors of

G. Scanniello et al. (Eds.): PROFES 2025, LNCS 16361, pp. 479–488, 2026.
https://doi.org/10.1007/978-3-032-12089-2_33

applications in exceptional cases, e.g., operational mistakes, are also essential to avoid unexpected failures. Because testing Web applications requires operating Web browsers, it can become costly and make negative testing more challenging.

There have been tools to automate Web browser operations, such as Selenium [4], and they can be helpful in efficiently testing Web applications. Once test engineers record their Web browser operations using Selenium, it can automatically re-execute the entire series of operations. However, we should note that such a tool only automatically re-executes test cases created by test engineers, but does not automatically generate those test cases. To facilitate automated negative testing of Web applications, we propose a novel method for generating executable negative test cases in this paper.

2 Negative Test Script Generation and Categorization

2.1 Related Technologies and Key Ideas

We give brief descriptions of technologies that our proposed method leverages.

Selenium IDE and Selenium WebDriver: Selenium is a tool that enables automated manipulation of a Web browser. Its core technologies include Selenium IDE [5] and Selenium WebDriver [10]. Selenium IDE is an add-on or extension for a Web browser that records user operations and reruns them automatically. Selenium IDE can also export the recorded operations as a test script written in a programming language, such as Python. Selenium WebDriver is an API for controlling Web browsers, and the exported scripts leverage that API. We utilize the exported Python scripts in this study.

Program Mutation: Mutation testing is a well-established testing technique that injects faults into the system under test and examines whether the test cases successfully detect these failures. However, we leverage the program mutation technique in "another context" rather than mutation testing in this paper. We consider a mutant to be a human error case, where a user makes a mistake during their Web browser operations. That is the key idea of this study: Although Leotta et al. [6] recently proposed a novel tool for Web mutation testing, we apply program mutation to "test code" rather than "production code" in this paper, aiming to generate negative test code automatically. For example, when we make a mutant by deleting a line of test code that clicks a hyperlink, the mutated test mimics a human error in which the user fails to click that link.

Tree Edit Distance Between HTMLs: After we perform negative tests using the automatically generated test scripts, we need to verify if any failures occurred during the tests. Because each negative test script simulates an operational error, the expected behavior of the Web application is to alert the user and not proceed with processing. To help the testers check the results of those negative tests, we categorize the generated test scripts by their final screens. We focus on the distance of the final screen from the original positive test's final screen because we can expect that the negative test's final screen differs from the positive test's final screen due to a failure occurrence caused by a mutant. We leverage the tree edit distance [7] to quantify the distance between the HTMLs of the final screens. The tree edit distance is an edit distance corresponding to the fewest operations required to change the node structure to another's structure. The edit operations include adding, deleting, and replacing a node.

2.2 Proposed Method

We now propose a method for generating and categorizing negative test scripts:

(1) Preparing a Positive Test Script. A test engineer performs and records a test using a positive test scenario on Selenium IDE. Then, we obtain a Python script corresponding to the recorded test case using Selenium IDE's export function. The exported test script is a "positive" test script and can serve as a seed for "negative" ones that we will automatically generate below.

(2) Converting a Test Script. Given an exported Python script, we divide it into functions so that each function corresponds to a specific Web page, allowing us to generate mutants for each one easily. Moreover, we also extract the location information of Web elements, such as clickable buttons, from the script and store them separately as a "locator" file. These conversions are inspired by the Page Object Model [3], a helpful concept for maintaining the readability and maintainability of Web application test programs [9].

(3) Generating Negative Test Scripts. We developed Python programs to perform the following mutations and create mutants of the original (positive) test scripts, mimicking common human errors in Web browser operations [8].
a) Deleting a test statement. Delete a statement within a function in a test script. This mutation corresponds to a human error, where a user missed an operation, such as failing to click a checkbox.
b) Rotating test statements. Rotate the statements within a function in a test script. This mutation mimics a wrong order of operations, e.g., a user mistakenly clicking a button before entering the e-mail address into a text field.
c) Rotating the locators. When we replace a locator with another one, the test script mimics a case where a user performs the same action as the original positive test, but the target Web element of the action differs. For example, a user enters the e-mail address into the wrong text field. We perform those mutations by rotating the locators, i.e., the list of target IDs, in a locator file.

(4) Running and Categorizing all Test Scripts. We run all of the above mutants using the `pytest` command. That corresponds to an automated negative test, and we can expect them to show different results from the original positive test because of those mutations. We capture the final screen's HTML of each test script and compute their tree edit distances from the original test's one. Then, we categorize the generated scripts by their distances to help detect failures.

3   Experiment

3.1   Aim

In this study, we address the following two research questions (RQs).

- RQ1: How efficiently does the proposed method automatically generate and run negative test scripts?
- RQ2: Do the mutation operations and categorization of final screens contribute to successful negative test generation and result checking?

RQ1 is on the efficiency of the proposed method in terms of test effort reduction. The key issues are how many negative test scripts the proposed method can automatically generate and how much effort the test engineer can reduce.

RQ2 is on the usefulness of our proposal. It is worth examining if the generated test scripts mimic unexpected use cases, such as human operation errors, and cause failures. Furthermore, the more test scripts a test engineer runs, the more tediously the engineer checks all test results. Examining whether the categorization helps test engineers check the results is also beneficial.

3.2   Studied Web Application and Procedure

We prepared a simple Web application to make an appointment for an online internship interview and conducted an experiment to answer the above RQs. This application has three screens. First, a student enters the required information to make an appointment (Table 1) in the appointment form and clicks the "next" button. Then, the application shows the confirmation screen. Finally, when the student clicks the "send your request" button, the application sends the interview request to the human resource manager.

Table 1. Information required to make an appointment.

Item	Input type	Item	Input type	Item	Input type
name	text box	department	text box	date	drop-down list
gender	radio button	grade	drop-down list	start time	drop-down list
e-mail	text box	background	radio button	end time	drop-down list
university	text box	fields of interest	check box	message	text box
faculty	text box				

We injected the following two faults into the application.

1. It accepts empty e-mail addresses.
   Although the student's e-mail address is required to contact them, the application wrongly accepts the request even if the e-mail address is empty.

2. It accepts inconsistent time slots.
   Students convey their available time slots by selecting the start and end times. However, the application erroneously accepts the request even if the selected end time is earlier than the start time (an inconsistent time slot).

In this study, we use the Web application under a positive test scenario: *Tomoya Yamashita (the first author of this paper) makes an appointment for an internship interview between 13:00 and 14:00 on April 15th, 2025.* We record all our Web browser operations using Selenium IDE and export them as a Python script. Then, we create mutants of the above positive test script as negative test scripts. After that, we automatically run the generated test scripts using the `pytest` command. For each run, we also record the screenshot image and the HTML code of the final screen automatically. Finally, we categorize those scripts by their final screens. We examine whether the mutation-based test script generation contributes to detecting the failures caused by the injected faults.

3.3   Results

We report our experimental results below.

Automatic Generation and Execution of Negative Test Scripts: Through our proposed method, we obtained 97 automatically generated negative test scripts (see Table 2). After that, we ran all the test scripts using the `pytest` command and measured the time to complete that execution. Furthermore, to examine the proposed method's contribution to the reduction of testing effort, we estimated the time to run all of those negative test cases manually. For each type of mutation, we randomly extracted three samples from the negative test scripts corresponding to the mutation type and performed those tests manually. We regarded the average time of three manual test runs as an estimation of the time required to manually run a negative test case corresponding to the mutation type. Then, we estimated the total time to complete manual negative tests by summing the corresponding average times for all test scripts.

As a result, the proposed method could complete 97 negative tests in 918 s (about 15 min). On the other hand, the estimated time to manually run all those negative tests is 5,458 s (about one hour and 31 min). Because the estimated manual testing time does not include the resting time for a test engineer, manual testing would require a longer time to complete, e.g., two or three hours, in the real world.

Table 2. Number of generated negative test scripts.

Mutation			
Deleting a statement	Rotating statements	Rotating locators	Total
37	34	26	97

Categorization of Test Scripts Using Their Final Screens: By running 97 negative test scripts, we obtained the final screens' HTML code. Then, we computed their edit distances from the final screen of the original positive test case, and those distances were 0, 26, or 104. Thus, we could classify our negative test scripts into three categories (Table 3).

Table 3. Number of generated negative test scripts by the performed mutation operations within the categories.

Category	Mutation			Total
	Deleting a statement	Rotating statements	Rotating locators	
1	15	2	1	18
2	1	1	1	3
3	21	31	24	76
Total	37	34	26	97

The first category (Category-1) is the set of 18 negative test scripts whose final screens have no edit distance from the original positive test's final screen. No edit distance means that those test scripts could reach the final screen without encountering any errors. Because a negative test script has an operation mistake on the Web application, we expected that they would encounter an error and could not proceed to the same final screen as the original positive test. Hence, we may efficiently detect a latent fault by checking those cases.

The second category (Category-2) consists of three negative test scripts whose final screen's edit distance from the normal one is 26. Their final screen was the confirmation screen, i.e., they encountered an error under a negative test scenario and could not proceed to the request sending. Because those mutants mimicking operational mistakes caused errors, they are the "successful" results of negative tests. The third category (Category-3) has the remaining 76 negative test scripts whose final screen's edit distance from the normal one is 104. In those test cases, the Web application displays error messages on the first page (input screen): for example, a negative test case fails to enter the university name. They are also successful results of negative tests because the Web application correctly prevents proceeding with erroneous input data.

Fault Detection: The studied Web application has two injected faults, as we mentioned above. We examined whether the proposed method helps detect those faults by generating and categorizing negative test scripts. As a result, we could detect a failure caused by one of the injected faults from a negative test case in Category-1. Figure 1(a) shows the screenshots corresponding to the failure, and Fig. 1(b) presents the execution result after fixing the fault. For instance, although the user missed entering their e-mail address, as shown in Fig. 1(a), the Web application proceeded to the confirmation page without error. Then, the user could make an appointment.

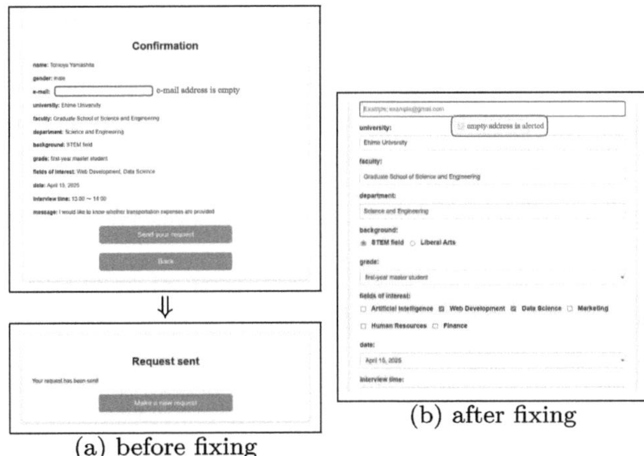

(a) before fixing

(b) after fixing

Fig. 1. Screenshots before and after fixing a fault.

Figure 1(b) shows a screenshot when rerunning the negative test script after we fixed the corresponding fault. After fixing the fault, the Web application successfully alerted to an input error for the empty e-mail address in that text field. However, the proposed method could not detect the remaining injected fault (one out of two faults)—the application could accept inconsistent interview time slots—through the above 97 negative tests. It would be a limitation of our proposed method to utilize only three types of mutation operations.

3.4   Discussions

We discuss the obtained results from the perspectives of our RQs below.

RQ1 (How Efficiently Does the Proposed Method Automatically Generate and Run Negative Test Scripts?)

We prepared a faulty Web application to make an appointment for an internship interview. Based on a positive test case in which a student sends a request for an interview via that application, we applied our proposed method to generate and run various negative test scripts. As a result, the proposed method could automatically generate 97 negative test scripts. Although not all of those scripts are useful in detecting failures, each test script might correspond to a human error in the Web browser operations, and they are worth checking if the Web application exhibits unexpected behaviors due to those human errors.

Moreover, the proposed method could automatically generate and run those scripts in about 15 min, while manual testing would require at least 91 min. The more complex the Web application under test becomes, the more negative test scripts we should prepare and run. Therefore, although it is trivial that automated test runs are much faster than manual tests, the above difference in testing times would become much larger in a real testing context.

> **Our answer to RQ1**: Once we prepare a single positive test case using Selenium, the proposed method automatically generates 97 negative test scripts mimicking human operation mistakes on the studied Web application. Generating and running all negative test scripts by the proposed method is four or more times faster than manual testing. Because thorough negative testing by hand would become harder as the system under test is more complex, the proposed method would help perform more efficiently negative tests.

RQ2 (Do the Mutation Operations and Categorization of Final Screens Contribute to Successful Negative Test Generation and Result Checking?)

Although generating various test scripts helps perform negative tests, whether the generated ones contribute to revealing latent faults is also significant. To examine their usefulness, we have injected two faults into the studied application. As a result, 18 out of 97 generated scripts were categorized into Category-1, in which their final screens are the same as the original positive test's final screen. Because a negative test contains an operational mistake, we can expect to find a failure by checking Category-1 scripts. Then, one of those 18 test scripts leads to detecting one of the injected faults, such that the Web application wrongly accepts an empty e-mail address. Hence, we could detect a fault earlier by preferentially checking about 19% (=18/97) of the negative test scripts; running those 19 test scripts took about three minutes. In those tests, a mutation, "removing a statement," helps detect a fault. Mutations removing test statements mimic an operation missing—a common human error—and would contribute to an efficient detection of latent faults.

On the other hand, our method missed another injected fault—the application wrongly accepts inconsistent time slots—due to the limitations of the mutation operators used in the study. The proposed method performed a simple mutation that rotates the statements or the locators in a test script as a code replacement mutation operation. Therefore, such a rotation-based mutation could not generate a test script corresponding to an inconsistent time slot input. We would successfully generate a negative test script to detect that fault if we adopted richer mutation operations, which include not only rotating statements/locators but also replacing each pair. Because more varied mutation operators may increase the number of scripts and make the test harder, we need to examine a proper selection of mutation operators in our future work.

As we saw in Table 3, the "removing a statement" mutation operation may generate negative test scripts that reach the same final screen as the original positive test, whereas "rotation" mutation operators rarely do. Rotating statements or locators can lead to incorrect operation flows (e.g., clicking "next" button before entering mandatory information) or incorrect actions (e.g., trying to enter text into a checkbox). Consequently, generated negative test scripts may cause errors, as shown in Fig. 1(b), and have larger edit distances from the original positive test's final screen. If the Web application has faults that overlook error checks, the corresponding negative test scripts' final screens have no edit distance from the positive test's screen and may be categorized into Category-1. Hence, although rotation mutations did not work well to detect faults in this study, those mutations might also be valuable to prevent the unexpected overlooking of error checks. As we mentioned above, enriching the set of mutation operators is our significant future work.

Notice that the selection of the original positive test also affects the effectiveness of the generated negative test scripts. When we choose a positive test scenario under which fewer Web elements and state transitions appear, our method can generate fewer mutants, resulting in a lower chance of detecting latent faults. Exploring a suitable set of positive test scripts as seeds for negative test scripts is also our significant future work.

> **Our answer to RQ2**: The mutation operation, "removing a statement," would work well to generate useful negative test scripts that may find a failure caused by human error. Moreover, categorizing the generated scripts by their final screens would help narrow them down to the ones that may lead to failure detection. Because we observed the above trend from a single experiment, we need further studies to ensure its practicality in our future work.

4 Conclusion and Future Work

We have proposed applying the program mutation technique to generate Python test scripts corresponding to human operation mistakes on Web applications. The generated test scripts are negative test cases for the Web application under test and are automatically runnable on the Selenium framework. Moreover, the proposed method can categorize the generated test scripts by their final screen contents to help test engineers notice the failures efficiently.

Through an experiment of testing a faulty Web application, we have demonstrated that the proposed method could generate many negative test cases, and the mutation "deleting a statement" would contribute to uncovering a latent fault. However, because the experiment is on a single and simple application, we have just shown the applicability but not the practicality of our method. Moreover, we missed validating whether each generated negative test case truly corresponds to an actual human error case. We need to examine the degree to which mutation-based negative test cases mimic real human errors through a developer survey in the future. Furthermore, enhancing our set of mutation operators and performing a further analysis using more general applications are also significant future work.

Acknowledgments. This study was supported by JSPS KAKENHI #23K11382, #25K15059, and #25K15062.

References

1. Andersson, E.A., Greenspun, P., Grumet, A.: Software Engineering for Internet Applications. MIT Press, Cambridge (2006)
2. Balsam, S., Mishra, D.: Web application testing—challenges and opportunities. J. Syst. Softw. **219**, 112186:1–112186:20 (2025). https://doi.org/10.1016/j.jss.2024.112186
3. Leotta, M., Clerissi, D., Ricca, F., Spadaro, C.: Improving test suites maintainability with the page object pattern: an industrial case study. In: Proceedings of the 6th International Conference on Software Testing, Verification and Validation Workshops, pp. 108–113 (2013). https://doi.org/10.1109/ICSTW.2013.19
4. Leotta, M., García, B., Ricca, F., Whitehead, J.: Challenges of end-to-end testing with selenium webdriver and how to face them: a survey. In: Proceedings of the 2023 IEEE Conference on Software Testing, Verification and Validation (ICST), pp. 339–350 (2023). https://doi.org/10.1109/ICST57152.2023.00039
5. Leotta, M., Molinari, A., Ricca, F.: Assessor: a PO-based webdriver test suites generator from selenium ide recordings. In: Proceedings of the 2022 IEEE Conference on Software Testing, Verification and Validation (ICST), pp. 389–399 (2022). https://doi.org/10.1109/ICST53961.2022.00045
6. Leotta, M., Paparella, D., Ricca, F.: Mutta: a novel tool for e2e web mutation testing. Software Qual. J. **32**, 5–26 (2024). https://doi.org/10.1007/s11219-023-09616-6
7. Nierman, A., Jagadish, H.V.: Evaluating structural similarity in xml documents. In: Proceedings of the 5th Int'l Workshop Web & Databases. pp. 61–66 (2002)
8. Norman, D.: The Design of Everyday Things. New York (2013)
9. Padhy, P., Nayak, P., Vaidya, S.: Web performance engineering — finding best data structure for automatically collected html locators. In: Proceedings of the 2nd International Conference on Computational Systems and Communication (ICCSC), pp. 1–6 (2023). https://doi.org/10.1109/ICCSC56913.2023.10142973
10. Raghavendra, S.: Python Testing with Selenium: Learn to Implement Different Testing Techniques Using the Selenium WebDriver. Apress, New York (2020)

MAPS-AI – A Tool for AI-Assisted Model-Driven Generation of IT Project Plan and Scope

Oksana Nikiforova[1] (✉), Rihards Bobkovs[1], Megija Krista Miļūne[1], Kristaps Babris[1], Oscar Pastor[2], and Jānis Grabis[1]

[1] Institute of Information Technologies, Riga Technical University, Riga, Latvia
`oksana.nikiforova@rtu.lv`
[2] Universitat Politècnica de València, Valencia, Spain

Abstract. Early phases of IT project management require well-structured plan and scope documents, which are often created manually and prone to inconsistencies. This paper presents MAPS-AI, an AI-assisted tool for model-driven generation of project initiation artefacts. It transforms high-level conceptual models into structured plans and scopes, combining large language models with model transformation rules. MAPS-AI integrates modelling, AI-assisted text generation, and prompt engineering techniques to enhance content relevance and consistency. This paper demonstrates the tool prototype, showcasing its potential to improve content traceability in early project phases.

Keywords: IT Project Management · Model-Driven Engineering · IT Project Plan and Scope · Large Language Models (LLMs) · Tool Demonstration

1 Introduction

Information technology (IT) projects have become complex, multi-layered endeavors requiring careful planning and coordination from the earliest stages. The project initiation phase—including defining objectives, planning resources, and scoping requirements—plays a decisive role in project success [1]. However, producing comprehensive, consistent, and standards-compliant documentation at this stage is often time-consuming and error-prone [2]. Agile practices [3] have accelerated delivery cycles, yet balancing speed with thorough documentation remains a challenge [4]. Incomplete project plans and scope definitions can lead to misaligned expectations, increased risks, and costly overruns [1], driving organizations to seek automation solutions that reduce manual effort while maintaining quality.

Model-Driven Engineering (MDE) provides a structured approach to capture requirements through multi-level models [5], improving traceability and generating artefacts in early phases [6]. Still, traditional MDE demands significant manual work to transform abstract models into complete documentation [7]. Meanwhile, generative artificial

G. Scanniello et al. (Eds.): PROFES 2025, LNCS 16361, pp. 489–497, 2026.
https://doi.org/10.1007/978-3-032-12089-2_34

intelligence (AI) and large language models (LLMs) have reshaped project management practices [8], offering automated generation of structured, domain-specific content. However, challenges remain in ensuring contextual accuracy, compliance with standards, and maintaining traceability [9]. This paper introduces MAPS-AI, a Model-driven AI-assisted tool for generating IT project plan and scope documents. Building on research in model-driven AI-assisted artefact generation [10-13], MAPS-AI integrates conceptual models with LLM-based text generation to produce structured, reusable, and standards-compliant artefacts. The main contribution is the demonstration of the MAPS-AI prototype and its workflow, showing how it supports efficient, traceable documentation generation in IT project initiation.

2 Conceptual Framework and Transformation Process

MAPS-AI development follows the Design Science Research (DSR) methodology as proposed by Hevner et al. [14]. In line with the Hevner's framework, this research is divided into three phases: Relevance, Design, and Rigor. In the Relevance phase, requirements for the artifact were elicited through a systematic literature review and mapping study to identify key artefacts in early IT project management and their interdependencies, published in [6]. This phase also analyzed transformations among project artefacts and input-output relationships [10]. Based on these insights, a source model representing initial project data (e.g., business process models, stakeholder requirements) and a target model for project plan and scope documents were developed [11]. In the Design phase, transformation rules were created to map source model elements to target model components, combining model-driven principles with AI-assisted methods for semantic enrichment and narrative generation via large language models [13]. The MAPS-AI tool's user interface was also designed, providing structured forms for model input, configuration, and document preview. The ongoing Rigor phase focuses on implementing the MAPS-AI prototype, integrating transformation rules with LLM-assisted content generation. A case study will be used to evaluate the tool's ability to produce consistent, traceable, and standards-aligned documentation, leading to iterative refinements of the framework and tool.

2.1 Solution Concept

The methodology underlying MAPS-AI builds on the two-hemisphere model [15], a conceptual framework widely applied in model-driven software development for organizing domain knowledge into two complementary components: a process model, which captures the behavioral logic of the business domain, and a concept model, which represents the static structure of data entities. The synergy between these models enables the automated transformation of domain analysis into system design artefacts, such as UML use case, class, sequence, and activity diagrams. In the context of this research, the two-hemisphere model serves as the conceptual foundation for structuring early-phase project information and guiding model-driven transformations toward documentation artefacts. While the full two-hemisphere model integrates both process and concept models, this study emphasizes the process model component, as it provides the necessary semantic richness to derive actionable elements for project documentation. These elements are essential for constructing structured content for the Project Management Plan and Scope Statement, which are the key outputs of MAPS-AI. By leveraging the process model as the primary input, MAPS-AI applies a combination of formal model-to-model transformations and AI-assisted text generation to produce structured, standards-aligned documents. The model elements serve as anchors for generating document sections, ensuring traceability and reducing ambiguity, while large language models provide the narrative and descriptive content needed for comprehensive and human-readable documentation.

2.2 Transformation Workflow

The transformation workflow implemented in MAPS-AI is designed to systematically convert early-phase project artefacts into structured, standards-aligned Project Management Plan and Scope documents. It combines formal model-driven transformations with AI-assisted content generation, ensuring that the final outputs are both semantically accurate and human-readable.

Stage 1: Model preprocessing. At this stage, problem domain process model and general project data are created. The transformation workflow operates on: (1) business process models – the primary source of structured project information, capturing activities, roles, events, and decision points within the project domain; (2) project parameters – preliminary requirements, project proposals, stakeholder lists and preliminary estimations for budget, timeline, and resource allocation, as well as project IDs, sponsor details, start and completion dates, and related parameters.

Stage 2: Model-to-project artefacts transformation. In the second stage, transformation rules are applied to translate the two-hemisphere model and project parameters into a structured set of project artefacts. The transformation relies on two complementary techniques: model transformation rules, which directly map structured artefacts to target elements using predefined logic, and LLM-assisted enrichment, which processes semi-structured data using guided prompts to extract or rephrase project-relevant content. Based on these techniques, the following mapping points are implemented:

MP1: Business process models and initial project parameters are mapped to establish the problem domain boundaries and contextual framing for the project scope.

MP2: Requirements are derived from the process model through model-driven transformations, represented as UML use case diagrams.

MP3: Product Backlog's User Stories are extracted directly from the process model: roles are mapped to the "As a [user]" clause, activities to the "I want to [task]" clause, and the "so that" clause is completed using LLMs to express business value or intent.

MP4: User Story Prioritization and Estimation is enhanced by LLMs, which incorporate contextual project parameters such as time constraints, team capacity, technical complexity, and budget limits to produce risk-informed outputs.

MP4: Project Scope information including purpose, background, deliverables, etc. is generated with LLM assistance.

The generated content is editable, allowing users to review, revise, or refine the proposed narrative text to ensure clarity, correctness, and alignment with project-specific needs. Through this mapping points MAPS-AI automatically generates artefacts for the project plan and scope, while also producing a traceable product backlog that can be further refined during later phases of project planning.

Stage 3: AI-assisted generation of documentation content.

Once the core project artefacts (e.g., stakeholder requirements, user stories, risks) are derived through model transformations, they serve as the basis for a standard-aligned document structure [16–18]. Using software engineering standards MAPS-AI defines essential sections of the Project Management Plan and Scope. With the document structure established, LLMs are employed to generate the narrative and descriptive content for each section. The LLMs operate within a guided prompt framework, leveraging the transformation outputs and predefined templates to produce coherent, contextually accurate, and standards-compliant text. This minimizes inconsistencies and enhances the clarity, readability, and practical applicability of the generated documents.

In order to overcome the key limitations of existing AI-based documentation methods, which are LLMs' token capacity and the need for contextual precision to ensure that generated content remains grounded in project artefacts and avoids hallucinated information, MAPS-AI employs a hybrid generation process that combines model-driven input with structured, dynamic prompt engineering techniques. A central innovation is the use of meta-prompts (also known as prompt-for-prompt generation). In this approach, higher-level "instruction prompts" are used to generate refined sub-prompts tailored for specific sections of the document. These meta-prompts define the structure, tone, and scope of each sub-prompt, ensuring consistency and reducing the cognitive load of prompt design [13].

To achieve this, prompt construction in MAPS-AI follows a multi-layered process:

1. Meta-prompts generate step-wise, context-aware sub-prompts. These are based on predefined schemas (e.g., JSON templates) that define expected sections of the document, such as objectives, deliverables, and constraints.
2. Semantic enrichment is applied through Retrieval-Augmented Generation (RAG). Relevant fragments (e.g., stakeholder goals, deliverables, risk factors) retrieved with the model transformations are injected into the prompts.
3. Iterative refinement ensures continuity across sections: each newly generated section is appended to the context, enabling the model to build on prior outputs while maintaining global coherence.

As the document structure is defined by standard guidelines, the meta-prompt framework maps extracted artefacts into standards-aligned sections. LLMs then generate narrative content using structured templates and enriched input artefacts. This approach reduces hallucinations by clearly separating missing information from confidently generated content and ensures traceability, as all outputs are grounded in the source models. As a result, MAPS-AI produces a consistent set of project initiation artefacts—including the Project Management Plan, Scope Statement, and Project Backlog. These artefacts can be exported to MS Word or Excel for traditional use, or delivered as API-ready outputs for direct integration with platforms like Jira [19] and Leantime [20], enabling automated creation of backlog items and scope records.

3   Tool Demonstration

A brief demonstration generates project artefacts for the Bachelor Thesis topic selection project. Figure 1 illustrates the process model designed using the two-hemisphere modeling approach. The model was created in draw.io and imported into the MAPS-AI tool as an XML file. Based on this input, the system applies model transformation to extract structured project artefacts. This corresponds to MP1, where business process models are used as described in the previous section.

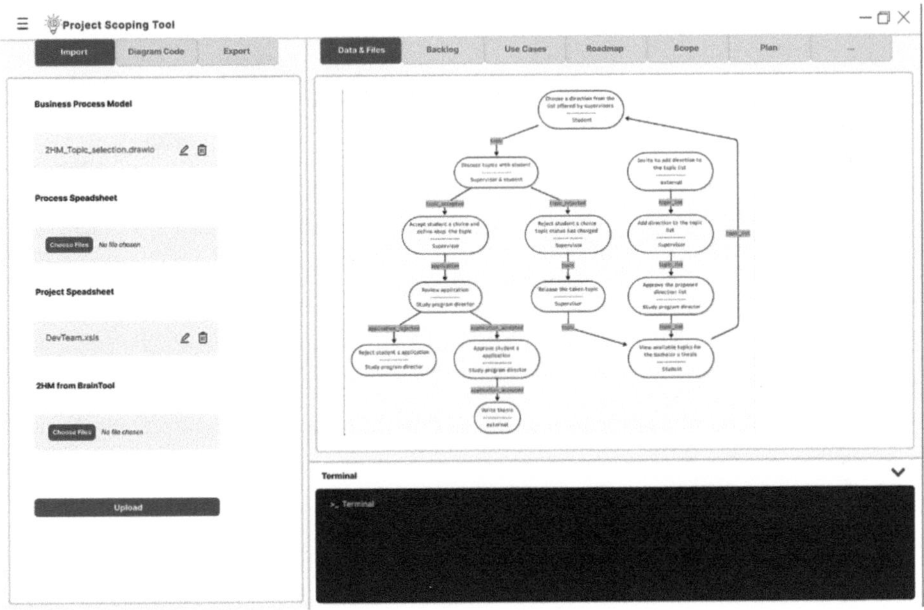

Fig. 1. Tool's UI form with import of the files containing project data and showing the process model of the experimental example.

Figure 2 presents the list of user stories automatically derived from the process model. These user stories form the basis of the project backlog (MP3) and can be exported to project management platforms. For each selected user story, detailed metadata are displayed: the actor and title are extracted from the process model (MP3), while the priority and effort estimation are generated by LLMs based on contextual project parameters such as time constraints, team capacity, and complexity (MP4). Although not shown in this paper, MAPS-AI also generates a UML Use Case Diagram to represent stakeholder requirements (MP2).

Figure 3 shows elements of the Project Scope (MP4), where all fields except for the project title and identifier are generated using LLMs based on structured prompts and enriched input data. Together, these artefacts serve as a constrained content base for the automated generation of structured and standards-aligned IT Project Management Plan and Scope documents.

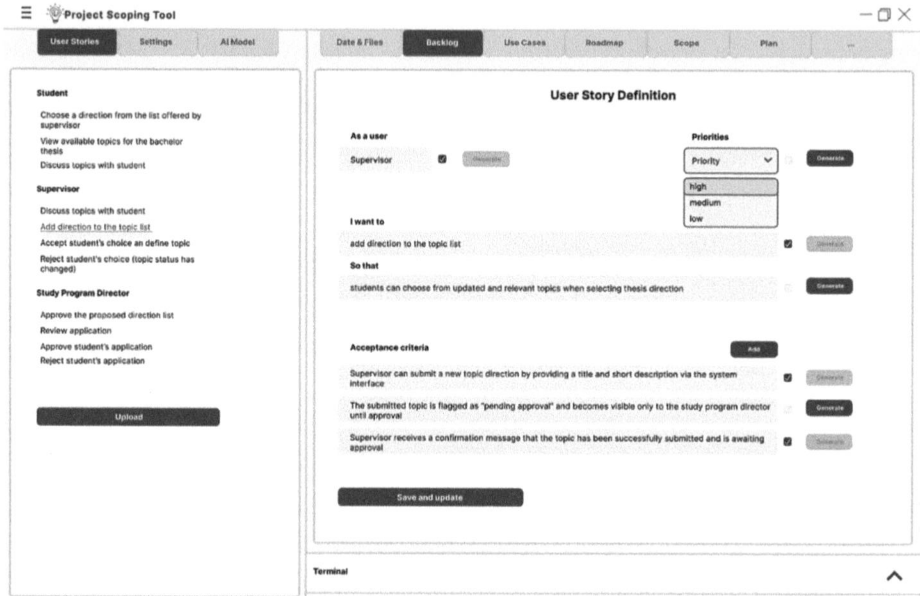

Fig. 2. Tool's UI form with obtaining user stories from the process model and refining them with AI-assistance.

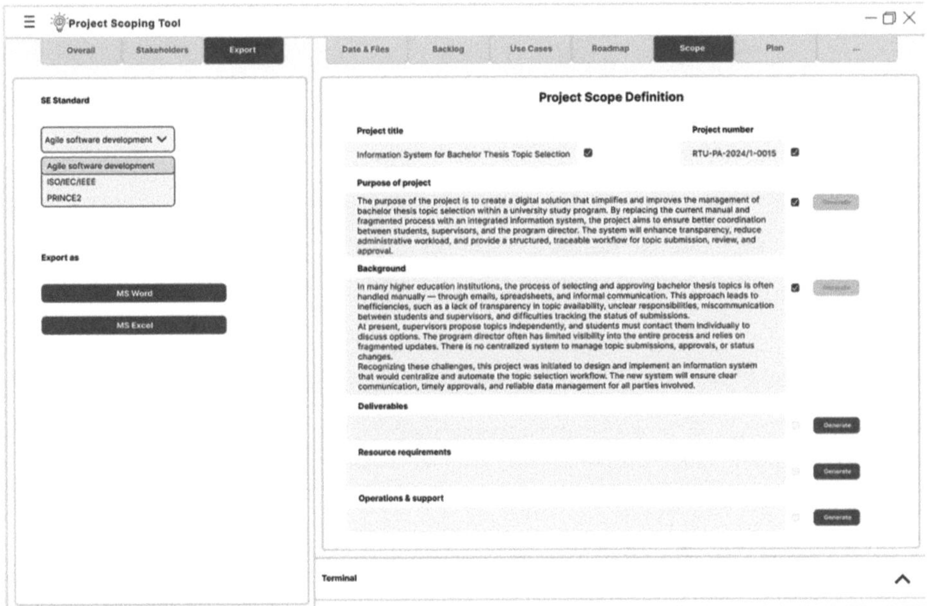

Fig. 3. Tool's UI form with LLM-assisted project scope elements generation based on project parameters.

4 Conclusions

This study presented MAPS-AI, a novel tool that integrates model-driven engineering principles with generative AI to automate the creation of Project Management Plan and Scope documents, as well as backlog-ready artefacts, during the initiation phase of IT projects. By combining the structural rigor of formal models with the expressive capabilities of large language models, the proposed approach ensures that the generated documentation is standards-aligned, semantically consistent, and traceable to its source artefacts. The use of meta-prompt engineering and semantic retrieval enables AI outputs to remain context-aware and reduces common challenges such as hallucinations or incoherence. From a theoretical perspective, this work contributes to the design science research body of knowledge by introducing an artefact that constrains and guides LLM behavior through model-based scaffolding. In practice, the solution offers project teams—especially those in resource-constrained environments—a way to accelerate and standardize project initiation workflows without compromising methodological integrity, while also facilitating integration with tools like Jira or Leantime for direct backlog population. Ultimately, MAPS-AI demonstrates that uniting business modeling with AI-assisted automation can streamline the early phases of IT project planning, improving documentation quality, enhancing communication among stakeholders, and supporting more structured, transparent, and Agile-aligned project initiation.

Acknowledgments. This research has been supported by Research and Development grant No RTU-PA-2024/1–0015 under the EU Recovery and Resilience Facility funded project No.

5.2.1.1.i.0/2/24/I/CFLA/003 "Implementation of consolidation and management changes at Riga Technical University, Liepaja University, Rezekne Academy of Technology, Latvian Maritime Academy and Liepaja Maritime College for the progress towards excellence in higher education, science, and innovation".

Disclosure of Interests..   The authors have no competing interests to declare that are relevant to the content of this article.

References

1. Kerzner, H.: Project Management: A Systems Approach to Planning, Scheduling, and Controlling, 13th edn. Wiley, Hoboken (2022)
2. Habib, B., Romli, R.: A systematic mapping study on issues and importance of documentation in agile. In: 2021 IEEE 12th International Conference on Software Engineering and Service Science (ICSESS), pp. 198–202. IEEE, Beijing (2021). https://doi.org/10.1109/ICSESS52187.2021.9522254
3. Manifesto for Agile Software Development. https://agilemanifesto.org/
4. Ehrlinger, L., Rusz, E., Wöß, W.: A survey of data quality measurement and monitoring tools. Front. Big Data **5**, 850611 (2022)
5. Noël, R., Panach, J.I., Ruiz, M., Pastor, O.: Stra2Bis: A model-driven method for aligning business strategy and business processes. In: Ralyté, J., Chakravarthy, S., Mohania, M., Jeusfeld, M.A., Karlapalem, K. (eds.) Conceptual Modeling. ER 2022, LNCS, vol. 13607, pp. 285–299. Springer, Cham (2022). https://doi.org/10.1007/978-3-031-17995-2_18
6. Nikiforova, O., et al.: Model Transformations used in IT project initial phases: systematic literature review. Computers **14**(2), 40 (2025). https://doi.org/10.3390/computers14020040
7. Ataman, A.: Data quality in AI: challenges, importance & best practices. https://research.aimultiple.com/data-quality-ai/
8. Brown, T.B., et al.: Language models are few-shot learners. In: Advances in Neural Information Processing Systems (NeurIPS 2020), vol. 33, pp. 1877–1901 (2020). https://doi.org/10.48550/arXiv.2005.14165
9. Nafz, F., Krajinovic, M., Ley, M.: Artificial intelligence in software documentation: embracing the documentation as code paradigm. In: Ernst, G., et al. (eds.) Go Where the Bugs Are. LNCS, vol. 15765, pp. 175–190. Springer, Cham (2025). https://doi.org/10.1007/978-3-031-92196-4_14
10. Nikiforova, O., Babris, K., Miļūne, M.K., Tanguturi, N., Pastor, Ó.: Key artefacts in the initial phases of IT project management: systematic mapping study. In: 20th International Conference on Evaluation of Novel Approaches to Software Engineering (ENASE), pp. 773–781. SciTePress, Lisbon (2025). https://doi.org/10.5220/0013471000003928
11. Nikiforova, O., Miļūne, M.K., Babris, K., Pastor, O.: Generation of IT project Documentation elements from a model transformation chain. In: 20th International Conference on Software Technologies – ICSOFT, pp. 336–345. SciTePress, https://doi.org/10.5220/0013568300003964
12. Nikiforova, O., Grabis, J., Pastor, O., Babris, K., Miļūne, M.K., Bobkovs, R.: Model-based methodology for development of IT project management plan and scope using artificial intelligence: project in progress. In: CEUR Workshop Proceedings, vol. 3987, pp. 1–7 (2025). https://ceur-ws.org/Vol-3987/paper7.pdf

13. Blaževics,R.,Nikiforova,O.,Pastor,O.:Aframeworkformodel-drivenAI-assistedgener-ationofITprojectmanagementplanandscopedocuments.In: 20th Conference on Computer Scienceand Intelligence Systems (FedCSIS), M. Bolanowski, M. Ganzha, L. Maciaszek, M. Paprzycki, D. Slezak (eds). ACSIS, Vol. 43, pp. 121–132 (2025). http://dx.doi.org/10.15439/2025F8736
14. Hevner, A.R., March, S.T., Park, J., Ram, S.: Design science in information systems research. MIS Q. **28**(1), 75–105 (2004). https://doi.org/10.2307/25148625
15. Nikiforova, O., Kirikova, M., Pavlova, N.: Two-hemisphere driven approach: application for knowledge modeling. In: 7th International Baltic Conference on Databases and Information Systems, pp. 244–250 (2006). https://www.scopus.com/inward/record.uri?eid=2-s2.0-34250753483
16. ISO/IEC/IEEE: Systems and Software Engineering — Life Cycle Processes — Requirements Engineering. ISO/IEC/IEEE 29148:2018. In: International Organization for Standardization, Geneva (2018)
17. ISO/IEC/IEEE: Systems and Software Engineering — Life Cycle Processes — Project Management. ISO/IEC/IEEE 16326:2019. In: International Organization for Standardization, Geneva (2019)
18. Project Management Institute: A Guide to the Project Management Body of Knowledge (PMBOK® Guide). 7th edn. Project Management Institute, Newtown Square (2021)
19. Atlassian: Jira Software [Software]. https://www.atlassian.com/software/jira
20. Leantime: Open Source Project Management System https://leantime.io

Ticket-Augmented Just-In-Time Defect Prediction

Emanuele Gentili[1,2]([envelope]) [iD], Daniele LaProva[1] [iD], and Davide Falessi[1] [iD]

[1] University of Rome "Tor Vergata", Via del Politecnico 1, Rome 00132, Italy
daniele.laprova@hotmail.it, falessi@ing.uniroma2.it
[2] MBDA Italy S.p.a, Via Monte Flavio 45, Rome 00131, Italy
emanuele.gentili@mbda.it

Abstract. Context: With the aim to focus software testing where it is most needed, Just-In-Time Defect Prediction (JIT) consists of predicting the likelihood of a set of changes, i.e., commits, to be buggy. As a commit is intended to implement a (set of) ticket(s), the intuition in this paper is that ticket-level information could support the bugginess prediction of the commits implementing it. **Aim**: In this paper we propose and validate an approach called Ticket Augmented JIT, i.e., TA-JIT, which complements the standard 13 features used in JIT with 58 ticket-level features. **Method**: We compared the prediction accuracy of JIT vs TA-JIT using a sliding-window, balancing, feature selection, and three machine learning (ML) classifiers on about 10,000 tickets of two Apache open-source projects. Moreover, we investigate which of the 58 ticket features contributed to improving JIT prediction accuracy. **Results**: Our results show that the ticket-level information supports JIT. Specifically, TA-JIT was statistically significantly more accurate than JIT in about 75% of cases with large effect size in about 80% of cases. Regarding the importance of ticket-level features, results show that at least three ticket-level features are selected in each window and the type of selected ticket-level features varies across windows. **Conclusions**: By reducing false-positive alarms, TA-JIT enables teams to re-allocate verification effort, shortening feedback loops in continuous-delivery pipelines.

Keywords: Defect prediction · Ticket · Mining software repositories

1 Introduction

In industrial settings, a single defect can stall release trains, inflate remediation budgets, and—where safety is at stake—expose organisations to high risk. Consequently, much effort has been spent on bug prediction. In practice, high false-positive rates in JIT predictions cause unnecessary code reviews and test executions, diverting scarce verification effort from truly risky changes. These inefficiencies inflate engineering hours and extend CI/CD feedback cycles. The main purpose of bug prediction is to minimize the testing effort. This is achieved

G. Scanniello et al. (Eds.): PROFES 2025, LNCS 16361, pp. 498–505, 2026.
https://doi.org/10.1007/978-3-032-12089-2_35

by focusing testing on specific software artifacts, such as classes, methods, commits, or lines of code predicted to be buggy. Consequently, significant progress has been made in developing prediction models at the class, method, commit, and line levels [2–5,9–11,13–15,20,20]. Specifically, Just-In-Time Defect Prediction (JIT) is a commit-level prediction model that predicts the likelihood of a commit to be buggy [2,15]. Yet, prevailing JIT models operate without ticket-level information, thereby missing contextual information, such as ticket type, priority, or discussion dynamics, that may influence defect risk. As a commit is intended to implement a (set of) ticket(s), the intuition in this paper is that ticket-level information could support the bugginess prediction of the commits implementing it. Thus, in this paper we propose and validate an approach called Ticket Augmented JIT, i.e., TA-JIT, which complements the standard 13 features used in JIT with 58 ticket-level features.

Falessi et al. [2] uncovered the detrimental effect of dormant defects on defect prediction. Kamei and Shihab [5] provided an overview of accomplishments and challenges in defect prediction, suggesting richer contextual information. On the same vein, Zhao et al. [20] in their recent systematic survey identified the integration of artefact and process data as an important aspect in future research efforts. We directly supported these suggestions by complementing JIT data with ticket data. McIntosh and Kamei [10] observed that JIT predictors changes over time, implicitly suggesting the use of a sliding-window approach as applied in our evaluation technique. Falessi et al. [3] showed that method-level and class-level defect prediction increase accuracy if augmented with JIT predictions.

In this paper we compared the prediction accuracy of JIT vs TA-JIT using a sliding-window, balancing, feature selection, and three machine-learning classifiers on about 10,000 tickets of two Apache open-source projects. Moreover, we investigate which of the 58 ticket features helped in JIT prediction.

In the remainder of this paper, we first present our methodology in Sect. 2, followed by the results of our experiments in Sect. 3. Finally, we discuss and conclude the paper in Sect. 4.

2   Methodology

Figure 1 shows the TA-JIT dataset creation process. We took the JIT features from the ApacheJIT repository and the ticket-level features from the TLP repository. We used the commit ID as a unique identifier to link the JIT features with the corresponding ticket-level features.

As ticket-level features, we used the 72 features available in La Prova et al. [8]. Our final dataset is available online[1].

To measure the accuracy of classifiers we performed two independent evaluations, one using JIT features only and one using both JIT and ticket-level features (i.e., TA-JIT). Therefore, we propose our Null Hypothesis (**H10**): the accuracy of commit-level prediction does not change when augmenting JIT with ticket-level features.

---

[1] https://doi.org/10.5281/zenodo.15680865.

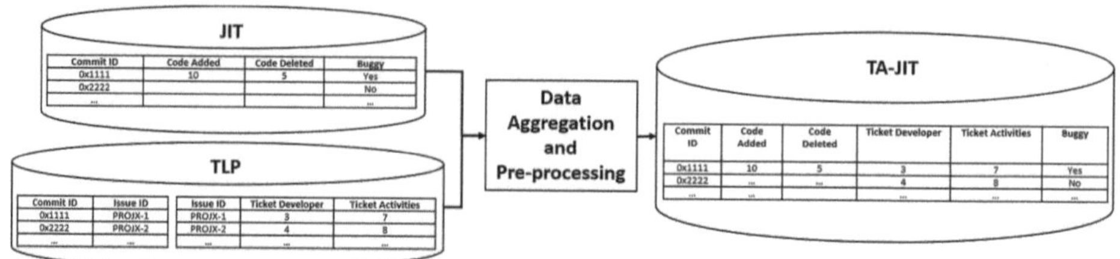

Fig. 1. TA-JIT dataset creation process.

The experimental design closely mirrors previous studies [8,12]: we adopted the same evaluation technique, i.e., a balanced sliding window of 1,000 commits advanced by 200, the same set of classifiers, i.e., Random Forest, Decision Tree, and a Feed-Forward Neural Network, and the same accuracy metrics, i.e., AUC, F1, Precision, Recall, G-Mean, and Specificity.

As feature selection techniques we combined a Symmetrical-Uncertainty filter with a backward Correlation-based Feature Selection wrapper which has been shown to retain, or improve, predictive accuracy while cutting the cost of exhaustive wrappers and hence it fits our context of high-dimensional feature selection tasks [19]. Moreover, we measured the selection frequency of feature families, e.g., ticket type, priority, and comments, across windows to assess which ticket-level information supports observed improvements. To test our null hypothesis, we used the Wilcoxon Signed-Rank Test (WRST) for each pair of JIT-versus-TA-JIT on each dataset, classifier, and accuracy metric combination. The WSRT is a distribution-free alternative to the paired t-test that requires only the symmetry of paired differences [17] and is therefore recommended when normality cannot be assured, as is typical for windowed performance metrics in software-engineering experiments [1]. To analyse the effect size, we measured the rank-biserial correlation, i.e., rrb [7]. To interpret the magnitude of the effect size, we followed widely adopted guidelines for rank-based correlations [16]. Specifically, we classified effects as follows: $|r_{\mathrm{rb}}| < 0.10$ (negligible), $0.10 \leq |r_{\mathrm{rb}}| < 0.30$ (small), $0.30 \leq |r_{\mathrm{rb}}| < 0.50$ (medium), and $|r_{\mathrm{rb}}| \geq 0.50$ (large).

3   Results

3.1   Does Leveraging Ticket-level Information Increase the Accuracy of Just-In-Time Defect Prediction?

Figure 2 reports the distribution of specific accuracy metrics over different windows and three classifiers of the JIT and TA-JIT approach. Table 1 reports the effect size interpretation and the statistical significance difference between TA-JIT and JIT in each specific combination of classifier and accuracy metric.

According to Fig. 2 and Table 1, for every performance metric considered, the median score of TA-JIT beats the corresponding median of JIT, confirming a systematic shift in central tendency in favour of the proposed approach. Regarding statistical test, we rejected H10 in 31 out of 42 pairwise comparisons, indicating that TA-JIT outperforms JIT in the majority of metric-classifier-dataset combinations. The largest effect sizes occur with Random Forest, whereas the smallest occur with the Neural Network. We note that Random Forest showed higher accuracy than the Neural Network across all metrics and projects, thus TA-JIT seems to help when used by accurate classifiers. We note that both aggregate metrics, AUC and F1, show large and statistically significant improvements across datasets and classifiers, aside from Neural Network on HIVE. It is important to highlight that the increase is more noticeable in Precision rather than Recall.

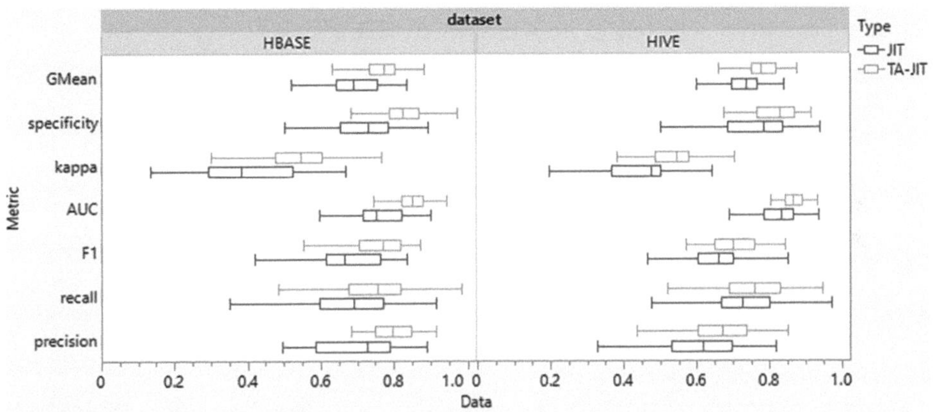

Fig. 2. Distribution of specific accuracy metrics over different windows and three classifiers of the JIT and TA-JIT approach.

Table 1. Effect size (Large, Medium, Moderate, Small) and statistical significance difference (*) between TA-JIT and JIT for each combination of classifier and accuracy metric.

	HBASE			HIVE		
	LR	NN	RF	LR	NN	RF
AUC	Large*	Large*	Large*	Large*	Moderate	Large*
F1	Large*	Large	Large*	Large*	Large*	Large*
G-Mean	Large*	Small	Large*	Large*	Large*	Large*
Kappa	Large*	Small	Large*	Large*	Large*	Large*
Precision	Large*	Large	Large*	Large*	Large*	Large*
Recall	Small	Small	Large*	Moderate	Small	Large*
Specificity	Large*	Moderate	Large*	Large*	Large*	Large

3.2 What is the Predictive Power of Ticket-level Features in Just-In-Time Defect Prediction?

Figure 3 reports the percentage of selected features in a specific window related to specific families. According to Fig. 3, the percentage of JIT features selected are in the [30,60] range, thus in some windows most of the selected features are ticket level. Figure 4 reports the percentage of windows with at least one feature selected of specific families. According to Fig. 4, at least one JIT feature is selected in all windows. Moreover, different projects select different features over different windows. External temperature features have been selected at least once in most of the windows in HBASE, and Internal temperature features have been selected at least once in most of the windows in HIVE. Finally, developer features have been selected in no windows in HBASE.

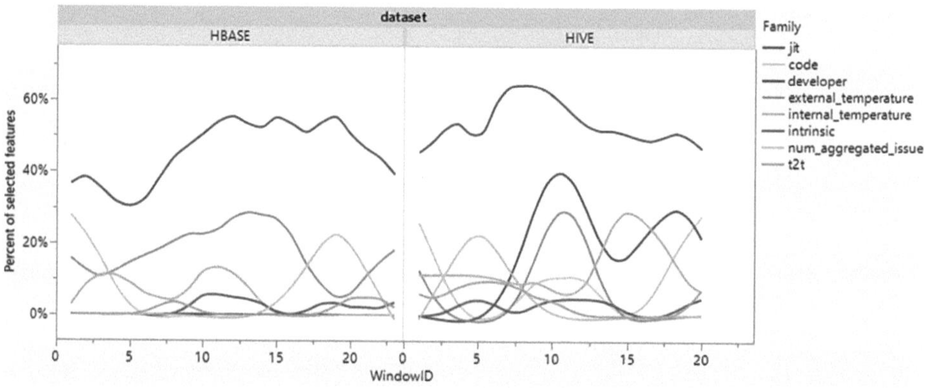

Fig. 3. Percentage of selected features in a specific window related to specific families.

4 Discussion, Practical Implications, and Conclusions

Our results show that the ticket-level information supports JIT. Specifically, TA-JIT outperforms JIT in all 42 metric–classifier–dataset combinations at the level of median performance; this superiority was statistically significant in 74% of those comparisons, with large effect sizes in 80% of the significant cases. These findings indicate that enriching commit-level models with ticket-level aggregation is beneficial across evaluated metrics and classifiers within the two studied projects; we note that establishing broader applicability will require a wider and cross-project validation. We note that both aggregate metrics, AUC and F1, show large and statistically significant improvements across datasets and classifiers, aside from Neural Network on HIVE. It is important to highlight that the increase is more noticeable in Precision rather than Recall. We note that a higher Precision reduces false alarms, enabling more focused reviews and test

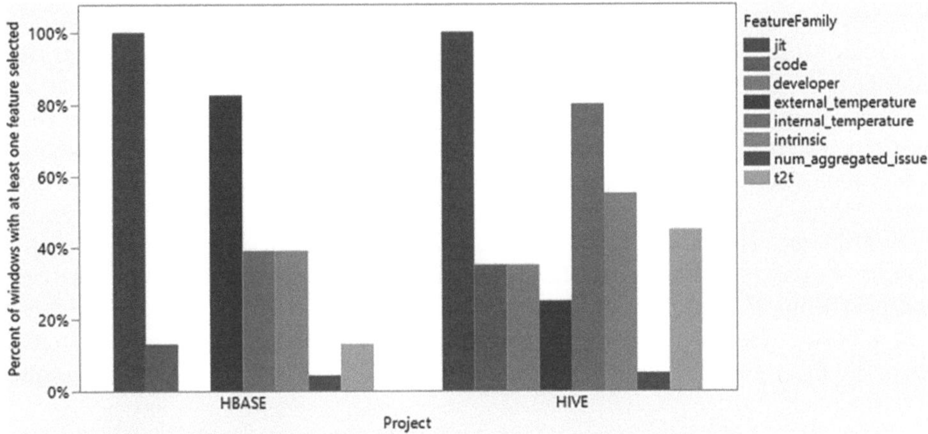

Fig. 4. Percentage of windows with at least one feature selected of specific families.

selection, and thereby shortening CI/CD feedback loops. This is confirmed by the statistical analysis and effect size, which for Precision is statistically significant in both projects and all classifiers other than NN in HIVE. Given that buggy commits constitute the majority class in both projects, Recall is already inflated by chance, whereas Precision remains sensitive to false positives; thus, TA-JIT primarily reduces false alarms while maintaining an already high hit-rate. This reasoning is confirmed by the significant improvements observed in G-Mean and Specificity.

Regarding the importance of ticket-level features, results show that at least three ticket-level features are selected in each window and the type of selected ticket-level features varies across windows. The consistent inclusion of at least one JIT feature in all windows (see Fig. 3) reinforces the foundational assumption of JIT models that recent changes contain valuable predictive signals. However, the fluctuating proportion of selected features (see Fig. 4) indicates that their utility is neither uniform nor static. This confirms findings by McIntosh and Kamei [10], who observed that the importance of JIT metrics may drift over time, necessitating frequent model updates or adaptive feature selection strategies. The absence of one dominant ticket-level feature underscores that TA-JIT adapts to project-specific contexts rather than imposing a one-size-fits-all model, a property valued by organisations operating multiple product lines. This heterogeneity underscores the importance of context-aware model customization, aligning with the conclusions of Kamei et al. [6] suggesting to customize models to specific project characteristics. Our results also show that the percentage of JIT features selected is higher than the percentage def ticket-level features selected in most windows. This suggests that JIT features are more relevant than ticket-level features in most contexts. However, the percentage of ticket-level features selected is still significant, indicating that ticket-level information can complement JIT features in some contexts. Finally, the selection frequency of ticket-level features is heterogeneous across projects and temporal windows. No single ticket-level feature family is consistently selected in all contexts, suggesting feature importance is both project- and time-dependent.

Regarding the practical implication of this study, the dynamic and context-sensitive selection of ticket-level features suggests that industrial organisations can enhance defect prediction by customising models to specific temporal contexts. Moreover, the absence of a universally dominant ticket-level feature underscores the importance of continuous monitoring and adjustment of feature selection strategies to maintain optimal model performance across diverse projects and over time. Potentially, given that TA-JIT outperforms JIT by 20% in Precision, a team reviewing about 400 commits in a two-week sprint can expect to save about 80 false-positive alerts; this could translate in saving about 35-man-hours per two-week sprint.

Regarding threats to validity [18], the main limitation is the evaluation on only two open-source projects, without cross-project testing, which constrains external validity. The choice to restrict the dataset to two projects was intentional: to support internal and construct validity. The main limitation of the TA-JIT approach, as with any approach based on ML, where garbage in results in garbage out, is that it requires high-quality ticket information; the ApacheJIT repository from which we gather the data contains only two (high-quality) projects. In the future we plan to extend the dataset to industrial context since we expect that a more rigorous process would lead to high quality data which in turn would benefit the prediction models.

References

1. Demsar, J.: Statistical comparisons of classifiers over multiple data sets. J. Mach. Learn. Res. **7**, 1–30 (2006). https://jmlr.org/papers/v7/demsar06a.html
2. Falessi, D., Ahluwalia, A., Penta, M.D.: The impact of dormant defects on defect prediction: a study of 19 apache projects. ACM Trans. Softw. Eng. Methodol. **31**(1), 4:1–4:26 (2022). https://doi.org/10.1145/3467895
3. Falessi, D., Laureani, S.M., Çarka, J., Esposito, M., da Costa, D.A.: Enhancing the defectiveness prediction of methods and classes via JIT. Empir. Softw. Eng. **28**(2), 37 (2023). https://doi.org/10.1007/S10664-022-10261-Z
4. Fu, W., Menzies, T., Shen, X.: Tuning for software analytics: is it really necessary? Inf. Softw. Technol. **76**, 135–146 (2016). https://doi.org/10.1016/J.INFSOF.2016.04.017
5. Kamei, Y., Shihab, E.: Defect prediction: accomplishments and future challenges. In: Leaders of Tomorrow Symposium: Future of Software Engineering, FOSE@SANER 2016, Osaka, Japan, March 14, 2016. pp. 33–45. IEEE Computer Society (2016). https://doi.org/10.1109/SANER.2016.56
6. Kamei, Y., et al.: A large-scale empirical study of just-in-time quality assurance. IEEE Trans. Software Eng. **39**(6), 757–773 (2013). https://doi.org/10.1109/TSE.2012.70
7. Kerby, D.S.: The simple difference formula: an approach to teaching nonparametric correlation. Comprehensive Psychology **3**, 11.IT.3.1 (2014)

8. La Prova, D., Gentili, E., Falessi, D.: Anticipating bugs: ticket-level bug prediction and temporal proximity effects. arXiv preprint arXiv:2506.14290 (2025)
9. Li, Z., Du, Q., Zhang, H., Jing, X., Wu, F.: An empirical study of data sampling techniques for just-in-time software defect prediction. Autom. Softw. Eng. **31**(2), 56 (2024). https://doi.org/10.1007/S10515-024-00455-8
10. McIntosh, S., Kamei, Y.: Are fix-inducing changes a moving target? a longitudinal case study of just-in-time defect prediction. IEEE Trans. Software Eng. **44**(5), 412–428 (2018). https://doi.org/10.1109/TSE.2017.2693980
11. Ozakinci, R., Tarhan, A.: Early software defect prediction: a systematic map and review. J. Syst. Softw. **144**, 216–239 (2018). https://doi.org/10.1016/J.JSS.2018.06.025
12. Patel, H., Adams, B., Hassan, A.E.: Post deployment recycling of machine learning models. Empir. Softw. Eng. **29**(4), 100 (2024). https://doi.org/10.1007/S10664-024-10492-2
13. Song, L., Minku, L.L.: A procedure to continuously evaluate predictive performance of just-in-time software defect prediction models during software development. IEEE Trans. Software Eng. **49**(2), 646–666 (2023). https://doi.org/10.1109/TSE.2022.3158831
14. Tantithamthavorn, C., Hassan, A.E., Matsumoto, K.: The impact of class rebalancing techniques on the performance and interpretation of defect prediction models. IEEE Trans. Software Eng. **46**(11), 1200–1219 (2020). https://doi.org/10.1109/TSE.2018.2876537
15. Tantithamthavorn, C., McIntosh, S., Hassan, A.E., Matsumoto, K.: The impact of automated parameter optimization on defect prediction models. IEEE Trans. Software Eng. **45**(7), 683–711 (2019). https://doi.org/10.1109/TSE.2018.2794977
16. Tomczak, M., Tomczak-Łukaszewska, E.: The need to report effect size estimates revisited. An overview of some recommended measures of effect size. Trends Sport Sci. **21**, 19–25 (01 2014)
17. Wilcoxon, F.: Individual comparisons by ranking methods. In: Breakthroughs in Statistics: Methodology and Distribution, pp. 196–202. Springer (1992)
18. Wohlin, C., Runeson, P., Höst, M., Ohlsson, M.C., Regnell, B., Wesslén, A.: Experimentation in software engineering. 2nd Edn. Springer (2024). https://doi.org/10.1007/978-3-662-69306-3
19. Yu, L., Liu, H.: Feature selection for high-dimensional data: a fast correlation-based filter solution. In: Fawcett, T., Mishra, N. (eds.) Machine Learning, Proceedings of the Twentieth International Conference (ICML 2003), August 21-24, 2003, Washington, pp. 856–863. AAAI Press (2003). http://www.aaai.org/Library/ICML/2003/icml03-111.php
20. Zhao, Y., Damevski, K., Chen, H.: A systematic survey of just-in-time software defect prediction. ACM Comput. Surv. **55**(10), 201:1–201:35 (2023). https://doi.org/10.1145/3567550

How Well Small Language Models Can Be Adapted for Software Maintenance and Refactoring Tasks

Gabija Asvydyte[1]([✉]), Sushant Kumar Pandey[1], and Sivajeet Chand[2]

[1] University of Groningen, Groningen, Netherlands
gabi.asvydyte@gmail.com
[2] Technical University of Munich, Munich, Germany

Abstract. Software maintenance and refactoring can help programmers keep a clean code base. Recently, there has been a growing interest in applying Large Language Models (LLMs) to assist with this task. Their large costs to train and deploy have sparked interest in using Small Language Models (SLMs) instead, especially in resource-constrained environments. To help us understand the capabilities of SLMs (specifically LLMs under 8 billion parameters) in software maintenance and refactoring, we perform a Systematic Literature Review (SLR) with a focus on code refactoring and code smell detection. We searched multiple databases and defined an inclusion/exclusion criterion to help us answer six Research Questions (RQs), which led to 40 papers. We have found that the software refactoring field is not well explored, which includes SLMs. We also found that 19 out of 40 collected literature do not list parameter counts, and SLMs are usually fine-tuned with datasets. Further research revealed that LLMs have longer times to train, higher costs to run and train, and introduce challenges with data privacy. Baseline SLMs usually perform worse than LLMs and achieve lower metrics. However, we can see that this field is evolving. SLMs, due to their lower costs, can be used to continue research in bias and safety when using models and in domain-specific fields.

Keywords: Software engineering · LLM · SLM · Code maintenance · Code refactoring

1 Introduction

Code refactoring is the enhancement of code while keeping its functionality the same and reducing code smells and code bugs [2]. Code smells are an indication that there might be trouble with the code; however, it is not definite [2]. In recent years, programmers have started using LLMs to help refactor code and maintain a cleaner code base. LLMs' parameters have grown in size, and they can complete more tasks. For instance, GPT-2 had 1.5 billion parameters and GPT-3, released less than a year later, had 175 billion. SLMs became a possible

G. Scanniello et al. (Eds.): PROFES 2025, LNCS 16361, pp. 506–515, 2026.
https://doi.org/10.1007/978-3-032-12089-2_36

replacement. However, the number of their parameters is not concrete. Some define them as less than 10 billion [3], others as less than 1 billion [9]. Following a study by Fali Wang et al. [8], who chose 7 billion as their cutoff based on recent literature, we have chosen 8 billion parameters to allow inclusion of slightly larger models.

A clean code base is important for a productive workflow. One of the main ways to do so is by code refactoring, which can reduce code smells and code bugs [2]. There are various studies and surveys that cover refactoring and maintenance tasks using LLMs, some surveys include: [1, 4, 7, 10]. However, these and many other studies focus on LLMs or, otherwise, models with more than 8 billion parameters. On the other hand, SLMs have fewer parameters and can be overall more efficient, but there is no comprehensive survey for these tasks with SLMs. Conducting an SLR can provide a comprehensive overview of the tasks in which SLMs excel and identify areas where their performance remains limited. We hope to close this research gap and contribute to the conversation of how well SLMs compare to LLMs. This paper continues with the SLR methodology in Sect. 2, followed by an analysis of the collected literature in Sect. 3, Sect. 4 includes threats to validity, and finally the future works and conclusion in Sect. 5.

2 Systematic Literature Review

We conducted an SLR following the guidelines proposed by B. Kitchenham and S. Charters [6]. Three steps were taken: first, planning, second, conducting the review, and third, reporting the review. The first stage includes identifying the need for the review, specifying research questions, and developing and evaluating the research process. The second stage includes the selection of primary studies and data extraction. The final third step, reporting the review, includes formatting the main report and evaluating the main report.

2.1 Search Process

The goal of the search query was to find papers for the chosen Software Engineering (SE) task. To do so, various spellings and tenses were included to retrieve more (e.g., for "refactoring" we can have "refactorisation" and "refactor"). The full search queries can be found in Table 1. The databases selected for this SLR are IEEExplore, ACM, WebOfScience, Springer, Scopus, and Google Scholar. Papers were excluded if they were not written in English or were written before 2020-01-01. We chose 2020 as the cut-off to align with the release of GPT-3 and the maturation of transformer-based LLMs, ensuring a focus on research developed after these advances. The papers were further analyzed (beyond the abstract) to see if they met any of the following:

(i) Evaluates or compares SLMs (<8B parameters) and/or LLMs on code refactoring or code smell detection.

(ii) Provides empirical results (metrics, benchmarks, comparisons) on code refactoring or code smell detection.
(iii) Addresses ethical and environmental considerations when deploying LLMs for maintenance or refactoring tasks.

If they met any of the inclusion criteria, the papers were further analyzed to see if conclusions could be drawn about the models used or the sizes of the models.

Table 1. Search queries for chosen SE tasks involving language models

SE Task	Search Query
Code refactoring	(`"language models" OR "small model" OR LLM OR SLM OR "small language models"`) AND (`code refactorisation OR code refactorization OR code refactor OR code refactoring`)
Code smell detection	(`"language models" OR "small model" OR LLM OR SLM OR "small language models"`) AND (`code smell refactor OR code smell detect OR code smell (identification OR identify OR identifying) OR code smell (recognition OR recognise OR recognize OR recognising OR recognizing)`)

To help us understand the current state of SLMs and answer the main question of this paper, "How Well Small Language Models Can Be Adapted for Software Maintenance and Refactoring Tasks", we propose 6 Research Questions (RQ):

RQ1: What Small Language Models are used in the task of software maintenance and refactoring?

RQ1.1: What are the gaps in research for maintenance and refactoring tasks for Small Language Models?

RQ1.2: What fine-tuning techniques have been used with Small Language Models for maintenance and refactoring tasks?

RQ2: Is there a way to replace Large Language Models with Small Language Models?

RQ2.1 What are the trade-offs in using Small Language Models instead of Large Language Models?

RQ2.2 What are the trade-offs in using Large Language Models instead of Small Language Models?

The collection of papers was done throughout April and May 2025 until the 07/07/2025. We picked out 40 papers that met the inclusion/exclusion criteria and gave interesting insights. The papers were evaluated on whether they answered the RQ or not (Yes or No). Some papers received a rating of 0, and thus their results were not included in the Results section, but were kept for consistency's sake. The full list of references and analysis of the SLR and papers (ratings, metadata, and metrics) can be found under this link[1].

3   Results

This section analyzes the collected literature. Each paper is referenced with an ID: CFx or SFx. CF means it was collected using the code refactoring search query; SF means it was collected using the code smell detection search query. Some of the questions were split into two sections: **"Code refactoring"** and **"Code smell detection"**. The respective sections include information that is strictly from papers related to that task.

3.1   RQ1 : What Small Language Models Are Used in the Task of Software Maintenance and Refactoring?

For this question, we have gathered the SLMs along with models for which the parameter count was not listed, used in the collected literature, in a dataset (available on FigShare titled SLMs_and_other_models.pdf). In total, 51 models are included in the table, but 20 of them do not have a clear parameter count due to missing or inconsistent sources. Almost half (19/40) of the collected literature did not list any parameter counts, which limits analysis on model size impact. Developers of the (presumably) larger models also keep their parameter counts hidden, notably the Gemini models. The most referenced SLMs are (at least 4 references): CodeBERT (7 studies), Code-T5 (6 studies), CodeLlama-7B (4 studies), CuBERT (4 studies), GraphCodeBERT (4 studies). The table includes 17 confirmed SLMs and 3 potential SLMs (with parameter ranges).

3.2   RQ1.1 : What Are the Gaps in Research for Maintenance and Refactoring Tasks for Small Language Models?

In this subsection, we discuss the research gaps related to model sizes, focusing on smaller models, for maintenance and refactoring tasks in the collected literature. The programming languages used in each paper (full table on FigShare in document titled SLR_appendix.pdf) have been plotted in Fig. 1. The three top-most popular programming languages are Java, Python, and C++. We can define research in other languages as research gaps.

Code Refactoring: The scaling law [5] states that, generally speaking, the larger the models are, the better the results are achieved. However, some studies (e.g., CF5, CF19) found smaller models outperforming larger ones, challenging this assumption. There is ongoing research into finding the optimal size of models while keeping them accurate. CF2 and CF24 mention the high costs and energy consumption of larger models. Some studies were restricted by the expensive running costs of larger models and had to use smaller models instead (CF5, CF8).

---

[1] https://doi.org/10.6084/m9.figshare.29681093.v2.

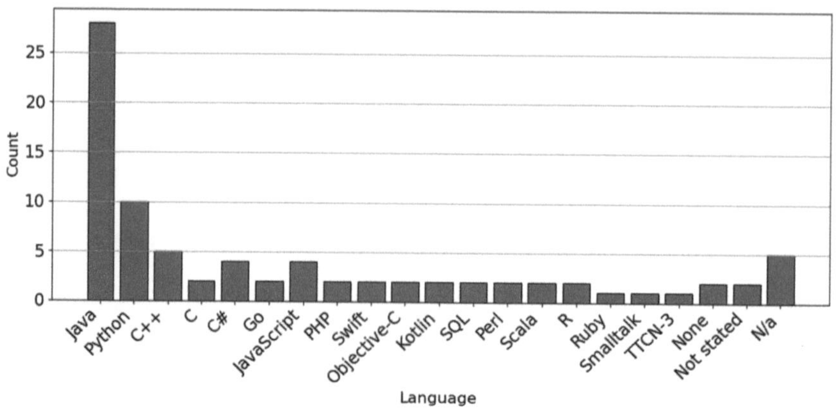

Fig. 1. Count of programming languages across all collected literature

Even when using larger models like GPT-3.5-turbo, code refinement results fall short of industry standards (CF21). Overall, the code refactoring field is under-explored (CF12), but the rising number of publications suggests a promising future for this field.

Code Smell Detection: In the field of code smell detection, researchers bring even more attention, compared to the code refactoring field, to the need for smaller models to use in resource-constrained environments (SF6, CF7). Increasing the model size does not guarantee better results, as performance varies between syntactic and semantic tasks (SF9). Similar to code refactoring research, SF8, SF12, and SF15 were restricted in their research by the large costs of larger models, forcing them to use smaller models, which impacts generalizability. Recent studies (SF6, SF10) argue that the current metrics may not represent the capabilities of models well, failing to consider interpretability, robustness, etc. This shows that future research should investigate optimizing smaller models and improving evaluation metrics.

3.3 RQ1.2 : What Fine-Tuning Techniques Have Been Used with Small Language Models for Maintenance and Refactoring Tasks?

In SF11, the SLMs were fine-tuned on a dataset of code smells, and in CF22, the SLMs were fine-tuned on the MLCQ dataset. In SF15, they say they "convert the code pairs of methods and classes into token sequences, feed them to the pre-trained model, and fine-tune the pre-trained model to detect feature envy and recommend the methods with feature envy to the appropriate classes". SF12 used various Parameter-Efficient Fine-Tuning (PEFT) methods like prompt tuning, prefix tuning, Low-Rank Adaptation (LoRA), and (IA)3. The SF6 study contains a large number of fine-tuning techniques with their definitions, but they do not perform any of the fine-tuning techniques themselves or provide an explicit comparison.

> **RQ1 RQ1.1 RQ1.2 answer summary**
>
> The most referenced SLMs are (at least 4 references): CodeBERT (7 studies), Code-T5 (6 studies), CodeLlama-7B (4 studies), CuBERT (4 studies), GraphCodeBERT (4 studies). Almost half (19/40) of the collected literature did not list any parameter counts. The code refactoring field using SLMs/LLMs is underexplored. There is a need for better evaluation metrics that better represent the capabilities of models. There are some studies that were restricted by the expensive running costs of larger models and had to use smaller models instead, which impacts generalizability. Overall, there is a very small number of studies (8/40) that have performed fine-tuning on SLMs. This can be categorized as a research gap. They were often used out-of-the-box, or only LLMs were used in studies.

3.4   RQ2 : Is There a Way to Replace Large Language Models with Small Language Models?

Code Refactoring: The CF5 study suggests that the larger size of ChatGPT helps get a better EM score - other studies show that SLMs can match or even outperform LLMs in refactoring tasks (CF2, CF15, CF19, CF20). The researchers in CF15 say that the training purpose of a model may have greater influence than the size of the model, as GPT-3.5 performed similarly to much smaller models. CF19 found that closed-source models outperform open-source models irrespective of size, and opencodeinterpreter-ds-6.7B (openci-ds-6.7B) surpassed models with 34B parameters in few-shot scenarios. This challenges the idea that larger always means better. In CF14, medium-sized models sometimes performed the best; thus, the size of the models was not a determining factor. CF13 showed that high-quality data can compensate for smaller parameter counts. Larger models can also incur massive energy and compute costs (CF24); SOTA models saw a factor of 300,000 increase in computational costs between 2012 and 2018. According to CF20, the larger models are more computationally expensive, but the transforms synthesized by all models perform equally well, suggesting a compute/inference budget tradeoff. Scalability and deployment favor SLMs (CF2, CF13), and CF24 emphasizes LLMs' sustainability challenges due to energy demands.

Code Smell Detection: SLMs can compete or outperform in certain tasks (SF1, SF12, CF22). In SF1, the CodeT5-small model outperforms the CodeT5-base, while in SF12, SLMs had comparable performance in detecting complex conditional and complex method smells, and GraphCodeBERT significantly outperformed all other models, including LLMs. LLMs showed superiority in detecting feature envy. Fine-tuning and PEFT help SLMs catch up to LLMs (SF10,

SF12). A study referenced in SF10 was able to reduce the number of parameters from 13B to 25M while keeping metrics consistent. Energy, memory, and cost also strongly favor SLMs (SF6, SF8, SF12), as training a 176 billion parameter model like BLOOM on a 1.5 TB dataset is estimated to consume 1,082,880 GPU hours. Quantization (as shown in SF8) reduces memory usage with minimal performance difference. SLMs exhibit substantially lower peak GPU memory consumption compared to LLMs, according to the results shown in SF12. Nonetheless, LLMs show an advantage in complex reasoning (SF9, SF10, SF8). For example, GPT-4 identified nearly double the vulnerabilities than GPT3.5 (SF10) and consistently outperformed the smaller Llama models (SF8). But still, GPT-4's performance was considered poor in the wide scheme of things.

3.5   RQ2.1 : What Are the Trade-Offs in Using Small Language Models Instead of Large Language Models?

Code Refactoring: Some studies (CF9, CF11, CF17) mention that even LLMs do not perform code refactoring to a satisfactory extent. The biggest concern is that because of the smaller parameter count, smaller models may lack in understanding a full code base and making useful code refactoring suggestions. Smaller models also understand fewer tokens at a time (CF8, CF21), which can lead to hallucinations; however, this is possible in larger models as well (CF13, SF10). Multiple studies that tested models note that smaller models perform worse, achieving lower accuracy (CF13), struggling to recognize style changes and have precision issues (CF2), getting lower EM scores (CF5), and having lower overall performance (CF20, CF21). CF2 suggests that the reason for that is that SLMs can sometimes rely on code comments for summarizing code. CF24 shows that smaller task-specific models are trained, on average, on 1.3 languages while larger task-agnostic models are trained, on average, on 3.6 - this makes general applicability more challenging.

Code Smell Detection: SF8 shows that even with few-shot prompting, smaller models achieved much lower results than GPT-4. SF9 and SF10 also show that baseline models will usually underperform larger models at a certain threshold. As shown in SF12, for the future envy smell, LLMs substantially outperformed SLMs. The results found in these papers follow the scaling law.

3.6   RQ2.2 : What Are the Trade-Offs in Using Large Language Models Instead of Small Language Models?

Code Refactoring: Larger models are more challenging to adapt in resource-constrained environments (CF2). They come with higher performance costs as shown in several studies (CF5, CF8, CF13, CF19, CF20, CF21, CF24). In CF20, they show that using smaller models (Llama 3.1 8B) is also possible to achieve good results without using as much energy as the larger models (Llama 3.1 70B and 405B). GPT-3.5-turbo was used in the CF16 study, and processing the data took a "considerable amount of time". CF24 found that 42% of their collected studies do not show hardware details and 50% do not provide training times, making it challenging to understand the real costs of using the models. Nonetheless, they found that larger models have higher energy costs, longer training times, and higher financial costs. Besides the high costs, larger datasets, used by larger models, introduce data ownership, privacy concerns, and ethical concerns (CF5, CF21). Both SLMs and LLMs struggle with longer code contexts.

Code Smell Detection: LLMs have high costs and computational complexity (SF6, SF9, SF10). The researchers of SF8, SF12, and CF4 had to use smaller models because of their lower costs. Full fine-tuning on LLMs is unfeasible because of their high computational complexity and financial costs (SF12). Collecting large amounts of data to train large models can lead to privacy issues and ethical concerns about where the data came from (SF6, SF9, CF7). There is a higher chance of poison in the data, leading to incorrect or harmful results (SF10). Understanding internal decision making and causes for hallucinations is more difficult with larger models because of their, so to speak, "black box" (SF10, CF13).

> **RQ2 RQ2.1 RQ2.2 answer summary**
>
> SLMs can outperform or match LLMs in refactoring tasks. Model sizes do not always mean best performance. Fine-tuning and PEFT help SLMs catch up to LLMs. Scalability and deployment favor SLMs. LLMs consume far more energy, but they show an advantage in complex reasoning. SLMs can, at times, make extra suggestions because they are not capable of taking in as many tokens as LLMs at a time. SLMs tend to be trained on fewer languages (1.3 instead of 3.6 in larger task-agnostic models). If SLMs are not properly fine-tuned, LLMs will tend to outperform SLMs in the detection of many code smells. LLMs have higher computational costs, longer training times, and higher financial costs. Obtaining large amounts of data to train LLMs on can introduce privacy issues and ethical concerns. Full fine-tuning on LLMs is unfeasible because of their high computational complexity and financial costs.

4   Threats to Validity

This study is subject to several threats to validity. **Internal validity** may be affected by the limited comparison of model performance metrics across studies. While we compiled a list of all metrics used (available in Appendix B via FigShare), our analysis emphasized general trends over specific quantitative results to reduce interpretation bias. This may limit the depth of performance-based conclusions. **Construct validity** is threatened by the relatively small number of fine-tuning techniques identified for SLMs, which restricts our ability to fully characterize fine-tuning practices in software maintenance and refactoring tasks. **External validity** is limited by the scope of our review, which focused primarily on SLMs and a narrow subset of SE tasks. As such, the findings may not generalize to other SE tasks or LLMs without further investigation. **Conclusion validity** may also be impacted due to the heterogeneity of datasets, evaluation metrics, and experimental setups across the studies reviewed, making direct comparisons challenging.

5   Conclusions

In this paper, we have explored the question "How Well Small Language Models Can Be Adapted for Software Maintenance and Refactoring Tasks" by performing an SLR of the current literature, specifically for code refactoring and code smell detection. Our analysis has revealed that SLMs have the ability to outperform LLMs when using properly selected fine-tuning techniques. This can be especially important in research about bias and safety when using models and in specific coding tasks since LLMs are usually general-purpose. Research focusing on improving SLMs with various resource-efficient techniques, such as PEFT and LoRA, can be beneficial for the environment. In practice, we can see that SLMs production should be prioritized because of their lower costs and good performance. This is especially the case in smaller organizations where inference costs, privacy, and latency matter more than cutting-edge performance. However, this field still has various research gaps, including the lack of understanding in what is the optimal size of models that reduces costs yet keeps up with metrics, the lack of understanding of how we can reduce model sizes, the lack of proper evaluation metrics that can properly represent the capabilities of models, and the code refactoring field itself being underexplored. The understanding surrounding LLMs and SLMs is getting more extensive. Seeing the large amount of literature we collected from the year 2025, it is fair to say that this field is evolving. SLMs have the potential to assist programmers in software maintenance and refactoring tasks in the near future.

Future work includes expanding research to all other SE tasks and providing a concrete comparison of SLMs vs LLMs on the most common metrics.

References

1. Fan, A., et al.: Large language models for software engineering: survey and open problems. In: 2023 IEEE/ACM International Conference on Software Engineering: Future of Software Engineering (ICSE-FoSE), pp. 31–53
2. Fowler, M.: Refactoring: Improving the Design of Existing Code. Addison-Wesley Professional, Boston (2018)
3. Fu, Y., Peng, H., Ou, L., Sabharwal, A., Khot, T.: Specializing smaller language models towards multi-step reasoning. In: International Conference on Machine Learning, pp. 10421–10430. PMLR (2023)
4. Hou, X., et al.: Large language models for software engineering: a systematic literature review. ACM Trans. Softw. Eng. Methodol. **33**(8), 1–79 (2024)
5. Kaplan, J., et al.: Scaling laws for neural language models. arXiv preprint arXiv:2001.08361 (2020)

6. Kitchenham, B., Charters, S.: Guidelines for performing systematic literature reviews in software engineering **2** (2007)
7. Liu, J., et al.: Large language model-based agents for software engineering: a survey. arXiv preprint arXiv:2409.02977 (2024)
8. Wang, F., et al.: A comprehensive survey of small language models in the era of large language models: techniques, enhancements, applications, collaboration with LLMs, and trustworthiness. arXiv preprint arXiv:2411.03350 (2024)
9. Zhang, B., et al.: A comprehensive evaluation of parameter-efficient fine-tuning on method-level code smell detection. arXiv preprint arXiv:2412.13801 (2024)
10. Zheng, Z., et al.: Towards an understanding of large language models in software engineering tasks. Empir. Softw. Eng. **30**(2), 50 (2025)

Cost of Artificial Intelligence: A Survey in Finnish Software Companies

Antti Klemetti[1]([envelope]) [ORCID], Anssi Sorvisto[2], Mikko Raatikainen[1] [ORCID], and Jukka K. Nurminen[1] [ORCID]

[1] University of Helsinki, Helsinki, Finland
{antti.klemetti,mikko.raatikainen,jukka.k.nurminen}@helsinki.fi
[2] University of Jyväskylä, Jyväskylä, Finland
anssi.j.sorvisto@student.jyu.fi

Abstract. Artificial intelligence (AI), particularly deep learning (DL) and large language models (LLMs), has rapidly gained prominence across industries. Training and serving deep neural networks (DNNs)—the core of LLMs—requires substantial computational resources, often provided by costly specialized hardware such as Graphics Processing Units. Cloud computing enables flexible access to such hardware but raises cost concerns. This study reports the significance of AI-related costs for Finnish software companies, based on a thematic subset of the 2025 Finnish Software Industry Survey. Of the 411 respondents, 64 reported developing or fine-tuning AI models, with 61% considering AI costs a significant or very significant concern. Respondents estimated AI-related expenses to rise from under 10% of cloud or hardware costs in 2025 to 10–25% in 2026 and 25–50% by 2028. These findings indicate that AI is expected to become a major driver of infrastructure costs, highlighting the importance of cost-efficient adoption strategies.

Keywords: Cost-efficiency · Infrastructure costs · Cloud computing · Artificial Intelligence · Deep Learning · Survey

1 Introduction

Artificial intelligence (AI) and its subfield deep learning (DL) have become prominent part of software systems across industries, driven by advances in natural language processing (NLP) with large language models (LLMs) such as GPT [1] and LLaMa [15]. There are early indications that AI and LLMs could significantly reduce the need for human labor and reshape society [3,4]. Deep neural networks (DNNs), the core technology behind LLMs, had already transformed computer vision [12,14] and have been applied to domains such as genomics [18], materials science [17], and climate science [5].

DNNs require substantial computational power, with industrial-scale models needing over an order of magnitude more resources than linear models [7]. Computer vision DNNs can have millions of parameters [12], while recent LLMs

G. Scanniello et al. (Eds.): PROFES 2025, LNCS 16361, pp. 516–524, 2026.
https://doi.org/10.1007/978-3-032-12089-2_37

contain billions [15], and sizes continue to grow. DNN parameters are stored as numeric matrices whose size often exceeds the on-chip memory capacity of general-purpose processors. Off-chip memory access consumes orders of magnitude more energy than on-chip access [9] and dominates execution time due to the memory wall of the prevailing Von Neumann computer architecture [16]. To address these limitations, specialized hardware for matrix operations is required.

Graphics Processing Units (GPUs), and other accelerators, are well-suited for such parallel computations and are commonly accessed through cloud providers (e.g., Amazon, Google, Microsoft). However, using cloud GPUs is typically at least an order of magnitude more expensive than using general-purpose processors. In fact, the most compute-intensive workloads in cloud data centers are related to DL [10]. Using a cloud allows fast adoption of new types of specialized hardware, e.g., new more powerful GPUs, instead of constantly buying the latest hardware. In addition, cloud offers elastic scaling of the computational resources [2].

Given these trends, infrastructure and especially computing costs in software systems are, or will become, a major expense for AI-focused companies. This study examines how prevalent AI model development is among Finnish software companies and whether AI-related costs are a significant concern. We also investigate the role of cloud services versus in-house hardware in shaping cost perceptions.

To address these questions, we included and report AI cost-related items in the 2025 Finnish Software Industry Survey[1], which received 411 responses. Of these, 64 companies reported developing or fine-tuning AI models. Key findings include:

- 61% view AI costs as a significant or very significant concern.
- AI-related costs are expected to rise from less than 10% of cloud or hardware spending in 2025 to 25–50% by 2028.

2 Research Questions and Methodology

2.1 Research Questions

Our research problem addresses the relevancy of AI costs in Finnish software companies. Specifically, our goal was to answer the following research questions (RQ):

RQ1: How significant topic the cost of AI is for Finnish software companies?

RQ2: How Finnish software companies are expecting the costs of AI to develop in the future?

RQ3: How does the use of cloud infrastructure versus own or customer-provided hardware influence the perception of AI-related costs in Finnish software companies?

---

[1] https://sites.app.jyu.fi/softwareindustrysurvey/en.

2.2   Method

The data were collected as part of the recurring Finnish Software Industry Survey, with AI as a focus area in 2025. The survey, promoted in collaboration with the Confederation of Finnish Industries (EK) and Software Finland, was mailed to 8,948 Finnish companies listed by Statistics Finland[2] with annual revenue exceeding 100,000 euros. Recipients received a cover letter and reminder card directing them to an online questionnaire.

Companies were selected using industry codes relevant to software activities: **TOL 58210**: *Publishing of computer games*, **TOL 62**: *Computer programming, consultancy, and related activities*, **TOL 70220**: *Other management consultancy activities*. While not all were formally classified as software firms, the materials targeted the software sector, and responses were accepted only from companies self-identifying as having significant software-related operations or employing software developers. This also included firms from other industries (e.g., mechanical engineering or chemistry) developing software as part of their core business. All such respondents were classified as software companies for this study.

A total of 411 companies responded, a rate consistent with previous editions of the survey. We included the following background questions on AI adoption to filter responses.

SQ1: Are you developing or using AI in your company? (1) We do not use or develop AI in any form (2) We use off-the-shelf AI products in product development or other business activities (3) We are fine-tuning AI models developed by others (4) We are developing our own AI models (5) Don't know (6) Other, what?

SQ2: Where are the AI models you are developing trained or run(executed)? (1) In a self-paid cloud service: Trained (2) In a self-paid cloud service: Run (3) In a customer-paid cloud service: Trained (4) In a customer-paid cloud service: Run (5) In own equipment: Trained (6) In own equipment: Run (7) In customer's equipment: Trained (8) In customer's equipment: Run (9) Don't know: Trained (10) Don't know: Run (11) Somewhere else, where?: Trained (12) Somewhere else, where?: Run

Concerning the actual costs of AI, we asked the following questions:

SQ3: The cost of using or developing AI is a significant topic for our company (1) Strongly disagree (2) Disagree (3) Neutral (4) Agree (5) Strongly agree (6) Don't know

SQ4: What percentage of your cloud service or hardware costs is currently related to AI models, and what do you estimate the percentage will be in one year and in three years? (1) 0% (2) Less than 10% (3) 10–25% (4) 25–50% (5) More than 50% (1) Don't know

---

[2] https://stat.fi/en.

Most responses included a business identifier, enabling determination of company size by employee count; this was not possible for respondents without an identifier.

3   Results

This section presents AI cost-related findings from the 2025 Finnish Software Industry Survey. Based on SQ1 responses, we excluded companies not developing or fine-tuning AI models (90 remaining), those without a business identifier (9), and single-employee companies, which in Finland typically operate as individual consultants (19). After filtering, 64 relevant responses remained from the original 411. Their employee counts are shown in Fig. 1.

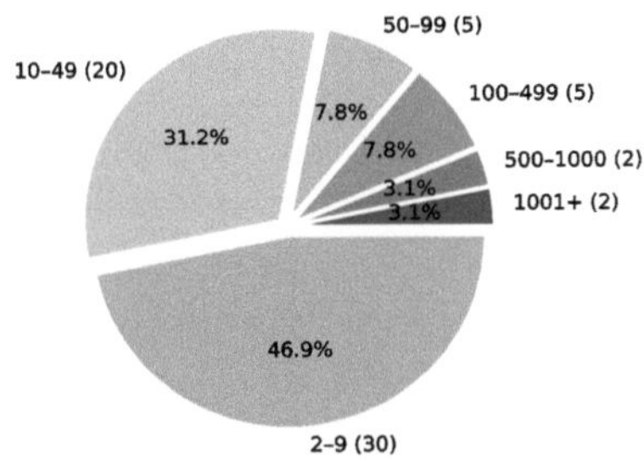

Fig. 1. AI developers by employee count. Number of companies in parentheses.

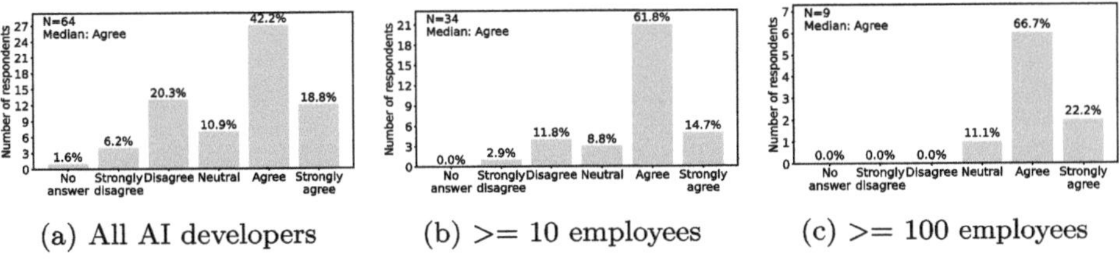

(a) All AI developers   (b) >= 10 employees   (c) >= 100 employees

Fig. 2. Significance of AI cost for companies developing or finetuning AI models

The following subsections analyze the data by grouping respondents according to SQ2, which distinguishes between cloud infrastructure and own or customer hardware. These categories are not mutually exclusive; some companies develop models on their own hardware but deploy them in the cloud.

3.1 SQ3: The Cost of Using or Developing AI is a Significant Topic for Our Company

Figure 2a presents responses from companies developing or fine-tuning AI models. As no significant differences were found between those using cloud infrastructure and those using own or customers' hardware, separate figures are not shown.

Cost relevance increases with company size: only 14.7% of firms with at least 10 employees disagreed with the statement (Fig. 2b). Among companies with at least 100 employees, 8 of 9 agreed or strongly agreed that AI costs are significant, and one was neutral (Fig. 2c).

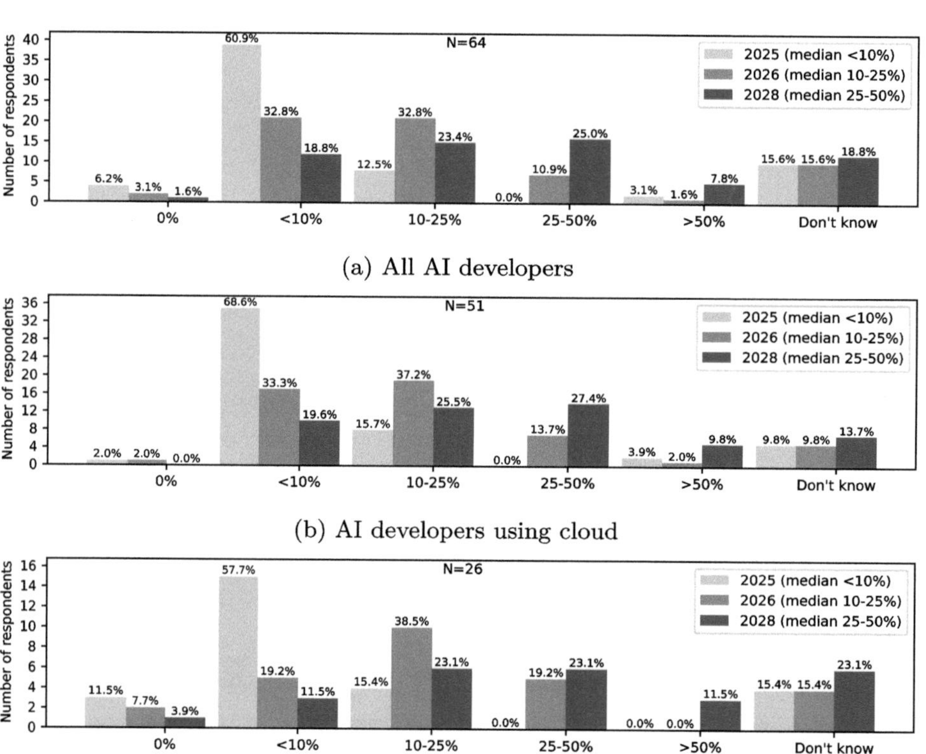

(a) All AI developers

(b) AI developers using cloud

(c) AI developers using own or customer's hardware

Fig. 3. AI's share of hardware or cloud costs

3.2 SQ4: What Percentage of Your Cloud Service or Hardware Costs is Currently Related to AI Models, and What Do You Estimate the Percentage Will Be in One Year and in Three Years?

Figure 3 presents AI cost shares for all AI developers (Figs. 3a–3c). The survey was conducted in 2025, so projections for "one year" and "three years" correspond to 2026 and 2028, respectively; explicit years are used in the figures for clarity. Across all infrastructure types, respondents anticipate rising AI-related costs toward 2026 and 2028, with cloud users expecting larger increases. No significant differences were found between cases where the respondent or their customer pays for the infrastructure, so results are not subdivided further.

In Fig. 3a, costs rise from 2025 to 2026, with "<10%" and "10–25%" each receiving 32.8% of responses in 2026; the median[3] falls in "10–25%" as it is central in the ordered distribution.

4   Discussion

In this section, we present the answers to our research questions and take a critical view on the validity of our research.

4.1 Answer to RQ1: How Significant Topic the Cost of AI is for Finnish Software Companies?

Among AI-developing companies, 61% viewed AI costs as a significant concern, while 27% disagreed. None of the firms with 100+ employees expressed disagreement (Fig. 2c). We attribute this to rising AI and DL costs with business scale, driven by larger datasets, more frequent retraining to address concept drift [13], and increased inference demand. Although Finnish firms operate on a smaller scale than global leaders such as Meta [7], similar trends are likely as they grow.

4.2 Answer to RQ2: How Finnish Software Companies are Expecting the Costs of AI to Develop in the Future?

In 2025, AI accounted for less than 10% of total cloud or hardware costs among companies developing or fine-tuning AI models. This share is projected to rise to 10–25% in 2026 and 25–50% by 2028 (Fig. 3).

4.3 Answer to RQ3: How Does the use of Cloud Infrastructure Versus Own or Customer-Provided Hardware Influence the Perception of AI-Related Costs in Finnish Software Companies?

Companies developing AI models in the cloud show greater confidence in projecting rising costs through 2026 and 2028 (Fig. 3b), whereas those using their own

---

[3] The median here refers to the middlemost response category when ordered by increasing AI cost share.

or customers' hardware express more uncertainty (Fig. 3c). While both groups anticipate increases, 25% of non-cloud users versus 18% of cloud users report not knowing their 2028 AI-related costs, suggesting that cloud usage may provide more predictable cost structures.

4.4 Threats to Validity

While most AI-developing companies in Finland view AI costs as significant and expect increases within three years, survey design limitations affect interpretation. SQ1 did not distinguish between model types, despite DL models often being far costlier than linear ones [7]. The broad industry scope limited cost-specific questions, and some executive-level respondents may have lacked detailed technical insight.

API-based LLM usage (e.g., Claude[4], GPT[5]) billed per token was not explicitly captured, preventing separation of in-house model development from external API consumption.

The survey reached 8948 companies, with 411 responses (4.6%), including 64 AI-developing firms. The small, geographically limited sample and possible self-selection bias constrain generalizability. The Finnish software industry is predominantly B2B, lacking global-scale B2C tech giants where inference costs are often more critical due to the large number of customers they serve.

Out of AI-developing companies, 61% viewed AI costs as significant or very significant; with $n = 64$, the 95% confidence interval is $\pm 11.9\,\%$ (49.1%–72.9%), indicating a clear trend but limited precision.

These results offer insight into Finnish firms' perceptions of AI costs, but broader generalization should be made cautiously.

4.5 Practical Approaches to Cost-Efficient AI

This study examined AI-related costs based on the 2025 Finnish Software Industry Survey. While cost-control measures were not addressed, future surveys could provide valuable insights into such practices. Our recent systematic literature review [11] outlines established methods for reducing DL costs, including model compression (pruning, quantization [6], knowledge distillation [8]) and optimizing the use of suitable hardware accelerators such as GPUs, Tensor Processing Units (TPUs), or custom Application-Specific Integrated Circuits (ASICs).

5 Conclusion

This study integrated AI cost-related questions into the 2025 Finnish Software Industry Survey and analyzed the responses. Of the 411 respondents, 64 reported developing or fine-tuning AI models, with 61% identifying AI-related costs as a

---

[4] https://docs.anthropic.com/en/docs/about-claude/models/all-models.
[5] https://platform.openai.com/docs/pricing.

significant or very significant concern. Respondents projected a rise in AI-related expenses from under 10% of cloud or hardware budgets in 2025 to 10–25% in 2026 and 25–50% by 2028. These results indicate growing awareness of the financial impact of AI development, particularly in DL, one of the most resource-intensive AI domains.

Future research should incorporate more detailed technical questions, distinguishing between DL and other ML approaches, and explicitly address service-based AI usage such as LLM APIs. A more targeted approach—including qualitative methods and technically oriented respondents rather than solely executives—would enable deeper analysis of technical and cost-related factors.

Disclosure of Interests. The authors have no competing interests to declare that are relevant to the content of this article.

References

1. AI, O.: GPT-4 Technical Report (2023). https://arxiv.org/abs/2303.08774
2. Armbrust, M., et al.: A view of cloud computing. Commun. ACM **53**(4), 50–58 (2010)
3. Brynjolfsson, E., Li, D., Raymond, L.: Generative AI at Work. Q. J. Econ. (2025)
4. Eloundou, T., Manning, S., Mishkin, P., Rock, D.: GPTs are GPTs: labor market impact potential of LLMs. Science **384**(6702), 1306–1308 (2024)
5. Ham, Y.G., Kim, J.H., Luo, J.J.: Deep learning for multi-year ENSO forecasts. Nature **573**, 568–572 (2019)
6. Han, S., Mao, H., Dally, W.J.: Deep compression: compressing deep neural networks with pruning, trained quantization and Huffman coding (2016). http://arxiv.org/abs/1510.00149
7. Hazelwood, K., et al.: Applied machine learning at facebook: a datacenter infrastructure perspective. In: IEEE International Symposium on High Performance Computer Architecture (HPCA), pp. 620–629 (2018)
8. Hinton, G., Vinyals, O., Dean, J.: Distilling the Knowledge in a Neural Network. Technical report (2015). https://arxiv.org/abs/1503.02531
9. Horowitz, M.: 1.1 Computing's energy problem (and what we can do about it). In: IEEE International Solid-State Circuits Conference Digest of Technical Papers (ISSCC), pp. 10–14 (2014)
10. Jouppi, N., et al.: In-datacenter performance analysis of a tensor processing unit. In: Proceedings of the 44th Annual International Symposium on Computer Architecture, ser. ISCA 17. New York, NY, USA: Association for Computing Machinery, pp. 1–12 (2017)
11. Klemetti, A., Raatikainen, M., Myllyaho, L., Mikkonen, T., Nurminen, J.K.: Systematic literature review on cost-efficient deep learning. IEEE Access **11**, 90158–90180 (2023)
12. Krizhevsky, A., Sutskever, I., Hinton, G.E.: ImageNet classification with deep convolutional neural networks. In: Advances in Neural Information Processing Systems, vol. 25 (2012). https://proceedings.neurips.cc/paper/2012/hash/c399862d3b9d6b76c8436e924a68c45b-Abstract.html
13. Lu, J., et al.: Learning under concept drift: a review. IEEE Trans. Knowl. Data Eng. **31**(12), 2346–2363 (2019)

14. Redmon, J., Divvala, S., Girshick, R., Farhadi, A.: You only look once: unified, real-time object detection. In: 2016 IEEE Conference on Computer Vision and Pattern Recognition (CVPR), pp. 779–788 (2016)
15. Touvron, H., et al.: LLaMA: open and efficient foundation language models (2023). http://arxiv.org/abs/2302.13971
16. Wulf, W.A., McKee, S.A.: Hitting the memory wall: implications of the obvious. ACM SIGARCH Comput. Archit. News **23**(1), 20–24 (1995)
17. Xie, T., Grossman, J.C.: Crystal graph convolutional neural networks for an accurate and interpretable prediction of material properties. Phys. Rev. Lett. **120**(14) (2018)
18. Zhou, J., Troyanskaya, O.G.: Predicting effects of noncoding variants with deep learning-based sequence model. Nat. Methods **12**, 931–934 (2015)

Exploring the Performance of ML Model Size for Classification in Relation to Energy Consumption

Andreas Bexell[1,2]([✉]), Lo Gullstrand Heander[1], Emma Söderberg[1], Sigrid Eldh[2,3,4], and Per Runeson[1]

[1] Lund University, Lund, Sweden
`{andreas.bexell,lo.heander,emma.soderberg,per.runeson}@cs.lth.se`
[2] Ericsson AB, Stockholm, Sweden
`{andreas.bexell,sigrid.eldh}@ericsson.com`
[3] Mälardalen University, Västerås, Sweden
[4] Carleton University, Ottawa, Canada

Abstract. The use of large language models (LLMs) is being explored for a multitude of tasks in software engineering (SE), ranging from code generation to bug report assignment. Although LLMs provide impressive results, they require more time and energy than some other machine learning models. For some tasks, simpler models may be more sustainable than LLMs. In this paper, we construct natural language classifiers of different complexity for a use case in the SE domain: commit message classification. We compare the performance of each model with the state-of-the-art with regard to energy consumption for training and inference. We find that simpler models based on Naïve Bayes and LSTM perform similarly to LLMs, while using a fraction of the energy, suggesting that choosing a small model can lead to significant reduction in power usage without compromising performance.

Replication package: https://doi.org/10.5281/zenodo.15641782.

Keywords: software engineering · natural language processing · commit message classification · large language models · energy consumption

1   Introduction

The use of Large Language Models (LLMs) has gained broad adoption, especially for natural language processing (NLP) tasks. In the software engineering (SE) context, we see NLP classifiers that provide automation throughout the software development pipeline, e.g., for toolchain optimization [21], test selection [10], issue report classification [11,12], and analysis of code review comments [14].

However, LLMs are associated with high energy consumption and expensive hardware requirements [3]. When choosing which machine learning (ML) model

G. Scanniello et al. (Eds.): PROFES 2025, LNCS 16361, pp. 525–532, 2026.
https://doi.org/10.1007/978-3-032-12089-2_38

to use, it is easy to assume that LLMs will compensate for their energy consumption with good performance, but is this always the case? Studies focused on models for NLP tasks in the SE domain (e.g., [11,12,14]) typically focus on performance in isolation and leave out concerns such as energy consumption. To our knowledge, only one study by Rigutini et al. [16], set in a legal context, examines both model performance and energy consumption. We are unaware of similar studies in the SE context.

In this paper, we seek to provide initial insight into how to balance performance and energy consumption when selecting models for classification in the SE context. We focus our investigation on the performance-to-energy ratio of a selection of ML models for an NLP classification task in the SE context; commit message classification. Our objective is to provide an answer to the research question *What is the performance-to-energy ratio for different ML model sizes for commit message classification?*. To this end, we select five ML models of different sizes (three LLM variants and two smaller models, LSTM and Naïve Bayes), and we train and evaluate these models using data sets composed of commit messages from three selected open-source projects. Our models perform similarly to previous state-of-the-art [9].

Our results indicate no significant differences in performance between the larger and smaller ML models, but we do find a significant difference in energy consumption, resulting in a much higher performance-to-energy ratio for the smaller models.

2   Method

Data Sets We collect tagged commit messages from the open source projects Angular[1], Vue[2] and Vuejs[3]. We selected these projects because the contribution guidelines of these projects [2,19] dictate that commit messages must have a prefixed tag describing their type. The tag is selected by the author of a commit. Angular defines 7 base tags. The tag taxonomy is extended in the Vue and Vuejs projects, where developers are allowed to use "Other prefixes [...] up to your discretion" [19]. The Vuejs project does not provide definitions of extended types, but provides some examples of their use. The three projects are written in JavaScript and contain in total 43k commits tagged by the commit author. The commit messages from the three projects are randomly divided into a 80% training portion and a 20% test portion kept isolated during training.

Classification We employ the modified Swanson classes used by Gharbi et al. [7] and Sarwar et al. [17] and add the "Not Sure" class inspired by Hassan et al. [8] and Fu et al. [6]. The 1st and 2nd authors mapped the tags to classes by reading example commit messages for each tag, comparing them with class definitions, and discussing until they reached interpretative convergence (see Table 1).

---

[1] https://github.com/angular/angular/.
[2] https://github.com/vuejs/vue/.
[3] https://github.com/vuejs/core/.

Table 1. The classification scheme used in automated classification of the open data sets. Each tag is mapped to one of the Modified Swanson classes as defined by Gharbi et al. [7] or to "Not sure".

Class	Commit Tag
Adaptive	`feat(ure)`
Corrective	`fix, bug`
Perfective	`refact(or), build, chore, test, ci, perf, release, style, types, workflow, clean, restructure, polish`
Not Sure	`doc, revert, wip, merge, dx, example, (... everything else)`

The balance ratio (the size of the smallest class divided by the size of the largest class) for the training and test data sets is 0.20.

Model Selection and Training. We used cross-entropy-loss as the loss function during training of all models. To compensate for the uneven balance between classes, the loss function is given the inverse relative frequency of the classes as weights [15].

To sample different sizes of LLMs, we select the following models: DistilBERT (67 million parameters)[4], Microsoft Phi-3 Mini 4K (3.8 billion parameters) [1], and Meta Llama 3 8B (8 billion parameters)[5]. All LLMs are used out-of-the-box with their original pre-training and without fine-tuning[6]. On top of the language pre-training, Microsoft Phi-3 Mini 4K is delivered instruct-trained by the vendor [1]. Since we classify the commits based only on the human-language text in the commit message, and not any part of the source code, we use generic language models rather than models, e.g. Codestral or Qwen2.5-Coder, trained specifically for source code.

We employ the approach used for classification tasks within the Huggingface source code for Llama 3 [5]: to replace the token generation layer with a custom classification head (see Figure 1) using the latent representation of the final LLM layer to classify commit messages. Creating a classification layer in this way has been shown to give

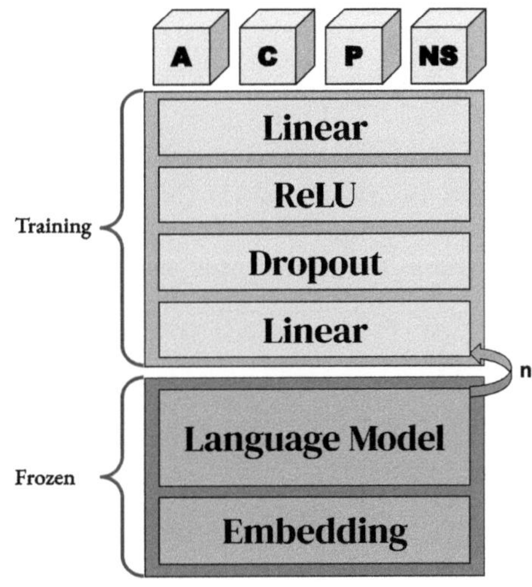

Fig. 1. Network architecture of the complete classifier and language model complex. Top linear layer in the classifier reduces the dimensions down to the four classes; **A**daptive, **C**orrective, **P**erfective and **N**ot **S**ure.

---

[4] https://huggingface.co/distilbert/distilbert-base-uncased.

[5] https://huggingface.co/meta-llama/Meta-Llama-3-8B.

[6] Experiments with fine-tuning did not yield better results, but increased training energy use several orders of magnitude.

good performance in cases where precise label prediction is desired from a small set of labels [13,18]. The input to the LLM is the raw commit message, giving the lowest possible memory consumption. This approach gives the highest classification F1 scores and allows comparison of models with or without instruct training, since the model is used only to create an abstract representation of the commit message. Since this method gives the best result for this task, we argue that it best represents the potential of each language model for commit classification and use the results from this architecture.

The classifier layer is built up by a neural network with an input dimension equal to the output dimensions of the latent space of the language model. Internally, the classifier has an initial linear layer with an output dimension of 2048, a ReLU activation layer, and a dropout layer with a factor of 0.2. A final linear layer transforms the hidden 2048 dimensions to the 4 output classes (see Figure 1). We train a classifier layer separately for each LLM. Hyper-parameters such as learning rate, batch size, and optimizer choice are varied. The test portion of the data set is used to pick the best classifier parameters for each LLM, based on the epoch and hyperparameters with the highest F1-score.

To compare LLMs with traditional NLP architectures, we create a Long-Short Term Memory (LSTM) classifier and a Bernoulli Naïve Bayes classifier. To create the LSTM tokenizer, we select all tokens that occur 10 times or more in the entire vocabulary of our training data set. These 4566 tokens are then assigned random 100-dimensional embeddings. The embeddings feed into a bidirectional LSTM-layer that then forwards its output to a classifier layer identical to the one used in the LLM cases, see Figure 1. For the Bernoulli Naïve Bayes classifier, we use the following relation:

$$p(\mathbf{x}|C_k) = \prod_{i=1}^{n} \begin{cases} p_{ki}, & x_i = 1 \\ (1 - p_{ki}), & x_i = 0 \end{cases}$$

Each dictionary word indicates, or counter-indicates, a class. We train the classifier by incremental optimization of the dictionary over the training data set.

Measuring Performance and Energy Consumption. Following the tradition of previous work on commit message classification, we validate the performance of the models based on accuracy (A)[7] and F1 Score[8], according to established practice [9]. We measure the energy consumption of training and inference separately. All models are trained and executed on an NVIDIA A100 GPU. We monitor the power consumption on the GPU over the training time to calculate the energy consumption for training using the relation $e = Pt$. When validating, we measure the energy consumption of the GPU for inference by monitoring the power consumption during the validation time and divide by the size of the validation data set.

---

[7] Accuracy is the ratio of correct classifications. $A = \frac{TP+TN}{TP+FP+FN+TN}$.

[8] F1 score is the harmonic mean of precision and recall. $F1 = 2 \times \frac{P \times R}{P+R}$ where $P = \frac{TP}{TP+FP}$ and $R = \frac{TP}{TP+FN}$.

3   Results

Table 2 presents the models ranked after number of parameters along with performance measurements for the test data set. The sizes of the models range from thousands (10^3) to billions (10^9) of parameters. Despite this, we see only small differences in performance on the test data set: $A \in (0.68, 0.72)$ and $F1 \in (0.64, 0.67)$. The second smallest model has the best F1 score, whereas the second largest model is tied with the smallest model for the worst F1 score. Detailed performance data is presented in the confusion matrices in Figure 2. In summary, we see no clear trend between the size of a language model and its performance in the classifier case. In contrast, we find that the simpler models rival the performance of the LLMs (Fig. 2) (Table 2).

Table 2. The Accuracy and F1 scores for each of the models on the test data set, along with the training and inference energy required. See also Figure 3.

Model	Size	Performance		Energy	
		A	F1	Training	Inference
Bernoulli NB	8.0×10^3	0.68	0.64	5 kJ	0.3 J
LSTM	1.1×10^6	0.72	0.67	10 kJ	1.0 J
DistilBERT	6.7×10^7	0.71	0.66	15 kJ	14 J
Phi-3 mini	3.8×10^9	0.71	0.64	220 kJ	319 J
Llama 3	8.0×10^9	0.72	0.66	260 kJ	384 J

Naïve Bayes

	NS	C	A	P
NS	2899	365	258	459
C	206	1260	215	271
A	88	92	499	98
P	236	264	233	1290

LSTM

	NS	C	A	P
NS	3142	321	146	372
C	241	1320	136	255
A	104	119	433	121
P	246	251	130	1396

DistilBERT

	NS	C	A	P
NS	3240	290	129	322
C	274	1334	129	215
A	139	116	411	111
P	381	261	137	1244

Phi-3 mini

	NS	C	A	P
NS	3458	227	70	226
C	365	1276	98	213
A	182	174	325	96
P	460	280	108	1175

Llama 3

	NS	C	A	P
NS	3389	269	71	252
C	279	1369	82	222
A	146	169	354	108
P	400	318	92	1213

Fig. 2. Confusion matrices for each model on the test data set. The abbreviations NS, C, A, P refer to the classes described further in Table 1. The imbalance between classes is clearly visible, but the models also predict the less represented classes to a high degree. Small and large models give very similar results.

The rightmost part of Table 2 shows the training and inference energy for each of the models. Generally, the more complex the LLM, the more energy is required to train the classification layer ($15 - 260$ kJ compared to $5 - 10$ kJ). DistilBERT stands out in our experiment, by requiring only 50% more energy than the LSTM model despite being ~ 60 times bigger. This might be because

DistilBERT is a very popular model that has been available long enough to become heavily optimized by the ML community. The inference energy required by the simpler models is several orders of magnitude smaller than with the LLMs (ranging from 0.3 J to 384 J); the larger the LLM, the more energy it requires for inference (Fig. 3).

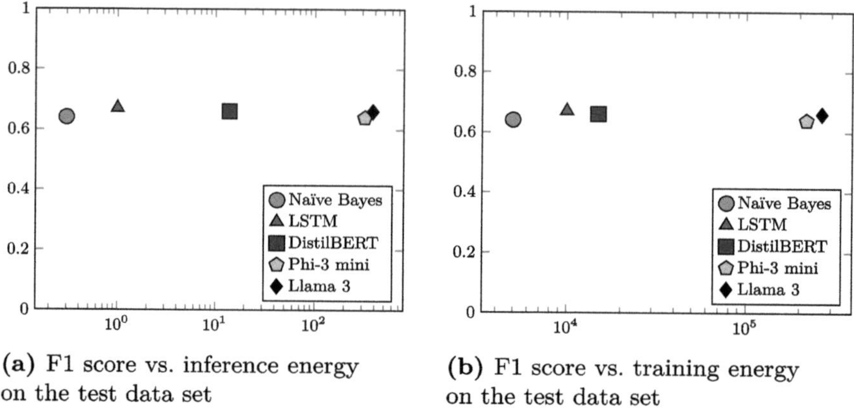

(a) F1 score vs. inference energy on the test data set

(b) F1 score vs. training energy on the test data set

Fig. 3. The F1 performance on the test data set on the y-axis plotted against the inference and training energy, respectively, in joules on the x-axis for all the models. Note the logarithmic scale of the x-axis. Despite ∼1000 times higher energy consumption, the large models do not have better performance.

Figure 3 shows the F1 score on the test data set plotted against the inference energy required for each of the models. While the models' performances form almost a horizontal line on the y-axis, they are spread over several orders of magnitude along the logarithmic x-axis, representing inference energy. The corresponding plot for the training energy is shown in Figure 3 and exhibits a similar pattern. In summary, we find the performance-to-energy ratio to be much higher for the smaller models in our experiment.

4   Threats to Validity

Here, we list threats to validity following the guidelines for software engineering research by Wohlin et al. [20]. *Internal validity*: The choice of training and test data is a concern in this regard [4]. We have chosen data sets for model training from open source projects, similar to the ones that are used in previous commit classification research. The projects are similar in terms of commit message guidelines and programming language, which decreases the risk of diffusing the relationships and the risk of relying on single data sets. *Construct validity*: The size of the models are measured in terms of the number of model parameters. There are magnitudes of difference between the different model sizes, implying that the factors of construct are easily distinguishable. Performance is measured as standardized accuracy and F1 scores, while energy is measured as power over time. The commit classification scheme and the classification as such are a threat to construct validity, as the classes are not fully orthogonal and vary between the data sets. We rely on common practice in previous research and provide a transparent mapping scheme to enable replication (see Table 1). *Conclusion validity*: The experimental setup uses standardized open source machine learning components. Our programs are written in Python and utilize commonly used frameworks such as `transformers`, `torch`, `ignite`, and `numpy`. *External validity*: We have prioritized external validity and practical relevance using independent data sets. The scope of validity of our findings may be limited to similar types of project and environment represented in the data.

5 Conclusions

We conducted an experiment to gain insight into the relationship between the size, performance, and energy consumption of ML models used for classification of commit messages, an example of an NLP task in the context of software engineering. We found that small and simple NLP models perform similarly to LLMs in the classifier task while using a fraction of the energy required by the LLMs. Our results suggest that the performance-to-energy ratio of ML models may be worthy of more attention when selecting ML models for classification tasks in the SE context.

Acknowledgments. This work was partially supported by the Wallenberg AI, Autonomous Systems and Software Program (WASP) funded by the Knut and Alice Wallenberg Foundation, and the Competence Centre NextG2Com funded by the VINNOVA program for Advanced Digitalisation with grant number 2023-00541.

References

1. Abdin, M., et al.: Phi-3 Technical Report: a highly capable language model locally on your phone (2024)
2. Angular community: angular conventional changelog (2024). https://github.com/conventional-changelog/conventional-changelog/tree/508bdf/packages/conventional-changelog-angular
3. Bartlett, K.: Google carbon emissions surge nearly 50% due to AI energy demand (2024). https://www.cnbc.com/2024/07/02/googles-carbon-emissions-surge-nearly-50percent-due-to-ai-energy-demand.html
4. Borg, M., Runeson, P.: IR in software traceability: from a bird's eye view. In: In Proceedings Empirical Software Engineering and Measurements (ESEM), pp. 243–246. IEEE (2013)
5. EleutherAI, the HuggingFace Inc. team: modeling_llama.py (2025). https://github.com/huggingface/transformers/blob/1ce0e29/src/transformers/models/llama/modeling_llama.py#L890

6. Fu, Y., Yan, M., Zhang, X., Xu, L., Yang, D., Kymer, J.D.: Automated classification of software change messages by semi-supervised latent Dirichlet allocation. Inf. Softw. Technol. **57**, 369–377 (2015)

7. Gharbi, S., Mkaouer, M.W., Jenhani, I., Messaoud, M.B.: On the classification of software change messages using multi-label active learning. In: Proceedings of the 34th ACM/SIGAPP Symposium on Applied Computing, pp. 1760–1767 (2019)

8. Hassan, A.E.: Automated classification of change messages in open source projects. In: Proceedings of the 2008 ACM Symposium on Applied Computing, pp. 837–841. SAC '08, ACM, New York, NY, USA (2008)

9. Heričko, T., Šumak, B.: Commit classification into software maintenance activities: A systematic literature review. In: 2023 IEEE 47th Annual Computers, Software, and Applications Conference (COMPSAC), pp. 1646–1651. IEEE (2023)

10. Hindle, A., German, D.M., Godfrey, M.W., Holt, R.C.: Automatic classication of large changes into maintenance categories. In: 2009 IEEE 17th International Conference on Program Comprehension, pp. 30–39. IEEE (2009)

11. Köksal, Ö., Öztürk, C.E.: A survey on machine learning-based automated software bug report classification. In: 2022 International Symposium on Multidisciplinary Studies and Innovative Technologies (ISMSIT), pp. 635–640. IEEE (2022)

12. Laiq, M., Dobslaw, F.: Automatic techniques for issue report classification: A systematic mapping study. arXiv preprint arXiv:2505.01469 (2025)

13. Li, Z., et al.: Label supervised LLaMA finetuning (2023), version Number: 1

14. Ochodek, M., Staron, M., Meding, W., Söder, O.: Automated code review comment classification to improve modern code reviews. In: International Conference on Software Quality, pp. 23–40. Springer (2022)

15. Rezaei-Dastjerdehei, M.R., Mijani, A., Fatemizadeh, E.: Addressing imbalance in multi-label classification using weighted cross entropy loss function. In: 2020 27th National and 5th International Iranian Conference on Biomedical Engineering (ICBME), pp. 333–338. IEEE (2020)

16. Rigutini, L., Globo, A., Stefanelli, M., Zugarini, A., Gultekin, S., Ernandes, M., et al.: Performance, energy consumption and costs: a comparative analysis of automatic text classification approaches in the legal domain. Int. J. Natural Lang. Comput. **13**(1), 19–35 (2024)

17. Sarwar, M.U., Zafar, S., Mkaouer, M.W., Walia, G.S., Malik, M.Z.: Multi-label classification of commit messages using transfer learning. In: IEEE International Symposium on Software Reliability Engineering Workshops (ISSREW), pp. 37–42. IEEE (2020)

18. Sheikhaei, M.S., Tian, Y., Wang, S., Xu, B.: An empirical study on the effectiveness of large language models for SATD identification and classification. Empir. Softw. Eng. **29**(6), 159 (2024)

19. Vuejs Community: Vuejs git commit message convention (2024). https://github.com/vuejs/core/blob/8a99f9/.github/commit-convention.md

20. Wohlin, C., Runeson, P., Höst, M., Ohlsson, M.C., Regnell, B., Wesslén, A.: Experimentation in Software Engineering. Springer, 2nd Springer Edn. (2024)

21. Zhou, Y., Sharma, A.: Automated identification of security issues from commit messages and bug reports. In: Proceedings of the 2017 11th Joint Meeting on Foundations of Software Engineering, pp. 914–919 (2017)

Towards Understanding the Developer Experience in Quantum Software Development

Ronja Heikkinen[(✉)], Majid Haghparast, and Tommi Mikkonen

University of Jyväskylä, Jyväskylä, Finland
{ronja.k.heikkinen,majid.m.haghparast,tommi.j.mikkonen}@jyu.fi

Abstract. In this thematic analysis, we study how quantum software development challenges can be framed in terms of general developer experience and how these connections can enhance our understanding of quantum developer experience. As a result, general developer experience categories, quantum software development challenges, and the connections and parallels between the two are identified. These novel results help to understand quantum developer experience better than before, thus offering guidance to future research and practical implementations.

Keywords: Developer experience · quantum software · quantum software development challenges · quantum developer experience · quantum computing · thematic analysis

1 Introduction

Quantum software development, while sharing foundational principles with classical software development, is distinguished by unique challenges arising from its basis in quantum mechanics and the current immaturity of its tooling and ecosystems [16,33]. These challenges include limited abstraction in development tools, lack of standards, vendor lock-in, and the need for specialized expertise [3]. Developer experience has been extensively studied in classical settings, with research highlighting factors such as tool usability, cognitive load, motivation, and social context as influences on productivity and satisfaction [14,32]. However, there is a notable gap in research connecting these findings to the specific challenges faced in quantum software development. Addressing this gap is critical to guide the creation of effective tools, processes, and practices that support quantum software developers, thereby advancing both academic understanding and practical outcomes in this emerging field.

In this paper, we explore the connections and parallels between quantum software development challenges and developer experience through a thematic analysis of relevant literature. Our goal is to identify categories linking these two areas to inform both research and practice.

The results enable practitioners to identify quantum software development challenges that affect specific aspects of the developer experience. Furthermore, researchers working on quantum software development and practical implementations can use these findings to guide their work.

The rest of this paper is structured as follows. Section 2 provides the background of the study, and Sect. 3 outlines the methodology. Preliminary findings are presented in Sect. 4, followed by a discussion of the research questions and proposed actions in Sect. 5. Finally, Sect. 6 concludes the paper.

2   Background and Related Works

Quantum Software Development. Quantum software development shares similarities with classical software development processes such as design, testing, and maintenance, but is fundamentally grounded in quantum mechanics [31,33]. Key computational distinctions include the use of qubits that exploit superposition and entanglement, enabling quantum computers to perform especially parallel computations more efficiently than classical computers [38]. These fundamental differences between classical and quantum computing mean that traditional software development tools and processes cannot be directly applied to quantum software development [25]. The dominant programming framework supporting such computations is the quantum circuit model, which manipulates qubits through quantum gates represented as unitary matrix transformations [16]. However, the tools available for this model often provide limited abstraction, requiring developers to operate close to hardware or gate-level details [16]. Furthermore, challenges such as immature tooling, lack of standards, vendor lock-in, limited availability of specialized skills, and the fragmented nature of available information hinder efficient quantum software development [3,33]. These issues highlight the urgent need for new solutions that can better support quantum software developers [21,38].

Developer Experience. Developer experience (DX) encompasses developers' perceptions and experiences of their everyday work, and is recognized as a distinct category of user experience [14,32]. DX is influenced by a range of factors including cognitive load, emotional states, social and technical skills, and the quality of tools and workflows available [18,36]. Improving developer experience has been shown to enhance individual, team, and organizational performance, as well as project outcomes [14,34]. While DX is well-studied in classical software development, there is a lack of research focused on how the unique challenges of quantum software development affect developer experience.

3   Research Design

The goal of this research is to study how quantum software development challenges within the general developer experience categories enhance our understanding of quantum software developer experience. To address this goal, we formulated three research questions, outlined below:

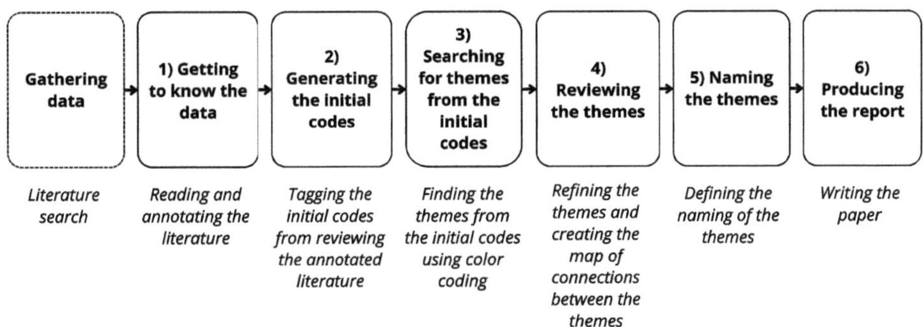

Fig. 1. Used research method [8] and its implementation details.

RQ$_1$: What are the groups of features affecting general developer experience?

RQ$_2$: What are the categories of commonly experienced challenges in quantum software development?

RQ$_3$: How can quantum software development challenges be framed in terms of general developer experience categories?

This study follows Braun and Clarke's six-step thematic analysis framework [8] (see Fig. 1). Since no existing framework for quantum developer experience was available, the analysis is primarily data-driven, deriving insights directly from the literature. Data for the analysis was collected through two systematic keyword searches in IEEE, Google Scholar, Scopus, and ACM Digital Library. Keywords included (("developer experience" OR "dx" OR "user experience") AND ("tool" OR "workflow" OR "programming")). The term "quantum" was added in the second round. Both forward and backward citation searches were used to complement the initial set, along with relevant literature known to the authors. In total, the search yielded 17 sources on general developer experience and 20 on quantum software development challenges, amounting to 37 articles (see Table 1). Papers were chosen based on abstract and keywords.

4   Preliminary Findings

The reviewed literature was classified into two subcategories: general developer experience and quantum software development challenges. From these, initial codes were identified and grouped into six preliminary themes per category. The themes for general developer experience were subsequently consolidated into three main themes, and further integration was carried out to connect quantum development challenges with these themes. The resulting developer experience categories and the related quantum software development challenges are presented below (see Fig. 2).

Coordination, Practices, and Governance. Organizational knowledge management, release systems, and product management directly impact developers'

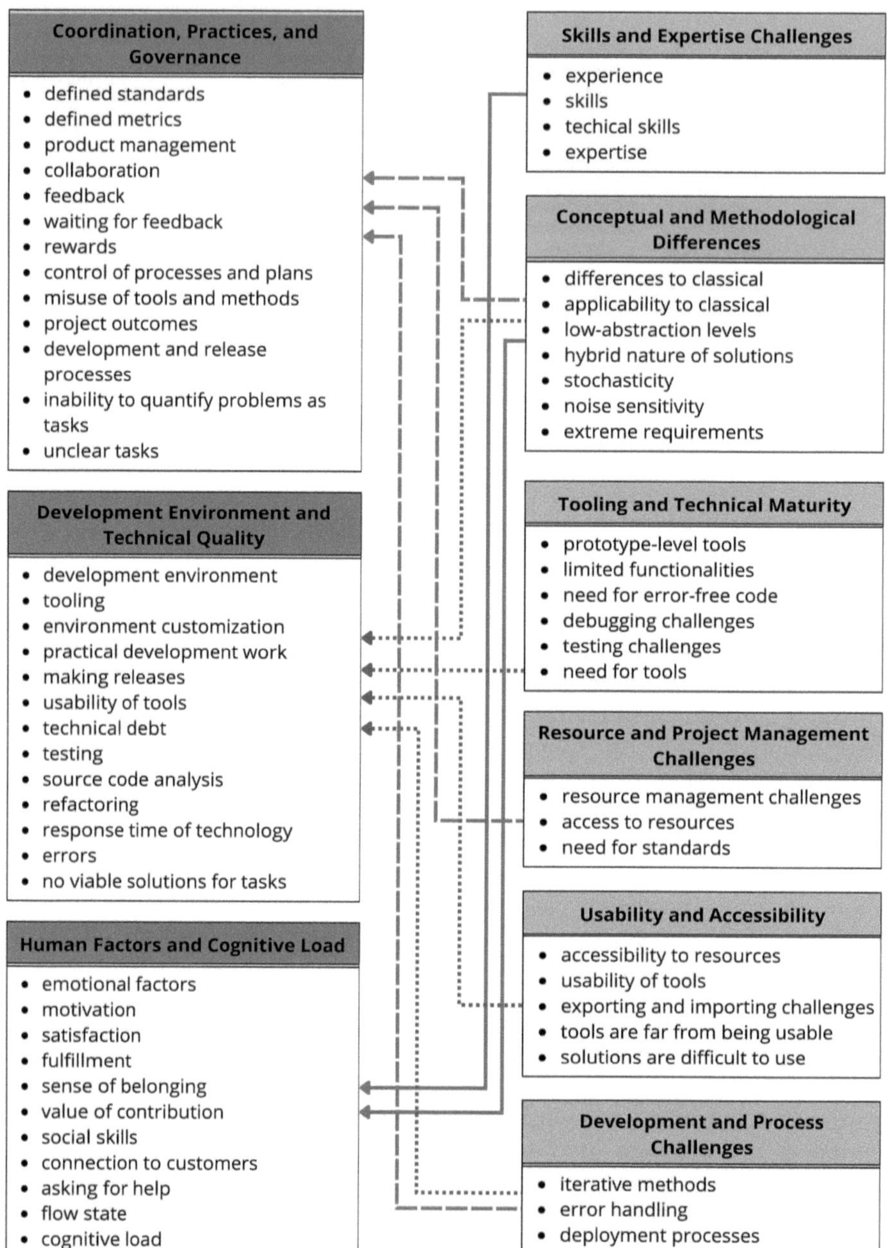

Fig. 2. Visual map of connections from quantum software development challenges to general developer experience topics. General developer experience topics are displayed on the left, while categories of quantum development challenges appear on the right. Coloring and arrow design are used to enhance clarity and support visual interpretation.

Table 1. Papers for the literature review grouped as in Fig. 2. DX = developer experience, Q = quantum software development challenges.

Theme	Topic	Papers
DX	Governance, Practices, and Governance	[5,7,10,11,14,20,36,43]
DX	Development Environment and Technical Quality	[6,9–11,14,20,32,34,37,44]
DX	Human Factors and Cognitive Load	[7,9–11,14,18–20,32,34,36,42,43]
Q	Skills and Expertise Challenges	[2,24,26,41]
Q	Conceptual and Methodological Differences	[12,15,17,22,23,25,27,29,40,41,46]
Q	Tooling and Technical Maturity	[1,22–25,27,35,39,45,46]
Q	Resource and Project Management	[1,4,15,17,28,29,40,41,46]
Q	Usability and Accessibility	[2,22,24,39–41,45]
Q	Development and Process Challenges	[23,27,41]

work and motivation [10,14,20]. Challenges include low prioritization, unclear processes, and organizational politics [20]. Communication and timely feedback significantly affect productivity and developer satisfaction [10,14]. In quantum computing, development complexity and lack of standardization pose major challenges [38]. Well-maintained documentation helps mitigate these issues [13,30].

Development Environment and Technical Quality. Tools and development environments shape developers' daily experiences [32]. Many quantum tools remain prototypes with limited robustness, causing usability and accessibility issues [31,39]. Vendor lock-in restricts interoperability and access in quantum software development tools [33]. Openness and universality in quantum tool design are critical for wider adoption [16].

Human Factors and Cognitive Load. Motivation, job satisfaction, and a sense of belonging are central for developer experience [14,20]. Quantum software development demands high technical expertise and interdisciplinary skills, increasing cognitive load [3].

Differences Between Classical and Quantum Computing. Fundamental differences between classical and quantum computing heavily influence developer experience [21,31]. Integration of classical computing concepts into quantum environments is challenging [33].

The analysis revealed connections between quantum software development challenges and general developer experience themes. Quantum software development challenges relate to three main categories within general developer experience, including (i) Human factors: skills, expertise, cognitive load; (ii) Coordination, practices, and governance: project and resource management, teamwork; and (iii) Development environment and technical quality: tools, technical maturity, usability. Figure 2 illustrates how quantum software development challenges relate to general developer experience themes. Skills and expertise challenges align with human factors, tooling and usability issues correspond to the development environment, and project and resource management relate to coordination and governance. One overarching theme, capturing the fundamental differences between quantum and classical computing, cuts across all categories, influencing every aspect of developer experience. Overall, developer experience in this context spans individual, collaborative, and technological dimensions, with quantum-specific challenges mapping onto these domains.

5   Discussion and Future Directions

To answer to the proposed research questions, each question is addressed below:

RQ_1: What are the groups of features affecting general developer experience?

– As a result of this thematic analysis, the main groups for developer experience influences are coordination, practices and governance, development environment and technical quality, and human factors and cognitive load.

RQ_2: What are the categories of commonly experienced challenges in quantum software development?

– The identified categories of quantum software development challenges include skills and expertise, conceptual and methodological differences, tooling and technical maturity, resource and project management, usability and accessibility, as well as development and process.

RQ_3: How can quantum software development challenges be framed in terms of general developer experience categories?

– As a result of our analysis, quantum challenge category skills and expertise corresponds to the developer experience theme of human factors and cognitive load; tooling and technical maturity, usability and accessibility, and development and process challenges are relevant to the theme of development environment and technical quality; and resource and project management relate to the theme of coordination, practices, and governance. Beyond these specific mappings, the theme of conceptual and methodological differences cuts across all categories, shaping every aspect of developer experience.

DX has been studied extensively and is often compared to user experience, but with a focus on developers and interactions within the work environment [11,14,32,34]. Several frameworks exist: Fagerholm and Münch [11] highlight the balance between abstraction and practicality, Schlichtig [37] focuses on developers using static analysis tools, and Noda et al. [34] emphasize feedback loops, cognitive load, and flow states. Google's developer survey also identifies many factors influencing DX, though without deep analysis [10]. Quantum software development challenges have been explored mainly to motivate research or provide broad overviews. For example, Awan et al. [3] used fuzzy analytic hierarchy to identify challenges, while Ferreira and Campos [13] surveyed quantum developers. However, few studies focus specifically on these challenges, and none address the quantum developer experience directly. This study's thematic analysis linking quantum software development challenges to general developer experience is a novel contribution to the field.

To address the concerns surrounding quantum software, we urge the research community, cloud providers, and policymakers to pursue the following directions:

- **Develop Comprehensive Developer Experience Frameworks.** Build on existing developer experience research by creating frameworks specifically tailored to quantum software development. This includes addressing the unique cognitive, technical, and social challenges quantum software developers face, as identified in the thematic analysis.
- **Invest in Tooling and Technical Maturity.** Accelerate the development and standardization of robust, user-friendly quantum software tools and environments. Prioritize interoperability and openness to reduce vendor lock-in and enhance usability and accessibility for broader developer community.
- **Enhance Education and Skill Development.** Support interdisciplinary training programs that equip developers with both classical and quantum computing skills, bridging the expertise gap highlighted as a challenge.
- **Foster Collaboration and Knowledge Sharing.** Encourage collaborative frameworks and communication practices that improve coordination and governance in quantum software projects, mitigating challenges related to project management and information flow.
- **Conduct Further Empirical Research.** Promote studies on quantum developer experience to deepen understanding of human factors and cognitive load, guiding design of better processes and tools tailored to quantum software development.

6 Conclusion

This paper presents a thematic analysis of quantum developer experience challenges based on existing literature, situating these challenges within the broader framework of general developer experience. By doing so, it identifies key quantum software development issues across themes of cognition and human factors, development environment and technical quality, and coordination, practices, and governance. The study offers new insights into how specific quantum challenges impact developer experience, providing a connections map that can guide researchers in addressing targeted issues.

Acknowledgments. This work has been supported by the Research Council of Finland through project DEQSE (349945).

Disclosure of Interests. The authors have no competing interests.

References

1. Altman, E., et al.: Quantum simulators: architectures and opportunities. PRX Quant. **2**(1), 017003 (2021)
2. Amato, F., et al.: QuantuMoonLight: a low-code platform to experiment with quantum machine learning. SoftwareX **22** (2023). https://doi.org/10.1016/j.softx.2023.101399
3. Awan, U., Hannola, L., Tandon, A., Goyal, R.K., Dhir, A.: Quantum computing challenges in the software industry. a fuzzy AHP-based approach. Inf. Softw. Technol. (2022). https://doi.org/10.1016/j.infsof.2022.106896
4. Basu, S., Das, A., Saha, A., Chakrabarti, A., Sur-Kolay, S.: FragQC: an efficient quantum error reduction technique using quantum circuit fragmentation. J. Syst. Softw. **214**, 112085 (2024)
5. Besker, T., Ghanbari, H., Martini, A., Bosch, J.: The influence of technical debt on software developer morale. J. Syst. Softw. **167**, 110586 (2020)
6. Besker, T., Martini, A., Bosch, J.: Software developer productivity loss due to technical debt-a replication and extension study examining developers' development work. J. Syst. Softw. **156**, 41–61 (2019)
7. Borrego, G., Cinco, R.R.P., Rodríguez, L.F., et al.: Agile software engineers' affective states, their performance and software quality: a systematic mapping review. J. Syst. Softw. **204**, 111800 (2023)
8. Braun, V., Clarke, V.: Using thematic analysis in psychology. Qual. Res. Psychol. **3**(2), 77–101 (2006). https://doi.org/10.1191/1478088706qp063oa
9. Cornejo, O., et al.: A family of experiments about how developers perceive delayed system response time. Software Qual. J. **32**(2), 567–605 (2024)
10. D'Angelo, S., et al.: Measuring developer experience with a longitudinal survey. IEEE Softw. **41**(4), 19–24 (2024). https://doi.org/10.1109/MS.2024.3386027
11. Fagerholm, F., Munch, J.: Developer experience: concept and definition. In: IEEE International Conference on Software and System Process (ICSSP) (2012). https://doi.org/10.1109/ICSSP.2012.6225984
12. Feitosa, S.S., Vizzotto, J.K., Piveta, E.K., Du Bois, A.R.: A monadic semantics for quantum computing in an object oriented language. Sci. Comput. Program. **173**, 37–55 (2019). https://doi.org/10.1016/j.scico.2018.03.003
13. Ferreira, F., Campos, J.: An exploratory study on the usage of quantum programming languages. Sci. Comput. Program. **240** (2025). https://doi.org/10.1016/j.scico.2024.103217
14. Forsgren, N., Kalliamvakou, E., Noda, A., Greiler, M., Houck, B., Storey, M.: DevEx in action: a study of its tangible impacts. ACM Queue **21**(6), 47–77 (2023). https://doi.org/10.1145/3639443
15. Garcia-Alonso, J., Rojo, J., Valencia, D., Moguel, E., Berrocal, J., Murillo, J.M.: Quantum software as a service through a quantum API gateway. IEEE Internet Comput. **26**(1), 34–41 (2022). https://doi.org/10.1109/MIC.2021.3132688
16. Gill, S.S., et al.: Quantum computing: a taxonomy, systematic review and future directions. Softw. Pract. Exp. **52**(1), 66–114 (2022). https://doi.org/10.1002/spe.3039
17. Giortamis, E., Romão, F., Tornow, N., Lugovoy, D., Bhatotia, P.: Orchestrating quantum cloud environments with qonductor. arXiv preprint arXiv:2408.04312 (2024)
18. Gonçales, L.J., Farias, K., da Silva, B.C.: Measuring the cognitive load of software developers: an extended systematic mapping study. Inf. Softw. Technol. **136** (2021). https://doi.org/10.1016/j.infsof.2021.106563

19. Graziotin, D., Fagerholm, F., Wang, X., Abrahamsson, P.: What happens when software developers are (un)happy. J. Syst. Softw. **140**, 32–47 (2018). https://doi.org/10.1016/j.jss.2018.02.041
20. Greiler, M., Storey, M., Noda, A.: An actionable framework for understanding and improving developer experience. IEEE Trans. Software Eng. **49**(4), 1411–1425 (2023). https://doi.org/10.1109/TSE.2022.3175660
21. Meijer van de Griend, A.: A comparison of quantum compilers using a DAG-based or phase polynomial-based intermediate representation. J. Syst. Softw. **221** (2025). https://doi.org/10.1016/j.jss.2024.112224
22. Grossi, M., et al.: A serverless cloud integration for quantum computing (2021). arXiv preprint arXiv:2107.02007 (2021)
23. Haghparast, M., Mikkonen, T., Nurminen, J.K., Stirbu, V.: Quantum software engineering challenges from developers' perspective: mapping research challenges to the proposed workflow model. In: 2023 IEEE International Conference on Quantum Computing and Engineering (QCE), vol. 02, pp. 173–176 (2023). https://doi.org/10.1109/QCE57702.2023.10204
24. Hevia, J.L., Peterssen, G., Piattini, M.: QuantumPath: a quantum software development platform. Softw. Pract. Exper. **52**(6), 1517–1530 (2022). https://doi.org/10.1002/spe.3064
25. Jones, T., Brown, A., Bush, I., Benjamin, S.C.: Quest and high performance simulation of quantum computers. Sci. Rep. **9**(1), 1–11 (2019). https://doi.org/10.1038/s41598-019-47174-9
26. Juárez-Ramírez, R., et al.: Skills required for quantum computing: a comprehensive review of recent studies. Program. Comput. Softw. **50**(8), 844–874 (2024). https://doi.org/10.1134/S0361768824700804
27. Khan, A.A., et al.: Embracing iterations in quantum software: a vision. ACM (2022). https://doi.org/10.1145/3549036.3562057
28. Li, T., Zhao, Z.: Moirai: optimizing quantum serverless function orchestration via device allocation and circuit deployment. In: 2024 IEEE International Conference on Web Services (ICWS), pp. 707–717. IEEE (2024)
29. Lublinsky, B., Jennings, E., Spišaková, V.: A Kubernetes bridgeoperator between cloud and external resources (2022). https://arxiv.org/abs/2207.02531
30. Matthews, D.: How to get started in quantum computing. Nature (London) **591**(7848), 166–167 (2021). https://doi.org/10.1038/d41586-021-00533-x
31. Mondal, A.K., Nadim, M., Roy, C.K., Roy, B., Schneider, K.A.: Quantum software engineering and potential of quantum computing in software engineering research: a review. Autom. Softw. Eng. **32**(1), 27 (2025). https://doi.org/10.1007/s10515-025-00493-w
32. Morales, J., Rusu, C., Botella, F., Quinones, D.: Programmer experience: a systematic literature review. IEEE Access **7**, 71079–71094 (2019). https://doi.org/10.1109/ACCESS.2019.2920124
33. Murillo, J.M., et al.: Quantum software engineering: roadmap and challenges ahead. ACM Trans. Softw. Eng. Methodol. (2025, just accepted). https://doi.org/10.1145/3712002
34. Noda, A., Storey, M., Forsgren, N., Greiler, M.: DevEx: what actually drives productivity: the developer-centric approach to measuring and improving productivity. ACM Queue **21**(2), 35–53 (2023). https://doi.org/10.1145/3595878
35. Quetschlich, N., Burgholzer, L., Wille, R.: MQT bench: benchmarking software and design automation tools for quantum computing. Quantum **7**, 1062 (2023)

36. Salido O., M.G., Borrego, G., Palacio Cinco, R.R., Rodríguez, L.: Agile software engineers' affective states, their performance and software quality: a systematic mapping review. J. Sys. Softw. **204** (2023). https://doi.org/10.1016/j.jss.2023.111800

37. Schlichtig, M.: Building a framework to improve the user experience of static analysis tools. In: Proceedings of the ACM (2024). https://doi.org/10.1145/3639478.3639813

38. Sepúlveda, S., Pérez-Castillo, R., Piattini, M.: A software product line approach for developing hybrid software systems. Inf. Softw. Technol. **178** (2025). https://doi.org/10.1016/j.infsof.2024.107625

39. Serrano, M.A., Cruz-Lemus, J.A., Perez-Castillo, R., Piattini, M.: Quantum software components and platforms: overview and quality assessment. ACM Comput. Surv. **55**(8), 1–31 (2022). https://doi.org/10.1145/3548679

40. Singh, P.: A survey on available tools and technologies enabling quantum computing. IEEE Access **12**, 57974–57991 (2024). https://doi.org/10.1109/ACCESS.2024.3388005

41. Stirbu, V., de Griend, A.M.v., Muff, J.: Exposing the hidden layers and interplay in the quantum software stack. In: 2024 IEEE 21st International Conference on Software Architecture Companion (ICSA-C), pp. 24–25 (2024). https://doi.org/10.1109/ICSA-C63560.2024.00010

42. Sánchez-Gordón, M., Colomo-Palacios, R.: Taking the emotional pulse of software engineering - a systematic literature review of empirical studies. Inf. Softw. Technol. **115**, 23–43 (2019). https://doi.org/10.1016/j.infsof.2019.08.002

43. Tessem, B.: Individual empowerment of agile and non-agile software developers in small teams. Inf. Softw. Technol. **56**(8), 873–889 (2014). https://doi.org/10.1016/j.infsof.2014.02.005

44. Yusop, N.S.M., Grundy, J., Schneider, J.G., Vasa, R.: A revised open source usability defect classification taxonomy. Inf. Softw. Technol. **128**, 106396 (2020)

45. Zayas Gallardo, J., Moguel, E., Canal-Velasco, J.C., García-Alonso, J., et al.: Quirk+: a tool for quantum software development based on quirk (2024)

46. Zhao, P., Miao, Z., Lan, S., Zhao, J.: Bugs4Q: a benchmark of existing bugs to enable controlled testing and debugging studies for quantum programs. J. Syst. Softw. **205**, 111805 (2023)

On the Use of Agentic Coding Manifests: An Empirical Study of Claude Code

Worawalan Chatlatanagulchai[1](✉), Kundjanasith Thonglek[1], Brittany Reid[2],
Yutaro Kashiwa[2], Pattara Leelaprute[1], Arnon Rungsawang[1],
Bundit Manaskasemsak[1], and Hajimu Iida[2]

[1] Faculty of Engineering, Kasetsart University, Bangkok, Thailand
`worawalan.c@ku.th`
[2] Nara Institute of Science and Technology (NAIST), Nara, Japan

Abstract. Agentic coding tools receive goals written in natural language as input, break them down into specific tasks, and write/execute the actual code with minimal human intervention. Key to this process are agent manifests, configuration files (such as `Claude.md`) that provide agents with essential project context, identity, and operational rules. However, the lack of comprehensive and accessible documentation for creating these manifests presents a significant challenge for developers. We analyzed **253** `Claude.md` files from **242** repositories to identify structural patterns and common content. Our findings show that manifests typically have shallow hierarchies with one main heading and several subsections, with content dominated by operational commands, technical implementation notes, and high-level architecture.

Keywords: Agentic Coding · Autonomous Programming · Documents

1 Introduction

"The hottest new programming language is English," stated OpenAI founding member Andrej Karpathy,[1] capturing a fundamental shift in how software development is evolving. The rise of Large Language Models (LLMs) has enabled the deployment of Artificial Intelligence (AI) agents capable of facilitating or executing autonomous software engineering tasks through natural language interactions. This novel approach, termed `Agentic Coding`, interpret natural language goals, decompose them into subtasks, and autonomously plan and execute code with minimal human intervention. Unlike vibe coding, which focuses on describing desired feelings or essence, agentic coding provides concrete objectives and lets AI independently determine implementation through multi-step planning, tool usage, and self-correction.

Notable implementations of agentic coding tools include Claude Code, Cursor, Aider, GitHub Copilot, and Devin AI. Most of these tools rely on `Agentic`

---

[1] https://x.com/karpathy/status/1617979122625712128.

`coding manifests` to function effectively, which are specialized configuration files that define AI agent behavior within specific projects. Loaded at the start of each session, they equip AI agents with project-specific knowledge, behavioral guidelines, and operational rules that determine how well the agent can understand codebases, interpret developer intent, and execute tasks autonomously. However, despite `agentic coding manifests` being crucial for the performance, there is little research on how to design them effectively. The lack of comprehensive documentation means developers resort to trial-and-error approaches, resulting in suboptimal agent behavior and missed opportunities to fully leverage these tools' capabilities.

This study aims to reveal common structural patterns and their contents. Our empirical study on 253 `Claude.md` files from 242 repositories revealed (i) they follow a shallow hierarchical structure with a single main heading and moderate subsections; and (ii) the most common content patterns include instructions for `Build and Run`, `Implementation Details`, and `Architecture`, highlighting the critical role of contextual information for AI-assisted software development and how action-oriented focus of `agentic coding manifests`.

2   Agent Coding Manifests

Agentic coding tools can be configured through specialized Markdown files that define how AI coding assistants should operate within specific projects. These configuration files, such as `Claude.md` for Claude Code or `AGENTS.md` for Codex, establish the AI agent's identity, capabilities, and operational workflows.[2] We refer to these configuration files as `Agentic Coding Manifests` (ACMs). By documenting project-specific context and conventions, `ACMs` eliminate the need for repetitive explanations and reduces misunderstandings between developers and AI assistants. When stored in version control alongside the codebase, these files ensure that AI agents maintain a consistent understanding of each project's unique requirements and characteristics throughout the development lifecycle.

There are official documents for each agentic coding tool that introduce setup for `ACMs` to pull context into prompts automatically. However, it is not comprehensively written. For example, the official documents of Claude Code indicate only that `ACMs` can be used to share instructions for the project, such as project architecture, coding standards, and common workflows.

This fragmentation and lack of explicit, standardized guidance can delay developers' ability to effectively define, orchestrate, and leverage the Claude agent's behavior, therefore creating a substantial barrier to exploiting the full potential of agentic coding and potentially leading to inconsistencies in agent performance and a steeper learning curve for integration. Consequently, this gap in practical guidance for the creation of `ACMs` served as a primary motivation for our current research. We aim to address this challenge by systematically investigating existing `Claude.md` files within open-source repositories. Our study is specifically designed to infer common structural patterns, typical instructions,

---

[2] An   example   can   be   seen   here: https://github.com/fschutt/azul/blob/3fe83b9d4c8004ebe96ea0a77660c777fcd05bc8/CLAUDE.md.

and general practices in how developers configure these crucial `agentic coding manifests` and maintain them.

3   Data Collection

This study used a systematic data collection methodology using the GitHub API[3] to identify and analyze "`Claude.md`" files in open-source software repositories. The data collection process began by searching for repositories containing files named `Claude.md` (insensitive to case) using the GitHub API. The search focused on files created between February 24, 2025, when Claude MCP[4] was released, and June 16, 2025. This initial search identified 838 `Claude.md` files distributed in 806 different repositories.

To exclude projects that had only recently adopted Claude Code, we applied a filtering requiring repositories to have at least 20 commits after introducing their `Claude.md` file. This threshold corresponds to an average of five commits per month during the four months between the release of Claude Code and the start of data collection. After applying this filter, our dataset comprised 253 `Claude.md` files from 242 repositories. We cloned these repositories and retrieved 1,249 commits in total.

4   Results

RQ_1: How Are Agent Manifest Files Organized?

Motivation. Prior work on software documentation has noted that developer docs often use hierarchical section structures [10]. For example, Treude *et al.* observed that technical documentation "usually follows a hierarchical structure with sections and subsections" [10]. Empirical studies of project documentation (*e.g.*, `README` and `CONTRIBUTING` files) also find that early versions tend to be very minimal and focused on basic usage or contribution procedures [4]. However, `agentic coding manifests` files such as `CLAUDE.md` represent a novel documentation artifact specifically designed for AI-assisted coding. To the best of our knowledge, no prior research has systematically analyzed their structural characteristics (*e.g.*, how many and what levels of instructions they contain). We first investigate common organizational patterns that developers use when structuring instructions for AI coding agents.

Approach. We extracted each `Claude.md` file from the cloned repositories and measured the number of markdown headers that multiply nest. Specifically, we identified each header level, ranging from H1 (*i.e.*, #) to H6 (*i.e.*, ######). A header's section includes all subsequent lines until the next header of the same level is found. We counted every non-empty line within these sections. Lines within code blocks (*i.e.*, demarcated by ``` ``` ```) were not included in our count.

---

[3] https://docs.github.com/en/rest?apiVersion=2022-11-28.
[4] https://docs.anthropic.com/en/release-notes/claude-code.

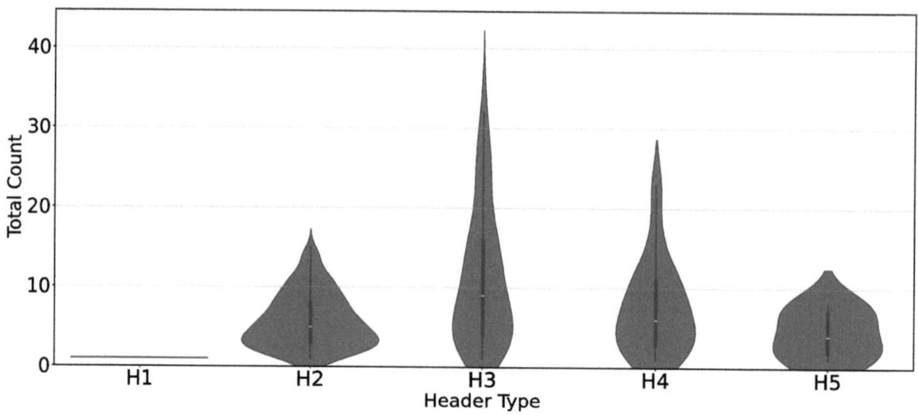

Fig. 1. Distribution of header counts across `Claude.md` files (outliers removed)

Results. Figure 1 depicts the distribution of header levels in `Claude.md` files. The distributions indicate that most documents begin with a single primary heading (H1), with a median of 1.0. This typically branches into a moderate number of subsections (H2), showing a median of 5.0, followed by more granular points (H3), which have a median of 9.0.

Header usage declines sharply as depth increases. Deeper levels such as H4 and H5 occur infrequently, with H4 appearing in only 37 documents and H5 in just 5 among the 253 files analyzed. The median counts per document are 6 for H4 and 4 for H5, which indicates their limited use. We observed H6 only once in the entire corpus; given this extremely low frequency, we exclude it from further analysis. Overall, deeply nested structures are rare, indicating a preference for straightforward organization.

This organizational pattern in `agentic coding manifests` is further confirmed by the statistics for nested headers, which show a similar distribution to the overall heading counts. For example, the median for H2 headings directly nested under an H1 heading (Median = 5.0) is nearly identical to the overall statistics for all H2 headings (Median = 5.0). This consistency suggests a predictable structural approach across the dataset, where the main topics are broken down in a similar fashion. We observed distinct purposes for different heading levels. H1 headings typically encapsulate the main content topic of the `agentic coding manifests`. H2 headings commonly describe broader aspects such as coding style, project structure, command-line instructions, or overall testing strategies. As the hierarchy deepens, H3 headings become more granular, detailing specific methods of testing or how to apply those methods. Further details on the content will be addressed in the next research question.

> **Answer to RQ1:** Agent manifest files are typically organized using a shallow hierarchical structure, with most documents starting from a single top-level heading and branching into a moderate number of H2 and H3 subsections.

RQ_2: What Instruction Are Included?

Motivation. Prior work shows that clear, structured instructions, such as stepwise task descriptions or templated formats, significantly improve LLM-generated outputs [13], with performance fundamentally shaped by the contextual information provided [7]. Despite this, there is little empirical research on `agentic coding manifests` intended to configure and guide AI agents. RQ2 addresses this by identifying prevalent instruction patterns in these manifests, revealing how developers structure context to align AI behavior in practice.

Approach. We adopted a two-stage manual content classification approach comprising a label creation phase followed by a label assignment phase. This separation was necessary due to the extensive structure and diversity of instructional content in `Claude.md`, which made simultaneous label generation and assignment impractical.

In the first phase, we focused on constructing a robust and comprehensive label set. We began by extracting all the H1 and H2 titles from the `Claude.md` files. Subsequently, we prompted three popular large language models (LLMs), Claude, Gemini, and ChatGPT, to generate candidate labels. One of the authors then selected the most appropriate label from these suggestions or created a new label when none were suitable. The use of LLMs was motivated by findings from prior research [1], which demonstrated that recent LLMs perform comparably to human annotators in manual labeling tasks while significantly reducing effort. To ensure label quality, two authors independently reviewed the initial label set. This process yielded 80 distinct labels. In the final step, three inspectors collaboratively refined the label set by merging semantically similar entries, resulting in a consolidated set of 20 core labels.

In the second phase, two inspectors assigned the labels generated in the first phase to each `Claude.md` file, allowing multiple labels per file. Initially, both inspectors independently labeled the content of each file. This process resulted in 1,228 total label assignments across the 253 files, with 113 instances of disagreement. To resolve these conflicts, a third inspector joined the discussion and collaborated with the initial two to reach a consensus on the final labels. During this reconciliation process, a new and more descriptive label (*i.e.,* `Build and Run`) was introduced. This refinement finalized our classification scheme with 15 distinct labels. All three inspectors involved in the labeling process have programming experience ranging from 4 to 17 years.

Results. Table 1 presents the distribution of documentation categories, where percentages indicate the proportion of `Claude.md` files containing instructions for each category. The most prevalent was `Build and Run` (77.1%), containing

Table 1. Categories, descriptions, and their prevalence.

Category	Label	Description	%
General	System Overview	Provides a general overview or describes the key features of the system.	48.2
	AI Integration	Contains instructions or notes specifically for integrating with or interacting with the agentic coding tools.	15.4
	Doc.&Refs	Lists supplementary documents, links, or references for additional context.	13.8
Impl.	Architecture	Describes the high-level structure, design principles, or key components of the system's architecture.	64.8
	Impl. Details	Provides specific details for implementing code or system components, including coding style guidelines.	71.9
Build	Build and Run	Outlines the process for compiling source code and running the application, often including key commands.	77.1
	Testing	Details the procedures and commands for executing automated tests.	60.5
	Conf.&Env.	Instructions for configuring the system and setting up the development or production environment.	26.5
	DevOps	Covers procedures for software deployment, release, and operations, such as CI/CD pipelines.	9.5
Management	Development Process	Defines the development workflow, including guidelines for version control systems like Git.	37.2
	Project Management	Information related to the planning, organization, and management of the project.	11.1
Quality	Maintainance	Guidelines for system maintenance, including strategies for improving readability, detecting and resolving bugs.	19.8
	Performance	Focuses on system performance, quality assurance, and potential optimizations.	12.7
	Security	Addresses security considerations, vulnerabilities, or best practices for the system.	8.7
	UI/UX	Contains guidelines or details concerning the user interface (UI) and user experience (UX).	8.3

command-line instructions, scripts, and procedures for compiling and running code. This was followed by Implementation Details (71.9%) with development guidance (*e.g.*, code style) and Architecture (64.8%) describing high-level system design.

While the most prevalent instructions (Build and Run, Implementation Details, Architecture, Testing) address functional aspects, meta-level or non-functional categories like Performance (12.7%), Security (8.7%), and UI/UX

(8.3%) appear far less frequently. This pattern suggests that manifests are primarily optimized to help agents execute and maintain code efficiently rather than address broader quality attributes or user-facing aspects.

Beyond functional factors, we observed notable instances where developers provide contextual information. For example, half of the `Claude.md` files contain system overview explanations (*i.e.*, `System Overview`). Additionally, 15.4% of manifests (*i.e.*, `AI Integration` label) explicitly define the agent's role and describe its responsibilities within the project (*e.g.*, reviewers). This indicates that manifests serve not only as technical guides but also as means of establishing an AI agent's understanding, responsibilities, and collaborative alignment.

> **Answer to RQ2:** The most common content categories in `agentic coding manifests` are `Build and Run`, followed by `Implementation Details` and `Architecture` descriptions. These patterns reflect the action-oriented focus and specificity of the files.

5 Future Direction

Our future work will pursue the following two directions as well as involving more different agentic coding tools, such as Codex and Copilot.

Maintenance: The long-term efficacy and relevance of `agentic coding manifests` may be inherently tied to their maintenance. Previous research on documentation maintenance, such as Gaughan *et al.* [4] observed "burst-then-taper" effect in documentation changes. Future work could examine the evolution and decay of `Claude.md` files, revealing update frequencies, change-prone sections, and correlations with project development cycles or agent performance.

Impact: A critical direction for future research is to empirically assess the direct impact of `Claude.md` files on the performance of the Claude agent and the productivity of developers utilizing it. This could involve controlled experiments where agents are tasked with identical coding challenges, but with varying qualities or completeness of `agentic coding manifests`. Metrics such as task completion time, code quality (*e.g.*, bug count, adherence to style guides), number of iterations, and developer satisfaction could be measured. Additionally, qualitative studies, such as developer interviews or surveys, could explore how developers perceive the utility and influence of well-crafted manifests on their workflow, debugging efforts, and overall experience with agentic coding.

6 Related Work

Instructions for AI: A growing body of work investigates how developers formulate instructions for AI tools (prompt engineering) and categorizes AI agent tasks. Schulhoff *et al.* [9] investigates a wide array of prompt techniques and best practices. Kumar *et al.* [6] examine recurring instruction patterns and found that roughly 50% of developer prompts to an AI agent requested code changes, while others sought code explanations, test execution, or reviews. These studies examine typical instruction patterns that directly order AIs, while our study focuses on the contexts written in documents behind the instructions.

Contexts for AI: Many studies consistently highlight the critical role of contextual information such as codebase [3], documentation [12], and dependencies [5] for effective AI software development assistance. Akhoroz *et al.* [2] observed that programmers often note *"inaccuracies [and] lack of contextual awareness"* in AI outputs. Tufano *et al.* [11] points out that existing assistants like Copilot *"exhibit limited functionalities and lack contextual awareness"*. Our work directly addresses this need, as `agentic coding manifests` are designed to encapsulate this crucial context.

Documents for Human: Previous studies provide a strong foundation for understanding the structure and evolution of documentation. Gaughan *et al.* [4] found that initial README files are typically concise and function-focused, often expanding over time. Similarly, Prana *et al.* [8] observed that over 90% of GitHub READMEs they studied mentioned basic information like project name, description, and usage instructions. Our work extends this by quantifying the structure of the documents for AIs, like `Claude.md`.

7 Conclusion

This study analyzed `253 Claude.md` files and found that developers prefer a shallow hierarchical structure, typically using a single primary heading with a moderate number of subsections. Additionally, manual analysis revealed that manifests prioritize operational commands, followed by technical implementation notes and architecture descriptions. Many manifests also include AI role definitions to guide agent behavior. These patterns demonstrate how manifests serve dual purposes in agentic coding workflows: as execution guides for technical tasks and as frameworks for human-AI collaboration.

Acknowledgments. We gratefully acknowledge the financial support of JSPS KAKENHI grants (JP24K02921, JP25K21359), as well as JST PRESTO grant (JPMJPR22P3), ASPIRE grant (JPMJAP2415), and AIP Accelerated Program (JPMJCR25U7).

References

1. Ahmed, T., Devanbu, P.T., Treude, C., Pradel, M.: Can LLMS replace manual annotation of software engineering artifacts? In: Proceedings of MSR 2025, pp. 526–538 (2025)
2. Akhoroz, M., Yildirim, C.: Conversational AI as a coding assistant. CoRR arXiv:abs/2503.16508 (2025)
3. Athale, M., Vaddina, V.: Knowledge graph based repository-level code generation. In: Proceedings of LLM4Code 2025, pp. 169–176 (2025)
4. Gaughan, M., Champion, K., Hwang, S., Shaw, A.: The introduction of README and CONTRIBUTING files in open source software development. In: Proceedings of CHASE 2025, pp. 191–202 (2025)

5. Hai, N.L., Nguyen, D.M., Bui, N.D.Q.: On the impacts of contexts on repository-level code generation. In: Proceedings of NAACL 2025, pp. 1496–1524 (2025)

6. Kumar, A., Bajpai, Y., Gulwani, S., Soares, G., Murphy-Hill, E.R.: Sharp tools: how developers wield agentic AI in real software engineering tasks. CoRR arXiv:abs/2506.12347 (2025)

7. Min, S., et al.: Rethinking the role of demonstrations: what makes in-context learning work? In: Proceedings of EMNLP 2022, pp. 11048–11064 (2022)

8. Prana, G.A.A., Treude, C., Thung, F., Lo, D., Jiang, L.: Categorizing the content of GitHub readme files. Empir. Softw. Eng. **24**(3), 1296–1327 (2019)

9. Schulhoff, S., et al.: The prompt report: a systematic survey of prompt engineering techniques. CoRR arXiv:abs/2406.06608 (2024)

10. Treude, C., Robillard, M.P., Dagenais, B.: Extracting development tasks to navigate software documentation. IEEE TSE **41**(6), 565–581 (2015)

11. Tufano, M., Agarwal, A., Jang, J., Moghaddam, R.Z., Sundaresan, N.: AutoDev: automated AI-driven development. CoRR arXiv:abs/2403.08299 (2024)

12. Wang, Y., et al.: Towards an understanding of context utilization in code intelligence. CoRR arXiv:abs/2504.08734 (2025)

13. Zamfirescu-Pereira, J.D., Wong, R.Y., Hartmann, B., Yang, Q.: Why Johnny can't prompt: how non-AI experts try (and fail) to design LLM prompts. In: Proceedings of CHI 2023, pp. 437:1–437:21 (2023)

Detecting and Characterizing Low and No Functionality Packages in the NPM Ecosystem

Napasorn Tevarut[1], Brittany Reid[2(✉)], Yutaro Kashiwa[2], Pattara Leelaprute[1], Arnon Rungsawang[1], Bundit Manaskasemsak[1], and Hajimu Iida[2]

[1] Faculty of Engineering, Kasetsart University, Bangkok, Thailand
[2] Nara Institute of Science and Technology (NAIST), Ikoma, Japan
`brittany.reid@naist.ac.jp`

Abstract. Trivial packages, small modules with low functionality, are common in the npm ecosystem and can pose security risks despite their simplicity. This paper refines existing definitions and introduce data-only packages that contain no executable logic. A rule-based static analysis method is developed to detect trivial and data-only packages and evaluate their prevalence and associated risks in the 2025 npm ecosystem. The analysis shows that 17.92% of packages are trivial, with vulnerability levels comparable to non-trivial ones, and data-only packages, though rare, also contain risks. The proposed detection tool achieves 94% accuracy (macro-F1 0.87), enabling effective large-scale analysis to reduce security exposure. This findings suggest that trivial and data-only packages warrant greater attention in dependency management to reduce potential technical debt and security exposure.

Keywords: Software Libraries · Npm Ecosystem · Security vulnerability

1 Introduction

JavaScript is one of the most widely used programming languages. It's associated package manager, which enables the download, installation and updating of third-party dependencies, NPM (Node Package Manager), host over 3.5 million packages as of July 2025 and continues to grow rapidly[1]. While library use accelerates development, it also introduces risks by creating longer dependency chains that increase indirect vulnerabilities and maintenance overhead. Node.js developers often rely on small, low-functionality ('trivial') packages. Despite their apparent simplicity, such packages can create deep dependency chains [1,6], increasing vulnerability and maintenance risks [6], as seen in the `left-pad` incident [1,4,6] that disrupted major platforms.

---

[1] https://replicate.npmjs.com/.

Prior research has defined trivial, low functionality packages based on lines of code and cyclomatic complexity [1], or function count [6], and shown they can be as risky as larger ones due to transitive dependencies [4,5]. However, existing work has not investigated the security of trivial packages themselves. Additionally, The study identified a set of packages that contain no functionality – data-only packages. These contain no executable logic and serve solely as containers for static values or datasets, such as `color-names`, which maps color names to hex codes and `const-log10e`, which exports a single numeric constant. While seemingly harmless, they can still introduce risks through bundled metadata, configuration content, or dependency chains–similar to trivial packages. However, no systematic study has addressed data-only packages in the npm ecosystem or proposed automated detection methods for them.

This gap matters since many developers are unaware that trivial or data-only packages increase security risks [1]. In some cases, developers may include these packages in their dependency chain without realizing it. To address this issue, The study propose a rule-based detection method and conduct an empirical study on their prevalence and risks in the npm ecosystem in 2025. The result indicate that 17.92% of npm packages are trivial and remain widely uses today, with vulnerability levels similar to non-trivial ones. This paper also define data-only packages as those with no functions, complexity per file ≤ 1, and no import statements; although logic-free, they can still carry vulnerabilities. Using both definitions, our detection tool achieved 94% accuracy, enabling effective large-scale analysis.

2   Related Work

In this section, we discuss studies related to this work, primarily on trivial packages in the npm ecosystem. Abdalkareem et al. [1] defined trivial packages as those with ≤ 35 lines of code and cyclomatic complexity ≤ 10, while Kula et al. [6] focused on micro-packages, identifying them by function count ≤ 1. Both studies emphasize that, despite their minimal functionality, such packages can create deep dependency chains. Chowdhury et al. [4] extended this perspective by showing that trivial packages can have non-trivial impacts on security and stability in large-scale JavaScript projects. Similarly, Decan et al. [5] examined how vulnerabilities propagate through npm's dependency network, revealing that security issues can affect both small and large packages via transitive dependencies. These findings highlight that trivial packages can present significant risks despite their minimal features.

While these studies address the prevalence and risks of small or trivial packages, none explicitly characterize data-only packages–packages that contain no executable logic. Our work extends this research by defining data-only packages, assessing their prevalence and risks, and proposing an automated detection method.

3   Dataset

To support our study on low functionality and no functionality packages in the NPM ecosystem, we constructed a dataset by randomly sampling packages from the public NPM registry (Table 1).

Table 1. Overview of the dataset.

Subset	Number of Packages
NPM Packages as of July 2025	3.5 million
Random Sample	3281
Low Functionality (Trivial)	577
No Functionality (Data-only)	40
Vulnerability Count	5660

A total of 3,281 packages were randomly selected using data from **npms.io**.[2]

The selection was designed to encompass a wide range of functionality, sizes, and popularity levels. The dataset includes both newly published and long-standing packages, reflecting the current state of the ecosystem as of July 2025.

For each package, the name, GitHub repository link, download count, and score were obtained from the npms.io API. In addition the repository source files were retrieved using the `npm install` command, and the dataset excludes irrelevant files such as tests, type declarations, and distribution/build directories to ensure consistency.

Furthermore, 61 packages that contained no measurable source code were filtered out, as they did not provide any implementation logic and would not contribute meaningfully to the analysis.

The dataset also contains five calculated package metrics for the remaining 3,220 packages; 1) lines of code (LOC), 2) cyclomatic complexity, 3) function count, 4) dependency count, and 5) known vulnerabilities. First, LOC was calculated using `cloc`,[3] excluding comments and empty lines. Cyclomatic complexity and function count were calculated using `typhonjs-escomplex` [7]. The dependency count was calculated as the total number of transitive dependencies (both direct and indirect) by recursively traversing the dependency graph of each package [1]. Finally, known vulnerabilities were collected using the `npm audit` command in JSON output mode, capturing the number and severity of known vulnerabilities for each package.

---

[2] https://npms.io/.
[3] https://www.npmjs.com/package/cloc.

4   Results

4.1   RQ1: How Prevalent Are Trivial Packages in the Ecosystem?

The analysis examined the prevalence, popularity, and download counts of trivial libraries within the sample of 3,220 mined NPM packages. To effectively explore and detect trivial packages, a clear definition of what constituted a trivial package was established. Following the definition from Abdalkareem et al. [1], classifying packages as trivial if they had LOC ≤ 35 and complexity ≤ 10. Among the 3,220 mined NPM packages, 577 packages (17.92%) were identified as trivial. This indicated that nearly 1 in 5 packages in the NPM ecosystem could be considered trivial, highlighting their relative prevalence.

To further understand the significance and prevalence of trivial packages, their real-world usage was explored by examining download counts between June and July 2025. The analysis revealed that 12.3% of trivial packages had over 1,000,000 downloads per month, and 28.2% had more than 1,000 downloads per month. These statistics suggest that many trivial packages are widely used, emphasizing their importance despite their simplicity. Beyond download counts, the npms.io popularity score was also considered, which accounts for community signals like stars and forks, making it a more reliable indicator of real-world adoption [2]. The popularity score assigned by npms.io paints a more conservative picture. Only 6.3% of trivial packages scored above 0.6, and a mere 0.9% scored above 0.8 in popularity.

Taken together, these findings indicate that trivial packages are not only prevalent in the NPM ecosystem but also widely adopted, despite potentially being underrated by scoring systems that rely heavily on community interaction metrics.

4.2   RQ2: Are Trivial Packages More Likely to be Vulnerable?

Previous studies have shown that trivial packages often introduce long dependency chains, which many developers cite as a major drawback of using them [1]. Such dependency trees increase vulnerability exposure [5], but prior work has not examined trivial packages directly. Motivated by these observations, we conducted an empirical study to examine whether trivial packages are more likely to be vulnerable by looking at vulnerability reports via `npm audit`.

Using the dataset of 3,220 npm packages, the relationship between package type (trivial vs. non-trivial) and known vulnerabilities was analyzed. The distribution plots shown in Fig. 1b reveal that although most packages in both categories have fewer than five vulnerabilities, some trivial packages are outliers, with vulnerability counts exceeding 100. Overall, both package types exhibit very similar distributions, as illustrated in Fig. 1a.

To statistically assess the difference, we performed a Mann–Whitney U test, which yielded a p-value of 0.0000000013–indicating a statistically significant difference between the two groups ($p < 0.05$). However, when Cliff's Delta was calculated to evaluate the effect size, the result was -0.1091, which indicates a

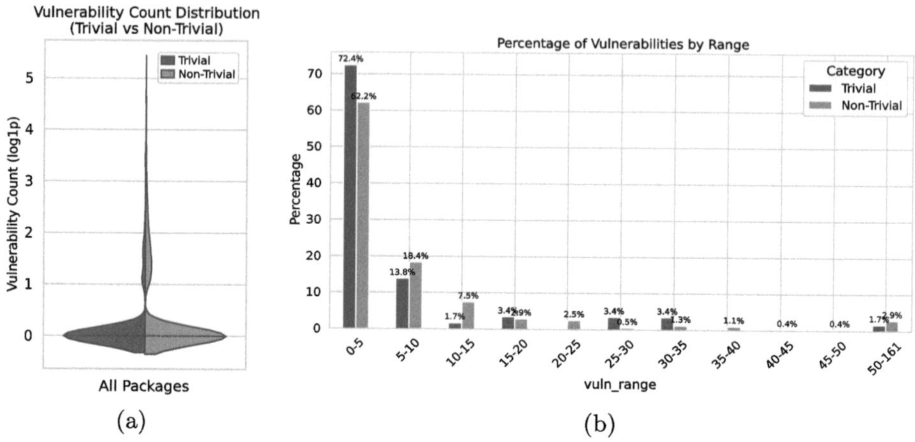

Fig. 1. Trivial vs. non-trivial vulnerability distribution (a) and percentage (b).

negligible difference. Although Non-trivial packages have slightly more vulnerabilities on average, but the difference is negligible. Trivial packages can pose similar security risks, so their inclusion may be unjustified given their potential impact on dependency chains and ecosystem stability.

4.3 RQ3: How Can We Identify Data-Only Packages Automatically?

To support further analysis, we propose a rule-based heuristic grounded in static code analysis to automatically identify both trivial and data-only packages, aligning with the study's goal of scalable detection and risk assessment in the npm ecosystem. The assumption is that data-only packages contain no user-defined functions, based on their logic-free nature. Starting with 80 packages having zero functions, manual inspection categorized them as 40 data-only, 27 trivial, and 13 normal packages.

However, the function count alone proved insufficient. Several edge cases were encountered, including facade packages that re-export from other libraries and packages that use external dependencies without defining functions. To address this, cyclomatic complexity (normalized by file count) and dependency usage patterns were examined. Instead of relying on declared metadata, actual import behavior was analyzed by parsing source files for import and require statements, excluding internal references. Packages importing external libraries were assumed to use external logic and excluded from data-only classification. This filtering effectively removed all trivial and normal packages while retaining verified data-only packages. **Final Rule:** Data-only packages must satisfy: **(1) function count = 0, (2) average cyclomatic complexity per file ≤ 1, (3) no import/require statements referring to external modules.** This rule-based method enables automated detection without requiring runtime analysis or full AST parsing.

4.4   RQ4: What are the Types of Data-Only Libraries?

Following automated identification, the 40 data-only packages (1.24% of the dataset) were manually classified by a single author using the zero-function, no-logic definition. Given the clarity of this definition, the process was straightforward. To understand their nature and roles, we observed two main categories:

Static JSON Data Exporters: Packages exporting predefined JavaScript objects via module.exports, including large datasets and configuration modules (e.g., brittanica-r, color-name,).

```
1    module.exports = {
2        aliceblue: [240, 248, 255],
3        ...
4    }
```

Listing 1.1. Static JSON data exporter example from `color-name`

Constant Value Containers: Packages exporting reusable constants like numbers or strings, designed for direct use in application logic (e.g., const-e, const-log2e).

```
1  module.exports = 2.718281828459045235360287471352662497757247093699959574966;
```

Listing 1.2. Excerpt from the `const-e` package exporting only a constant value

Despite differences in size and format, all data-only packages share common characteristics: they contain no functions, do not perform any computation or side effects, and exclusively provide static values for consumption by other packages.

4.5   RQ5: Are Data-Only Libraries More Likely to be Vulnerable?

To complement the investigation of risks associated with trivial packages, this study analyzes the vulnerability exposure of data-only packages. Vulnerability data are extracted using the npm audit API, and the results are compared between data-only and non-data-only packages.

Table 2. Vulnerabilities in Data-only and Non-Data-only npm Packages

npm Packages	Min.	Median	Mean	Max
Data-only	0.00	0.00	1.10	9.00
Non-Data-only	0.00	0.00	1.76	161.00

As shown in Table 2, data-only packages exhibit fewer vulnerabilities in raw numbers and mean values (max = 9 vs. 161, mean = 1.10 vs. 1.76), although the median remains zero for both groups. However, while the raw numbers suggest that data-only packages tend to have fewer reported vulnerabilities, statistical tests reveal no significant difference. The Mann–Whitney U test yields a non-significant result, and the effect size measured by Cliff's Delta is negligible (0.0164).

To further confirm this result, given the large sample size imbalance (40 data-only packages vs. 3,180 non-data-only packages), bootstrapping was applied [3]. In 1,000 iterations, only 1.1% of the samples showed a statistically significant difference ($p < 0.05$). This reinforces the conclusion that the difference is not statistically significant. Data-only packages, though logic-free, still carry risks from configuration or metadata, potentially exposing the ecosystem to vulnerabilities.

4.6 RQ6: How Effective is a Tool to Detect Trivial and Data-Only Packages?

We implemented a command-line, rule-based analysis tool[4] designed to automatically detect trivial and data-only packages in npm projects based on our defined criteria. (LOC $\leq$35 and complexity $\leq$10) and data-only packages (function count = 0, average complexity per file $\leq$1, no external imports) (Fig. 2).

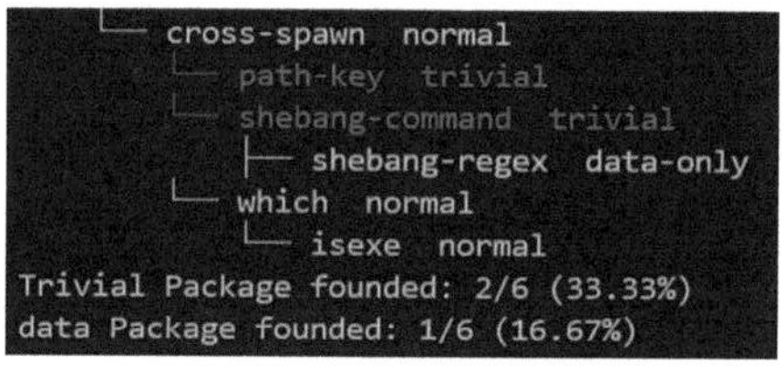

Fig. 2. Example tool UI.

The tool analyzes packages by calculating LOC, cyclomatic complexity, function count, and dependency usage, then classifies each as Normal, Trivial, or Data-only with a dependency tree highlighted output and summary statistics.

For evaluation, 250 samples were randomly selected using Cochran's formula (90% confidence). A single researcher labeled them, with ambiguous cases cross-checked by two LLMs (GPT-4o, Gemini 2.5 Flash) for additional validation and to reduce bias. The tool achieved 94% accuracy and 0.93 weighted F1. It performed strongly for normal and trivial packages (precision 0.93–1.00, recall 0.76–0.99) but had lower recall for data-only (0.67) due to the small sample size. Overall, the rule-based tool is effective for large-scale analysis, though data-only detection needs refinement with larger datasets.

---

[4] https://github.com/tnnpp/Trivial-package-detection-tool.

5   Threats to Validity

Construct Validity: The tool has certain limitations. First, typhonjs-escomplex cannot detect some newer JavaScript syntax. Second, it does not measure lines of code or complexity in other programming languages, which may cause some packages to be misclassified. In RQ3, we evaluated the tool only on packages it could analyze. Moreover, the definition of data-only packages used in this study is a rule-based heuristic; we did not perform deeper dynamic or runtime behavior analysis. The small number of data-only cases in the dataset also limits confidence in the results for this category. **Internal validity:** The accuracy of ground truth labeling may affect results. Although we reduced bias by consulting two LLMs for ambiguous cases, misclassifications may still occur. **External validity:** The dataset was randomly sampled from the npm registry, but it represents only a small portion of the ecosystem and may not cover all package types.

6   Conclusion

Trivial and data-only packages pose overlooked risks in the npm ecosystem. In this study, our analysis found that 18% of packages are trivial and 1.24% are data-only, yet both can expose projects to vulnerability levels comparable to larger packages. This illustrates how package usage accelerates development time but increases maintenance and security risks. The proposed rule-based detection tool achieved 94% accuracy, showing the feasibility of scalable static analysis. Future work will enhance detection with AST and runtime analysis, expand dataset coverage, and compare across ecosystems such as PyPI and Maven to better understand supply chain risks.

Acknowledgments. We gratefully acknowledge the financial support of JSPS KAKENHI grants (JP24K02921, JP25K21359), as well as JST PRESTO grant (JPMJPR22P3), ASPIRE grant (JPMJAP2415), and AIP Accelerated Program (JPMJCR25U7).

References

1. Abdalkareem, R., et al.: Why do developers use trivial packages? An empirical case study on NPM. In: Proceedings of the 2017 11th Joint Meeting on Foundations of Software Engineering, pp. 385–395. ESEC/FSE (2017). https://doi.org/10.1145/3106237.3106267
2. Abdellatif, A., et al.: Simplifying the search of NPM packages. Inf. Softw. Technol. **126**, 106365 (2020). https://doi.org/10.1016/j.infsof.2020.106365
3. Afzal, W., et al.: Resampling methods in software quality classification. Int. J. Softw. Eng. Knowl. Eng. **22**(02), 203–223 (2012). https://doi.org/10.1142/S0218194012400037

4. Chowdhury, M.A.R., et al.: On the untriviality of trivial packages: an empirical study of NPM Javascript packages. **48**(8), 2695–2708 (2022). https://doi.org/10.1109/TSE.2021.3068901
5. Decan, A., et al.: On the impact of security vulnerabilities in the NPM package dependency network. In: Proceedings of the 15th International Conference on Mining Software Repositories, MSR 2018, pp. 181–191 (2018). https://doi.org/10.1145/3196398.3196401
6. Kula, R., et al.: On the impact of micro-packages: an empirical study of the NPM Javascript ecosystem (2017). https://doi.org/10.48550/arXiv.1709.04638
7. Tarner, H., et al.: Visually analyzing the structure and code quality of component-based web applications. In: 2021 Working Conference on Software Visualization (VISSOFT), pp. 160–164 (2021). https://doi.org/10.1109/VISSOFT52517.2021.00031

PostItFlow: An Early Study on Agent-Based Workflow for Enhancing and Visualizing User Stories

Oshani Weerakoon[1]([✉]) [ID], Juuso Rytilahti[1] [ID], Tuomas Mäkilä[1] [ID], Erkki Kaila[1] [ID], and Shola Oyedeji[2] [ID]

[1] University of Turku, Turku, Finland
`osweer@utu.fi`
[2] LUT University, Lappeenranta, Finland

Abstract. Incomplete or missing requirements are a primary cause of project failure. During the initial phase of requirements elicitation, shortcomings frequently arise due to stakeholders' differing perspectives and the predominance of elicitation methods that emphasize textual extraction. To address this challenge, we introduce PostItFlow, an AI agent-based workflow designed to provide a simple, easy-to-generate, and holistic visual overview of requirements. PostItFlow visualizes events and interactions among components, systems, and entities within a collection of user stories under an epic. Its objective is to reduce missed and incomplete requirements at the early stages of elicitation by offering a practical visual aid that can be utilized by both customers and requirements engineering (RE) practitioners. The visual output is produced through four progressive steps using GPT-5: (i) finalizing the given epic by adding supplementary stories where necessary, (ii) integrating a potential timeline that reflects the phases of the user story flow, (iii) enriching events related to entities or components with additional details, and (iv) generating the HTML-based visual output. We also demonstrate our workflow using a selected case study. This workflow will undergo industrial testing, with further enhancements guided by evaluations of usability, accuracy, and relevance to the information visualized. The prototype has been published as open source on Zenodo.

Keywords: Requirement engineering · Requirement elicitation · Requirement visualization · Visual workflow · User story · Large language model · GPT-5

1 Introduction

Business clients frequently struggle to articulate clear requirements at the outset of a project, as they often lack a clear understanding of what they require. Studies in requirements engineering show that clients may not fully know or express their own business needs during early elicitation [6], tend to have a limited

G. Scanniello et al. (Eds.): PROFES 2025, LNCS 16361, pp. 561–570, 2026.
https://doi.org/10.1007/978-3-032-12089-2_42

perspective, often aware of only the issues in their immediate domain, which means they identify only a subset of the true requirements [2] or they discover new possibilities as a project progresses; exposure to prototypes or discussions can reveal options they had not considered [15]. These factors explain why initial requirements are frequently incomplete or missing, and it is a serious issue that causes projects to fail [9].

User stories remain the paramount format for specifying software requirements in industry [24]. In practice, poorly written user stories can be overly lengthy, vague, or biased, and thus lack quality, making them difficult to use in downstream development tasks and meeting client expectations [22]. On the other hand, as the number of user stories in a project grows, stakeholders struggle to maintain an accurate mental model of the system from these scattered descriptions. Together, they can manifest as missed dependencies, redundancies, or conflicts among requirements that are hard to detect by reading text alone.

One approach to mitigate these problems is to derive more structured, visual representations from user stories and aim to uncover missing, unclear requirements based on them during the elicitation stage itself. According to prior research, automatically extracting conceptual models or other diagrams from requirements can provide a better mental image of the relationships between different entities and systems [13] than text. In principle, such visual models improve requirements comprehension and support analysis by offloading cognitive burden from stakeholders' memory onto an external diagram. However, the development of tools to achieve this for user stories has been limited, and current tool support for visualizing existing NL requirements is minimal [24].

Emerging AI technologies, like large language models (LLMs), offer new pathways to address this gap. Their strength in natural language (NL) processing responds to one core challenge of NL requirements the ambiguity and variability of human language. Current studies already indicate that LLM-driven tools can expedite different requirements engineering activities [1,17], particularly for generating user stories from documents [18,22], enhancing user story quality [21,22], and user story and test case generation [18]. Researchers also caution that LLMs are not a silver bullet for RE since they lack a true understanding of the software's context and goals, therefore might miss subtle nuances or trade-offs that a human analyst would catch [1]. LLMs have other downsides as well, most notably hallucinations [28], shortcuts [26], tendency to repeat patterns present in their training data [7], and their potential to cause long-term harm to one's creativity and cognition [10,11,14].

In this paper, we explore the aforementioned gap through the research question, ***RQ: How can large language models, within a multi-agent architecture, be harnessed to automatically structure and visualize user story requirements for improved understanding?*** To address it, we propose PostItFlow, a post-it-note style AI agent-based workflow that improves a given set of user stories and visually represents different relationships with stakeholders, systems, and other entities. Our goal is to bridge the gulf between early and actual requirements by providing clients and RE engineers with a simple, modifiable visual that may lower the cognitive burden for users [13] than current existing requirement visualizing and modeling-based approaches [5], and more fitting for the early requirement elicitation stage. We will pilot this workflow as a part of an AI-based multi-agent collaboration system that will manage a complete requirement engineering workflow of one of the author's PhD projects in the future. Therefore, this workflow will be under continued improvement and will soon be ready for its first test pilot. The contributions of this work are summarized as follows:

- PostItFlow: An AI agent-based workflow for improving and visualizing user stories to better understand and identify missing or unclear requirements at an early stage of requirement elicitation.
- Part of the AI-based multi-agent RE workflow that handles RE activities from elicitation to management.
- Current version of the PostItFlow, and additional materials are available with an open-source license in Zenodo [1].

2   Related Work

Early requirement elicitation largely depends on client input. However, many requirements are tacit, implicitly understood by the client but left unstated, resulting in important needs being overlooked during initial interviews [20]. Prior studies have examined approaches to streamlining requirement elicitation so as to enhance the value contributed to subsequent project phases [6,12,20]. Proposed remedies from the RE practitioners' side include the use of requirement elicitation prompting technique during interviews [4] and client learning through collaborative elaboration [15].

Researchers have also long explored requirements visualization as a means to improve understanding and decision-making in RE, which can range from simple graphical models (such as UML diagrams or goal models) to complex interactive dashboards. A comprehensive survey by Cooper et al. [5] found that a wide variety of visualization formats have been applied to RE, including tabular, relational, sequential, hierarchical, and metaphorical (quantitative) under different RE activities (elicitation, modeling, negotiation, etc.). These formats have shown potential to highlight relationships and new patterns that are not obvious in other forms [19] like text alone. Prior work has also proposed automated approaches, for example, Lucassen et al.'s [13] Visual Narrator tool demonstrated that it is possible to generate a conceptual model from user story requirements. Some limitations of this tool include cognitive overload for human analysts and a user story processing algorithm that lacks support for certain human expressions, such as adjectives and adverbs [13]. Relatively few of these methods have achieved broad practical uptake or delivered clear end-to-end value for end users [19] and remain at the prototype stage, and traditional barriers that hinder wider adoption.

---

[1] https://doi.org/10.5281/zenodo.16886981.

In summary, the state of the art suggests that (i) visualizing and improving requirements (we will focus on user stories) remains an underdeveloped area with known limitations in existing solutions, and (ii) emerging AI techniques (LLMs) have not yet been fully harnessed to both improve and produce intuitive visual representations in the RE context. There is a clear need for research to fill this gap.

3   Experimental Design

3.1   Design Philosophy behind PostItFlow

PostItFlow consists of an autonomous agent pipeline that generates an HTML file with the proposed visualization of entities and their relationships. The pipeline is illustrated in the Fig. 1, and an example of the visual output in HTML format is shown in Fig. 2. The project code, along with the input for the example flow (epic and user stories) and other related materials, is available at our repository [2].

Autonomous Agent Pipeline: The autonomous one-way pipeline generates the visualization and completes the user stories through a four-step process (Fig. 1), utilizing GPT-5 as the underlying model. The only input provided to the model is the epic and its user stories, without additional context such as acceptance criteria. The model is prompted three times, once for each of the first three steps. In steps 2 and 3, the input additionally includes the full chat history from the preceding steps to preserve contextual information. Nevertheless, the process remains explicitly separated into distinct steps to ensure that the LLM adheres closely to the instructions for each stage. The final step of HTML file generation is performed using a Python script to guarantee a consistent visual appearance across different runs.

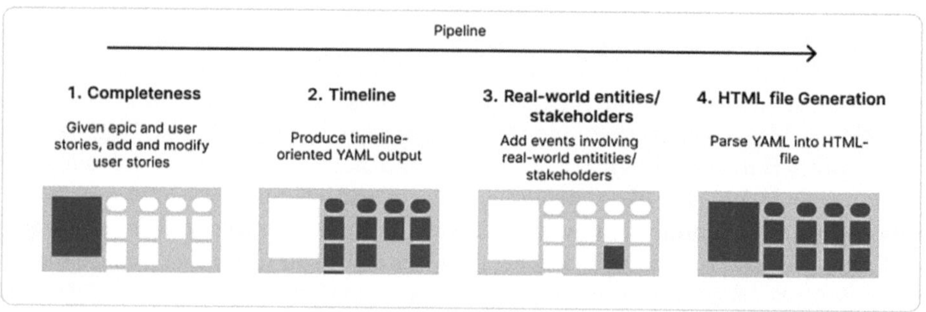

Fig. 1. Overview of the autonomous agent pipeline. The visualization is generated in the final (fourth) step of the process.

---

[2] https://doi.org/10.5281/zenodo.16886981.

The four steps of the pipeline are explained in detail below:

1. **Completeness**: In the first step (prompt 1), the model receives as input an individual epic and a set of user stories without any additional context. The model is instructed to ensure the completeness of the epic by revising the existing user stories and, where necessary, adding new ones. The output is required to be in JSON format and contains the improved list of the epic and associated user stories without additional descriptive text.

2. **Timeline**: In the second step (prompt 2), the model receives as input the JSON output from the first step and is instructed to generate a timeline-oriented representation of the user stories by dividing them into multiple phases, each comprising several events. In the final output, phases are presented as columns.

   Each event must include a timeline sequence number, labels of the related user stories, entities responsible for the event's actions, and details regarding the required UI and server interactions. Events are represented as individual notes in the final output, which is formatted in YAML.

3. **Real-world entities/stakeholders**: In the third step (prompt 3), the model receives as input the output from the previous step and is instructed to augment the epic by adding events involving real-world entities or stakeholders not explicitly mentioned in the original user stories. This step captures interactions in practice that are often not directly related to the application itself.

4. **HTML-file Generation**: In the fourth and final step, the generated YAML file is processed by a Python script that converts the information into a partially interactive HTML file.

This pipeline enabled the model to achieve the desired output in each step, ultimately leading to the final HTML output file.

Output Design: When designing the PostItFlow, the design philosophy ("what is being modeled") is inspired by the service design blueprint [3], that aim to visualize the process of the events, such as key interactions between entities and related support activities, including e.g. phases of a process that are invisible to customers [3]. This is especially helpful in software development, as often there is a need to model interactions between things that the user can not see, like API calls between different servers. The visual outlook ("how information is displayed") of this workflow is inspired by the post-it note-like appearance of Kanban [8] board. Kanban is an agile development methodology that helps manage workflow by using visual aids [8] on a board and increase work visibility [23], making it a good design choice for user story modeling. However, PostItFlow is different from Kanban. It shows the process that the collection of user stories under the given epic describes, not the workflow of an ongoing project.

In summary, PostItFlow visualizes the interactions between entities and components from the perspective of implementing the given epic and user stories, under a four-step pipeline leading to an HTML output.

3.2 Case study

To demonstrate the visualization workflow in practice, we selected Mentcare, a case study concerning a clinical information system, as presented in the Software Engineering textbook by Ian Sommerville [25]. We generated epics and their corresponding user stories based on this case study and used them as inputs for producing the visualization flows. An example visualization flow, including one post-it note, is shown in Fig. 2.

In the Fig. 2, the epic and user stories are listed on the left of the visualization. Any new user stories generated by the LLM are displayed at the bottom of the list. The phases of the user story flow are depicted as columns, and Post-it notes are individual events. The different stakeholders are presented by having a different background color for easy differentiation. Each user story is numbered, and these numbers are displayed on the post-it notes to easily distinguish which note is related to which user story. The timing of the events in the flow is read from left to right, from top to bottom, one phase (column) at a time. There may also be additional phases added by the LLM that relate to the epic's implementation. The appearance can also be easily understood, as the post-it note-like appearance makes it intuitive for non-technical stakeholders as well. We propose that showing the early requirements as a user story flow in this way can help to identify possible gaps, especially if done in unison for all of the stakeholders included. In this preliminary test example, we observed the addition of new and relevant user stories, as well as the inclusion of more realistic details about entities and their relationships, compared to the original user stories.

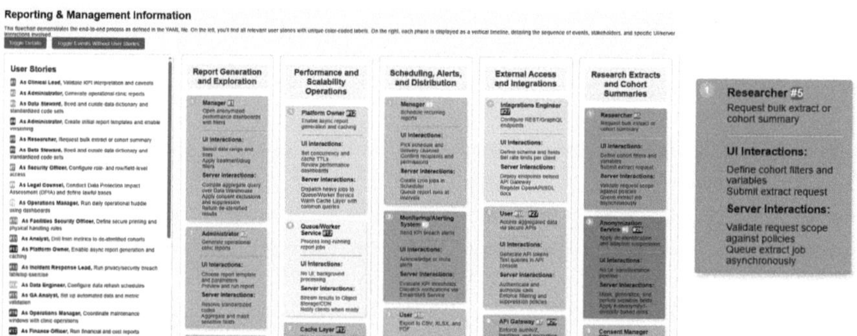

Fig. 2. PostIFlow visualization flow: On the left is a truncated version of the whole flow, and on the right is a magnified version of a single card. The output is produced from one epic ("Reporting and management information"), consisting of 5 user stories, without additional details such as acceptance criteria. The model used was OpenAI's GPT-5.

4   Key Observations

In this paper, we present PostItFlow, a novel AI agent-based workflow visualizing events and interactions between entities, systems, and components in a set of given user stories belonging to an epic. Our goal for PostItFlow is to provide a practical visualization tool for both RE practitioners and clients to use during the requirement elicitation, with the aim of minimizing missing or unclear requirements at the early stages, an important objective, as prior research has demonstrated that missing or incomplete requirements are a major cause of project failure [9].

Our workflow is backed by GPT-5 and user stories of a single epic act as the input. Relevant instructions are provided to the model in order to achieve a meaningful and information-enriched visualization of different interactions of the entities involved. The visual output is generated through four incremental steps: (i) completing the epic with additional relevant stories, (ii) incorporating a potential timeline that illustrates the flow of the user stories, (iii) enriching entities or stakeholders with associated events and further details, and (iv) generating the HTML-based visual output. We propose that this visualization flow can be used by RE practitioners (e.g., Requirement Engineers) during elicitation rounds with clients to uncover hidden or missing requirements. This will also act as a working visual for both parties before a prototype comes to life.

While PostItFlow is primarily expected to be used in the requirements elicitation process, it could also be used as a testing and quality assurance tool to ensure the completeness of an epic. This approach is also supported by the early research results on a study conducted by Kosmyna et al. that suggests that rewriting an essay using AI tools (after prior AI-free writing) could be beneficial, while utilizing AI directly in the writing process could potentially be harmful in the long-term [10].

As discussed in the Sect. 1, when it comes to the introduction of gen-AI to different workflows, there are many challenges, some related to human cognition, and some to the capabilities of the large language models. But we contend that this does not preclude the use of LLMs, given their continually increasing potential. Moreover, we note that generating a complete visualization for each epic would be highly resource-intensive if done manually from the ground up. Utilizing LLMs in producing the visualization reduces the manual work required significantly, thus making such an approach feasible for more use cases.

5   Limitations

The current prototype of PostItFlow is intentionally designed to be simple and accessible, even for non-technical users, and has demonstrated feasibility within the visual workflow (Fig. 2) generated from the case study presented in Subsect. 3.2. However, it has not yet been tested in industrial project scenarios, which will reveal next set of improvements needed.

To generate the desired visual outputs, we employed structured prompting, with potential hallucination effects to be assessed in real-world testing. Additionally, the current pipeline input is restricted to an epic and its related user stories, limiting the model's contextual understanding. These constraints may affect both the completeness and reliability of the generated artifacts. While the limitations with all large language modelbased approaches may never be fully resolved, we propose that PostItFlow can still stimulate discussions with stakeholders, leading to a more comprehensive understanding of the requirements during elicitation and beyond.

6   Future Work

Future work will address these limitations and advance the development of the final multi-agent system. We aim to enhance flexibility in modifying context, regenerating notes, and enabling visual edits during stakeholder discussion rounds. Currently, the pipeline input is limited to an epic and its associated user stories. Expanding it to incorporate additional sources, such as meeting notes and business documents, is a key direction for extending the system's capabilities. Moreover, providing the model with broader contextual information may improve the quality of the generated artifacts [16].

To mitigate hallucinations and improve domain adaptation, fine-tuning the underlying large language model for the specific requirements engineering context is a promising direction. While the current prototype utilizes GPT-5, future iterations will also explore open-source models, such as LLaMA and DeepSeek, to enable greater flexibility for fine-tuning and adaptation.

7   Conclusion

PostItFlow has been developed as a prototype and will undergo empirical evaluation in real-world industrial settings to assess and improve its usability, accuracy, and output relevance. This evaluation will follow a lab-to-field generalization approach [27], scaling up the workflow for pilot deployment in industry. As outlined in Sect. 1, the long-term goal is to integrate this workflow into a broader AI-based multi-agent system for requirements engineering tasks, ensuring alignment with the overarching objectives of the envisioned system.

Acknowledgments. This work has been supported by FAST, the Finnish Software Engineering Doctoral Research Network, funded by the Ministry of Education and Culture, Finland.

Disclosure of Interests. The authors have no competing interests to declare that are relevant to the content of this article.

Declaration on Generative AI. During the preparation of this work, the authors employed OpenAI's language models as a supportive tool for developing the pipeline. Following their use, the authors thoroughly reviewed and edited the content and take full responsibility for the final version.

References

1. Arora, C., Grundy, J., Abdelrazek, M.: Advancing requirements engineering through generative AI: assessing the role of LLMS (2023). https://doi.org/10.48550/arXiv.2310.13976, arXiv:2310.13976
2. Arthur, J.D., Groner, M.K.: An operational model for structuring the requirements generation process. Requirements Eng. **10**, 45–62 (2005)
3. Bitner, M.J., Ostrom, A.L., Morgan, F.N.: Service blueprinting: a practical technique for service innovation. Calif. Manage. Rev. **50**(3), 66–94 (2008)
4. Browne, G.J., Rogich, M.B.: An empirical investigation of user requirements elicitation: comparing the effectiveness of prompting techniques. J. Manag. Inf. Syst. **17**(4), 223 (2001)
5. Cooper, J.R., Lee, S.W., Gandhi, R.A., Gotel, O.: Requirements engineering visualization: a survey on the state-of-the-art. In: 2009 Fourth International Workshop on Requirements Engineering Visualization, pp. 46–55. IEEE, Atlanta, GA (2009). https://doi.org/10.1109/REV.2009.4
6. Davey, B., Parker, K.R.: Requirements elicitation problems: a literature analysis (2015)
7. Jiang, B., et al.: A peek into token bias: Large language models are not yet genuine reasoners. arXiv preprint arXiv:2406.11050 (2024)
8. Junior, M.L., Godinho Filho, M.: Variations of the KANBAN system: literature review and classification. Int. J. Prod. Econ. **125**(1), 13–21 (2010)
9. Kalinowski, M., et al.: Preventing incomplete/hidden requirements: reflections on survey data from Austria and Brazil, pp. 63–78 (2016). https://doi.org/10.1007/978-3-319-27033-3_5
10. Kosmyna, N., et al.: Your brain on ChatGPT: accumulation of cognitive debt when using an ai assistant for essay writing task. arXiv preprint arXiv:2506.08872 (2025)
11. Kumar, H., Vincentius, J., Jordan, E., Anderson, A.: Human creativity in the age of LLMS: randomized experiments on divergent and convergent thinking. In: Proceedings of the 2025 CHI Conference on Human Factors in Computing Systems. CHI 2025, Association for Computing Machinery, New York, NY, USA (2025). https://doi.org/10.1145/3706598.3714198
12. Loucopoulos, P.: Engaging stakeholders in defining early requirements, pp. 37–42. Springer-Verlag, Heidelberg (2006). https://doi.org/10.1007/1-4020-3675-2_5
13. Lucassen, G., Dalpiaz, F., Van Der Werf, J.M.E.M., Brinkkemper, S.: Visualizing user story requirements at multiple granularity levels via semantic relatedness. In: Comyn-Wattiau, I., Tanaka, K., Song, I.Y., Yamamoto, S., Saeki, M. (eds.) Conceptual Modeling, LNCS, vol. 9974, pp. 463–478. Springer International Publishing, Cham (2016). https://doi.org/10.1007/978-3-319-46397-1_35
14. MacArthur, M.: Large language models and the problem of rhetorical debt. AI and Soc., 1–14 (2025). https://doi.org/10.1007/s00146-025-02403-w
15. Majchrzak, A., Beath, C.M., Lim, R.A., Chin, W.W.: Managing client dialogues during information systems design to facilitate client learning. MIS Q. **29**(4), 653 (2005)
16. Mei, L., et al.: A survey of context engineering for large language models (2025). arXiv:2507.13334
17. Nguyen-Duc, A., et al.: Generative artificial intelligence for software engineering – a research agenda (2023). https://doi.org/10.48550/arXiv.2310.18648, arXiv:2310.18648

18. Rahman, T., Zhu, Y.: Automated user story generation with test case specification using large language model (2024). https://doi.org/10.48550/arXiv.2404.01558, arXiv:2404.01558
19. Reddivari, S., Rad, P., Bhowmik, T., Cain, N., Niu, N.: Visual requirements analytics: a framework and case study. Requirements Eng. **19**(3), 257–279 (2014). https://doi.org/10.1007/s00766-013-0194-3
20. Robertson, S.: Requirements trawling: techniques for discovering requirements. Int. J. Hum Comput Stud. **55**, 405–421 (2001)
21. Ronanki, K., Cabrero-Daniel, B., Berger, C.: ChatGPT as a tool for user story quality evaluation: trustworthy out of the box?, Lecture Notes in Business Information Processing, vol. 489, pp. 173–181. Springer Nature Switzerland, Cham (2024). https://doi.org/10.1007/978-3-031-48550-3_17
22. Sami, M.A., Waseem, M., Zhang, Z., Rasheed, Z., Systä, K., Abrahamsson, P.: AI based multiagent approach for requirements elicitation and analysis (2024). https://doi.org/10.48550/arXiv.2409.00038
23. dos Santos, P.S.M., Beltrão, A.C., de Souza, B.P., Travassos, G.H.: On the benefits and challenges of using KANBAN in software engineering: a structured synthesis study. J. Softw. Eng. Res. Dev. **6**(1), 13 (2018)
24. Slob, G.J., Dalpiaz, F., Brinkkemper, S., Lucassen, G.: The interactive narrator tool: effective requirements exploration and discussion through visualization
25. Sommerville, I.: Software Engineering. Pearson, 10th edn. (2015). https://software-engineering-book.com/case-studies/mentcare/
26. Song, R., Li, Y., Shi, L., Giunchiglia, F., Xu, H.: Shortcut learning in in-context learning: a survey. arXiv preprint arXiv:2411.02018 (2024)
27. Wieringa, R., Daneva, M.: Six strategies for generalizing software engineering theories. Sci. Comput. Program. **101**, 136–152 (2015). https://doi.org/10.1016/j.scico.2014.11.013
28. Xu, Z., Jain, S., Kankanhalli, M.: Hallucination is inevitable: an innate limitation of large language models. arXiv preprint arXiv:2401.11817 (2024)

An Empirical Study of Security-Policy Related Issues in Open Source Projects

Rintaro Kanaji[1]([✉]), Brittany Reid[1], Yutaro Kashiwa[1], Raula Gaikovina Kula[2], and Hajimu Iida[1]

[1] Nara Institute of Science and Technology, Nara, Japan
`kanaji.rintaro.kq8@naist.ac.jp`
[2] The University of Osaka, Osaka, Japan

Abstract. GitHub recommends that projects adopt a `SECURITY.md` file that outlines vulnerability reporting procedures. However, the effectiveness and operational challenges of such files are not yet fully understood. This study aims to clarify the challenges that `SECURITY.md` files face in the vulnerability reporting process within open-source communities. Specifically, we classified and analyzed the content of 711 randomly sampled issues related to `SECURITY.md`. We also conducted a quantitative comparative analysis of the close time and number of responses for issues concerning six community health files, including `SECURITY.md`. Our analysis revealed that 79.5% of `SECURITY.md`-related issues were requests to add the file, and reports that included links were closed, with a median time that was 2 days shorter. These findings offer practical insights for improving security reporting policies and community management, ultimately contributing to a more secure open-source ecosystem.

Keywords: Documentation · Open source software · Vulnerability reporting · Security.md

1 Introduction

Most modern systems rely on Open Source Software (OSS), and a single security vulnerability can spread widely to multiple systems through webs of interconnected dependencies. However, if a developer who discovers a vulnerability reports it using public channels such as GitHub's Issues feature, the information runs the risk of being exploited by malicious third parties. Therefore, establishing a policy to properly and safely report vulnerabilities is crucial to reducing security risks for all projects that also rely on that software.

An effective solution for avoiding this risk is the introduction of a `SECURITY.md` file. This file was proposed at the GitHub Satellite held in May 2019 [1] and specifies secure reporting methods for vulnerabilities (e.g., specific email addresses or external forms) and information about supported versions. This allows vulnerability discoverers to report vulnerabilities directly to development teams without disclosing confidential information. GitHub has also published a SECURITY.md template in order to promote its use.

Despite these recommendations, previous work found that the adoption rate of SECURITY.md files remains low at 7% [2], and its adoption has not yet become widespread. The disconnect between GitHub's strong promotion of SECURITY.md and its limited adoption suggests there may be underlying barriers that prevent developers from implementing this security practice. Understanding these barriers is essential for developing strategies to improve adoption rates and ultimately enhance the security of the software supply chain. One valuable source of insight into these challenges is the discussions happening within the developer community itself–specifically, the GitHub issues where developers propose, debate, and implement SECURITY.md files. Figure 1 illustrates an example of a common issue related to SECURITY.md files, where it is proposed that vulnerability reporting instructions be added to the project via a security policy.

In this study, we aim to clarify the problems developers may face in regards to SECURITY.md files, before and after adoption, through analysis of related issues. We analyzed 711 issues regarding SECURITY.md files and found that the most common request was for additions to SECURITY.md, accounting for 79.5% of the total. Among these additional requests, issues that included detailed links related to SECURITY.md, such as documentation, took two days less to close. Our findings suggest an increased awareness of security policies by the community, and the effectiveness of providing example documentation.

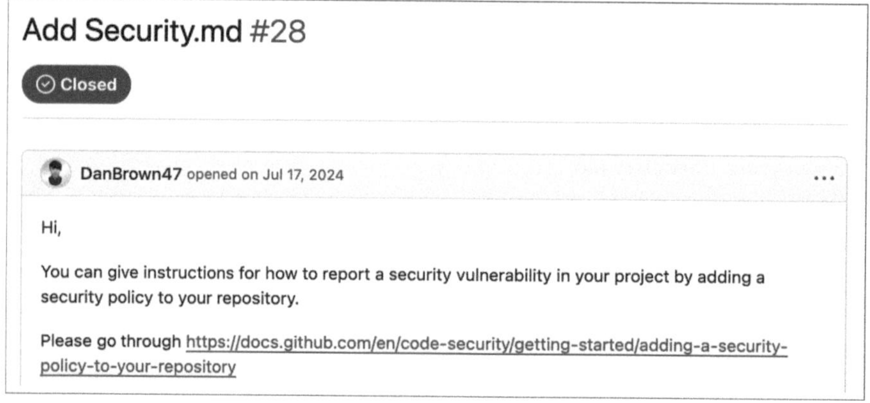

Fig. 1. SECURITY.md-related issue (https://github.com/incidentalhq/incidental/issues/28.

2 Related Work

Kancharoendee et al. [3] investigated the relationship between the presence of a SECURITY.md file and a project's security score on GitHub. Their findings reveal that projects lacking a `SECURITY.md` file tend to have lower security scores from OpenSSF. Similarly, the work by Bühlmann et al. [4] focused on how developers handle security issue reports on GitHub, noting an increasing trend in security-related issue reports and a decrease in their average resolution time. These findings suggest that the adoption of `SECURITY.md` contributes to maintaining repository health and indicates a rising security awareness across the developer community. However, prior research [3,4] has not sufficiently addressed the factors hindering the adoption of `SECURITY.md` files or the specific challenges faced after implementation. Furthermore, while there has been research on analyzing issues for `README.md` files [5], there has been no research on issues related to `SECURITY.md`. Therefore, to bridge this gap in the literature, this study investigates and analyzes the challenges associated with `SECURITY.md` by focusing on the content of its related issues and the close time.

3 Research Questions

This study addresses the following two research questions (RQs).

RQ1: How long does it take to close `SECURITY.md` related issues?

For this RQ, we investigate the close time of `SECURITY.md` related issues. Security-related issues are an area that requires early response, and so we ask how seriously developers take these issues. To answer this question, we compare:

RQ1.1: Close time vs. other documentation
RQ1.2: Close time with links
RQ1.3: Number of responses to issues

First, we evaluate how quickly issues related to `SECURITY.md` are addressed compared to other community health files (e.g., `CONTRIBUTING.md`, `SUPPORT.md`, etc.). Then we compare issues that include links providing detailed information about `SECURITY.md` with those that do not, and quantitatively evaluate whether the presence or absence of links to information about the installation of `SECURITY.md` has an effect on reducing the time required to close issues. Issues related to the addition of `SECURITY.md` need to be resolved more quickly. To provide more practical guidelines, it is necessary to analyze how differences in content affect resolution times, which is why this RQ was established. Finally, we quantitatively evaluate the level of community interest in security-related topics by comparing the "number of responses," such as the number of comments and frequency of exchanges on an issue, between `SECURITY.md` and other files. Since this issue is related to security, we established this RQ based on the assumption that it would be discussed more than other files.

RQ2: What security policy related issues do developers create?

This RQ focuses on the content of issues related to SECURITY.md. In order to clarify the actual usage and issues of SECURITY.md in OSS, we investigated what kinds of issues are reported in GitHub Issues that mention SECURITY.md. Examples include requests to add or modify SECURITY.md, but we also investigated what other issues there are and what percentage of them are included.

4   Data Collection

In this study, we collected issues related to SECURITY.md or similar documents on GitHub. We utilized the GitHub REST API (v3) [6] to search public repositories for closed issues created between May 1, 2019 (i.e., the date GitHub introduced SECURITY.md), and June 30, 2025 (i.e., the date our data collection started). The search targeted issues that included any of the following documentation files in their titles or descriptions: SECURITY.md, SUPPORT.md, LICENSE.md, GOVERNANCE.md, CONTRIBUTING.md, and CODE_OF_CONDUCT.md. To accommodate API rate limits and ensure processing efficiency, data collection was continued until a total of 10,000 issues for each file type had been retrieved.

To ensure the quality of the collected issues, we applied the following filtering criteria:
- Issues from repositories with fewer than 20 stars were excluded
- Non-English issues were filtered out using the *langdetect* library to ensure consistent analysis.
- When multiple issues from the same repository were found, only the first instance was retained to avoid overrepresentation.
- Issues without a recorded close date were excluded to enable analysis of resolution times.

After applying these filters, we obtained 15,192 issues. Table 1 summarizes the number of issues collected. For each issue, we collected metadata including creation and closure dates to support our analysis of response times.

For the manual classification of SECURITY.md files (i.e., RQ2), we randomly sampled 711 issues from a total of 3,323. Two authors independently reviewed and manually categorized each issue report according to its reporting purpose, employing an open card sorting methodology. The two inspectors classified in the same way 97.5% of the inspected issues, with a Cohen's kappa coefficient of 0.958, which demonstrates an almost perfect agreement. The conflicting cases between the two inspectors were resolved through discussion, facilitated by a third author who acted as an adjudicator.

5   Results

RQ1.1: Do Developers Close SECURITY.md Related Issues Faster Than Other Documentation?

Table 2 summarizes the statistics of closing time across different documentation file types. Issues associated with SECURITY.md exhibited a median close time

Table 1. Number of issues related to each community health file.

	# of issues
`GOVERNANCE.md`	240
`SUPPORT.md`	478
`LICENSE.md`	2,042
`CODE_OF_CONDUCT.md`	2,089
`SECURITY.md`	**3,323**
`CONTRIBUTING.md`	7,020

of 7 days and a mean of 81.1 days, placing them among the relatively shorter durations observed. However, similar resolution times were found for other documentation types such as `LICENSE.md` and `CONTRIBUTING.md`, suggesting that the close time for `SECURITY.md` is not exceptionally brief in comparison.

In contrast, issues linked to `GOVERNANCE.md` stand out as a significant exception. These issues required substantially more time to resolve, with a median of 34 days and an average of 135.5 days. This finding implies that governance-related concerns may be inherently more complex or deprioritized in terms of timely resolution.

Table 2. Days until close statistics for community health files.

	Min.	Median	Mean	Max.
`CODE_OF_CONDUCT.md`	0	5	71.4	2,007
`LICENSE.md`	0	5	82.1	1,991
`SECURITY.md`	**0**	**7**	**81.1**	**1,977**
`CONTRIBUTING.md`	0	8	83.4	2,189
`SUPPORT.md`	0	11.5	112.2	2,007
`GOVERNANCE.md`	0	34	135.5	1,532

RQ1.2: Do Developers Close SECURITY.md Related Issues Faster When They Contain Links?

We investigated whether the presence of additional information via links in the issue text influences the resolution time of issues. During data collection, two issues containing broken URLs were identified and excluded from the analysis because the broken links prevented accurate classification, thereby preserving the integrity and validity of our findings.

Table 3 presents the close-time statistics for issues with and without links. The median close time for issues without links was 9 days, whereas issues that included links were resolved in 7 days, suggesting that providing links enables maintainers to access relevant information more efficiently and to reduce communication overhead such as verification steps or follow-up inquiries. However, a formal comparison between issues with links ($n = 315$) and without links ($n = 97$) using the Mann–Whitney U test (two-sided, $\alpha = 0.05$) detected no statistically significant difference between the distributions ($U = 15{,}177.5$, $p = 0.9223$). This suggests that we need to investigate this research question deeper, such as using a bigger sample or investigating the different types of links.

Table 3. Days until close statistics with link vs without link.

	# issues	Min.	Median	Mean	Max.
With link	315	0	7	82.9	1,309
Without link	97	0	9	66.4	764

RQ1.3: Do Developers Discuss SECURITY.md More Actively Than Other Documentation?

Table 4 shows the number of responses received for issues associated with various documentation files. Issues related to SECURITY.md had a median of 2 responses and an average of 3.1, indicating relatively active engagement. This level of interaction is comparable to LICENSE.md and CODE_OF_CONDUCT.md, which also had median values of 2 and slightly lower average responses.

Notably, GOVERNANCE.md and SUPPORT.md issues received the highest average responses, at 4.6 and 4.7, respectively, suggesting that these topics may require more discussion or clarification. In contrast, CONTRIBUTING.md issues had the lowest median (i.e., 1) and average (i.e., 2.6) response counts, implying that contribution-related issues may be more straightforward or less debated. Overall, the data suggests that issues involving governance, support, and security tend to generate more community interaction, possibly due to their complexity or importance.

> **Answer to RQ1:** Issues containing security-related URLs were closed two days earlier than those that did not, although no significant difference was observed in the overall close time or the number of responses for SECURITY.md issues compared to other document files.

RQ2 What security policy related issues do developers create?

We manually and independently classified the purposes of 711 issues randomly sampled from a total of 3,323 issues that contained the term SECURITY.md.

Table 4. Number of issue responses for each file.

	Min.	Median	Mean	Max.
`SUPPORT.md`	0	2	4.7	374
`GOVERNANCE.md`	0	2	4.6	131
`SECURITY.md`	**0**	**2**	**3.1**	**374**
`CODE_OF_CONDUCT.md`	0	2	2.9	357
`LICENSE.md`	0	2	2.8	77
`CONTRIBUTING.md`	0	1	2.6	85

Table 5. Classification results of SECURITY.md-related issues.

Category	Description	#	%
Creation Request	Request to add a file, or report that a file does not exist.	414	79.5
Revision Request	Internal links, email revision requests, and content update requests.	61	11.7
Reference	Refer to Security.md or their contents.	36	6.9
Educational Campaign	Recommendation to use SECURITY.md.	2	0.4
Other	Requests to delete files, contributors' opinions, etc.	8	1.5

Table 5 summarizes the distribution of issue purposes. During manual inspection, we excluded 190 issues that were not directly related to `SECURITY.md`. For example, those referencing directories or logs, or those automatically generated by bots such as `allstar-app` and `google-cloud-policy-bot`. After this filtering, 521 issues (73.3%) remained for analysis.

The most prevalent category was "Addition Requests," comprising 414 issues. Notably, 250 of these were submitted via the bug bounty platform `huntr.dev` [7], which specializes in OSS. On this platform, security researchers are rewarded for identifying and reporting vulnerabilities in OSS projects, thereby enhancing OSS security while incentivizing white-hat contributions.

The second most common category was "Revisions" (61 issues), which included requests to revise internal links, translate or update content, correct email addresses, relocate files for better accessibility, and fix content errors. Among the issues referencing `SECURITY.md`, 36 explicitly mentioned the file, with 25 directly referring to it—often with phrases like *"Please see SECURITY.md for details."* Of these, six discussed the file's contents, such as version information or usage instructions, five raised questions about how to report vulnerabilities, indicating confusion about the appropriate reporting channel. Some GitHub users pointed out that there is also a reporting method called "Report a security vulnerability," and it was unclear which reporting channel should be used. Two issues served educational purposes, such as promoting best practices for community health files, discouraging the use of issue trackers for vulnerability disclosure, and advocating for the adoption of SECURITY.md. Finally, eight issues were categorized as "Other." These included discussions about the file's directory location, suggestions to synchronize or delete some community health files.

> **Answer to RQ2:** The types of issues related to SECURITY.md were 79.5 % add requests, followed by revision requests and issues describing SECURITY.md.

6   Threats to Validity

With respect to internal validity, our analysis of resolution times may be influenced by unobserved factors such as repository size, popularity, ownership (organization vs. individual), or ecosystem. In addition, by considering only closed issues, the dataset may be biased toward more easily resolvable cases. Regarding external validity, our dataset was restricted to English-language issues from public GitHub repositories with at least 20 stars. Consequently, the findings may not generalize to smaller or private projects, non-English-speaking communities, or other platforms such as GitLab.

7   Conclusion

This study investigated SECURITY.md files, which are crucial for outlining secure vulnerability reporting procedures in open-source projects. We studied 711 randomly sampled issues related to SECURITY.md, finding that the most common type, at 79.5% of requests, was to add the file. A significant portion of these addition requests, 48.0%, originated from huntr.dev, an OSS-specialized bug bounty platform, while only 11.7% were requests for revisions. This distribution indicates that SECURITY.md is still in its diffusion stage, not yet widely adopted. Additionally, our findings indicate that while SECURITY.md helps clarify matters for developers, it can also increase confusion and burden.

Acknowledgments. We gratefully acknowledge the financial support of JSPS KAKENHI grants (JP24K02921, JP25K21359), as well as JST PRESTO grant (JPMJPR22P3), ASPIRE grant (JPMJAP2415), and AIP Accelerated Program (JPMJCR25U7).

References

1. Clark, B.: Open source security: advisories and workflows to keep open source secure. In: GitHub Satellite 2019. GitHub (2019). https://github.blog/2019-05-23-introducing-security-md/. Accessed 10 Aug 2025

2. Ayala, J., Garcia, J.: An empirical study on workflows and security policies in popular GitHub repositories. In: Proceedings of the 1st IEEE/ACM International Workshop on Software Vulnerability, pp. 6–9 (2023)
3. Kancharoendee, S., et al.: On categorizing open source software security vulnerability reporting mechanisms on GitHub. In: Proceedings of the IEEE International Conference on Software Analysis, Evolution and Reengineering (SANER), pp. 751–756 (2025)
4. Bühlmann, N., Ghafari, M.: How do developers deal with security issue reports on GitHub? In: Hong, J., Bures, M., Park, J.W., Cerný, T. (eds.) Proceedings of the 37th ACM/SIGAPP Symposium on Applied Computing, pp. 1580–1589 (2022)
5. Ikeda, S., Ihara, A., Kula, R.G., Matsumoto, K.: An empirical study on README contents for JavaScript packages (2018). CoRR vol. arXiv:abs/1802.08391
6. GitHub: GitHub rest API documentation (2025). https://docs.github.com/en/rest. Accessed 10 Aug 2025
7. huntr.dev (2025). https://huntr.dev. Accessed 10 Aug 2025

Author Index

A

Abrahamsson, Pekka 408
Adamov, Oleksandr 253
Amalfitano, Domenico 153
Aman, Hirohisa 479
Amasaki, Sousuke 479
Anwar, Hina 461
Astekin, Merve 334
Asvydyte, Gabija 506
Awan, Wardah Naeem 186
Aydemir, Fatma Başak 269

B

Babris, Kristaps 489
Berntsson Svensson, Richard 369
Bexell, Andreas 525
Bobkovs, Rihards 489
Borg, Markus 20
Bosch, Jan 319

C

Calder, Ella 52
Carrión, Emilio 397
Çelikmasat, Gökberk 269
Chand, Sivajeet 506
Changizi, Amirali 153
Chatlatanagulchai, Worawalan 543
Coppola, Riccardo 153

D

Dalpiaz, Fabiano 102
Dashti, Meelad 153
Distante, Damiano 153
Dorrani, Kimia 153
Drews, Paul 36

E

Eldh, Sigrid 525
Engström, Emelie 20

F

Fagerholm, Fabian 169

Falessi, Davide 498
Fischbach, Jannik 470
Fucci, Davide 253
Fulcini, Tommaso 153

G

Gao, Dongmei 169
Gentili, Emanuele 498
Gilson, Fabian 52
Giobergia, Flavio 153
Goknil, Arda 334
Gonzalez-Huerta, Javier 285, 353, 451
Grabis, Jānis 489
Gullu, Ali Ihsan 461
Güllü, Ali Ihsan 69
Gupta, Rushali 20

H

Haghparast, Majid 533
Hamza, Muhammad 186
Hasan, Md Mahade 408
Heander, Lo Gullstrand 525
Heikkinen, Ronja 533
Heller, Gerald 440
Hernández López, José Antonio 203
Hess, Anne 440
Heyn, Hans-Martin 119
Higo, Yoshiki 3
Holmström Olsson, Helena 319
Horkoff, Jennifer 119

I

Iacovou, Kypros 86
Iida, Hajimu 543, 552, 571
Inayat, Irum 369

K

Kaasik, Eliisabet 387
Kaila, Erkki 561
Kanaji, Rintaro 571
Kapitsaki, Georgia 86, 429
Karras, Oliver 440

Kashiwa, Yutaro 543, 552, 571
Kawahara, Minoru 479
Kemell, Kai-Kristian 408
Khan, Fauzia 461
Kilamo, Terhi 237
Klemetti, Antti 516
Korn, Alexander 470
Kula, Raula Gaikovina 571

L
LaProva, Daniele 498
Leelaprute, Pattara 543, 552

M
Mäkelä, Kalle 408
Mäkilä, Tuomas 561
Manaskasemsak, Bundit 543, 552
Mårtensson, Torvald 203
Martini, Antonio 137
Mehraj, Ali 237
Mendez, Daniel 253, 470
Mikkonen, Tommi 533
Miļūne, Megija Krista 489
Molenaar, Sabine 102
Mori Serra, Vitor 319

N
Neal, Daniel 52
Nguyen, Phu 334
Nikiforova, Oksana 489
Novikov, Oleksii 253
Nurminen, Jukka K. 516

O
Oyedeji, Shola 561
Özgövde, Atay 269

P
Pandey, Sushant Kumar 506
Parveen, Risha 237
Pastor, Óscar 397
Pastor, Oscar 489
Paudel, Bhuwan 285, 451
Pautasso, Cesare 220
Peng, Yi 119
Pfahl, Dietmar 69, 387, 461
Philippou, Anna 429
Pir Muhammad, Amna 369

R
Raatikainen, Mikko 516
Rasheed, Zeeshan 408
Rasku, Jussi 408
Reid, Brittany 543, 552, 571
Ricca, Filippo 153
Riggio, Edoardo 220
Runeson, Per 20, 525
Rungsawang, Arnon 543, 552
Rytilahti, Juuso 561

S
Saari, Mika 408
Sabir, Muhammad Waheed 186
Sadrnezhaad, Masoud 203
Schmitt, Hartmut 440
Sears, Dillan Wyatt 303
Sen, Sagar 334
Seraphin, Cornelia 440
Shah, Faiz Ali 69, 387
Shimizu, Sasara 3
Shivashankar, Karthik 137
Siddeeq, Shahbaz 408
Söderberg, Emma 20, 525
Song, Qunying 20
Sorvisto, Anssi 516
Stotz, Nils 36
Sundelin, Anders 419
Systä, Kari 237

T
Terho, Henri 408
Tevarut, Napasorn 552
Thonglek, Kundjanasith 543
Tsilionis, Konstantinos 303
Tverdal, Simeon 334

V
Valderas, Pedro 397
Vanezi, Evangelia 86, 429
Varró, Dániel 203
Villamizar, Hugo 470
Vogelsang, Andreas 470

W
Wagner, Matthias 20
Waseem, Muhammad 408
Wautelet, Yves 303
Weerakoon, Oshani 561

Y

Yamashita, Tomoya   479
Yokogawa, Tomoyuki   479

Z

Zabardast, Ehsan   285, 353, 451
Zhang, Zheying   237

If you have any concerns about our products,
you can contact us on
ProductSafety@springernature.com

In case Publisher is established outside the EU,
the EU authorized representative is:
Springer Nature Customer Service Center GmbH
Europaplatz 3, 69115 Heidelberg, Germany

Printed by Libri Plureos GmbH
in Hamburg, Germany